A

# CATALOGUE OF BOOKS,

IN ALL BRANCHES OF LITERATURE,

## BOTH ANCIENT & MODERN;

IN THE

**Greek and Latin, English, French, Italian, Spanish, German, and the Oriental Languages;**

IN

THEOLOGY, (INCLUDING A VALUABLE AND CURIOUS COLLECTION OF BIBLES AND TESTAMENTS,) HISTORY, VOYAGES & TRAVELS, OLD POETRY, NATURAL HISTORY, LAW, LANGUAGE, BIBLIOGRAPHY, &c., &c., &c.,

THE RAREST OF WHICH DATE

## FROM 1479 TO 1603,

The end of the Reign of QUEEN ELIZABETH, which period, both as regards this and other countries, is very particularly illustrated.

Later, the Reigns of CHARLES I. and II., including the Usurpation, have many curious articles, and a most singularly rare, and, in many instances, UNIQUE collection of BROADSIDES, relating to the Great Duke of Marlborough and other celebrities of the time of QUEEN ANNE.

ON SALE AT

## E. JEANS'S,

BOOKSELLER,

WHITE LION STREET, NORWICH.

---

☞ *A Discount of* 10 *per cent. will be allowed on all orders from this Catalogue, for cash, and the carriage paid to all parts of the kingdom.*

---

MDCCCLX.

About nine years ago there were disposed of by auction in Norwich a quantity of books, many of which had belonged to Sir Christopher Hatton; who, as Sir Harris Nicolas, in his Memoirs of him, says, was "Gentleman Pensioner, Captain of the Guard, Vice-Chamberlain, and Lord Chancellor to Queen Elizabeth, and distinguished personal Favourite, of whom less was known than of almost any other statesman of that period. This neglect of a very remarkable person," Sir Harris further says, "probably arose from the notion that he was a mere Courtier, whose life presented no incidents to instruct, and few to amuse mankind;" and further, "so far from being a vain, idle 'scapegrace,' with few acquirements and less talents, and the mere ornament of a Court, Hatton took a prominent part in all state affairs; and his opinion on public transactions received great consideration from Lord Burghley, Leicester, Walsingham, and all the other ministers. He was for many years what is now termed the Leader of the House of Commons; and if he did not adorn the woolsack, to which he was unexpectedly raised, by great legal learning, he had the modesty and good sense to consult *eminent lawyers* in cases of magnitude, and obtained the respect of the public by the equity and impartiality of his decisions." This extract I have transcribed as it proves my case, as regards the books formerly possessed by Sir Christopher Hatton. One of them, No. 32 in the Catalogue, has his autograph; and a great many the initials of his name, C. H., stamped in gold outside the covers: one of the old law books has the name of Dr. Swabey, an *eminent civilian*, in it, whom it is known Sir Christopher consulted; and the old Italian books, of which there are a great many rare and uncommon ones, prove that he studied the elegant literature of that day—in which language, as well as many others, Queen Elizabeth was a proficient—it was reasonable, therefore, that her very handsome favourite (for the Queen is recorded to have had a partiality for handsome men) should obtain a knowledge of a fashionable language, if only in compliment to his mistress.

There are other books in this Catalogue which should have a passing remark—for besides many black letter volumes which illustrate Elizabeth's period, there are a great many others which are equally singular, relating to more recent history. For instance, in the reign of Charles the First there are the very broadsides (see Nos. 985 and 6) put forth by the Parliament, complaining of the "arrest of the five Members," about which *Mr. Forster* has *re-written* "a Chapter of English History." Under the head of both the Charles's are many extremely curious things; but, perhaps, more singular than all are those lampoons under Queen Anne's reign, (collected by Sir Edmund Bacon, M.P. for Norwich in 1710,) the titles of which, referring to the great Duke of Marlborough, explain themselves, and which would have afforded Lord Macaulay, had he been still amongst us, infinite pleasure to have turned over. His lordship, Mr. Hallam, Mr. Prescott, and Washington Irving, all great men, but recently departed, would have thoroughly appreciated such curiosities as these.

Further, let those who are fond of the history of France look to those little ephemeral things of four pages each, here collected into volumes, relating to the murder of Henry IV. of France, by Ravaillac, and say if they are not of much interest; and altogether, I think I may venture to say, that for the *number* of books, there are more curious articles in this Catalogue than are ordinarily to be found in the same number of pages. This arises from the circumstance of the books having been *treasured,* if I may so say, for a number of years, and they are now offered to the public; when once dispersed, it will be difficult to put them together again.

And, in conclusion, I have but to say, that inasmuch as I have had much pleasure in compiling the Catalogue, which I think it will be conceded to me is done with some care; so I trust the public will partake liberally of its contents. My end will then be answered. If it does, I promise that public—always bountiful where it sees a good object in view—that if it helps me to the means, I will endeavour to cull for its future contentation a more rich and a more varied collection. My aspirations being to a hundred thousand instead of ten thousand volumes; and thus "I humbly take my leave;" and with regard to books, will say with *Horace Walpole* :—

"Visions, you know, have always been my pasture; and so far from growing old enough to quarrel with their emptiness, I almost think there is no wisdom comparable with that of exchanging what is called the realities of life for dreams. Old castles, old pictures, old histories, and the babble of old people, make one live back into centuries that cannot disappoint one. One holds fast and surely what is past. The dead have exhausted their power of deceiving."

# E. JEANS'S

## CATALOGUE

OF

# NEW AND SECOND-HAND BOOKS,

## 1860.

---

1 ABANO (Pierre dict Conciliateur) Traicté des Venims, ensemble un traicté de Theophraste, Paracelsus des Vertus et proprietez merveilleuses des Serpents, Arraignes, Crapaux et Cancres, le tout trad. en François par L. Boet, 16mo. *old binding, curious*, 5*s* *Lyon*, 1593

2 ABBOTSFORD LIBRARY: a Catalogue of Sir Walter Scott's Library there, drawn up by Mr. Cochrane, and published with the sanction of Mr. Lockhart, Sir Walter's Son-in-law, 4to. *boards*, VERY SCARCE, £3 3*s* .. .. .. *Edinburgh*, 1838

I have always esteemed this volume (one of the Bannatyne Club Books) as a very valuable acquisition to Literature, and shews more than anything else the peculiar bent of Sir Walter Scott's reading. There is an immense collection of very curious Tracts on Witchcraft, Sorcery, and Magic. Old Tracts on the Civil Wars, Antiquarian Tracts, History, Poetry, the Drama, Fiction, &c., &c. extending over 464 pages.

3 ABBOTT'S (Jacob) Young Christian; or the Principles of Christian Duty, by Cunningham, 12mo. *cloth*, 2*s* 6*d* (*cost* 5*s*) 1833

"I feel it to be truly a fascinating book."—*Rev. W. Innes, Edinburgh.*

4 — Corner Stone; the Principles of Christian Truth; with a Preface by Dr. John Pye Smith, 12mo. *cloth*, 2*s* 6*d* (*pub. at* 5*s*) 1834

5 ABERCROMBIE'S (John) Harmony of Christian Faith and Character, 18mo. *cloth*, 1*s* .. .. *Edinburgh*, 1838

6 ABERDEEN'S (George, Earl of) Inquiry into the Principles of Beauty in Grecian Architecture; with an historical view of the rise and progress of the Art in Greece, post 8vo. *boards*, 5*s* 1822

"The Travelled Thane, Athenian Aberdeen."

7 ABOUT'S (Edmond) Tolla; a Tale of Modern Rome, translated by L C. C., post 8vo. *cloth*, 2*s* 3*d* (*pub. at* 3*s* 6*d*) 1855

8 ACCOMPLISHED Youth: the Principles of Morality and Politeness, *frontispiece*, 18mo. *boards*, 1*s* .. .. 1811

9 ADAM'S (Dr. Alexander) Summary of Geography and History, Ancient and Modern, *maps*, 8vo. *neat*, 3*s* 6*d* .. .. 1802

10 — Roman Antiquities; with Notes by Dr. J. Boyd, *map and* 100 *plates*, 12mo. *cloth*, 3*s* (*pub. at* 7*s*) .. .. 1842

11 ADAMS'S (George) Description and Use of the Celestial and Terrestrial Globes; with a Comprehensive View of the Solar System, by Dudley Adams, *plates*, 8vo. *boards*, 4*s* .. 1810

12 ADAMS'S (George) Geometrical and Graphical Essays, corrected and enlarged by W. Jones, 34 *plates*, 2 vols. 8vo. *boards*, 7*s* (*pub. at* 16*s*) 1813

13 ADDISON'S (Hon. Joseph) Christian Poet; a Miscellany of Divine Poems, with Memoirs of his Life and Writings, *E. Curll*, 1728;—Rapin's Sufferings of Christ, a Poem, *E. Curll*, 1720;—Doomsday, by William Alexander, Earl of Sterline;—Large Catalogue of Books (16 pages) printed by *H. Curll*—in 1 vol. 8vo. *neat*, 4*s*. *v. y.*

14 — Remarks on Several Parts of Italy in 1701-3, 12mo. *neat*, 2*s* 1726

15 — Plays: Cato, The Drummer, and Rosamond, 12mo. *old calf neat*, 2*s* . .. .. *Glasgow, Foulis*, 1748-51

16 — Evidences of the Christian Religion; with Discourses against Atheism and Infidelity, 12mo. *calf, gilt*, 2*s* 6*d* *Oxford*, 1801

17 — Life, by Lucy Aikin, *portrait*, 2 vols. post 8vo. *cloth*, 4*s* 6*d* (*pub. at* 18*s*) .. .. .. .. 1843

"A very amusing and instructive book."

18 ADDISON'S (L. Dean of Lichfield) Christian's Manual: 1. The Catechumen; 2. Introduction to the Communion Table; 3. Necessity of Catechising, *frontispiece*, 12mo. *old calf, scarce*, 3*s* 1691

19 ADRIANI (Giovambatista) Istoria de' suoi Tempi, *portrait*, thick folio, of above 1,000 pages, *half bound neat*, 25*s* *In Firenze, Giunti*, 1583

First edition and rare —Collates by *Brunet*. The period comprehended is from 1536 to 1574. See also *Haym*.

20 ADVENTURER, 4 vols. 18mo. *calf, neat*, 4*s* .. 1774

21 ADVICE to Young Gentry, by the Author of Youths Grand Concern, by J. G., *calf neat*, 2*s* 6*d* .. 1711

Anecdotes of eminent virtuous persons. Dedicated to Sir John Hobart.

22 ÆLFRICUS ABBAS Saxon Treatise concerning the Old and New Testament, written about the time of King Edgar (seven hundred years ago), published in Anglo-Saxon and English by William Lisle, of Wilburgham, 4to. *half morocco*, 15*s* *John Haviland*, 1623

At the end is "a Testimonie of Antiquitie touching the Sacrament of the Bodie and Bloud of the Lord," by the said Ælfricus. A Treatise of Elfrike's out of the Liber Penitentialis, and the Lord's Prayer, Creed, and Commandments, all in Anglo-Saxon and English.

23 ÆLIANI Varia Historia, Gr. et Lat., cum notis variorum et Gronovii, 2 vols. 4to. LARGE PAPER, *old calf neat*, £1 1*s* *Lugd. Bat.*, 1731

Fuhrmann calls this a very splendid and excellent edition. Rabelais, who was a man of too much imagination not to be delighted with a gossiping book of legends and prodigies, like the *Varia Historia*, quotes Ælian frequently. This curious and entertaining compilation, contains extracts from Greek authors whose writings are no longer extant.

24 ÆLIAN'S TACTIKS; or, Art of Embattailing an Army after ye Grecian Manner, by Capt. JOHN BINGHAM, *engraved title and numerous plates*, folio, *both parts old calf, rare*, £1 1*s*
*London, at the Charges of the Author*, 1631

"From whence is derived ye military exercise of ye English in ye Lowe Countries set on foote by that great General, Maurice, Prince of Orange."

25 ÆMILIUS PROBUS, see Cornelius Nepos.

26 ÆSCHYLUS, Græcè et Latinè, Stanleii et Butleri notis, 8 vols. 8vo. *boards, scarce*, £2 5*s* .. .. *Cantabrigiæ*, 1809

"This edition contains the entire of Stanley's folio, besides various collations. It is now entirely out of print and become a scarce book."—See *Museum Criticum and Dibdin*.

27 ÆSOPI Fabulæ Selectiores, Gr. et Lat., et vocum omnium explicatio, 8vo. *fine copy in vellum*, 4s 6d *Parisiis, apud C. Morellium*, 1625

A remarkably fine Greek type, with a Latin interlineary translation.

28 — Fabulæ, Græcè, 12mo. *old calf, neat*, 2s *Londini, R. Daniel*, 1657

29 — Fables, in English and Latin, Interlineary, by John Locke, 8vo. *sheep, very clean, scarce*, 5s .. .. 1723

30 AFRICA.—Scenes and Occurrences in Albany and Caffirland, South Africa, *coloured frontispiece*, post 8vo. *boards*, 2s 6d 1827

31 AGOSTINO (Gio.) La Staffetta privata Lettere, 12mo. *parchment*, 2s *Genova, per B. Guasco*, 1656

32 AGRICOLA (Rodolpho, *Frisio*) della Invention Dialettica, tradotto da Oratio Toscanella, 4to. *limp vellum, with autograph of Sir Christopher Hatton, rare*, £1 1s *Venetia, G. Bariletto*, 1567

At the end is a Tract on the same subject. "Dialettica di Georgio Trapezontio, con le Interpretat. del Neomago et del Latomo, tradotta da Oratio Toscanella, *Venetia, G. Bariletto*, 1567." This is the only book I have with the AUTOGRAPH of *Sir Christopher Hatton*. There are many with C. H. stamped on the outsides of the volumes in gold, but this is the only *Autograph* I possess of his. Erasmus gives a very exalted character of the learning and abilities of Agricola.

33 AGRICULTURE.—Reports of the Harleston Farmers' Club, from 1838 to 1849, 8vo. *cloth*, 2s .. .. 1850

34 AGRIPPA (Hen. Corn.) de Incertitudine et Vanitate Scientiarum, In artem brevem Raymundi Lullii Commentaria, Epistolæ, etc., *portrait*, 8vo. *fine copy, in the original stamped calf*, 12s *Lugduni, per Beringos fratres, absque nota anni*

This is Vol. 2 "of the most esteemed edition of Agrippa's Works; it is in *Italics*."—*Dr. Adam Clarke*. The date is about 1550.
"Bonne édition, et le plus rare de ce livre."—*Fournier*.

35 — Vanity of Arts and Sciences, *fine portrait by Thos. Burnford (not in Granger)*, small 8vo. *original binding*, 8s .. 1676

H. C. Agrippa was in England in 1510 and in 1529 was invited by Henry VIII. to settle here.—See *Baker's Reflections on Learning*.

36 — another copy, *portrait*, 8vo. *neat*, 9s .. .. 1676

37 AIKIN'S (Edmund) Essay on the Doric Order of Architecture, *seven plates*, imperial folio, *boards*, 15s .. *Bensley*, 1810

Published by the London Architectural Society, with a Table of the Proportions of the Examples contained in the plates.

38 AIKIN'S (Dr. John) Essays on Song Writing; with a Collection of such Songs as are most eminent for Poetical Merit, 12mo. *calf neat*, 3s 6d .. .. .. *Warrington*, 1774

39 — Woodland Companion: a Brief Description of British Trees, 28 *plates*, 12mo. *calf neat*, 3s .. .. 1815

40 — Letters from a Father to his Son, 12mo. *purple morocco gilt, gilt edges*, 5s .. .. .. .. 1838

41 AINSWORTH'S (Robert) English-Latin and Latin-English Dictionary, by Dr. Thomas Morell, 2 vols. 4to. *strongly bound*, 7s 6d 1773

42 — another copy, thick 4to. (wants title), 5s .. 1783

43 — another copy, abridged for School Use by Morell and Duncan, 8vo. *bound*, 9s .. .. .. .. 1854

44 AINSWORTH'S (W. H.) Magazine, *plates by Cruikshank*, vol. 1 only, 8vo. *half calf neat*, 3s 6d .. .. 1842

45 AITON'S (William) Hortus Kewensis; a Catalogue of the Plants cultivated in the Royal Botanic Garden at Kew, *plates*, 3 vols. 8vo. *old calf, very neat*, 10*s* 6*d* .. .. 1789

"A most curious, instructive, and excellent Botanical Work, which for Scientific arrangement has never been surpassed."—*Lowndes.*

46 AKENSIDE'S (Dr.) Pleasures of Imagination, a Poem, 8vo. *half calf neat*, 2*s* .. .. .. .. 1754

47 ALAIN de Rohan et Rollon de Coucy, 2 vols. 12mo. *half bound*, 2*s* 6*d* *Paris*, 1813

48 ALANI ab Insulis Parabolæ, et ad easdem And. Senftlebii notæ Philologicæ, 12mo. *old calf*, 5*s* .. *Lipsiæ*, 1663

Alain de L'Isle, surnamed the Universal Doctor from his extensive knowledge, was born about the middle of the 12th century. There is a Life of him attached to this volume.

49 ALBERICI (Giacomo) Catalogo breve de Gl'illustri et famosi Scrittori Venetiani, 4to. *old boards*, 15*s* *Bologna, G. Rossi*, 1605

"L'Autore era Agostiniano. *Il Catalogo è sommamente ristretto, e scarso.*"—*Haym.* It is dedicated to Marino Grimani, Doge of Venice, and has five leaves of complimentary Poetry.

50 ALBERTI (Gio. Batt.) Discorso dell' Origine delle Accademie publiche, e private, e sopra l'Impresa de gli affidati di *Pavia*, small 8vo. *sewed*, 3*s* .. .. *Genova*, 1639

Not in Haym.

51 ALBERTI (Leon Baptista) of Architecture, Painting, and Statuary, Italian and English, by C. Bartoli and James Leoni, *numerous plates*, 3 vols. in 1, large folio, *binding indifferent*, 15*s* *London*, 1726

52 ALBINI (Joannis) de Gestis Regum Neapo. ab Aragonia qui extant libri IV., 4to. *old calf, rare*, 12*s* .. *Neapoli*, 1589

With Joseph Cacchius, the printer's, fine device at the end.

53 ALBITES (F.) Morality of all Nations, Proverbs in English, French and Italian, to be learnt by heart, 8vo. *sewed*, 3*s* 1850

"A treasury of beautiful maxims is superior to any mass of riches."—*Isocrates.*

54 ALCIATI Emblemata, *above* 100 *cleverly engraved woodcuts*, small 8vo. 142 pages, (wants title) *neatly half bound*, 6*s* 1531

"Edition rare et très peu connue." .. *Brunet.*

55 ALCIATI (Andreæ) Notitia Provinciarum Imperii Romani, Descriptio Urbis Romæ, et Constantinopoleos, de Militaribus civilibusque officiis, de Rebus Bellicis, &c, folio, *limp vellum*, £1 1*s* *Basileæ, apud H. Frobenium*, 1552

This book is illustrated throughout by a great number of very curious woodcuts.

56 ALCORAN, various curious Tracts relating to, see Mahomet, also Coran.

57 ALCUIN'S Life, by Dr. F. Lorenz, Englished by Jane M. Slee, 12mo. *half cloth*, 3*s* (*pub. at* 6*s*) .. .. 1837

Alcuin at the Court of Charlemagne in 790.

58 ALDOBRANDINI (Silvestri. *Jureconsult Florentini)* in primum Institutionum Justiniani librum, Annotationes, 4to. 330 pages, besides 72 of introductory matter, *old parchment*, rare, 10*s* 6*d* *Venetiis, in Off. hæredum Luceantonii Junte Florentini*, MDXLVIII.

This Sylvester Aldobrandini was the father of Pope Clement VIII. and died in 1558; none of his works are mentioned by De Bure or Brunet.

59 ALEXANDER VII. and CLEMENT IX.—Account of the Life and Death of Pope Alexander VII., with the Ceremonies performed at the Coronation of the present Pope Clement IX.; with a Catalogue of all the Cardinals, by P. A. Gent, *fine portrait of Clement IX, by Gaywood,* 4to. *sewed, scarce,* 7*s* 6*d* *Moses Pitt,* 1667

60 ALEXANDER'S (Capt. J. E.) Travels to the Seat of War in the East, through Russia and the Crimea, in 1829, *map and coloured plates,* 2 vols. 8vo. *cloth,* 7*s* 6*d* (*pub. at* £1 8*s*) 1830

"Captn. Alexander's productions are pleasant and useful, his style and manner are brisk and rattling."—*Spectator.*

61 ALEXANDRE I. de Russie; Bon Mots et Paroles Remarquables, pendant son séjour dans Paris, *portrait,* 18mo. *sewed,* 2*s* *Paris,* 1815

62 ALGAROTTI (Conte) Congresso di Citera, accresciuto del alcune Lettere e del giudizio d'Amore, 12mo. *old calf, gilt leaves,* 3*s* *Parigi, Marcello Prault,* 1768

63 ALI BEY'S Travels in Morocco, Tripoli, Cyprus, Egypt, Arabia, Syria, and Turkey, in 1803 to 1807, *portrait, maps, and numerous fine plates,* 2 vols. 4to. *calf, neat,* £1 5*s* (*pub. at* 6 *guineas*) 1816

"Ali Bey (Domingo Badia y Leblich, a Spaniard) obtained access to many places to which Christians were not permitted to go."—*Stevenson.*

64 ALISON'S (Sir Archibald) England in 1815 and 1845, or, a sufficient and a contracted Currency, 2nd edition, with an Answer to Sir Robert Peel, 8vo. *cloth,* 2*s* 6*d* .. .. 1845

65 — History of Europe, from 1789 to 1815, epitomized, post 8vo. *cloth* 4*s* (*pub. at* 7*s* 6*d*) .. .. 1849

66 — History of Europe from 1815 to 1852, vols. 1 and 2, 8vo. *cloth,* 20*s* (*pub. at* 30*s*) .. .. .. 1853

67 — Future; or, the Science of Politics, post 8vo. *cloth, new,* 2*s* 6*d* (*pub. at* 5*s*) .. .. .. 1852

68 ALL ABOUT IT; or, the History and Mystery of Common Things, 12mo. *cloth, gilt,* 2*s* 6*d* .. .. 1859

69 ALLEINE'S (Joseph) Alarm to Unconverted Sinners, 12mo. *bound,* 1*s* 6*d* .. .. .. .. 1819

70 ALLIBONE'S (S. Austin) Critical Dictionary of English Literature, and British and American Authors, living and deceased; with 40 Indexes of Subjects, vol. 1, A to J, imperial 8vo, all yet published, *cloth new,* £1 4*s* .. *Philadelphia,* 1859

Contains 30,000 Biographies and Literary Notices.

"The work is conducted on what to me is an entirely novel principle, and presents the reader not simply with the opinions of the author, but with those of the best critics on every writer whose character he discusses."—*W. H. Prescott.*

71 ALMANACK, by John Partridge, for 1701, being the 12th year after our deliverance from Popery, small 8vo. *curious,* 3*s* 6*d*

With a Poetical Dialogue between a red-hot Jeroboam Tory and a Jerusalem Whig, about the Calves at Dan and Bethel, published in the year King William III. died.

72 — de Gotha, 1819, 1821, 1822, 1823, 1824, 1829, 1832, 1834, 1836, 1839, 1840, 1848, 1850, *boards,* 1*s* 6*d* *each* (*pub. at* 5*s* *each.*)

These contain Portraits of many Foreign Potentates not easily elsewhere obtainable.

73 ALMANZAIDE, Histoire Afriquaine, 12mo. *old red morocco, gilt edges,* 10*s* 6*d* .. .. *Amsterdam,* 1766

Nice specimen of old red morocco binding, with Autograph of the Dowager Mrs. Catharine Nassau.

74 ALTAR, Companion to the, with an Essay on the Lord's Supper, by Dr. Hugh Blair, *portrait*, 24mo. *bound, gilt edges*, 1*s* 1826

75 ALTAR SERVICE, with Prayers for the Communion of the Sick, by Isaacson, 18mo. *morocco, gilt edges*, 3*s* (*cost* 5*s*) 1830

76 ALTESSERÆ (Antonii Dadini, *Professoris Univers. Tolosanæ)* in libros Clementinarum Commentarii, 4to. *calf, very neat*, 6*s* *Parisiis*, 1680

77 ALVAREZ de Colmenar (D. Juan) Delices de l'Espagne et du Portugal, *maps, views of cities, plates of costume, &c.* 6 vols. 12mo. *old calf, very neat*, 10*s* .. .. .. *Leide*, 1715

An edition not mentioned by Brunet.

78 AMARANTH; or Religious Poems, consisting of Fables, Visions, Emblems, &c. *portraits and plates*, by W. Hibbart, 8vo. *half calf*, 4*s* .. .. .. .. 1767

79 AMERICAN OCEAN; Reasons to show that there is a great probability of a navigable passage to the Western American Ocean through Hudson's Streights, and Chesterfield Inlet, 8vo. *sewed*, 4*s* 1749

80 — Short Narrative and Justification of the proceedings of the Committee appointed by the adventurers, to prosecute the discovery of the passage to the Western Ocean of America, 8vo. *sewed*, 3*s* 1749

81 — Short State of the Countries and Trade of North America claimed by the Hudson's Bay Company, under pretence of a charter for ever, 8vo. *sewed*, 4*s* .. .. 1749

To this Tract is appended a "Standard of Trade," and "an Abstract of the Weather taken at Montague House, near York-Fort, Hudson's Bay, from August, 1746, to September, 1747."

82 — Baily's (J.) Central America, describing each of the States of Guatemala, Honduras, Salvador, Nicaragua, and Costa Rica, *plates*, post 8vo. *cloth*, 3*s* (*cost* 5*s*) .. .. 1850

83 — Bartram's (William) Travels through North and South Carolina, Georgia, the Cherokee Country, &c. *plates*, 8vo. *calf, neat*, 7*s* 1792

"A most interesting work to lovers of Natural History, especially Botany, the manners of the Indians, &c."—*Stevenson.*

84 — Buccaneers of America, History of the, *portrait of Francis Lolonois*, vol. 2 only, 12mo. *calf, neat, scarce*, 8*s* .. 1741

85 — Carey and Lea's Geography, History, and Statistics of America and the West Indies, *coloured maps and plates*, 8vo. *half calf, neat*, 7*s* 6*d* .. .. .. .. 1823

86 — Carver's (J.) Travels through the Interior parts of North America in 1766, 1767, 1768, *coloured maps and plates*, 8vo. *calf, very neat, scarce*, 7*s* 6*d* .. .. .. 1778

"This valuable work lately attracted much attention, from its description of parts near to the supposed N. W. Passage."—*Lowndes.*

87 — Dwight's (Theodore) Travels in America, 12mo. *cloth*, 2*s* *Glasgow*, 1848

88 — Hall's (Hon. Judge) Letters from the West; Sketches of the Scenery, Manners and Customs of the first settlements of the Western Sections of the United States, 8vo. *boards*, 5*s* (*pub. at* 12*s*) 1828

89 — Haverford School, An Account of, from its Institution to 1835, *View and Plan of the School*, 8vo. *cloth*, 3*s* *Philadelphia*, 1835

Presentation copy to Mr. Joseph John Gurney.

90 AMERICA.—Hunter's (John D.) Memoirs of a Captivity among the Indians of North America, from childhood to the age of nineteen, with Anecdotes of their Manners and Customs, *portrait*, 8vo. *boards*, 7*s* 6*d* (*pub. at* 14*s*) .. .. 1824

"An authentic, most amusing, and accurate narrative."—*Lowndes.*

91 — Hutchinson's (Lieut. Governor) History of the Colony of Massachusets Bay, from the year 1628 to 1691, 2 vols. 8vo. *calf, fine copy, scarce,* £1 1*s* .. .. .. 1760

92 — North American Boundary—Map of New Brunswick and Lower Canada, in reference to the dispute by the United States Government, Col. Mudge and Mr. Featherstonhaugh, Commissioners, ordered by Lord Palmerston in 1839—45 in. by 27 in. folded, 2*s* 6*d* .. .. .. .. 1840

93 — Men and Manners in America, by the author of Cyril Thornton, 2 vols. post 8vo. *boards*, 6*s* (*pub. at* 21*s*) .. 1834

94 — North American Indians. Some account of the conduct of the Society of Friends towards the Indian Tribes of Jersey and Pennsylvania, from 1682 to 1843, large map, 8vo. *boards*, 3*s* 1844

95 — Oregon, the claim of the United States to Oregon, as stated by Mr. Calhoun, Mr. Buchanan, and the Rt. Hon. R. Pakeham, our Plenipotentiary, *map, shewing the boundary line*, 8vo. *cloth*, 2*s* 6*d* 1846

96 — Prince's (Thomas) Thanksgiving Sermon, July 18th, 1745, at South Church, Boston, N. E., for the taking of the City of Louisbourg, Isle of Cape Breton, 1746; another by him, November 27th, 1746, wherein the most remarkable Salvations of the year past, both in Europe and North America, are considered, 1747—in 1 vol. 8vo. *very neat and clean*, 6*s* .. 1745—6

This volume also contains seven Thanksgiving Sermons, by Owen, Farmer, Townsend, Smith of Sheffield, Butler, Warburton, and Watkins, for the suppression of the late unnatural (Scotch) Rebellion of 1745-6.; with "Britain's Remembrancer," 1747; and "An Impartial Enquiry into the true cause of our present National Troubles." 1746.

97 — Popple's (Henry) Map of the British Empire in America, with the French and Spanish Settlements adjacent thereto, engraved on twenty sheets, *coloured*, by William Henry Toms, imperial folio, *old calf gilt, scarce*, £1 11*s* 6*d* .. .. 1733

This very nicely engraved Atlas is not to be found in *Lowndes.*

98 — Robertson's (Dr. William) History of America, Books 9 and 10, containing the History of Virginia to 1688, and of New England to 1652, 4to. *half calf neat, scarce*, 5*s* .. 1796

This fragment was published by the Author's Son after his father's death, being left in MS. by him.

99 — Stork's (William) Description of East Florida, with a Journal kept by John Bartram, of Philadelphia, with Botanical Notes, *map and two plans*, 4to. *boards, scarce*, 7*s* 6*d* .. .. 1769

100 — Ulloa's Voyage to South America, describing the Spanish Cities, Towns, &c., with Reflections on the Customs and Trade of the Inhabitants, and Natural History of the Country, *plates*, 2 vols. 8vo. *calf neat*, 7*s* 6*d* .. .. .. 1758

101 — Views and Reviews in American Literature, History, and Fiction, post 8vo. *cloth*, 3*s* 6*d* .. *Wiley and Putnam*, 1846

102 AMERICA.—Wansey's (Henry) Journal of an Excursion to the United States of North America in 1794, *portrait of General Washington, plate*, 8vo. *calf neat*, 3*s* 6*d* *Salisbury*, 1796

103 — Washington's (George, *First President of the United States*) Life, by Aaron Bancroft, 8vo. *calf neat, scarce*, 6*s* 1808

104 — Weld's (Isaac) Travels through North America and the Canadas in 1795, 1796, 1797, *maps and plates*, 2 vols. 8vo. *half russia, neat*, 8*s* .. .. .. .. 1800

105 — Worsley's (Israel) View of the American Indians, their Character, Customs, Language, Traditions, &c., 12mo. *boards*, 2*s* 1828

Shews them to be descendants of the ten tribes of Israel. Other books about the two Americas will be found in various parts of this catalogue.

106 AMHURST'S (Nicholas) Terræ-Filius; the Secret History of the University of Oxford, with Remarks on Dr. Newton's Book, University Education, *plates by Hogarth*, 12mo. *calf neat, scarce*, 6*s* .. .. .. .. 1726

"An ingenious but intemperate satire."—*Lowndes*.

107 AMMIANO MARCELLINO della Guerre de Romani, tradotto per M. Remigio Fiorentino, small thick 8vo. 676 pages, *fine copy in vellum, rare*, 15*s* *Vinetia, Gabriel Giolito di Ferrarii*, 1550

The only translation of this historian in Italian; held in considerable estimation by the Italians, and forms part of their "Collana."—See *Moss. Classical Manual*.

108 AMMONIUS de Adfinium Vocabulorum differentia, Græcè, Notis Valckenaer, 4to. *editio optima, boards*, 5*s* *Lugd. Bat.*, 1739

"An excellent work and now rare."—*Dibdin*.

109 AMORY'S (John) Memoirs; containing the Lives of Several Ladies of Great Britain, vol. 2, 12mo. *neat*, 2*s* .. 1776

110 AMSTERDAM.—Proclamation by the Lords of the Council of the City for the Apprehension of the Ruffians who endeavoured to Assassinate their Burghemaster, *Van Beuningen*, March 16th, folio broadside, *curious*, 5*s* .. *Thos. Malthus*, 1684

111 — Description de l'Hotel de Ville d'Amsterdam, 4 *plates*, 12mo. *half bound, neat*, 2*s* .. .. *Amsterdam*, 1745

112 ANACREON, Gr. et Lat., Opera et Studio J. Barnes, 3 *portraits*, 12mo. *fine copy in old calf gilt*, 4*s* 6*d* *Cantabrigiæ*, 1721

The best Cambridge edition, more correct than the London one.
"Barnes has explained many things in a very learned and useful manner."—*Dibdin*.

113 — Odæ, Græcè, accedunt selecta quædam e Lyricorum Reliquiis, cura Brunckii, 32mo. *old blue morocco, extra gilt, gilt edges, by Walther*, 15*s* .. *Argentorati, Treuttel*, 1786

This is a thick, fine, and large paper copy of a highly esteemed edition.

114 ANANIA (Gio Lorenzo) L'Universale Fabrica del Mondo, overo Cosmografia, 4to. *very fine large and clean copy, in white Italian vellum, scarce*, 12*s* .. *Venetia, Jacomo Vidali*, 1576

First edition of a very beautifully printed volume, dedicated "Alla Seren. Caterina Sforza d'Arogonia, Reina di Suetia." Sir Christopher Hatton's copy with the initials of his name.

115 ANASTASII Bibliothecarii de Vitis Romanorum Pontificum, a B. Petro Apostolo ad Nicolaum I., vol. 1 only, folio, LARGE PAPER, *old calf neat*, 15*s* .. .. *Romæ*, 1718

A very sumptuously printed volume, has also the lives of Hadrian II. and Stephen VI., and is illustrated with some very beautiful engravings by Maximilian Limpach after Passarus.

116 ANCHORAN'S (John) Gate of Tongues Unlocked and Opened, in Latine, English, and French, 8vo. *old calf, scarce,* 6s 1637

"Brought to light, in behalfe of the most illustrious Prince Charles and of British, French, and Irish youth." This is the third edition. No mention of this author by *Lowndes.*

117 ANDERSON'S (Dr. James) Recreations in Agriculture, Natural History, Arts, and Miscellaneous Literature, 6 vols. 8vo. *half calf neat,* £1 4s .. .. .. 1799

"A copious list of this eminent Agricultural writer's works will be found in Watt's Bibliotheca Britannica."—*Lowndes.*

118 ANDREWS'S (James Pettit) Anecdotes, Ancient and Modern, *plate,* 8vo. *calf neat,* 6s .. .. .. 1789

"An amusing and humorous collection."—*Lowndes.*

119 — Continuation of Dr. Henry's History of Great Britain, vol. 1 only, 8vo. *half calf neat,* 3s 6d .. .. 1796

120 ANDREWS'S (Dr. John) History of the War with America, France, Spain, and Holland, 1775 to 1783, *portraits, maps, and charts,* 4 vols. 8vo. *half calf neat,* 12s .. .. 1785

121 ANDREWS'S (Bishop Lancelot) Nineteen Sermons concerning Prayer, 12mo. *purple morocco, by Hayday,* £1 1s *Cambridge, Roger Daniel,* 1641

122 ANGLING.—Best's (Thomas) Art of Angling, with Nobbs's Complete Troller, *frontispiece,* 12mo. *sewed,* 2s 6d .. 1814

123 — Biographical Catalogue of English Writers on Angling and Ichthyology, post 8vo. *stiff cover,* 2s *J. R. Smith,* 1856

124 — Gentleman Fisher; or, the whole Art of Angling, 2nd Edition, *frontispiece by Hulsbergh,* 1727.—Essay on Criticism, by Alexander Pope, with Notes by Warburton, 1749.—Pleasures and Felicity of Marriage, by Lemuel Gulliver, *plates,* 1745.—Art of Drawing and Painting in Water Colours, *plates,* 1763.—Artists' Assistant in Drawing, Perspective, Etching, Mezzotinto Scraping, and Painting on Glass, *plates, no date*—5 Tracts in 1 vol. small 8vo. *half calf,* 12s

125 — Rennie's (James) Alphabet of Scientific Angling, for the Use of Beginners, *portrait and plates,* 12mo. *cloth,* 2s 1833

126 — Taylor's (Samuel) Angling in all its Branches, with the complete Fly Maker, small 8vo. *half calf neat,* 3s 6d .. 1800

127 — True Art of Angling, 1770.—Dean Nickoll's Letter on the Abolition of the Slave Trade, 1787.—Summary View of the Slave Trade, 1787.—Trenchard's Private Soldier's and Militia Man's Friend, 1786.—Essay on Laughter, dedicated to Samuel Foote (wants title)—5 Tracts, in 1 vol. 12mo. *half bound,* 3s

128 — Williamson's (John) British Angler; or, Pocket Companion for Gentlemen Fishers, *plates by Bickham and Cole,* 12mo. *old calf neat,* 5s .. .. .. .. 1740

Sold in Haworth's Sale for 7s 6d

129 ANGUS'S (W.) Seats of the Nobility and Gentry in Great Britain and Wales, with a description of each, 32 *plates,* oblong 4to. *half calf, very clean and neat,* 15s .. .. 1787

An original copy with very fine impressions of the plates.

QUEEN ANNE, the DUKE and DUCHESS of MARLBOROUGH, and DR. HENRY SACHEVERELL.—A COLLECTION of VERY CURIOUS BROADSIDES and TRACTS relating to these MEMORABLE PERSONAGES, as follows:—

130 ANNE.—The Restauration; or, a Change for the Better, being a Paper of VERSES in Memory of the City of London's Gratitude in choosing Sir William Pritchard, Sir Francis Child, Sir John Fleet, and G. Heathcot, Esq., for their Members in Parliament, folio broadside, *curious*, 6*s* *For B. D., in Fleet Street*, 1702

131 — Whitehall, August 19th.—Express arrived this day with Letters from the Army in Germany, folio broadside, 10*s* 6*d* *Edw. Jones, in the Savoy*, 1704

This is the original account of the Battle of Blenheim, fought 13th August, sent from the Duke of Marlborough's camp at Steinheim, August 17, N.S., with a list of the chief Prisoners taken.

132 — Windsor, August 13th, 1704.—Lord Tunbridge arrived here this morning, bringing the Duke of Marlborough's Letter to Mr. Secretary Harley, reporting the Victory over the French and Bavarians at Hochstet; also Sir George Rooke's Account of the taking Gibraltar, folio broadside, *curious*, 6*s* *Edw. Jones, in the Savoy*, 1704

133 — Whitehall, August 10th.—Duke of Marlborough's Dispatch, by his Aide-de-Camp Colonel Park, of his Victory over the French at Hochstetten, Aug. 13, folio broadside, 5*s* *Edw. Jones*, 1704

134 — True Account of the Stopping of the D—e of M. and my L—d G—d—hin, on Tuesday last, as they were going for Holland, and bringing them back again to London, folio broadside, 3*s* *J. Middleton, no date*

135 — Jack Ketch; Letter to — P—tts, M.P., and First President of the March Club, in relation to a *Preface* which has made some noise (in reference to Bp. Hoadly) folio broadside, 3*s*

136 — List of those worthy Patriots, who, to prevent the Church of England being undermined, voted that the Bill to prevent Occasional Conformity might be Tackt to the Land-tax Bill, folio broadside, *curious*, 6*s* .. .. *Oxford*, 1705

This is the original List of what were popularly called the Tackers.

137 — Health to the Tackers, a New Song, with the Music, folio broadside, 5*s* .. .. .. *Oxford*, 1705

At the back is another in MS. called the Aylesbury Ballad, and another "Upon the Tackers, spoke by the K. of France."

138 — List of the 134 Tackers, in Manuscript, folio broadside, 2*s* 6*d*

139 — Letter from the States-General to his Grace the Duke of Marlborough, in French and English, folio broadside, 2*s* *M. Jones*, 1706

140 — New Ode; or, Dialogue between Mars, God of War, and Plutus, or Mammon, God of Riches, performed in an Entertainment made for his Grace the Duke of Marlborough at Vintner's Hall, City, December 19th, folio broadside, 5*s* *J. Bland*, 1706

141 ANNE.—The Newberry Skirmish; a relation of the Fight that happened there, between the Towns-men and Soldiers, about Pressing Men, folio broadside, 3*s* 6*d* .. *T. Curtis*, 1706

Contains also an account of the murder of Lieut. Blake, by a butcher at Market Drayton, Shropshire, who clove the Lieut.'s head with his cleaver for Listing his brother.

142 — London.—True Copy of the Last Will and Testament of Mr. Benjamin Dod, Citizen and Linen Draper, who lately fell from his Horse, and Died soon after, folio broadside, *curious*, 6*s* 1706

"I will have no Presbyterians, Moderate Low-Churchmen, or Occasional Conformists, to be at my Funeral."

143 — Mr. J. Wight's Speech to the Queen at Somerset House, Dec. 31, for the Victory obtained over the French at Ramillies, folio broadside, 2*s* .. .. .. *J. Read*, 1707

144 — Elegy on the Death of the most valiant Sir Cloudesley Shovel, Admiral of the Fleet in the Mediterranean, drowned Oct. 10, 1707, folio broadside, 3*s* .. .. 1707

145 — The Save-alls, *Poetry*, folio broadside, *curious*, 5*s* *In writing*, April, 1710

Archbishop Sharp, Bishops Compton, Crew, Sprat, Hooper, Dawes, and Burnet are here immortalized.

146 — Dr. Henry Sacheverell's Answer to the Impeachment against him for High Crimes and Misdemeanors, 6 leaves, folio, *manuscript, in a good hand*, 10*s*

The Articles against him were for Two Sermons he preached at Derby Assizes in August, 1709, and before the Lord Mayor of London, in November, the same year.

147 — List of the Peers who gave Judgment in Dr. Sacheverell's Trial, Mar. 20, 1709-10, folio broadside, 2*s* .. 1710

148 — Alphabetical List of the Names of the Lords and Commons who were for Dr. H. Sacheverell, *portrait in an oval*, folio broadside, 7*s* 6*d* .. .. .. .. 1710

VERY RARE, this Portrait is *not mentioned* by Noble in his continuation of Granger. It has no engraver's name, but is a very pretty portrait.

149 — Impartial Account of what passed in the Last Session of Parliament relating to Dr. Henry Sacheverell, *fine portrait*, folio, *sewed*, 3*s* 6*d* .. .. .. *Jacob Tonson*, 1710

150 — List of the Mobb sent to the Savoy for breeding Riots and Disorders in and about London, pulling down Meeting Houses, &c., folio broadside, 2*s* .. .. *R. Hawkins*, 1710

This was a Sacheverell riot, 255 incarcerated; with all their names given.

151 — Bishop of Salisbury, Oxford, Lincoln, and Norwich's Speeches on the 1st and 2nd Articles of Impeachment of Sacheverell, folio, 2*s* .. .. .. *J. Morphew*, 1710

152 — Speech of a Noble Peer in the Lords, containing the Tryal of Sacheverell, folio broadside, 2*s* .. *P. Crawley*, 1710

153 — Tale of a Disbanded Courtier, POETRY, folio broadside, 5*s* *Private*, 1710

Dr. H. Sacheverell and Sir George Rook, Admiral, alluded to.

154 — List of the Parliament summoned at Westminster, Nov. 25, 1710, folio broadside, 5*s* .. .. *John Nutt*, 1710

155 — Tale of a Kettle, by a Person of Quality, POETRY, folio broadside, 4*s* .. .. .. *Cambridge*, 1710

156 ANNE.—Tub and Pulpit, a Dialogue between an Old Cloak of Forty-one and a Rusty Gown of Eighty-eight, written by the Man in the Moon, POETRY, folio broadside, *curious*, 5s. *Private*, 1710

The Cloak is Bishop Burnet.

157 — The Westminster Combat, 22 *verses*, folio broadside, *curious*, 6s. .. .. .. .. No date

Margins annotated, Lord Wm. Poulet, General Stanhope, Spencer, Cooper, Mountague, Attorney General, Sir Joseph Jekell, lampooned.

158 — Advice to the Queen, POETRY, folio broadside, 4s *In writing*, April, 1710

159 — The Court Lady's Tale; or, a Tale from the D(uke) of M(arlborough), POETRY, folio broadside, 5s .. *Private*, 1710

At the back is an "Address from the City of London to Her Majesty on the late tumultuous Assemblies."—*John Morfew*, 1710.

160 — Proclamation Commanding all Papists to Depart from London and from within 10 miles of it, dated March 15th, folio broadside, *black letter*, 5s .. .. *Hills' Assigns*, 1710-11

161 — Proclamation for encouraging Seamen to Enter themselves on Board Her Majesty's Ships of War, folio broadside, *black letter*, 5s .. .. *Hills' Assigns, Jan.* 21, 1710-11

162 — Proclamation for the Suppressing of Riots in London, Mar. 17th, folio broadside, *black letter*, 5s .. *John Baskett*, 1711

163 — Marlborough Turned Out; or, the Downfall of a Great Favourite, with a List of all the New Promotions at Court, with POETRY, folio broadside, *curious*, 6s .. .. *J. Tomson*, 1711

At the back is "Prince Eugene's Speech to the Queen and Parliament, Dec. 13, 1711."

164 — Resolutions Without Doors upon the Resolutions Within Doors, 5th March, folio broadside, 3s 6d .. *Private*, 1711

165 — The W(in)ds(o)r Prophecy, *Prose and Poetry*, folio broadside, *curious*, 6s .. .. .. *Private*, 1711

Writing on the Margins "John Bishop of Bristol, L. P. S., Earl of Nottingham, Dutchess of Somerset, Mrs. Hill, Lady Massam," refer to characters in the Poetry.

166 — The Thanksgiving, a New Protestant BALLAD, 18 verses, folio broadside, *curious*, 5s .. .. .. 1711

167 — Toast for A(nn)e and Robin (Robert Walpole) in the French Wine POETRY, folio broadside, *rare*, 7s 6d *John Turnham*, 1711

168 — Report from the Committee of the House of Commons to Enquire how far the Imprest Accountants have passed their Accounts, with the Resolutions of the House thereon, folio, 8 leaves, 4s *S. Keble*, 1711

169 — Duke of Marlborough's Speech in the House of Lords, December 8th, on the Prospect of Peace, folio broadside, 3s 6d 1711

170 — Song sung at the Bowling Green House, April 30th, 1711, on the Anniversary of the Duke of Ormond's Birth-day, folio broadside, *curious*, 5s .. .. *Dublin, F. Dickson*, 1711

171 — An Excellent New Song, being the intended Speech of a famous Orator against Peace, POETRY, folio broadside, *very curious*, 10s .. .. .. *No Place or Name*

Allusion made to Daniel Finch, Earl of Nottingham, (who had the nick-name of the Dismal Orator) and the Duke and Duchess of Marlborough.

172 ANNE.—T(o)l(an)d's Invitation to Dismal, to Dine with the Calves' Head Club, Poetry, folio broadside, *very curious*, 10*s* *Jan.* 29, 1711

Margins annotated by a Contemporary, Dismal is Daniel Finch, Earl of Nottingham, Earls Godolphin, Scarborough, Cholmley, Robert Walpole, and many others alluded to.

173 — Exact List of those worthy Patriots who have, in one Session, Detected the Mismanagements of the late M—ry, discovered the Abuses in the Victualling and other Public Offices, Overturned the Fanaticks, added 50 New Churches to London, &c., folio broadside, *curious*, 6*s* .. .. *John Baker*, 1711

Those with this mark + before them are of the October Club.

174 — List of the Voters taken at Aylesbury, Buckinghamshire, Oct. 4 and 5, 1710, Viscount Fermanagh and Sir Edmund Denton returned, folio, 27 leaves, 5*s* .. .. 1711

175 — Full and True Account of the Notorious and Bloody Murder designed upon the Lord Treasurer (Harley) by Guiscard, folio broadside, *rare*, 10*s* .. .. *R. Newcomb*, 1711

176 — The Dangerous Present; an Account of a barbarous designed Plot against the Lord High Treasurer (Harley, Earl of Oxford), folio, *three leaves, rare*, 10*s* *J. Reed, in White Fryers, no date*

This Present was a box containing three Pistols loaded with slugs and bullets, and so contrived that on the opening they would discharge.

177 — The Examiner (by Swift), Sept. 14 to 21, 1710; ditto, May 31 to June 7, 1711; ditto, April 10 to 17, 1712; Daily Courant, Dec. 5, 1711, folio, 4 *leaves, curious*, 5*s* *John Morphew*, 1710-12

178 — Some Reasons, which may serve as a Vindication of a certain Pat(rio)t for leaving his Friends, folio broadside, 2*s* *Private*, 1711-12

179 — Copy of a Letter taken up in the Court of Requests, and directed to a W—g M—b—r (Earl of Nottingham pointed at), folio broadside, 3*s* .. *No Printer, Jan.*, 1711-12

180 — Letter from the States-General to Queen Anne about the Duke of Ormond's Orders not to Fight, folio broadside, 2*s* 6*d* 1712

181 — Jack Ketch.—Speech of John Ketch, Esq., at the Burning of a late Scandalous and Malicious *Preface*, folio broadside, 3*s* 1712

A lampoon on Hoadley, Bishop of Bangor. See No. 135.

182 — Remarks on the Letter sent by the D—— of M—— to the Commissioner of Accounts, folio broadside, 3*s* *J(ohn) D(unton)*, 1712

183 — Treaty between Her Majesty and the States-General, for Securing the Succession to the Crown of Great Britain, and for Settling a Barrier for the States-General against France, folio, 36 pages, 7*s* 6*d* .. .. .. *Sam. Keble*, 1712,

184 — The D(uk)e and D(uches)s of M(arlboroug)h's loss; being an Estimate of their former yearly Income, folio broadside, *curious*, 7*s* 6*d* .. .. .. .. 1712

185 — True Copy of a Paper stuck upon the D(uke) of M(arlborough)'s Gate at St. James's, on Saturday last, being the day of Her Majesty's Accession to the Crown, POETRY, folio broadside, *curious*, 6*s* .. .. .. *R. Mott*, 1712

186 ANNE.—Substance of the Depositions taken at the Coroner's Inquest, in November, on the Bodies of Duke Hamilton and My Lord Mohun, engaged in a Duel, folio, one leaf, *curious*, 5*s* *A. Baldwin*, 1712

187 — Beware of the Pretender; or, a Great Hurricane at Court; for they are all fallen out at last, folio, 3 *leaves*, *rare*, 6*s* *J. Reed*, 1712

Relates the disgrace of Lady Massam and Lord Bolingbroke.

188 — Account of a Great Duel fought between Mr. Henry Pine, son to the late Lord Chief Justice of Ireland, and Theophilus Biddulph, Esq., with the Apprehending the Seconds, and their Examination before Justice Medlicot, folio, 3 leaves, rare, 10*s* *J. Reed*, 1712

On the back of one leaf is printed—"The London Miracle, being a Strange Account of a Scroll of Vellum found in the White of an Egg, predicting the Peace, 29th September, 1712." Written by Dr. Partridge, with his opinion thereon.

189 — It's Ten to One we're all Undone: or the Tories all Bewitch'd, folio, 3 leaves, *curious*, 6*s* .. *R. Newcomb*, 1713

Sacheverell, Marlborough, Sunderland, Godolphin, Wharton, Prior, mentioned.

190 — Tryal of Geo. Redpath, Gent. Author of the Flying Post, Feb. 19, 1712, for Libels against the Government, before Lord Chief Justice Parker, folio, 3 leaves, 5*s* .. *J. Read*, 1713

191 — The Merchant A-la-mode, POETRY, to the Tune of "Which nobody can deny," folio, 3 leaves, RARE, 6*s* *R. Newcomb*, 1713

192 — The Merchant A-la-mode, to the Tune of the "Commons and Peers," POETRY, folio, *manuscript*, 5*s*

To this is added another Poem in manuscript called "*The British Ambassadress' Speech to the French King.*"

193 — Full Account of a Horrid and Barbarous Plot against the Queen and Government, with the Apprehending 4 of the Plotters, and their Commitment to Newgate, folio, 3 leaves, 6*s* *J. Read*, 1713

With "Lord M——n's Ghost to the D—— of R——nd on Sunday night last, concerning the murder of Duke Hamilton and the Peace." A piece of *Poetry*.

194 — True Copy of Mr. Richard Noble's Original Paper, which he designed for his last Speech, with an Account of his behaviour before his Execution, folio, 3 leaves, 3*s* *Sam. Keble*, 1713

*Some of the most eminent Authors of this period were engaged in these lampoons,* SWIFT, POPE, GAY, DR. ARBUTHNOT, *and the celebrated* MRS. MANLEY.

195 QUEEN ANNE and KING GEORGE I.—The Art of Restoring; or the Piety and Probity of General Monk in bringing about the last Restoration, 1714.—The Art of Canvassing at Elections (a curious piece), 1714.—Method for Executing the Powers relating to the Militia and Trained Bands, 1684.—Mr. Walpole's case, in a Letter from a Tory M.P. to his Friend in the Country, 1712.—Brockwell's Chronological History of Great Britain, 1719-20.—Memoirs relating to the Restoration of King James I. of Scotland—in 1 vol. small 8vo. *half bound, clean and neat*, 12*s*

Collected by Sir Edmund Bacon, with his Autograph on the title page of one of the Tracts; has also a Sermon by Abp. Tillotson, a 5th of November Sermon by Bradshaw, 1714, and Webster's Essay on Book-keeping, 1721, with his Directions for the Writing School, 1721.

For a number of other very curious and scarce pamphlets and broadsides, collected by SIR EDMUND BACON, who was MEMBER for NORWICH during the greater part of the Reign of QUEEN ANNE. See CHARLES I. and II., CROMWELL, JAMES II., WILLIAM and MARY, and K. GEORGE I.

196 ANNONII *(Monachi Benedictini)* de Regum procerumq. Francorum origine Gestisq. libri V., *nunc primum impressi,* small folio, *vellum,* 12*s* .. *Parisiis, I. Badius Ascensius,* 1514

With Jehan Petit's Device, the Title page in a compartment cut in wood.

197 ANNUAL BIOGRAPHY and OBITUARY, 1818, 1819, 1820, 1826, 1828, 1829, 1830, 1832, 1833, 1834, 8vo. *cloth,* 3*s* 6*d* per volume, (*published at* 15*s each.*)

These may be considered Supplemental to Chalmers' Biographical Dictionary, 32 vols. 8vo. which was completed in 1817.

198 ANSON'S (George, Lord) Voyage round the World in 1740 to 1744, compiled by Richard Walter, 42 *maps, charts, and plates,* 9th edition, 4to. *old calf, neat,* 14*s* .. .. 1756

199 — Another copy; 4to. *russia extra,* £1 11*s* 6*d* 1756

"Anson's Voyage will contribute more to call forth genius, and open the blossoms of the mind, than a dull didactic treatise of the most sagacious philosopher."—*Knox's Essays.*

200 — Life, by Sir J. Barrow, *portrait,* 8vo. *cloth,* 6*s* (*published at* 14*s*) .. .. .. .. 1839

201 ANSTED, Smith, Breen, Scoffern, and Lowe's Natural History of the Inanimate Creation, *numerous plates,* thick 8vo. *cloth, gilt, new,* 8*s* 6*d* .. .. .. 1856

202 ANSTEY'S (Christopher) New Bath Guide, Memoirs of the B-n-r-d Family, Poetical Epistles, *plate,* small 8vo. *calf, gilt,* 3*s* 6*d* 1772

Very clever, amusing, and witty, hitting off with admirable dexterity the follies of his day.

203 ANTHOLOGIA; seu, Florilegium Græco-Latinum, hoc est Veterum Græcorum Epigrammata, latino carmine a doctissimis Viris conversa, et recens edita ab Hier. Megisero, 2 vols. in 1, thick 8vo. 1110 pages, *old binding,* 8*s* *Francofurti, sumptibus authoris,* 1602

"Edition peu commune."—*Brunet.*

204 ANTIQUARIAN SOCIETY, Catalogue of the Printed Books in the Library of the Society of Antiquaries of London, 4to. *sewed,* 7*s* 6*d* *Bensley,* 1816

"This valuable Catalogue of the Society's Library will be found most useful to persons writing on Antiquarian subjects."

205 ANTONINI (Marci, *Imperatoris)* de Rebus suis, libri XII., Gr. et Lat., Gatakeri, necnon M. A. Vita, aucta G. Stanhope, *portrait,* 4to. *old calf, neat,* 6*s* .. .. *Londini,* 1697

"A good edition."—*Lowndes.*

206 ANTONINO, Vita, Gesti, Costumi, Discorsi et Lettere di Marco Aurelio Imperatore, small 8vo. *nice copy in calf,* 8*s* *Venetia, Heredi del Bonelli,* 1574

An edition of the Life of the Emperor Marcus Aurelius Antoninus, (probably from the Spanish of Antonio de Guevara, Bishop of Cadiz), not mentioned by Haym. The name of the translator of this Italian version is not given.

207 ANTWERP, Historia Episcopatus Antverpiensis, continens Episcoporum Seriem, et Capitulorum Abbatiarum, et Monasteriorum Fundationes; *many views of cathedrals by Harrewyn, the arms emblazoned,* small 4to. *vellum,* 10*s* 6*d* *Bruxellis, F. Foppens,* 1717

Exhibita pro Schemate Historiæ Ecclesiasticæ Omnium Episcopatuum Belgii.

208 APOLLONII Pergæi Conicorum libri VIII., et Sereni Antissensis de Sectione Cylindri et Coni libri II., Gr. et Lat., Edente Edw. Halley, fol., LARGE PAPER, *good copy, in old calf,* £1 1*s* *Oxoniæ,* 1710

This is the best edition."—*Dr. Adam Clarke.*

209 APOLLONII RHODII ARGONAUTICA, Græcè, cum notis Variorum et Brunckii, small 8vo. *fine copy, in russia,* 5*s* *Argentorati,* 1780

210 — Idem, small 8vo. *calf, very neat,* 4*s* 6*d* *Argentorati,* 1780

"Brunck has performed the part of a skilful interpreter of the Text; the notes and emendations are superior to those of preceding editors."—*Dr. Dibdin.*

211 APOLLONIUS TYANÆUS, his Life. See Houtteville.

212 APTHORPE'S (East) Letters on the prevalence of Christianity before its Civil Establishment, 8vo. *bds.* 3*s* 6*d*—*calf, neat,* 5*s* 1778

Contains also an answer to Gibbon's Rome, and a "Large and useful Catalogue of Historians."—*Gibbon,* who writes very flatteringly of him.

213 APULEIUS, Cupid and Psyche, a Mythological Tale, from the Golden Ass of Apuleius, (by Hudson Gurney, Esq.) 2 *plates,* royal 8vo. *boards,* 6*s* .. .. *Bulmer,* 1800

Most elegantly printed. "An excellent Poetical Translation of the most beautiful Story which antiquity has left to us."—*Lowndes.*

214 ARABIAN NIGHTS' ENTERTAINMENTS, Englished from the French of Galland, by G. S. Beaumont, *plates,* 4 vols. royal 12mo. *boards,* 12*s* (*pub. at* 36*s*) .. .. 1811

Valuable for "accurately describing the Manners, Customs, Laws, and Religion of the Eastern Nations."

215 — Another edition, translated by Forster, 600 *engravings,* large 8vo. *cloth,* 12*s*

216 — Tales from ditto, 40 *plates,* square 18mo. *cloth,* 2*s* 1841

217 ARAM (Eugene) his Trial and Life, with his Letters and Poems, and Anglo-Celtic Lexicon, 12mo. *bds.* 2*s* (*pub. at* 3*s*) *Richmond,* 1832

218 ARBUTHNOT (Dr. John) Tables of the Grecian, Roman, and Jewish Measures, Weights, and Coins, reduced to the English Standard, oblong 4to. VERY SCARCE, *sewed,* 6*s* *London, Ralph Smith, no date*

Dedicated to "His Royal Highness the Prince," (George of Denmark) to whom he was Physician. These tables are engraved by *Sturt* on 14 leaves, and are not mentioned by *Lowndes,* the *Retrospective Review,* or elsewhere, that I can find; they are anterior to 1727, when the Doctor published his "Tables of Ancient Coins," 4to.

219 ARCANI Politici de i Prencipi d'Italia, 12mo. *old vellum,* 6*s* *Villa Franca, no Printer's name,* 1669

This is an earlier book, by two years, than any mentioned by *Dr. Cotton* in his *Typographical Gazetteer,* as printed at either of the *Villa Francas,*—"The contents of which were of such a nature as to make it necessary for the Authors and Publishers to disguise themselves as much as possible."

220 ARCHÆOLOGIA: Tracts relating to Antiquity, vol. 1 to 26, with Index to the first 15 vols. *plates,* 4to. good set, *half bound in russia,* £15 15*s* .. .. 1770-1835

Two of these volumes are so scarce, having accidentally been burnt, that alone they have been known to produce £8 at auction.

221 — Vols. 13 to 23, 4to. *sewed,* £3 .. 1800-1831

222 — Vol. 17, *sewed,* 6*s*; Vol. 18, Part 2, 4*s* .. 1814-1817

223 — Index to the 1st 15 Vols. of ditto, 4to. *sewed,* 8*s* 1809

224 ARCHÆOLOGICAL JOURNAL, published by the British Archæological Association for the Encouragement of Researches into the Arts and Monuments of the Early and Middle Ages, *numerous plates,* vols. 1, 2, and 3, 8vo. *half calf, gilt, cost two guineas,* £1 1*s* .. .. .. 1845—46

225 ARCHÆOLOGIST and Journal of Antiquarian Science, edited by James O. Halliwell, Esq., 8vo. *cloth neat,* 6*s* 6*d* (pub. at 10*s* 6*d*) 1842

226 ARCHBOLD'S Summary of the Law relative to Pleading and Evidence in Criminal Cases, by Jervis, 12mo. *bound,* 3*s* 6d 1838

227 ARCHITECTURE.—Rudiments of Ancient Architecture, containing Extracts from Vitruvius, Pliny, &c., with a Dictionary of Terms, *plates, and portrait of James Stuart,* royal 8vo. *boards, scarce,* 6*s* 1794

"A very useful work."—*Lowndes.*

228 — Architectural Notes on the German Churches, with Remarks on the Origin of Gothic Architecture, 4 *plates by the Storers,* 8vo. *cloth,* SCARCE, 9*s* (*pub. at* 16*s*) .. *Cambridge,* 1830

229 — Glossary of Terms used in Grecian, Roman, Italian, and Gothic Architecture, the fifth edition, enlarged, 3 vols. 8vo. *with* 1,700 *woodcuts, cloth,* £1 18*s* (*pub. at* £2 8*s*) .. 1850

230 ARETINO (Pietro) Lettere, *fine portrait in title page,* small 8vo. *old calf, stained,* 12*s*
*In Vinegia, per Nicolo d'Aristotele detto Zoppino,* 1538

The principal part of these letters are dated 1537; there are a few as early as 1524. On the title is "A Podio et amicorum."

231 ARETINO.—Libro Secondo delle Lettere scritte al Signor P. Aretino, da Molti Signori, dedicate al Rev. Signor Lodovico Beccatelli, small 8vo. *fine copy in the original binding,* £1 1*s*
*In Venetia, per Francesco Marcolini,* 1551

"Ce recueil de Lettres est rare et recherché."—*Peignot.* The Capital letters have a singular appearance, and the volume looks as if it were written. The letters are dated 1539 to 1551. "Pietro Aretino, Paolo Manuzio and Bonfadio are also celebrated for their style."—*Hallam.*

232 ARGALUS and PARTHENIA, the Unfortunate Lovers: or, the Famous and Renowned History of Argalus and Parthenia, *wood cuts,* 12mo. *half calf,* CURIOUS, 5*s* *Printed by W. Onley,* 1703

Both Sir Philip Sidney and Francis Quarles wrote a History of Argalus and Parthenia, but this differs from both; there are four books all separately paged. Not in *Lowndes.*

233 ARGENTI (Borso, *Nobile Ferrarese*) la Prigione, Comedia, 12mo. *parchment, scarce,* 10*s* *Vinetia, Marchio Sessa,* 1587

"In carattere molto bello. E'una delle migliori Commedie, che si abbiano in nostra Lingua."—*Haym.* The title page presents us with Sessia's Cat., a passport for its scarcity. See *Liburnio.*

234 ARISTOTELIS de Arte Rhetorica, libri III., Græcè, small 8vo. *old calf,* 6*s* .. .. *Basileæ, apud Isingrinium,* 1546

This is an early edition and rare, I cannot find it mentioned anywhere.

235 — de Mundo, Græcè, cum duplici Interp. Latinâ, cum Scholiis et Castigat. B. Vulcanii, 8vo. *old calf,* 3*s* *L. Bat., Plantin,* 1591

236 — Poetica, ab Antonio Riccobono Latine Conversa, ejusdem Riccoboni Paraphrasis et Ars Comica, 4to. *fine copy in old calf gilt, scarce,* 7*s* 6*d* .. .. .. *Patavii,* 1587

237 ARISTOTELIS et THEOPHRASTI scripta quædam, Græcè, small 8vo. *old calf neat,* 6*s* .. *Parisiis, H. Stephani,* 1557

"A very rare and valuable book."—*Thomas Taylor, the Platonist.*

238 ARISTOTLE'S Metaphysics, translated from the Greek, with Notes, and a Dissertation on Nullities and diverging Series, by Thomas Taylor, 4to. *boards*, SCARCE, £1 1*s* (*pub. at* £2 2*s*) 1801

This is the first edition containing the elaborate *Introduction*, 55 pages, and Essay on *Nullities*, both omitted in the second. The best translation.

239 — Ethicks and Politics, translated, with an Analysis of his Speculative Works by Dr. John Gillies, 2 vols. 8vo. *calf, very neat*, 7*s* 6*d* 1804

240 — POETICA, vulgarizzata et sposta per Lodovico Castelvetro, small thick 4to. of 392 leaves, *old vellum, rare*, £3 3*s* *Stampata in Vienna d' Austria, par Gaspar Stainhofer*, 1570

"Rarissima."—*Haym*. "Edit. originale et assez rare, d'une traduction qui est regardée comme le meilleur ouvrage de son auteur." Vend 120 fr.—*Brunet*.

241 — Les Politiques d'Aristote, trad. en François par Louis Le Roy, folio, fine copy, *old calf*, 12*s* *Paris, par M. de Vascosan*, 1576

At the end of this volume is "De la Vicissitude ou Varieté des choses en l'Unnivers," par Loys Le Roy. *Paris*, 1579. Sir Christopher Hatton's Copy.

242 — Golius (Theoph.) Epitome Doctrinæ Politicæ ex Octo libris Politicorum Aristotelis collecta, small 8vo. *old binding*, 4*s* *Argentorati*, 1622

243 ARIOSTO (Lodovico) Orlando Furioso, with Memoirs and Notes by Antonio Panizzi, Esq,, now Principal Librarian of the British Museum, 4 vols. 8vo. *cloth, scarce*, £1 8*s* (*pub. at* £2 8*s*) *W. Pickering*, 1834

244 — con Note e dilucidazioni grammaticali da R. Zotti, 4 vols. 12mo. *half bound, neat*, 12*s* .. .. *Londra*, 1814

245 — Le Satire di Ariosto, small 8vo. 32 leaves, *paper cover, rare*, 7*s* 6*d* *In Vinegia, per F. Bindoni et M. Pasini*, 1537

"The Satires of Ariosto are worthy of a place by the side of those of Horace; he produced those Poems (master pieces) towards the end of his life."—See *Quarterly Review*, No. 42. This edition was published close to his death which happened in 1533.

246 ARITHMETIQUE, théorique et pratique, par Eysséric et Gautier, 12mo. *boards*, 1*s* .. .. *Paris*, 1848

247 — Décimale, 12mo. *vellum*, 1*s* 6*d* .. *Paris*, 1850

248 ARMENIAN DICTIONARY, small 8vo. *newly bound*, 14*s* 1698

249 — Poetry on the Birth, Passion, and Death of Jesus Christ, in Armenian, *plates*, small 8vo. *neat*, 10*s*

250 — Psalms of David, *plates*, 8vo. *foreign impressed binding, scarce*, 12*s*

251 — Psalms of David, in Armenian, 24mo. 321 pages, *bound*, 4*s*

252 — Armenian Religious Instruction, in Armenian, 12mo. *bound*, 4*s*

253 — Explanation of the Armenian Religion, in the Armenian Language, small 4to. *foreign binding*, 10*s* 6*d*

Autograph of T. Arratoon.

254 — Book of Prayers, in the Armenian Language, 8vo. *foreign binding*, 12*s* .. .. .. 1790

"T. Arratoon.—This book was the gift of my dear father, 1790."

255 ARNAUDI (Andreæ) Joci, Epistolæ, Rara, P. Guirandi Alosiani Margarita, Epigrammata, Tumuli, Apologiæ, 12mo. *vellum wrapper*, 5*s* .. .. .. *Parisiis*, 1609

I can no where find this Author or the Work mentioned. It wants a leaf at the end.

256 ARNISÆI (Henningi, *Halberstadiensis*) de Jure Majestatis libri III.; de autoritate Principum in Populum semper inviolabili; de Jure Connubiorum; de Subjectione et exemtione Clericorum, 4 vols. in 1, thick 4to. of, collectively, 1,200 pages, *fine clean copies in vellum*, 12*s* .. *Argentorati*, 1635—6

"These Political Writings are written to counteract the opinions of Althusius, who wrote in favor of the Sovereignty of the People; Arnisæus contends for their allegiance. Boecler and Grotius speak of Arnisæus with respect."—*General Dictionary.*

257 ARNOLD'S Chronicle of the Customs of London, containing, among divers other matters, the original of the NUT-BROWN MAID, 4to. *boards*, £1 5*s* .. .. .. 1811

Edited by Mr. Douce, "A faithful Reprint with a judicious Introduction."—*Lowndes.* Contains one of the most exquisite Old Poems in our language—The "Nut Brown Maid."

258 ARNOLD (T. K.) Eclogæ Horatianæ, pars II. Sermones, 12mo. *half calf neat*, 3*s* (*cost* 7*s*) .. .. *Rivington*, 1843

259 ARNOTT'S (Dr. N.) Elements of Physics or Natural Philosophy, explained independently of Technical Mathematics, 8vo. *boards*, SCARCE, 14*s* .. .. .. 1828

260 ARRIANI de Expedit. Alex. Magni Historia, lib. VIII., Gr. et Lat., edidit B. Vulcanii, folio, *calf, very neat*, 7*s* 6*d* *Excudebat H. Stephanus*, 1575

This is the first *critical* edition of Alexander's Expedition by Arrian.

261 ARRIANO di Nicomedia, chiamato nuovo Xenofonte de i fatti del Magno Alessandro Re di Macedonia, trad. in Italiano per Pietro Lauro, small 8vo. *nice clean copy in vellum*, RARE, 10*s* *Venetia, Michele Tramezino*, 1544

The only Translation into Italian of Arrian. Re-printed at Verona in 1730.

262 ARTICULI LAMBETHANI, curâ F. G., *Londini*, 1651.—Fur Prædestinatus, 1651, 12mo. *calf, very neat, scarce*, 9*s* 1651

Abp. Sancroft, the author of Fur Prædestinatus. See his Life.

263 ARTICLES agreed upon by the Archbishop and Bishops of both Provinces and the whole Clergy in the Convocation, holden at London, 1562, small 4to. *sewed, uncut, rare, clean*, 7*s* 6*d* *Bill and Barker*, 1675

264 ARTICLES of Religion of the Church of England, temp. King Edward VI. and Queen Elizabeth, *fine portrait of Cranmer*, 4to. *boards, scarce*, 10*s* 6*d* .. .. *Nicholls*, 1811

Only a few of these printed for presentation by the late Dr. Burney. The Articles of 1553, 1562, MS; 1563 and 1571 are presented parallelwise on each opening. Six different editions.

265 ARTICLES of Lincoln Diocese, see *Lincoln*

266 ARTHUR.—La Mort d'Arthure; the History of King Arthur and of the Knights of the Round Table, by Sir Thomas Malory, Knt., 3 vols. 12mo. *cloth*, 15*s*—and L. P. £1 2*s* 6*d* *J. R. Smith*, 1858

Edited from the rare edition of 1634, with Introduction and Notes by Thos. Wright, Esq., F.S.A.

"This is good stuffe for wise men to laugh at, or honest men to take pleasure at."—*Roger Ascham.* "Sir Thomas Malory compiled from various French Authorities his celebrated 'Morté d'Arthur,' indisputably the best Prose Romance the language can boast."—*Sir Walter Scott.*

267 — his Life, by Joseph Ritson, crown 8vo. *boards*, 9*s* *W. Nicol*, 1825

"No more our long-lost Arthur we bewail."—*Gray*

This curious Work, compiled from ancient Historians and authentic documents, was prepared for the press by Mr. Ritson a short time before his death.—See *Advertisement.*

268 ARUNDELL'S (Fr. V. J.) Visit to the Churches of Asia, with an Excursion into Pisidia, &c., *map and 22 plates of Inscriptions*, 8vo. *half calf neat*, 5s 6d .. .. 1828

269 ASCHAM'S (Roger) Scholemaster; a Plain and Perfect Way of Teaching the Learned Languages, revised by James Upton, 8vo. *calf, very fine clean copy*, 6s .. .. 1714

Roger Ascham, Tutor to Queen Elizabeth. "Ascham is a great name in our National Literature; he was one of the first founders of a true English style in Prose composition."—*Retrospective Review.*

270 ASH'S (Dr. John) Dictionary of the English Language, 2 vols. 8vo. *calf, neat, scarce*, 10s .. .. 1775

271 — Another copy, 2 vols. 8vo. *sheep*, 8s .. 1775

Contains many obsolete words used by Shakspere and his contemporaries, and many other words not to be found in modern Dictionaries.

272 ASHE (Tho.) Fasciculus Florum: or, a Handfull of Flowers, gathered out of Sir Edward Coke's Bookes, 18mo. *neat, scarce*, 4s 1618

273 ASHMOLE'S (Elias) History of the most noble Order of the Garter, &c., *portrait of the Prince of Wales, and plates*, 8vo. *old calf, scarce*, 6s .. .. .. 1715

An account of the Town, Castle, Chappel, and College of Windsor, with their several Officers, Habits, Ensigns, &c.

274 ASIATIC ANNUAL REGISTER, by Lawrence Dundas Campbell, 12 vols. 8vo. *calf, neat*, £2 2s .. 1799-1811

275 ASIATIC JOURNAL and Monthly Register for British India and its Dependencies, 12 vols. 8vo. *half russia, very neat*, £1 4s 1816 to 1821

276 ASIATIC RESEARCHES, into the History and Antiquities, Arts, Sciences, and Literature of Asia, vols. 1 to 10, 8vo. *plates, boards*, £1 11s 6d .. .. 1806-1811

"They are full of the most curious and valuable intelligence in every possible form, and on every possible subject."—*Dr. Dibdin.*

277 ASTLE (Thomas) on the Origin and Progress of Writing, as well Hieroglyphic as Elementary, *illustrated by Engravings taken from Marbles, MSS. &c., portrait*, 4to. BEST EDITION, *fine copy, in calf*, £1 16s *(pub. at* £3 13s 6d) .. 1803

Mr. Astle was keeper of the Records in the Tower of London.

278 ASTRY'S (Sir James) General Charge to all Grand Juries, and other Juries, with advice to those of Life and Death, Nisi Prius, &c., and a Discourse of the Antiquity, Power, and Duty of Juries, 8vo. *vellum, neat*, 3s .. .. 1725

"The very learned Sir J. Astry, Knight, was in the Commission of the Peace for Bedfordshire, and this Charge was considered so very excellent that it was deemed worth republishing." Autograph of *W. Rawlinson*," and *Book Plates.*

279 ASTRONOMY, Découverte de Deux Nouvelles Planetes autour de Saturne, 8 *astronomical plates*, folio, *old red morocco, royal arms on the sides*, £1 5s *Paris, Sebast. Mabre-Cramoisy*, 1673

Dedicated "Au Roy" par Cassini, not in Brunet. A nice specimen of old red Morocco binding.

280 ATHENÆUM, Catalogue of the Library of the Athenæum, London, with the Supplement, 2 vols. royal 8vo. *half morocco, good as new*, 25*s* .. *Printed for the Members*, 1845-51

Has a Classified Index of Subjects.

281 ATHENÆUS, Natale de Comitibus Veneto nunc primum è Græca in Latinam linguam vertente, folio, *limp vellum*, 10*s* *Venetiis, apud A. Arrivabenum*, 1556

282 ATHENAGORÆ Atheniensis Apologia pro Christianis et de Resurrectione Mortuorum, Gr. et Lat., 8vo. *old calf, neat*, 7*s* *Parisiis, H. Stephani*, 1557

A very beautifully printed volume, RARE, *Harles*. This is the FIRST edition of the Apology.

283 ATKINSON'S (James) Account of the State of Agriculture and Grazing in New South Wales, *View of Sydney, and coloured plates*, 8vo. *half calf, neat*, 3*s* 6*d* .. 1826

284 ATLAS, Chambers' Atlas for the People, 32 quarto and 4 folio maps, in 1 vol. 4to. *coloured*, 15*s* .. .. 1858

285 ATTERSOLL'S (William) Commentarie on the Epistle of St. Paule to Philemon, small folio, *newly hf. bd. in calf, very neat*, 12*s* 1612

At the back of the title is "*John Cooke* (of Holkham), 1711, *his booke, given to him by Mrs. Manley*." For an account of Mrs. Manley, a most celebrated woman, who assisted Dean Swift in the *Examiner*, and was the author of the *Memoirs of the New Atlantis*, for writing which she was confined.—See *Baker's Biog. Dramat.*

286 AUBERY (Le Sieur) de la Pre-eminence de nos Roys et de leur Preseance sur l'Empereur et le Roy d'Espagne, 4to. *limp parchment, clean and neat, scarce*, 10*s* 6*d* .. *Paris*, 1650

Appended is 1.—Relation Italienne de Michel Suriano Venetien touchant son Ambassade de France, an. 1562; and 2.—Relation Italienne de Bernard Navagero, Venetien et depuis Cardinal, touchant son Ambassade de Rome, an. 1558. Two very curious Treatises.

287 AUBREY'S (John) Letters of Eminent Persons in the 17th and 18th Centuries, with Hearne's Journey to Reading, and Lives of Eminent Men, &c., 3 vols. 8vo. *boards*, 10*s* 6*d* 1813

Edited by John Walker with Biographical and Literary Illustrations.

288 — Miscellanies upon various subjects, with his Life, *portrait and plate*, foolscap 8vo. *cloth, new*, 4*s* *J. R. Smith*, 1857

Treats of Day-Fatality, Dreams, Omens, Apparitions, Impulses, Angels and Spirits, Second-sighted Men, one of the most curious Books of its kind.

289 AUGUSTIN, Les Confessions de S., traduites en François par M. Arnauld D'Andilly, 12mo. *fine copy, in old red morocco, gilt edges, scarce*, 8*s* .. *Paris, Jean Camusat*, 1649

A very elegantly printed little volume, of 600 pages.

290 AULUS GELLIUS, NOCTES ATTICÆ, folio, 196 *unpaged leaves* (Capitulæ 15 leaves, 1 blank, noctes 180 leaves,) *vellum*, £4 4*s* *Venetiis, per Andream Jacobi Catharensem*, 1477

This early edition of Aulus Gellius is described by Beloe in his "Anecdotes of Literature and Scarce Books." It is a fine specimen of Printing, on beautiful paper, interspersed with some very elegantly formed Greek; on the margins is some very old writing. Each book, of which there are nineteen, commences with a handsome ILLUMINATED Capital letter in gold and colours; unfortunately it wants a leaf at the beginning and one at the end, so that the Printer's Name does not appear, however it is sufficiently described by Brunet to identify it. From Lord Leicester's Library at Holkham.

"Belle édition faite sur d'autres MSS. que les trois précédentes (described by Brunet), et plus correctement imprimée."—*Brunet*. "This edition is very scarce and beautiful."—*Moss*. Thysius praises it in the most unqualified terms.

291 AUSTIN'S (William of *Lincolne's Inne*, Esq.) Devotionis Augustinianæ Flamma. Certaine devout, godly, and learned Meditations, set forth by his deare wife, Mrs. Anna A., as a surviving monument of her ever-honoured husband, who changed his life, Jan. 16th, 1633, small folio, *old calf neat*, 7*s* 6*d* *Ralph Mab*, 1635

Interspersed with POETRY, Christmas Carols, &c., and the Author's Epicedium, made by himself upon himself, in Verse.

292 AUTOGRAPH of BEN JONSON, Dramatist, temp. Eliz. and Jac. I., see *Hayward*

293 AUTOGRAPH of LORD TREASURER BURLEIGH, temp. Eliz., see *Zenobius*

294 AUTOGRAPH of Charles Cotton, Isaac Walton's Friend and Coadjutor in his Angler, see *Pinto*

295 AUTOGRAPH Mourning Letter from Sir George Naylor to the Duchess of Wellington, dated Earl Marshall's Office, July 14, 1830, 5*s*

Regretting that the Earl Marshall had already disposed of all the organ-loft Tickets. King George IV. died June 26th this year.

296 BABINGTON'S (Charles C.) Manual of British Botany, 12mo. *cloth*, 6*s* 6*d* (*pub. at* 10*s*) .. .. *Van Voorst*, 1847

Contains the Flowering Plants and Ferns arranged according to the Natural Orders.

297 BABINGTON'S (Bp. Gervase) Comfortable Notes upon every Chapter of Genesis, edited by Miles Smith, afterwards Bishop of Gloucester, small 4to. *wants title, old calf* .. 1596

With Autograph of WILL. SHAKSPERE, as I conjecture.—See *Shakspeare*.

298 BACCII (Andreæ) de Thermis, Libri VII., in quo agitur de Universa Aquarum Natura, de Lacubus, Fontibus, Fluminibus, de Balneis totius orbis, etc., folio, *a fine copy in vellum*, £1 11*s* 6*d* *Venetiis, apud V. Valgrisium*, 1571

"Belle et rare édition d'un ouvrage estimé."—*Brunet*.
A copy sold at the White Knight's sale for £5 10s., and at the La Valliere for £3 4s. It is very beautifully printed by Valgrisius.

299 BACON'S (Lord Chancellor) Wisedome of the Ancients, Englished by Sir Arthur Gorges, Kt., 12mo. *original calf, very scarce*, 10*s* 6*d* *John Bill*, 1619

Dedicated to the Lady Elizabeth, daughter of K. James I., with the Autograph of Edmund Horrex, who had a very curious Library.—See *Blandy* and *Verstegan*.

299*— Sylva Sylvarum; or, Natural Historie, published by Dr. W. Rawley, 2nd edit., folio, *fine clean copy, old calf, neat*, 10*s* 6*d* 1628

This Second Edition is not noticed by Lowndes, it has an engraved title by Thomas Cecill which is dated 1629.

300 — Sylva Sylvarum, a Naturall History, in Ten Centuries—New Atlantis—with the History of Life and Death (of the Prolongation of Life), published by Dr. Will. Rawley, small folio, *old calf*, 8*s* 1651

301 — Essayes or Counsels, Civill and Moral, 4to, *original calf, a fine clean copy*, £1 11*s* 6*d* .. *John Haviland*, 1629

"This edition, dedicated to the Duke of Buckingham, collates by that of 1625 given in Lowndes, but it has at the end, in addition to the 58 Essays, "A TABLE OF THE COLOURS OF GOOD AND EVILL," *a Fragment*, on nineteen *unpaged leaves*. This Fragment does not appear to be contained in any of the former editions, nor is it noticed by Lowndes at all.

302 BACON, Sermones Fideles, Ethici, Politici, Œconomici; accedunt Faber Fortunæ, Colores boni et mali, &c., *engraved title*, 18mo. *old calf gilt*, 4*s* .. .. *L. Bat.*, *Hackius*, 1644

303 — Historia Naturalis de Ventis, de Forma Calidi, de Motu, &c., 18mo. *old calf neat*, 3*s* .. *Amst.*, *Elz.*, 1662

304 — Historia Regni Henrici VII., Angliæ Regis, 18mo. *vellum, neat*, 5*s* .. *Lugd. Bat.*, *apud F. Hackium*, 1647

"Bacon's Henry VII. betrays too much of the Apologist for Arbitrary Power, but is otherwise of great value; it is written from original, and now lost materials, with vigour and philosophical acuteness."—*Drake's Shakspeare and his Times.*

305 — On the Advancement of Learning, 24mo. *half calf neat*, 2*s*—12mo. *boards*, 5*s* .. .. .. 1828

"The Advancement of Learning, though much less read than the superficial works o later times, is one of the most entertaining and instructive books in the language."—*Knox*

306 — Letters, Memoirs, Parliamentary Affairs, State Papers, &c., and Life, by Robert Stephens, late Historiographer Royal, *very fine portrait by Vertue*, 4to. *old calf neat*, 7*s* 6*d* .. 1736

"Bacon is elaborate, sententious, often witty, often metaphorical; nothing could be spared; his analogies are generally striking and novel; his style is clear, precise, forcible."—*Hallam.*

307 BACON'S (John) Liber Regis; vel Thesaurus Rerum Ecclesiasticarum (an Account of the Valuations of the Ecclesiastical Benefices in England and Wales), with proper Directions and Precedents relating to Presentations, Institutions, Inductions, &c., very thick 4to. *boards, uncut*, 16*s* .. *John Nichols*, 1786

"A very valuable and useful work, entirely superseding Ecton."—*Lowndes.* Mr. Nassau's copy sold for £2 10s

308 [BACON (Nathaniel)] Rights of the Kingdom; or Customs of our Ancestors, or the Duty, Power, Election or Succession of our Kings and Parliaments, 4to. *old calf, neat*, 4*s* 6*d* 1682

This was secretly printed in 1672 and again in 1682, for these editions the publishers were prosecuted.

309 BACON'S (Rich. M., *of Cossey, near Norwich*) Elements of Vocal Science, 12mo. *boards*, 3*s* 6*d* *Norwich, Bacon*, 1824

310 BADGER'S (George Percy) Description of Malta and Gozo, *map and many lithographed plates*, 12mo. *cloth, scarce*, 7*s* 6*d* *Malta*, 1838

Printing and Lithography by *M. Weiss.* Books printed at Malta are rare.—See *Dr. Cotton.*

311 BAILEY'S (Henry J.) Liturgy Compared with the Bible, thick 12mo. *cloth*, 3*s* (*pub. at* 5*s*) .. .. 1839

312 BAILEY'S (N.) English Dictionary, with all the words in all Arts and Sciences, Ancient Charters, Statutes, &c., 500 *woodcuts*, 2 thick vols. 8vo. *good copy in old calf*, SCARCE, 10*s* 1759

313 BAILLY (C.) Manuel complet du Jardinier, 2 thick vols. 18mo. *sewed*, 2*s* .. .. .. *Paris*, 1829

314 BAILLY.—Vray Discours des Interrogatoires faits à Roch Bailly, surnommé la Riviere, *Paris*, 1579.—Sommaire defence de Roc le Baillèf, aux demandes des docteurs, et faculté de Med. de Paris, 1579, *with some* POETRY and other Tracts on the same subject,—in 1 vol. 8vo. *limp vellum*, SCARCE, 9*s* *Paris*, 1579

Roc le Baillif, Sieur de la Riviere, was Physician to King Henry III. of France.

315 BAKER'S (Thos.) Reflections upon Learning, 8vo., *old calf, neat,* 3*s* 6d .. .. .. .. 1738

A very ingenious work, once one of the most popular books in our language.

316 BAKER'S Companion to the Play-house; an Historical Account of all the Dramatic Writers and their Works, 2 vols. 12mo. *calf, neat,* 3*s* 6*d* .. .. .. 1764

317 BAKER, REED, and JONES'S Biographia Dramatica; Historical and Critical Memoirs of British and Irish Dramatic Writers, with Lists of their Works, 4 vols. 8vo. *boards,* 12*s* (*pub. at* £2 2*s*) 1812

This is a very useful work, and the best of its kind.

318 BAKEWELL'S (Frederick C.) Great Facts of the Present Century, Steam Navigation, Railways, Photography, the Stereoscope, Electric Telegraph, Paper Printing, *plates,* post 8vo. *cloth, gilt, new, gilt edges,* 3*s* 6*d* .. .. .. 1859

319 BAKHTYAR NAMEH: or, Story of Prince Bakhtyar and the Ten Viziers; a Series of Persian Tales, in Persian and English, from a MS. in Sir W. Ouseley's Collection, royal 8vo. *half russia, neat,* 6*s* .. .. .. .. 1801

320 BALDUINI (Francisci, *Jurisconsult.*) libri II. ad Leges Romuli et ad Leges XII. Tabularum, folio, *old calf, neat, scarce,* 10*s* 6*d*
*Lugduni, apud S. Gryphium,* 1550

From the Leicester Library; formerly Sir Christopher Hatton's copy.

321 — ad Paulum de Cautione Lecta in Auditorio Papiniani, 4to. *limp vellum,* £1 1*s* *Lugduni, apud A. Vincentium,* 1554

With Autograph of "P. de St. Andre" in a very old hand. This curious volume contains also the following Tracts.—

I.—Goveani (Antonii Jureconsulti) Lectionum Variarum Juris Civilis lib. 1. .. .. *Tolosæ, Guido Boudevillæus,* 1554
II.—Ex Libro Lectionum Juris Variarum Ant. Goveani Jureconsulti *Tolosæ, Guido Boudevillæus,* 1552
III.—Ant. Goveani ad L. Gallus liber, .. *Tolosæ, ib.,* 1554
IV.—Ant. Goveani ad tit. de Vulg. et Pupil. subst. liber. *Tolosæ, ib.,* 1554
V.—Ant. Goveani de Jurisdictione Libri II., adversus E. Baronem Jureconsultum .. .. .. *Tolosæ, ib.,* 1551

"This Anthony Govea, the youngest and most eminent of all of them, wrote several pieces on Philosophy and Law, and is mentioned with great encomiums by Thuanus, Ronsard, and all the learned."—See *Moreri.*

322 — Juris Civilis Catechesis, *Basileæ, per Jo. Opporinum, no date.*—Commentarius de Jurisprudentia Muciana, *Basileæ,* 1558.—Edicta Principum Romanorum de Christianis, *Basileæ, no date*—in 1 vol. 8vo. *fine clean copies,* £1 1*s* .. .. *v. y.*

All these three works of the celebrated Jurisconsult, Balduinus, are from the Press of Oporinus. On the title page is the Autograph of "*Socinus.*"

323 BALDWIN'S Hist. of England, for the Young, *portraits,* 12mo. *bound,* 2*s* .. .. .. 1836

324 BALFOUR'S (Clara) Sketches of English Literature, from the Fourteenth to the Present Century, 12mo. *cloth,* 4*s* 6*d* (*pub. at* 7*s*)
*Longmans,* 1852

325 BALLADS (Old), with Introductions and Notes, by Thomas Wright, F.S.A., 4 small volumes, *black letter, sewed, scarce,* 15*s* *W. Pickering,* 1836

Contents—I. The Nutbrowne Maid, from the earliest edition of Arnold's Chronicle, 1502. II. The Turnament of Totenham and the Feest, two early Ballads. III. The Tale of the Basyn and the Frere and the Boy, two other early Ballads. IV. Songs and Carols from a MS. in the British Museum.

326 BALLARD'S (George) Memoirs of several Celebrated Learned Ladies of Great Britain, 4to. *old calf neat,* 10*s* 6*d* *Oxford, for the Author,* 1752

"An entertaining Work, comprising notices of the Lives and Writings of sixty-two Ladies, commencing with Juliana, Anchoret of Norwich, and ending with Constantia Grierson."—*Lowndes.*

327 BAMPTON LECTURES, Bp. Mant's, for 1812, 8vo. *boards, edges cut smooth,* 3*s* .. .. *Oxford,* 1813

328 — Bp. Mant's, for 1812, 8vo. *boards,* 5*s* .. 1816

329 — Morgan's (Hector Davies) for 1819, 8vo. *half calf neat,* 5*s* *Oxford,* 1819

330 — Vogan's (Thomas S. L.) Sermons and Bampton Lectures, 8vo. *half cloth, neat,* 4*s* 6*d* (*pub. at* 12*s*) .. *Oxford,* 1837

331 — White's (Dr. Joseph), for 1784, 8vo. *boards,* 3*s* 6*d* *Reprint,* 1811

"Elegant and eloquent."—*Butler, Horæ Biblicæ.*

332 BANDELLO (Matteo) Il terzo Volume delle Novelle del Bandello, nuovamente ristampato, e con diligenza corretto dal S. Ascanio Centorio de Gli Hortensii, small 8vo. *old binding, rare,* £1 1*s* *In Milano, G. Antonio,* 1560

This volume contains 60 Novellæ. On the title page is written "*W. Unwyn.*" "*Sum Caroli Le Gros.*" Would this be Charles IX. of France? who reigned from 1550 to 1574; and "*Alta 'l pensiero Mabassa la speranza Jacomo Chirtono.*"

333 — Novelle, novamente corretto et illustrato dal Sig. Alfonso Ulloa, 3 vols. in 1, thick 4to, *half bound, clean and neat, rare,* £1 5*s* *Venetia, appresso Camillo Franceschini,* 1566

"In point of composition, these Novels, although much inferior to those of Boccaccio, are written with a degree of vivacity and nature which seldom fails to interest the reader, and which, combined with the singularity of the incidents, will probably secure a durable, although not a very honourable reputation to the author."—*Roscoe.*

334 BANIER'S (Abbé) Mythology and Fables of the Ancients, explained from History, 4 vols. 8vo. *calf, very neat,* £1 1*s* 1739-40

"A work containing an immense store of important information."—*Lowndes.*

335 BARBARO (Daniel) La Pratica della Perspettiva, Opera molto utile a Pittori, a Scultori & ad Architetti, folio, *numerous plates, fine, clean copy in vellum,* £1 1*s* *In Venetia, appresso C. & R. Borgominieri,* 1569

This Daniel Barbaro was the translator of the rare edition of Vitruvius, of 1556, folio, which see in this Catalogue.

336 BARBARY.—History of the Piratical States of Barbary, Algiers, Tripoli, and Morocco, *map and plan,* 8vo. *calf neat,* 3*s* 6*d* 1750

337 BARBAULD'S (Mrs.) Legacy for Young Ladies; Miscellaneous Pieces in Prose and Verse, 12mo. *half calf, neat,* 2*s* 6*d* 1826

338 — Selections from the Spectator, Tatler, Guardian, and Freeholder, with a Preliminary Essay, *portraits,* 2 vols. post 8vo. *cloth,* 4*s* (*cost* 7*s*) .. .. .. *E. Moxon,* 1849

339 BARBIER (A. A.) Dictionnaire des Ouvrages Anonymes et Pseudonymes, avec Notes historiques et critiques, 2 vols. 8vo. *bound*, 8*s* .. .. .. *Paris*, 1806

"An admirably well executed work."—*Dibdin*.

340 BARCLAII (Joannis) Argenis, cum Clave, thick 12mo. *old calf gilt*, 7*s* 6*d* .. .. *L. Bat.*, *Elzevir*, 1630

"Coleridge has pronounced an ardent and rather excessive eulogy on the language of the Argenis, preferring it to that of Livy or Tacitus. It is a Latin Romance, superior to those which the Spanish or French language could boast."—*Hallam*.

341 — Argenis, cum Clave, thick 18mo., of above 700 pages, *good copy in old calf*, 6*s* .. .. *L. Bat.*, *Elz.*, 1630

With the Book-plate of "Francis Blomefield," the Norfolk Historian. Cowper, the celebrated Poet, pronounced this the most amusing Romance ever written. The Latin style has been much praised.

342 — Argenis, cum Clave, small 8vo. *old calf, neat*, 5*s* *Cantabrigiæ, Jo. Creed*, 1673

"It is said that Cardinal Richelieu was extremely fond of reading this work, and that from thence he derived many of his political maxims."—*Chalmers*.

343 — Satyricon lib. V., accessit Conspiratio Anglicana, 12mo. *old calf*, 3*s* 6*d* .. .. *Amst.*, *Elzevir*, 1658

344 BARETTI'S (Joseph) Account of the Manners and Customs of Italy, 2nd edit., 2 vols. 8vo. *old calf gilt*, 5*s* 1769

345 — Spanish and English and English and Spanish Dictionary, 4to. *old calf*, 8*s* .. .. .. 1794

346 — Dictionary of the Italian-English and English-Italian Languages, 2 vols. 8vo. *half vellum*, 10*s* 6*d* .. .. 1824

347 BARGAGLI (G.) Dialogo de Giuochi che nelle Vegghie Sanesi si usano di fare del Materiale Intronato (Girolamo Bargagli) small 8vo. *old vellum, stained*, 5*s* *Venetia, A. Gardane*, 1581

"Dialogo bello, e curioso."—*Haym*.

348 BARONIS (Eguinarii, *Jurecons.*) Variarum Quæstionum pub. tractat., ad Digesta Juris Civilis I., de Jurisdictione, *Lugduni, apud S. Gryphium*, 1548.—Antidotum ad postulata de interim authore D. Roberto, Episcopo Abrincatensi, *Lugduni, apud M. Bonhomme*, 1548—in 1 vol. small 8vo. *old vellum*, 6*s*

349 BARRETT'S (Thomas, *of Lee, Essex*) Catalogue of his Library, sold by Sotheby, Dec., 1818, 8vo. *calf (prices and purchasers' names), neat*, 3*s* .. .. .. .. 1818

350 BARRINGTON'S (George) History of New South Wales, including Botany Bay, &c., *coloured plates*, 8vo. *half calf, neat*, 4*s* 6*d* 1802

351 BARROW'S (Dr. Isaac) Sermons on Contentment, Patience, and Resignation to the Will of God, *portrait*, 12mo. *calf*, 2*s* 1714

352 BARROW'S (John) Travels in Southern Africa, *coloured plates*, 2 vols. 4to. *calf, very neat*, £1 1*s* .. .. 1806

353 — Travels in China, *coloured plates*, 4to. *calf*, 12*s* 1804

"Whoever will follow our traveller through his valuable works will derive both pleasure and entertainment. His remarks are the result of deep and extensive research."—*Stevenson*.

354 BARRY'S (Sir Edward) Observations on the Wines of the Ancients, and the Analogy between them and the Modern Wines, 4to. *old calf, neat*, 10*s* 6*d* .. .. .. 1775

Further illustrated with observations on the principles and qualities of waters, particularly those of Bath.

355 BARRY'S (James, *Historical Painter*) Works, with his Life, *portrait and plates*, 2 vols. 4to., *half calf, very neat*, £1 11*s* 6*d* (*pub. at* £5 5*s*) .. .. .. .. 1809

356 BARRY (Martinus, *Anglus, Chirurgus*) Dissertatio inauguralis de Animalium Temperie, 8vo. *calf extra, gilt leaves*, 5*s* *Edinburgi, Jac. Walker*, 1833

Presentation copy from "*The Author to his friends, Joseph John and Mary Gurney.*"

357 — Ascent to the Summit of Mont Blanc, 1834, *plates*, 8vo. *boards*, VERY SCARCE, 5*s* .. .. .. 1834

PRIVATELY PRINTED, not in Mr. Martin's list of privately printed books. From "*the Author to his friend Catherine Gurney, Earlham, 26th of 9th month, 1834.*"

358 BARTAS, his Devine Weekes and Works, translated and dedicated to the King's Most Excellent Maiestie by Joshua Sylvester—Fragments and other small Works of Bartas—the Quadrains of Pibrac, *Arms of the Earl of Essex, and woodcuts*, small 4to. LARGE PAPER, *fine clean copy, this early edition* VERY RARE, £2 2*s* *London, by Humfrey Lownes*, 1605

"Perused Feb. 1788. Pathetic praises fail me to give incomparable Bartas the distinguish'd character he justly deserves."—*Satchy.*

"He that with comprehension, profit, and delight would peruse him, ought first to study the GLOSSARY or explanation of some names and other difficult terms made use of through the whole, page 662. But should any leave that task to be the last, he may be said to have cunningly learnt to put his cloak on after the Rain."—*MS. in the Volume.*

359 BARTHELEMY Voyage du Jeune Anacharsis en Grèce, 7 vols. 8vo., *the maps and plates in* 4to. *sewed*, 18*s* *Paris*, 1822

360 — le meme, et Memoires sur la Vie de J. J. Barthelemy, 7 vols. 12mo. *calf, neat*, 10*s* .. .. *Paris*, 1810

361 — Maps, Plans, Views, and Coins Illustrative of Anacharsis's Travels, in English, *portrait*, 4to. *boards*, 6*s* .. 1817

362 BARTHOLINI (Thomæ) de Luce Hominum et Brutorum libri III., 12mo. 600 pages, 8vo. *old calf*, 3*s* 6*d* *Hafniæ*, 1669

363 BARTON'S (Bernard) Napoleon and other Poems, 8vo. *boards*, 5*s* 6*d* (*pub. at* 12*s*) .. .. .. 1822

Book-plate of "*Mr. Joseph John Gurney, Earlham,*" to whom these belonged.

364 — New Year's Eve and other Poems, *frontispiece*, 8vo. *boards*, 3*s* 6*d* (*pub. at* 9*s*) .. .. .. 1828

365 BARTON'S (Lucy) Life of Christ, a gospel history for the use of children, *plate*, 12mo. *cloth, new*, 3*s* 6*d* .. 1857

366 BARWICK (Joannis) Vita, a Petro Barwick, M.D. conscripta, *portraits of John and Peter Barwick*, 8vo. *old calf, neat*, 5*s* *Londini*, 1721

"A work of great interest and amusement, particularly of the period of the Restoration of K. Charles II."—*Lowndes.* Autograph of *Caros. Umfreville.*

367 BASNAGE, Histoire de la Religion des Eglises Reformées, depuis Jesus Christ jusqu'a present, 2 vols. 4to. *good copy, old calf, gilt*, £1 1*s* .. .. .. *Rotterdam*, 1725

An Answer to Bossuet's *Hist. des Variations.* "Quod inter reliqua argumenti hujus scripta a reformatis composita, principatum tuetur."—*Walch. Book Plate of Lord Walpole of Woolterton.*

368 BASTINGIUS (Jeremias) his Exposition or Commentarie upon the Cathechisme of Christian Religion, taught in the Lowe Countries and Countie Palatine, 4to. *old calf*, 3*s* *John Legatt*, 1614

Imperfect, but may do to complete another copy.

369 BASTIUS. Excerpta ex F. J. Bastii Commentatione Palæographica, cum *Tabulis Lithographicis* XX. a Johanne Hodgkin transcriptis, 8vo. *boards*, 5*s* .. .. .. 1835

"*To his dear friend, Joseph John Gurney, in token of unfeigned Respect, from the Editor.*"

370 BATES'S (Dr. William) Harmony of the Divine Attributes in the contrivance of man's Redemption, 4to. *old calf*, 4*s* 6*d* 1674

"Dr. Bates was, beyond comparison, the most beautiful and elegant writer among the Nonconformist Divines."—*Dr. Williams.*

371 BATHER'S (Ven. Archdeacon) Sermons on Old Testament Histories, 8vo. *cloth*, 4*s* .. .. . 1850

372 BATHURST (Henry, Bishop of Norwich) Memoirs of, by his Son, vol. 2 only, 8vo. *cloth*, 3*s* .. .. 1837

373 BATLEY'S (E. C.) Ecclesiastical Digest of all writers of the Church from A.D. 34 to this time, with a Secular Chronology, 4to. *half cloth*, 9*s* (*pub. at* 14*s*) .. .. 1834

This is a very useful work, and must have cost much labour.

374 BATTELY (Joan.) Antiquitates Rutupinæ, *plates of coins, &c. by M Burghers*, 8vo. LARGE PAPER, *old calf, neat*, 7*s* 6*d* *Oxoniæ*, 1711

"An elegant posthumous Discourse."—*Bp. Nicolson.* This account of the ancient state of the Isle of Thanet, composed in elegant Latin, was published by Dr. Thomas Terry, Canon of Christ Church, Oxford.

375 BAUDII (Dominici) Epistolæ; accedunt ejusdem Orationes et libellus de Fœnore, *portrait*, 12mo. LARGE PAPER, *good copy*, 6*s* *Amst., Elzevirii*, 1654

These letters are considered the most entertaining of the Works of Baudius, the Latinity is very pure and elegant. He came to this country and was intimate with Sir Philip Sidney, and many other distinguished persons.

376 — idem, thick 18mo. *old calf*, 3*s* 6*d* *Amst., L. Elzevirii*, 1662

377 BAXTER'S (Andrew) Matho: the Principles of Natural Religion demonstrated from the Phœnomena of the Material World, 2 vols. 12mo. *old calf, neat*, 2*s* 6*d* .. .. 1765

378 BAXTER (Richard) Second Sheet for the Ministry; Justifying our calling against Quakers, Seekers, and Papists, small 4to. 8 *leaves, uncut, very scarce*, 6*s*
*By R. White, for Nevil Simmons, Bookseller, in Kederminster*, 1657

379 — Reasons of the Christian Religion, *fine impression of the portrait*, 4to. *old calf, neat*, 6*s* .. .. 1667

First meditated for the Wel-setling of his own belief, and now published for the benefit of others.

380 — Life and Times, with an Account of his Writings, by William Orme, *portrait*, thick 8vo. *half cloth*, 10*s* (*pub.at* 18*s*) *Liverpool*, 1837

A valuable acquisition to the literary History of the period, 1615—1691. Baxter was the Author of the astonishing number of 168 Works.

381 BAXTER (Will.) Glossarium Antiquitatum Britannicarum; accedunt Edv. Luidii Fluviorum, Montium, Urbium, &c. in Britanniâ nominibus adversariæ, Edit. 2nda, *fine portrait, by Vertue*, 8vo. *fine copy, in calf*, 7*s* 6*d* .. .. *Londini*, 1733

"A curious Work."—*Bp. Nicolson.*

382 BAYFIUS (Lazarus) de Re Navalis,—de Re Vestiaria, de Vasculis,—Antonii Thylesii de Coloribus libellus, small 4to. *a very fine copy, in old calf, gilt*, 10*s* 6*d* *Parisiis, R. Stephanus*, 1536

A beautiful old volume from Lord Orford's Library at Wolterton. Illustrated with Cuts of Ancient Ships, Vestments, Vases, &c.

383 BAYFIUS, alia Editio, 4to. *half vellum*, 6*s* *Lutetiæ, R. Stephani*, 1549

This learned gentleman was educated under Budæus and Musurus, from whom he learnt Greek, in 1531 Francis I. sent him Ambassador to Venice.

384 BAYLE. Examen de la Theologie de M. Bayle, répandue dans son Dictionnaire, &c. 12mo. *half calf, neat, scarce*, 4*s* 6*d* *Amst., l'Honoré*, 1706

"Par Izaac Jacquelot."—*Barbier, Dict. des Anonymes.*

385 BEALE'S (Thomas) Natural History of the Sperm Whale; with a Sketch of a South-sea Whaling Voyage, *plates*, post 8vo. *half calf, neat*, 7*s* 6*d* *(pub. at* 12*s)* *Van Voorst*, 1839

386 [BEAR'S (N.)] Resurrection founded on Justice; a Vindication in Answer to the objections of the learned Dr. Hody, small 8vo. *old calf*, 2*s* 6*d* .. .. .. 1700

387 BEATIANO (Cavalier Giulio Cesare *de Mondeserto*) La Corona Imperiale, 12mo. *sewed*, 2*s* .. *Ferrara*, 1689

388 BEATTIE'S (Dr. James) Essays on Poetry and Music, and the utility of Classical Learning, 8vo. *calf, very neat*, 4*s* *Edinb.* 1778

389 — Poetical Works, with Life, by Alex. Dyce, *fine portrait*, 12mo. *morocco extra, gilt edges*, 9*s* *W. Pickering*, 1831

390 — Account of his Life and Writings, including many of his original Letters, by Sir William Forbes, *fine portrait by Gaugain, after Sir Joshua Reynolds*, 2 vols. 4to. *boards*, 8*s* (*pub. at* £1 11*s* 6*d*) *Edinburgh*, 1806

391 BEAUCLERK.—Catalogue of the Library of the Honble. Topham Beauclerk, F.R.S., 50 Days' Sale, sold by Mr. Paterson, April, 1781, royal 8vo. *boards, uncut*, 4*s* .. 1781

392 BEAUFORT'S (Margaret, *Countess of Richmond and Derby, Mother of King Henry VII.*) Life, by Caroline A. Halsted, *portrait*, 8vo. *cloth*, 5*s* 6*d* (*pub. at* 12*s*) .. .. 1839

393 BEAUMONT, Le Magasin des Enfans, *plates*, 2 vols. 12mo. *calf, neat*, £1 1*s* .. .. .. *Paris*, 1801

With this Autograph, "*Mary Nugent Buckingham, Stowe, August* 7, 1810, *given to her dear little friend, Emma.*" This Lady Mary Nugent was daughter of Robert, Earl Nugent, wife of George, the first Marquis, and mother of the present Duke of Buckingham.

394 BEAUSOBRE, Sermons sur le XII. Chap. de Romains, vol. 2 only, 8vo. *old calf, neat*, 2*s* 6*d* .. *Lausanne*, 1744

395 BEAUSOBRE and LENFANT'S New Version of St. Matthew's Gospel, with a Literal Commentary, 8vo. *boards*, 3*s* 6*d* *Cambridge*, 1779

"A work of extraordinary merit."—*Bp. Watson.*

396 BEAVER'S (Capt. Philip) African Memoranda; relative to an Attempt to Establish a British Settlement on the Island of Bulama, in 1792, with a Notice of the Neighbouring Tribes, *map*, 4to. *boards*, 7*s* 6*d* (*pub. at* £1 11*s* 6*d*) .. .. 1805

397 BECKET.—Vita di S. Tomaso (à Becket) Arcivescovo di Cantuaria, e Martire, tradotta dalla Lingua Francese nell' Italiana per Gio. Battista Cola, *plate of the Murder of the Archbishop, by Isabella Picini, inserted*, thick 4to. of 520 pages, *old parchment*, RARE, 10*s* 6*d* .. *In Lucca, Marescandoli*, 1696

Dedicated to "Rinaldo I., Duca di Modena." Thomas à Becket, Abp. of Canterbury, was born in 1119, and slain by William de Tracy at Canterbury, in 1170, in the Reign K. Henry II.

398 BECKFORD'S (Peter) Thoughts on Hunting, in Letters to a Friend, *frontispiece by Bartolozzi, and plates,* FIRST EDITION, 4to. *old calf, neat,* 8*s* .. .. .. *Sarum,* 1781

For a notice of this esteemed work, see *Retrospective Review,* Vol. 13.

399 — another edition, *frontispiece by Bartolozzi, and plates,* 4to. *nice copy in calf,* 7*s* 6*d* .. .. .. 1802

400 BECKMANN'S (John) History of Inventions and Discoveries, from the German by W. Johnston, best edition, 4 vols. 8vo. *bds.* 18*s* 1814

"A most interesting and valuable work."—*Lowndes.*

401 — another edition. 2 vols. post 8vo. *cloth,* 7*s* *H. G. Bohn,* 1850

402 BEDDOES'S (Tho. Lovell) Poems, with a Memoir of him, thick 12mo. *cloth,* 4*s* (*pub. at* 7*s* 6*d*) .. *Pickering,* 1851

Son of the celebrated Dr. Thomas Beddoes, of Clifton, the friend of Sir Humphrey Davy.

403 BEDÆ (Venerabilis) Axiomata Philosophica, quibus accessere Theses Philosophicæ, 18mo. *old binding,* 2*s* *Coloniæ,* 1605

404 — Ecclesiastical History of the English Nation, from Julius Cæsar to 731, Englished by John Stevens, 8vo. *old calf, neat,* 7*s* 6*d* 1723

"This work is scarce, the translation is well done, and the Notes very useful."—*Dr. Adam Clarke.*

405 BEECHY'S (Capt. F. W. and H. W.) Expedition to explore the Northern Coast of Africa, from Tripoly eastward, in 1821 to 22, with an Account of the Greater Syrtis and Cyrenaica, and the Ancient Cities composing the Pentapolis, 22 *maps and plates,* 4to. *boards,* 18*s* (*pub. at* £3 3*s*) .. .. 1828

406 BELL'S (Currer) Jane Eyre, an Autobiography, 3 vols. post 8vo. *cloth, neat,* 7*s* 6*d* (*pub. at* £1 11*s* 6*d*) .. 1848

407 — Professor, a Tale, 2 vols. post 8vo. *cloth,* 8*s* 6*d* (*pub. at* 21*s*) 1857

408 BELL'S Lives of the English Dramatists, 2 vols. 12mo. *cloth,* 5*s* *Lardner's Cyclopædia,* 1839

409 — Lives of the British Poets, 2 vols. 12mo. *cloth,* 5*s* *Lar. Cyclo.* 1839

410 BELL'S (Thomas) Anatomy, Physiology, and Diseases of the Teeth, *plates,* 8vo. *half cloth,* 5*s* 6*d* (*pub. at* 16*s*) . 1829

411 BELL'S (Will.) Enquiry into the Divine Missions of John the Baptist and Jesus Christ, 8vo. *boards,* 3*s* 6*d* 1761

Bp. Watson highly commends the Works of this Author.

412 BELLAMY'S (D.) Family Preacher; Practical Discourses for every Sunday throughout the year, Christmas Day, Good Friday, and other Solemn Occasions, 2 vols. in 1, 4to. *fine copy, in calf,* 9*s* 1776

413 BELLAMY'S (John) History of all Religions, *portraits,* 12mo. *boards,* 3*s* .. .. .. 1813

414 BELLENDENI (Gulielmi) de Statu libri III., editio Secunda, edente S. Parr, *portraits of Burke, Fox, and Lord North,* 8vo. *calf, neat,* 6*s* .. .. *Londini,* 1787

The Preface by Dr. Samuel Parr, a fine specimen of Latinity,—see *Mr. Hallam's History of Literature.* Bellenden, a Scotchman, dedicated his book, de Statu, to Prince Charles in 1615. Dr. Parr thought it worth re-editing in 1787.

"Bellenden's learning is considerable, and without that pedantry of quotation which makes most books of the age intolerable."—*Hallam.*

415 BELLICARD'S Antiquities of Herculaneum, 42 *plates,* 8vo. *calf, neat,* 4*s* .. .. .. 1753

"An ingenious work." Has also Reflections on the Painting and Sculpture of the Ancients.

416 BELLORIUS (Petrus) Selecti Nummi duo Antoniniani, (Antonini Pii et Commodi,) 8vo. *vellum, neat,* 3*s* *Romæ,* 1676

With this writing, "*Liber Z. Isham, ex dono Cl. Authoris.—Romæ,* 1677."

417 [BELOE'S (William)] Sexagenarian; or Recollections of a Literary Life, 2nd edition, 2 vols. 8vo. *boards,* 5*s* 1818

"A very amusing performance, filled with anecdotes and characters of the Author's literary contemporaries."

418 BEMBI (Petri) Epistolarum Leonis X. Pontificis Max. nomine Script. libri XVI., ad Paulum III. Pont. Max. Romam missi, thick 8vo. of 743 pages, *vellum, rare,* 10*s* 6*d* *No place where printed or date given.*

Some of these letters, from and to some of the most eminent persons of that time, are dated as early as 1513, the latest, 1546.

419 BENGAL.—Timely Retreat; a Year in Bengal before the Mutinies, by two Sisters, *plates,* 2 vols. post 8vo. *cloth,* 8*s* (*pub at* £1 1*s*) *R. Bentley,* 1858

A fearful but faithful narrative.

420 BENJAMINIS (de Tudela) Itinerarium, Latine redditum operâ Const. l'Empereur, 32mo. *old calf, neat,* 6*s* *L. Bat. Elzevir,* 1633

"This work is no doubt a curiosity as the production of a Jewish Rabbi in the 12th Century."—*Chalmers.*

421 BENSON'S (C.) Discourses on the Evidences of Christianity, his Hulsean Lectures for 1820, 8vo. *bds.* 4*s* 6*d* (*pub. at* 12*s*) 1824

422 BENTHAM'S (James) History and Antiquities of Ely Cathedral, *numerous finely engraved plates,* royal 4to. *fine copy in the original calf binding,* £1 11*s* 6*d* .. *Cambridge,* 1771

423 — Supplement to, by Mr. William Stevenson, F.S.A., *numerous plates,* royal 4to. *boards,* 16*s* .. *Norwich,* 1817

424 BENTIVOGLIO (Cardinale) Relationi delle Provincie Unite di Fiandra, publicate da Erycio Puteano (Henry Dupuy) in Anversa, 4to. *engraved title, neat,* 5*s* .. *Colonia,* 1630

Book Plate of "Edward Coke, of Norfolk, Esq., 1701." Dedicated to Isabella, Infant of Spain. "These Historical Memoirs are amusing and illustrative of the characters and events of his times."—*Moreri.*

425 — Raccolta di Lettere scritte dal Cardinal B., 4to. *vellum,* 7*s* 6*d* *Colonia,* 1631

These Letters were written to many eminent persons during the time the Cardinal was Nuncio to Flanders and France, 1607 to 1621.

426 — Historicall Relations of the United Provinces of Flanders, 1652; Bentivoglio's History of the Warrs of Flanders, 1559 to 1609, both Englished by Henry (Carey), Earl of Monmouth, *map and* 24 *portraits,* 2 vols. in 1, folio, *old binding,* 10*s* 6*d* 1652-54

These are both 1st editions, there are two Portraits, engraved by Crosse and Vaughan, belonging to the English Series, Queen Elizabeth and Robert Dudley, Earl of Leicester.

427 BENTLEY'S (The very learned Dr. Richard) Works; viz., Dissertations upon the Epistles of Phalaris, Themistocles, Socrates, Euripides, Æsop, and Boyle Lectures, edited with Notes by the Rev. Alexander Dyce, 3 vols. 8vo. *bds.* £1 1*s* (*pub. at* £1 18*s*) 1836

"The greatest of English Critics in this, or possibly any other age, was Richard Bentley."—*Hallam.*

"We have carefully looked through these volumes, and can safely say, that Mr. Dyce is a good scholar and a careful editor. Bentley could not have fallen into better hands."—*Literary Gazette.*

428 BENTLEY'S Dissertations upon the Epistles of Phalaris, with an Answer to the Objections of the Honble. Charles Boyle, 8vo. *old calf, neat,* 3*s* 6*d* .. .. .. 1699

429 — Dissertation upon the Epistles of Phalaris, Themistocles, Socrates, Euripides, and Æsop's Fables, 8vo. *boards,* 5*s* (*pub. at* 12*s*) 1817

430 — Remarks on Collins's Discourse on Free Thinking, 8vo. 8*th edition, neat,* 4*s* 6*d* .. .. *Cambridge,* 1743

"Best edition of a most valuable work, which should be studied by every man who is desirous of forming just notions of Biblical Criticism."—*Lowndes,* from *Bp. Herbert Marsh.*

431 — Bentleii et Doctorum Virorum Epistolæ, royal 4to. *fine copy, calf,* £1 1*s* .. .. .. .. 1807

Only 200 copies of this sumptuous volume printed by Bulmer. Copies have sold from 8 to 10 guineas.

432 BENTLEY'S STANDARD NOVELS, *plates,* 12mo. *cloth, gilt,* 2*s* 6*d each* (*pub. at* 6*s*)

Tales of the Alhambra, by Washington Irving.—De L'Orme, by James.—Adventures of Hajji Baba, of Ispahan, by Morier.—Cooper's Bravo.—The Adventures of Hajji Baba, of Ispahan, in England, by Morier.—Zohrab the Hostage, by Morier.—Fleetwood, by Godwin.—Ayesha, the Maid of Kars, by Morier.—Canterbury Tales, by Sophia and Harriet Lee, 2 vols.—Tylney Hall, by Thomas Hood.—St Leon, by William Godwin.—Lawrie Todd, or the Settlers in the Woods, by John Galt.—Discipline, by Mary Brunton.

433 BENTLEY'S MISCELLANY, Feb., April, June, July, Aug., Nov., Dec., 1851, Seven Months, 3*s* 6*d* (*pub. at* 24*s* 6*d*)

434 BENZONIS (Hieron.) Novæ Novi Orbis Historiæ, lib. III., U. Calvetonis Opera et Italicis, et de Gallorum in Floridam expeditione, et insigni Hispanorum in eos sævitiæ exemplo, Brevis Historia, 8vo., *a fine copy in vellum, rare,* £1 1*s* *Genevæ,* 1578

At the end is "Lycophronis Cassandra, Latinè, per Bernardum Bertrandum, *Basiliæ, per I. Oporinum,* 1558."

435 BEOLCHI (Carlo) Saggio della Poesia Italiana, 12mo. *calf elegant, gilt edges,* 5*s* 6*d* .. .. *Londra,* 1825

A very pretty little book, with some Italian Verses in MS.

436 BERANGER'S Songs, Englished, 12mo. *cloth,* 3*s* 6*d* *Pickering,* 1837

437 BERENS'S (Edw.) Lectures on the Liturgy of the Church of England, abridged from Waldo, 12mo. *half calf, neat,* 5*s* *Oxford,* 1821

Has also Lent Lectures on the Catechism, 1823. VIII. Lectures on the Offices, 1822, and VI. Lectures on the Penitential Psalms, 1823, all by Berens, in one volume.

438 — Sermons on Sickness and Sorrow, 12mo. *bound,* 1*s*

439 BERGAMO (Giacopo Filippo da) Chroniche Universale, della creatione del mondo all' anno ti tempi suoi, bound in 2 vols. 4to., *old calf, neat,* 18*s* .. *Vinegia, per H. Calepino,* 1554

"In quest' ultima Edizione vi sono le aggiunte del Giovio, del Bembo, del Carlone e di Marco Guazzo."—*Haym.* For a Supplement to this work, see *Sansovino.* In MS. at back of title we read—

Ben spè felice quel, amici cari
Eh' esser accorto à l'altrui spese impari.—*George Watsonn.*

440 BERGAMO.—Chroniche, tradotta, riformata et ampliata da M. FRANCESCO SANSOVINO, 2 thick vols. 4to. *old vellum,* RARE, £1 11*s* 6*d* *Vinegia, Altobello Salicato,* 1581

Sir Christopher Hatton's Copy, with the Initials of his Name stamped in gold on the vellum, also the Autograph of his Nephew and Heir, William Hatton. This is Sansovino's continuation of Bergamo's Chronicle to 1581.

441 BERKENHOUT'S (Dr. John) Biographia Literaria; Biographical History of Literature, containing the Lives of English, Scotch, and Irish Authors, from the Fifth to the end of the Sixteenth Century, Vol. 1, all published, 4to. *half calf, very fine copy, uncut,* 7*s* 6*d* .. .. .. .. 1777

"Of this judicious and useful compilation, only one of three volumes was published."—*Lowndes.*

442 — Botanical Lexicon, in which all the Terms occurring in Linnæus are Alphabetically arranged, small 8vo. *calf, neat,* 4*s* 1789

Second edition of a very useful work, with a Calendarium Botanicum at the end.

443 BERLIN and its Treasures, 13 *plates, nicely engraved,* 4to. 4*s*

444 BERNARDI (Edvardi S.T.P.) Orbis Eruditi Literatura à charactere Samaritico deducta, ed. Carolus Morton, M.D., 8vo. *nicely written,* £1 1*s* .. .. .. .. 1759

This appears to be the ORIGINAL MANUSCRIPT of Dr. Morton, who, in 1759, printed an improved edition of the learned Edward Bernard's Table of Oriental and other Alphabets. Dr. Morton was a Fellow of the Royal and Antiquarian Societies and principal Librarian of the British Museum in 1776 to 1799. There are above 170 distinct Alphabets here.

445 BERNOUILLI (Jacobi) Dissertatio de Gravitate Ætheris, *plates,* 12mo. *old calf, neat,* 4*s* .. *Amst., Wetstein,* 1683

A little before the publication of this work on the Weight of the Air, this great man came to England, contracting the acquaintance of our Savans, and attending the Philosophical Societies held at Mr. Boyle's house.—See *Chalmers.*

446 BEROSI (Chaldæi Sacerdotis) de Antiquitate Italiæ ac totius orbis, cum F. Joan. Annii Commentatione, *tomus prior,* thick 18mo., *fine copy, old calf gilt, ruled throughout with red lines, scarce,* 10*s* 6*d* *Lugduni, apud J. Temporalem,* 1555

Contents, Xenophon de Æquivocis.—De temporibus ante Diluvium.—Genealog. primorum Ducum post Diluvium.—De Regibus Babyloniæ.—De Regibus Assyriorum.—Manethonis Supp. ad Berosum.—Metasthenes de Judicio Temporum.—Philonis de Temporibus liber.—De Regibus Hispaniæ —De Antiquitate et Regibus Ethruriæ.

447 BERQUIN, Idylles, *numerous plates by De Ghendt, Le Beau, Le Gouar, and others,* 12mo. *old mottled calf, gilt,* 6*s* 1776

A very pretty book, on large paper, with plates, after Marillier, very nicely engraved.

448 BERRINGTON'S (Joseph) Literary History of the Middle Ages, *portrait of Chaucer,* 12mo. *cloth,* 3*s* *Bogue,* 1846

449 — History of the Lives of Abeillard and Heloisa, from 1079 to 1163, with their Genuine Letters, 4to. *boards,* 7*s* 6*d* *Birmingham,* 1788

"A valuable and accurate work, composed from authentic materials."—*Lowndes.*

450 BERRUTI (Amadei) Dialogus, in quo precipue tractat: An amico sepe ad scribendum provocato: ut scribat: non respondenti sit amplius scribendum; et hinc incidenter multa pulcra. De Amicitia Vera, de Amore Honesto, de Amicis Veris, &c., small 4to. *vellum, in a very fine state, clean as new,* £2 12*s* 6*d* *Romæ, per Gabrielem Bononiensem,* 1517

46 leaves. A copy of this EXTREMELY RARE Tract sold at Sir Mark Sykes's sale for 20 guineas; but it had Marc Antonio's Engraving of Amadeus, which has been purloined from the title of this copy, which has also a blank leaf after the Dedication to Claude de Seysell, Archbishop of Turin.

451 BERTHOLLET'S (C. L.) Elements of the Art of Dyeing, &c., Englished with Notes by Dr. A. Ure, *plates,* 2 vols. 8vo. *boards,* 7*s* 6*d* 1824

452 BERWIK (Marechal de, *Duc et Pair de France)* Memoirs, vol. 1, 12mo. *neat*, 2*s* .. .. *La Haye*, 1737

Marshal Berwik was Generalissimo of all the forces under Louis XIV.

453 — Memoirs of the Marshal Duke of Berwick, by himself, from 1670 to 1734, *map*, 2 vols. 8vo. *calf, neat*, 4*s* .. 1779

454 BERZELIUS Analisi Chimica d'ogni specie di Minerali, tradotta in Italiano dal Prof. Gazzeri, *plates*, 8vo. *half bound in parchment*, 3*s* 6*d* .. .. .. *Firenze*, 1822

455 — Instructions for the use of the Blowpipe, and Chemical Tests, by J. Mawe, *plates*, 16mo. *cloth*, 2*s* (*pub at* 4*s*) 1825

456 BETTS'S Geological Map of England and Wales, 34 inches by 42, *Coloured*, and mounted on canvas, in a cloth case, with Explanatory Companion, by G. F. Richardson, F.G.S., of the British Museum, 12mo. *cloth*, 15*s (pub. at* £1 11*s* 6*d*)

457 BEUDANT (F. S.) Traité Elémentaire de Mineralogie, *plates*, thick 8vo. *bound in parchment*, 5*s* .. *Paris*, 1824

458 BEVAN (Dr. Edward) On the Honey Bee, its Natural History, Physiology, and Management, 12mo. *boards*, 5*s* (*pub. at* 9*s*) 1827

459 BEVAN (Rev. Fred.) Visitation Sermon, at the Cathedral, June 16th, 1845, 8vo. *sewed*, 1*s* *Norwich, C. Muskett*, 1845

460 BEVERIDGE'S (Bp.W.) Thesaurus Theologicus; a Complete System of Divinity, 2 vols. 8vo. *half cloth*, 10*s (pub. at* 24*s*) 1832

461 BEZÆ (Theodori) Confessio Christianæ Fidei, et ejusdem collatio cum Papisticis Hæresibus, small 8vo. *original binding, scarce*, 6*s* *Genevæ*, 1573

462 BIANCHINI (Giuseppe) della Satira Italiana Trattato, con una Dissertazione dell' Ipocrisia degli Uomini letterati, 4to. *sewed, uncut*, 4*s* .. .. *Firenze, G. Manni*, 1729

This is the 2nd edition, not noticed by Haym, who dates the 1st, 1714, but that has not the *Dissertation*. Dr. Bianchini was a Member of the Academy at Florence.

## BIBLES IN VARIOUS LANGUAGES.

463 BIBLIORUM GRÆCO-LATINORUM, 4 vols. in 3, thick 8vo. *very fine clean copy, in the original calf*, £2 2*s* *Basiliæ, ex Officina Brylingeriana*, 1582

"The Greek and Latin are printed in opposite columns, the Greek Text from the Aldine, the Latin from the Complutensian; the type is distinct and neat; rare, in a fine state of preservation."—*Dibdin*. But this copy is valuable on account of having the Autograph of the very learned Hadrian Beverland —thus, "*Hadriani Beverlandi et Amicorum Lugduni in Batavis*, 1678," in it. Also on the title page is written, "*Paulus Colomesius Rupellensis, notas in Margine adjecit, R. Gipps.*" And at the end of two of the volumes, "*Deus cornu salutis meæ Henr. Ainsworth*," the learned Annotator on the Pentateuch.

464 BIBLIA, Gr. ex Versione Septuagintā interpretum, thick 12mo. *old morocco, gilt*, 3*s* 6*d* .. *Cantabrigiæ J. Field*, 1665

"The very learned Preface, of 19 pages, to this edition by the celebrated Bishop Pearson will interest the Biblical student."—*Dibdin*.

465 BIBLIA SACRA LATINA, **Black Letter**, folio, *remarkably fine large and clean copy*, £4 4*s* *Biblia Impressa Venetiis opera atque impressa Nicolai Jenson, Gallici*, MCCCCLXXIX

Jenson's second edition,—"A beautiful book, and is remarkable for presenting us with a Specimen of Jenson's large gothic type: his Bible of 1476, being printed in his small letter."—*Dibdin's Bibliographical Decameron.*

466 BIBLIA LATINA, breves in eadem annotationes, ex doctiss. interpretationibus, et Hebræorum commentariis, thick folio, *old oak covers*, £1 11*s* 6*d* *Antverpiæ, Martinus Cæsar*, 1534

This edition, which was prohibited, and which was printed in the same year that Luther published his translation into German, is a reprint of Robert Stephens's of 1532; it is printed in long lines, with the same Concordances and marginal Notes; the Title is enclosed within a well-executed Wood-cut Border.—See *Cat. of Duke of Sussex's Bibles.*

At the end is a memorandum "by me Thomas Wattes, 24 Oct. 1602," about the restoration of some books to him by Mrs. Mary Brudenell.

467 BIBLIA LATINA, thick folio, *old calf, neat*, 12*s* *Hanoviæ*, 1624

Immanuel Tremellius did the Canonical Books; F. Junius, the Apocryphal; and Theodore Beza The New Testament.

468 — small 8vo. *no Title Page*, 2*s* .. .. *No date*

469 — Old and New Testament in ARABIC, 4to. *bound, neat*, 15*s* *Newcastle*, 1811

470 — The Old and New Testaments in the BENGALI Language, 4to. *rough calf*, £1 1*s* *Calcutta*, 1845

471 — Old and New Testaments, and Singing Psalms, set to Music, in DUTCH, thick 12mo. *bound in velvet, edges gilt*, 6*s* *Amst.*, 1774

472 — Bible, l'ancien et le nouveau Testament, 12mo. *nice copy in old blue morocco, gilt edges*, 6*s* *Amst., Wetsteins*, 1710

473 — Traducidos al ESPANOL, de la Vulgata Latina, por el Rmo. P. P. Scio, 8vo. *bound*, 5*s* .. *Londres*, 1828

474 — Old and New Testaments in SYRIAC, 2 vols. 4to. *neat, scarce*, £1 5*s* .. .. *Londini*, 1816-23

"Dr. Buchanan and Professor Lee edited these beautiful editions of the Scriptures, printed at the expense of the Bible Society. They were received with much gratitude by the Syrian Christians in India."—See *Horne's Introduction.*

## BIBLES IN ENGLISH.

475 BIBLE, complete from GENESIS to MALACHI, 410 pages.—The NEWE TESTAMENT, complete, p. 2—129. Table of principal things, 18 pages, 4to. *Geneva, printed by John Crespin*, MDLXVIII

Contains all the Bible and New Testament, but not the Apocrypha. Wants the Title page to the Bible and some of the Introductory leaves, but has the *Title Page* to the NEW TESTAMENT, which identifies this EXCESSIVELY RARE 2nd 4to edition of the Genevan version, collates by *Dr. Cotton's List*, p. 301. It appears that there is only ONE OTHER COPY *known to exist* of this 1568 edition, in the possession of *Mr. Pinchard of Taunton, Somersetshire*, not *Devon*, as Dr. Cotton says, p. 35.

476 BIBLE—ABP. PARKER'S 1st Edition, 1568, **Black Letter**, folio; *portraits of Lords Leicester and Burleigh.* Wants the Title Page, the Introductory part, six leaves in sheet K, in Leviticus, and folios 142 to 157 at the end of the New Testament, £15. *Richard Jugge*, 1568

The remarkably fine and clean state of this truly magnificent volume is worthy of especial remark; a perfect copy, which is of the utmost rarity, lately produced £60 at Mr. Pickering's sale. The most interesting memorial of the reign of Elizabeth.

477 — ABP. PARKER'S 2nd Edition, 1572, **Black Letter**, *with the portraits of Lords Leicester and Burleigh*, also slightly deficient, 3 vols. folio, *half russia, very neat*, £6 6*s* *Richard Jugge*, 1572

This 2nd edition is usually priced 25 guineas. It contains a double version of the Psalms, namely, that of the Great Bible, in addition to that by the Bishops.

478 BIBLE, Apocrypha, and New Testament, 2 Concordances and Sternhold and Hopkins's Psalms, in 1 vol. thick 4to. **Black Letter**, *very fine state of preservation*, £2 15s *C. Barker*, 1594

This is a very fine clean copy of the Breeches Bible, in old oak impressed boards, with brass bosses and clasps, stout russia back. It belonged to the family of Aldridge, and has some of their births and deaths recorded in MS. from 1661 to 1734.

479 — Old Test., Apocrypha, and New Testament, *Robert Barker*, 1610. Two Tables, 1611.—Sternhold and Hopkins's Psalms, 1610.—Common Prayer, 1609, in 1 vol. 4to. *modern binding, very neat*, £1 1s

The Bible is in Roman, the Common Prayer in Black letter, in this copy.

480 — Old Test., Apocrypha, and New Testament, *Robert Barker*, 1614. Sternhold and Hopkins's Psalms, 1615, in 1 thick vol. 4to. *a remarkably fine clean copy, the Titles in handsome compartments, newly bound in the old style, with bevilled edges*, £1 11s 6d

481 — Old Test., Apocrypha, and New Testament, Common Prayer, and Sternhold and Hopkins's Psalms, *finely engraved Title, by J. Payn*, folio, *ruled throughout with red lines, rough calf*, £1 11s 6d *Cambridge, Tho. and John Buck*, 1629

Copies in the Bodleian Library and Mr. Lea Wilson's Collection. Mr. Wilson remarks that "the Text appears to have undergone a complete revision for this *beautiful edition*," &c. See *Dr. Cotton's List of Editions of the Bible*, p. 65, 1852.

482 — Old Test., Apocrypha, and New Testament, *Cambridge, Thomas and John Buck*, 1629—Sternhold and Hopkins's Psalms 1629.—Book of Common Prayer, 1629, in 1 vol. folio, *fine and large paper*, RARE, £3 3s .. .. .. V. Y.

483 — Old Test., Apocrypha, and New Testament, *Buck, Cambridge*, 1635; Concordance or Table; Sternhold and Hopkins's Psalms, 1636; Common Prayer, 1635; in 1 thick vol. 4to. *remarkably fine copy, ruled throughout with red lines, and bound in old blue morocco, extra, with gilt edges, and massive silver clasps*, £5 5s

The binding of this handsome old volume is in an unusually fine state of preservation.

484 — Bible, faithfully translated out of Latin into English, by the English College of Doway, vol. 1, 4to. *old calf, new back, rare*, 15s .. .. *Permissu Superiorum*, 1635

Translated by Cardinal Allen, Gregory Martin, and Richard Bristow.

485 — Bible, containing the Old and New Testaments, the Genevan Version, translated by L. Tomson, folio, *a remarkably fine tall copy, in old calf, gilt, gilt leaves*, £2 12s 6d *Amsterdam, by Thomas Stafford*, 1640

"According to the copy printed at Edinburgh, by Andro Hart, in 1610." At the end of this Bible are the two leaves of "Admonition concerning the Apocrypha-Books, shewing why they are here omitted," which Dr. Cotton, in his list of editions of the Bible, says are in the edition of 1644, printed at Amsterdam by the same printer. At the end are "Sternhold and Hopkins's Psalms," printed by R. Badger, 1632.

Mr. Lea Wilson had two copies of *Stafford's* edition, of 1640, in 4to but not this folio, which is a very handsome book. "It follows the Geneva translation in the Old Test., but the New is that of 1576, by Laurence Tomson, with Annotations from Beza, Camerarius, and Villerius."—See *Mr. Bohn's Edit. of Lowndes.*

486 — Old Test., (wants Title) and New Testament, in a very small type, 12mo. *old morocco*, 10s *London, Stationers' Company*, 1646-47

This edition of the Bible is dated at the end of the New Testament, 1646, but was issued in 1647. Dr. Cotton says that there was no edition in 1646, or 1647, but here it is; at the end is a SCOTCH VERSION of the singing PSALMS, printed at *Glasgow, by J. Robertson*, 1775, an edition which has escaped Dr. Cotton's researches too.

487 BIBLE, Apocrypha, and New Testament, in a beautiful very small clear type, with marginal references, 1650.—Common Prayer, *Robert Barker*, 1642; Sternhold and Hopkins's Psalms in meeter, 1651, in 1 vol. 8vo. *very fine copy in old purple morocco, gilt, gilt leaves*, £1 11s 6d. .. .. V. Y.

488 — Bible, Apocrypha, and New Testament, with Sternhold and Hopkins's Psalms, small thick 12mo. *old purple morocco, gilt leaves* £1 1s .. .. *Printed in the year* 1664

This Bible is printed in a small Diamond type. As it has no Printer's name mentioned it was probably printed abroad, but as it has not Canne's Marginal Notes it cannot be his. Not in *Lewis's* or *Dr. Cotton's* Lists.

489 — Bible, Apocrypha, and New Testament, *Cambridge, John Hayes*, 1673; Sternhold and Hopkins's Psalms, *ib.* 1673; Common Prayer, *ib.* 1673, in 1 thick vol. 4to. *in old purple morocco, gilt leaves*, £1 11s 6d .. .. .. 1673

In MS., "Alice Martin, her booke, 1673."
"Once was I lost, but now am founde,
Unto the Church I stand for ever bownde."—*Alice Martin.*

490 — Bible, containing the Old Testament and the New, with most profitable Annotations, large folio, bound in 2 vols. LARGE PAPER, *ruled throughout with red lines, bound in rough calf, the edges gilt*, RARE, £3 3s .. .. *London*, 1679

This book which belonged to *Lady Scarsdaile*, is very scarce on LARGE PAPER, it has, besides the printed, an *engraved Title Page*, with a *View of Old London* on it *previous to the Great Fire*. It is the Genevan Translation, and was printed simultaneously at Amsterdam and in London. It is illustrated with Maps by Joseph Moxon, one of which he dedicates to Gilbert [Sheldon], then Abp. of Canterbury. Dr. Cotton tells us *he has seen it*, but he does not say *where one is to be found*. The APOCRYPHA is inserted, but it does not belong to this edition of the book. Lord Scarsdale had a fine collection of books on large paper, and this may have been one of them

491 — Bible, Apocrypha, New Testament, Common Prayer, and Sternhold and Hopkins's Psalms, in 1 vol. thick 8vo. *calf neat*, 5s 1711

492 — Bible, BASKETT'S SPLENDID EDITION, royal folio, large paper, *with the large Vignettes, which are not in the small paper copies, old russia*, £4 4s .. .. 1717

A copy of this remarkably fine volume, commonly called the VINEGAR BIBLE, from the error of the "Parable of the Vineyard" being called "the Parable of the Vinegar," and the existence of which on large paper has been doubted by some eminent bibliographers, lately produced above £6 at Lord Alvanley's sale.

"Large paper copies of this magnificent edition are so scarce, that Dr. Dibdin and other bibliographers have doubted their existence. They are, however, easily distinguished by the large vignettes, which, in the small paper copies are replaced by fluerons."

493 — Bible, containing the Old and New Testaments, 18mo. *old purple morocco, gilt, gilt edges*, 5s *Oxford, Baskett*, 1743

Not in Dr. Cotton's List.

494 — Bible, explained by Question and Answer, from the writings of the most eminent Historians, Divines, and Commentators, *maps and numerous plates, by Vdr. Gucht, Carwitham, &c.*, 8vo. *old calf, scarce*, 6s .. .. .. 1748

An early book published by the Christian Knowledge Society.

495 — Bible, Genesis to end of Joshuah, by Dr. Geddes, vol. 1. royal 4to. *boards*, 5s .. .. .. 1792

496 — Bible, containing the Old and New Testaments, thick 8vo. *morocco, gilt edges, bound by Hayday*, £1 10s *Cambridge Pitt Press*, 1838

NEW TESTAMENTS in various languages will be found under *Novum Testamentum.*

497 BIBLE OF EVERY LAND, a History, with Specimens, Alphabets, *coloured maps, &c.*, of the Scriptures, as printed throughout the world, 4to. *elegantly bound in morocco, gilt edges,* £2 10*s* *S. Bagster,* 1848

In this valuable volume are specimens of 271 Languages and Dialects, divided into VIII. Classes; I. Monosyllabic; II. Shemitic; III. Indo-European; IV. Ugro-Tartarian; V. Polynesian or Malayan; VI. African; VII. American; VIII. Mixed or Patois.

498 BIBLIOGRAPHICAL MISCELLANIES; being a selection of curious Pieces in Prose and Verse, *Oxford,* 1813—Pieces of ancient Poetry, from unpublished MSS. and scarce Books, *Bristol,* 1814, in 1 vol. 4to. *half bound in morocco, uncut, top edges gilt, choice copies,* £1 4*s* .. .. 1813-14

Of the first of these little Treatises, published by Dr. Philip Bliss, there were 104 copies printed; of the second, edited by Mr. Fry, of Bristol, there was likewise a limited impression of only 102 copies.

499 BIBLIOSOPHIA; or, Book-Wisdom, containing some account of the Pride, Pleasure, &c., of that glorious vocation, Book Collecting, by an aspirant, [the Rev. James Beresford,] 12mo. *boards,* 3*s* *Bulmer,* 1810

500 BIBLIOTHECA AMERICANA; a Catalogue of American Publications, including Reprints and Original Works, from 1820 to 1848, inclusive, by O. A. Roorbach, royal 8vo. *cloth,* 6*s* *New York,* 1849

501 BIBLIOTHECA ANGLO-POETICA; a Descriptive Catalogue of a rare and rich collection of Early English Poetry, on sale at Longman's, with Critical and Biographical Remarks, by A. F. Griffiths, *portraits,* royal 8vo. *boards, uncut,* £1 4*s* 1815

"This extremely useful Catalogue is deserving of a place in every good library from the interesting information it affords of the works of our early Poets."—*Lowndes.*

502 BIBLIOTHECA PARISIANA; a Catalogue of a Collection of Books formed by a Gentleman in France, sold by Mr. Edwards, March, 1791, neatly priced, small 8vo. *fine paper, nice copy in calf,* 7*s* 6*d* .. .. .. 1791

The produce of this fine collection of Books was £6610 6*s.* 6*d.*

503 BICKERSTETH'S (Edward, *Rector of Watton,*) Christian Student, with lists of Books adapted to the various Classes of Society, thick 12mo. *half cloth,* 5*s* (*pub. at* 9*s* 6*d*) .. 1829

504 — Christian Student, 3rd Edition, 12mo. *half cloth,* 5*s* 6*d* 1832

505 — Four Sermons on the Advent of Christ, 18mo, *cloth,* 1*s* 1834

506 — Memoirs of, by the Rev. T. R. Birks, 2 vols. 8vo. *cloth, neat,* 9*s* (*pub. at* 16*s*) .. .. .. 1852

507 BINCHII (Johan.) Mellificium Theologicum ad Disputandum et Concionandum proficuum, *fine portrait,* 5 vols. in 1, very thick 4to. of 1350 pages, *old calf, neat,* 8*s* *Amstelodami, Janson,* 1658

"A valuable work with Arminian Views."—*Bickersteth.*

508 BINGLEY'S (Rev. Will.) Biography of 68 Celebrated Roman Characters, *plates,* 12mo. *half cloth,* 3*s* 6*d* (*pub. at* 7*s*) 1824

509 BIOGRAPHIA BRITANNICA; the lives of the most eminent persons who have flourished in Great Britain, by Dr. Kippis, 5 vols. folio, A. to F. all published, *nice set in half russia, uncut,* £2 2*s* .. .. .. 1777-93

"An exceedingly valuable work, which it is necessary to possess as well as the former edition."—*Lowndes.*

510 BIOGRAPHIA CLASSICA, the Lives and Characters of all the Classical Authors, with the best editions of their Works, 2nd Edition, 2 vols. 12mo. *old calf, neat,* 4*s* 6*d* .. 1750

A very useful little work.

511 — Biographical Dictionary of the Living Authors of Great Britain and Ireland, with the Supplement, 8vo. *half cloth,* 6*s*.—*Another copy, half calf,* 7*s* 6*d* .. .. 1816

Comprises notices of nearly 10,000 living authors, with correct lists of their publications, a perfect originality in English literature.

512 — Biography, Sketches of Ancient Poets, Orators, and Historians, 18mo. *cloth,* 2*s* .. .. *Darton,* 1832

513 — Cyclopædia of Biography, *numerous cuts,* thick 8vo. *cloth, new,* 10*s* 6*d* .. .. .. 1858

By Sir A. Alison, Sir David Brewster, Professors Eadie, Ferguson, Nichol, and others.

514 BION et Moschus, Græcè, illustrabat et emendabat Gilb. Wakefield, 12mo. *fine paper, purple morocco, by Kalthoeber, gilt edges,* 9*s* *Londini, Bensley,* 1795

"A beautiful and correct edition, printed with great care and delicacy by Bensley. It is commended by Foreign Critics."—*Dr. Dibdin.*

515 BIONDI (Cavaliere Gio. F.) l'Historia delle Guerre Civili d'Inghilterra, trà le due Case di Lancastro e Iorc, 3 vols. in 1, 4to. *old calf, neat,* 10*s* 6*d* .. *Bologna, per C. Zenero,* 1647

Period embraced 1377 to 1509. "This elegant History gained the Author great reputation." Sir Henry Wotton introduced him to the notice of K. James I. who made him Gentleman of the Bedchamber, and sent him on a Secret Mission to the Duke of Savoy, to whom this book is dedicated.

516 BIRKS (Anthony and John) Arithmetical Collections and Improvements, 8vo. *calf, neat, scarce,* 6*s* .. 1774

One of the best books ever published on Arithmetic. Both Birks were born in Norwich.

517 BISHOPS, Catalogue of all the Archbishops and Bishops, from 1688 to 1812, 8vo. *sewed,* 2*s* .. .. 1812

518 — Chart of the Episcopacy of England and Wales, beginning at Henry VIII. to Geo. IV., *mounted on canvas, in case,* 5*s* 1821

Shews, at one view, Lists of all the Bishops under their several Sees, in each Reign, separately.

519 BIZARI (Petri) Senatus populique Genuensis Rerum Domi forisque Gestarum Historiæ atque Annales, folio, *old calf, neat,* 15*s* *Antwerpiæ, C. Plantini,* 1579

This History extends from 1100 to 1578. At the end are Treatises De Syriaca Expeditione, De Bello Pisano, De Bello Veneto, &c. Sir Christopher Hatton's copy.

520 BLACK'S Life of Tasso, 2 vols. 4to. see *Tasso.*

521 BLACK and ARMSTRONG'S Catalogue of Foreign Books, 8vo. *boards,* 2*s* 6d .. .. .. 1840

522 BLACKMORE'S (Sir Richard) Creation, a Philosophical Poem, 8vo. *old calf, neat,* 3*s* 6*d* .. .. .. 1712

Presentation copy from "The Author to his worthy Friend Dr. Dl. Duncan, 1714."
"This work was undertaken with so good an intention, and executed with so great a mastery, that it deserves to be looked upon as one of the most useful and noble productions in our English verse."—*Addison.*

523 BLACKSTONE'S (Sir William, Judge) Commentaries on the Laws of England, 4 vols. 4to. *old calf, gilt,* 12*s* *Oxford, Clarendon Press,* 1770

524 BLACKSTONE'S (Sir William, Judge) Commentaries on the Laws of England, by Archbold, 4 vols. royal 8vo. *boards* 16*s* 1811

525 — another edition, *portrait*, 4 vols. 8vo. *boards*, 10*s* *London*, 1825

526 — Biographical History of his Life, Catalogue of his Works, and Nomenclature of Westminster Hall, 8vo. *boards*, 4*s* 1782

527 BLACKWOOD'S Edinburgh Magazine, vols. 20 to 38 and 40, 20 vols. 8vo. *neatly half bound*, £2 5*s* .. 1826-36

528 — Edinburgh Magazine, March to December, 1854, 4*s*

529 — Edinburgh Magazine, complete for 1855, in 12 numbers, 6*s*

530 — Edinburgh Magazine, complete for 1856, in 12 numbers, 6*s*

531 BLAIR'S Chronological and Historical Tables, from the Creation, with Continuation supervised by Sir Henry Ellis, then chief Librarian to the British Museum, royal 8vo. *half bound, quite new*, £1 11*s* 6*d* .. .. *Longman's*, 1851

"Dr. Blair's Chronological Tables have long been the favourite Manual of readers of History. The present volume has been re-constructed from the folio edition by a Literary friend. The thorough revision of the MS. and its transit through the press having been intrusted to myself, will justify my signature to the Preface, and may be taken to express my perfect confidence in its general accuracy and character."—*Henry Ellis.*

532 — Chronological Tables, revised and enlarged to the Russian Treaty of Peace, 1856, by J. W. Rosse, double vol. post 8vo. *cloth new*, 10*s* .. .. .. *H. G. Bohn*, 1856

The repeating column of dates is a useful novelty of Mr. H. G. Bohn's invention, indeed the plan and arrangement of this edition are exclusively his own.

533 — Rosse's (J. W.) Index of Dates, alphabetically arranged, being an Index to the above Tables, by J. W. Rosse, 2 vols. post 8vo. *cloth, new*, 10*s* .. .. *H. G. Bohn*, 1858

This is an indispensable adjunct to the Chronological Tables, both of which should find a place on the shelves of every Historical enquirer.

534 BLAIR'S (Dr. Hugh) Sermons, with his Life, by Dr. J. Finlayson, *portrait*, 8vo. *half cloth*, 5*s* (*pub. at* 12*s*) .. 1826

535 — Lectures on Rhetoric and Belles Lettres, *portrait*, 3 vols. 8vo. *calf, neat*, 6*s* .. .. .. 1793

536 BLANDY (Rev. Adam) Chronological Tables, from the Creation to Christ's Nativity, digested with those of Col. W. Parsons, with the characters of the High Priests, &c., by Will. Blandy, Fellow of Pemb. Coll. Oxford, small 4to. *old calf, rare*, 10*s* 6*d* *No date*

The whole of this curious Book is engraved by HULETT. Not to be found in *Lowndes*. *Book Plate of Edmund Horrex*, engraved by Dent, Bell Alley, Lombard Street.

537 BLAKESLEY'S (Rev. Jos. W., *Fellow of Trin. Coll. Camb.*) Four Months in Algeria, with a Visit to Carthage, *maps and plates*, 8vo. *cloth*, 7s (*pub. at* 14*s*) .. .. 1859

538 BLENHEIM, the Seat of the Duke of Marlborough, a description of, *plates*, 8vo. *half calf, neat*, 2*s* 6*d* *Oxford, no date*

539 BLISS.—Catalogue of the Valuable Library of Dr. Philip Bliss, sold by Auction, June, 1858, by Messrs. Sotheby and Wilkinson, *priced*, 8vo. *sewed*, 10*s* .. .. 1858

540 BLOME'S (Alexander, Gentleman) Songs and other Poems, *portrait*, small 8vo. *clean copy, old calf, rare*, £1 1*s* .. 1668

These are the Songs which used to amuse the young gentlemen of Charles the 2nd's Court.

541 BLONDEAU, Manuel de Minéralogie, *plate*, thick 18mo. *sewed*, 2*s* 6*d* *Paris*, 1827

542 BLOSIUS (Louis) Instruction Spirituelle, et Pensées Consolantes pour les ames affligées, trad. du Latin par le Père Brignon, 12mo. *bound*, 2*s* 6*d* .. .. *Nancy*, 1737

543 BLOUNT'S (Charles, Esq.) Miscellaneous Works, Oracles of Reason, Man's Soul after this Life, Priestcraft and Idolatry, &c., and an account of his Life, thick 12mo. *old calf*, SCARCE, 5*s* 1695

"In point of learning, judgment, and freedom of thought, these Essays are in no way inferior to those of the celebrated Montaigne."—*Chalmers*.

544 BLUMENBACH'S (J. F.) Manual of Comparative Anatomy, Englished, with Notes by W. Laurence and W. Coulson, 8vo. *half calf, neat*, 6*s* (*pub. at* 18*s*) .. 1827

545 BLUNDEVIL, his Exercises, VIII. Treatises on Cosmographie, Astronomie, Geographie, and Navigation, 7th edit. enlarged by R. Hartwell, *plates*, thick 4to. of above 800 pages, *old calf, neat*, 10*s* 6*d* .. .. .. 1636

In BLACK LETTER. The former editions contained but Six Books; specially written for the furtherance of the Art of NAVIGATION.

546 BLUNT'S (Henry) XII. Lectures on the History of St. Paul, during Lent, 1831, at Chelsea, vol. 1, 12mo. *cloth*, 3*s* (*pub. at* 5*s* 6*d*) 1832

547 — Lectures on the History of St. Paul, 2 vols. 12mo. *cloth*, 6*s* (*pub. at* 11*s*) .. .. .. 1832-3

548 — Discourses on some of the doctrinal Articles of the Church of England, 12mo. *cloth*, 2*s* 6*d* (*pub. at* 5*s* 6*d*) 1835

549 — another edition, 12mo. *cloth*, 3*s* .. 1842

550 — Practical Exposition of the Epistles to the VII. Churches of Asia, 12mo. *cloth*, 3*s* (*cost* 5*s* 6*d*) .. .. 1838

551 — Lectures on the History of Elisha, 12mo. *cloth*, 3*s* (*cost* 5*s* 6*d*) 1839

552 — another copy, 12mo. *cloth*, 3*s* 6*d* (*pub. at* 5*s* 6*d*) 1846

553 BLUNT'S (I. J.) Sketch of the Reformation in England, 18mo. *cloth*, 2*s* 6*d* (*cost* 5*s*) .. .. *Fam. Lib.*, 1833

554 BOCCATIO (Messer Johanne, *da Certaldo*) Incomincia il libro Primo di Florio et di Bianzafiore chiamato Philocolo, folio, *old bds. rare*, £1 1*s* *Impressio in Venetia per Augustino de Zanni*, MDXIIII.

This appears to be the last folio edition of "Il Philocolo," it has a Life of Boccaccio at the end "Composto per Hieronymo Squarzefico de Alexandria."

555 BOCCACCIO (Giovanni) Il Decamerone, con la Dichiaratione d'i Vocaboli difficili, 4to. *good copy, in old calf, gilt*, £1 5*s*
*Vinegia, per Francesco Bendoni e Mapheo Pasini*, 1541

This edition is dedicated to Cardinal Bembo, by Lodovico Dolce.

556 — Il Decamerone.—Dichiaratione di Tutti i Vocaboli, detti Proverbii el voghi difficili, che nel presente libro si trovano con lautorità di Dante, del Villani, del Cento, e d' altri Antichi per M. Francesco Sansovino, 4to. *rough calf*, £1 5*s*
*Vinetia, Gabriel Giolito di Ferrarii*, 1550

This elegant edition, dedicated to "la Delphina di Francia," has a portrait of Boccaccio, and a Life of him, by Sansovino, and is otherwise adorned with cleverly designed cuts in wood, as well as four of Gabriel Giolito's Devices.

557 — Il Decameron, (Cento Novelle), thick 12mo. 811 pages, *nice copy, in old gilt parchment*, 9*s* .. .. *Date cut off.*

I think this is the Amsterdam edition of 1703, priced by Mr. John Bohn, One Guinea. The Title page has a Sphere on it.

558 BOCCACCIO (Giovanni), Il Decamerone di, nuovante corretto et con diligentia stampato, per Paolo Rolli, 2 vols. 12mo. *nice copy in calf gilt, gilt edges,* 15*s* .. *Londra,* 1727

The Decameron is an enchanting work; it contains more good Tales of the gay and facetious kind than had then been produced by all other writers. Chaucer and Fontaine though they lived almost 300 years apart, are equally indebted to Boccaccio. He flourished in the middle of the XIVth Century.

559 BOCCALINI (Trajani) Lapis Lydius Politicus, Latinitate donavit E. J. Creutz, 18mo. *old calf, neat,* 5*s* *Amst., Lud. Elzevir,* 1640

"Boccalini was received into the Academies of Italy, where he gained great applause by his Political Discourses, and his elegant criticisms."—See *Chalmers.*

560 BOCCHI (Francesco) Bellezze della Citta di Firenze, e da Giovanni Cinelli ampliate, thick 8vo. 660 pages, *old parchment,* 8*s* *Firenze, G. Gugliantini,* 1677

With a Portrait of Cardinal Nerli, Archbishop of Florence, to whom the book is dedicated. *Mr. Coke's* copy.

561 BOCHARTI (Sam.) de Quæstione num Æneas unquam fuerit in Italia Dissertatio, 18mo. 2*s* .. *Hamburgi,* 1672

562 BODONI (Jo.) de Republica libri VI., folio, *unbound,* 8*s* *Lugduni,* 1586

This is a very good book on the subject, and scarce. See *Brunet,* who has given too long a note for transcription.

563 BOERHAAVE'S Medical Correspondence, containing Symptoms of Chronical Distempers, 8vo. *calf neat,* 3*s* .. 1745

564 BOEZIO Severino della Consolazione della Filosofia, trad. in Volgare Fiorentino da Benedetto Varchi, small 8vo. *vellum, scarce,* 7*s* 6*d* .. .. *Fiorenza, Filippo Giunti,* 1589

This version of Varchi's was thought worthy to be reprinted by Bodoni, at Parma, in 1798.

"It is a common expression in Italy, that if Jupiter wished to speak Italian he would use the Idiom of Benedetto Varchi."—*Mills's Theodore Ducas.*

565 BOETIUS'S Consolation of Philosophy, Englished by Will. Causton, 8vo. *old calf, scarce,* 4*s* .. *Printed for the Author,* 1730

566 BOHEMIAN CONFESSION.—The utmost Fury of Anti-Christ against the Reformed Church of the Bohemian Confession in Poland, set down in a brief Narrative, folio, 4 *leaves,* 6*s* *Hills and Field, Printers to his Highness,* 1658

567 BOHN'S (Henry G.) Guinea Catalogue of Books, very thick 8vo. *half morocco, as good as new,* 12*s* *York Street, Covent Garden,* 1841

This most extraordinary Catalogue is 5 inches thick; it consists of 23,208 articles, and is one of the most remarkable productions of the age. It contains an immense amount of information, and the books are remarkably well, and most correctly described. I would on no account part with it had I not two.

568 — Guide to Pottery, Porcelain, and other Objects of Vertu in the Bernal Collection, *numerous engravings,* 12mo. *cloth,* 5*s* 1857

569 — Standard Library, a number of the volumes at 2*s* 3*d* each *(pub. at* 3*s* 6*d)*

570 BOHN'S (James) Catalogue of Ancient and Modern Books in all Languages, thick 8vo. 792 pages, *half morocco, neat,* 7*s* 6*d* 1840

571 BOHN'S (John) Catalogue of French, Spanish, Portuguese, and Italian Books, 8vo. *half calf, neat,* 6*s* .. 1833

572 — Catalogue of Books, Natural History, Agriculture, Gardening, Mining, Hunting, Hawking, Fishing, &c. 8vo. *half calf, neat,* 3*s* 1835

573 — Catalogue of Ancient and Modern Theological Works, in the Learned and other Foreign Languages, 8vo. *boards,* 4*s* 6*d* 1842

574 BOHN'S (John) another copy, *half morocco*, 7*s* .. 1842

575 BOILEAU-DESPREAUX (Nicolas) ses Œuvres, avec des Eclaircissemens Historiques, donnez par lui-meme, *plates by B. Picart*, 4 vols. 12mo. *calf, neat*, 12*s* .. *La Haye*, 1729

With this Autograph "*William Nasmith, Glasgow, Dec.* 14, 1754."

576 BOLINGBROKE (Lord) Letters on the Study and Use of History, 2 vols. royal 8vo. *half bound, calf*, 2*s* 6*d* .. *Lond.* 1852

577 BOLTON'S (Robert, *of Broughton, Northamptonshire*) Discourse of True Happiness, 1631; his Directions for a Comfortable Walking with God, 1630; his Instructions for a Right Comforting Afflicted Consciences, 1631; 3 Treatises in 1 vol. thick 4to. 1244 pages, *old calf, neat*, 10*s* .. .. .. V. Y.

578 — Some General Directions for a Comfortable Walking with God, small 4to. *half calf, neat*, 3*s* 6*d* .. .. 1638

"Bolton had been a notorious sinner, reclaimed by a great work of terror, therefore is excellent both for conviction and consolation; his most useful works are his 'Directions for walking with God,' and for 'comforting afflicted consciences.'"—*Williams's Christian Preacher*.

579 BOMHOFF'S (D.) English-Dutch and Dutch-English Dictionary, 2 vols. square 12mo. *half bound, very neat*, 7*s* 6*d* *Nimmegen*, 1832

580 BONAR'S (Horatius) Night of Weeping: Words for the Suffering Family of God, 12mo. *cloth*, 2*s* .. .. 1847

581 BONEFONIUS'S Altar of Love, the whole Art of Kissing, 8vo. *old calf, neat*, 6*s* .. .. .. 1731

Besides the above, this volume contains,—1. Popeana, *no date*;—2. Young's Force of Religion, or Vanquished Love, a Poem, 1714;—3. Jacob's Rape of the Smock, 1736;—4. Four Poems in Praise of Tobacco;—5. Jesus Grove, Night, in Imitation of Milton;—6. Duck's Thresher's Miscellany, &c., 1731;—7. Apology for the Writings of Walter Moyle, 1727.

582 BONFADIUS (Josephus) Dicaeologia omnium rerumpub. adversus Paræneticam orationem H. Chunradi ad Reges et Principes, 4to, *limp vellum, scarce*, 6*s* .. *Venetiis*, 1620

I cannot find this Author mentioned in Biographical Dictionaries.

583 BONNECHOSE (Emile de) History of the Reformers before the Reformation, John Huss and the Council of Constance, from the French, by Campbell Mackenzie, 2 vols. in 1, cr. 8vo. *cloth, gilt*, 5*s* (*pub. at* 12*s*) .. .. *Edinb.* 1844

584 BONNYCASTLE'S (John, *of the Roy. Military Acad. Woolwich*) Introduction to Astronomy, *plates*, 8vo. *calf, neat*, 4*s* 6*d* 1796

585 BONOMI'S (Joseph) Nineveh and its Palaces, 240 *Engravings*, post 8vo. *cloth*, 4*s* 6*d* .. .. .. 1857

The Discoveries of Botta and Layard, applied to the Elucidation of Holy Writ.

586 BOOKBINDING, The Handbook of Taste in, *plates*, 8vo. *sewed*, 1*s* 6*d* .. .. *E. Churton, no date.*

587 — A curious specimen of inlaid old binding taken from the cover of an *old morocco* book, 2*s*

588 BOOK of the Fathers, containing the Lives of Celebrated Fathers of the Christian Church and the Spirit of their Writings, 8vo. *boards, uncut*, 2*s* .. .. *Lond.* 1837

589 BOOK Collector's Handbook, a Modern Library Companion, 8vo. *cloth*, 2*s* .. .. *E. Churton*, 1845

590 BOOKS—An Essay on the Illustration of Books, royal 8vo. *boards*, 2*s* 6*d* .. .. .. 1824

591 BOOKSELLERS' CATALOGUES, Messrs. Arch, 1817, 21, 23, 25, 28, 30.—Baynes, 1833.—Cock, 1833.—Leslie, 1833.—John Bohn, English, 1829, Bohn, Foreign, 1833.—Henry G. Bohn, 1831.—Arch, 1834, and 5 Auction Catalogues.—Harding, 1829. —Jennings, 1832.—Longman, 1822.—Jennings, 1823.—Parsons, 1831.—Longman, 1832, 1833.—Payne and Foss, 1837, and Arch, 1836, in 10 vols. 8vo. *half calf, gilt, very neat, quite clean,* £2 10*s* V. Y.

592 BOOTH'S (David) Analytical Dictionary of the English Language, Part 1, 4to. *boards,* 4*s* (*pub. at* 7*s* 6*d*) .. 1828

This edition is not mentioned by either Lowndes or Mr. Bohn.

593 BORGHINI (Don Vincenzio) Discorsi (dell' origine di Firenze, di Fiesole, della Toscana, &c.) dell' arme delle Famiglie Fiorentine, *arms emblazoned,* 2 vols. 4to. *fine copy, old calf, gilt,* 18*s* *Fiorenza, Giunti,* 1584-5

"Ouvrage recherché des Italiens. Il faut voir si le traité *della Chiesa e Vescovi Fiorentini.*"—*Brunet.*

594 BORRICHII (Olai) Lingua Pharmacopæorum; sive, de Accuratâ Vocabulorum in Pharmacopoliis usitatorum pronunciatione, 4to. *sewed,* 4*s* .. *Hafniæ, Matt. Godicchenii,* 1670

With E. Bartholinus's approbation.

595 — de Sommo et Somniferis maximè papavereis dissertatio, 4to. *sewed,* 2*s* 6*d* .. *Hafniæ, D. Paulli,* 1681

596 BORROW (George) The Romany Rye, a Sequel to "Lavengro," 2 vols. post 8vo. *cloth,* 8*s* (*pub. at* £1 1*s*) *Murray,* 1857

597 BORUWLASKI, Memoirs of the celebrated Dwarf Joseph Boruwlaski, a Polish gentleman, by himself, French and English, by M. Des Carrieres, *portrait by W. Hinks,* 8vo. *boards,* 4*s* 1788

598 BOSSANGE, Barthes et Lowell, Catalogue des Livres Français, Italiens, Espagnols, &c., royal 8vo. *half calf, very neat,* 8*s* *Londres,* 1843

599 BOSSI (Luigi) Dizionario portatile di Geologia, Litologia e Mineralogia, *plates,* 12mo. *sewed,* 3*s* 6*d* *Milano,* 1819

600 BOSSU'S Treatise of the Epic Poem, useful for judging of the excellencies of Homer and Virgil, 2nd edit., 2 vols. 12mo. *calf, neat,* 2*s* 6*d* .. .. *J. Knapton,* 1719

601 BOSSUET (Evesque de Meaux) Discours sur l'Histoire Universelle, 2 vols. 12mo. *fine copy, in old red morocco, gilt leaves, by De Rome,* £1 1*s* .. .. .. *Paris,* 1682

This is a very choice copy of this book.

602 — Suite de l'Histoire Universelle, A.D. 800 to 1700, vol. 2 only, 12mo. *bound,* 2*s* .. .. *Paris,* 1736

"The Honble. Edward Coke, Esq., his book, Anno Domini, 1739, Memento Mori."

603 — Survey of Universal History, Englished by Mrs. Jenkins, 12mo. *boards,* 2*s* .. .. .. 1819

604 — Recueil des Oraisons Funebres, 12mo. *hf. cf., neat,* 2*s* *Rouen,* 1790

605 — le même, 12mo. *old French calf, gilt,* 3*s* 6*d* *Paris,* 1774

"His Funeral Orations, and his Discourse upon Universal History, have conducted him to Immortality."—*Voltaire.*

606 BOSWELL'S (James) Account of Corsica, and Memoirs of General Pascal Paoli, *map*, 8vo. *calf, neat, 4s 6d* .. 1768

"This book was received with extraordinary approbation, and has been translated into almost every European Language."—*Nichols's Anecdotes*, vol. 2, p. 402. Dr. Samuel Johnson highly commends it.

607 — Life of Dr. Samuel Johnson, exhibiting a View of Literature and Literary Men in Great Britain for near half a Century, *portrait*, 3 vols. 8vo. 2nd Edition, *old calf, gilt, 10s 6d* 1793

"Boswell's Life of Johnson is the richest Treasury of Wit and Wisdom any language can boast."—*Quarterly Review*.

608 — Journal of a Tour to the Hebrides with Dr. Samuel Johnson, 8vo. *boards, 4s 6d* .. .. 1807

Contains an authentic account of the Distresses and Escape of the Grandson of K. James II. in 1746.

609 BOSWORTH'S (J.) Elements of the Anglo-Saxon Grammar, with Notes, a grammatical praxis, Anglo-Saxon and English, &c., 8vo. *boards, 10s 6d (pub. at 16s)* .. .. 1823

Has also an Introduction on the Origin and Progress of Alphabetic Writing.

610 — another copy, 8vo. *half calf, gilt, 15s* .. 1823

611 — another copy, 8vo. LARGE PAPER, full edition, *half calf, very neat, 18s* .. .. .. .. 1823

612 — Compendious Grammar of the Anglo-Saxon Language, 8vo. *boards, 3s (pub. at 5s)* .. .. 1826

613 BOSWORTH'S (Newton) Accidents of Human Life, with hints for their prevention, 18mo. *boards, 2s (pub. at 4s 6d)* 1813

On Accidents from Fire, at Sea, at Plays, Travelling, &c.

614 BOUGAINVILLE'S (Lewis de) Voyage to the Malouine or Falkland Islands, 1763-4, and two Voyages to the Streights of Magellan, with an Account of the Patagonians, *maps & plates*, 4to. *bds. 5s* 1771

615 — Voyage round the World, 1766 to 69, Englished by John R. Forster, *maps and charts*, 4to. *calf, gilt, neat, 7s* 1772

616 BOUILLY, Conseils à ma Fille, *plates*, 12mo. *neat, 2s* *Lond.*, 1813

617 BOUNTY—Eventful History of the Mutiny of the Bounty, *etchings by Col. Batty*, 18mo. *cloth, 2s 6d (cost 5s)* *Fam. Lib.*, 1831

618 BOURGOING—Modern State of Spain, (The Atlas to) 4to. *swd. 3s* 1808

619 BOUTERWEK'S (Frederic) History of Spanish and Portuguese Literature, Englished by Thomasina Ross, 2 vols. 8vo. *cloth, 9s (pub. at 24s)* .. .. .. 1823

620 — History of Spanish Literature, Englished, with Notes, by T. Ross, *portrait*, 12mo. *cloth, 3s* .. *Bogue*, 1847

621 BOWDEN'S (James) Covenant Right of Infants, on Baptism, 12mo. *cloth, 2s* .. .. .. 1823

622 BOWDEN'S (John) Epitaph Writer, consisting of six hundred original Epitaphs, with an Essay on Epitaph Writing, 12mo. *half bound, 3s* .. *Chester, J. Fletcher*, 1791

623 BOWDICH'S (T. Edward) Excursions in Madeira and Porto Santo, in 1823, with Mrs. Bowdich's continuation of his 3rd African Voyage, until his Death, *coloured plates*, 4to. *half calf, very neat, 14s (pub. at 2 guineas)* .. .. 1825

Mr. Joseph John Gurney's copy, with his Book-plate.

624 BOWYER'S (Will.) Origin of Printing, the substance of Dr. Middleton's and Mr. Meerman's accounts, 8vo. *boards, uncut, scarce,* 10*s* 6*d* .. .. .. 1776

The 2nd and best edition, with the Supplement, dated 1781.

625 — Critical Conjectures and Observations on the New Testament, 4to. *very good copy in grained calf,* 16*s* *J. Nichols,* 1782

"This work cannot but be acceptable to every critical reader of the New Testament; it is the best collection of conjectural emendations and remarks which has yet appeared."—*Critical Review.* "A book which ought to be read by every scholar, and every rational Christian."—*Dr. Parr.*

626 BOXIANA; Sketches of Ancient and Modern Pugilism, by P. Egan, *portraits,* 3 vols. 8vo. *calf, gilt rolls on the sides,* 15*s* 1818-21

627 BOY'S BIRTHDAY BOOK; a Collection of Tales, Essays, and Narratives of Adventure, by Mrs. Hall, William Howitt, and others, *numerous plates,* 12mo. *cloth gilt, gilt edges,* 5*s* .. 1859

628 BOYER, Dictionnaire François-Anglois et Anglois-François, thick 4to. *old calf,* 6*s* .. .. *Londres,* 1764

629 BOYS'S (Dr. John) Exposition of all the Principal Scriptures used in our English Liturgie, with a Reason why the Church did chuse the same, 4to. *old calf,* 5*s* *Felix Kyngston,* 1610

630 BOYS'S (William) Collections for an History of Sandwich, in Kent, with Notices of the other Cinque Ports and Members, and of Richborough, *with all the plates,* very thick 4to. *fine clean copy half bound in russia,* £1 11*s* 6*d* .. *Canterbury,* 1792

Contains both the Lists of Subscribers, which Mr. Upcott thought were generally cancelled when the volume was completed.

631 BRACCIOLINI'S (Poggio) Life, by Dr. Wm. Shepherd, *frontispiece,* 8vo. *cloth,* 7*s* (*pub. at* 12*s*) .. .. 1837

"Another important acquisition to the knowledge of Italian Literature in the Middle Ages."—*Dibdin.* "Very interesting."—*Dr. Samuel Parr.*

632 BRADLEY'S (Richard, F.R.S.) History of Succulent Plants, with their Descriptions and Manner of Culture, Latin and English, 50 *plates engraved by Sturt,* 4to. *old calf, gilt,* 10*s* .. 1716-27

A curious specimen of binding, the book in 5 Decades, all published.

633 BRADY'S (John) Clavis Calendaria; a Compendious Analysis of the Calendar, illustrated with Ecclesiastical, Historical, and Classical Anecdotes, 2 vols. 8vo. *boards,* 9*s* (*pub. at* £1 1*s*) 1815

"A useful work."—*Lowndes.*

634 BRADY'S (Dr. Robert) History of England, during the Reigns of Edward I. II. and III. and Richard II., *portraits by White,* folio, *old calf, neat,* 8*s* .. .. .. 1700

635 BRAGGE'S (Francis) Practical Observations upon the Miracles and Parables of our blessed Saviour, 4 vols. 8vo. *very fine copy in old calf, gilt,* 18*s* .. .. .. 1710

"I would likewise recommend Bragge on the M. & P. especially if he (the Student) would learn to emancipate himself from the slavery of using Notes."—*Dr. Wotton.*

636 BRAMSTON'S (Sir John, *of Skreens*) Autobiography, now first published from the MS. by T. W. Bramston, Esq., his descendant, thick 4to. *cloth,* 8*s* .. *Camden Soc.,* 1845

637 BRAND'S (John) Observations on Popular Antiquities, including the whole of Mr. Bourne's Antiquitates Vulgares, 8vo. *very fine copy in old calf,* 7*s* 6*d* .. *Newcastle upon Tyne,* 1777

638 BRAND'S (John) another edition, 8vo. *half russia, scarce,* 6s 6d 1810
639 — another edition, enlarged, &c. by Sir Henry Ellis, *frontispiece,* 3 vols. post 8vo. *cloth,* 15s .. *H. G. Bohn,* 1849
640 — Catalogue of his Rare Collection of Books, sold by Mr. Stewart, in May, *with prices and purchasers' names,* 8vo. *boards,* 7s 6d 1807

Inserted is a Note from the Rev. W. Bentinck Hawkins, of 23, Gt. Marlborough St. June 20, 1835, thanking Mr. Pickering for the loan of this Catalogue.

641 BRANDEBOURG, Memoires pour servir a l'Histoire de, *portrait of Frederic le Grand,* 2 vols. in 1, 12mo. *calf, neat,* 3s 6d *No place or printer's name,* 1751
642 BRANDOLESE (Pietro) Pitture, Sculture, Architetture ed altre cose notabili di Padova, *plan,* 12mo. *half bound,* 2s *Padova,* 1795
643 BRANDT'S (W.) Treatise on the Law of Divorce and Matrimonial Causes, 12mo. *boards, new,* 7s 6d .. 1858
644 BRANT (Sebastian) Titulorum omnium Juris tam Civilis quam Canonici Expositiones, 8vo. *calf neat,* 5s *Lugduni, Gryphii,* 1560
645 BRENTON'S (Capt. Edward Pelham) Naval History, *portraits, maps, and plates,* 2 vols. 8vo. *half calf, gilt, new,* £1 5s 1837

"This important work has long been an esteemed Chronicle of the triumphant Exploits of the British Navy."—*Globe.*

646 — Memoir of his Life, by his brother, Vice-Admiral Sir J. B., 8vo. *cloth,* 4s (*pub. at* 7s) .. .. 1842
647 BRENTON'S (Vice-Admiral Sir Jahleel) Memoir of his Life and Services, edited by Chancellor Raikes, thick 8vo. *cloth,* 7s (*pub. at* 16s) .. .. .. .. 1846
648 BREREWOOD (Edv.) Tractatus de Prædicabilibus et Prædicamentis; item, Tractat. de Meteoris, de Cometis, de Mari, et de Oculo, thick 8vo. *old calf, neat,* 6s *Oxoniæ,* 1631

The first two Treatises in this volume, which occupy 431 pages, are not mentioned by Lowndes.

649 BRETI (Car.) Ordo Perantiquus Judiciorum Civilium eorumque Solennia, 4to. *old vellum, very clean,* 6s *Parisiis,* 1604

With Autograph of "C. Bretaigne," in a very old hand.

650 BRETT'S (Thomas) Tradition necessary to explain the Holy Scriptures, with remarks on Mr. Toland's Nazarenus, 8vo. *old Cambridge panelled calf, neat,* 3s .. .. 1718
651 BREWER'S (Dr.) Guide to the Scientific Knowledge of Things Familiar, thick 18mo. *cloth,* 2s .. 1850
652 BRIDGES'S (Rev. Charles) Christian Ministry, 12mo. *boards,* 3s (*pub. at* 6s 6d) .. .. .. 1829
653 — Exposition of the 119th Psalm, as Illustrative of the Character and Exercise of Christian Experience, 14th edition, 12mo. *purple morocco, extra gilt edges,* 12s .. .. 1839
654 — another copy, 12mo. *cloth,* 4s (*pub. at* 7s 6d) 1843
655 BRIDGEWATER TREATISES.—Chalmers (Dr. Thos.) on the Power, Wisdom, and Goodness of God, with Biography by Dr. Cumming, post 8vo. *cloth,* 3s (*pub. at* 5s) *H. G. Bohn,* 1853
656 — Kidd's (Dr. John) Physical Condition of Man, post 8vo. *cloth,* 2s 6d .. .. .. .. *ib.* 1852
657 — Whewell's (Dr. William) Astronomy and General Physics, *portrait,* post 8vo. *cloth,* 2s 6d .. .. *ib.* 1852

658 BRIGHT (Benjamin H., Esq., of Bristol,) Catalogue of his Valuable Library, sold by Mr. Sotheby, March 1845, with the 24th day's Sale of Natural History, &c., 8vo. above 400 pages, *sewed,* 6s 1845

659 BRIGHTMAN'S (Thomas) Revelation of St. John, Illustrated with an Analysis and Scholions, 3rd edition much enlarged, very thick 8vo. of 1143 pages, *engraved frontispiece, fine clean copy in vellum, rare,* 15s *Imprinted at Leyden, by John Classon Van Dorpe,* 1616

Fuller, the Church Historian, gives this Puritan Divine a most exalted character for Piety and Learning.

660 [BRIGHTWELL'S (Thomas)] Journal of a Tour through Belgium to Frankfort, &c. and to Paris, by T. B., *frontispiece,* 8vo. *sewed, scarce,* 6s .. .. *Norwich, Wilkin,* 1828

"*Mrs. Opie, with T. B.'s kind regards.*

"With a View of Huy Castle, lithographed by Johnson, from a Sketch by the Author, Thomas Brightwell, Esq., a Solicitor at Norwich, and a great promoter of the Study of Natural History."—J. Martyn's Catalogue of *Privately printed Books,* p. 362, 2nd edition.

661 BRISMAN (Suen) Engelskt och Suenskt samt Sucnskt och Engelskt Hand-Lexicon, 4to. *hf. cf. nt.,* 15s .. *Upsala,* 1815

662 BRISSEAU-MIRBEL (C. F. *de l'Institut.*) Elémens de Physiologie Végétale et de Botanique, 3 vols. 8vo. *sewed,* 15s *(pub. at 24s) Paris,* 1815

One vol. consists of 72 plates.

663 BRISSONIUS (Bar.) de Regno Persarum, cura J. H. Lederlini, thick 8vo. *old calf,* 5s .. .. *Argentini,* 1710

664 BRISTOL TRACTS.—1, Rebuke to the Informers, w. a Plea for the Nonconformist Ministers, 1675.—2, An Exercitation upon a Momentous Question, whether it be Lawful for a Person to Act Contrary to the Opinion of his own Conscience, 1675.—3, Reply to the Bristol Narrative, a more just Account of the Imprisonment of Mr. John Thompson, 1675.—4, In obitum Domini Joannis Thompson, *Bristoliensis,* 2 *leaves of Verse in English,* 1674.—5, Sober Answer to an Address of the Grand Jurors of the City of Bristol, 1675.—6, Some Reasons which have Prevailed with the Dissenters in Bristol to Continue their Open Meetings, 1675.—In 1 vol. 4to. *old binding,* VERY SCARCE, £1 1s 1674-75

No Printer's name to either of these rare Tracts.

665 BRISTOL CHURCHES, engraved by Lander, Miller, and Willis, 25 *plates on India paper,* 4to. *half bound, very neat,* £2 2s *Bristol, George Davey, Broad Street, no date*

Presented by Mr. George Davey, the publisher, to the late Mr. Charles Muskett.

666 BRISTOL.—Catalogue of the Books in the City Library, by Charles Tovey, with the History of its Founders and Benefactors, *plans and plate,* 8vo. *cloth,* 2s 6d .. .. 1853

Dr. Evans, with Charles Tovey's compliments.

667 BRITISH Almanack and Companion, 1858, 12mo. *cloth,* 2s

668 BRITISH Catalogue of Books from 1837 to 1852, with the Prices and Publishers' names, compiled by Sampson Low, with 3 Supplements, 8vo. *half morocco, neat,* £1 1s .. 1853

669 BRITISH ESSAYISTS, with biographical prefaces, by Ferguson, *portraits,* 45 vols. 12mo. *boards,* (*pub. at* £10 10s) £2 2s 1819

670 BRITISH ESSAYISTS.—The Rambler, *portrait*, vols. 1 & 2, 12mo. *calf, neat*, 5*s* .. .. .. 1823

671 — The Adventurer, *portrait*, 3 vols. 12mo. *calf, very neat*, 7*s* 6*d* 1823

"But the most memorable consequence of Swift's frolic was the establishment of the Tatler, the first of that long series of Periodical works, which from the days of Addison to those of Mackenzie, have enriched our literature with so many effusions of genius, humour, wit, and learning."—*Sir W. Scott.*

672 BRITISH Martial; an Anthology of English Epigrams, 2 vols. 12mo. 4*s* .. .. .. 1806

673 BRITISH MUSEUM, Synopsis of the Contents of, 12mo. *sewed*, 1*s* 1842

674 — Handbook to the Library of, by Richard Sims, *map*, 12mo. *cloth, new*, 5*s* .. .. *J. R. Smith*, 1854

This little volume has been most highly extolled, and very deservedly so, it is a most useful Manual.

675 — List of the Books of Reference in the Reading Room of the British Museum, *plan of the room*, 8vo. *boards*, 7*s* 6*d* *Printed by order of the Trustees*, 1859

A valuable book of reference, with a very interesting and lucid Preface, by Mr. J. Winter Jones, its compiler.

676 BRITISH Physicians, Lives of, *portraits*, 18mo. *cloth*, 2*s* 6*d* 1830

677 BRITISH REMAINS.—1. A Concise History of the Lords' Marchers.—2. Arms of the Ancient Nobility and Gentry of N. Wales.—3. On Jeffrey of Monmouth's British History.—4. On the Discovery of America by the Welsh more than three hundred years before Columbus.—5. Celebrated Poems of Taliesin, in Sapphic verse.—6. Memoirs of Edward Llwyd, antiquary, by Rev. J. Owen, 1777.—Dr. S. S. Smith, on the Causes of the Variety, Complexion, and Figure in the Human Species, with Strictures on Lord Kames on the original diversity of mankind, *Edinburgh*, 1788.—Whiter's Specimen of a Commentary on Shakspeare, 1794—in 1 vol. 8vo. *clean copies, calf, neat, scarce*, 12*s* .. .. .. .. V. Y.

This is a very nice volume, and the Tracts are uncommon.

678 BRITTON'S (John, F.S.A.) Catalogue Raisonné of the Pictures belonging to the Marquis of Stafford, in Cleveland House, 8vo. *boards*, 3*s* 6*d* .. .. .. 1808

679 — Dictionary of the Ancient Architecture of Great Britain, and Archæology of the Middle Ages, royal 8vo. *numerous plates, half morocco, uncut*, £1 10*s* (*pub. at* £2 16*s*) 1838

680 — Auto-biography, Part I. Personal and Literary Memoir of the Author. II. Account of his Literary Works. III. Biographical, Topographical, Critical, and Miscellaneous Essays, *portraits and plates*, 2 vols. royal 8vo. *cloth*, £1 10*s* .. 1850

681 — Britton Testimonial. Account of a Public Dinner given to him at the Castle Hotel, Richmond, July 7th, 1845, with the Toasts and Speeches, 8vo. *stiff cover*, 3*s* 6*d* .. 1846

Printed for the Subscribers to the Testimonial.

682 BROADLEY'S (Robert) Lectures on the Services, Creeds, and Offices of the Ch. of England, 8vo. *cloth*, 3*s* 6*d* (*pub. at* 7*s*) 1836

683 BROCHANT (Signor) Elementi di Mineralogia, compendiosamente tradotti ed aumentati di nuovo Scoperte, *plates*, 2 vols. 12mo. *sewed*, 4*s* .. .. .. *Milano*, 1823

684 BRODIE'S (George, *Advocate)* History of the British Empire, from the accession of Chas. I. to the Revolution, 4 vols. 8vo. *boards*, 18*s* (*pub at* £2 12*s* 6*d*) .. *Edinburgh*, 1822

"Mr. Brodie is a man of research and independence of mind; his History is a work of weight and learning."—*Professor Smyth.*

685 BROICKUVY (Antonii) in IV. Evangelia enarrationum, pars 2nda, 8vo. *fine old copy with clasps*, £1 1*s* *Parisiis, apud J. Dupuys*, 1554

A remarkably beautiful specimen of contemporaneous impressed wooden binding, with the date, 1554, on it.

686 BROMLEY'S (Henry) Catalogue of Engraved British Portraits, from Egbert the Great to 1793, 4to. *half calf, very neat*, 8*s* 1793

687 BRONGNIART (Alex.) Classification et caractères Mineralogiques des Roches, homegènes et hétérogènes, 8vo. *sewed*, 2*s* *Paris*, 1827

688 BROOKE'S (Arthur de Capell) Winter in Lapland and Sweden; with Observations on Finmark, *vignettes, but no plates*, 4to. *calf, gilt edges, very fine copy*, 15*s* .. .. 1827

689 BROOKE'S Examination of Middleton's Free Inquiry into the Miraculous Powers of the Primitive Church, 8vo. *cf*, 1*s* 6*d* *Camb.*

690 BROOKE'S (H. J.) Familiar Introduction to Crystallography, 400 *wood cuts*, post 8vo. *boards*, 8*s (pub. at* 16*s)* 1823

691 BROOKES'S (Dr. R.) General Gazeteer, *maps*, 8vo. *bound*, 2*s* 6*d* 1797

692 — another copy, *maps*, 8vo. *half bound, neat*, 2*s* 6*d* 1802

693 BROOKIANA, with a bibliographical account of all the Ana's, *portrait of Henry Brooke, Esq.*, 2 vols. 12mo. *hf. cf. neat*, 5*s* 1804

694 BROUGHAM'S (Henry, Lord) Statesmen of the time of Geo. III. vols. 1 and 2, 18mo. *cloth*, 2*s* .. *Knight*, 1845

695 — Rhetorical and Literary Dissertations and Addresses, post 8vo. *cloth, neat*, 5*s* .. .. .. 1856

696 — Lives of the Philosophers of the time of George III. 8vo. 3*s* *(pub. at* 5*s)* .. .. .. *Lond.* 1855

697 — Historical Sketches of Statesmen who Flourished in the Time of George III., 6 vols. in 3, 18mo. *cloth, gilt edges*, 6*s* *Lond.* 1845

698 BROWN'S (Richard) Sacred Architecture, its rise, progress, and present state, Parts 1 to 7 only, 21 *plates*, 4to. *sewed*, 6*s* (*pub. at* 14*s*) .. .. *Fisher & Co.*, 1845

699 BROWN'S (Thomas) Observations on Dr. E. Darwin's Zoonomia, 8vo. *half vellum*, 5*s* .. *Edinburgh*, 1798

700 BROWN (Dr. Thomas) on the Physiology of the Human Mind, 8vo. *cloth*, 3*s* 6*d* .. .. *Edinburgh*, 1820

701 BROWN'S (Capt. Thomas) Dictionary of the Scottish Language, 12mo. *cloth, gilt*, 2*s* 6*d* .. .. 1845

Useful for reading Scott, Burns, Ramsey, and other popular Authors.

702 — Conchologist's Text Book, with Glossary, 19 *plates*, 12mo. *boards*, 3*s* (*pub. at* 5*s*) .. .. *Glasgow*, 1835

703 BROWNE'S (Sir Thomas) Works, edited by S. Wilkin, *portrait*, 3 vols. post 8vo. *cloth*, 15*s* .. *H. G. Bohn*, 1852

704 — Religio Medici, with Observations by Sir Kenelm Digby, small 8vo. *a fine copy in old calf*, 5*s* .. .. 1682

"This little book made a remarkable impression, and is highly extolled by Conringius and others."—*Hallam.* See, also, Dr. Johnson's Life of him.

705 BROWN'S (Tom) Works, Serious and Comical, in Prose and Verse, *plates*, vols. 2 and 4, 12mo. *old calf, very cln. and neat, 7s 6d* 1719-20

706 BRUCE (Lord) The Abstract of Lord Bruce's Bill, and the Lady Elizabeth his wife, as to the mannor of Amesbury, &c., to the use of Sir John Talbott and John Fitz-herbert, Esq. for 99 years, &c., folio, *single leaf, printed both sides, 5s* *Dated July,* 1684

707 BRUCE'S (James) Travels into Abyssinia to discover the Source of the Nile, abridged by S. Shaw, 12mo. *calf, neat, 2s* 1790

708 — Life, by Major Head, *portrait and maps*, 18mo. *cloth, 2s 6d (cost 5s)* .. .. .. *Fam. Lib.*, 1830

709 BRUCE'S (Peter Henry) Memoirs, containing his Travels in Germany, Russia, Tartary, &c., 4to. *boards, 5s* 1782

Sold at the Fonthill Sale for 15s. Contains private anecdotes of Peter I., of Russia. Mr. Bruce was a military officer in the services of Prussia, Russia, and G. Britain, 1704 to 1745.

710 BRUMMERI (Friderici, *Lipsiensis)* Commentarius ad Legem Cinciam, 4to. *old binding, rare, 10s 6d* *Lut. Parisiorum,* 1668

Dedicated to the Illustrious Minister of Louis XIV., Jean Baptiste Colbert, with a very fine portrait of him by Landry after Mignard.

711 BRUMOY'S (Father) Greek Theatre, translated by Mrs. Charlotte Lennox, 3 vols. 4to. *half russia, neat, 15s* .. 1759

Mrs. Lennox was assisted in this work by the Earl of Cork and Orrery, and Dr. Samuel Johnson. The preliminary Essay on the Ancient Drama is highly esteemed.

"Brumoy's Théâtre des Grecs is esteemed the best and most perfect work of the kind."—*Voltaire.*

712 BRUNET (Jacq. Ch.) Manuel du Libraire, et de l'amateur de Livres, 4 vols. 8vo. LARGE PAPER, *uncut, nice old French boards,* £1 11*s* 6*d* *Paris,* 1814

"Only 50 copies were printed of this large paper, at £4 14*s* 6*d*."—I. H. perhaps *Joseph Hazlewood.*

713 — Manuel du Libraire et de l'ameteur de Livres, contenant. 1. Un Nouveau Dictionnaire Bibliographique. 2. Une Table en forme de Catalogue Raisonné, 5 vols. royal 8vo. *half bound in green morocco, uncut, top edges gilt,* .. *Paris,* 1842

The 4th and best edition, of one of the best books a bibliographer can be possessed of. It is not now obtainable, being entirely out of print.

714 BRUNNMARK'S (Gustavus) Swedish Grammar, 12mo. *sewed, 2s* 1805

715 BRYAN'S (Margaret) Lectures on Natural Philosophy, with a great number of Astronomical and Geographical Problems, some useful Tables, and a Vocabulary, *portrait by Heath, and* 36 *plates*, 4to. *half calf, very neat,* 12*s* *(pub. at £2 12s 6d)* 1806

716 BRYANT'S (Jacob) Treatise upon the authenticity of the Scriptures and the Truth of the Christian Religion, 8vo. *half cloth, 3s* *Cambridge,* 1793

717 — another edition, 8vo. *boards, 3s 6d* .. 1810

"Bryant brings forward some valuable treasures of classical and historical learning, and shews how admirably these divine interpositions were adapted to put to confusion the idolators of the heathen world."—*Van Mildert.*

718 BUCCANIERS of America, History of, *portrait of Francis Lolonois,* vol. 2, 12mo. *old calf, neat, 8s* .. 1741

719 BUCHANAN'S (Dr. Claudius) Christian Researches into Asia, with Notices of the translation of the Scriptures into the Oriental Languages, 8vo. *calf, neat, 4s* .. .. 1811

720 BUCHANAN'S Life and Writings, by Hugh Pearson, *portrait*, 2 vols. 8vo. *boards*, 5*s* 6*d* .. .. *Oxford*, 1817

Best edition of a very interesting Memoir. Dr. Buchanan was Vice-Provost of the College of Fort William, Bengal.

721 BUCHANAN'S (Dr. Francis) Journey from Madras through Mysore, Canara, and Malabar, *map and plates*, 3 vols. 4to. *boards*, 25*s* 1807

"Contains more valuable matter than almost any other book of Travels. Dr. Buchanan was sent into the Countries he surveyed, by order of Government, and enjoyed singular advantages."—*Renouard.*

722 BUCHANANI (Georgii, Scoti) Opera Omnia, curante Thoma Ruddimanno, 2 vols. folio, *old calf*, £1 1*s* *Edinburgi*, 1715

723 — Paraphrasis Psalmorum Davidis poetica, small 8vo. *old calf*, 2*s* 6*d* *Glasguæ, R. Urie*, 1750

A beautifully printed edition.

724 BUCHANAN'S (William of Auchmar) Genealogy of Ancient Scottish Surnames, with the origin and descent of the Highland Clans and Family of Buchanan, 8vo. *calf, neat, scarce*, 7*s* 6*d* *Edinburgh*, 1775

725 BUCHLERI (Joan.) Elegantiarum Centum et undesexaginta Regulæ, item Medulla Eloquentiæ per F. N. Baxium, 12mo. *old binding*, 3*s* *Antwerpiæ*, 1640

With the Autographs of Alexander Nowell, Robert Parker, and Elizabeth Dugdale.

726 — Thesaurus Phrasium Poeticarum, adjecta est institutio Poetica ex I. Pontani libris desumpta, 18mo. *old vellum*, 3*s* *Amst., Jansonii*, 1650

727 BUCKINGHAM.—Manifestation or Remonstrance of the most Honble. the Duke of Buckingham, declaring his Maiesties intention for this present arming, given aboard the ship Admirall, July 21st, 4to. *sewed, scarce*, 6*s* .. 1627

In English and French, this edition not in *Lowndes*.

728 BUCKINGHAM Restored, being two Essays which were castrated from the Works of the late Duke of Buckingham, 4to. *sewed*, 2*s* *Hague*, 1727

729 BUCKINGHAMSHIRE—Congratulatory Address from the County, to Queen Anne, presented by the Lord Viscount Fermanagh and other influential persons, about the French King's surrendering Dunkirk, folio, 4 *leaves, MS. curious*, 10*s* 6*d* 1712

730 BUDÆI Epistolæ Græcæ, per Ant. Pichonium Latinæ factæ, 4to. *old calf, neat*, 6*s* and 9*s* *Parisiis, apud I. Benenatum*, 1574

"His knowledge of Greek was so great that John de Lascaris, the most learned Grecian of his time, declared that Budé might be compared with the first Orators of Ancient Athens." He was an intimate of Erasmus's, who called him *portentum Galliæ*.—See *Jortin's Erasmus.*

731 BUFFON'S Natural History, 100 *plates, shewing several hundred subjects*, 2 vols. 8vo. *half cloth*, 8*s* (*pub. at* £1 11*s* 6*d*) 1827

732 BUGG'S (Francis) Quakerism Exposed to Publick Censure, a Narrative of the Proceedings of some of the Norfolk Clergy and the Quakers at West Dereham, Norfolk, *plate*, 1699.—Quakerism Withering, *J. Dunton*, for the Author, 1694.—And 6 other Tracts, by F. Bugg, against the Quakers, in 1 vol. 12mo. *old calf, neat, scarce*, 8*s* 6*d* .. .. .. V.Y.

One of these Tracts is entitled "George Whitehead turned Topsie-Turvy," 1700. Bugg was originally a Quaker; these Tracts shew him to have been very virulent against them.

733 BUGNYON (Philebert, *Docteur 'es Droicts*) Traicté des Loix Abrogees et inusitees en toutes les cours, terres, jurisdictions et seigneuries du Royaume de France, thick 4to. above 600 pages, *limp vellum*, 6s .. .. .. .. *Paris*, 1605

Dernière edition, augmentie d'un sixiesme livre par Pierre Guenois, Conseiller du Roy.

734 BUISSON (Ludov. du) et Ez. Sureau. Omnibus orbis terrarum mortalibus Hercules Chymicus morborum debellator, sive, Aurum Philosophorum Potabile, 4to. *sewed*, 3s *Francof. ad Mænum*, 1661

735 BULL (Bishop George) Some Important Points of Primitive Christianity Maintained and Defended in Sermons, *fine portrait, by Van der Gucht*, 3 vols. with his Life, by Robert Nelson, 4 vols. 8vo. *calf, good clean copy*, 14s .. .. .. 1713

"His style is strong and manly, yet plain and intelligible; he abhorred all affectations of pompous Rhetoric, and yet expressed himself with great spirit and life."—*Nelson.*

736 — Life, by Robert Nelson, with the History of those Controversies in which he was engaged, *portrait*, 8vo. *old calf, neat*, 5s 1714

"One of the finest pieces of Theological Biography in the English language."—*Appendix to Williams.*

737 BULWER'S (Sir E. L.) Student, and England and the English, *plates*, 12mo. *cloth*, 3s .. .. 1840

738 — Pilgrims of the Rhine, *plates*, 12mo. *cloth*, 3s *(pub. at 6s)* 1840

739 — Last Days of Pompeii, *plates*, 12mo. *cloth*, 3s .. 1848

740 BULWER'S (Mr.) Ascent of Mont Blanc, See *Mont Blanc.*

741 BUNNY'S (Edmund) Booke of Christian Exercise, thick 12mo. 491 pages, *calf, neat, wants title*, 5s . 1584

Dedicated to Edwin Sandys, Abp. of Yorke, from Bolton Percie in the Ancientie of York, the 9 of Julie, 1584.

742 BUNOMIKON, sive de Jurisperitis libri II., autore Joanne Bertrando Præside Tolosano, 4to. *old vellum, scarce*, 6s *Tolosæ, Raymundi Colomerii*, 1617

With a Life of John Bertrand, by his son Francis.

743 BUNYAN'S (John) Pilgrim's Progress from this World to that which is to Come, an Allegory, with Notes by Mason, *plates*, 8vo. *cloth, gilt*, 4s .. .. .. .. 1858

744 — another edition, with Life by Dr. Cheever, *numerous elegant cuts by Dalziel after Harvey*, crown 8vo. *tinted paper, morocco extra, gilt leaves*, 12s *(cost 18s)* .. .. .. 1856

"Bunyan's natural talents and evangelical principles and piety are admirable."—*Edw. Bickersteth.*

745 BUNIAN (Jean) Le Voyage du Chrétien vers l'Eternité, traduit de l'Anglois, *quatriéme edition, frontispiece*, small 8vo. *old calf, gilt, a remarkably fine clean copy*, RARE, £2 12s 6d *Rotterdam, Abraham Archer*, 1738

At the end of this rare edition of BUNYAN'S PILGRIM'S PROGRESS are some "Cantiques par B. Pictet, *Pasteur et Professeur à Geneve.*"

746 BUONARROTI (Filippo) Osservazioni istoriche sopra alcuni Medaglioni Antichi, 33 *plates*, 4to. *a fine copy in vellum*, 12s *In Roma*, 1698

"Dissertation très estimée."—*Brunet.*

747 BURCKHARDT'S (John L.) Travels to Syria and the Holy Land, *portrait, maps, and plans,* 4to. *half calf, neat, scarce,* £2 5s 1822

"Few travellers have done more for Geography than this author; Antiquities, Manners, Customs, &c., were examined and investigated by him with a success which could only have been insured by such zeal, perseverance, and judgment as he evidently possessed."—*Stevenson.*

748 BURDETT (Sir Francis) Memoirs of his Life, *portrait,* 1810, Narrative of the Proceedings in the House of Commons relative to his Commitment to the Tower, 1810, 2 Tracts, *sewed,* 3s

749 BURKE'S (Rt. Hon. Edmund) Works, 6 vols. 4to. *good copy, in calf,* £2 12s 6*d* .. .. .. 1792

Mr. J. J. Gurney's copy, with his book-plate.

"He was a writer of the first class, and excelled in almost every kind of prose composition. He reminds us of Bacon's multifarious knowledge and the exuberance of his learned fancy; while his many-lettered diction recalls to mind the first of English poets, and his immortal verse, rich with the spoils of all sciences and all times."—*Edinburgh Review.*

750 — Public and Domestic Life, by Peter Burke, *engravings,* post 8vo. *cloth,* 2s 6*d* .. .. .. 1854

751 BURKE'S (William) Greek-English Derivative Dictionary, in English Characters, 12mo. *boards,* 2s 6*d* .. .. 1806

752 BURKITT'S (William) Expository Notes, with Practical Observations on the New Testament, folio, *old calf,* 12s .. 1752

"A very useful Commentary; it is both pious and practical."—*Dr. Adam Clarke.*

753 — Help and Guide to Christian Families, 12mo. *neat,* 1s 6*d* 1822

754 BURLEIGH, Prime Minister to Queen Elizabeth, his Autograph, see *Zenobius.*

755 BURN'S (Richard) Justice of the Peace and Parish Officer, the 25th edition, by Chetwynd and Marriott, 5 vols. 8vo. *cf. very neat,* 15s

756 BURNET'S (Bp. Gilbert) History of the Reformation of the Church of England, *illustrated with portraits,* 6 vols. 8vo. LARGE PAPER, *very nice set in calf, gilt, marbled edges,* £3 3s 1820

"His talents gave him an unusual degree of consequence both in Church and State. He obtained the thanks of both Houses of Parliament on the appearance of the first volume of his History of the Reformation."—*Chalmers.*

757 — Abridgment (by himself) of the History of the Reformation, 1520-1567, *frontispiece,* 8vo. *old calf, neat,* 3s 6*d* 1683

758 — another edition, 8vo. *half calf, neat,* 5s *Oxford, the Clarendon,* 1808

759 — Historie de la Reformation de l'Eglise d'Angleterre, traduite par M. de Rosamond, 2 vols. 4to. *old calf, neat,* 10s 6*d* *Lond.,* 1683

760 — Memoirs of the Lives and Actions of James and William Dukes of Hamilton, 3 *portraits, by R. White,* folio, *fine clean copy, in old calf, gilt,* 12s .. .. .. 1677

This is an account of the Civil Wars of Scotland from 1625 to 1652, with many Letters of K. Charles I. never before published.

761 — History of his own Time, from the Restoration (1660) to the Peace of Utrecht, 1713, and the Bishop's Life, 2 vols. folio, *old calf,* 12s .. .. .. 1724-34

Prefixed is a recapitulation of affairs in Church and State from K. James Ist's time.

762 — another edition, *portrait,* 4 vols. 8vo. *bound,* 18s 1753

763 — Memoires pour servir a Hist. de la Grande-Bretagne, sous les Regnes de Charles II. et de Jaques II., *fine portrait by Houbraken,* 3 vols. 12mo. *good copy, in calf,* 15s *à La Haye,* 1725

764 BURNET'S (Bp. Gilbert) Exposition of the XXXIX. Articles of the Church of England, folio, *old calf, neat,* 3*s* 6*d* 1737
765 — another copy, 8vo. *boards, uncut,* 5*s* .. *Oxford,* 1831
766 — another copy, *half-bound, calf neat,* 4*s* 6*d* *London,* 1833
767 — Lives of Sir Matthew Hale, the Earl of Rochester, Abp. Leighton, Hon. Robert Boyle and others, with Notes by Bp. Jebb, 12mo. *nice copy in calf,* 11*s* .. .. .. 1833

"All that is controversial, indeed, is nearly forgotten; but the history of the Reformation, and of his Own Time, his Lives of Rochester, Bedell, Hale, &c. afford a fair prospect that his fame will be prolonged."—*Dr. Johnson.*

768 BURNET and ATTERBURY.—XI. Original Sermons by Bishop Burnet, 1680 to 1706.—Bishop Burnet's Modest Survey of "Naked Truth," 1676.—Bp. Burnet's Funeral Sermon for Abp. Tillotson, 1694.—Parsons's Sermon for the celebrated John, Earl of Rochester, 1680.—XI. Original Sermons by Francis Atterbury, afterwards Bishop, 1692; No. 7, is a Funeral Sermon for Mr. Thomas Bennett, Aug. 30th, 1706; No. 8, a Latin Concio ad Clerum Londinensem, Maii 17, A.D., 1709, in 1 vol. 4to. *half calf, neat,* 10*s* 6*d* .. .. .. V.Y.
769 BURNET'S (Rev. Richard, *of Bungay, Suffolk*) Various English and Latin Poems, with an Essay on the Composition of Latin Verse, with particular Reference to Prosody, 2*s* 6*d* *Norwich, Bacon,* 1808
770 BURNET'S (Thomas) Sacred Theory of the Earth, *portrait by White, and plates,* fifth edition, 2 vols. 8vo. *old calf, neat,* 6*s* 1722

"This celebrated book will ever continue to charm the reader by the eloquence of its style, and the grandeur of its imagery."

771 — de Statu Mortuorum et Resurgentium, accesserunt Epistolæ duæ circa libellum de Archæologiis Philosophicis, 8vo. *half bound,* 2*s* *Londini,* 1726
772 BURNETT'S (George) Specimens of English Prose Writers, to the Close of the XVII. Cent., with Sketches, Biographical and Literary, including an Account of Books, 3 vols. post 8vo. *half cloth,* 15*s* *(pub. at 24s)* .. .. .. 1807

"An elegant and judicious compilation, forming a companion to Ellis's Specimens."—*Lowndes.*

773 BURNHAM'S (Richard) Pious Memorials of Eminent Persons, 8vo. *old calf, neat,* 4*s* .. .. .. 1754

With Dr. Hervey's recommendatory Preface.

774 BURNS'S (Robert) Poems, chiefly in the Scottish Dialect, *portrait,* 2 vols. small 8vo. *boards,* 4*s* .. *Edinburgh,* 1798
775 — Poetical Works, *portrait,* 3 vols. 12mo. *cloth, new,* 15*s* *W. Pickering,* 1839
776 — Works and Life, edited by Robert Chambers, 4 vols. 12mo. *cloth, new,* 12*s* *Edinburgh,* 1851

The opinions of the many are concentrated in that of Lord Byron, who said, "The rank of Burns is the very first of his Art." He is said to "rival all but Shakspeare's name below."

777 — Life, by J. G. Lockhart, Sir Walter Scott's son-in-law, 8vo. *cloth, scarce,* 7*s* 6*d* .. .. *Edinburgh,* 1828

This edition is out of print, it has a full-length Portrait of Burns, by Miller, after Nasmyth, on India paper.

778 — another edition, *frontispiece,* 18mo. *cloth,* 2*s* .. 1828

779 BURRHI (F. J.) Epistolæ duæ.—I. De Cerebri ortu et usu Medico. II. De Artificio oculorum humores restituendi, 4to. *sewed,* 2*s* 6*d* *Hafniæ, D. Paulli,* 1669

780 BURTON'S (Dr. Edward) Lectures on the Ecclesiastical History of the First Century, 8vo. boards, *scarce, out of print,* 7*s* 6*d* *Oxford,* 1831

781 BURTON'S (Robert) Anatomy of Melancholy, *engraved title page by C. Le Blon, containing his portrait,* folio, *half russia, nice clean copy,* £1 1*s* .. .. *Oxford, Henry Cripps,* 1628

782 — another edition, with an Account of his Life, 2 vols. 8vo. *good copy, in calf, gilt,* 16*s* .. .. .. 1813

"Writing fortunately in English, and in a style not by any means devoid of point and terseness, with much good sense and observation of men as well as of books, and having, also, the skill of choosing his quotations for their rareness, oddity, and amusing character, without losing sight of their pertinence to the subject, he has produced a work of which, as is well known, Dr. Johnson said, it was the only one which had ever caused him to leave his bed earlier than he had intended."—*Hallam.*

783 BURTON'S (Thomas) Diary of the Parliaments of Oliver and Richard Cromwell, 1654 to 1659, edited with Notes by J. T. Rutt, *plates,* 4 vols. 8vo. *half calf, very neat,* 24*s* (*pub. at* £2 16*s*) 1828

"Every library, which pretends to contain an historical collection, must possess itself of this Diary, it is as indispensable as Burnet, or Clarendon."—*Atlas.*

"One of the best and fullest views which we have of Cromwell's Parliaments. It shows us more of the working of the Protector's system than any former publication had done." —*Orme's Life of Baxter,* p. 138.

784 BURTONI (Guil.) Veteris Linguæ Persicæ Historia, small 8vo. *old calf, neat, scarce,* 4*s* 6*d* .. .. *Lubecæ,* 1720

At the end is an Epistle from M. Z. Boxhornius to M. Blancardus, "de Persicis Curtii Vocabulis."

785 BUSBEQUII (A. Gislenii, *Legationis Turcicæ*) Opera Omnia, 18mo. *old calf, very neat,* 3*s* 6*d* .. *L. Bat., Elzevir,* 1633

786 — Epistolæ, de Itineribus Turcico, et Amasiano, thick 24mo. *vellum,* (no title page) 2*s* 6*d*

The relation which he wrote of his Two Journeys to Turkey is much commended by Thuanus. See *Saxii Onomasticon.*

787 BUSBY'S (Dr. Thomas) Dictionary of Music, with an Introduction to the First Principles, 12mo. *boards,* 3*s* 6*d* (*pub. at* 7*s* 6*d*) 1817

788 BUTEONIS (Joan.) Opera Geometrica, 9 Tractat.; in Jure Civili, 6 Tractat., 4to. *vellum, scarce,* 6*s* *Lugduni, apud T. Bertellum,* 1570

15 Curious Treatises. De Arca Noæ, cujus formæ, capacitatisq. fuerit, —Confutatio quadraturæ Circuli,—De fluentis aquæ mensura,—De pretio margaritarum, &c.

789 BUTLER'S (Charles) Horæ Juridicæ Subsecivæ; Notes Respecting the Geography, Chronology, and Literary History of the Principal Codes and Original Documents of the Grecian, Roman, Feudal, and Canon Law, royal 8vo. *boards,* 5*s* 6*d* .. 1807

790 — Notes on the Chief Revolutions of the Principal States of the Empire of Charlemagne, (Germany,) from 814 to 1806, royal 8vo. *half calf,* 5*s* .. .. .. 1807

791 — Reminiscences, 8vo. *boards,* 5*s* 6*d* .. 1822

792 — The Author's Works, and some of his Reminiscences, 8vo. *boards,* VERY RARE, 10*s* .. .. .. 1821

"*Mrs. Thomlinson with the Author's respects,*" in MS. This brochure, which consists of 52 pages, is called vol. 3, and appears to be introductory to a 3rd *intended* vol. of Reminiscences, but is evidently *privately printed;* not mentioned in *Mr. Bohn's Lowndes.* It is a list of his works, of which he enumerates 17, with Anecdotes concerning them.

793 BUTLER'S (Bp. Joseph) Whole Works, complete in 1 vol. 12mo. *cloth*, 4*s* 6*d* .. .. .. 1852
794 — Analogy of Religion to the Constitution and Course of Nature, with select Sermons, fcap. 8vo. *cloth, new*, 2*s* 6*d* *Edinb.* 1850
795 — Analogy, with Dissertations of Personal Identity and of the nature of Virtue, 12mo. *cloth*, 2*s* 6*d* .. 1855

"Able and argumentative, a work of incalculable value."—*Bickersteth.*

796 BUTLER'S (Samuel) Hudibras, a Poem, *with portrait and plates by W. Hogarth*, 12mo. *old calf*, SCARCE, 10*s* 6*d* 1726

FIRST EDITION with *Hogarth's cuts.* Dr. Samuel Johnson used this edition when he compiled his Dictionary.

797 — Hudibras: written in the time of the late wars, with large annotations, by Dr. Zachary Grey, *fine portrait by G. Vertue, and plates by Hogarth*, 2 vols. 8vo. *old calf*, £1 4*s* *Camb.*, 1744
798 — Hudibras, with a Life of Butler, and a Discourse of the Civil War, notes, &c., *plate*, 2 vols. 18mo. *boards*, 4*s* 6*d* (*pub. at* 9*s*) 1812
799 — Hudibras, 18mo. *boards*, 2*s* *Chiswick, Whittingham*, 1828
800 BUTLER'S (William) Exercises on the Globes and Maps, with the Constellations and Fixed Stars, by T. Bourne, 12mo. *neat*, 3*s* 1837
801 BUXTON (Sir Thomas F.) On the African Slave Trade, 8vo. *cloth*, 3*s* 6*d* .. .. .. .. 1839
802 — African Slave Trade and its Remedy, *map*, 8vo. *cloth*, 4*s* 6*d* 1840
803 BYRON'S (Lord) Works and Life, by Thomas Moore, *plates*, 17 vols. 12mo. *cloth*, £2 5*s* (*pub. at* £4 5*s*) 1832
804 — another copy, *nicely half bound in morocco, gilt leaves*, £3 10*s* 1832

This is the best edition, and now quite out of print. Same size as Scott's Waverley Novels, and Southey's Cowper.

805 — Poetical Works complete, *Thorwalsden's Statue of him*, post 8vo. *cloth*, 9*s* .. .. .. *Murray*, 1857
806 — Don Juan, with Life and Notes by A. C. Cunningham, *plates*, 12mo. *cloth, gilt edges*, 5*s* .. .. 1852
807 — English Bards and Scotch Reviewers, 8vo. *boards*, 2*s* 6*d* 1810
808 — Sardanapalus, a Tragedy; The Two Foscari, a Tragedy; Cain, a Mystery, 8vo. *sewed*, 5*s* .. *Murray*, 1821
809 — Island, or Christian and his Comrades, 8vo. *sewed*, 2*s* 1823

The foundation of this Story is the Mutiny of the Bounty, 1789, and Mariner's Tonga Islands, both of which see.

810 — Childe Harold, Thirty Illustrations of, done expressly for the Art Union of London, *portrait, fine impressions*, 4to. *boards*, 10*s* 1855
811 — Journal of his Conversations at Pisa, in 1821-22, with Thomas Medwin, *portrait, and fac-simile of Byron's Writing*, 2 vols. 12mo. *sewed*, 5*s* .. .. .. *Paris*, 1824
812 — Correspondence with a Friend, forming an original Memoir of his Life, from 1808 to 1814, by the Rev. A. R. C. Dallas, 3 vols. 12mo. *sewed*, 15*s* .. .. *Paris*, 1825

Sir John Cam Hobhouse, (now Lord Broughton) caused an Injunction to be issued against the publication of these volumes, which are very scarce, only a few having got into circulation.

813 — Letters on the Character and Poetical Genius of Lord Byron, by Sir Egerton Brydges, post 8vo. *boards*, 4*s* 6*d* (*pub. at* 10*s* 6*d*) *Longmans*, 1824

814 CÆSARIS Commentarii, small 8vo. *old calf, neat,* 3*s* 6*d* *Parisiis, ap. I. Bladium,* 1533

815 — Commentarii de Bello Gallico et Civili, *map and plates,* 8vo. *old stamped calf, rare,* £1 1*s* *Lugd. Bat., Christ. Plantini,* 1586

This is a remarkably fine specimen of old oak stamped binding, by Grolier, with his initials, F. G. stamped on it.

816 — quæ extant, ex emendatione Jos. Scaligeri, 18mo. *remarkably fine clean copy in white vellum,* 18*s* *L. Bat. Elzevir,* 1635

"This is the genuine Elzevir edition, an *extremely scarce* book, page 149 marked 153.—This little book has sold so high as £5 5*s* in Paris."—*Dr. Adam Clarke's Bibliog. Dict.*

817 — ex emendatione Jos. Scaligeri, 18mo. *neat,* 12*s* *Ludg. Bat. Elzevir,* 1635

This is a fine clean copy of the Editio Vera.

818 — cum notis variorum et J. Scaligeri, *map,* 8vo. *good copy in old calf,* 5*s* .. .. *Amst. Elzevir,* 1670

819 — ex emendatione Jos. Scaligeri, 18mo. *old calf, neat,* 3*s* 6*d* *Amst. Elz.* 1675

820 — et Hirtii Commentarii, 12mo. *old calf, very neat,* 5*s* *Londini, Tonson,* 1716

"*Tho. Dillingham Donum Tho. Tooke, S. T. P.,* 1719." Edited by the erudite Michael Maittaire.

821 — Commentari, fatte da ANDREA PALLADIO, *con le figure in Rame,* 4to. *very fine copy in old calf, gilt,* 25*s* *Venetia, Pietro de Francheschi,* 1575

Dedicated "Al Excellentiss. Sig. il Signor Giacomo Bon Compagno, Generale di Santa Chiesa." "This *first* edition is extremely rare and valuable; it is adorned with numerous elegant engravings."—*Moss.* This is a particularly fine copy and the impressions of the plates are brilliant.

822 — Discourse of the Portus Itius, see *Godmond.*

"The Greek and Latin languages have nothing in their kind more perfect than those admirable performances, the Expedition of Cyrus and the Commentaries of Cæsar."—*Spelman.*

823 CAGNATI (Marsilii *Veronensis*) Variarum Observationum lib. IV., ejusdem disputatio de ordine in cibis servando, small 8vo. *old binding,* 5*s* 6*d* *Romæ, apud B. Donagellum, permiss. Superiorum,* 1587

"This eminent Roman Physician was one of the most learned men of his time. These Lectures abound with Quotations from the Greek and Latin Classics, on which account they acquired particular interest."—See *Chalmers.*

824 CAIN, Death of Cain, after the manner of the Death of Abel, (see *Gessner*) by a Lady, 18mo. *boards,* 1*s* 6*d* 1812

825 CAIRD'S (John) Sermon before the Queen, Oct. 1855, the Religion of Common Life, 8vo. *sewed,* 1*s* .. *Edinb.,* 1855

826 CALAMY—Master Edmund Calamy's Leading Case, small 4to. *eight leaves,* SCARCE, 8*s* .. *No Printer's name,* 1663

Calamy was Curate of St. Mary Aldermanbury, London; he was suspended, and for contumaciousness to the Bp. of London was committed to Newgate;—this is his examination before the authorities.

827 — Godly Man's Ark; or City of Refuge in the day of his distress, in Sermons; also contains Mrs. Moore's Evidences for Heaven, and her Funeral Sermon, 18mo. *bound,* 2*s* 6*d* 1672

828 — Nonconformist's Memorial; An Account of those who were ejected by the Act of Uniformity, Aug. 24th, 1662—abridged by S. Palmer, *numerous portraits,* 2 vols. thick 8vo. *calf, neat,* 12*s* 1775

829 CALF'S Head Club—The Whig's Unmask'd, being the Secret History of the Calf's Head Club, *satirical plates*, 8th edition, 8vo. *old calf, scarce*, 8*s* .. .. .. 1713

Contains all the treasonable Songs and Ballads; several characters by Sir John Denham; a vindication of Charles I. by Butler, &c. Milton is said to have been the principal founder of this club.

830 CALIFORNIA, A Natural and Civil History of, *map and plates*, 2 vols. 8vo. *calf*, 6*s* .. .. 1759

831 CALLET (Francois) Tables Portatives de Logarithmes, des nombres 1—108000, et des Sinus et Tangentes, 2 vols. royal 8vo. *boards*, 20*s* .. .. .. *Paris, Didot*, 1795

832 CALLIMACHUS, Cleanthes, Proclus, Græcè, curante J. F. Boissonade, 24mo. *green morocco, extra, gilt leaves*, 4*s* 6*d* *Parisiis, Lefevre*, 1824

An elegantly printed little edition with short notes at the end.

833 CALMET'S Dictionary of the Bible, by Mr. Charles Taylor, *maps and plates*, royal 8vo. *half calf, new*, 14*s* (*cost* 20*s*) 1833

834 CALVERT (Sir Peter) Speech preparatory to adjudging a Decree in favour of Mrs. Inglefield, 8vo. *sewed*, 1*s* 1786

835 CALVINI (Joannis) de Prædestinatione et Providentia Dei, libellus, small 8vo. 356 pp. *neat, rare*, 9*s* *Genevæ, apud I. Crispinum*, 1550

836 — Declaration pour maintenir la vraye foy que tiennent tous Chrestiens de la Trinité des personnes en un seul Dieu, small 8vo. *a fine clean copy in calf*, 15*s* *Geneve, Iean Crespin*, 1554

This Tract of Calvin's against Servetus, who was burnt at Geneva in the previous year, is written in justification of the proceedings of the Synod there, signed by Calvin and 14 ministers of the reformed Church, and is extremely scarce and valuable.

837 — Sermons on the Epistles of S. Paule to Timothie and Titus, translated out of French, by L. T., 4to. *old calf, rare*, 25*s* *G. Bishop and T. Woodcoke*, 1579

A very considerable volume of 1248 pages.

838 — Harmonie upon the 3 Evangelistes, Matthew, Marke, and Luke, with the Commentarie, translated by Eusebius Paget, 1610.—Commentarie on S. John, Englished by Christopher Fetherstone, in 1 thick vol. *old calf*, £1 1*s* *Thomas Dawson*, 1610

Portrait of Calvin inserted.—The 1st Treatise is dedicated to Francis, Earle of Bedford, 1584, 806 pages.—The 2nd to Robert Dudley, Earle of Leycester, 464 pages.

839 — Institution of Christian Religion, Englished with Notes, &c., by Thomas Norton, thick folio, *unbound*, 10*s* *John Norton*, 1611

840 — another edition, Englished by Thomas Norton, *fine mezzotint portrait of Calvin inserted*, folio, *newly bound in calf extra*, 15*s* 1634

841 — the same abridged, by William Lawne, translated out of Latin into English by Christopher Fetherstone, small 8vo. *original calf, very neat, scarce*, 7*s* 6*d* .. *Printed at Edinburgh*, 1587

Dedicated to the "Ladie Judith Pelham, by Christopher Featherstone, from Maighfield, in Sussex, this xvii. of April, 1586."

842 — Christian Theology, with his Life by Samuel Dunn, *portrait*, 12mo. *cloth*, 3*s* 6*d* .. .. .. 1837

"I hold the memory of Calvin in high veneration; his works have a place in my library, and, in the study of the Holy Scriptures, he is one of the Commentators whom I frequently consult."—*Bp. Horsley.*

843 CALVINI (Joannis) Histoire de la Vie, Mœurs, Actes, Doctrine, et Mort de Jean Calvin, recueilly par M. Hierosme Hermes Bolsec, small 8vo. *clean and neat, in old calf, gilt, scarce*, 9*s* *Paris, G. Chaudiere*, 1578

At the end is "Calvinodie, ou Hymne sur le Tombeau de Jean Calvin." A Poem occupying 9 pages.

844 CAMBRIDGE Problems, from 1801 to 1810 inclusive, 8vo. *boards*, 2*s* .. .. .. *Cambridge*, 1810

845 — University Calendar, large 12mo. *cloth*, 4*s* (*pub. at* 6*s* 6*d*) 1858

846 — Catalogue of Abp. Parker's MSS. in C. C. C., Camb., see *Nasmith*

847 — Collett's (W. R.) List of the Early Printed Books in the Library of Gonville and Caius College, Cambridge, 8vo. *cloth*, 4*s* *Cambridge*, 1850

848 — Graduati Cantabrigienses ab anno 1659, usque ad 1823, 8vo. *boards, scarce*, 8*s* (*pub. at* 12*s*) .. *Cantabrigiæ*, 1823

849 — Horne's (Thos. Hartwell) Catalogue of the Library of Queen's College, methodically arranged, 2 vols. royal 8vo. *boards*, SCARCE, £1 10*s* .. .. .. .. 1827

In MS. "J. L. Hubbersty, Fellow of Queen's College." "From an affectionate brother, in the Gospel of Christ, to Rev. George Ingram, 20 Feby., 1839."

850 — MS. volume, relating to the University Lands, Burwell St. Mary, Pecuniæ et Scaccariæ, Crane's Lands, University Courts, Civil Jurisdiction, Clerkship of the Market, Wine Licenses, &c., &c. 8vo. *half-bound, uncut*, 5*s*

From the Library of Dr. Thomas Sutton.

851 — Masters's History of Corpus Christi College in Cambridge, 4to. *large paper, plates, and a private portrait of the author inserted*, RARE, £1 10*s* .. .. .. .. 1753

852 — Memorials of Cambridge, by Wright and Jones, *with Views of the Colleges, Halls, and Public Buildings, by Le Keux, nicely engraved*, 2 vols. 8vo. *cloth, gilt*, £1 4*s* .. .. 1847

853 — Musæ Seatonianæ; a complete Collection of the Cambridge Seatonian Prize Poems, from 1750, small 8vo. *old calf, neat*, 4*s* 1772

854 — Poem on Stirbich Fair, Miscellanies to the Norwich Ladies, with the following Tracts .. *Norwich, W. Chase*, 1736

Opposition no Proof of Patriotism, 1735.—Some Considerations on the Public Funds, the Revenue and Parliamentary Supplies, 1735.—Letter from a M.P. on the Wine and Tobacco Duties, 1733.—Smith's Curiosities of Common Water, by Ralph Thoresby, 1723.—The Grand Accuser the Greatest of all Criminals, 1735, in 1 vol. 8vo. *boards*, 6*s* .. 1733-36

855 — Wilson's (Joseph) Memorabilia Cantabrigiæ; an Account of the Colleges in Cambridge, with Biographical Sketches of the Founders and Eminent Men, *numerous portraits and plates*, 8vo. *half calf, neat*, 5*s* .. .. .. .. 1803

856 CAMDENI (Gulielmi) Rerum Anglicarum et Hibernicarum Annales, regnante Elizabetha, thick 8vo. *good copy in calf*, 6*s* *Lugd. Bat., Elzevir*, 1639

"A most exquisite history, undertaken by the special directions and command of the great Lord Cecil."—*Bp. Nicolson.*

857 — idem, *fine portrait of the Queen, by Crisp. Van Queboren*, 1625, 8vo. *very good copy in old calf*, 8*s* *L. Bat. Elzevirii*, 1639

"It has had many editions and in several languages, though 'tis pity it should be read in any other than its author's polite original Latin."—*Bp. Nicolson.*

858 CAMDENI (Gulielmi) et Illustrium Virorum Epistolæ, *fine portrait, by R. White*, 4to. *nice copy in old calf*, 7*s* 6*d* *Londini*, 1691

Added are,—I. Annals of the Reign of K. James I., 1603-1623.—II. A Treatise on the Antiquity, Dignity, and Office of Earl Marshall of England, and Camden's Life by Dr. Thomas Smith, all in Latin.

859 CAMDEN SOCIETY.—Autobiography of Sir John Bramston, of Skreens, edited by Lord Braybrooke, thick 4to. *cloth*, 8*s* 1845

860 — Private Diary of Dr. John Dee and Catalogue of his Library, edited by James O. Halliwell, 4to. *cloth*, 4*s* .. 1842

861 — Correspondence of Robert Dudley, Earl of Leycester, during his Government of the Low Countries, 1585-86, Edited by John Bruce, thick 4to. *cloth*, 7*s* 6*d* .. .. 1844

862 — Hayward's (Sir John) Annals of the First Four Years of the Reign of Queen Elizabeth, Edited by John Bruce, 4to. *cloth*, 4*s* 1840

863 — Kemp's Nine Daies Wonder, performed in a daunce from London to Norwich, with Introduction and Notes, by Alexander Dyce, 4to. *cloth*, 4*s* .. .. .. 1840

864 — Proceedings against Dame Alice Kyteler, prosecuted for Sorcery, 1324, Edited by Thomas Wright, 4to. *cloth*, 5*s* 6*d* 1843

865 — Letters from James, Earl of Perth, to his sister, the Countess of Errol, Edited by W. Jerdan, 4to. *cloth*, 6*s* 1845

866 — Rutland Papers; Original Documents Illustrative of the Courts and Times of Henry VII. and VIII., Edited by W. Jerdan, F.S.A., 4to. *cloth*, 3*s* 6*d* .. .. 1842

867 — Verney Papers; Notes of Proceedings in the Long Parliament, Temp. Charles I., Edited by John Bruce, Esq., 4to. *cloth*, 6*s* 1845

868 — Warkworth's (Dr. John) Chronicle of the First Thirteen Years of the Reign of King Edward IV., Edited by James O. Halliwell, 4to. *cloth*, 4*s* .. .. .. 1839

869 CAMILLI (Camillo) Imprese Illustri di diversi, coi Discorsi di, et *con le figure intagliate in rame di* GIROLAMO PORRO, *parte prima*, 4to. *fine clean copy in old vellum*, 15*s* *Venetia, Francesco Ziletti*, 1586

With the Book-plate of "the Rt. Hon. Charles Lord Halifax, 1702." 59 *exquisite Plates* by GIROLAMO PORRO, on the letter press, in form of EMBLEMS.

870 CAMPAN'S (Madame) Memoirs of the private Life of Marie Antoinette, *portrait*, vol. 1, 8vo. *boards*, 2*s* 1823

871 CAMPBELL'S (Lord) Speeches at the Bar, and in the House of Commons, 8vo. *cloth*, 9*s* (*pub. at* 12*s*) *Edinburgh*, 1842

872 CAMPBELL'S (George) Modern India; a Sketch of the System of Civil Government, with some Account of the Natives and Native Institutions, 8vo. *cloth*, 8*s* (*pub. at* 16*s*) .. 1852

873 CAMPBELL'S (John) Lives of the Admirals and other Eminent British Seamen, 2nd edition, 4 vols. 8vo. *old cf., very nt.*, 7*s* 6*d* 1750

874 — another edition, by Yorke, *portraits*, 8 vols. 8vo. *large paper, boards*, £1 16*s* (*pub. at* £7 4*s*) .. .. 1812

875 CAMPBELL'S (Thomas) Philosophical Survey of the South of Ireland in Letters to John Watkinson, M.D., *plates*, 8vo. *half calf, uncut*, 5*s* .. .. .. .. 1777

"An interesting and valuable work."—*Lowndes*.

876 CAMPBELL'S (Thomas) Poetical Works, *portrait and plates, after Harvey*, 12mo. *morocco, extra gilt edges*, 11*s* *Moxon*, 1849

877 CAMPBELL'S (Thomas) Essay on English Poetry with Notices of the British Poets, post 8vo. *cloth, neat,* 3*s* 6*d* (*pub. at* 6*s*) 1848

878 CANADAS (The) in 1841, by Sir Rich. H. Bonnycastle, *maps and plates,* 2 vols. post 8vo. *cloth,* 5*s* 6*d* (*pub. at* £1 1*s*) 1841

879 CANNING'S (Rt. Hon. George) Speeches delivered on Public occasions at Liverpool, *portrait,* 8vo. *half calf, neat,* 4*s* *Liverpool,* 1825

880 CAPELL'S (Edward) Prolusions; or Select Pieces of Ancient Poetry, compil'd with great care from their several originals, small 8vo. *old calf, gilt, a nice copy,* 12*s* .. .. 1760

Contents.—I. The exquisite old ballad, The Notbrowne Maid; Master Sackville's Induction; and Overbury's Wife.—II. Edward the Third, a Play, thought to be writ by Shakespeare.—III. Those excellent didactic Poems, intitl'd Nosce Teipsum written by Sir John Davies.

"Given as specimens of the integrity that should be found in the editions of worthy authors."

881 CAPEL'S (Richard) Temptations, their Nature, Danger, Cure, with a Treatise on Usury, thick 12mo. *old calf,* 4*s* 1636

882 CAPELLI (Jacobi, *Parrhisiensis*) Fragmenta ex Variis Authoribus pressim concinata, 4to. *vellum,* (*some of the margins gnawed*) 6*s* *Parisiis, Jehan Petit,* 1517

With Jehan Petit's beautiful wood-cut Device on the title-page, and the Autograph, "Thou," perhaps the historian, De Thou, or Thuanus.

883 CAPGRAVE'S (John) Chronicle of England, to 1417, with his Metrical Life of Saint Katharine, edited by the Rev. F. C. Kingeston, royal 8vo. *half morocco,* 8*s* 6*d* *Longmans,* 1858

Published under the direction of the Master of the Rolls. Capgrave was born at Lynn, in Norfolk, in 1393, and excelled all his companions in his zeal for learning. This is a capitally edited book, with a complete Glossary and Index compiled with much care and labour.

884 CAPOA (Lionardo di) Lezioni intorno alla Natura delle Mofete, small 4to. *old parchment, clean,* 3*s* 6*d* *Napoli, per S. Castaldo,* 1683

885 CAPPER'S (B. P.) Topographical Dictionary of the United Kingdom, 47 *maps,* thick 8vo. *half vellum,* 10*s* (*pub. at* £1 11*s* 6*d*) 1825

886 CARACCIOLUS (Galeacius, *the Noble Marquesse of Vico*) his Life, by W. Crashaw, small 4to. (wants title) *sewed,* 4*s* 1608

887 CARBONARI—Memoirs of the Secret Societies of the South of Italy, particularly the Carbonari, *portraits and plates,* 8vo. *boards,* 4*s* 6*d* (*pub. at* 12*s*) .. .. 1821

Autograph of Mrs. "*Catherine Nassau.*"

888 CARD'S (Henry) XI. Literary Recreations; Moral, Historical, and Religious Essays, 8vo. *old calf, gilt,* 4*s* *Liverpool,* 1811

889 CARLETON'S (Bp. George) Thankfull Remembrances of God's Mercy, in an Historicall Collection of the Mercifull Deliverances of the Church and State of England from the beginning of Q. Elizabeth's Reign, small 4to. *half calf, neat,* 10*s* 6*d* 1624

First edition of a very curious collection of facts wholly unnoticed by any other Historians.

890 CARLISLE'S (Antony) Essays on the Disorders of Old Age, and how to prolong Life, 8vo. *boards,* 2*s* 6*d* 1818

891 CARLISLE'S (Frederic Howard, Earl of) Poems, *plate of arms, Bulmer,* 1807—Stepmother, a Tragedy, *Bulmer,* 1812—Father's Revenge, a Tragedy, *Bulmer,* 1812—in 1 vol. small 8vo. *nice clean copies, half bound in russia,* 15*s* 1807-12

Privately printed, and most elegantly executed on a thick vellum paper by Bulmer.

892 CARNARVON'S (Earl of) Portugal and Gallicia, post 8vo. *calf, gilt, very nice copy,* 5*s* .. .. 1848

893 CARNE'S (John) Recollections of Travels in the East, post 8vo. *boards,* 3*s* 6*d* (*pub. at* 10*s* 6*d*) .. .. 1830

894 CARNEVALE (Dottor Gioseppe) Historie et Descrittione del Regno di Sicilia, 4to. *much injured by damp, old calf, gilt,* 6*s*
*Napoli, Horatio Salviani,* 1591

895 CARO (Annibal) Gli Straccioni, Comedia, 1st edition, 12mo. *sewed,* 3*s* 6*d* *In Vinegia, Aldo Mannucci,* 1582

Historia vere Gregorio de Ferrari.

896 — delle Lettere Familiari, colla Vita dell' Autore scritta dal Signor A. F. Seghezzi, 3 vols. 8vo. *Italian vellum, a very nice copy,* 15*s*
*Padova,* 1743

"They (the Italians) took infinite pains with their letters, those of Annibal Caro are among the best known."—*Hallam.*

897 CARR'S (George *of Edinburgh*) Sermons, 2 vols. 8vo. *calf neat,* 5*s* 6*d*
*Edinburgh,* 1791

"Exhibit the most useful and important truths of the gospel, not only with plainness and perspicuity, but in a language always eloquent."—*Sir W. Forbes.*

898 CARREL'S (Armand) History of the Counter-Revolution in England under Chas. II. and James II., with Fox's History of the Reign of James II., *portrait,* post 8vo., *cloth,* 2*s* (*cost* 3*s* 6*d*) *Bogue,* 1846

899 CARRINGTON'S (Rev. James, *Senior Prebendary of Exeter Cathedral*) Sermons, 8vo. *boards,* 3*s* .. *Exeter,* 1826

900 CARTER'S (Eliz.) Poems on Several Occasions, 2nd edition, small 8vo. *beautiful copy in old red morocco, gilt edges,* 6*s* 1766

Printed by the desire of the Earl of Bath, the authoress says in her dedication to his Lordship.

901 CARTER (Harry Lee, Esq., *of the Carabineers,*) Dead of Ennui, a Comedietta, translated from the French, 8vo. *sewed,* 3*s* 6*d*
*Norwich, C. Muskett,* 1846

"This little trifle was printed almost solely for private circulation."—*Preface.*

902 CARY'S (H. F.) Lives of the English Poets, from Johnson to Kirke White, 12mo. *cloth,* 3*s* 6*d* .. .. 1846

Designed as a continuation of Dr. Johnson's Lives.

903 — Early French Poets, with a History of French Poetry by his Son, 12mo. *cloth,* 4*s* (*pub. at* 7*s*) .. .. 1846

904 CARY.—Memoirs of the Life of Robert Cary, Baron of Leppington, and Earl of Monmouth, written by himself, *plate of Queen Elizabeth in Procession,* 8vo. *half calf, neat,* 6*s* .. .. 1759

Edited by John, Earl of Corke, with Explanatory Notes, this book illustrates the Reigns of Q. Elizabeth and James I.

905 CARY'S Atlas of England and Wales, with a General Description of each County, 45 *coloured maps,* 4to. *calf, neat,* 15*s* 1793

906 CASA (Giovanni della) Rime et Prose, small 8vo. *a nice copy in calf,* 12*s* .. .. .. *Fiorenza, i Giunti,* 1564

"Raro."—*Gamba.* "No poet of his time enjoyed more reputation. His style is pure Tuscan, and his Sonnet, *Son queste Amor,* is a delightful expression of Love."—*Mills's Theodore Ducas.*

907 CASELLÆ (P. L.) de Primis Italiæ Colonis, de Tuscorum Origine et Republica Florentina, Elogia Illustrium Artificum, Epigrammata et Inscriptiones, 8vo. *old calf, very neat,* 6*s* *Lugduni,* 1606

Grævius has thought this book worthy of a place in his *Thesaurus Antiquitat. Italiæ.*

908 CASIMIRI (Mathiæ) Lyricorum libri IV. et Epigrammata, 24mo. *calf,* 2*s* and 3*s* .. .. *Cantabrigiæ,* 1684

909 CASSAN (Jacques de, *Conseiller du Roy)* Le recherche des Droicts du Roy, et de la couronne de France, sur les Royaumes, Duchez, Villes, et Pais occuppez par les Princes estrangers, thick 4to. 696 pages, *limp vellum,* 6*s* .. .. *Paris,* 1632

910 CASTALIONIS (Josephi, *Juris-consulti)* Observationum in criticos, Decades X., small 8vo. *old calf,* 3*s* 6*d* *Lugduni,* 1608

Book-plate of William Kennett, Bp. of Peterborough.

911 CASTELLANI (Petri) Syntagma de Festis Græcorum, de Mensibus Atticis, et de Græcorum et præcipue Atheniensium Mensibus et Anno, small 8vo. *old calf,* 3*s* 6*d* *Antwerpiæ, H. Verdussii,* 1617

912 CASTELLETTI (Christoforo) Le Stravaganze d'Amore, Comedia, 12mo. *sewed,* 2*s* 6*d* .. *Venetia, Bertano,* 1613

913 CATALOGUES of Libraries, the Art of Making; a method to obtain a satisfactory printed Catalogue of the British Museum Library, by a reader therein, 8vo. *sewed,* 2*s* .. 1856

914 CATALOGUE des Livres de M. Gluc de Saint-Port, Conseiller honoraire au Grand Conseil, disposé par J. Boudot, Libraire, *priced,* 8vo. *nice copy in calf, gilt edges,* 4*s* 6*d* *Paris,* 1749

This is a systematized Catalogue.

915 — des Livres rares et precieuses de F. Goutard, par G. de Bure, *Priced, Paris,* 1780.—Catalogue des Livres du Cardinal de Loménie, *Paris,* 1797.—Catalogue des Livres le C. Camus de Limare, *Paris,* 1795.—Prix des Livres rares, (de M. de Limare) dont la sente s'est faite de Lundi 20 Mars, 1786, in 1 vol. 8vo. *calf, very neat,* 10*s* V. Y.

With the Book-plates of *T. F. Dibdin,* and *John Trotter Brockett, F.S.A.* Three capital Catalogues.—See *Horne's Bibliography.*

916 — of Saunders and Otley's Public Library, Conduit Street, Hanover Square, 8vo. with the Supplement, 2 vols. 8vo. *cloth,* 3*s*

917 CATALONIA—Histoire de tout ce qui s'est passé en la Catalogne, depuis qu'elle a secoüé le joug de l'Espagnol, 4to. *limp parchment,* 4*s* .. .. .. *Rouen,* 1642

Contenant le progrez de la Guerre en 1640 et 1641, avec la Signalée Victoire de Monjuique.—Les Secrets Publics de la Catalogne, 1642.—et l'Appuy de la Verité Catalane, 1642.

918 CATULLUS Tibullus, et Propertius, Scaligeri, thick 12mo. *vellum, neat,* 4*s* .. .. .. *Lyons,* 1607

Barthius says, this edition, edited by Grasserus, was unknown to literary men. "Scaliger's merits in regard to Catullus should be received with gratitude, as he has often by his own divine talent, restored the true reading."—*Sillig.*

919 — Opera, 12mo. *old calf, very neat,* 5*s* *Londini, J. Tonson,* 1715

"*Theo. Dillingham, Donum Thomæ Tooke. S.T.P.,* 1719."—Michael Maittaire's edition esteemed very correct.

920 CAULFIELD'S (James) Calcographiana; The Printseller's Chronicle and Collector's Guide to the Knowledge and Value of Engraved British Portraits, *port. of the author,* 8vo. *hf. morocco, uncut,* 6*s* 1814

921 CAVALCANTI—Rosso (Paolo del) Comento sopra la Canzone di Guido Cavalcanti, small 8vo. *old boards, the edges all rough*, 7s 6d *Fiorenza, Bartolomeo Sermartelli*, 1568

Dedicated to Cosmo de Medici, with the Autograph of *Niccola Francesco Haym*, the celebrated Italian Bibliographer, who says of this book—"Comenti assai buoni."

922 CAVALLO'S (Tiberius) Treatise on Air and other permanently elastic Fluids, with an Introduction to Chemistry, thick 4to. *half calf, very neat*, 9s .. *For the author*, 1781

923 CAVE'S (Dr. Will.) Primitive Christianity; the Religion of the Ancient Christians in the first ages of the Gospel, thick 8vo. *neat*, 3s 6d .. .. .. .. 1673

924 — Scriptorum Ecclesiasticorum Historia Literaria, ad Sæc. XIV. 2 vols. folio. *old calf, gilt*, £2 5s .. *Oxonii*, 1740

Best edition of "A very capital performance, discovering great reading."—*Orme*.

925 CAWDREY'S (Daniel, *of Billing Magna)* III. Sermons, small 4to. *sewed*, 3s 6d .. .. .. 1641

Dedicated to "Sir Christopher Yelverton, Kt., High Sheriff of the Countie of Northampton."

926 CECIL'S (Rev. Richard) Life, Character, and Remains, collected by Josiah Pratt, *portrait*, 8vo. *half calf, neat*, 6s 1812

927 CELESTINO (F. *Sacerdote Capuccino)* Historia di Bergomo et suo territorio, thick 4to. of 614 pages, *vellum, neat*, 10s 6d *Bergomo, per Valerio Ventura*, 1617

"*Raro.*"—*Haym*. The history of Bergamo, an ancient city in Italy. This contains XI. Books.

928 CELLARII (Christ.) Epistolæ Selectiores et Præfationes conlegit I. G. Walchius, qui et copiosiorem diatriben de Dedicationibus Librorum Vet. Latinorum præmisit, *portrait*, 12mo. *sewed, uncut*, 5s .. .. .. *Lipsiæ*, 1715

929 CELLINI (Benvenuto, *Florentine artist)* Memoirs of, written by himself, containing information on the Arts and History of the 16th Century, with Notes, &c., by T. Roscoe, *portrait*, 2 vols. 8vo. *boards*, 9s (*pub. at* 24s) .. .. 1822

"Cellini was one of the most extraordinary men of an extraordinary age; his Life, written by himself, is more amusing than any novel I know."—*Horace Walpole*.

930 — another edition, *portrait*, 12mo. *cloth*, 2s 6d 1847

931 CELSUS, de re Medica; Sereni Samonici Præcepta Medica, Versibus Hexametris; Rhemnii Fannii Palæmonis de Ponderibus et Mensuris, in 1 thick vol. small 8vo. *old calf, neat*, 7s 6d *Haganoæ, per I. Secerium*, 1528

"Liber rarus et utilissimus." "For elegance, terseness, learning, good sense, and practical information Celsus stands unrivalled."—*Anthon*.

932 CERVANTES—Don Quixote, translated by Motteaux and Ozell, *plates*, 4 vols. 12mo. *old calf, neat, scarce*, 12s 1725

"On the whole, I am inclined to think the version of Motteaux is by far the best we have yet seen of the romance of Cervantes, and that, if corrected in its licentious observations and enlargements, we should have nothing to desire superior to it in the way of translation."—*Tytler*.

933 For other editions, see *Don Quixote*.

934 CHALMERS'S (Alexander) General Biographical Dictionary, 32 vols. 8vo. *good set in calf, grained*, £7 10s 1812

This is the very best Biographical Dictionary extant.

935 CHALMERS'S (Alex.) Biog. Dict., vol. 2 only, 8vo. *boards*, 6*s* 1812
936 — History of all the Colleges and Halls of Oxford University, with the Lives of the Founders, *plates by Storer and Greig*, 2 vols. 8vo. *calf*, 9*s* .. .. .. *Oxford*, 1810

"This work contains much information which will be useful and amusing to the generality of readers, and which could not be procured, except in works which are now become both scarce and expensive."—*Quarterly Review.*

937 CHALMERS'S (George) Estimate of the Comparative Strength of Great Britain during the present and 4 preceding Reigns, and of the losses of her Trade from every war since the Revolution, 3rd edition, 8vo. *boards*, 7*s* 6*d* .. .. 1794

"One of the most useful and conclusive books, both for the extent and accuracy of its researches, and the force of its reasonings."—*Lowndes.*

938 CHALMERS (Dr. Thomas) on the Use and Abuse of Literary and Ecclesiastical Endowments, 8vo. *boards*, 3*s* (*cost* 6*s*) *Glasgow*, 1827
939 — Lectures on the Establishment and Extension of National Churches, 8vo. *cloth*, 2*s* 6*d* .. .. .. 1838
940 CHAMBERLAIN'S (John) Present State of Great Britain, 8vo. *portrait, old calf*, 4*s* 6*d* .. .. .. 1716
941 — another edition, with Remarks upon its Ancient State, *portrait*, 8vo. *old calf, neat*, 6*s* .. .. .. 1737

Autograph of "*Dan Fromanteel*, 1739." A valuable work, Lord Macaulay has made much use of it in his History.

942 CHAMBERS'S (Robert and William) Cyclopædia of English Literature; a History of British Authors with Extracts from their Works, *portraits and plates*, 2 vols. royal 8vo. *cloth*, 14*s* *Edinb.*, 1858
943 — Information for the People, 2 vols. royal 8vo. *cloth*, 16*s* *ib.* 1858
944 — Domestic Annals of Scotland from the Reformation to the Revolution, 2 vols. 8vo. *cloth*, 24*s* .. .. *ib.* 1858
945 — History of the English Language and Literature, 12mo. *cloth*, 2*s* .. .. .. .. *ib.* 1836
946 — another edition, 12mo. *cloth, new*, 2*s* 6*d* .. *ib.* 1857
947 — Exemplary and Instructive Biography, 12mo. *cloth, new*, 2*s* 6*d* *ib.* 1855
948 — Educational Course, Astronomy, 12mo. *cloth*, 1*s* *ib.* 1854
949 — on Infant Education, from 2 to 6 years, 12mo. *cloth*, 1*s* *ib.* 1837
950 — Commercial Tables consisting of Interest, Measures, &c. 12mo. *cloth*, 3*s* .. .. .. *ib.* 1856
951 — History and Adventure, *numerous engravings*, 12mo. *cloth*, 2*s* 1855
952 — Select Poetry, *numerous engravings*, 12mo. *cloth*, 2*s* *ib.* 1855
953 — Rudiments of Zoology, *cuts*, 12mo. *cloth, new*, 3*s* 6*d* *ib.* 1855
954 — Cookery and Domestic Economy, *illustrated*, 12mo. *cloth*, 1*s* 6*d* 1856
955 — Youth's Companion and Counsellor, *portrait of B. Franklin*, square 16mo. *cloth, gilt*, 4*s* 6*d* .. .. *ib.* 1857
956 — new edition, *portrait*, 16mo. *cloth, new*, 5*s* .. *ib.* 1858
957 — Popular Rhymes of Scotland, with Original Poems, *plate*, f.cap 8vo. *cloth*, 4*s* .. .. .. *ib.* 1847
958 — Traditions of Edinburgh, *plate*, 12mo. *cloth*, 4*s* *ib.* 1856
959 — Encyclopædia; a Dictionary of Useful Knowledge for the People, parts 1 to 10, imperial 8vo. *all published*, 7*d* per part *ib.* 1859

960 CHAMBERS'S (R. & W.) Library for Young People.–The Whisperer, by Mrs. Hall—Steadfast Gabriel, by Mary Howitt—Alfred in India—Orlandino, by Miss Edgeworth—Uncle Sam's Money Box, by Mrs. Hall, 5 vols. 18mo. *cloth, 1s each* .. 1858

961 CHAMPION'S (Anthony) Miscellanies, in Verse and Prose, English and Latin, edited by William Henry Lord Lyttelton, royal 8vo. *calf, very neat, 5s* .. .. .. 1801

Finely printed by Bensley, there is a Memoir of the Author.

962 CHANDLER'S (Dr. Richard) Travels in Asia Minor and Greece, Tours made at the expense of the Society of Dilettanti, *maps and plans*, 2 vols. 4to. *calf, very neat, 10s 6d* 1776

Lord Walpole's autograph on each Title Page.
"These are valuable Travels to the antiquarian: the author, guided by Pausanias as respects Greece, Strabo for that country and Asia Minor, and Pliny has described with wonderful accuracy and perspicuity the ruins of the Cities of Asia Minor, its Temples, Churches, &c."—*Stevenson.*

963 CHANDLER'S (Samuel) Vindication of the Christian Religion, 8vo. *boards, uncut, 2s* .. *For the Author*, 1725

A Discourse on Miracles, and in answer to Collins's Grounds.—"*Donum Auctoris.*"

964 CHANNING'S (Dr. W. E.) Literary Works, 8vo. *cloth, 4s 6d* 1854

On the character and writings of Milton, Napoleon Buonaparte, and Fenelon—a National Literature, Education, Slavery, Temperance, Self-culture, &c.

965 — Character of Napoleon, and other Essays, *plate*, 2 vols. 24mo. *cloth, gilt edges, 3s* .. .. 1837

966 — Funeral Sermon for him, Nov. 6th, 1842, by Dr. Jos. Hutton, 8vo. *sewed, 1s* .. .. .. 1842

967 CHANSONS—Recüeil de Trois Cent Chansons Françoises, 8vo. *old calf, neat, 6s* .. *Londres, G. Smith*, 1737

"Vend. 16 fr. Labédoy; 20 fr. en 1843."—*Brunet.*

968 CHAPONE'S (Mrs.) Letters on the Improvement of the Mind, addressed to a Young Lady, 2 vols. 12mo. *old calf, gilt, 4s* 1773

969 — another edition, 18mo. *green morocco, gilt edges, 3s 6d (cost 7s)* 1829

Sharpe's pretty edition, with Westall's plates.

970 CHARLEMAGNE; An Anglo-Norman Poem of the XIIth Century, 12mo. *cloth, new, 9s* .. *W. Pickering*, 1836

*Only* 10 *Copies for Sale.* This is now for the first time published with a Literary Introduction and Glossary, by F. Michel.

971 CHARLES I.—The King's Majesties Proceeding to St. Paul's Church, 26 March, 1620, showing the order of Procession, MS. folio, *broadside, 5s*

972 — A Prayer for the King's Maiestie, in his Northern Expedition, folio, *broadside*, Black Letter, *curious, 3s 6d* *R. Barker*, 1639

Done when the King was going to Scotland to settle the Liturgy—Laud's Liturgy, which the Scots refused. See *Common Prayer.*

973 — Declaration of the Daily Grievances of the Catholiques Recusants of England, with Protestations to the same for their Loyaltie, &c. small 4to. *stiff covers, clean as new, 6s* *John Thomas*, 1641

974 — Proclamation 23 Dec. 1641, in Black Letter, for a Fast, 20 Jan. next, folio, *broadside, in a handsome compartment, 4s* *R. Barker*, 1641

975 — Message sent to H. Majesty by both Houses, concerning present dangers, folio, *broadside, 2s* *Joseph Hunscott*, 1641

976 CHARLES I.—H. Maiesties Speech and Mr. Speaker's, on passing the Bill for Tonnage and Poundage, fol., *broadside*, 4*s* 22 *June*, 1641

977 — Rudyerd's (Sir Benjamin) Speech, concerning Bishops, Deans, and Chapters, at a Committee of the whole House, small 4to. 4 leaves, *sewed*, 4*s* .. .. 1641

978 — Verney's (Sir Ralph) Notes and Proceedings in the Long Parliament, temp. Charles I., Edited by John Bruce, 4to. *cloth, new*, 5*s* *Camden Soc.* 1845

979 — Short View of the Life and Reign of K. Charles (the Second Monarch of Great Britain) from his Birth to his Burial, *portrait by Marshall*, 12mo. *half calf, neat, scarce*, 6*s* 1658

980 — Salmasius, Defensio Regia, pro Carolo I., 1649—Miltoni (Joan.) pro populo Anglicano defensio, contra Salmasii, *Londini*, 1650, in 1 vol. thick 12mo. *old calf*, 5*s* .. V. Y.

981 — Eikon Basilike, le Pourtraict du Roy de la Grand Bretagne, durant sa solitude et ses souffrances, *portrait*, 12mo. *morocco, gilt leaves, rare*, 7*s* 6*d* .. .. *Paris*, 1649

982 — Fac Simile of the Death Warrant of K. Chas. I., with the Signatures of all the Regicides, 1*s* 6*d* .. 1827

983 — The Rotterdam Quakers Excommunication, and Damning of GEORGE JOYCE, who was formerly known by the stile of CORNET JOYCE; Notorious for his carrying away of King CHARLES the First from *Holmby House*, to the *Isle of Wight*, faithfully translated out of Dutch into English, licensed according to the order by Roger Lestrange, 4to. *four leaves, sewed*, £4 4*s*
*London, Printed and Sold by Joseph Moxon, on Ludgate Hill, right against the Old Baly, at the sign of Atlas* 1671

The answer of the King to Joyce, upon his Majesty's asking him to show him his *Commission* for forcibly carrying him off, is differently given in this EXCESSIVELY RARE AND POSSIBLY UNIQUE TRACT, (which is not to be found in *Lowndes*,) to the quotation made by *Hume* from *Whitlocke*. And the King's answer here seems to be so extremely natural that it is very likely to be the correct one. "*This is indeed the only Commission of these times.*" Upon Joyce's requesting H. M to look out of the window where he could see 500 horse, this happened June 3, 1647. This tract says he was governor of the Isle of Wight, (a circumstance not mentioned by *Hume*,) where he conducted himself so tyrannically that he was obliged to fly to *Holland*, where he turned *Quaker*. And this tract was published by that fraternity to disacknowledge him as one of their sect.

984 — Matthews (William) Observations upon a Pamphlet entitul'd the Letter which Pope Gregory XV. wrote to Charles I. of England concerning his Marriage to the Infanta of Spain, and that Prince's Answer, 4to. *sewed*, 3*s* *Ipswich, J. Bagnall*, 1729

985 — Declaration of the Committee of the H. of Commons to consider the safety of the Kingdom and of the City of London, folio, *broadside, curious*, 5*s* *Joseph Hunscott*, 6 *Jan.*, 1641

In consequence of Mr. Hollis, Sir Arthur Haslerige, Pym, Hampden, &c's, chambers, studies, and trunks, by colour of His Majestie's warrant, have been sealed up by Sir Will. Kilegrey and others.

986 — Declaration of the House of Commons touching a late breach of their Privileges, fol., *broadside, rare*, 10*s* *J. Hunscott*, 17 *Jan.*, 1641

Has immediate reference to the preceding Article, "And we declare that if any person shall arrest M. Hollis, Haslerigg, Pym, Hampden, &c., he is guilty of a breach of the liberties of the subject," &c.

987 — Declaration of both Houses touching the Government and Liturgy of the Church, folio, *broadside*, **Black Letter**, 3*s*
*R. Barker*, 9 *Ap.*, 1642

988 CHARLES I.—Mysterie of the two Juntos, Presbyterian and Independent, small 4to. *stiff cover, clean as new, scarce,* 6*s* 1647

989 — A MS. commencing "The King is the Fountaine of Mercy as well as of Justice," small 8vo. *beautifully written, limp white vellum,* 10*s* .. .. .. *No Date*

990 — The Life and Reigne of King Charles, or the Pseudo-Martyr Discovered, 12mo. *vellum, rare,* 6*s* .. 1651

In MS. "A d—d libell made by a villaine who eate the K's bread," then "a silly reflection made by a blockhead who knew not the happiness of our constitution."

991 — Ashburnham's (John) Narrative of his attendance on K. Cha. I. never before printed, with a Vindication of him from Lord Clarendon's misrepresentations, *portrait,* 2 vols. 8vo. *cloth,* 5*s* 6*d* (*pub. at* £1 1*s*) .. .. .. 1830

"This work is valuable from throwing much light on a portion of history which has hitherto been involved in unusual obscurity."—*Athenæum.*

992 — Histoire des Troubles de la Grand Bretagne, par R. M. D. S., thick 4to. 815 pages, *fine copy, in vellum,* 10*s* *Paris, Antoine Vitré,* 1649

This is a finely printed volume, the History extends from 1633 to 1646.

993 — History of the Reign of K. Charles I., by M. de Larrey, Englished, *portrait,* 2 vols. 8vo. *old calf, neat,* 5*s* .. 1716

Autograph of "John Gurney, Earlham," and book plate of Mr. "Joseph John Gurney."

994 CHARLES II.—A Collection of 32 Tracts published between 1661 and 1631, being original editions of Speeches in Parliament by the King and others, in 1 vol. folio, *half bound, in an original state, many of them uncut, very clean,* £5 5*s*

Principal Contents. Ogilby's Entertainment of his Majesty in his passage through London to his CORONATION, with a Description of the Triumphal Arches and Solemnity, 1661, RARE.—His Majesty's Commission concerning the reparation of the CATHEDRAL CHURCH OF ST. PAUL, in London, 18 *leaves,* VERY RARE, 1663.—*Lowndes, who enumerates many Commissions for the reparation af the Cathedral, does not mention this, which just preceded the Great Fire of London.* There are 20 other speeches by the King, all relating to the History of the Country—the Declaration of War against the States General, &c., &c. An earlier Tract by BEN JONSON on TIMBER, 1641.—And 10 others from 1700 to 1717, on occasional Conformity, repealing the Triennial Act, &c. 42 original Tracts in all, a very curious and valuable volume.

This collection was made by Sir Edmund Bacon, who was member for Norwich in the time of Queen Anne, about 1711. Several of them have the initials of his name on them as well as that of Sir Robert Bacon his father.

995 — Grand Memorandum: or a true and perfect copy of the *Secluded Members* of the H. of Commons, sitting 16 March, 1659, being the day of their *Dissolution.* Also a perfect Catalogue of the RUMPERS, and the names of the *King's Judges who condemned him to death,* marked with a *hand,* folio, *broadside, very curious and rare,* £1 1*s* .. *Edward Husbands,* 1660

996 — A List of his late Majesties unjust Judges and others, who are to be tried for their Horrid Treasons, at the Old Bayly, Oct. 10, 1660, a *broadside, curious,* 5*s* *London, for John Stafford,* 1660

997 — H. Majesties gracious Commission to search into and examine the pretended sale of Mannors, Lands, &c. belonging to him, his Royal Mother, the Abps., Bps., Deans and Chapters, &c., folio, **Black Letter**, *sewed,* 5*s* .. .. 1660

This was almost the first act of the King's at his Restoration.

998 CHARLES'S II.—His Maj. gracious Commission to search into the pretended sales and purchases of the Honours, Mannors, Lands, &c. belonging to H. Maj., his Royal Mother, Deans and Chapters, &c., folio, 4 *leaves*, **Black Letter**, 7*s* 6*d* *Rich. Marriott*, 1660

999 — Speaker's Speech to the King at Whitehall, Nov. 9, 1660, folio, 3 *leaves*, 2*s* .. .. *John Bill*, 1660

1000 — List or Roll of the King's Majesties Royal Proceedings from the Tower through London to Whitehall, folio, *broadside*, RARE, 10*s* *For Richard Williams*, 1661

1001 — King's Speech to both Houses, July 30, 1661, on their adjournment, 4 *leaves*, folio, 2*s* .. *Bill and Barker*, 1661

1002 — Fourteen Stanzas of French Poetry, addressed "Sur l'heureuse arrivée de la tres haute Princesse Catherine Reigne de G. Bretagne," par Claude Mauger, Professeur de le Langue Fr. à Londres, folio, *broadside*, RARE, 10*s*

May 14, 1662, Catharine the Infanta of Portugal, arrived at Portsmouth, where she was married to K. Ch. II.

1003 — Votes of the Commons, Feb. 25, 1662, upon reading H. Maj. gracious Declaration and Speech, 4to. *sewed*, 1*s* 6*d* 1662

1004 — Speaker's (Sir Edw. Turnor's) Speech to H. Majesty on the Prorogation of Parl., 20 July, 1663, folio, *six leaves*, 3*s* *Robert Pawlet*, 1663

1005 — His Majesties and Sir Edw. Turnor's Speeches, on the Prorogation, May 17, 1664, folio, 6 *leaves*, 3*s* *C. Barker*, 1664

1006 — Sir Edw. Turnor's Speech to the King and Parl., Feb. 9, 1664, on granting a Royal aid, folio, 4 *leaves*, 3*s* *C. Barker*, 1664

1007 — Proclamation touching Mariners, Seamen, and Souldiers to serve in H. Maj. Navy, folio, *broadside*, **Black Letter**, 5*s* *C. Barker*, 23 *Nov*. 1664

1008 — His Majesties' Charge to all the Justices of the Peace of Middlesex, upon his going to meet his Parliament at Oxford, folio, *single leaf*, *curious*, 6*s* .. *about* 1669

In 1666 the King was suspected of leaning to Romanism, but, this broadside expressly declares that "it is his firm resolution to stick to the Church of England."

1009 — Lord Chancellor's Speech in the Exchequer to Baron Thurland, on his taking his Oath, 24 Jan., 1672, folio, 2 *leaves*, 3*s* 1672

1010 — Advice to the Patrons of the Test, folio, *single leaf*, 2*s* *No Date, about* 1673

1011 — Particular and exact List of such Officers of his Highness the Prince of Orange's Army, as were killed, wounded, &c., in the late fight, August, 1674, between him and the Prince of Condé, with a List of the French killed, folio, *broadside*, *curious*, 6*s* *Tho. Newcomb*, 1674

1012 — King's and Lord Keeper's Speeches to both Houses, Oct. 13, 1675, 5 *leaves*, folio, *sewed*, 2*s* *Bill and Barker*, 1675

1013 — A Letter from a Person of Quality to his Friend in the Country, folio, MS. of 34 *pages*, 10*s* 6*d* .. 1675

A beautifully written MS. about the Five Mile Act, the Act of Uniformity, &c.; the Lord Treas, Southampton, Lords Wharton and Ashley, took part in these proceedings.

1014 — King's and Lord Chancellor's Speeches to both Houses, Feb. 15, 1676-7, 10 *leaves*, folio, *sewed*, 2*s* *Bill and Barker*, 1677

1015 CHARLES II.—Proclamation for the apprehending of Aron Smith, for speaking Seditious Words, dated June 6, *Royal arms*, folio, *broadside*, **Black Letter**, 6*s* .. *C. Barker*, 1677

1016 — King's Speech to both Houses, Jan. 28, 1678, 4 *leaves*, folio, 4*s* *Bill, Barker, Newcomb, and Hills*, 1678

1017 — Proclamation, An order of the King in Council, to enforce former Proclamations against Papists, who were very troublesome, folio, *broadside*, 5*s* *C. Barker, dated* 31 *Jan.*, 1678

1018 — His Majesties Speech and the Lord Chancellor's to the Parliament, Oct. 21, 1678, folio, 20 *pages*, 2*s* *C. Barker*, 1678

1019 — England's Lamentation for the Duke of Monmouth's departure, folio, *broadside*, POETRY, signed J. F., 5*s* 1679

1020 — Commons Address to H. M. to remove Sir George Jeffreys out of all publick Offices, 1 *leaf*, 3*s* 6*d* .. 1680

1021 — Articles of Impeachment against Edward Seymour, Esq., 1 *leaf*, 2*s* .. .. .. 1680

1022 — Proclamation, or order of Council concerning those that endeavoured to assassinate Mr. Arnold, (a Justice of the Peace for Monmouthshire,) £100 reward, folio, *broadside*, **Black Letter**, 10*s* .. .. *Henry Hills, Ap.* 16, 1680

The three assassins said "Damme yee Dog, now pray for the soul of Captain Evans." *Quotation from Proclamation.*

1023 — H. Majesties Speech to both Houses, at the Opening of the Parliament at Oxford, Nov. 21, 1680, folio, 4 *leaves*, *scarce*, 6*s* *Printed at the Theatre in Oxford*, 1680

1024 — King's Gracious Letter to his Parliament of Scotland, conveened at Edinburgh, July 28, 1681, with the High Commissioner's (the Duke of Albany) Speech to the Parliament on that Letter, 1 *leaf*, 4*s* 6*d* .. .. *John Smith*, 1681

1025 — The Two Associations, one subscribed by 156 M.P.'s in 1643, the other seized in the closet of the Earl of Shaftesbury, with a List of the Grand Jury that found the bill against the Earl of Danby, on the evidence of Fitz-Harris, with S. College's, Rouse's and other Grand Juries, folio, 6 *leaves*, *curious*, 4*s* 1681

1026 — PORTSMOUTH.—Articles of Impeachment for High Treason and other Crimes against (Louise de Querouaille) the DUCHESS of PORTSMOUTH, 4 *leaves*, folio, *in Manuscript*, *curious and rare*, 21*s* .. .. .. *No Date*

For diseasing the King, and conspiring with the French King (Louis XIV.) against this country's interests.

1027 — LOUISE DE QUEROUAILLE, DUCHESS OF PORTSMOUTH, and NELL GWYN, 2 companion cabinet PORTRAITS in OIL of these CELEBRITIES, three-quarter lengths, very beautifully painted by some pupil of SIR PETER LELY'S; size 17 by 13 inches, in gilt frames, at least a century old, 50 Guineas

Of Louise de Querouaille it is said, "This lady's polite manners and agreeable temper riveted the chains which her personal charms had imposed upon the King. She had the first place in his affections, and he continued to love her to the day of his death."—*Granger's Biographical Hist. of England.*

Of Mistress Eleanor Gwynn it may be only necessary to observe that she was one of the most witty and agreeable of Charles's favourites. It is seldom that authentic portraits of Charles's Mistresses occur, when they do, they obtain large prices. The value of these are enhanced by their being known to have come from the collection of Blomfield, the Norfolk Historian.

1028 CHARLES II.—Sentence of Nathaniel Thompson and others at the Court of King's Bench, 3 July, 1682, for publishing Letters and Libels purporting that Sir Edmundbury Godfrey murthered himself, folio, *single leaf*, 3*s* .. *J. Heathcott*, 1682

1029 — Matters of Fact in the present Election of Sheriffs (for London) for the year ensuing, faithfully reported, and the miscarriages of my Lord Mayor, and some other persons in this matter, briefly declared, folio, 2 *leaves*, *(a very curious London Tract)* 21*s* *J. Johnson*, 1682

*Curious*. The names of those where initials only are given are written in full on the margins, Sir Dudley North, Sir Lyonell Jenkins, Sir G. Jefferies, since Lord Chancellor, and others are mentioned.

1030 — Character of a true Protestant, *a leaf*, 1*s* *For T. S.*, 1682

1031 — List of all the CONSPIRATORS that have been seized since the discovery of the horrid and bloody PLOT, contrived by the Phanaticks against the lives of his Majesty, and his Royal Highness, with the names of the three famous *Ignoramus Juries*, folio, *broadside, printed both sides*, 6*s* 1683

1032 — Proclamation granting Protection to Merchantmen against Ships of War and Privateers in our Ports and Harbours, folio, *broadside*, Black Letter, 5*s* *Newmarket, dated March* 12, 1683

1033 — Proclamation in reference to that at Newmarket of Mar. 12, folio, *broadside*, 4*s* *March* 26*th*, 1683

1034 — True Spirit and Elixir of Cant, folio, *broadside, very curious*, 10*s* *Printed for information of Distemper'd Protestants*, 1684

"At the sign of the *Groaning Board*, in *Plot Alley*, in *Equity Street*, there lives an eminent *Scotch* DOCTOR, student in *Schism* and *Sedition*," &c. This Scotch Doctor is Dr. Gilbert Burnet, afterwards Bishop of Salisbury, it is a most singularly curious lampoon on him.

1035 — True relation of the late King's Death, folio, *broadside*, 5*s* *No date, but* 1685

Narrates how the Roman Catholicks were attempted to be introduced to the King's chamber. The King died Feb. 6th.

1036 CHARLES XII., Roi de Suede, Historie de, par Voltaire, *portrait*, 12mo. *neat*, 3*s* .. .. *Basle*, 1732

1037 — the same, in English, 8vo. *calf, neat*, 2*s* 6*d* 1732

1038 CHARLES Louys, Comte Palatin du Rhin, MANIFESTE du tres haut et Serenissime Prince, Grand Seneschal et Electeur du St. Empire Romain, Duc de Baviere, &c. Contenant ses droits hereditaires, &c. Traduit de l'Original Alleman, et la PROTESTATION de son altesse Palatine, small 4to. *limp vellum, nice clean copy*, 6*s* .. .. .. *No place*, 1639

This Manifesto and Protestation are both dated "Fait à Londres, le 2 Feburier, 1637," but the book is evidently printed abroad.

1039 CHARLETON'S (Dr. Walter) Enquiries into Human Nature, in VI. Anatomic Prælections, *plates*, 4to. *old calf*, 4*s* 6*d* 1680

Fellow of the Roy. Coll. of Physicians, before whom these were delivered.

1040 CHARNOCK'S (John) Biographia Navalis; Memoirs of the Lives and Characters of the Officers of the British Navy, from 1660 to 1794, *portraits by Bartolozzi, and maps*, 4 vols. 8vo. *calf, gilt, neat*, 10*s* 6*d* .. .. .. 1794

1041 CHARNOCKE'S (Dr. Stephen) Works, several Discourses on the Being and Attributes of God, and other Discourses, *fine portrait,* 2 vols. large folio, *good copy in calf,* £1 18*s* .. 1682-4

Best Edition, usually sells for £3 3*s*.

1042 — Discourses on the Attributes, abridged by G. Williams, 8vo. *half calf, neat,* 3*s* 6*d* .. .. 1797

1043 CHART of the North and Baltic Seas, by Philips, folded into 12mo. *stiff cover,* 1*s* .. .. *Liverpool,* 1854

1044 CHATEAUBRIAND (F. A. de) Atala, les amours de deux Sauvages dans le Désert, 18mo. *half calf, neat,* 2*s* *Paris,* 1801

1045 — Itinéraire de Paris à Jerusalem, *large map,* 3 vols. 8vo. *sewed* 6*s* *Paris,* 1812

1046 — Travels in Greece, Palestine, Egypt, and Barbary, in 1806 and 1807, 2 vols. 8vo. *half calf,* 6*s* .. .. 1812

1047 CHATHAM'S (Earl of) Letters to his Nephew, Thomas Pitt, Esq., afterwards Lord Camelford, then at Cambridge, crown 8vo. *half calf, neat,* 3*s* 6*d* .. .. *Bensley,* 1804

Chiefly on Literary subjects, edited, with a long preface, by Lord Grenville.

1048 CHAUCER'S Canterbury Tales, with an Essay on his Language and Versification: Notes and Glossary by Tyrwhitt, *portrait,* 2 vols. 4to. *half bound in russia, extra, scarce,* £1 11*s* 6*d* *Oxford, Clarendon Press,* 1798

The very best edition of Chaucer.

"In elocution and elegance, in harmony and perspicuity of versification, Chaucer surpasses his predecessors in an infinite proportion; his genius was universal, and adapted to themes of unbounded variety."—*Warton.*

"The Prologue to the Canterbury Tales is one of the finest specimens of the pourtraiture of character and persons that the English language possesses."—*Turner.*

1049 — Canterbury Tales, with Notes, by Thomas Wright, 8vo. *sewed,* 2*s*

1050 — Life, including Memoirs of his near kinsman, John of Gaunt, by W. Godwin, *portrait,* 4 vols. 8vo. *calf, very neat,* £1 1*s* 1804

With sketches of the manners, opinions, arts, and literature of England in the XIVth Century. "The production of a man who has read poetry with taste and feeling."—*Edinb. Review.*

1051 CHEKI (Joannis, *Angli*) de pronuntiatione Græcæ potissimum linguæ disputationes cum Stephano Vintoniensi Episcopo, small 8vo. 349 pages, *fine copy in old stamped vellum,* £1 1*s* *Basileæ, per N. Episcopium,* 1555

In the same volume with this rare treatise against Bp. Gardiner, by the celebrated and learned Sir John Cheke, first professor of Greek in the University of Cambridge, and afterwards tutor to Edward VIth, are, I. Ex Scriptis Herodiani excerpta, Græcè, *Basiliæ, ap. C. Wechelum,* 1542. II. Græcorum Veterum selectæ brevesque Epistolæ, *Parisiis, apud G. Morelium,* 1557.

1052 CHELSUM'S (Dr. James) Remarks on the two last Chapters of Gibbon's History, small 8vo. *calf, neat,* 3*s* 6*d* *Oxford,* 1778

At the end, "A moral demonstration of the truth of the Christian Religion," 1775, First printed in 1660—the author Bp. Jer. Taylor, the editor Dr. Halifax, Bp. of Gloucester.

1053 CHELTENHAM Poetical Alphabet, by several Authors, 18mo. *stiff cover,* 1*s* .. *Cheltenham, Williams,* 1832

1054 CHENIER'S (M.) State of the Empire of Morocco, its Animals, Products, &c., translated into English, *map,* 2 vols. 8vo. *calf, neat,* 6*s* .. .. .. 1788

1055 CHESELDEN (W., F.R.S.) Anatomy of the Human Body, 40 *plates*, royal 8vo. LARGE PAPER, *old cf.*, *a fine old book*, 7*s* 6*d* 1740

Best Edition of "a Valuable Work."—*Lowndes.*

1056 CHESTER—Petition to the Lords, by Sir Thomas Aston, Bart., from the County Palatine of Chester, concerning Episcopacie, *a broadside, curious*, 3*s* 6*d* .. .. 1641

1057 — A Walk round its Walls, *wood cuts*, 8vo. *half calf, neat*, 2*s* 6*d* *Chester, no date*

"30 copies only are printed on this paper."

1058 CHETHAM (Humphrey) Bibliotheca Chethamensis: sive Bibliothecæ publicæ Mancuniensis ab. H. Chetham Armig. fundatæ Catalogus, exhibens Libros in Varias Classes, *fine portrait, by Heath*, 3 vols. 8vo. *a very fine copy in half russia*, £1 11*s* 6*d* *Mancunii, (Manchester)* 1792-1826

This well-arranged Catalogue, compiled by J. Radcliffe and the Rev. Parr Greswell, is privately printed. This copy is printed on WRITING PAPER.

1059 CHEYNE'S (Dr. Geo.) Essay on Regimen, with five Discourses, Medical, Moral, and Philosophical, 8vo. *old calf, neat*, 3*s* 1740

1060 — English Malady: a Treatise on Nervous Diseases, with the Author's own case, 8vo. *old calf, neat*, 3*s* 6*d* 1733

1061 CHILD'S (Sir Josiah) Discourse of Trade, 4th Edition, 12mo. *old calf, very neat*, 2*s* .. .. .. 1730

1062 CHINESE Tales, the Wonderful Adventures of the Mandarin Fum-Hoam, 18mo. *neat*, 1*s* 6*d* .. 1800

1063 CHINESE—a Book in the Chinese Language, in red (which shews it to be official) and black, 8vo. *sewed*, 6*s*

1064 CHOUL (Guglielmo, *Gentilhomo Lionese)* Discorso sopra la Castrametatione et Disciplina Militare de Romani, con i Bagni et essercitii Antichi de Greci et Romani et tradotti in Lingua Toscana per M. Gabriel Symeoni, *numerous plates*, large 4to. *fine copy in vellum*, 16*s* .. .. *Lione*, 1556

Haym mentions no earlier edition of this rare book than that of 1569.

1065 CHRISTIAN Doctrine and Practice in the Second Century, fcap. 8vo. *cloth*, 2*s* 6*d* .. .. *W. Pickering*, 1844

1066 CHRISTIAN'S Prayer, with Notes, by a Lay Member of the Ch. of England, 8vo. *cloth*, 2*s (pub. at* 4*s* 6*d)* 1831

1067 CHRONICLE from Brute to 1571, small thick 8vo. Black Letter, imperfect, fol. 1 to 216 and Table 20 leaves, but wanting Title and 9 leaves, *in a bad state*, 10*s* .. 1572

The last notices in this volume are the arraignment of Thomas Duke of Norfolk, Jan. 16, 1571, and the executions Feb. 11, 1571, of Mather, Barney, and Rolfe.

1068 CHRONICLES of the Crusades, being contemporary narratives of the Crusades of Richard Cœur de Lion and St. Louis, by Richard of Devizes, Geoffery de Vinsauf and Lord John de Joinville, *illuminated plate*, post 8vo. *cloth*, 3*s* 6*d* *H. G. Bohn*, 1848

1069 CHRONOLOGICAL Tables, Ancient and Mediæval History, A.M. 1 to A.D. 1500, *map*, post 8vo. *cloth, new*, 5*s* *Ency. Metropolitana*, 1857

1070 — Modern History, A.D. 1501 to A.D. 1856, *map*, post 8vo. *cloth, new*, 5*s* .. .. .. *ib.* 1857

1071 CHRONOLOGY of Remarkable Occurrences from 1770 to 1820, with a General Chronology to 1770, thick 12mo. *boards,* 3*s* 6*d* *Sir Richard Phillips, n. d.*

1072 CHRYSOSTOMI (Joannis) Homiliæ ad populum Antiochenum, Græcè, ed. Jo. Harmari, 12mo. *old calf,* 2*s* 6*d* *Londini, G. Bishop,* 1590

1073 CHURCHILL'S (Charles) Poems, 2nd Edition, 2 vols. in 1, 4to. *calf, very neat,* 5*s* .. .. .. 1765

Printed for John Churchill, (C. Churchill's executor) whose autograph is at the end, has also the autograph of "*James Hare, e dono Ld. Carlisle,* 1766."

1074 — Poetical Works, with Notes and Life, by W. Tooke, of Gray's Inn, *portrait,* 2 vols. 8vo. *boards,* 7*s* .. 1804

"The best (library) edition, ably and usefully illustrated."—*Lowndes.* "Churchill has an exclusive right to the title of the British Juvenal."—*Headley.*

1075 CHURCHILL'S (Sir Winston, Kt.) Divi Britannici; Remarks upon the Lives of all the Kings of this Isle, from 2855 to A.D. 1660, *arms,* folio, *old calf, neat,* 12*s* .. 1675

"This work, written by the father of the great Duke of Marlborough, shows the author to have been well-read in our ancient historians, and is considered very accurate as to dates and authorities."—*Lowndes.* Bp. Nicolson says it is a "diverting view of the arms and exploits of our kings." See Blenheim, Marlborough, and Queen Anne in this Catalogue for many remarkably curious Tracts about the great Duke.

1076 CHYMICAL, Medicinal, and Chyrurgical Addresses, made to Samuel Hartlib Esquire, 12mo. *old calf, neat, curious,* 6*s* *For Giles Calvert,* 1655

Contains 9 several Treatises, Sir George Ripley's Epistle to K. Edward unfolded; Gabriel Plat's Caveat for Alchemists; On the Philosopher's Stone; Metals, &c.

1077 CHYMICAL Physic, Marrow of; or, Practice of making Chymical Medicines, by W. T., 18mo. *old boards, curious,* 3*s* 6*d* 1669

With book-plate of Reuben Melmoth, W. T. acknowledges himself indebted to Dr. Bolnest for help in this work, which teaches the art of making artificial Rubies, Jacinths, &c.

1078 CHYTRÆI (Nathan) Variorum in Europa Itinerum deliciæ, ex variis MSS. selectiora, thick 8vo. 846 pages, *old calf, scarce,* 9*s* *Herbornæ Nassoviorum,* 1594

All the various Monuments, Inscriptions, Libraries, &c., in all the great cities in Italy, Germany, Belgium, France, England, Poland, &c., are here described.

1079 CIACCONIUS (Petrus *Toletanus*) de Triclinio: sive de modo Convivandi apud Priscos Romanos, et de Conviviorum apparatu, accedit F. Ursini appendix et. H. Mercurialis Dissertatio de accubitu antiquorum, *plates,* 12mo. *old calf, neat, scarce,* 6*s* *Amst., Wetstein,* 1689

Pope Gregory XIII. employed this very learned Spanish critic in correcting the Calendar, revising an edition of the Bible, &c. This little work is particularly noticed in *Morhoff Polyhistor.*

1080 CIBBER'S (Colley) Apology for his Life, written by himself, with an historical view of the Stage during his time, 8vo. *old calf,* 3*s* 6*d* .. .. .. .. 1740

"Cibber wrote bad Odes; but then he wrote the *Careless Husband* and his *own Life,* which both deserve immortality."—*Horace Walpole.*

1081 CICERONIS Opera Omnia, D. Lambini, vols. 1, 2, 4, (vol. 3 missing) folio, *large copy, but wormed, in old impressed vellum,* £1 1*s* *Parisiis, Rouillii,* 1566

"This FIRST of Dionysius Lambinus's excellent editions is now very scarce and the most valuable."—*Dibdin.*

1082 CICERONIS Opera, ex emendatione Dionys. Lambini, 9 vols. 8vo. *old calf*, £1 1*s* .. *Lutetiæ, Jacobi Dupuys*, 1572-85

With the autograph of "William Hatton, Anno Domini, 1579, 18o. Augusti,"—written in a very nice old hand. This William, was the nephew of Sir Christopher Hatton, of Elizabethan memory, and heir to his estate.

1083 — Opera, post Naugerianam et Victorinam correctionem, emendatum à I. Sturmio, 8 vols. 8vo. *old calf, neat*, £1 1*s* *Argentorati*, 1574

1084 — Opera, editio ad Manutianum et Brutinam conformata, 10 vols. 8vo. *old binding, neat*, £1 1*s* *Francofurti, apud A. Wecheli*, 1590

"A very good edition with learned notes and commentaries."—*Dibdin.*

1085 — Opera, the best edition by Olivet, 9 vols. 4to. *old sprinkled calf*, £4 14*s* 6*d* .. .. .. *Parisiis*, 1740

This is the very best Library Edition of Cicero, and usually sells for 9 Guineas.

1086 — Opera, recensuit J. N. Lallemand, *portrait*, 14 vols. 12mo. (vol. 7 missing) *fine copy, French calf, edges gilt*, £2 2*s* *Parisiis, Barbou*, 1768

Usually priced 4 Guineas. 10s. would be given for the missing volume. "A beautiful and correct edition, well spoken of by Ernesti, the Bipont Editors and Harles. Dr. Harwood said he read it carefully through, and considered that Lallemand, its editor, had done himself much credit as a scholar."—See *Dibdin.*

1087 — Consolatio, vel de luctu minuendo, fragmenta ejus à Carolo Sigonio et And. Patritio exposita, small 8vo. *parchment*, 3*s* 6*d* *Bononiæ*, 1583

1088 — Epistolarum ad Atticum, ad Brutum, ad Quintum fratrem, libri XX., small 8vo. *old stamped binding*, 10*s* 6*d* *Venetiis, Ædibus Aldi*, 1513

The first Aldine Edition, 662 pages, besides 32 unpaged Introductory.

1089 — Epistolæ ad Familiares, Lambini et P. Manutii Annotationes, small 8vo. *old binding*, 2*s* .. *Londini*, 1607

1090 — Orationes, vol. 1, 12mo. *vellum*, 2*s* *Lugduni, Gryphius*, 1585

1091 — Orationes Selectæ, de Senectute et de Amicitia, in usum Delphini, 8vo. *bound*, 3*s* 6*d* .. *Londini*, 1813

1092 — OPERA PHILOSOPHICA (de natura Deorum, de Divinatione, de Legibus, Academicæ Questiones, de Finibus Bonorum et Malorum, de Fato, Somnio Scipionis, etc.) folio, *half bound, stained, rare*, £1 1*s* *Venetiis, p. Cristoferum de Pensis de Mandello*, 1494

With MS. marginal remarks in a very old hand.—Printed in the first age of the art.

1093 — Opera Philosophica, 8vo. imperfect, commences at page 9, then perfect to the end, p. 179, *with the Aldine Anchor on a separate leaf, vellum*, 4*s* 6*d* *Venetiis, apud Aldi filios*, 1546

1094 — de Officiis de Senectute et de Amicitia, *portrait*, 64mo. *purple morocco, gilt edges*, 6*s* .. *W. Pickering*, 1821

Exquisitely printed by C. Corrall, in Diamond type, for W. Pickering, for the waistcoat pocket.

1095 — de Officiis libri III., Cato Major, Lælius, Paradoxa, Somnium Scipionis, small 8vo. *old vellum, neat*, 3*s* 6*d* *Venetiis, apud Gryphium*, 1575

1096 — de Oratore, corrigente Paolo Manutio, Aldi filio, small 8vo. *limp vellum*, 4*s* .. *Venetiis, Aldus*, 1546

Has the Aldine anchor on the title, but wants leaves 122 to 137.

1097 CICERONIS Tusculanæ Disputationes, accedunt Lect. Var. et Doctorum præcipue C. Bouherii conjecturæ, 12mo. *calf, neat,* 3*s* 6*d* .. .. *Glasguæ, Foulis,* 1744

1098 — de Re Publica, quæ supersunt, edente Angelo Maio, 8vo. *boards,* 5*s* (*pub. at* 12*s*) .. .. *Londini,* 1823

1099 — de Claris Oratoribus liber, qui dicitur Brutus, cum notis Var. et F. Ellendt, 8vo. *sewed,* 4*s* *Reg. Prussorum,* 1825

1100 — Le Orationi di Cicerone, tradotte de M. Lodovico Dolce, 2 parts in 1 vol. 4to. *very fine clean copies in old calf, gilt,* £1 1*s* *Vinegia, Gabriel Giolito,* 1562

Has Giolito's beautiful devices at the beginning and end of each volume, and a fine head of Cicero.

1101 — Locutioni dell' Epistole di Cicerone Scielte da Aldo Manutio, 8vo. *badly stained,* 3*s* .. *In Venetia,* 1575

"Utilissime al comporre nell' una, e l'altra Lingua."—*Haym.*

1102 — Rhetorica, tradotta di Latino in Lingua Toscana per Antonio Brucioli, small 8vo. *old limp vellum, rare,* 6*s* *Venetia, per Gabriel Iolito di Ferrarii,* 1542

"Gli Eruditi vogliono, che quest' opera non sia di Cicerone."—*Haym.* Most *elegant wood-cut title page,* containing Giolito's device, different from any other I have seen.

1103 — Epistres Familiaires de, traduictes en Francoys par Estienne Dolet, natif d'Orleans, small 8vo. *old stamped binding, curious,* 10*s* 6*d* .. *Paris, pour Jehan Ruelle,* 1544

This appears to be a very rare, and probably the 2nd Edition, not mentioned even by Brunet, who cites those of 1542, 1547, and 1549.—There are very old autographs on the title, of *Thomas Brounne* and *Jaques Wrenche.*

1104 — Cato; an Essay on Old Age, with Remarks by Melmoth, the translator, 8vo. *old calf,* 3*s* .. .. 1773

1105 — Cato; or an Essay on Old Age, and on Friendship, with Remarks by William Melmoth, *portraits,* 2 vols. 8vo. *calf, nice copy,* 6*s* 1777

1106 — on the Nature of the Gods, translated, with notes, and an Enquiry into the Astronomy and Anatomy of the Antients, by Thos. Francklin, 8vo. *old calf, neat,* 2*s* 6*d* 1741

1107 — on the Complete Orator, Englished with notes, by Geo. Barnes, 8vo. *neat,* 4*s* 6*d* .. *For the Author,* 1762

1108 — Letters to several of his Friends, translated, with remarks by Will. Melmoth, 3 vols. 8vo. *old calf, gilt,* 7*s* 6*d* 1753

With the book-plate of Lord Walpole, of Woolterton.

1109 — another copy, translated by William Melmoth, 3 vols. 8vo. *calf, gilt,* 15*s* .. .. .. 1778

This is on Large Paper, and a very fine copy. "Translations are in general the bane of every language; but such translations as those of Melmoth, bring both our language and our learning in their debt."—*Monthly Review.*

1110 — Epistles to Brutus, and of Brutus to Cicero, Latin and English, by Dr. Conyers Middleton, 8vo. *old calf, neat,* 3*s* 1743

With a Prefatory Dissertation answering Tunstall's Objections.

1111 — another copy, 8vo. *old calf, gilt,* 3*s* 6*d* .. 1743

1112 CICERO.—Markland's (Jer.) Remarks on (Middleton's) Epistles of Cicero to Brutus, and of Brutus to Cicero, 1745.—Dissertation after the manner of Markland, *no date.*—Markland, Epistola Critica, ad Fr. Hare, *Cantabrigiæ,* 1723, 3 Treatises in 1 vol. 8vo. *calf, neat,* 6*s* .. .. .. V. Y.

The second Treatise is anonymous, but is by Dr. Ross, afterwards Bp. of Exeter, see *Nichols's Anecdotes of Bowyer,* p. 189.

1113 — Ciceronis Filii Vita, Simone Vallamberto auctore; accessit A. Schotti, Cicero, Pater, a calumniis vindicatus, cum præfatione J. A. Fabricii, small 8vo. *calf, neat,* 3*s* *Hamburgi,* 1733

1114 — Life, by Dr. Conyers Middleton, 3 vols. 8vo. *old cf, very neat,* 9*s* 1755

"The style of Middleton is considered to be as pure English as can be read."—*Dibdin.*

"Cicero brought together all the good things he could find in the books of the Greek writers and teachers. 'When I read Brutus' writings,' says Cæsar, 'then I take myself to be eloquent; but when I read the orations of Cicero, then I am ineloquent. I loll like a child.'"—*Luther.*

1115 CICUTA (Aurelio *Sig. Cavalliere)* Disciplina Militare, *plates showing the Marshalling of Armies,* small 4to. *fine clean copy in limp vellum,* 12*s* *In Venetia, appresso Lodovico Avanzo,* 1572

In vain we look for this book in Brunet, De Bure, or Haym.

1116 CIVILIUM apud Belgas bellorum initia, progressus, finis optatus: in quam rem remedia a ferro et pace præscripta, small 8vo. *parchment,* 3*s* .. *No place, or Printer's name,* 1627

1117 CLAPMARII (Arnoldi) de Arcanis Rerumpublicarum libri VI., 4to. *limp vellum, (few leaves at the end gnawed)* 4*s* 6*d* *Bremæ,* 1605

"Ce livre sous un titre specieux contient peu de choses utiles et curieuses."—*Dufresnoy.*

1118 CLARENDON'S (Edward, Earl of) History of the Rebellion and Civil Wars in England, 1641 to 1660, *portrait,* 6 vols. 8vo. (vol. 4 missing) *old calf, neat,* 8*s* *Oxford,* 1721

1119 — new edition, with an Historical View of the Affairs of Ireland, and Notes, by Bishop Warburton, 7 vols. medium 8vo. *cloth,* £2 10*s* .. *Oxford University Press,* 1849

This is the last and best edition of this valuable historical work.

"Clarendon's History of the Rebellion is one of the noblest historical works of the English nation."—*Edinburgh Review.*

1120 — Collection of Tracts from his Lordship's Original Manuscripts, folio, *old calf, neat,* 7*s* 6*d* .. .. 1727

CONTENTS.—Vindication of himself from the Charge of High Treason, 1668; on Drunkenness, Envy, Pride, Anger, War and Peace, on the respect due to Age, Education, the Psalms, &c.

1121 — Characters of Eminent Men, in the Reigns of Charles 1 and 2, from the Works of Lord Clarendon, small 8vo. *half calf,* 3*s* 1793

"Lord Clarendon particularly excels in characters. He is, in this particular, as unrivalled among the moderns as Tacitus is among the ancients."—*Granger.*

1122 — Ellis (Honble G. A.) Historical Enquiries respecting the character of Edward Hyde, Earl of Clarendon, post 8vo. *boards,* 3*s* (*pub. at* 6*s* 6*d* .. .. .. 1827

1123 CLARKE'S (Dr. Adam) Bible, the Old and New Testament, with Notes, 6 vols. 1836.—Carpenter's Biblical Companion, 1 vol. 1836.—Calmet's Dictionary of the Bible, by Taylor, 1 vol. 1837. —Cruden's Concordance, 1 vol. *portrait,* 1849; together 9 vols. imperial 8vo. *calf, extra, marbled leaves,* £6 6*s* V. Y.

A very valuable and complete set of Books.

1124 CLARKE'S Bibliographical Dictionary and Miscellany, 8 vols. bound in 4 thick vols. 12mo. *half calf, new and neat,* £1 11*s* 6*d* *Liverpool,* 1802-1806

The *Dictionary* contains a Summary of the Life of each author, the time when he lived, and a list of his works.—The *Miscellany* contains an account of the English Translations of the Greek and Latin Classics, with the principal works of the best Arabian and Persian writers. Remarks on the Origin of Language. Various Essays on Bibliography. Places where Printing was carried on, &c., &c. A very useful little work, to which I have frequently been much indebted for information not easily elsewhere attainable.

1125 — Concise View of the Succession of Sacred Literature, in a Chronological Arrangement of Authors and their Works, to 345, 12mo. *boards,* 5*s* .. .. .. 1807

"A little volume equally interesting to the biblical and the bibliographical student."—*Horne.*

1126 — Concise View of the Succession of Sacred Literature, from A.M. 2513 to A.D. 1300, the 2nd vol. by Dr. Clarke's Son, 2 vols. 8vo. *half cloth,* 12*s* (*pub at* 30*s*) .. 1830-31

1127 CLARKE'S (Dr. E. D.) Life and Remains, by Rev. W. Otter, *portrait,* 4to. *half russia, very neat,* 9*s* .. 1824

1128 — another edition, by Otter, *portrait,* 2 vols. 8vo. *boards,* 8*s* (*pub. at* 21*s*) .. .. .. 1825

1129 CLARKE'S (Rev. R.) Prophetic Records of the Christian Era, with a familiar illustration of the Prophetic Symbols, 8vo. *boards,* 5*s* (*pub. at* 10*s* 6*d*) .. .. .. 1812

Chronologically arranged from Thomas à Becket, 1170 to 1812.

1130 CLARKE'S (Dr. Samuel) Discourse on the Being and Attributes of God, and the Truth of the Christian Revelation, 8vo. *old calf, neat,* 3*s* .. .. .. 1738

1131 CLARKE (Will.) Repertorium Bibliographicum; some account of the most celebrated British Libraries, *plates,* royal 8vo. *fine copy, in half russia, uncut, top edges gilt,* £1 5*s* 1819

"A work containing much curious bibliographical information, to which the Editor of these pages has frequently been indebted."—*Lowndes's Bibliographer's Manual.*

1132 CLASSICAL Collector's Vade Mecum; an Introduction to the Knowledge of the best editions of the Greek and Roman Classics, 18mo. *nicely interleaved, and half bound in morocco,* 8*s* 1822

A very useful little work by R. E. Poole, under the heads Editiones Principes, Aldine, Stephens's, Delphin, Elzevir, Foulis, Brindley, Editiones optimæ, &c.

1133 — another copy, *in boards, quite thin for the pocket,* 3*s* 6*d* 1822

1134 CLASSICAL Museum, No. 14 to 18, 5 Nos. 7*s* 6*d* (*pub. at* 17*s* 6*d*)

1135 CLAUDERI (Gabriel.) Methodus Balsamandi Corpora Humana, 4to. *half bound,* 3*s* 6*d* .. *Altenburgi,* 1679

1136 CLAUDIANI Opera, recensuit ac notas addidit N. Heinsius, 18mo. *sound copy, in calf,* 8*s* .. *L. Bat., Elzevir,* 1650

1137 CLAVIS Calendaria; the Liturgy-Calendar of the Church of England explained, by W. C., 12mo. *bound, curious,* 2*s* 6*d* *John Nutt,* 1700

1138 CLAYTON'S (Capt. J. W.) Ubique; or English Country Quarters, and Eastern Bivouac, 8vo. *cloth,* 3*s* 6*d* (*cost* 7*s* 6*d*) 1857

1139 CLEAVELAND'S (John) Genuine Poems, Orations, Epistles, &c., purged from the many spurious ones, 8vo. *neat,* 10*s* 6*d* 1677

Fuller says of Cleaveland that he was "a general artist, pure latinist, exquisite orator, and excellent poet." It seems Bp. Pearson "preached his Funeral Sermon, and made his death glorious." Priced £1 11*s* 6*d* in the Bibliotheca Ang. Poetica.

1140 CLEMENTIS VII. Literæ, 1526.—Responsio Cæsaris Pontifici, 1526.—Pro invictissimo Cæsare Carolo Augusto Hisp. Rege Epist. Franci Regis ad Principes Imp. transmissæ ac Apologiæ Madritiæ conventonis dissuasoriæ refutatio, small 8vo. 5*s* 1527

1141 CLEOPATRA, (Regina d'Egitto) Vita, scritta dal Conte Giulio Landi, 12mo. *neat*, 3*s* 6*d* .. *Parigi*, 1788

This is a reprint of the rare Venice edition of 1551.

1142 CLERCK (Caroli) Aranei Suecici (Swedish and Latin) 6 *plates, containing numerous coloured figures of spiders*, 4to. *foreign binding, gilt back, good copy*, £1 11*s* 6*d* *Stockholmiæ*, 1757

A copy of this rare book brought £3 10*s* at Evans's in 1833.

1143 CLERGY List for 1847, 8vo. *cloth*, 2*s* 6*d*; for 1856, 5*s*

1144 CLERGYMAN'S Intelligencer, a Complete List of all the Patrons in England and Wales, with the Livings in their gift, 8vo. *old calf*, 3*s* .. .. .. 1745

1145 CLERKS, Advice to Clerks, and Hints to Employers, by an Experienced Clerk, 18mo. *sewed*, 1*s*

1146 COBBETT'S Parliamentary History of England, from 1066 to 1803; 36 vols. royal 8vo. 10 vols. *half bound in russia, the others in boards*, £6 6*s* .. .. 1806-1820

Published at £56 14*s*, and usually priced 18 Guineas.

1147 — Political Annual Register, from 1802 to 1816, 31 vols. in 17, royal 8vo. *half bound in russia*, £2 2*s* 1802-1816

This may be considered a continuation of his Parliamentary History.

1148 — Peter Porcupine's Works; exhibiting a faithful picture of the United States of America, from the end of the War in 1783 to the Election of the President in March, 1801, 12 vols. 8vo. *a nice clean set, gilt*, £1 11*s* 6*d* .. .. 1801

1149 COCHRANE'S (Capt. J. D.) Narrative of a Pedestrian Journey through Russia and Siberian Tartary, from the Frontiers of China to the Frozen Sea and Kamtschatka, *portraits, maps, and plates*, 2 vols. post 8vo. *boards*, 7*s* 6*d* (*pub. at* £1 1*s*) 1825

"A novel and amusing work."—*Lowndes.*

1150 COCHRANE'S (John G.) Catalogue of the London Library, 12, St. James's Square, 8vo. *cloth, uncut, top edges gilt*, 8*s* 1847

1151 COCKER'S (Edward) Young Clerk's Tutor enlarged, a collection of the best Precedents of Recognizances, &c.—Latin names of Men and Women, and their several trades, all the Kings' reigns, &c., 12mo. *curious and very scarce*, £1 11*s* 6*d* 1693

With plates showing various specimens of Court and Chancery Hands; this is the 13th Edition, and not mentioned by Lowndes or his continuator.

1152 — Decimal Arithmetic, by John Hawkins, 8vo. *neat, scarce*, 16*s* 1695

1153 — Arithmetic, by Hawkins and Fisher, *portrait*, 53rd Edition, 12mo. *original sheep binding, scarce*, 8*s* 1750

1154 COCKMAN'S (Dr. Thos.) Select Theological Discourses, by Tipping Silvester, *portrait*, 2 vols. 8vo. LARGE AND THICK PAPER, *old calf, neat*, 10*s* .. .. .. 1750

Dr. Cockman was master of University College, Oxford. These Discourses are so arranged as to make a "Treatise on the Prevalent Infidelity, Corruptions, and Errors."

1155 CODINUS Curopalata (Georgius) de Officiis et Officialibus Magnæ Ecclesiæ et aulæ Constantinopolitanæ, Gr. et Lat., cum notis J. Gretseri, accessit dissertatio de Imaginibus non Manufactis, folio, *a fine copy in calf,* 12*s* .. *Parisiis,* 1625

This is a "very curious work," see Dr. A. Clarke's account of the Byzantine Historians.

1156 COGHLAN'S (Francis) Hand Book for Central Europe, (Belgium, Holland, the Rhine, Germany, Switzerland, France, the Channel Islands, &c.) 12mo. *cloth,* 3*s* 6*d* (*pub. at* 8*s*) 1844

Autograph of the late Earl of "Orford."

1157 COINS, Gold and Silver.—Renovatie van't Placcaet vande Munte vanden 21en Julii, 1622, 4to. *half bound, neat,* 5*s* *In's Graven-Haghe,* 1626

This Tract in Dutch, is on 54 leaves, representing some hundreds of coins, Dutch, Danish, English, Saxon, &c.

1158 COINS, Medals, &c.—The truths of Revelation demonstrated by an appeal to existing Monuments, Sculptures, Gems, Coins, and Medals, by a Fellow of several learned Societies, *plates,* 12mo. *cloth,* 5*s* (*pub. at* 10*s*) .. *Longmans,* 1831

1159 COLERIDGE'S (Samuel Taylor) Life, by James Gillman, vol. 1 (all published) 8vo. *cloth,* 5*s* (*pub. at* 10*s* 6*d*) *W. Pickering,* 1838

1160 COLES'S (E.) English Dictionary, small 8vo. *sheep,* 1*s* 6*d* 1701

1161 COLLETT'S (W. R.) List of Early Printed Books in Caius College Library, Cambridge, 8vo. *cloth,* 5*s* *Cambridge,* 1850

1162 COLLIER'S (J. Payne) Poetical Decameron; Ten Conversations on English Poets and Poetry, particularly of the Reigns of Elizabeth and James I., 2 vols. post 8vo. *calf, gilt, nice copy,* 12*s* (*pub. at* £1 1*s*) .. .. .. .. 1820

1163 COLLIGNY, (Admiral of France) Memoirs of, with an account of the Bartholomew Massacre, Aug. 24, 1572, 12mo. *cloth,* 2*s* 6*d* *Edinburgh,* 1844

1164 COLLINS'S (Arthur) Life of Edward the Black Prince, and of his brother, John of Gaunt, 8vo. *old calf,* 6*s* 1740

1165 COLLINS'S Historical and Critical Essay on the 39 Articles of the Church of England, 8vo. *old calf, neat, scarce,* 6*s* 1738

1166 COLLINSON'S (John) Beauties of British Antiquity, from esteemed Antiquaries, 8vo. *calf, neat,* 5*s* .. 1779

In the same volume is "Barber's Tour through South Wales and Monmouthshire," *map and plates,* 1803.

1167 COLLOQUIA et Dictionariolum octo Linguarum, Latinæ, Gallicæ, Belgicæ, Teutonicæ, Hispanicæ, Italicæ, Anglicæ, et Portugallicæ, oblong 12mo. *the English part in* Black Letter, *neat,* 6*s* *Delphis,* 1598

1168 COLLYER'S (John) Criminal Statutes of England, enlarged and arranged alphabetically, with notes, thick 12mo. *law calf,* 5*s* (*pub. at* 18*s*) .. .. .. 1832

1169 COLONNA, (D. Giovan Battista Romano) della Congiura de i Ministri del Re di Spagna, contro le fedelissima, ed esemplare Citta di MESSINA, Racconto istorico, *map and plates,* 2 vols. 4to. *old calf,* 12*s* .. *Messina, Matteo la Rocca,* 1676

Lord Leicester's arms impressed on the sides.

1170 COLTON'S (C. C.) Lacon; Many things in few Words, 2 vols. 8vo. *boards*, 6*s* .. .. .. 1826

1171 COLOMBO, Historie del Sig. Don Fernando Colombo, della patria, origine et nome dell' ammiraglio Christoforo Colombo, nuovamente di lingua Spagnuola tradotte nell' Italiana dal S. Alfonso Ulloa, 12mo. 246 leaves, besides 19 of Tavola, &c., *very fine copy in old calf, gilt, very rare*, £1 11*s* 6*d* 1571

Wants the title, but the Dedication by Gioseppe Moleto is dated "Venetia il di 25 d'Aprile del 1571." This curious Life of Columbus by his son, who entered the Ecclesiastical State, and founded the Columbine Library at Seville, is made use of by Washington Irving in his Life of Columbus. Who says of it, that "it is an invaluable document, entitled to great faith, and is the corner stone of the History of the American Continent." v. 4, p. 116.

1172 COLUMBUS, (Christopher) Hist. of his Life and Voyages, by Washington Irving, 4 vols. 8vo. *boards*, 16*s* (*pub. at* £2 2*s*) 1828

"This is an excellent work, it possesses all the interest of a novel invention, with the startling and thrilling assurance of its actual truth and exactness."—*Edinburgh Review*. "This work gives Mr. Irving prodigious increase of fame."—*Literary Gazette.*

1173 — Life and Voyages, by Washington Irving, *portraits*, 18mo. *cloth*, 2*s* 6*d* (*cost* 5*s*) .. *Fam. Lib.*, 1830

1174 — Voyages and Discoveries of the Companions of Columbus, by Washington Irving, 18mo. *cloth*, 2*s* 6*d* (*cost* 5*s*) *Fam. Lib.*, 1831

1175 — Life, Voyages, and Discoveries, 12mo. *cloth*, 2*s* 1845

1176 COLUMELLA—On Husbandry and Trees, Englished, with illustrations from Pliny, Cato, Varro, and other ancient and modern authors, 4to. *calf, gilt, very good copy*, 10*s* 6*d* 1745

"Columella. Born at Cadiz, in Spain, flourished circa, A.D. 42. His works very valuable, not only on account of the style, which is formed on the model of the Augustan age, but also on account of the precepts it contains."—*Dr. Adam Clarke.*

1177 COMBE (Taylor) Catalogue of his Numismatic and Classical Library, sold by Mr. Sotheby, Dec. 7, 1826, *with the prices and purchasers' names*, 8vo. *boards*, 4*s* .. 1826

1178 COMBER (Dr. Thomas, *Dean of Durham)* Memoirs of his Life and Writings, by his great grandson, *portrait*, 8vo. *boards*, 5*s* 1799

1179 COMEDIES, Garrick's Guardian; She Stoops to Conquer, Goldsmith; Belle's Stratagem, Mrs. Cowley; West Indian, Cumberland; Macklin's Man of the World; Gay's Beggars' Opera; Lionel and Clarissa, and Sheridan's Critic, in 2 vols. 18mo. *neatly half bound*, 3*s*

1180 COMINES, Memoires de Messire Phillipe de Comines, 1461-1498, folio, *remarkably fine copy in old calf, gilt*, large paper, £2 12*s* 6*d* *Paris, de l'imprimerie Royale*, 1649

This is a very beautiful volume, and Philip de Comines is one of the most interesting of the old French Historians.

1181 — Historie of Philip de Commines, Knight, Lord of Argenton, translated by Thomas Danett, folio, *old binding*, 10*s* 6*d* *London, Ar. Hatfield*, 1596

Dedicated to Lord Burleigh, by the Translator, who says he was urged to the work by Sir Christopher Hatton, late Lord Chancellor, and since his death by other gentlemen, at the end are the pedigrees of many great houses.

"Above all men in this kind of writing, in my opinion, may be accounted the plain, sincere, unaffected, and most instructive Philip de Commines."—*Dryden.*

1182 COMMENTARY on the Old and New Testament, by Patrick, Lowth, Arnald, Whitby, and Lowman, 4 vols. royal 8vo. *cloth, uncut*, 45*s* (*pub. at* £4 10*s*) .. *London*, 1842

1183 COMMENTARIORUM de Statu Religionis et Reipublicæ in Regno Galliæ, part 3, containing Books 7, 8, 9, 8vo. *limp vellum*, 3*s* *Absque loco, (Genevæ)* 1571

"Hic liber pertinet ad Gulielmum Heveningham." Period embraced, 1563 to 1569 temp. Car. IX.

1184 — parts 3 and 4, being books 7 to 12, in 1 vol. 8vo. *old vellum*, 5*s*

Period embraced, 1563 to 1574. "Cet ouvrage très curieux est de Jean de Serres, écrivain Calviniste."—*Brunet.*

1185 COMMERCIAL Tables, consisting of reckoning, interest, annuity, money, weights, measures, and other tables, 12mo. *half bound, new*, 3*s* .. .. .. 1858

1186 COMMON PRAYER BOOK, called the Elizabethan Prayer Book, *elegant wood cut border round every page*, 8vo. *morocco*, £1 5*s* *W. Pickering*, 1853

Very scarce, difficult now to procure, it is a most elegant volume.

1187 — for the use of the Church of Scotland, with King James's translation of the Psalms, ending at Psalm 146, folio, *wants* 2 *leaves at the end*, £2 12*s* 6*d* *Edinburgh, Robert Young*, 1637

This is called Abp. Laud's Liturgy, which was very unpopular, and was the means of causing much disturbance in Scotland; the following book was intended to allay the irritation.

1188 — A Large Declaration concerning the late Tumults in Scotland, by the King, (Charles I.) *of whom there is a fine portrait*, folio, 430 pages, *fine copy, hf. bd. in morocco*, £1 1*s* *Robert Young*, 1639

There is also a portrait of Sir Francis Bacon inserted.

1189 — An ORIGNAL COPY of the SEALED BOOK of COMMON PRAYER, folio, on LARGE PAPER, *very rare, ruled throughout with red lines*, £7 7*s* .. .. 1669

A very fine volume, bound in red russia, extra, grained. A large paper copy is of extreme rarity.

1190 — and Brady and Tate's Singing Psalms, *plates by Sturt*, 12mo. *old purple morocco*, 5*s* 6*d* *John Baskett*, 1717-19

1191 — *with 55 Historical cuts by Sturt, including portraits of K. James I., Cha. I. and II., and K. George II.*, 1729.—Companion to the Altar, 1725.—Sternhold and Hopkins's Psalms, 1729, in 1 vol. 12mo. *old red morocco, gilt edges, rare*, £1 1*s* 1729

Archdeacon Cotton in his List of Bibles, &c., says, there was "no edition" of these Psalms issued in 1729, but here it is. "Printed by Kath. Wilmer, for the Company of Stationers." Notwithstanding his indefatigable researches, the Archdeacon had not happened on it. On the outside is stamped "Elizabeth Tully, 1730."

1192 — with Sternhold and Hopkins's Psalms, 8vo. LARGE PAPER, *fine copy in old red morocco, gilt, gilt edges*, 10*s* 6*d* *Oxford, Thomas Baskett*, 1745

The Psalms not in Dr. Cotton's List, there is this peculiarity in this edition, that the Psalms which are usually in 4 line verses are here in two.

1193 — with the Companion to the Altar, and Sternhold and Hopkins's Psalms, 8vo. *fine copy in old morocco, gilt, gilt edges*, 6*s* *Oxford, Tho. Baskett*, 1754

1194 — with Sternhold and Hopkins's Psalms, 8vo. *old morocco*, 3*s* 6*d* *Oxford, Mary Baskett*, 1762

1195 — Bp. Mant's Common Prayer Book, with Notes, royal 4to. large paper, *very fine copy in russia extra, grained*, £1 16*s* *Oxford*, 1820

1196 COMMON PRAYER BOOK, with Brady and Tate's Psalms, Large Letter Edition, 8vo. *calf, neat,* 4*s* 6*d* *Cambridge,* 1830

1197 — minion 32mo. *purple morocco, gilt edges,* 6*s* *Oxford University Press,* 1843

1198 — adapted for general use in other Protestant Churches, 12mo. *cloth,* 4*s* .. .. *W. Pickering,* 1852

1199 — (American) with the Psalms, 12mo. *old binding, very scarce,* £1 1*s* *Charleston, for W. P. Young,* 1799

"*Rebecca Carson, Exmouth, July* 28*th*, 1804."

1200 — of the Church of England, translated into the Bengali Language, 8vo. *half bound, neat,* 7*s* 6*d* .. *Calcutta,* 1846

"Not published."

1201 COMPLETE Family-Piece, and Country Gentleman and Farmer's Best Guide, in 3 parts, 12mo. *original binding, scarce,* 5*s* *T. Longman, at the Ship,* 1776

Part I. 800 Family Receipts in Physick, Surgery, Cookery, Drinks, &c. Part II. Hunting, Coursing, Shooting, Dogs, Fishing, Gardening, &c. Part III. On Farming, Cattle, &c.

1202 COMTE'S (Auguste) Philosophy of the Sciences, by G. H. Lewes, post 8vo. *cloth,* 3*s* (*cost* 5*s*) .. *H. G. Bohn,* 1853

1203 CONÆI (Georgii) de duplici statu Religionis apud Scotos libri duo, 4to. *limp vellum, rare,* £1 1*s* *Romæ, typis Vaticanis, superiorum permissu,* 1628

A very interesting volume, containing much valuable matter relating to the History of Scotland. It is dedicated to Cardinal Barberini, afterwards Pope Urban VIII, "*Magnæ Britanniæ Protectorem.*"

1204 CONCIONES et Orationes ex Historicis Latinis excerptæ, 18mo. *old calf,* 2*s* .. .. *Amst., Elzevir,* 1662

1205 CONDAMINE (M. de la) Journal of a Tour to Italy, Eruptions of Vesuvius, Curiosities at Herculaneum, Leaning Towers of Pisa, &c. 12mo. *neat,* 3*s* .. .. 1763

1206 CONDÉ, Memoirs of the Life of the Great Condé, 1621-1680, written by his Serene Highness Louis Joseph de Bourbon, Prince de Condé, translated by N. Holcroft, 8vo. *bds.,* 3*s* 6*d* 1811

1207 — Life, by Lord Mahon, 1621-1675, square 12mo. *boards,* 3*s* 6*d* (*pub. at* 6*s*) *Murray's Colonial Library,* 1846

1208 CONNOISSEUR (The) 4 vols. 12mo. *old calf, gilt,* 8*s* *Oxford,* 1774

1209 CONRINGII (Hermanni) Dissertationes Academicæ, *portrait,* 12mo. *boards, uncut,* 5*s* .. .. *Lugduni,* 1686

Conringius an eminently learned man, was consulted by Christina, Queen of Sweden, the Elector Palatine, the Elector of Mentz, Louis XIV. of France, &c., all of whom conferred upon him honours and rewards.

1210 CONSTABLES, Whole Duty of Constables, Headboroughs, Tythingmen, &c., by a late Acting Magistrate of the County of Norfolk, 8vo. *boards,* 3*s* .. .. *Norwich,* 1830

1211 CONSTITUTIONS and Canons Ecclesiastical, treated on in the Convocation of 1603, in the 1st year of James 1st's Reign, 4to. *sewed,* 6*s* .. .. *Reprinted,* 1673

1212 — and Canons Ecclesiastical, treated on in the Convocation of 1640, 16th Charles I., 4to. ORIGINAL EDITION, *sewed, scarce,* 6*s* *Barker and Bill,* 1640

1213 CONTANSEAU'S (Leon) French-English and English-French Dictionary, post 8vo. *cloth,* 10*s* 6*d* .. 1858

1214 CONTINUATION of the present State of the Controversy between the Church of England and the Church of Rome, small 4to. *newly half bound, scarce,* 6*s* *Ric. Chiswell,* 1688

This is a full account of the books that were written on both sides.

1215 CONVERSIONS Incomplètes, par un Magistrat, 18mo. *sewed,* 1*s* 6*d* *Paris,* 1848

1216 CONYBEARE'S (Bp. John) Sermons, 2 vols. 8vo. *calf,* 5*s* 1757

1217 CONYBEARE'S (W. D.) and Phillips's Outlines of the Geology of England and Wales, *coloured maps,* 8vo. part 1, all published, *half cloth, scarce,* 12*s* .. .. 1822

1218 — Elementary Course of Theological Lectures, in three parts; 1, On the Evidences of Religion; 2, On the Interpretation of the Bible; 3, On the peculiar Doctrines of Christianity, *frontispiece,* 12mo. *cloth,* 3*s* 6*d* (*pub. at* 6*s*) .. 1836

1219 COOK'S (Sir Edward) Reports, abridged by Sir John Davis, Atturney General in Ireland, 12mo. *old binding,* 2*s* 6*d* 1651

1220 COOK'S (Dr. George) History of the Reformation in Scotland, 3 vols. 8vo. *half bound in calf,* 15*s* *Edinburgh,* 1811

1221 COOK'S (Captain James) 1st Voyage round the World, by Dr. Hawkesworth, 3 vols. 4to. *original edition, old cf., gilt,* £1 1*s* 1773

Mr. Joseph John Gurney's copy, with his Book-plate and this autograph, "J. and C. Gurney."

1222 — Voyages et Aventures du, par Henri Lebrun, *plate,* 12mo. *boards,* 1*s* 6*d* .. .. *Tours,* 1852

1223 — Life, by Andrew Kippis, *fine portrait, by Heath,* 4to. *boards, uncut,* 5*s* .. .. .. 1788

"The spirit, disinterestedness, penetration, physical and intellectual energies of Capt. James Cook, fitted him in an especial manner for the various and extraordinary discoveries which he so successfully accomplished, and to which, alas, he fell a victim and a sacrifice."—*Dibdin.*

1224 COOKE'S (Will.) Bankrupt Laws, by George Roots, 2 vols. royal 8vo. *law calf,* 12*s* (*pub. at* 38*s*) .. 1823

1225 COOKERY and Domestic Economy, for Young Housewives, including Directions for Servants, by the Mistress of a Family, 12mo. *cloth, new,* 1*s and* 1*s* 6*d* *Chambers,* 1858

1226 COOLEY'S History of Maritime and Inland Discovery, 3 vols. 12mo. *cloth,* 7*s* 6*d* *Lardner's Cyclopædia,* 1839

1227 COOROO, *(a native of the Pellew Islands)* his Adventures, by C. D. L. Lambert, 8vo. *boards,* 3*s* *Norwich, Stevenson,* 1805

Dedicated to the Rt. Hon. Lady Harriet Berney.

1228 COOPER'S (American Novelist) Novels—Deerslayer, Spy, Water Witch, and 15 others, together 18 of his novels in 18 vols. 12mo. (Bentley's Standard Novels,) *nice clean copies in cloth,* £2 14*s* .. .. .. 1853, &c.

Published at £5 8*s*, out of print, not now procurable.

1229 COOPERI (Thomæ) Thesaurus Linguæ Romanæ et Britannicæ, thick folio, *old binding,* 12*s* .. *Londini,* 1578

This Dictionary was so much esteemed by Queen Elizabeth, that she promoted him first to the Bishopric of Lincoln, then to Winchester. It is founded on Sir Thomas Eliot's Bibliotheca, Stephens's Thesaurus, and Frisuis's Latin and German Dictionary.

1230 COOPERI (Thomæ) Thesaurus, *arms of Dudley, Earl of Leicester on Title, to whom the Book is dedicated,* thick folio, *old calf,* 12*s* 1584

1231 COOTE'S (Charles, *Pemb. Coll., Oxford)* Elements of the Grammar of the English Language, 8vo. *old binding,* 2*s* 1788

1232 — History of Ancient Europe from the Earliest times, 3 vols. 8vo. *half calf, gilt,* 15*s* .. .. .. 1815

Designed as an accompaniment to Russell's Modern Europe, which see.

1233 COPEMAN (Dr. Edward, *of Norwich)* Brief Essays on an all-powerful, wise, and good Being, and on the Religion of Geology, 8vo. *sewed,* 1*s* .. .. *Norwich,* 1856

1234 — Records of Obstetric Consultation Practice, and a translation of Busch and Moser on Uterine Hæmorrhage, *plates,* 12mo. *cloth,* 3*s* (*pub. at* 5*s*) .. .. .. 1856

1235 COPLEY'S (Esther) Catechism of Domestic Economy, 24mo. *cloth,* 1*s* .. .. .. 1851

1236 COQUEREL (Athanase) Jean Calas et sa Famille, Dépèches, Lettres, Bibliographie, &c. *plate,* 12mo. *sewed,* 2*s* 6*d* (*sells* 5*s*) *Paris,* 1858

1237 CORAN, traduit de l'Arabe, avec notes, et la Vie de Mahomet, par M. Savary, 2 vols. 12mo. *neat,* 6*s* *Amsterdam,* 1786

1238 CORBET'S (Richard, *late Bp. of Oxford and Norwich)* Poems, with Notes and Life, by O. Gilchrist, post 8vo. *cloth, scarce,* 6*s* 1807

"Best edition, ably edited."—*Lowndes.* With, to this fourth edition, an "Oratio in Henrici Principis."

1239 CORII (Bernardini) Mediolanensis Patria Historia, large folio, a remarkably fine volume, *in old calf, gilt,* £3 3*s* *Mediolani, apud Manutianum,* MDIII

"Edition originale."—*Brunet.* Sold at Gaignat's sale for 151 francs. This early History of Milan is a very rare book.
"All these historians, except Corio, wrote in Latin. His book is written in Italian." *Mills's Theodore Ducas.* Although the title page would indicate that it is in Latin.

1240 CORMERII (Thomæ, *Alenconii)* Rerum Gestarum Henrici II., Regis Galliæ libri V., 4to. *old parchment, clean,* 6*s* *Parisiis, Sebast. Nivellii,* 1584

1241 CORMON e Manni Dizionario Francese-Italiano ed Italiano-Francese, 2 vols. 8vo. *neat,* 8*s* *In Lione,* 1813

1242 CORNELIUS NEPOS.—Æmilii Probi, seu Cornelii Nepotis liber de Vita excellentium Imperatorum, cum Commentariis Dionys. Lambini, thick 4to. *old binding,* 8*s* *Lutetiæ,* 1569

"A very excellent edition, accompanied with a very learned and critical Commentary, and a copious and useful Index."—*Moss.*

1243 — alia editio, cum notis variorum, 8vo. *very fine prize copy in vellum,* 10*s* 6*d* .. .. *Amstelodami,* 1687

1244 — alia editio, 12mo. *old calf, gilt edges,* 5*s* *Parisiis, Barbou,* 1767

A very pretty book.

1245 — alia editio, small 8vo. *calf, neat,* 3*s* 6*d* *Glasguæ, Foulis,* 1777

This is a finely printed book, with a large type.

1246 — et Phædrus, *profusely illustrated with spirited wood cuts,* royal 8vo. *cloth,* 7*s* 6*d* .. *Parisiis, R. Bregeaut,* 1837

1247 — Lives of Illustrious Men, Englished by several gentlemen of Oxon, 8vo. *sewed,* 1*s* 6*d* .. .. 1685

1248 CORNWALL—Guide to the Mount's Bay and the Land's End, by a Physician, *plates and wood cuts*, post 8vo. *bds*, 5*s* (*pub. at* 10*s*) 1824

Comprehends a full account of the Climate, Geology, Antiquities, Botany, Manners, and Customs, &c., of the District.

1249 CORONATIONS.—Account of the Ceremonies observed in the C. of the Kings and Queens of England, *cuts and plate*, 4to. *sewed*, 4*s* .. .. .. 1761

1250 — Collections relative to Claims at the Coronations of several of the Kings of England, beginning with K. Richard II., 8vo. *boards, scarce*, 6*s* .. .. *Nichols & Son*, 1820

Supplemental to Taylor's Glory of Regality, and Thomson's Coronation of Geo. III.

1251 CORSI (Faustino) delle Pietre Antiche, 8vo. *half vellum, very neat*, 6*s* .. .. .. *Roma*, 1828

476 authors are cited at the end as having been used in compiling this work.

1252 CORVINI (I. A.) Enchiridium; seu Institutiones Imperiales, per Erotemata digestæ lib. IV., thick 12mo. *calf, very neat*, 8*s* *Amst. Elzevir*, 1640

1253 COSIMO III.—Il Mondo Festeggiante Balletto a Cavallo fatto nel Teatro congiunto al Palazzo del Sereniss. Gran Duca, per le reali Nozze de' Ser. Principi Cosimo Terzo di Toscana e Margherita Luisa d'Orleans, 2 *large folding plates*, 4to. *limp vellum, nice clean copy*, 6*s* .. .. *Firenze*, 1661

1254 COSIN'S (Bp. John) Scholastical History of the Canon of Scripture, *frontispiece by Hollar*, 4to. *old binding*, 6*s* 1657

"A satisfactory induction of the Evidence for the authenticity of the Scriptures."—*Orme.*

1255 COSTARD'S (George) History of Astronomy, with its application to Geography, History, and Chronology, *plate*, 4to. *half vellum, neat*, 5*s* .. .. .. 1767

Costard was a very considerable oriental and classical scholar, which this book clearly shews.

1256 COSTIGAN'S (Arthur W.) Sketches of Society and Manners in Portugal in 1778-9, 2 vols. 8vo. *half calf, neat*, 8*s* 1787

A copy of this book sold for 28*s* at the Fonthill sale.

1257 COSTO (Tomaso) Apologia Istorica, del Regno di Napoli, 4to. *old boards, scarce*, 5*s* *Napoli, G. D. Roncagliolo*, 1613

1258 COTERÆI (Claudii *Turonensis Jurisconsulti*) de Jure et Privilegiis Militum libri III., de officio Imperatoris liber, folio, *old calf, neat*, 12*s* .. *Lugduni, apud S. Doletum*, 1539

Stephen Dolet, the printer, dedicates this book to Cardinal Bellay.

1259 COTMAN'S (M. E.) XI. Original Etchings, Imperial 8vo. *in stiff cover*, 5*s* .. *Norwich, C. Muskett*, 1846

Fine impressions, only a few printed.

1260 COTTIN, (Mad.) Elizabeth; ou les Exilés de Sibérie, 18mo. *boards*, 1*s* .. .. .. *Londres*, 1817

1261 COTTON (Charles) Planter's Manual; instructions for cultivating all sorts of Fruit Trees, *engraved frontispiece, by Van Hove*, small 8vo. *old calf*, 4*s* .. .. .. 1675

1262 COTTON'S Poetical Works, Virgil travestie, Wonders of the Peake, &c., View of the Duke of Devonshire's House at Chatsworth, and *plates*, 12mo. *calf, neat*, 3*s* 6*d* .. .. 1765

Walton's friend and coadjutor in his Angler, for an autograph of his, see *Pinto* in this Catalogue.

1263 COTTON'S (Archdeacon Henry) List of Editions of the Bible, from 1505 to 1820, first edition, *Oxford*, 1821.—MENDHAM'S (Joseph) Account of the Indexes, both Prohibitory and expurgatory of the Church of Rome, in 1 vol. 8vo. *half calf, very neat*, 7*s* 6*d* .. .. *Birmingham*, 1826

1264 — Editions of the Bible, from 1505 (i.e. 1525) to 1850, with Specimens of Translations and bibliographical Descriptions, 8vo. *cloth, new*, 12*s* .. *Oxford University Press*, 1852

This Second Edition is very much enlarged, it is a capital concise enumeration.

1265 — Typographical Gazetteer, 2nd Edition, much enlarged, 8vo. *cloth, new*, 12*s* .. *Oxford University Press*, 1831

A most valuable alphabetical list of Places where Books have been Printed, with the earliest known books mentioned, quite indispensable to the Bibliographer.

1266 COUNCIL. Acta Constantiensis Concilii, nunc primum ex Codicibus MSS. in lucem eruta ac dissertatione illustrata per Eman. a Schelstrate, 4to. *old parchment*, 6*s* *Antverpiæ*, 1683

"Ex libris Henrici Legoix."

1267 COUSIN (Jehan, Senonois, *Maistre Painctre à Paris*) Livre de Perspective, *plates*, folio, *sewed, uncut*, RARE, £1 1*s*
*Paris, Jehan le Royer*, 1560

This eminent French artist and mathematician was the earliest historical painter France produced, born near Sens, in 1530, died 1589; of this work Brunet says, that it is the "Edition originale et assez rare."

1268 COVENTRY'S (Henry) Philemon to Hydaspes; the History of False Religion in the Earlier Pagan World, 1st and 2nd parts, 1753-40.—Edmund Burke's Ironical Letter to Lord Bolingbroke, being a Vindication of Natural Society, 1757.—Bishop Hare's Difficulties and Discouragements attending the Study of the Scriptures, 1735, in 1 vol. 8vo. *half calf, neat*, 3*s* 6*d*

1269 COVERDALE, Certain most godly, fruitful, and comfortable Letters of such true Saintes and Holy Martyrs of God, as in the late bloodye Persecution here within this Realme, gave their Lyves for the Defence of Christ's Holy Gospel: written in the time of their Affliction and Cruell Imprysonment, small 4to. **Black Letter**, *antique calf*, VERY RARE, £5 5*s*
*Imprinted at London by Iohn Day*, 1564

The Original Edition of one of the most interesting books published in Elizabeth's reign, by Miles Coverdale, Bp. of Exeter.

1270 COWLEY'S (Abraham) Works, with an Account of his Life by Bp. Sprat, *portrait*, 3 vols. 12mo. *calf, neat*, 7*s* 6*d* 1721

"Lord Clarendon considered Cowley superior to Ben Jonson."

1271 COWPER'S (William, Poet) Works and Life, by Hayley; edited by Grimshaw, *plates*, 8 vols. 12mo.; *nice set, in half morocco, gilt edges*, £1 12*s* .. .. .. 1835

1272 COWPER'S Works and Life, by Southey, *plates*, 15 vols. 12mo. *boards, scarce, (pub. at £3 15s) £1 18s* .. .. 1836

1273 — Poetical Works, with Memoirs of him, *portrait*, 3 vols. 12mo. *morocco, gilt edges, by Hayday, £1 10s* *W. Pickering*, 1843

**Genuine copy, beautifully bound by Hayday.**

1274 — Works and Life, by Robert Southey, *portrait and plates*, vol. 1 only, post 8vo. *cloth, 2s cost 3s 6d* *H. G. Bohn*, 1853

1275 — Table Talk and other Poems, *plates, by Finden*, 12mo. *boards, 3s (pub. at 5s 6d)* .. .. .. 1817

1276 COX (George) Spectacle Secrets, *plates*, 12mo. *cloth, 1s* 1838

1277 COXE'S (Archdeacon W.) Travels in Poland, Russia, Sweden, and Denmark, *maps, portraits, and plates*, 4 vols. 8vo. *nice set in old calf, gilt, 15s* .. .. .. 1787

"This work confirmed the literary reputation of its author, and from the time of its first appearance it has been esteemed one of the most valuable sources of knowledge on the subject of Northern Europe."—*Quarterly Review.*

1278 — Memoirs of the Life and Administration of Sir Robert Walpole, Earl of Orford, *portrait*, 3 vols. 4to. *calf, neat, £1 18s* 1798

"A more judicious and instructive biographical work, or one more satisfactory to every rational desire of knowledge, is not found in our English Literature."—*Quarterly Review.*

1279 — History of the House of Austria from 1218 to 1792, 3 vols. 4to. *good copy, in calf, £1 16s* .. .. 1807

"Coxe's House of Austria must be diligently read."—*Professor Smyth.*

1280 — Memoirs of the Duke of Marlborough, *portrait*, 3 vols. post 8vo. *cloth, 10s 6d* .. .. *H. G. Bohn*, 1847

1281 COZZANDI (Leonardi) de Magisterio antiquorum Philosophorum libri VI., thick 12mo. *old calf, 4s 6d* *Genevæ*, 1684

1282 CRABB'S (George) English Synonymes explained, in Alphabetical order, thick 8vo. *boards, 10s (pub. at 21s)* 1816

1283 CRADOCK'S (Joseph) Account of some of the most Romantic parts of North Wales, *plates of arms*, 12mo. *boards, uncut, 3s* 1777

1284 CRADOCK'S (Samuel, *of North Cadbury, Somersetshire)* Knowledge and Practice; a plain discourse of the chief things necessary to be known, believed, and practised in order to salvation, thick 8vo. of 692 pages, *a fine copy, in old morocco, gilt leaves, scarce, 9s* .. .. 1659

With a recommendatory Preface by Dr. Edward Reynolds, afterwards Bishop of Norwich, "I commend unto the Christian reader this Manual, which I have read with great satisfaction and delight."

1285 CRADOCK'S (Sam.) Harmony of the IV. Evangelists, wherein the entire History of our Lord is methodically set forth, folio, *good copy, in old calf, 7s 6d* .. .. 1668

"I cannot but recommend this as among the most useful and judicious Expositions of the New Testament I have ever seen."—*Dr. Doddridge.*

1286 CRAIK'S (G. L.) History of the Literature and Learning in England, from the Norman Conquest to the present Day, 6 vols. in 3, 18mo. *cloth, new, 6s* .. .. 1844-5

1287 CRANMER (Abp. of Canterbury) His Life, by Prebendary H. J. Todd, *fine portrait*, 2 vols. 8vo. *boards, 12s (pub. at 24s)* 1831

1288 CRASHAW'S (William) Parable of Poyson, in V. Sermons of Spirituall Poyson, the poysonfull nature of sinne, and the spirituall antidotes, small 4to. *sewed*, 5*s* 1618

1289 CRAWSHAW'S (William) Poetical Works, edited by W. B. Turnbull, foolscap 8vo. *cloth*, 5*s* *J. R. Smith*, 1859

1290 CREIGHTON (Capt. J. N.) Narrative of the Siege and Capture of Bhurtpore, Agra, Upper Hindostan, under Lord Combermere, 1825-6, *plates*, 4to. *morocco gilt, gilt leaves*, 10*s* (*pub. at* £1 1*s*) *For the Author*, 1830

John Hunter's copy with his Book-plate.

1291 CRENNII (Th.) Fasciculi I—III. opusculorum quæ ad historiam et philologiam sacram spectant, 3 vols. small 8vo. *old binding*, 7*s* 6*d* *Rotterodami*, 1691-93

A re-print of many rare works tending to Philological enquiry, which would now be extremely difficult to procure in the originals.

1292 CRESHALD.—A Legacy left to the World, by (that able Lawyer) Richard Creshald, Serjant at Law; late one of the Judges of the Court of Common Pleas, addressed (in his life-time) to his foure sons in Lawes, small 4to. *sewed, scarce*, 5*s* 1658

"Very useful for all men to read and practice."—Not in *Lowndes*.

1293 CRESSY. (Serenus) An Epistle Apologetical of S. C. to a person of Honour; touching his Vindication of Dr. Stillingfleet, small 8vo. *half bound, clean and neat*, £1 11*s* 6*d* *Permissu Superiorum*, 1674

This curious little volume contains also the following Tracts:—

I.—The Several Ways of Resolving FAITH in the Roman and Reformed Churches .. .. *York, Stephen Bulkley*, 1677

II.—Reflection upon Mr. Varillas, his History of Heresy, as far as relates to English Matters, more especially those of Wicliff .. 1688

III.—Raillerie a la Mode considered; or, the Supercilious Detractor, a Joco-Serious Discourse, shewing the Impertinence and Degenerosity of publishing private Pecques .. *Henry Million*, 1663

IV.—Legend of St. Cuthbert, with the Antiquities of the Church of Durham, by B. R., Esq. [Robert Hegge,] *plate* .. 1663

V.—List of the House of Commons .. .. 1714

Norfolk then returned Sir Edmund Bacon, (to whom this book belonged, having his Initials on the title pages of some of the Tracts) and Sir Jacob Astley; Norwich, Richard Berney, Esq.; Lynn Regis, Robert Walpole, afterwards Prime-Minister; Castlerising, Horatio Walpole, Esq.

1294 CROCII (Johan.) Commentarius in S. Pauli Apost. Epist. ad Titum, 12mo. *vellum, neat*, 5*s* *Cassellis*, 1638

1295 CROFTS. Bibliotheca Croftsiana: a Catalogue of the curious Library of Thomas Crofts, Chancellor of Peterborough, sold by Auction in 1783, by Mr. Paterson, *partly priced*, 8vo. 420 pages, *boards, uncut*, 5*s* .. .. .. 1783

"An excellently well-arranged Catalogue, and, in my opinion, the Chef d'Œuvre of Patterson."—*Dr. Dibdin*.

1296 CROKE'S (Sir Alexander) Essay on the Origin, Progress, and Decline of Rhyming Latin Verse, with Specimens, post 8vo. *cloth*, 4*s* 6*d* (*pub. at* 7*s* 6*d*) *Oxford, Talboys*, 1828

1297 — Progress of Idolatry, a Poem in 10 books, with notes, 14 *etchings of Hindu Deities*, 12mo. *cloth*, 3*s* 6*d* (*pub. at* 7*s*) *Oxford, J. H. Parker*, 1841

"P. B. Duncan, Esq., from the Author, observantiæ ergo."—in MS.

1298 CROMWELL'S ACTS passed in the Parliament at Westminster, in 1656-7.—Some in **Black Letter**, folio, *new half calf, neat, rare*, £1 1*s* .. .. *Hills & Field*, 1657

1299 CROMWELL (OLIVER) A Catalogue of the names of those Honourable persons, who are now members of this present House of Lords, folio, *broadside*, VERY RARE, £5 5*s* *No date, but* 1657

This very curious document commences thus, "the Lord RICHARD CROMWELL; the Lord HENRY CROMWELL, Lord Deputy of Ireland; Nathaniel Fiennes, John Lisle, Lords Commissioners of the Great Seal; Henry Lawrence, Lord President of his Highness' Privy Council;" and 55 others, amongst whom is George Monke, Commander in Chief in Scotland;—this George Monke, afterwards Duke of Albemarle, had a principal hand in the Restoration of Charles II.

In Howell's excellent *Medulla*, 1766, we read, under 1657,—"And the better to strengthen himself at home, and to raise his family into esteem, he gave his eldest son (Richard) a command in the army, his younger son (see above) he made Lord Deputy of Ireland. And, that he might be as King-like as possible, he constituted an Upper House of *Parliament, instead* of the House of Lords, (they are, however, above called the House of Lords) 62 in number (Hume says 60, which is the number on this broadside) most of them his own creatures," &c. And Howell mentions Colonel Pride, Colonel Hewson, and the Earl of Warwick, all of whom are mentioned in this most rare broadside, which is, in point of fact, the ORIGINAL of CROMWELL'S HOUSE OF LORDS, published at the time of his being anew inaugurated at Westminster LORD PROTECTOR.

1300 — Catalogue of the Knights, Citizens, and Burgesses, elected to serve in Parliament now assembled at Westminster, 1659, folio, MS., *very nicely written*, 7*s* 6*d* .. .. 1659

The Members for Norfolk then were, Sir Horatio Townsend, Bart. and Sir William Doyley; for Norwich, Wm. Branham and John Hobart. This must have been RICHARD Cromwell's Parliament.

1301 — Historical and Critical Account of his Life, after the manner of Bayle, by William Harris, 8vo. *old calf, neat*, 4*s* 6*d* 1762

1302 — Noble's (Mark) Memoirs of the Protectoral House of Cromwell, and their allies, *portrait and plates*, 2 vols. 8vo. *very nice clean copy*, 8*s* .. .. *Birmingham*, 1787

1303 CROOKSHANKS (Will.) History of the State and Sufferings of the Church of Scotland, from 1660 to 1688, 2 vols. 8vo. *boards, scarce*, 10*s* 6*d* .. .. *Edinburgh*, 1812

1304 CROSS (Maurice) Selections from the Edinburgh Review, 6 vols. in 3, 8vo. *newly half bound in calf*, £1 4*s* 1835

This is a very nice, pleasant, and readable book, full of Literary Critical Essays; prefixed is an excellent Dissertation reviewing all the works of a similar description which had preceded it.

1305 CROSSE'S (Dr. J. G., *of Norwich)* Retrospective address upon Medical Science and Literature, delivered in Manchester, in July, 1836, 8vo. *cloth*, 2*s* 6*d* .. *Worcester*, 1836

1306 CROWTHER'S (Rev. Samuel) Vocabulary of the Yoruba Language, with Introductory Remarks, by Bp. Vidal, 8vo. *cloth*, 7*s* 6*d* .. .. .. .. 1852

1307 — Journal of an Expedition up the Niger and Tshadda Rivers, in 1854, with Vocabularies at end, *map*, 12mo. *cloth*, 2*s* 6*d* 1855

1308 CRUDEN'S (Alexander, M.A.) Complete Concordance of the Holy Scriptures, or a Dictionary and Alphabetical Index to the Bible, royal 8vo. *portrait, cloth*, 12*s* 6*d* .. 1857

1309 — another edition, by Dr. J. Eadie, with an Introduction, by Dr. David King, 8vo. *cloth, new*, 5*s* .. 1857

1310 CUDWORTH (Dr. Ralph) True Intellectual System of the Universe, wherein all the reason and philosophy of Atheism is confuted, 2 vols. in 1, thick 4to. *good copy, in calf,* £1 1s *(usually sells for* £2 2s) .. .. .. 1743

"Best edition (with an account of Dr. Cudworth's Life by Dr. Birch) of a complete storehouse of Ancient Literature and a work of the first merit."—*Lowndes.*
"A valuable storehouse for inquiries into Ancient Philosophy."—*Dr. Burton.*

1311 — abridged by Dr. Tho. Wise, 2 vols. small 4to. *good copy, in calf,* 8s .. .. .. .. 1706

"A very excellent abridgment."—*Lowndes.*

1312 CULMANNI (Leonhardi) Contiones in Evangelia, vols. 2 and 3, small 8vo. *old curious stamped binding,* 8s *Norimbergæ, I. Montani et Ulrici Neuber,* 1550

At the ends of these volumes are some leaves on vellum and paper, on which is old music and caligraphy.

1313 CULPEPER'S English Physician enlarged, with the Family Physician, *coloured plates,* 12mo. *boards,* 4s (*pub. at* 7s 6d) 1809

1314 CUMBERLAND.—Speech of Ferdinando Huddleston, Esq., in the face of the County, at Baggry Election, Aug. 27, folio, *broadside,* 2s .. .. .. .. 1679

1315 CUMBERLAND (Richard) Memoirs of Himself, with anecdotes and characters of the most distinguished Persons of his time, *portraits,* 2 vols. 8vo. *calf, neat,* 5s .. 1807

A very amusing, anecdotical book. "It is, indeed, one of the Author's most pleasing works, and conveys a very accurate idea of his talents, feelings, and character, with many powerful sketches of the age which has passed away."—*Sir Walter Scott.*

1316 CUMMING (Dr. John) and Mr. French's Protestant Discussion at Hammersmith, in 1839, on the differences between it and Popery, post 8vo. *cloth,* 3s (*pub. at* 6s) 1848

1317 CUNDALL (Joseph) on Ornamental Art, applied to Ancient and Modern Bookbinding, *elegantly illustrated with specimens,* 4to. *boards,* 12s .. .. .. 1848

1318 CUNNINGHAM (Allan) Lives of the most eminent British Painters, Sculptors, and Architects, *portraits,* 6 vols. 18mo. *cloth,* 15s (*cost* 30s) .. .. *Fam. Lib.,* 1829

1319 CUNNINGHAM'S (Geo. G.) Lives of Eminent and Illustrious Englishmen, arranged in Periods, *portraits,* 8 vols. 8vo. *boards,* £1 10s (*pub. at* £3 12s) .. *Glasgow,* 1835

1320 CUNNINGHAM'S (Rev. F.) Selection of Psalms and Hymns, 18mo. *cloth,* 1s 6d .. .. .. 1850

1321 CURIONIS (Cælii Secundi) Schola, sive de perfecto Grammatico libri III., et Liberis pie Educandis libellus, *Basileæ, per I. Oporinum,* 1555.—C. S. Curionis de Omni artificio disserendi atque tractandi summa, *Basileæ, per Oporinum,* 1547.—Orationes in Gymnasio Altorfiano partim a Rectore I. Thoma Freigio recitatæ, partim Adolescentibus recitandæ traditæ, *Noribergæ,* 1578—in 1 vol. 8vo. *old binding,* 8s .. V. Y.

With Autograph and Book-plate of White Kennett, Bishop of Peterborough.

1322 — de Amplitudine beati Regni Dei, Dialogus, small 8vo. *old calf, scarce,* 7s 6d .. *Goudæ, And. Burier,* 1614

"A *curious* work. Cælius Secundus Curio was born in San-Chirico, in Piedmont, of a noble family, died 1569."—See *Clarke's Bib. Dict.*

1323 CURIOUS TRACTS in 1 vol., namely:—

I.—Catalogue of those composing the Parliament begun at Westminster Nov. 3, 1640

II.—Stephens's (Thos.) Three Sermons preached before the Judges at Bury St. Edmund's, Suffolk, 1660 *Cambridge, Field,* 1661

III.— —— Sacred Hymns upon the Gospels of the Hyemal Quarter, *ib.* 1661

IV.—Cotton (Charles) Scarronides; or Virgil's Æneis Travestie, a mock Poem, 1st EDITION .. .. .. 1664

Anonymous, but written by Charles Cotton, Izaac Walton's friend.

V.—Case of his Grace the D(uke) of M(arlborough), about Bread and Bread Waggons, in Vindication of himself .. 1712

VI.—One Word more and we have done; or, the Plain English of Indulgence, no Government, no Order, no Religion, .. 1663

VII.—Cowley's (Abraham) Foure Ages of England; or the Iron Age, with other Select Poems, FIRST EDITION .. 1648

VIII.—Casa (John, *Abp. of Benevento*) The Acts of Grandeur and Submission, Englished by Henry Stubbe, Physician at Warwick, 2nd EDITION .. .. .. 1670

On the behaviour of Great Men towards their Inferiours, and vice versâ.

IX.—Answer to the Reasons against an African Company 1711

X.—Short Character of His Ex(cellency) T. E(arl) of W(entworth) L(ord) L(ieutenant) of I(reland) .. .. 1711

XI.—Baxter's (Richard) One Sheet for the Ministry, against the Malignants of all sorts, 8 *leaves,* VERY RARE .. 1657

This is the 31st out of Baxter's 168 works as enumerated by his biographer, *Orme.*

XII.—Dunkirk, Reasons concerning the immediate demolishing of Dunkirk 1713

the above 12 Pieces in 1 vol. small thick 8vo. *half bound,* £2 2*s*

This volume was put together by Sir Edmund Bacon, M.P. for Norwich, temp. Queen Anne.

1324 CURTIS'S (William) Botanical Magazine, by Dr. Sims, 53 vols. in 28, *full bound in calf,* with Index vol. *in boards,* and vols. 1 to 5 of new series, by Sir W. Hooker, *in numbers,* £15 1787-1831

3122 beautiful coloured plates, published at 2 guineas per vol. Such a set as this is usually priced £35.

1325 — General Indexes to the first 53 volumes of Curtis's Botanical Magazine, *portrait,* royal 8vo. *half morocco, uncut,* 12*s* 1828

1326 — History of the Brown Tail Moth, the Caterpillers of which are now so numerous near the Metropolis, *coloured plates,* 4to. *sewed,* 4*s* .. .. . .. 1782

This is in MS. and appears to be the original work.

1327 CUVIER'S Fossil Remains of the Animal Kingdom, with additions by Edward Pidgeon, 49 *plates,* thick 8vo. *cloth,* 12*s (pub. at* 18*s)*

1328 — Essay on the Theory of the Earth, with Mineralogical Illustrations, by Professor Jameson, *plates,* 8vo. 3rd edition, *boards,* 4*s* *Edinburgh,* 1817

1329 — Essay on the Theory of the Earth, by Professor Jameson, *plates,* 8vo. 4th edition, *boards,* 5*s* .. .. *ib.* 1822

1330 CYCLOPÆDIA of Universal Biography, edited by Elihu Rich, *numerous illustrations,* 8vo. *cloth,* 10*s* 6*d* .. 1858

1331 DALGAIRN'S (Mrs., *i.e. Sir Walter Scott)* Practice of Cookery, adapted to the business of every day life, 12mo. *cloth, new,* 4*s* 1858

1332 DALLAS'S (W. S.) Natural History of the Animal Kingdom, *coloured frontispiece and numerous plates,* thick 8vo. *cloth, new,* 8*s* 6*d* .. .. .. .. 1856

1333 DANCES.—Sixty Favourite Dances, ten Cotillons, and ten Minuets, with Rondos, Airs, Marches, Songs, and Duetts, by Pleyel, Haydn, &c., adapted for the Harpsicord, Violin, and German Flute, oblong, *sewed,* 4*s* .. *Cambridge, M. Barford*

1334 DANYEL (Samuel) Collection of the Historie of England, 1st edition, folio, *old calf,* RARE, 18*s* *For the Author,* 1618

Dedicated to the Majesty of Anne of Denmark, Queene of England, to whom he was Groome of the Chamber. This Historie ends with the Reign of K. Edward III.
"Written with a freedom from all stiffness, and a purity of style which hardly any other work of so early a date (1618) exhibits."—*Hallam.*

1335 — another edition, small folio, *rough calf,* 8*s* 1626

1336 — another, with Continuation to the end of the Reign of Richard III., by Trussel, folio, *stained at the end, half calf, neat,* 6*s* 1685

This edition, by Dr. Trussel, continues the History from where Daniel ends to where Lord Bacon began.—See *Bacon.*

1337 DANIEL (William B.) Rural Sports, the Supplemental volume only, *portrait and plates,* 4to. *boards, clean copy,* £1 1*s* (*pub. at* £2 12*s* 6*d*) .. .. .. 1813

1338 D'ANOIS (The Countess) Fairy Tales and Novels, translated from the French, *plates,* 2 vols. 12mo. *boards,* 4*s* 6*d* (*pub. at* 8*s*) 1817

1339 DANTE, La Comedia di, con la nova Espositione di Alessandro Vellutello, thick 4to. *numerous remarkable wood cuts, a fine copy in old vellum,* £2 12*s* 6*d*
*Impressa in Vinegia per Francesco Marcolini,* 1544

"Raro. Edizione bellissima, ornata di eleganti intagli in legno."—*Gamba.*
"Une des meilleures éditions anciennes de Dante."—*Brunet.*
A copy produced £3 16*s* at Mr. Heber's sale.

1340 — La Divina Commedia, con nuovi argomenti, annotazioni, &c., da Pietro Cicchetti, thick 18mo. *boards,* 5*s* *Whittingham,* 1827

"I hold a familiar knowledge of Dante, to be next to Demosthenes."—*Lord Brougham to Lord Macaulay's Father, Mar.* 1823.

1341 — Discorso sul Testo e su le Opinioni diverse prevalenti intorno alla Storia e alla Emendazione Critica della Commedia di Dante, da Ugo Foscolo, crn. 8vo. 435 pages, *cloth,* 9*s* *W. Pickering,* 1825

1342 — Dante and Petrarch, Sketch of the Lives and Writings of, 18mo. *neat,* 2*s* 6*d* .. .. .. 1790

"An ingenious work written by M. Penrose."—*Lowndes.*
It has, also, an account of the Italian and Latin Literature of the 14th Century.

1343 D'ANVILLE'S Compendium of Ancient Geography, Englished, *with maps mounted on canvass,* 2 vols. 8vo. *boards,* 8*s* 1791

"A good translation of a work of the first authority, it has a map of Roman Britain from John Horsley's *Britannia Romana.*"—*Lowndes.*

1344 — another copy, *maps,* 2 vols. 8vo. *calf, neat,* 8*s* 1791

1345 D'ARBLAY'S (Madame) Diary and Letters, *portraits,* 7 vols. 12mo. *cloth,* 14*s* (*pub. at* £1 1*s*) .. 1854

"*Miss Burney's Diary,* sparkling with wit, lively anecdote, and delectable gossip, and full of sound and discreet views of persons and things."—*Athenæum.*

1346 DARLING'S (James) Bibliotheca Clericalis, at Little Queen St., Lincoln's Inn Fields, 8vo. *cloth,* 4*s* .. 1843

1347 DARLING'S Cyclopædia Bibliographica; a Library Manual of (chiefly) Theological and General Literature, and Guide to books for authors, preachers, students, and literary men, thick royal 8vo. *cloth*, £2 12*s* 6*d* .. .. 1854

This is a most stupendous volume of 1664 pages, extremely valuable, principally, to Clergymen, it being analytical, as well as biographical and bibliographical, must have cost its compiler an immense amount of labour. There is another "Companion" volume of "Subjects," published at 30*s* which enhances the value of this.

1348 DARWIN'S (Dr. Erasmus) Poetical Works, with philosophical Notes, *coloured plates*, 3 vols. royal 8vo. *boards*, LARGE PAPER, 15*s* .. .. .. .. 1806

Contains:—I. The Economy of Vegetation.—II. The Loves of the Plants.—III. The Temple of Nature.

1349 D'AUBIGNE'S (Dr. J. H. Merle) History of the Reformation in the XVI. Century, translated by Henry Beveridge, 4 vols. 12mo. *sewed*, 4*s* .. .. *Collins's Edit.*, 1846

1350 DAUBUZ (Charles) Perpetual Commentary on the Revelation of St. John, thick folio, *best edition, old calf, neat*, £1 5*s* 1720

1351 D'AVAUX (Count) Negotiations, 1679-1688, 4 vols. in 2, 12mo. *half calf, neat*, 8*s* .. .. .. 1754

A book much quoted by Lord Macaulay. Count D'Avaux was Ambassador from Louis XIV. to the States General, and this History contains, not only the Secret History of the Duke of Monmouth's Rebellion, but the Intrigues of the Court of France in favor of K. James II. against K. Will. III.

1352 D'AVENANT (Sir William) Gondibert, an Heroic Poem, small 8vo. *calf, gilt, very neat*, 7*s* 6*d* .. .. 1651

With the large preface of 51 pages addressed to Mr. Hobbes; and Mr. Hobbes's reply; also Complimentary Poems by Waller and Cowley.

1353 DAVIES'S (Edward) Celtic Researches on the Origin, Traditions, and Language of the Ancient Britons, with some Introductory Sketches of Primitive Society, royal 8vo. *boards*, SCARCE, 12*s* *For the Author*, 1804

1354 DAVIES'S (Sir John) Discoverie of the True Causes why Ireland was never entirely subdued until K. James Ist's Time, 12mo. *calf, gilt*, SCARCE, 6*s* .. .. .. 1747

Reprint of the rare edition of 1612. The author was Attorney-General of Ireland, temp. Jac. 1.

1355 DAVILA'S (H. C.) History of the Civil Wars of France, 1560-1598, from the Italian, folio, *fine copy, old calf, gilt*, 12*s* 1678

1356 DAVY'S (Sir Humphrey) Elements of Agricultural Chemistry, *plates*, 8vo. *calf, very neat*, 6*s* .. .. 1827

1357 — Consolations in Travel, *plates*, 12mo. *cloth*, 4*s* 6*d* (*pub. at* 6*s*) 1851

1358 — Salmonia; or Days of Fly Fishing, *plates*, 12mo. *cloth*, 4*s* 6*d* (*pub. at* 6*s*) .. .. .. 1851

1359 DAWES (Rich.) Miscellanea Critica, edidit Th. Burgess et G. C. Harless, 8vo. *half calf, neat*, 3*s* 6*d* *Lipsiæ*, 1800

1360 DAYES'S (Edward, *artist*) Works; Containing an Excursion through Derbyshire and Yorkshire, with Notes, by E. W. Brayley; Essays on Painting; Instructions for Drawing and Colouring Landscapes; and Sketches of Modern Artists, *portrait and plates*, 4to. *calf, gilt, very fine copy*, £1 1*s* 1805

The plates finely engraved by Angus and Smith; quite an Artist's book.

1361 DEALTRY'S (William) Principles of Fluxions, 8vo. *boards, 2s 6d* *Cambridge,* 1816

1362 DEAN'S (Rich.) Essay on the Future Life of Brute Creatures, 12mo. *stiff covers, 2s 6d* .. *Manchester,* 1767

1363 DE BURE (Guil. Fr.) Bibliographie Instructive: ou, Traité de la Connoissanee des Livres rares et singulieres, 7 vols. 8vo. *good copy, in old French calf, gilt, 21s* *Paris,* 1763-68

"One of the best executed and most intrinsically valuable Catalogues in existence."—*Dibdin.*

1364 — Catalogue des Livres du Cabinet de feu M. Louis J. Gaignat, 2 vols. 8vo. *uniform with the above, 9s* *Paris,* 1769

1365 — Catalogue des Livres rares et précieux de la Bibliothèque de feu M. le Comte de Mac-Carthy Reagh, *plates,* 2 vols. 8vo. *nice copy, in calf, 10s 6d* .. .. *Paris,* 1815

With list of the prices the books produced at the end.

1366 DECANDOLLE'S (M. Aug. P.) Vegetable Organography; or a Description of the Organs of Plants, 2 vols. 8vo. *nice copy, calf, gilt, 10s* .. .. .. .. 1841

1367 DE DIEU (Ludovici) Animadversiones in IV. Evangelia, in quo collatis Æthiopici, Syri, Arabis, Hebræi, Vulgati, Erasmi et Bezæ Versionibus, 4to. *vellum, neat, 7s 6d* *Lugd. Bat., Elzevir,* 1631

Autograph of "*C. Macro. Xti. Coll. Cant.*, 1702." "Perhaps no man ever possessed a more consummate knowledge of the Oriental languages than De Dieu, nor employed his knowledge to more useful purposes."—*Bibliog. Dict., Clarke.*

1368 DE DILUVII Universalitate Dissertatio prolusoria, 12mo. *old binding, 2s* .. .. .. *Genevæ,* 1667

1369 DEE'S (Dr. John) Private Diary, and a Catalogue of his MSS. by J. O. Halliwell, 4to. *cloth, new, 5s* *Camden Soc.,* 1842

1370 DEFENCE de la Religion Reformée, et de la Monarchie et Eglise Anglicane, contre l'Impieté et Tyrannie de la Ligue Rebelle d'Angleterre, small 8vo. *old calf, neat,* RARE, £2 12*s* 6*d* *L'an Second apres la Martyre de Charles I., Roy de la Grand Bretagne, &c.* 1650

*With a brilliant impression of the Portrait, by Hollar, of King Charles II.* when quite a young man and an exile.

A copy of this rare portrait of Chas. II. was in the Townley collection in 1818, and is thus described, "small etching, half length, after Vandyck, rare, not in Vertue." It sold for 4 guineas.

1371 DE FOE'S (Daniel) Jure Divino, a Satyr, 8vo. *original binding, scarce, 7s 6d* .. .. .. 1706

1372 — Further Adventures of Robinson Crusoe, 8vo. 2nd edition, *rare, indifferent copy, 15s* .. .. .. 1719

1373 — Secrets of the Invisible World Disclos'd, a Universal History of Apparitions, by Andrew Moreton, Esq., *plates,* 8vo. *original binding, scarce, 12s* .. .. .. 1729

1374 — System of Magic; a History of the Black Art, *frontispiece,* 8vo. *original binding, rare, 15s* .. .. 1727

1375 — Life and Adventures of Mrs. Christian Davies, during a Campaign under King William as a Foot Soldier and Dragoon, 8vo. *old calf, neat, scarce, 5s* .. .. .. 1740

1376 — Adventures of Robinson Crusoe, *plates,* 12mo. *cloth, new, 3s 6d* 1853

1377 — Another edition, with a Memoir of the Author, *and* 300 *engravings after Grandville,* 8vo. *cloth gilt, gilt edges, 6s* .. 1856

1378 DEGGE'S (Sir Simon) Parsons Counsellor, with the Law of Tithes, and Additions by C. Ellis, 8vo. *calf, neat,* 5s .. 1820

1379 DEIGHTON (Messrs.) Catalogue of English and Foreign Theology and Ecclesiastical History, 8vo. *half cloth,* 2s 6d *Cambridge,* 1841

1380 DE LA MAYNE (Thomas) Love and Honour, a Dramatic Poem taken from Virgil, *plate,* 12mo. *elegantly bound in red morocco, gilt edges,* 4s 6d .. .. *For the Author,* 1742

Dedicated to Philip, Earl of Chesterfield. Very favourably noticed in the *Biographia Dramatica.*

1381 DE LA MOTTE'S (Franc. *a Convert to the Ch. of Eng.*) Abominations of the Church of Rome, a Recantation Sermon, 4to. *sewed,* 2s 6d .. .. .. .. 1675

Contains "curious particulars of the practices of the Papists beyond the seas."

1382 DELANO'S (Amasa) Voyages and Travels Three times Round the World, *portrait and plates,* 8vo. *calf, scarce,* 6s *Boston, U. States,* 1817

1383 DELANY (Mrs.) Letters to Mrs. Hamilton, 1779 to 1788, containing anecdotes of the late Royal Family, with Memoir, *profile,* 12mo. *boards,* 2s .. .. .. 1820

1384 DE LA RUE (Pere, *de la Compagnie de Jesus)* ses Sermons, 4 vols. 12mo. *old calf, neat,* 12s .. .. *Lyon,* 1719

In Rivington and Cochrane's Catalogue at £1 4s.

1385 DELAVAL (Edward Hussey) Experimental Inquiry into the cause of the changes of colours in opake and coloured bodies, 4to. *very fine clean copy, in calf,* 8s .. .. 1777

This work, the production of a F.R.S., is omitted by *Lowndes,* as well as by his new editor, but a copy in 8vo. is in the library of the Royal Institution.

1386 DE LOLME'S (John L.) Constitution of England, 8vo. *calf, very neat,* 3s 6d .. .. .. 1775

1387 — another edition, with a Preface, Notes, Index, &c., by William H. Hughes, *portrait,* 8vo. *half cloth,* 6s *(pub. at* 12s) 1834

1388 — another edition, with Life and Notes, by J. Macgregor, M.P., post 8vo. *cloth,* 2s 6d .. *H. G. Bohn,* 1852

"An Account of the English Government as compared with Republican."

1389 DEL RII (Martini Antonii) Syntagma Tragœdiæ Latinæ, in III. partes distinctum, bound in 2 vols. 4to. *limp vellum, neat,* 7s 6d *Antverpiæ, Plantini,* 1593

The second part of this work is devoted to an edition of Seneca, which is said to be "a very excellent one." Delrio having successfully amended the text of his author.

1390 — alia editio, 3 vols. in 1, 4to. *Prize Copy to Joannes Quentelor, Castroportianus, in old morocco, profusely ornamented with fleurs-de-lis, and the College Arms,* 15s *Lut. Parisiorum,* 1620

"This is an edition of SENECA, annexed to the '*Fragmenta Veterum Tragicorum,* and illustrated with learned observations."—*Dr. Adam Clarke.*

1391 DEMOSTHENES, Græcè, 3 vols. small 8vo. *good clean copy, in old calf,* £1 4s *Corrigente Paulo Manutio Aldi filio, Venetiis,* 1554

One of the very few Greek Books edited by Paul Manutius.
"Cette édition est fort rare."—*Renouard.*

1392 DEMOSTHENES, Orationes de Republica XII., Gr. et Lat., cum notis historicis J. V. Lucchesinii, accessit Philippi Epistola, edidit Guil. Allen, *portrait and map*, 2 vols. 8vo. *fine copy, in old calf, gilt*, 10*s* .. .. *Londini*, 1755

The Greek text is in a fine bold character; the Latin version is that of Wolf. Dr. Dibdin says a fine copy could not be procured under a Guinea. A high character of it from the Monthly Review is given in Mr. Moss's Manual.

1393 — et Æschines, Gr. et Lat., edidit Io. Taylor, 2 vols. 8vo. *calf, neat*, 7*s* 6*d* .. .. *Cantabrigiæ*, 1769

Contains the Orations de Corona and de Falsa Legatione.

1394 DENNY'S (Henry) Monographia Pselaphidarum et Scydmænidarum Britanniæ: an Essay on the British Species of the Genera Pselaphus of Herbst, and Scydmænus of Latreille, *coloured plates*, 8vo. *boards, scarce*, 8*s* *Norwich*, 1825

Mr. Joseph John Gurney's copy with his book-plate.

1395 DEPARCIEUX (Ant.) Nouveaux Traités de Trigonometrie, Rectiligne et Spherique, avec un traité de Gnomonique, 17 *plates*, large 4to. *fine sound copy, in old calf, gilt*, 10*s* *Paris*, 1741

1396 DERBYSHIRE. 29 Engravings by Cooke, Le Keux and Blore, Illustrative of Peak Scenery, royal 4to. *half bound, neat*, 15*s* 1818

1397 DE RETZ, (Cardinal) Memoirs of his own Life, *portrait*, 4 vols. 12mo. *calf*, 10*s* .. .. .. 1774

Highly amusing. "The best Memoirs that I know of, are those of Cardinal de Retz,—I hardly know any book so necessary for a young man to read and remember."—*Lord Chesterfield*.

1398 DERHAM'S (W.) Astro Theology; a Demonstration of the Being and Attributes of God, from a Survey of the Heavens, 8vo. *old calf*, 2*s* 6*d* .. .. .. 1719

1399 DE SACY'S Discourse of Friendship, Englished by Daniel Bret, small 8vo. *old calf, neat*, 2*s* 6*d* .. .. 1707

1400 DESAGULIERS (Dr. J. T.) Newtonian System of the World the best model of Government, an Allegorical Poem; also Cambria's complaint against the intercalary Day in the Leap-Year, notes, 3 *astronomical plates*, 4to. *sewed*, 3*s* *Westminster*, 1728

1401 DES CARTES (Renati) Principiorum Philosophiæ, pars I. et II. more Geometrico demonstratæ, per Benedictum de Spinoza, accesserunt ejusdem Cogitata Metaphysica, 4to. *good copy, in old calf*, 12*s* .. .. *Amst., J. Riewerts*, 1663

VERY SCARCE. "*Ex Libris Thomæ Fuke, Feb.* 25, 1688, *Empt. Exoniæ. E Collegio Tauntoniensi*: .." in MS... It is a century only that produces such a man as Des Cartes.—See *Dr. Adam Clarke*.

1402 DESCOMBAZ Histoire de l'Eglise Chrétienne, 12mo. *sewed*, 1*s* 6*d* *Lyon*, 1852

1403 D'EST (Hyppolite) Negociations, ou Lettres d'affaires Ecclesiastiques et Politiques, escrittes au Pope Pie IV. et au Cardinal Borromee, depuis Canonizé Saint, 4to. *fine clean copy, in old vellum*, 10*s* 6*d* .. .. *Paris, S. Piget*, 1658

Finely engraved title-page, containing Portraits of Pope Pius IV., Cardinal Borromeo, and the Author, who was Cardinal of Ferrara, and Legat to France at the commencement of the Civil Wars, 1562. The value of this volume is further enhanced by the Autograph of that great scholar, "*Stephanus Baluzius, Tutelensis*."

1404 DEVARII (Matt.) liber de Græcæ Linguæ Particulis, 12mo. *old calf*, 2*s* 6*d* .. .. .. *Londini*, 1657

1405 DEVON.—An Act for the better enabling the Master, Wardens, &c. of Trinity House, to rebuild the Light House on the Eddystone Rock, folio, *broadside*, **Black Letter**, 5*s* *T. Newcome's Executrix*, 1705

1406 DE WITT (John) Political Maxims of the State of Holland, with Memoirs of him and his illustrious brother Cornelius, thick 8vo. *old calf, neat*, 5*s* .. .. .. 1743

1407 DIAZ (Capt. Bernal, *del Castillo)* True History of the Conquest of Mexico, written in 1568, translated by M. Keatinge, 4to. *half calf, neat*, 12*s* .. .. .. 1800

"Is indeed a delightful work, and the only account of that transaction on which we can rely."—*Southey*.

1408 DIBDIN'S (Dr. T. F.) Introduction to the Knowledge of rare and valuable editions of the Greek and Roman Classics, with Notes, 1st edition, 12mo. *boards*, 4*s* *Glocester*, 1802

1409 — 2nd edition, 8vo. *old calf, neat*, 6*s* .. 1804

This edition includes the Scriptores de Re Rustica, Greek Romances, and Lexicons and Grammars, and an Index Analyticus, an Account of Polyglot Bibles, Greek Septuagints, and Greek Testaments.

1410 — 3rd edition, much augmented, 2 vols. crown 8vo. *boards*, 6*s* 1808

1411 — another copy of the 3rd edition, 2 vols. 8vo. *fine copy, in russia, gilt*, 12*s* .. .. .. 1808

The *Index Analyticus* and the account of *Latin Editions of Greek Writers* are omitted in this edition, to make room for what Dr. Dibdin considers more important additions to other parts of the work; an opinion in which all persons will not coincide.

1412 — 4th edition, 2 vols. 8vo. *calf, neat*, 18*s* .. 1827

1413 — another copy, 2 vols. 8vo. *half cloth*, 12*s* .. 1827

To this fourth and last edition is added Polyglott Bibles, Hebrew Bibles, Greek Bibles and Testaments, and Greek and Latin Fathers; but the Scriptores de Re Rustica, Greek Romances, Lexicons, Dictionaries and Grammars, and Lists of the Delphin, Variorum, Elzevir and Aldine Classics, are omitted. As each edition, therefore, differs from each other, so, ALL are necessary for the Bibliographer to possess.

1414 — Bibliomania, or Book-Madness; containing its history and cure, an Epistle to Richard Heber, Esq., thin 8vo. 1st edition, *boards*, 5*s* .. .. .. .. 1809

1415 — Library Companion; or, the Young Man's Guide, and the Old Man's Comfort, in the choice of a Library, 2nd edition, thick 8vo. *calf, gilt*, 16*s* .. .. .. 1825

1416 — TYPOGRAPHICAL ANTIQUITIES; the History of Printing in England, Scotland, and Ireland, with Memoirs of our ancient Printers, down to 1590, *portraits and fac-similies*, 4 vols. 4to. *half calf, very neat*, £5 5*s* .. .. 1810-19

This is by far the most *useful* of all Dr. Dibdin's Publications, indeed it is a most *useful*, as it is an indispensable book for the prosecution of bibliographical pursuits.

1417 — Typographical Antiquities, *portraits*, vol. 4 only, 4to. *cloth*, £1 1*s* (*pub. at* £3 13*s* 6*d*) .. .. 1819

1418 — Sermons, Doctrinal and Practical, 8vo. *half cloth*, 5*s* 6*d* (*pub. at* 12*s*) .. .. .. .. 1820

1419 DICK'S (Thomas) Christian Philosopher; the connection of Science and Philosophy with Religion, *portrait and plates*, 2 vols. post 8vo. *sewed*, 2*s* .. *Glasgow, Collins*, 1846

1420 DICKENS'S (Charles) All the Year Round, 31 numbers, 5*s*

1421 DICKENS'S Bleak House, original edition, *with* 40 *illustrations, by H. K. Browne*, 8vo. *half calf*, 10*s* (*pub. at* 21*s*) 1853

1422 — Little Dorrit, *numerous plates*, 8vo. *new, in half calf, gilt*, £1 1*s*

1423 — Little Dorrit, Nos. 1 to 8, 12 and 14, *plates*, 8vo. *sewed*, 8*d per number*

1424 — Household Narrative of Current Events, from Jan. 1, 1850, to Dec. 29, 1851, 2 vols. royal 8vo. in numbers, all published, 4*s*

1425 — Browne's (Hablot K.) 8 Full-length Portraits Illustrative of Dombey and Son, 8vo. *sewed*, 2*s* .. 1848

1426 DICTIONARIUM Polygraphicum; the whole Body of Arts regularly digested, Designing, Drawing, Painting, Washing Prints, Limning, Japanning, Gilding, &c. *above* 50 *plates*, 2 thick vols. 8vo. *very fine copy, in old calf, gilt*, SCARCE, 12*s* 1735

This, being a very practical work, is usually much dirtied, this is a particularly nice clean copy.

1427 DICTIONARY of Latin and Greek Quotations, edited by H. F. Riley, post 8vo. *cloth, new*, 5*s* *H. G. Bohn*, 1856

1428 DICTIONARY of Dates, containing 20,000 Historical facts relating to all times and Countries, edited by S. Neil, small 8vo. *cloth*, 1*s*

1429 DICTIONNAIRE d'Anecdotes, de traits singuliers et caractéristiques, historiettes, Bons Mots, Näivetés, Saillies, Reparties ingenieuses, &c. [par Lacombé de Prezel.] 2 vols. 12mo. *old calf, gilt*, 6*s* .. .. .. *Paris*, 1766

1430 DICTIONNAIRE Portatif des Proverbes François et des Façons de Parler comiques, burlesques, et familieres, 12mo. *nice copy, in panelled calf, gilt*, 5*s* .. .. *Utrecht*, 1751

1431 DIDEROT, aux Manes de, 12mo. *boards*, 2*s* *Paris*, 1788

1432 DIDRON'S (M.) Christian Iconography, the History of Christian Art in the Middle Ages, translated from the French, by E. T. Millington, *numerous plates*, vol. 1 (all published) post 8vo. *cloth*, 3*s* 6*d* (*cost* 5*s*) .. .. *H. G. Bohn*, 1851

1433 DID you ever see such damned stuff? or, so-much-the-better, a story without head or tail, wit, or humour, 12mo. *bound, scarce*, 3*s* .. .. .. .. 1760

1434 DIGGES (Leonard) Geometrical Practise, named Pantometria, in 3 Bookes, Longimetra, Planimetra, and Stereometria, lately finished by Thomas Digges, his Sonne, *plates*, 4to. **Black Letter**, *old calf, neat*, 10*s* 6*d* .. .. *Henrie Bynneman*, 1571

"Dedicated to Sir Nicholas Bacon, Knight, Lord Keeper of the Great Seale of England," by Thomas Digges, who has added "A Mathematical Discourse of Geometricall Solides."

1435 DIGGES (Thomas) Geometrical Practical Treatize, named Pantometria, in 3 Bookes, Longimetra, Planimetra, and Stereometria, Rules for Mensuration of all Lines, Superficies and Solides, folio, **Black Letter**, *a very fine clean copy, in half calf*, £1 5*s* *Abell Jeffes*, 1591

Dcediated to the Lord Keeper, Sir Nicholas Bacon, Knight, with many curious cuts.

1436 DIGGS'S (Dudley, Gentleman,) Unlawfulness of Subjects taking up Armes against their Soveraigne, in what case soever, *engraved frontispiece*, small 4to. *half bound, clean and neat*, 6*s* 1647

1437 DIODORI Siculi Bibliotheca Historica, Græcè, folio, *very fine copy, in calf gilt, bound by old Johnson,* £1 1*s* *Henrici Stephani,* 1559

"Belle édition et très correcte."—*Brunet.* This is the Editio Princeps of the first five and the 11th to the 15th books, and, as such, should be found in every classical library of importance. From Lord Leicester's Library.

1438 DIODORUS Siculus's Historical Library, containing the Antiquities of Egypt, Asia, Africa, Greece, the Islands, and Europe, Historical Account of the Affairs of the Persians, Grecians, Macedonians, &c., Englished by G. Booth, *maps,* folio, *old calf, scarce,* £1 1*s* 1700

*The only Translation in English* of Diodorus Siculus. "Very scarce and in high reputation for its general correctness."—*Dr. Adam Clarke.*

1439 DIONIS Nicæi Rerum Romanarum Epitome, Græcè, a uthore Joanne Xiphilino, small folio, *a fine copy,* 18*s* *Lutetiæ, R. Stephani,* 1551

1440 — Alia editio, 4to. *old vellum,* 8*s* *Lutetiæ, ex Off. Rob. Stephani,* 1551

A beautifully printed Greek volume.

1441 DIONISIO Halicarnaseo delle cose Antichi della Citta di Roma, tradotto in Toscano per Messer FRANCESCO VENTURI, *Fiorentino, elegant wood-cut of a Sibyl on the title page,* 4to. *beautiful copy in white parchment,* RARE, £1 1*s* *Venetia, per Nicolo Bascarini,* 1545

"This version is very highly esteemed in Italy; it forms part of their *Collana.*"—See *Moss* and *Haym. De Bure* and *Brunet,* who all laud it. There could not be a more beautiful copy than this; in the original binding and as clean as new.

1442 D'ISRAELI'S (Izaac) Miscellanies; or, Literary Recreations, crown 8vo. *old calf, neat,* 5*s* .. *Cadell & Davies,* 1797

1443 — Narrative Poems, thin 4to. 55 pages, *boards, scarce,* 7*s* 6*d* *John Murray,* 1803

1444 — Curiosities of Literature, 3 vols. 8vo. *half calf, neat,* 12*s* (*pub. at* 36*s*) .. .. .. .. 1807

1445 — another edition, complete, *portrait,* 6 vols. 12mo. *cloth,* £1 4*s* *Moxon,* 1834

1446 — Quarrels of Authors; some Memoirs of our Literary History, including Specimens of Controversy to the Reign of Elizabeth, 3 vols. crown 8vo. *boards, clean as new,* 15*s* .. 1814

1447 — Calamities of Authors; including some Inquiries respecting their Moral and Literary Characters, 2 vols. crown 8vo. *half calf, neat,* 7*s* 6*d* .. .. .. .. 1812

"An amusing collection of Anecdotes."—*Lowndes.*

1448 — Amenities of Literature; consisting of Sketches and Characters of English Literature, edited by his Son, the Rt. Hon. B. D'Israeli, *frontispiece,* 2 vols. post 8vo. *cloth, new,* 9*s* .. 1859

1449 — Literary Character; the History of Men of Genius, 12mo. *morocco, elegant, gilt edges,* 10*s* .. *Moxon,* 1839

1450 DIXON'S (Henry, *Schoolmaster, Bath,*) English Instructor, or the Art of Spelling Improved, *View of School House,* 12mo. *bound, curious,* 2*s* 6*d* .. .. .. 1784

1451 DODDRIDGE (Dr. Philip) Practical Discourses on Regeneration, 10 Sermons preached at Northampton, with 2 on Salvation by Grace, through Faith, 8vo. *old calf, neat,* 4*s* .. 1742

1452 — Rise and Progress of Religion in the Soul, with a Sermon on its Care, 8vo. *boards, large letter edition,* 3*s* .. 1819

1453 — another edition, 18mo. *half bound,* 1*s* 6*d* .. 1827

1454 — Memoirs of his Life, Writings, and Character, by Job Orton, *portrait,* 8vo. *old calf, neat,* 3*s* 6*d* *Salop, Eddowes,* 1766

1455 DODONÆUS (Rembert) Purgantium aliarumque eo facientium, tum et Radicum, Convolvulorum ac deletiarum herbarum historiæ libri IV., cujus altera parte umbelliferæ exhibentur, *numerous plates of plants*, 8vo. *old calf*, 7*s* 6*d* *Antverpiæ, C. Plantini*, 1574

For another work by this author see Lyte, in this Catalogue.

1456 DODSLEY'S (Robert) Collection of Poems, *cuts*, 6 vols. 12mo. *calf, neat*, 9*s* .. .. .. 1766

1457 — another edition, *plates*, 6 vols. 12mo. (vol. 1 wants title page,) *old calf*, 6*s* .. .. .. 1775

1458 — Œconomy of Human Life, translated from an Indian MS., written by an ancient Bramin, 8vo. *calf, neat*, 5*s* 1795

"A moral piece of great popularity."—*Lowndes*. A very pretty edition with numerous plates by *Harding*.

1459 DOMENICHI (Lodovico) Historia di detti, e fatti degni di Memoria di diversi Principi, e Huomini privati antichi, et moderni, *fine portrait*, thick 4to. of 724 pages, *old calf, fine clean copy, rare*, £1 1*s* *Vinegia, Gabriel Giolito*, 1557

A very beautiful volume handsomely printed with Giolito's elegant devices at the beginning and end. Lord Leicester's arms on the sides.

1460 DONALDSON'S (John) Agricultural Biography; an account of the Lives and Writings of British Authors on Agriculture, from 1480 to this time, royal 8vo. *sewed*, 3*s* 6*d* *For the author*, 1854

1461 DONI (Anton. Francesco) I Mondi del Doni, libro primo, *full of very singular wood cuts, and* ALL *the fine portraits*, 4to. *old vellum, rare*, £1 1*s* *Vinegia, per Francesco Marcolini*, 1552

"Edition la plus complète et la plus rare de cet ouvrage singulier. La première partie est surtout remarquable à cause des figures en bois et des Portraits d'Italians célèbres dont elle est ornée. Ces portraits sont ceux de Doni, d'Aretin, Marcolini, Gabr. Simeoni, Fr. Sansovino, Burchiello, Machiavelli, Fr. Alunno, Nic. Tartaglia, J. G. Gelli." et Dolce omitted by *Brunet*.

"Belle édition, ornée de gravures en bois, et d'une exécution magnifique."—*De Bure*.

1462 — La Morale Filosophia, tratta da gli antichi scrittori, *curious wood cuts*, 4to. *old vellum*, 15*s* *Vinegia, per Francesco Marcolini*, 1552

"Ce recueil se compose de fables d'allegories, de nouvelles et de recits d'événements curieux, en partie tirés des anciens fabulistes et conteurs indiens, comme Bidpai, Lokman, Sendabar, &c."—*Brunet*.

1463 — Trattati diversi di Sendabar Indiano filosopho Morale, *wood cuts*, 4to. *old vellum*, 8*s* *In Vinegia Nell' Academia Peregrina*, 1552

Doni was a member of the Academy of the Peregrini, in which he took the Academical name of Bizarro, perfectly suitable to his satirical and humorous character. These three books are all first editions and the rarest of all.

1464 DONNE'S (Dr. John) Devotions and Sermons, with his Life, by Izaak Walton, *plate*, 12mo. *cloth, new*, 5*s* *W. Pickering*, 1840

With two Sermons, one on Lady Danvers, the other on himself, called Death's Duel.

1465 — Devotions upon Emergent Occasions, and several steps in my Sickness, 18mo. *nicely bound, gilt edges*, 3*s* 6*d* *Oxford, Talboys*, 1841

A reprint of the edition of 1624.

1466 — Selection from the Works of Dr. Donne, 18mo. *bound as above*, 3*s* 6*d* .. .. .. *ib*. 1840

"His fancy was inimitably high, equalled only by his great wit."—*Izaac Walton*.
This is a nice book of Aphorisms.

1467 DONNOVAN'S Natural History of British Insects, 360 *coloured plates*, vols. 1 to 10, royal 8vo. *old boards, uncut*, £3 10*s* (*pub. at* £12) .. .. .. 1792-1801

1468 DON QUIXOTE, in Spanish, edited by Fernandez, vols. 2, 3, and 4, 18mo. *boards*, 3*s* 6*d* .. .. *London*, 1808

1469 — translated by Thomas Shelton, (reprint of the edition of 1620) *plates by Vdr Gucht*, vols. 2 and 3, 12mo. *very neat*, 5*s* 1740

1470 — with a Life of Cervantes, by Charles Jarvis, *portrait, map, and plates, after Stothard*, 4 vols. *calf, neat*, 16*s* 1801

1471 DONZELLI (Gioseppe, *Dottor Napolitano)* Partenope Liberata, overo racconto dell' Heroica risolutione fatta dal Popolo di Napoli, parte prima (all published) 4to. *old parchment*, 6*s* *Napoli, per O. Beltrano*, 1647

"*Raro*, E' uno de' migliori Scrittori del tumulto di Massaniello."—*Haym.*

1472 DORCHESTER to Roos, True and Perfect Copy of a Letter written by the Lord Marquis of Dorchester to the Lord Roos, folio, *broadside, rare*, £1 1*s* .. .. 25 *Feb.*, 1659

"From the beginning to the end of your letter you falsely lie; and if you dare appear, I will cram it down your throat with my sword. I say, and resay, *you are a base coward*."—*Quotation from it.*

1473 D'ORLEANS Histoire des Revolutions D'Angleterre, 3 vols. 12mo. *old calf*, 4*s* .. .. .. *Paris*, 1695

1474 DORT SYNOD. Acta Synodi Nationalis Dordrechti Habitæ, 1618-19, thick 4to., *fine copy in vellum*, 12*s* *Dordrechti*, 1620

1475 D'ORVILLE (Jac. Phil.) Bibliotheca Dorvilliana, *interleaved and priced, with purchaser's names*, 8vo. *old calf*, 9*s* *Amstelodami*, 1764

"As M. D'Orville was one of the most eminent critics of the last century, this circumstance will give his Catalogue a place in every collection which relates to Classical Literature and Antiquities. He was Professor of History, Eloquence, and Greek, at Amsterdam, from 1736 to 1742, and filled that office with the greatest reputation. He died in 1751."—*Horne's Bibliography.*

1476 DOUGLAS'S (James) Errors regarding Religion, 8vo. *half calf, very neat*, 3*s* 6*d* .. .. *Edinburgh*, 1830

1477 DOWDESWELL'S (Lt. General) Catalogue of his British Portraits sold by Mr. Evans, *interleaved, with the prices and purchasers' names*, 8vo. *half calf, neat*, 3*s* 6*d* .. .. 1819

1478 DOWLING'S (John G.) Introduction to the Critical Study of Ecclesiastical History, 8vo. *cloth*, 6*s* (*pub. at* 9*s*) .. 1838

1479 DOWNAME'S (Dr. George, *Bp. of Derry*,) Covenant of Grace, an Exposition on Luke i, 73, 74, 75, small 4to. *old calf, neat*, 5*s* *Dublin*, 1631

1480 D'OYLY and MANT'S Bible and Common Prayer, *profusely illustrated with plates*, 4 vols. 4to. *russia extra, gilt edges*, £5 15*s* 6*d* *cost* £10 10*s* .. .. .. *Oxford*, 1820

So fine a copy as this seldom occurs for sale.

1481 DRACONIS et Solonis Leges, Pardulpho Prateio collectore et interprete, *Lugduni*, 1559.—Pauli (Junii) Sententiarum receptarum ad Filium lib. V., cum Interpretat. Aniani, opera C. Rittershusii, *Noribergæ*, 1594.—Veterum Jurisconsultorum adversus L. Vallæ reprehensiones defensio, I. C. P. I. C. A. *Parisiis*, 1583, in 1 vol. thick 8vo. *old calf, neat*, 15*s* .. .. V.Y.

1482 DRAKE'S (Sir Francis) Famous Voyage into the South Sea, and there thence about the whole Globe of the Earth, begun 1577, ended 1580, folio, *on 6 unpaged leaves*, EXCESSIVELY RARE, *suppressed*, £3 13*s* 6*d* .. .. .. 1588

These 6 unpaged leaves are found in some copies of Hakluyt's Voyages, but as they were rigidly suppressed they are in but few.

1483 DRAKE'S (Daniel) Natural and Statistical View of Cincinnati and the Miami Country, with Observations on Earthquakes, &c. *maps*, 12mo. *half calf, neat*, 3*s* 6*d* .. *Cincinnati*, 1815

1484 DRAKE'S (Dr. Nathan) Literary Hours, Sketches Critical and Narrative, 2 vols. 8vo. *half calf*, 5*s* .. *Sudbury*, 1800

1485 — Mornings in Spring; Retrospections, Biographical, Critical, and Historical, 2 vols. in 1, small 8vo. *boards*, 5*s* (*pub. at* 18*s*) 1828

Contains an Account of the Cliffords of Craven, with a reprint from the 1st edition of Arnold's Chronicle of the beautiful ballad, the Nut Brown Maid.

1486 — Evenings in Autumn; Essays, Narrative and Miscellaneous, 2 vols. small 8vo. *boards*, 5*s* (*pub at* 18*s*) .. 1822

1487 — Essays, Biographical, Critical, and Historical, Illustrative of the Tatler, Spectator, and Guardian, *portrait*, 3 vols. 12mo. *boards*, 7*s* 6*d* .. .. *C. Whittingham*, 1805

1488 — another copy, *portrait and plates*, 3 vols. 12mo. *old boards*, 7*s* 6*d* *Buckingham*, 1814

1489 — Essays on the Rambler, Adventurer, and Idler, *portrait*, 2 vols. 12mo. *old boards*, 5*s* .. .. *ib.* 1809

1490 — Shakspeare and his Times, including the Biography of the Poet, Criticisms on his Genius and Writings, and a History of the Manners, Customs, and Amusements, Superstitions, Poetry and Elegant Literature of the Elizabethan Era, *fine portrait*, 2 vols. 4to. LARGE PAPER, *half bound in morocco, uncut*, £2 2*s* (*pub. at* £7 17*s* 6*d*) .. .. .. 1817

"A masterly production. So abundant is the light thrown by it upon the singularly interesting period in which the poet lived, that every person who is curious on the subject of the literature of that age must resort to it for information."—*Gentleman's Magazine.*

1491 DREAMS.—The Theory of Dreams, an inquiry into the powers and faculties of the Human Mind, 2 vols. 12mo. *boards*, 4*s* 1808

Anonymous, but by Bishop Gray.

1492 DRELINCOURT (Charles) Consolations de l'ame fidele contre les frayeurs de la Mort, *engraved frontispiece, and fine portrait of Drelincourt*, 8vo. *old binding*, 3*s* *Berlin, R. Roger*, 1698

1493 — Les Visites Charitables, ou les Consolations Chrétiennes, pour toutes sortes de Personnes afligées, 3 vols. 8vo. *good copy, in calf*, 12*s* .. .. *Amst., Mortier*, 1731

This is the best edition by J. Brutel de la Riviere.

1494 — Christian's Defence against the fears of Death, *plate by Sturt*, 8vo. *old calf, neat*, 3*s* 6*d* .. .. 1721

With Daniel De Foe's "Relation of the Apparition of Mrs. Veal, which Apparition recommends the perusal of Drelincourt on Death."

1495 DRESDEN GALLERY—Payne's Royal Dresden Gallery, 136 *well-executed engravings, after pictures by the Great Masters*, with descriptions, 2 vols. 4to. *half calf, very neat*, £2 2*s* (*cost* £3 7*s*) .. .. .. .. 1858

1496 DREXELIUS (Hieremia) de Æternitate considerationes, thick 18mo. *old calf*, 5*s* .. .. *Monachii*, 1627

Fine impressions of the plates by Philip Sadeler.

1497 DRUMMOND'S (Dr. James L.) Letters to a Young Naturalist on the Study of Nature and Natural Theology, *plates*, 12mo. *boards*, 3*s* 6*d* (*pub. at* 7*s* 6*d*) .. *Longmans*, 1831

1498 DRUMMOND (William, *of Hawthornden)* Poetical Works, edited by W. D. Turnbull, *portrait*, fcap 8vo. *cloth*, 5*s* *J. R. Smith*, 1857

1499 DRYDEN'S (John) Works, ORIGINAL EDITIONS.—I. The Medall, a Satyre against Sedition, 1682.—II. Religio Laici, a Poem, 1682.—III. Absalom and Achitaphel, a Poem, 3rd edition, augmented and revised, 1682.—IV. The Hind and the Panther, a Poem, 1687, (*written after his reconciliation with Popery.*)—V. The Hind and the Panther, transversed, 1687, (*written by Charles Montague, afterwards Earl of Halifax, and Mr. M. Prior.*)—VI. The Spanish Fryar, a Play, 3rd edition, 1690.—VII. Religio Laici; or, a Layman's Faith, two Letters by J. R., a (pretended) Convert, 1688. In 1 vol. 4to. *clean and neat, in old calf*, 15*s* .. .. .. 1682-88

1500 — Miscellany Poems, Translations of the Ancient Poets and Original Poems, *plates*, 6 vols. 12mo. *old calf*, 6*s* .. 1716

1501 — Fables, translated into Verse from Homer, Ovid, Boccace, and Chaucer, with original Poems, 12mo. *bound*, 2*s* 6*d* 1721

1502 — Dramatick Works, with the Essay on Dramatick Poesy, *portrait by Vertue*, 6 vols. 12mo. *very nice copy, in old calf gilt*, 15*s* *Jacob Tonson*, 1735

1503 — Miscellaneous Works; containing all his Original Poems, Tales and Translations, with Explanatory Notes, and his Life, by S. Derrick, *fine portrait by I. de Leeuw*, 4 vols. 8vo. *nice clean copy in old calf*, £1 1*s* .. .. *Tonson*, 1760

1504 DU BOS (l'Abbé) Réflexions Critiques sur la Poësie et sur la Peinture, 3 vols. 4to. *a very nice copy, in old calf, gilt*, 15*s* *Paris*, 1755

"Ouvrage estimé."—*Brunet, Man. du Libraire.* "All our artists read with advantage his reflections upon poetry, painting, and music."—*Voltaire.*

1505 DUCK (Arthur) de Usu et Authoritate Juris Civilis Romanorum in Dominiis Principum christianorum, 8vo. *calf, neat*, 4*s* *Londini*, 1653

Autograph of "*J. Hawkins Browne.*"

1506 DUDLEY (Robert, *Earl of Leycester)* Correspondence, during his Government of the Low Countries in 1585-6, edited by Mr. Bruce, thick 4to. *cloth*, 10*s* *Camden Society*, 1844

1507 DUFIEF'S French Self Interpreter; or Pronouncing Grammar, square 18mo. *stiff cover*, 1*s* 6*d* .. *Exeter*, 1820

1508 DU FRESNOY'S Chronological Tables, see *Lenglet du Fresnoy*.

1509 DUGDALE (John, Esq., *Windsor Herald, Deputy to Sir Will. Dugdale*) Catalogue of the Nobility of England, with the Blazon of their Paternal Coats of Arms, and a List of the present Bishops, folio, *broadside*, RARE, £1 1*s* *For Robert Clavell*, 1685

"Jan. 21, 1684. I do order and appoint that this list be printed, and that none other be printed without my allowance."—*Norfolk and Marshall.*

1510 DUGDALE'S Baronage, Remarks on its numberless Errors and Defects, in 3 Letters, 8vo. *half calf, neat, scarce,* 9*s* *For the Author,* 1738

By Charles Hornby, Esq., Secondary of the Pipe Office; at Reed's sale a copy brought 27*s*. Has the plate containing the pedigree of Brus of Anandale.

1511 DULAU & Co.'s Catalogue of Foreign Books, thick 8vo. *half calf, neat,* 9*s* .. .. .. 1828

1512 — Catalogue of Foreign Books, with the 2 Supplements, *plates,* 2 vols. royal 8vo. *newly half bound,* 15*s* .. 1845-7

1513 — 1st Supplement to the Catalogue of Foreign Books, (duplicate) 8vo. *stiff cover,* 3*s*

1514 DUMERSAN, Notice des Monumens exposés dans le Cabinet des Médailles et Antiques de la Bibliothèque du Roi, 42 *plates,* 8vo. *sewed,* 6*s* .. .. .. *Paris,* 1822

1515 DUMESNIL'S Latin Synonyms, with their different significations, Englished, with additions by Gosset, 8vo. *calf, very neat,* 5*s* (*cost* 19*s*) .. .. .. 1809

1516 DUMONT, Corps Universel Diplomatic du Droit des Gens, avec le Supplement par Rousset, 8 vols. in 16, and 5 vols. of Supplement, large folio, *fine clean copy,* LARGE PAPER, £10 10*s* *Amsterdam,* 1726-39

This fine set of books dates from Charlemagne, and is an important historical work, containing all the European Treaties of Alliance, Peace, Commerce, &c., from his time to 1739. A copy on LARGE PAPER, according to *Brunet,* produced above £34 at Pelletiere de Saint-Fargeau's sale. From Lord Orford's Library, at Wolterton.

1517 DU MOULIN'S (Dr. Peter) X. Sermons, 8vo. *old calf, neat,* 2*s* 6*d* 1684

1518 DUNCUMB'S (John) Collections towards the History and Antiquities of the County of Hereford, *portraits and plates,* vol. 1, and part 1 of vol. 2, *boards, uncut,* £1 1*s* *Hereford,* 1804-12

The Duke of Norfolk was at the expense of publishing this valuable history, the only one of this County.

1519 DUNHAM'S Early Writers of Great Britain, 12mo. *cloth,* 2*s* 6*d* *Lardner's Cyclopædia,* 1850

1520 — History of Europe during the Middle Ages, 4 vols. 12mo. *cloth,* 10*s* .. .. .. *ib.* 1851

1521 DUNI (Thaddæi) et Francisci Cigalini, Joannisq. Pauli Turriani et Hieronymi Cardani disputationes, cui accessit, de Hemitritæo, sive, de febre semitertiana libellus, small 8vo. *old calf, scarce,* 6*s* *Tiguri, per Gesneros,* 1555

In MS., "*Liber Edoardi Lapworthi ex dono charissimi patris sui,* 1601." "*Mors Christi Vita Hominum.*"

1522 DUPIN'S (Lewis E.) History of Ecclesiastical Writers, their Lives and Writings, Century I. to VIII., by Dr. W. Wotton, *plates,* 3 vols. small folio. *old calf, neat,* £1 4*s* .. 1693

"Dupin's account of Ecclesiastical Writers is undoubtedly the best we have."—*Dr. Wotton on the Study of Divinity.*

1523 DU PLESIS, (Scipio) Resolver; or Curiosities of Nature, usefull and pleasant for all, *engraved title by W. Marshall,* 12mo. *original binding, curious,* 6*s* .. *N. & I. Okes,* 1635

1524 DURANT (Samuel) Anatomie du Chrestien, small 8vo. *old parchment, clean,* 4*s* 6*d* .. .. *Geneve,* 1629

On the title page, in writing, "*Jean Daillé,*" author of the work, de usu Patrum.

1525 DURER'S (Albert) Designs of the Prayer Book, *fine portrait and 43 plates*, folio, *half morocco, new*, 15*s* *R. Ackerman*, 1817

Mr. Ackerman says, "this *fac-simile* of a very valuable graphic monument," is the *first* production of his *Lithographic* press. It is a reprint of Theurdank's work, printed exactly 300 years before. There is a Bibliographical Introduction furnished by M. Bernhart, keeper of the Royal Library, Munich.

1526 DURET (I. *Jurisconsulte de Moulins)* Alliance des Loix Romaines avec le Droict François, contenu les Ordonnances des Rois, Arrests des Cours Souveraines, et Coustumes provincialles, thick 4to. *limp vellum*, 12*s* .. .. *Paris*, 1600

A huge volume of 1480 pages, dedicated to "Louyse de Lorraine, Roine douairiere de France, Duchesse de Berry."

1527 EADIE'S (Dr. John) Concordance to the Scriptures, on the basis of Cruden, 8vo. *cloth, new*, 5*s* .. .. 1857

1528 — Dictionary of the Bible, for the use of Young Persons, *map and numerous illustrations*, 12mo. *cloth, new*, 3*s*—*cloth, gilt*, 3*s* 6*d* 1858

1529 EARL'S (Geo. W.) Eastern Seas; Voyages and Adventures in the Eastern Archipelago, in 1832-4, Java, Borneo, the Malay Peninsula, Siam, Singapore, &c., *maps*, 8vo. *boards*, 6*s* (*pub. at* 12*s*) .. .. .. .. 1837

1530 EAST India Sketch Book, an account of the State of Society in Calcutta, Bombay, &c., 2 vols. small 8vo. *half calf, neat*, 7*s* 6*d* (*pub. at* £1 1*s*) .. .. .. 1832

1531 EBERT'S (F. A., *Librarian to the King of Saxony)* General Bibliographical Dictionary, translated from the German, 4 vols. 8vo. *boards*, £1 10*s* .. *Oxford University Press*, 1837

1532 ECCLESIASTICAL History, a brief view of, from the earliest period to the present time, 24mo. *cloth*, 1*s* 6*d* *Dublin*, 1838

1533 EDGEWORTH (Miss) Novels, Tales, and Miscellaneous Pieces, 15 vols. 12mo. *neatly half bound*, £2 2*s* .. 1825

1534 — Popolar Tales, Murad the Unlucky; Manufacturers; Contrast; Grateful Negro; To-morrow; 12mo. *cloth*, (*no title*) 2*s*

1535 EDINBURGH, Johnston's Plan of the City of, 1*s* 6*d*

1536 EDINBURGH Gazetteer, 6 vols. 8vo. *neatly half bound*, £1 1*s* (*cost* £6 6*s*) .. .. .. *Edinburgh*, 1822

1537 — another copy, 6 vols. 8vo. *boards*, 15*s* (*pub. at* £5 8*s*) *ib.* 1822

1538 EDINBURGH Review, 199 to 219, 221, 222, 23 numbers, £1 14*s* 6*d* (*pub. at* £6 12*s*)

1539 — Nos. 202 to 209, 1*s* 6*d each*, (*pub. at* 6*s each*)

1540 EDWARD II., History of the most unfortunate Prince King Edward the 2nd, with observations on him and his favourites Gaveston and Spencer, by the Rt. Honble. Henry (Cary) Viscount Faulkland, *portrait*, small 8vo. *old binding*, 4*s* 1680

1541 EDWARD V. and Richard III., Historie of the pittifull Life of King Edward V.—The Tragicall Historie of the Life and Reign of Richard III., by Sir Thomas More, 12mo. *half bound*, 4*s* 6*d* 1641

"An elegant history."—*Lowndes.*

1542 EDWARD (David B.) History of Texas: or, Emigrant's, Farmer's, and Politician's Guide to the Character, Climate, Soil, &c. of that Country, 12mo. *boards*, 2*s* 6*d* .. *Cincinnati*, 1836

1543 EDWARDS (Dr. Jonathan) on that Freedom of the Will which is essential to Moral Agency, 8vo. *boards*, 3*s* 6*d* (*pub. at* 8*s*) 1818

1544 EDWARDS (Dr. J.) Treatise concerning Religious Affections, with an Essay by David Young, *portrait*, thick 12mo. *cloth*, 3*s* 6*d* (*pub. at* 7*s*) .. .. *Glasgow*, 1831

1545 EGEDE'S (Hans) Description of Greenland, with his Life, *map and plates*, 8vo. *boards*, 4*s* .. .. 1818

This Danish Missionary was 25 years in Greenland.

1546 ELECTORAT.—Deux Lettres touchant le Neuviéme Electorat, 4to. *neat*, 3*s* .. .. *Rotterdam*, 1698

1547 ELEGANT Extracts; Poetry, Prose, and Epistles, selected for the improvement of Young Persons, *plates*, 6 vols. royal 8vo. *very nice copy, in old calf, gilt*, £1 4*s* .. 1801

1548 ELIOT'S (Archdeacon Edw.) Christianity and Slavery, Lectures preached at the Cathedral in Barbados, 12mo. *cloth*, 2*s* 6*d* (*pub. at* 4*s* 6*d*) .. .. .. 1833

1549 ELIZABETHAN Poetry.—Select Poetry, chiefly devotional, of the Reign of Q. Elizabeth, edited by Edw. Farr, 2 vols. 12mo. *cloth, new*, 8*s* .. .. *Parker Society*, 1845

1550 ELLIOTT'S (E. B.) Horæ Apocalypticæ; a Commentary on the Apocalypse, with an examination of the chief Prophecies of Daniel, 2nd Edition, 4 vols. 8vo. *cloth*, £1 4*s* (*pub. at* £2 5*s*) 1846

"The Horæ of Mr. Elliott does credit to the Theology of the Age."—*Times, Nov.* 3, 1859.

1551 [ELLIS'S (George)] Specimens of the Early English Poets, 8vo. *half calf, uncut*, 7*s* 6*d* .. *Privately printed*, 1790

A copy of this "much admired selection" sold at Mr. Strettell's sale for 15s.

1552 ELLIS (Hon. G. A.) Historical Inquiries respecting the Character of Edward Hyde, Earl of Clarendon, post 8vo. *boards*, 4*s* (*pub. at* 6*s* 6*d*) .. .. .. 1827

1553 ELLIS'S (Henry) Voyage to Hudson's Bay, for discovering a N. W. Passage, in 1746-7, *map and plates*, 8vo. *calf, neat*, 4*s* 6*d* .. .. .. .. 1748

"A valuable performance."—*Lowndes.*

1554 ELLIS'S (Will.) Narrative of a Tour through Hawaii, or Owhyee, with observations on the Natural History of the Sandwich Islands, *portrait, map, and plates*, 8vo. *boards*, 5*s* 6*d* (*pub. at* 12*s*) .. .. .. .. 1827

"An interesting work."—*Lowndes.*

1555 — Polynesian Researches, during an 8 years residence in the Society and Sandwich Islands, *plates*, vols. 2, 3, and 4, 12mo. *cloth*, 6*s* .. .. .. .. 1830

1556 ELLWOOD'S (Thomas) Davideis; the Life of David, King of Israel, a Sacred Poem, 3rd Edition, small 8vo. *neat*, 3*s* 6*d* 1749

Thomas Ellwood, the friend and pupil of Milton, was one of the early Quakers. The Author says, this Poem was first begun in 1688.

1557 ELPHINSTONE'S (Hon. Mountstuart) Account of the Kingdom of Caubul, and its dependencies in Persia, Tartary, and India, *plates*, 2 vols. 8vo. *boards*, 12*s* (*pub. at* £1 8*s*) 1842

Comprises also a view of the Afghaun Nation; a History of the Dooraunee Monarchy; and a Pushtoo Vocabulary.

"A work which places its author in the first rank of historians and travellers in the East."—*Dr. Dibdin.*

1558 ELSMERE'S (Dr. Sloane) Sermons on Important Subjects, 2 vols. 8vo. *calf, neat,* 6*s* .. .. .. 1767

1559 ELSNERI (Jacobi) Observationes Sacræ in Novi Foederis Libros, 2 vols. 8vo. *vellum, neat,* 9*s* .. *Trajecti,* 1720

Dr. Harwood says, "this is one of the most valuable books on Sacred Criticism," and Ernesti and Michaelis both speak well of it.

1560 ELSTOB'S (Elizabeth) Rudiments of Grammar for the English-Saxon Tongue, with an Apology for the Study of Northern Antiquities, 4to. *calf, neat, scarce,* 9*s* *W. Bowyer,* 1715

1561 — another copy, 4to. *half morocco, neat,* 10*s* 6*d* *W. Bowyer,* 1715

1562 — English-Saxon Homily on the Birth-day of St. Gregory, anciently used in the English-Saxon Church, Anglo-Saxon and English, with Notes, &c., *frontispiece by Gribelin,* 8vo. *old calf, neat,* 10*s* 6*d* .. .. .. *W. Bowyer,* 1709

1563 — another copy, *frontispiece and portrait of Queen Anne by Gribelin,* 8vo. *old calf, very neat,* £1 5*s* .. *W. Bowyer,* 1709

*Lowndes* does not mention any copy of this book on LARGE PAPER, which this decidedly is; it is most imperfectly described by him. There is a dedication to Queen Anne, 8 pages; a most interesting Preface, 60 pages; a Latin version as well as the English by William Elstob, her husband, 11 pages; and an Appendix containing several Epistles of St. Gregory, illustrative of the Homily, 49 pages.

1564 ELTON'S (Charles A.) Tales of Romance with other Poems and Selections from Propertius, *plates,* 12mo. *calf, extra,* 4*s* 1810

"These tales are grounded on the Gesta Romanorum, a famous old history book."—*Preface.*

1565 ENFIELD'S (Dr. William) History of Philosophy from the earliest period, with Biographical Chart, 2 vols. 8vo. LARGE PAPER, *boards,* £1 1*s* .. .. .. .. 1819

A valuable book drawn up from Brucker's Historia Critica Philosophiæ.

1566 — another edition, in 1 vol. 8vo. *half cloth,* 7*s* (*pub. at* 14*s*) 1837

1567 ENGLAND'S Gazetteer, an account of all the Cities, Towns, &c. with an Index Villaris, 3 vols. 12mo. *fine copy, old calf, gilt,* 6*s* *Knapton,* 1751

Points out the old Military ways, camps, castles, and other remarkable ruins of Roman, Danish, and Saxon Antiquity, and particularly shews the Estates that were formerly Abbey-lands.

1568 ENGLISH (George Bethune) Narrative of the Expedition to Dongola and Sennaar, *map,* royal 8vo. *boards,* 5*s* *Boston, U.S.* 1823

First American edition. Ismael Pasha commanded the expedition; undertaken by desire of Mehemed Ali Pasha, Viceroy of Egypt.

1569 ENGLISH CHURCHWOMEN of the XVII. Century, (Lady Falkland, Lady Digby, Mary Evelyn, Lady Hastings, and 28 others,) 12mo. *cloth,* 3*s* 6*d* .. .. 1846

1570 ENGLISH HEXAPLA; the Greek Text (in a very fine type) of the New Testament, with Wiclif's, Tyndale's, Cranmer's, the Genevan, Anglo-Rhemish, and authorized English versions on each page, thick 4to. *cloth,* £1 10*s* *(pub. at 2 guineas) Bagster,* 1841

1571 ENGLISH PREACHER, Sermons selected from the most eminent Divines of the Church of England, on the principal subjects of Religion and Morality, 9 vols. 12mo. *a choice set in calf, gilt,* £1 4*s* .. .. .. .. 1773

1572 ENGLISHWOMAN'S Views of Society and Manners in America, in 1818-20, 8vo. *boards*, 5*s* (*pub. at* 13*s*) *Longmans*, 1821

1573 ENGLISH REVIEW, Nos. 7 to 14, 8vo. *sewed, clean*, 12*s* (*pub. at* 48*s*) .. .. *Oct.* 1845 *to June*, 1847

1574 ENGRAVING, Sculptura Historico-Technica, the History and Art of Engraving, with Monograms of Engravers, List of Painters and Engravers from the XI. Century, &c. *plates*, 4th edition, 12mo. *neat*, 5*s* .. .. .. 1770

Best edition of a useful little work.

1575 — another copy, *with plates and Monograms*, 12mo. *calf, neat*, 5*s* 1770

1576 ENQUIRE WITHIN upon Everything, small 8vo. *cloth, new, gilt*, 2*s* 6*d* .. .. .. .. 1859

1577 ENS (Johannes) Bibliotheca Sacra; sive Diatribe de librorum Novi Testamenti Canone, thick 12mo. *old calf, very neat*, 5*s* *Amst.* 1710

Recommended by Mr. Prebendary Horne in his introduction to Sacred Philology.

1578 EPICTETI ENCHIRIDION et Cebetis Tabula, Gr. et Lat. 64mo. *old calf, neat*, 3*s* .. .. *L. Bat.*, 1651

A very small edition, although the type is not so, with notes.

1579 — et Theophrasti Characteres Ethici, Gr. et Lat., Edidit C. Aldrich, 8vo. *morocco, gilt edges*, £1 1*s* .. *Oxonii*, 1707

A LARGE PAPER copy, beautifully bound by Clarke. VERY RARE.

1580 — Cebetis Tabula; Prodici Hercules; Theophrasti Characteres Ethici, Gr. et. Lat., Notis illustrati à Simson, 8vo. *calf, very neat*, 3*s* 6*d* .. .. .. *Oxonii*, 1804

1581 EPIGRAMMATA et Poematia Vetera, quorum pleraque nunc primum ex Antiquis Codicibus et Lapidibus, etc. thick 12mo. 620 *pages, old binding*, 8*s* .. *Lugduni, apud J. Chouet*, 1596

"Ce recueil, donné par le savant P. Pithou."—*Brunet*. With this autograph, "*Roberti Stephens liber ex dono Mri. Sparke Cll Gaii et tutoris longe dignissimi.*"

1582 EPIGRAMS, a Collection of, with a Dissertation on this species of Poetry, 12mo. *calf*, 2*s* 6*d* .. .. 1735

1583 EPISTOLARUM LACONICARUM ac Selectarum farrago altera, in qua Latinæ tantum continentur, thick 12mo. 503 *pages, old calf, rare*, 12*s* .. *Basileæ, ex off. J. Oporini*, 1554

1584 EQUICOLA d'ALVETO (Mario) di Natura d'Amore, di nuovo ricorretto per Thomaso Porcacchi, small 8vo. *fine clean copy in vellum, scarce*, 12*s* *Vinegia, Gabriel Giolito de' Ferrari*, 1563

Sir Christopher Hatton's copy. Impressed on the side C. H. This edition, not mentioned by Haym, has a large table to assist the memory.

1585 ERASMUS de libero arbitrio diatribe, [no date]—De Servo Arbitrio Martini Lutheri ad D. Erasmum Roterodamum, *Norembergæ*, 1526—Phil. Melancthon, Loci Communes, *Argentorati*, 1523, in 1 vol. small 8vo. *an extremely curious volume, in old impressed vellum binding on wood, rare*, 18*s* .. 1523-6

Erasmus, Martin Luther, Philip Melancthon.—Three tracts by these great men, published in their lives time—very interesting.

1586 — de complexione, et cæteris argumentationum oratoriarum generibus, small 8vo. *sewed*, 3*s* *Parisiis, P. Calvarini*, 1543

1587 — Colloquia thick 18mo. *fine clean copy in vellum*, 9*s* *L. Bat., Elzevir*, 1636

1588 ERASMUS, Colloquia, 24mo. *MS. title, calf*, 1s 6d *Amst., Elz.*, 1679

1589 — Encomium Moriæ; sive declamatio in laudem Stultitiæ, 18mo. *calf, neat*, 3s .. .. *L. Bat., J. Maire*, 1641

1590 — Moriæ Encomium, or the Praise of Folly, Englished, with a Preface by Bishop White Kennett, *portraits of Erasmus and Sir Thomas More, and singular plates after Hans Holbein*, 12mo. *old calf, scarce*, 6s .. .. .. 1726

With the autograph of R. Farmer, and writing by him.

1591 — l'Eloge de la Folie, avec Notes de Listrius, traduite en François par M. Guedeville, *plates after Holbein*, 12mo. *old calf, scarce*, 6s *Leide*, 1713

1592 — Paraphrase upon Matthew, Mark, Luke, and John, and the Acts of the Apostles, being vol. 1, folio, Black Letter, *clean*, 15s *London, Edw. Whytchurch*, 1548

With the dedications by Thos. Key and Nicholas Udall, the translators, to the Queen Dowager (Henry VIIIth's divorced Queen), imperfect, commencing at folio 23.

1593 — another copy of another edition of vol. 1, but it does not appear to be the reprint of 1551, commencing at pages 45 of Matthew, and ending at 80 of the Acts, wanting 8 leaves at the end, folio, *unbound*, 10s

1594 — Christian's Manual, a Translation from the Enchiridion Militis Christiani of Erasmus, 12mo. *old calf, neat*, 3s .. 1752

1595 — Life by Dr. John Jortin, *portrait*, 3 vols. 8vo. *calf, very neat*, £1 1s .. .. .. .. 1808

Period embraced, 1467 to 1536. "The life of no author is better calculated to interest our curiosity than that of Erasmus. He lived at the first dawning of literature. Having been an object of universal admiration, it is a matter of surprise that his life has never been written with accuracy and judgment. This task was reserved for Dr. Jortin; and the avidity with which it is read by the learned, is a proof of the merit of the execution." —*Dr. Knox.*

1596 — Life, with Historical Remarks on the State of Literature between the 10th and 16th Centuries, by Charles Butler, 8vo. *boards*, 4s 6d (*pub. at* 7s 6d) .. .. .. 1825

1597 ERIZZO (Sebastiano) Discorso sopra le Medaglie de gli Antichi, con la Dichiaratione delle Monete Consulari, et dell Medaglie de gli Imperadori Romani, *numerous cuts of Coins*, thick 4to. 780 *pages, old binding, a fine clean copy, gilt edges*, 18s *Vinegia, Giov. Varisco*, 1571

"It is a singular fact in literary history, that Vigo and Erizzo, although of different ways of thinking, never mention each other in their respective works. They were either afraid of controversy, or the one was unwilling to bring the other into notice." —*Mills's Theodore Ducas*, p. 380, V. 2. Both Spanheim and Patin much praise this author. Autograph of "*Goislard.*"

1598 ESTLIN'S (John Prior) Sermons, 8vo. *calf, neat*, 1s 6d *Bristol*, 1802

1599 ESSAYS from the Times; a Selection of Literary Papers, 12mo. *cloth*, 3s .. .. .. .. 1855

1600 ESSEX, History, Gazetteer, and Directory of the County of Essex, by Wm. White, *map*, 12mo. *calf, very neat, scarce*, 15s *Sheffield*, 1848

1601 — Funeral Sermon for Thomas Porter, of Hatfield-Broad-Oak, Essex, Oct. 29, 1752, by John Richardson, sm. 4to. *sewed*, 2s 1752

1602 ETHIOPIC Dictionary, see *Wemmers*.—Ethiopic Testament, see *Nov. Test.*

1603 ETON.—Electa ex Ovidio et Tibullo, 12mo. *cloth*, 2s *Etonæ*, 1844

1604 EUCLIDIS Elementorum Sex libri priores, adornati opera et studio H. Coetsii, *engraved title*, small thick 8vo. *old vellum*, 5*s* *Ludg. Bat.*, 1691

1605 EUGENE'S (Prince of Savoy,) Memoirs, written by himself, Englished by T. Shoberl, *portrait*, 8vo. *half calf*, 3*s* 6*d* 1811

1606 EUPHORMIONIS Lusinii Satyricon nunc primum recognitum, 12mo. *old vellum clean and neat*, RARE, 12*s* *Parisiis, Francisci Huby*, 1605

This is the first edition of this Satire, dedicated to King James I., its author was John Barclay, a Scotchman.—See *Barclaii Argenis et Satyricon*, No. 340, &c.

1607 EURIPIDES, Græcè, ex recensione Dindorfii, 3 small vols. *cloth*, 4*s* 6*d* . .. .. *Oxonii*, 1846

1608 EUSEBII, Socratis, Theodoriti, Sozomeni et Evagrii, et aliorum Historiæ Ecclesiasticæ, Græcè, thick folio, *old calf, very neat rare*, £1 11*s* 6*d* .. *Lutetiæ, Rob. Stephani*, 1544

The 1st edition of the Ecclesiastical Historians, beautifully printed by Robert Stephens.

1609 EUSTATHIUS de Varia temporum in jure Civili observatione, Leges Rhodiorum Navales, Militares et Georgicæ Justiniani, Gr. et Lat., opera et studio S. Schardii, 8vo. *old vellum, scarce*, 8*s* .. .. *Basileæ, per I. Oporinum*, 1561

In writing, is "Hic Liber pertinet ad Guilelum Heveningham, 1671." This William Heveningham married into the Coke family.

1610 EVANS'S (George W.) History of Van Diemens Land, *frontispiece*, 8vo. *boards*, 2*s* 6*d* (*pub. at* 7*s* 6*d*) .. 1824

1611 EVANS'S (Dr. John) Christian Temper; 34 Discourses on the principal heads of Practical Religion, 2 vols. 8vo. *boards*, 6*s* 1770

"This excellent Treatise is the most complete summary of those duties which make up the Christian life, that hath been published in our age."—*Dr. Watts.*

1612 EVANS'S (Robert W.) Tales of the Ancient British Church, *frontispiece*, 12mo. *cloth*, 3*s* 6*d* (*pub. at* 6*s*) 1846

1613 EVANS (Theophilus, *St. David's*) History of Modern Enthusiasm, from the Reformation to the present time, 8vo. *half bound, wormed*, 3*s* 6*d* .. .. .. 1757

This is a very curious book and exhibits a vast amount of reading.

1614 EVELYN'S (John) Sylva; a Discourse of Forest Trees; with Pomona, on Fruit Trees in relation to Cyder; and Kalendarium Hortense, or Gardener's Almanack, folio, *old calf, neat*, 9*s* 1670

This is the 2nd edition, and in his dedication to the King, Evelyn tells us that the first edition of a thousand copies had been sold in less than two years.

1615 — Sylva, Dr. Hunter's original edition, *with notes, and fine impressions of the numerous plates*, 4to. *good copy, in calf*, £1 1*s* *York*, 1776

"A diligent perusal of this noble work may animate our nobility and gentry to improve their estates, by the never failing methods therein recommended."—*British Critic.*

1616 — Terra; a Philosophical Discourse of Earth, with Notes, by A. Hunter, 8vo. *calf, very neat*, 3*s* 6*d* .. *York*, 1778

1617 — Navigation and Commerce, their Original and Progress, small 8vo. *old binding, neat*, 3*s* 6*d* .. .. 1674

1618 — Acetaria; a Discourse of Sallets, 12mo. *old calf, neat*, 3*s* 6*d* 1699

1619 EVELYN Kalendarium Hortense; or, Gardener's Almanac, directing what he is to do monthly throughout the year, 10th edit. 12mo. *old binding*, 3*s* 6*d* .. .. .. 1706

With a dedication to Abraham Cowley, Esq., and a Poem, called the Garden, addressed by Cowley to Evelyn, dated Chertsea, 1666.

1620 EVIL, Free Inquiry into the Nature and Origin of Evil, 1757.—Advice from a Bishop to a Young Clergyman, 1759, in 1 vol. 12mo. *old calf, gilt*, 3*s* .. .. V. Y.

1621 EVREMOND—La Vie de M. Charles de St. Denis, Sieur de St. Evremond, par Des Maizeaux, 4to. *sewed, gilt edges*, 2*s* 6*d* *Londres*, 1709

1622 EXCERPTA Historica; or, Illustrations of English History, royal 8vo. *cloth*, 10*s* 6*d* (*pub. at* £1 1*s*) *London, S. Bentley*, 1833

This curious and really valuable volume consists of extracts from various rolls in the Tower, the British Museum, &c. from A.D. 1205, to 1586. Mr. Bentley acknowledges his obligations to Mr. Hardy of the Record Office in the Tower, Sir Harris Nicolas, C. G. Young, Esq., York Herald, and various other gentlemen occupying public trusts.

1623 EXEA, (Andreæ ab) de Aerario, Fiscoq. ac utriusq. ratiocinorum præfectura libellus, 4to. *old calf, neat*, 6*s* *Lugduni, Seb. Gryphius*, 1532

This curious little treatise of 47 pages is dedicated to Francis I. of France. Lord Leicester's Arms impressed on the sides.

1624 EXETER.—Essays by a Society of Gentlemen at Exeter, *plates*, 8vo. *half calf, neat*, 6*s* .. *Exeter, Trewman*, 1796

1625 — another copy, *plates*, 8vo. *half morocco*, 6*s* *ib.* 1796

These esteemed Essays are illustrative of British Antiquities, Cromlechs, Urns, Monuments, &c. found in Devonshire.

1626 — the Humble Reply of the Churchwardens of Bampfordspeke to his Honor the Bishop of Hexeter, in verse, (satirical,) 12mo. *sewed*, 2*s* .. *Privately printed, no place*, 1850

1627 EXMOUTH'S (Admiral, Viscount) Life, by Edward Ostler, *portrait*, 12mo. *cloth*, 3*s* 6*d* (*pub. at* 6*s*) .. 1841

1628 EXPERIENCES of a Goal Chaplain, Anecdotes of Criminals, vols. 1 and 3, post 8vo. *cloth*, 3*s* .. .. 1847

1629 EZRÆ primi libri, in Ethiopic, Latin and English, with general remarks, by Dr. R. Laurence, 8vo. *boards, scarce*, 7*s* 6*d* *Oxoniæ*, 1820

"Dr. (now Archbishop) Laurence has the honour of being the first editor of the Ethiopic version. There is an elaborate critical disquisition on the author of the book." —*Prebendary Horne.*

1630 EZZELLINO III. da Romano, Vita di, dall' Origine al fine di sua famiglia, dal 1100 sino al 1262, autore Pietro Gerardo, suo contemporaneo, small 8vo. *parchment*, 7*s* 6*d* *Venetia, Fr. Lorenzini*, 1560

Dedicated to "Il Signor Sforza Marchese Pallavicino," by Fausto de Longiano, who edited this edition.—See *Haym*.

1631 EYTON (J. Walter K.) Catalogue of his fine Collection of Privately Printed Books, sold by Mr. Sotheby, May, 1848, 8vo. *sewed*, 3*s* 6*d* .. .. .. .. 1848

1632 FABRI (Petri, *Regii Consiliarii*) Semestrium liber primus, 4to. *limp vellum, clean, scarce*, 6*s* *Lutetiæ Parisiorum, apud J. Benenatum*, 1570

1633 FABRI (Petri) Agonisticon; sive de Re Athletica, Ludisque Veterum Gymnicis, Musicis atque Circensibus Spicilegiorum tractatus, small folio, *old calf, much stained*, 6*s* *Lugduni*, 1592

1634 FABRICII (Jo. Alb.) Bibliographia Antiquaria, sive Introductio in Notitiam Scriptorum, qui antiquitates Hebraicas, Græcas, Romanas et Christianas scriptis illustraverunt, 4to. *good copy, old calf, gilt*, 9*s* .. .. *Hamburgi*, 1713

"A work of this kind in our own language would be very useful, and even entertaining; Fabricius has executed it in a masterly manner."—*Dibdin's Bibliomania.*

1635 FABYAN'S CRONYCLES of ENGLANDE and of FRAUNCE, untill the begynnyng of the Reyne of our moste redoubted Soverayne Lord Kynge Henry the VIII., 2 vols. in 1, folio, *wants the first title only, with the two tables*, **Black Letter**, £6 16*s* 6*d* *Prentyd at London, by Wyllyam Rastell*, 1533

This is the 2nd edition of Fabyan's Chronicle. It is a very nice specimen of old printing, interspersed with much Poetry.

1636 FACII (Bartholomæi) de Rebus Gestis ab Alphonso I., Neapolitanorum Rege Cemmentariorum libri X., Io. Mich. Bruti opera nunc primum editi, 4to. *old calf, neat*, 12*s* *Lugduni, Gryphii*, 1560

This is the 1st edition. "Facio was one of the numerous assemblage of scholars that rendered illustrious the Court of Alphonsus, King of Naples, by whom he was treated with distinguished honour."—*Shepherd's Life of Poggio.* Tiraboschi thinks Facio's style much more elegant than that of any of his contemporaries. He died about 1467.

1637 FACTUM de L'Instance d'entre Monsieur le Procureur General, demandeur en Requeste du 29 jour de Jan. 1647, &c., contre les Doyen, Chanoines et Chapitre de l'Eglise S. Jean de Lyon, qui sont defendeurs, 4to. *limp parchment*, 12*s* *Paris, a Vitré*, 1648

This is a considerable treatise of 474 pages, it contains the Lettres Patentes de Philipes le Bel, du mois de Septembre, 1307, and various other important acts relating to this subject, both before and after his time.

1638 FADEN'S (Wm.) Large Map of England and Wales, *coloured, mounted on canvas, in a case*, 10*s* 6*d* .. 1818

Book-plate of Mrs. "Elizabeth Berney, Relict, Bracon Ash, Norfolk."

1639 FAENZI (Valerio, *Academico Veneto)* I Dieci Circoli dell' Imperio nella GERMANIA; Entrate de Prencipe Ecclesiastici; Contrabutioni de Soldati; Descrittione della Repub. de NORIMBERGA; RINUNCIA di CARLO V. al Sereniss. suo figliuolo, Ottobre 25 1555; RINUNCIA dell' Imperio, fatta da CARLO V. al Sereniss. suo fratello, Settembre 7, 1556; 39 *leaves and* 1 *blank*, small 4to. *a very fine clean copy*, RARE, 15*s* *Nell' Academia Venetiana*, 1558

This rare tract from the ALDINE PRESS, (see *Renouard*) contains, as is mentioned above, the celebrated abdication of Charles V., but it wants, as usual the 3 leaves of title and preface.

1640 FAIRFAX'S (Thomas) Complete Sportsman; or Country Gentleman's Recreation in Bowling, Horse-racing, Hunting, Shooting, &c. *plate*, 12mo. *neat*, 3*s* 6*d* .. *No Date*

"C. Fitz-Roy, R. Burroughes, e dono Domini Caroli Fitz-Roy, July 25, 1778, A.D." in MS.

1641 FAIRY Tales—Popular and Wonderful Legends, 26 of them collected by Benj. Tabart, *coloured plates*, 12mo. *bds.*, 4*s* 6*d* 1834

Cinderella, Blue Beard, Fortunatus, Puss in Boots, Hop o' my Thumb, Beauty and the Beast, Tom Thumb, Jack and the Bean Stalk, &c.

1642 FALCKENBURGK (Jacobi) die D. Matthiæ Natalicorum celebrandorum more—Meditatio Sacra et Historica, de Sanctorum trium Regum solemnib. et Natali domini, 12 *leaves*, 4to. *sewed*, RARE, 12*s* .. *Antverpiæ, Andreas Bax*, 1578

Poems in honour of the natal day of Matthew, Archduke of Austria, Duke of Burgundy and Governor of lesser Germany; with this writing on the title-page, "Generoso Dn. Danieli Rogersio, Legato Anglico in Germaniam, Noys suiq. memoriæ ergò dabat autor."

1643 FALCONER'S (William) Poetical Works, with Life, 12mo. *morocco, gilt edges*, 6*s* (*cost* 10*s*) .. *W. Pickering*, 1836

1644 — Shipwreck, *plates by Neagle, after Stothard*, 12mo. *morocco, gilt edges*, 3*s* 6*d* .. .. .. 1794

1645 FALCONERII (Octavii) Inscriptiones Athleticæ nuper repertæ editæ et notis illustratæ, quibus accesserunt aliæ ex Africanis Marmoribus recens descriptæ, una cum dissertatione de Nummo Apamensi, 4to. *good clean copy, in old calf*, 7*s* 6*d* *Romæ*, 1668

1646 FALETI (Girolamo) delle Guerre di Alamagna, small 8vo. *vellum*, 5*s* .. .. *Vinegia, Gabriel Giolito*, 1552

Only this edition ever published, dedicated to "Hercole da Esti IV. Duca di Ferrara."

1647 FALKLAND'S (Viscountess) Chow-Chow; being Selections from a Journal kept in India, Egypt, and Syria, *plates*, 2 vols. 8vo. *cloth*, 14*s* (*pub. at* 30*s*) .. .. 1857

1648 FALKNER'S (Will. *of St. Nicholas, Lyn Regis*) Libertas Ecclesiastica; Vindicating the lawfulness of those things excepted against the Liturgy and Worship of the Church of England, 8vo. *old calf, neat*, 3*s* 6*d* .. .. 1674

Dr. Allured Clarke's copy 1720, with his book-plate and autograph.

1649 FAMILIERE Explication des Articles de la Foy, par l'Evesque de Valence.—Sermons de l'Evesque de Valence, sur l'Oraison Dominicale.—Instructions sur les X. Commandemens.—Instruction pour le Saints Sacremens.—Epistre sur les Processions et Penitences publiques; in 1 vol. small 8vo. *old vellum, rare*, 7*s* 6*d* *Paris, M. de Vascosan*, 1561

Very handsomely printed tracts in a fine large type. Drawn up by the Bishop for the use of the Dioceses of Valence and Dye; the last tract dated 1555.

1650 FAMILY LIBRARY:—Cunningham's Lives of British Painters, Sculptors, and Architects, *portraits*, 6 vols.; Lives of Scottish Worthies, 3 vols.; Life of Alexander the Great, 1 vol.; of Sir Isaac Newton, 1 vol.; of Bruce, 1 vol.; the Duke of Marlborough, 1 vol.; British Physicians, 1 vol.; Napoleon Buonaparte, 2 vols.; the Court and Camp of Buonaparte, 1 vol.; Columbus, 1 vol.; Voyages of the Companions of Columbus, 1 vol.; Tour through Holland, 1 vol.; Mutiny of the Bounty, 1 vol.; Blunt's Reformation in England, 1 vol.; Sir W. Scott's Demonology and Witchcraft, 1 vol.; Lander's Expedition to the Niger, 3 vols.; Venetian History, 2 vols.; Milman's History of the Jews, 3 vols.; *all in cloth*, (*pub. at* 5*s each*) 2*s* 6*d each volume.*

1651 FARONI (Massimo) I Sospetti, Comedia, 12mo. *sewed, rare*, 6*s* *In Venetia, G. B. Ciotti*, 1603

This author's name, "Massimo Faroni, Gentilhuomo et Academiço Mantouano," is not to be found in *Haym*.

1652 FASCICULUS Florum; or, a Nosegay of Flowers, translated out of the Gardens of Severall Poets, 12mo. *bound*, SCARCE, 10*s* *By A. M.*, 1636

At Sir Masterman Sykes's sale, 19*s*—Mr. Heber's, 16*s*

1653 FASCICULUS Temporum, cum pluribus additionibus, ad annum, 1518, 4to. Black Letter, *old vellum*, 10*s* *Parrhisiis, Johannis Parui*, 1518

Folio 1 to 93, but wanting folios 9, portions of 18 and 19, and all 32. Brunet records a French translation of this date, but not this Latin one. It is also deficient of the 1st and last leaf of the table. At folio 38 is a very fine wood-cut of the Crucifixion, and several Comets are recorded under the years 304, 454, 584, 814, 834, 1294, 1404, and 1484.

1654 FAXARDO (Didaci Savedræ) Symbola Politica, *many hundreds of emblems*, 12mo. 832 pages, *parchment (wants title)* 3*s* 6*d* 1650

1655 FAZELLIUS (Thoma) de Rebus Siculis, folio, 650 pages, *old calf, neat*, £1 5*s* *Panormi* (Palermo) *apud I. M. Maidam*, 1558

This is the first edition of this esteemed and rare book.

1656 FELIBIEN, Entretiens sur les Vies et sur les Ouvrages des plus excellens Peintres, avec la Vie des Architectes, 6 vols. 12mo. *nice clean copy, in calf*, 12*s* .. *Trevoux*, 1725

1657 FELLOWES'S (Robert) Picture of Christian Philosophy, *Warwick*, 1798.—Simpson's (John) Essay on Christianity, *Leeds*, 1782.—Pitt's Speech on the Abolition of the Slave Trade, 1792.—Essay on the Happiness of the Life to Come, 1793.—Donalson's Elements of Beauty, *Edinburgh*, 1780.; in 1 vol. small 8vo. *calf, neat*, 3*s* 6*d* .. .. .. V. Y.

1658 FELTHAM'S (Owen) Resolves, Divine, Moral, Political, with Lusoria, occasional Pieces in Verse, and a brief Character of the Low Countries and Letters, folio, *old calf, scarce*, 9*s* 1661

This is the edition used by the *Retrospective Reviewers*. "Bacon (Essays) has been much extolled for the splendour of his imagery; we doubt whether many metaphors could be produced from his works surpassing the beauty of those which we shall quote from the *Resolves*."—*Retrospective Rev.* v. 10, p. 346.

1659 FELTON (S.) on the Portraits of English Authors on Gardening, with Biographies, 8vo. *boards*, 5*s* .. 1830

This is a very amusing book.

1660 FENELON (Archevêque de Cambray) Lettres sur divers sujets concernant la Religion et la Metaphysique, 12mo. *neat*, 2*s* 6*d* *Paris*, 1718

1661 — Aventures de Télemaque, fils d'Ulysse, *plates, by Le Grand*, 2 vols. 12mo. *old calf*, 4*s* .. *Paris, Barbou*, 1763

1662 — de l'Education des Filles, 18mo. *neat*, 1*s* 6*d* *Lyon*, 1809

1663 — Instructions for the Education of a Daughter, also for the Conduct of Young Ladies of Rank, and Devotions, *plate by Vdr Gucht*, 12mo. *nice copy, in old calf*, 2*s* 6*d* *Jonah Bowyer*, 1708

Dedicated to her Grace the Duchess of Ormond, by Dr. George Hickes who revised the work.

1664 — Life, with the Lives of St. Vincent, of Paul, and Henri-Marie de Boudon, &c., by Charles Butler, 8vo. *calf, elegant*, 5*s* 6*d* 1819

1665 — Dr. Channing's Remarks on his Character and Writings, 8vo. *sewed*, 1*s* .. .. .. 1830

1666 FERANDI (Adduensis, *Jurisconsulti Medialanensis)* Explicationum libri duo, quorum primus est in Pandectas: secundus in alias Juris Civilis partes, 8vo. *old vellum, scarce,* 6s *Lugduni, Gryphius,* 1561

An author not to be found in Brunet or modern biographical dictionaries.

1667 FERGUSON'S (James) Astronomy Explained upon Sir Isaac Newton's Principles, *numerous plates,* 8vo. *old cf., gilt,* 3s 6d 1778

1668 FERISHTA'S History of the Dekkan, see *Scott.*

1669 FERRARA (Professore Abate Fr.) Guide dei Viaggiatori in Sicilia, *portrait, map and plates,* 12mo. *sewed,* 2s 6d *Palermo,* 1822

1670 FERRARII (Octavii) de Re Vestiaria libri VII., *numerous plates,* 2 vols. 4to. *fine copy, in old calf, gilt,* 8s *Patavii,* 1654

1671 — Analecta de Re Vestiaria, accessit Dissertatio de Veterum Lucernis sepulchralibus, *many plates,* 4to. *old vellum, a nice clean copy,* 6s .. .. .. *Patavii,* 1670

1672 — de Re Vestiaria libri VII., 2 vols., *Patavii,* 1654.—Analecta de Re Vestiaria, accessit Dissertatio de Veterum Lucernis sepulchralibus, together 3 vols. in 1, *numerous plates,* 4to. *nice copy, in old vellum,* 15s *Patavii, P. M. Frambotti,* 1670

Grævius thought so well of these learned Treatises that he has inserted them in his great work the Roman Antiquities.

1673 FERRIAR'S (Dr. John) Essay towards a theory of Apparitions, post 8vo. *boards,* 3s .. .. 1813

1674 FIAT LUX, a general Conduct to a right understanding and charity in the great Combustions and Broils about Religion here in England, betwixt Papist and Protestant, Presbyterian and Independent, 12mo. *old calf, neat,* 3s 6d *No place, or Printer,* 1662

Dedicated by J. V. C. to the Countess of Arundell and Surrey. Quoted by Foulis in his *Romish Treasons.*

1675 FICORONI (Francesco de) I Piombi Antichi, 25 *plates of seals and* 39 *of medals, &c.,* 4to. *vellum, neat,* 10s *Roma,* 1740

1676 FIELDING'S (Henry) Works, with his Life, *portrait,* 8 vols., 8vo: vols. 5 and 6 missing, *old calf,* £1 1s .. 1771

1677 — Tragedy of Tragedies; the Life and Death of Tom Thumb the Great, *plate after Hogarth,* 8vo. *calf,* 2s 6d 1737

One of the best burlesques that ever appeared.

1678 — Journal of a Voyage to Lisbon, 12mo. *original edition, calf, neat,* 3s .. .. .. .. 1755

1679 — History of Tom Jones, a Foundling, 4 vols. 12mo. *beautiful copy in old calf, gilt,* 12s .. .. 1763

1680 FIGLIUCCI (Felice) de la Filosofia Morale libri X. sopra li X. libri de l'Ethica d'Aristotile, thick 4to. of 504 pages, besides Index and introductory matter, 18 leaves more, *old vellum, rare,* 14s .. .. *Roma, Vincenzo Valgrisi,* 1551

Sir Christopher Hatton's copy, with C. H. impressed on the sides. This is the 1st edition.

1681 FILIPPE (Bartolomeo, *Dottore Portoghese)* Trattato del Conseglio et de' Consеglieri de' Prencipi, tradotto in lingua Italiana per il Rev. D. Giulio Cesare Valentino, 4to. *limp vellum, clean and neat,* 5s .. .. .. *Venetia,* 1599

1682 FINLAYSON'S (George) Mission to Siam, and Hué, the Capital of Cochin China, in 1821-2, with Memoir of the Author, by Sir Stamford Raffles, *plate*, 8vo. *boards*, 6*s* 6*d* (*pub. at* 15*s*) 1826

1683 FIRENZUOLA (Agnolo *Fiorentino*) La Trinutia, Comedia, 8vo. *sewed*, 6*s* .. *Fiorenza, Bernardo Giunti*, 1551

"L'Edizione del 1551, si allega dal Vocabolario."—*Haym.*

1684 — I Lucidi, Comedia, 8vo. *sewed*, 6*s* *Firenze, apresso i Giunti*, 1552

These two Comedies published under the editorship of Lodovico Domenichi, are the only Comedies written or printed by Firenzuola.

1685 — Prose, dedicated to Pandolfo Pucci, by Lorenzo Scala, 8vo. *original vellum, rare*, 15*s* *In Fiorenza, Lorenzo Torrentino*, 1552

"Few Italian writers have united equally with Firenzuola the most simple naïveté to a delicate sweetness, that diffuses itself over the heart of the reader."—*Hallam.*

1686 — another, *very fine copy, in red morocco, gilt leaves, rare*, £1 1*s* *ib. ib.* 1552

"Edition aussi rare que la précédente." (alluding to that of 1548.)—*Brunet.*

Contents:—1. Discorsi de Glianimali.—2. Ragionamenti Amorosi.—3. Epistola in lode della Donne.—4. Novelle otto.—5. Discacciamento delle Lettre.—6. Dialogo della bellezza delle donne.

1687 FISHER (Johan, *Bp. of Rochester*) Mornynge Remembrancer, had at the moneth minde of the noble Prynces Margarete Countesse of Richmonde and Darbye, moder unto Kynge Henry VII. 8vo. **Black Letter**, *vellum*, 5*s* .. *A. Bosvile*, 1708

Re-print of Wynkyn de Worde's edition.

1688 — Funeral Sermon for Margaret, Countess of Richmond and Derby, mother to K. Henry VII., 2nd Edit. edited by Thomas Baker, 8vo. **Black Letter**, *neat, wormed at end, scarce*, 5*s* 1708

This re-print of Wynkyn de Word's edition of 1508, has a large Preface containing some further account of the Countess's Charities and Foundations, with a Catalogue of her Professors both at Oxford and Cambridge.

1689 — another copy, *arms*, small 8vo. **Black Letter**, *old calf, very nice copy*, 7*s* 6*d* .. .. .. 1708

This was Dr. Sutton's copy, who has made many MS. additions to it.

1690 FLAGS—A Collection of the principal Flags of all Nations, 225 *coloured*, 4to. *sewed*, 3*s* .. .. *Bungay*

1691 FLECHIER (Esprit, *Evêque de Nismes*) Panegyriques et autres Sermons, 3 vols. 12mo. *calf, neat*, 12*s* *Paris*, 1711

1692 FLEETWOOD'S (Bp.) Chronicon Preciosum; account of English Gold and Silver Money, the Price of Corn, Wages, &c., in England, *plates*, 8vo. *calf, neat, best edition*, 6*s* .. 1745

1693 FLEURY—Les Mœurs des Chrestiens, 12mo. *old purple morocco, gilt leaves*, 3*s* .. .. *a La Haye*, 1682

1694 — Mœurs des Israelites, 12mo. *bound*, 2*s* 6*d* *Bruxelles*, 1722

1695 — History of the Manners, Customs, Laws, &c. of the Ancient Israelites, by Dr. A. Clarke, 12mo. *old calf, neat*, 2*s* 6*d* *Liverpool*, 1802

1696 FLLOYD (Thomas) Bibliotheca Biographica, a Synopsis of Universal Biography, Ancient and Modern, 3 vols. 8vo. *half calf, neat*, 10*s* 6*d* (*in Lowndes at* 15*s*) .. 1760

1697 FLORIAN'S (M.) Estelle, a Pastoral Romance Englished by Mr. Maxey, 7 *pretty plates by Mitan*, 12mo. *calf, neat*, 3*s* 6*d* 1803

1698 FLORUS et Lucius Ampelius, cum notis selectissimus et Min-Ellii, 12mo. 3*s* .. .. *Amst., S. Swart,* 1683

With autograph of T. Coke, (of the Holkham family,) Feb. 21, 1710-11, with a map drawn by him.

1699 — cum notis Variorum, 2 vols. in 1, 8vo. *old vellum, clean and neat,* 6*s* .. .. .. *Amstelodami,* 1702

1700 — cum notis variorum et Dukeri, thick 8vo. *prize vellum copy,* 8*s* *Lugd. Bat.,* 1744

Duker's best edition, spoken very highly of by Ernesti and other bibliographers.

1701 FLUGEL'S German-English and English-German Dictionary, by Feiling, Heimann, and Oxenford, 2 vols. large 8vo. *cloth, last edition,* £1 4*s* .. : .. *Dulau,* 1857

1702 — the same abridged, 12mo. *bound,* 7*s* 6*d* .. 1859

1703 FLUTE. Richard Carte's Sketch of the Successive Improvements made in the Flute, 8vo. *sewed,* 2*s* .. .. 1851

1704 FOLIETÆ (Uberti) Opera subsiciva, Opuscula Varia, de Linguæ Latinæ usu et præstantia, clarorum Ligurum Elogia, *Romæ, apud Fr. Zannetum,* 1579.—Ub. Folietæ de Sacro Foedere in Selimum libri IV., ejusdem Variæ Expeditiones in AFRICAM, cum obsidione MELITÆ, 2 vols. in 1, 4to. *good clean copies, in the original calf, neat,* 15*s* .. .. *Genuæ, H. Bartoli,* 1587

"Hubert Foglieta, a Genoese noble, was born in 1518, and died at Rome in 1581, having there acquired the patronage of Hippolyto, Cardinal d'Este. Most of his works are scarce; his Latin style is peculiar, elegant, and pure, and his judgment at once accurate and sound."—*Moreri and Tiraboschi.*

Of the first, *Brunet* says, "Recueil rare et qui mérite d'être recherché." The second, which is a very interesting work, he does not mention.

1705 FOLKES'S (Martin) Table of English Silver and Gold Coins from the Norman Conquest, with their Weights and Value, *no plates,* 4to. *old calf, neat,* 6*s* .. .. .. 1745

1706 — Tables of English Silver and Gold Coins, published by the Society of Antiquaries, 67 *plates,* 4to. *best edition, old calf, neat,* £2 2*s* 1762

Fine portrait of the author, by Wm. Hogarth, inserted.

1707 FONSECA'S (Christ.) Discourse of Holy Love, Englished by Sir George Strode, 12mo. *very neat,* 7*s* 6*d* .. 1652

With very fine impression of the engraved title, containing portrait of Sir George Strode.

1708 FONTAINE (Messire Jean Baptiste de la) Memoires, 471 pages, small 8vo. *bound,* 3*s* 6*d* .. .. *Cologne,* 1699

Chevalier Seigneur de Savoie et de Fontenai, Brigadier et Inspecteur General des Armées du Roi.

1709 FONTENELLE'S History of Oracles, Englished by S. Whatley, 12mo. *neat,* 3*s* .. .. .. 1750

"An excellent treatise."—*Dr. Middleton's* Examination of Bp. Sherlock on Prophecy.

1710 — Plurality of Worlds, Englished by Mr. Glanvill, small 8vo. *bound,* 2*s* .. .. .. .. 1688

1711 FORBES (Rt. Hon. Duncan) Works, Thoughts on Religion, on Incredulity with regard to it, &c. 12mo. *neat,* 3*s* 6*d* *Glasgow,* 1788

Russell says, in his History of Europe, that Duncan Forbes (who was Lord President of the Court of Session) was probably the means of keeping the present Royal family on the throne, by preventing the success of the Pretender.

1712 FORDYCE'S (Dr. James) Sermons to Young Women, 2 vols. 12mo. *neat,* 3*s* 6*d* .. .. .. 1766

1713 FOREST Promiscuous of several Seasons Productions, folio, *old calf, rare*, £1 1*s* .. .. *Daniel Pakeman*, 1659

Anonymous, "For my Alma Mater, Cantabrigia." The Dedication to the reader is dated, Feb. 10, 1644. The volume consists of Letters, written in 1638 to 1645, and in one addressed to the Queen of Bohemia, p. 191, he declares himself Sir ROBERT HONYWOOD, but no such author is to be found in *Lowndes*, or in the *Bibliotheca Anglo Poetica*, there is much POETRY interspersed.

"*Rare*, by Francis Dudley, 3rd Lord North. A collection of Poems, Letters, Characters, Songs, Meditations, &c. replete with sound sense and piety; very interesting and curious." —*Lilly*.

1714 FORGET ME NOT, for 1836, edited by Fred. Shoberl, *no plates*, 12mo. *morocco, gilt edges*, 2*s* 6*d*

1715 FORSYTH'S (William) Treatise on the Culture and Management of Fruit Trees, &c. *plates*, 8vo. *half calf, neat*, 5*s* 1803

1716 FORTESCUE (Sir John, Lord Chief Justice and Lord Chancellor temp. Henry VI.) on the Difference between an Absolute and Limited Monarchy, edited by Sir John Fortescue-Aland Kt. royal 8vo. *good copy, scarce*, 9*s* .. .. 1719

"This most excellent Treatise was written by the author in the language of those times in which he lived; participating much of the nature of the SAXON; but by the *Etymological* remarks of the *learned editor*, the author appears with great advantage in his *native dress*." See *Oldys's British Librarian*, p. 250.

1717 — De Laudibus Legum Angliæ, Latin and English, with Notes, &c. by Selden and the Editor, Mr. F. Gregor, royal 8vo. *good copy in calf*, 7*s* 6*d* .. .. .. 1775

This edition has the Summs of Sir Ralph de Hengham, Lord Chief Justice to K. Edw. I., called Hengham Magna and Hengham Parva.

"Bracton and Fortescue are the two most learned, and almost the only learned of the ancient lawyers."—*Bp. Warburton*.

1718 FORTIS'S (Abbe Alberto) Travels into Dalmatia, with Observations on the Island of Cherso and Osero, 20 *plates*, 4to. *calf, neat*, 7*s* 6*d* .. .. .. .. 1778

Containing observations on the natural history of Dalmatia and neighbouring Islands; remarks on the natural productions, arts, manners, and customs of the Inhabitants, as well as a very curious Iter by *Antonio Verantius*, entitled "*Iter Buda Hadrianopolim anno MDLIII exaratum, nunc primum editum.*"

1719 FOSBROKE'S (Rev. T. D.) Synopsis of Ancient Costume, Egyptian, Greek, Roman, British, Anglo-Saxon, Norman, and English, 71 *figures on* 4 *plates*, 4to. 47 *pages, boards*, RARE, 10*s* 1825

Extracted from his "Encyclopædia of Antiquities," with additional remarks, not mentioned by Lowndes.

1720 — Encyclopædia of Antiquities, and Elements of Archæology, Classical and Mediæval, *numerous plates*, 2 vols. royal 8vo. *half calf, extra gilt*, 18*s* (*cost* £2 2*s*) .. *Nattali*, 1843

1721 — Greek and Roman Antiquities, 2 vols. 12mo. *cloth*, 5*s* *Lardner's Cyclopædia*, 1852

1722 FOSCOLO (Ugo) Discorso sul Testo e su le opinioni diverse prevalenti intorno alla storia e alla emendazione critica della Commedia di Dante, crown 8vo. *cloth, scarce*, 9*s* *Londra, Guglielmo Pickering*, 1825

An elegantly printed volume.

1723 FOSTER (Dr. James) Discourses on all the principal branches of Natural Religion and Social Virtue, 2 vols. 4to. *a very nice clean copy, in old calf*, 9*s* .. *For the Author*, 1749

"Let honest Foster, if he will, excell
Ten metropolitans in preaching well."—*Pope*.

1724 FOSTER'S (Mrs.) Hand-Book of Modern European Literature, thick 12mo. *cloth*, 8*s* 6*d* .. .. 1849

Arranged in centuries and under countries; a useful little manual.

1725 FOURNIER (Fr. Ign.) Nouveau Dictionnaire portatif de Bibliographie, 8vo. *old boards*, 8*s* .. *Paris*, 1809

23,000 rare and curious books are here enumerated, with bibliographical critiques on them; at the end are lists of the Aldine, Variorum and other esteemed sets of Classics.

1726 FOVARGUE'S (Stephen, *Fellow of St. John's Cambridge)* New Catalogue of Vulgar Errors, 8vo. *half calf*, 3*s* 6*d* *Cambridge*, 1767

Intended as a Supplement to Sir Thomas Browne's Vulgar Errors.

1727 FOWLER (John) Journal of a Tour in the State of New York, in 1830, and Shipwreck at the Western Islands, coming home, 12mo. *boards*, 2*s* 6*d* .. .. 1831

1728 FOWLE'S (F. W.) Ten plain Sermons, 12mo. *cloth*, 2*s* 6*d* (*cost* 5*s* 6*d*) .. .. .. .. 1835

1729 FOX'S (Hon. Charles James) Letters to the Electors of Westminster, 8vo. *half calf, neat*, 5*s* .. .. .. 1793

Has also his Speech in the House, Mar. 24, 1795, on the "State of the Nation," with several tracts pro and con on his letter to his constituents.

1730 FOX, North, and Burke, their Beauties and Deformities, selected from their Speeches, *frontispiece containing portraits of all three*, 12mo. *half bound, neat*, 3*s* .. .. 1784

With 2 other tracts in the same vol.—I. The Friend; Essays on Important Subjects, 1774.—II. Dr. Fothergill's Rules for the Preservation of Health, 1765.

1731 FRACCI (Ambrosii Novidii, *Ferentinatis*) Sacrorum Fastorum libri XII., cum romanis consuetudinibus per totum annum, *portrait and wood-cuts*, 4to. *old vellum wrapper, rare*, £1 1*s*
*Romæ, apud M. Antonium Bladum*, 1547

This author, whose name it is extremely difficult to find in bibliographical works, has lavished above 11,000 lines of Latin Poetry on this subject.

1732 FRANCE, The History of the Revolution in France translated from the French of Rabaut, by James White, 8vo. *half bound, calf*, 1*s* 6*d* .. .. .. *London*, 1793

1733 — Abregé Chronologique de l'Histoire de France, depuis Clovis jusqu'à Louis XIV. les Guerres, les Batailles, &c., 2 vols. 12mo. *calf, gilt*, 6*s* .. .. *Paris*, 1749

1734 — Discours Veritable de la Victoire obtenue par le Roy, en la Bataille donnée pres le Village d'Ivry le 14 de Mars, 1590, plus la desfaite des Ligueurs, tant en Auvergne qu'en Gascoigne, au mesme temps, 8vo. 40 *pages*, 3 *of which are Poetry, sewed*, 5*s*
*Lyon, G. Jullieron*, 1594

1735 — Ecclesiastical History of, describing Councils, Canons, Learned Writers and their Works, the Universities and their Founders, &c. 4to. *calf, neat*, 6*s* .. .. .. 1676

1736 — Histoire du Regne de Louis XIII. par M. Le Vassor, *portraits*, vol. 1; vol. 3, parts 1 and 2; vol. 4, parts 1 and 2; vol. 6, parts 1 and 2; vol. 7, parts 1 and 2, in all 9 vols. 12mo. *old binding*, 6*s* .. .. .. *Amsterdam*, 1700-1705

With the book-plate, and Arms of "Edward Coke, of Norfolk, Esq., 1701." Lord Leicester's Arms on the sides.

1737 FRANCE—the same translated into English, vols. 1 and 2, parts 1 and 2,in 3 vols. 12mo. *old calf, gilt,* 5*s* .. 1701

With the same book-plate and Leicester Arms as on the other.

1738 — Histoire de Charles IX. 1560-63, par le Sieur Varillas, vol. 1 only, 12mo. *bound,* 1*s* 6*d* .. *Cologne,* 1684

1739 — Histoire de Louis XI., 1470-83, par M. Duclos, vol. 2 only, 12mo. *bound,* 1*s* 6*d* .. .. *Amst.,* 1746

1740 — Intrigues Galantes de la Cour de France, depuis le commencement de la Monarchie, 2 vols. 12mo. *neat,* 5*s* 6*d* *Cologne,* 1694

1741 — Journal, contenant tout ce qui s'est fait et passé en la Cour de Parlement de Paris, en 1648.—Procez Verbaux des deux Conferences, entre les Deputez du Roy et les Deputez du Parlement, &c., *Paris,* 1649.—Recueil de toutes les declarations du Roy, rendues pour la Police, 31 Mars, 1649; in 1 vol. thick 4to. *vellum, neat and clean,* 9*s* .. *Paris,* 1648-9

*Ex libris Matthœi Noyrat de Rouville.*

1742 — Lettera Mandata da Roma a Madama la Reina Madre del Re di Francia, nella quale si contiene uno utile ricordo per rassettare le cose presenti del regno (with a translation into French) small 8vo. *parchment, rare,* 7*s* 6*d* .. .. 1563

This letter, dated from Rome, June 2, 1563, is signed Gio. Marco Bruccio. It is on 47 unpaged leaves, and is evidently privately printed. The French translation is paged to 104. Not in *Haym.* This is about the time of the Huguenot war in France, whom Q. Elizabeth aids.

1743 — Articles of Peace between France and Spain, concluded at Aix-la-Chapelle, May 2, 1668, 4to. *sewed,* 3*s* .. 1668

1744 FRANCIS (G.) Catalogue of British Flowering Plants and Ferns, from Hooker's British Flora, on a broadside for easy reference, 1*s*

1745 FRANCO (Nicolo) Il Petrarchista, Dialogo, nel quale si scuoprono nuovi Secreti sopra il Petrarca, *portrait of Petrarch on the title page,* small 8vo. *vellum,* VERY RARE, £1 1*s*
*Venetia, Gabriel Gioli, di Ferrarii,* 1543

Giolito's wood-cut device at the end, and 6 pages of very old writing. Nicolo Franco was a man of real learning, but his writings teem with the grossest abuse; he was the avowed enemy of Aretino, and at last was hanged for maligning Pope Pius the Vth.

1746 FRANK Fairlegh, *with numerous illustrations by George Cruikshank,* 8vo. *half calf, new and very neat,* 10*s* 6*d* *(pub. at* £1 1*s.)* *No date*

1747 FRANKLIN (Benjamin) Essays, with his Life written by himself, *plates,* 18mo. *boards,* 2*s* .. .. 1824

1748 FRANKLIN'S Footsteps; a Sketch of Greenland, along the shores of which his expedition passed, *map,* 12mo. *sewed,* 1*s*

1749 FRANZII (Wolfgangi) Animalium Historia Sacra, thick 12mo. *old calf,* 4*s* .. .. *Amst., Janson,* 1643

1750 FRASER'S (James B.) Journal of a Tour to the Himalaya Mountains, and to the Rivers Jumna and Ganges, *with the large map, frequently missing,* 4to. *good copy, in half calf,* £1 1*s* *(pub. at* £3 3*s)* .. .. .. 1820

The late Mr. J. J. Gurney's copy.

1751 FRAZER'S Magazine, Dec. 1855, and Jan. to June, 1857, 3*s*

1752 FRENCH Poets—Cary (Henry F.) Early French Poets, a Series of Notices and Translations, with a Sketch of the History of French Poetry, by his Son, 12mo. *cloth,* 4*s* *(pub. at 7s)* 1848

1753 FRIENDSHIP—Discourse of Friendship, Englished by Daniel Bret, small 8vo. *old red morocco, gilt, gilt edges,* 6s 1707

Dedicated to William, Earl and Viscount Yarmouth, Baron of Paston, Co. Norfolk, with Fontenelle's approbation.

1754 FRONTONIS (Cornelii) Opera inedita, Latina et Græca, cum Epistulis item ineditis Ant. Pii, M. Aurelii, L. Veri et Appiani nec non aliorum Vet. Fragmentis invenit et comment. A. Maius, 2 vols. 8vo. LARGE PAPER, *sewed, uncut,* 12s *Mediolani,* 1815

1755 FROST'S (John, *of Philadelphia)* History of the United States of North America, 12mo. *cloth,* 2s 6d (*pub at* 5s) 1838

1756 FULBECK'S (William) Abridgement, or rather, a Bridge of Roman Histories to passe the nearest way from Titus Livius to Cornelius Tacitus, the space of sixe score years, 4to. *half bound, neat,* 7s 6d *Mathew Lownes,* 1608

1757 FULLER'S (Thomas, D.D.) Anglorum Speculum; or, the Worthies of England in Church and State, epitomized, small 8vo. *old binding,* 7s 6d .. .. .. 1684

"An abridgment of Fuller's Worthies, with a continuation."—*Lowndes.*

1758 — Historie of the Holy Warre, 4th edition, *engraved title and map by Marshall,* folio, *neat,* 7s 6d *Cambridge, Tho. Buck,* 1651

1759 — History of the Holy War, 1840.—Holy and Profane State, 1840.—Good Thoughts in Bad Times, Good Thoughts in Worse Times, Mixt Contemplations in Better Times, with the Cause and Cure of a Wounded Conscience, 1841.—Memorials of Dr. Tho. Fuller, by A. T. Russell, 1844; together 4 vols. foolscap 8vo. *cloth, quite new,* £1 4s .. *W. Pickering,* 1840-44

VERY SCARCE, not now procurable.

Of the "Good Thoughts," the *Athenæum*, No. 134, says, "we have read this little work with the most unqualified and unbounded delight. We think that the publisher deserves the thanks of every lover of literature for having re-printed these invaluable tracts; we hope to read them again and again."

1760 — History of the Holy War, 12mo. *cloth,* 5s *W. Pickering,* 1840

1761 — Holy State and Profane State, 12mo. *cloth,* 5s *ib.* 1840

1762 — Memorials of the Life and Works of Dr. Thomas Fuller, by the Rev. A. T. Russell, 12mo. *cloth,* 5s .. *ib.* 1844

1763 — An Essay on his Life and Genius, with Selections from his Writings, by Henry Rogers, square 12mo. *cloth,* 2s 6d 1856

1764 FULLER'S (Thomas, M.D.) Introduction to Prudence, a book of Maxims, 12mo. *boards,* 3s (*pub at* 5s) .. 1815

1765 FULLER (W.) Meteors; as well Fiery and Ayrie as Watery and Earthy, 12mo. *curious, old calf,* 6s .. 1670

1766 FULLOM'S (S. W.) Great Highway; a Story of the World's Struggles, 12mo. *cloth,* 2s .. .. 1855

1767 FULVIO (Andrea) Opera delle Antichità della Città di Roma e delli edificii memorabili di quella, tradotta in lingua Toscana per Paolo del Rosso, cittadino Fiorentino, small 8vo. *old vellum,* RARE, 9s *Vinegia, per Michele Tramezino,* 1543

The first Italian translation. Dedicated to Pope Paul III., it is a nice clean copy of a very scarce little book.

1768 FUNNY Dogs with Funny Tales, *humourous plates,* 4to. *cloth, gilt edges,* 5s .. .. .. 1857

1769 GADDII (Jacobi) de Scriptoribus, folio, *old boards, uncut,* SCARCE, 10*s* 6*d* .. *Lugduni, superiorum permissu,* 1649

1770 GAFFAREL (James) Unheard of Curiosities; concerning the Talismanical Sculpture of the Persians; the horoscope of the Patriarkes; and the reading of the Stars, Englished by Edmund Chilmead, 8vo. *fine copy, in old vellum,* SCARCE, 12*s* 1650

"This curious work is styled by Dr. Adam Clarke, 'a feast for an occult philosopher.' The author, a learned rabbinical writer, was librarian to Cardinal Richelieu."—*Lowndes.* At the end is Aristeus's Ancient History of the Septuagint, written in Greeke, 1900 yeares since; of his voyage to Hierusalem; concerning the first translation of the Bible by the 72 Interpreters, Englished by I. Done, 1st edition, 1633.

1771 GALE'S (Theophilus) Court of the Gentiles, a Discourse touching the original of Human Literature, both Philologie and Philosophie, vol. 1 and 2, 4to. *old calf, neat,* £1 1*s* *Oxford,* 1672

"Shews the author to have been well read in, and conversant with the writings of the Fathers, the old Philosophers, and those that have given an account of them and their works; as also to have been a good metaphysician and school divine."—*Anthony à Wood's Athenæ Oxon.*

1772 GALILÆO Systema Cosmicum; in quo IV. dialogis de duobus Maximis Mundi Systematibus, Ptolemaico et Copernicano, ex Ital. Lingua Latine conversum, *frontispiece,* small thick 8vo. of 704 pages, *clean copy, in the original calf,* 10*s* 6*d* *Londini, ap. Tho. Dicas,* 1663

This is the principal work published by Galilæo (originally in 1632,) during his lifetime; for publishing which he was cited before the Inquisition at Rome, imprisoned, and his book burnt.

1773 GALLINI'S (Giovanni Andrea) Treatise on the Art of Dancing, *plate,* 2 vols. 8vo. *calf, scarce,* 9*s* *For the Author,* 1772

1774 GALPINE'S (John) Synoptical Compend of British Botany, arranged after the Linnean System, 12mo. *boards,* 5*s* (*pub. at* 10*s* 6*d*) .. .. .. 1820

1775 GALT'S (John) Bachelor's Wife, a Selection of Curious and Interesting Extracts, 8vo. *calf, neat,* 3*s* 6*d* *Edinburgh,* 1824

1776 — Lawrie Todd, or the Settlers in the Woods, *plate,* 12mo. *cloth,* 2*s* 6*d* .. .. .. *Bentley,* 1840

1777 GAMBIER'S (Edward John) Treatise on Parochial Settlements, 8vo. *law calf,* 2*s* 6*d* .. .. .. 1828

1778 GANNAL'S (J. N.) History of Embalming, and of Preparations in Anatomy, Pathology, and Natural History, Englished, with Notes, by Dr. R. Harlan, 8vo. *boards, scarce,* 6*s* *Philadelphia,* 1840

"*Miss Eliza Kirkbride, from her friend the translator, Oct.* 19. 1840," in writing.

1779 GARDENER'S Chronicle, 1841, 1842, 1843, 1844, 1846, 5 vols. folio, *half bound, neat,* 5*s* per vol. (*cost* 30*s* per volume)

1780 GARDENER'S Monthly Volume; The Pine Apple, by Johnson and Barnes, 2 vols. *cloth,* 4*s.*—The Strawberry, by Johnson and Reid, 12mo. *cloth,* 2*s.*—The Cucumber and Gooseberry, by G. W. Johnson, 12mo. *cloth,* 2*s.*—The Grape Vine, by Johnson and Errington, 2 vols. 12mo. *cloth,* 4*s.*—The Auricula and Asparagus, by the same, *cloth,* 2*s* .. .. 1847

1781 GARDENER and Practical Florist, *plates,* vol. 1, royal 8vo. *cloth,* 3*s* .. .. .. .. 1843

1782 GARIDEL, Histoire des Plants qui naissent aux Environs d'Aix et dans plusieurs autres endroits de la Provence, 100 *finely engraved plates by H. Blanc, and frontispiece*, folio, *half calf, neat*, 14*s* *Aix*, 1715

This finely printed book is preceded by an account of all the Botanical authors who had preceded the author, with lists of their works.

1783 GARNETT'S (Dr. T.) Observations on a Tour through the Highlands, and part of the Western Islands of Scotland, *map and* 52 *aquatinta plates*, 2 vols. 4to. *boards*, 12*s* (*pub. at* £4 4*s*) 1810

Garnett's Scotland, containing a description of the country, manners and customs of the inhabitants, natural curiosities, antiquities, mineralogy, botany, agriculture, fisheries, local history, and biography.

1784 GATAKER (Thomas) Of the Nature and Use of Lots, a Treatise, Historicall and Theologicall, small 4to. *good copy in old calf, very neat, rare*, 10*s* 6*d* .. .. .. 1619

Mr. Beloe, in his "Anecdotes of Literature," has devoted a chapter to this curious little volume.

1785 GAUSSEN; It is Written, or the Scriptures the Word of God, Englished, 12mo. *cloth, neat*, 2*s* .. *No date*

1786 GAVALDA (Francisco) Memoria de Peste de Valencia, 1647-8, see *Ribelles*.

1787 GAY'S (John) Shepherd's Week, in Six Pastorals, *plates by Du Guernier, R. Burleigh*, 1714.—Gay's Trivia; or, the Art of Walking the Streets of London, *Bernard Lintot, no date*.—Mitchell's Jonah, a Poem, *plates by Pine*, 1720.—Loyal Mourner for the best of Princes, a Collection of Poems to the Memory of Queen Anne, published by Mr. Oldisworth, *portrait of the Queen*, 1716.—Gay's Petticoat, an Heroi-Comical Poem, *Burleigh, Amen Corner*, 1716.—Human Happiness, a Poem, by G. J., 1721.—In 1 vol. 8vo. *old calf, neat*, 6*s* .. .. V.Y.

First editions of Gay's Poems. No edition mentioned by Lowndes so early as these.

1788 — Fables, *plates by Vdr. Gucht*, 2 vols. 8vo. *old calf*, 6*s* 1737

1789 — Flowers of English Fable, 67 *engravings on wood*, 24mo. *cloth*, 1*s* 6*d* .. .. .. *No date*

1790 — Fabulæ Selectæ, Latine redditæ, (Latin and English, not in Lowndes) *Londini, Dodsley*, 1777.—Letters from a Tutor to his Pupils, 1780.—An Historical Rhapsody on Mr. Pope, 1782.—Farmer's Essay on the Learning of Shakespeare, 1789.—J. Courtney's, M.P., Poetical Epistles from Paris, Rome, and Naples, in 1792-3, on the Manners, Arts, and Politics of France and Italy, 1794, in 1 vol. 8vo. *calf, very neat*, 8*s* V. Y.

1791 — Beggar's Opera, 5th edit., with the Overture in Score, and the *Musick to each Song*, 8vo. *old calf, neat, scarce*, 6*s* 1742

Has, also, Milton's Comus, now adapted to the stage, 1750, altered from the edit. of 1634.—Œconomy of Love, a Poetical Essay, 1749.—Cibber's Letter to Pope, inquiring into his Motives for Satyrising him, 2nd edition, 1742.

1792 — Poems, *plates after Du Guernier*, 2 vols. 12mo. *calf, neat*, 4*s* 1775

1793 GAZÆ (Theodori) Introductionis Grammaticæ libri IV., Græce, simul cum interpretatione Latina, 4to. *old parchment*, 12*s* *Basileæ, apud V. Curionem*, 1529

Erasmus is said to have made the Latin translation. Scaliger used to say, that "Of all those who revived the belles lettres in Italy, there were not above three that he was inclined to envy—Theodore Gaza, Angelus Politianus, and Picus of Mirandula." In another place he calls Gaza "Doctissimus."

1794 GAZET, Histories de la Sacree Manne et de la Sainte Chandelle. 12mo. *old calf, gilt,* 7*s* 6*d* .. *Arras*, 1672

Has, also, "La Vie de S. Vaast Evesque et Patron d'Arras." "Ce petit ouvrage n'est pas commûn."—*Langlet.*

1795 GAZETTEER'S or Newsman's Interpreter, part 2, 12mo. 1*s* 1724

1796 GAZETTEER, London General Gazetteer, a Geographical Dictionary of the various countries of the known World, *numerous maps*, 3 vols. 8vo. *half vellum, very neat,* 15*s* .. 1825

1797 GEBUILERUS (Hieronymus) Epitome Regii ac Vetustissimi Ortus Sacræ Cæsareæ ac Catholicæ Maiestatis, Serenissimi quoq. Principis & Domini, Dn. FERDINANDI, Ungariæ ac Bohemiæ Regis, omniumq. ARCHIDUCUM AUSTRIÆ, ac HABSBURGENSIUM COMITUM, *illustrated with wood-cut portraits on the letter press throughout,* and 5 large Genealogical folded charts, containining 49 portraits of all the Kings of France, from Dagobert an. 312, to Francis in 1525, 4to. *original binding, much wormed,* £1 11*s* 6*d*
*Haganoæ, ex officina Johannis Secerii,* MDXXX.

It is curious to observe how industriously the worm has perforated this most rare volume, but, although it has pierced it through and through, it is quite readable. I have bestowed much time in endeavouring to find some account of this author, but with no success. The account commences with Noah and ends with the reigning Emperor, Ferdinand, to whom the book is dedicated. There is much Latin Poetry on the Charts at the end of the volume.

1798 GEDDES'S (Dr. Alex.) General Answer to the Queries about his New Translation of the Bible, 4to. *sewed,* 1*s* 6*d*
*For the Author,* 1790

1799 — Letter to John Douglass, Bishop of Centuriæ, 4to. *sewed,* 1*s* 6*d*
*For the Author,* 1794

1800 — Memoirs of his Life and Writings by John Mason Good, *portrait,* 8vo. *half cloth,* 5*s* .. .. .. 1803

"In this work some valuable criticism on Geddes's writings occurs, as well as other interesting information to the biblical student."—*Lowndes.*

1801 GEDDES'S (Dr. Michael) Miscellaneous Tracts, chiefly against Popery, 4 vols. 8vo. *old calf, very neat,* 18*s* .. 1730

The 4th volume is entitled "Several Tracts against Popery, together with the Life of Don Alvaro de Luna."

1802 GEER (Charles de) Memoires pour servir a l'Histoire des Insectes, 43 *plates,* vol. 2, parts 1 and 2, 4to *half bound and wholly uncut,* 18*s* .. .. .. *Stockholm,* 1771

This is the 2nd volume, complete, with all the plates belonging to it, of this exceedingly rare work.

1803 GELDART'S (Mrs. Thomas) Truth is Everything, 18mo. *cloth, new,* 1*s* 6*d* .. .. .. 1858

1804 GELLI (Giovan Batista, *Accademico Fiorentino)* i Cappricci del Bottaio, small 8vo. *old calf, neat,* 12*s*
*Senza Luogo e Stampatore,* 1619

At the end, is "Tavola delle Sentenze, Proverbi e Detti piu belli" to be found in these X. Ragionamenti of Bottaio; a book sanctioned by the Della Cruscan Academy.

1805 GENLIS (Mad. de) Discours Moraux, particulièrement sur l'Education, 12mo. *half calf, neat,* 2*s* .. *Paris,* 1802

1806 — Traveller's Companion, Conversations in English, German, French, Italian, Spanish, and Portuguese, square 18mo. *half russia, neat,* 2*s* 6*d* .. .. *Leipsig,* 1814

1807 GENLIS—Tales of the Castle, or, Stories of Instruction and Delight, translated by Holcroft, *plates*, 2 vols. 24mo. *boards*, 5*s* 1816

1808 GENTLEMAN'S Magazine, 2 vols. 8vo. *half calf*, 7*s*, 1818—2 vols. *half calf*, 7*s*, 1821—2 vols. *half calf*, 7*s*, 1827—2 vols. *half calf*, 7*s*, 1828—2 vols. *half calf*, 7*s*, 1829—then for 1829 in numbers, 6*s*—1830, in numbers, 6*s*—1831, in numbers, (May missing,) 5*s*

1809 — New Series, for 9 years, vol. 1 to 18, in numbers, £3 1834-42

1810 — Jan. and May, 1836, 1*s*—March, 1840, 6*d*—Nov. 1841, 6*d*—Jan. to Oct. 1842, 5*s*—Jan. to June, 1845, being vol. 23 of N. S., complete, 5*s*—July, 1845, 6*d*—Nov. 1846, 6*d*—Jan., Sept., Oct., 1847, 1*s* 6*d*—Jan. and Dec. 1851, 1*s*—Feb. and Mar. 1852, 1*s*—Jan. to Nov. 1853, 5*s*—July, 1853, 6*d*—Dec. 1857, 1*s*

1811 — List of Plates, Maps, &c., contained in the Gent's Mag. from 1731 to 1813 inclusive, 8vo. *half calf, neat, scarce*, 5*s* *Westminster*, 1814

1812 GEOGRAPHY—Epitome of Geographical Knowledge, Ancient and Modern, 12mo. *cloth*, 3*s* .. *Dublin*, 1849

For the use of Teachers and advanced classes of National Schools in Ireland.

1813 GEOMETRY, Plain, Solid, and Spherical, (Library of Useful Knowledge,) *half calf*, 1*s* 6*d* .. *London*, 1830

1814 GEORGE II.—Fog's Weekly Journal, Select Letters taken from, 2 *plates by Vdr. Gucht*, 2 vols. 12mo. *old calf*, 4*s* .. 1732

Written in opposition to the Government, commencing September, 1728, ending, 1731.

1815 — Most Important Transactions of the 6th Session of the First Parliament of King George the II. on the Excise and Tobacco Bills, the National Debt, &c. 4to. *sewed*, 3*s* .. 1733

1816 GEO. III.—Politics of the Georgium Sidus; Advice how to become Great Senators and Statesmen, by a late M.P., *coloured plates*, 12mo. *half calf, neat*, 2*s* .. .. 1807

1817 GEO. IV.—The Rising Sun, a Serio-Comic Satiric Romance, by Cervantes Hogg, *coloured plates*, 2 vols. in 1, 12mo. *hf. cf., neat*, 4*s* .. .. .. .. 1807

1818 GERALDINE; or, Modes of Faith and Practice, by a Lady, 3 vols 12mo. *boards*, 3*s* 6*d* (*pub. at* £1 1*s*) .. 1821

1819 GERMANY and Hungary.—Case of the Persecuted Protestants, presented at Vienna, by Count Oxensteirn, folio, 4 leaves, *sewed*, 6*s* .. .. .. .. 1675

1820 GERTRUDE of Wyoming, Compositions from Campbell's Poem, by G. E. Hicks, 13 *spirited outline plates*, oblong 4to. *half morocco*, 12*s* .. .. .. *Art Union*, 1846

1821 GÉRUZET, François-Hollandais-Nederduitsch-Fransch, 2 thick vols. square 12mo. *half bound, neat*, 6*s* *Amsterdam*, 1838

1822 GESSNER'S (Solomon) Death of Abel, from the German, 12mo. *calf, neat*, 2*s* .. .. .. 1762

1823 — New Idylles, Englished by Dr. W. Hooper, with a Letter to M. Fuslin on Landscape Painting, and the Two Friends of Bourbon, a Moral Tale, by M. Diderot, *plates*, 4to. *old calf, gilt edges*, 5*s* 1776

1824 GIANNONE, Istoria Civile del Regno de Napoli, et Opere Postume, 7 vols. 4to., *Italian vellum*, £2 2*s* .. *Napoli*, 1770

From the Wolterton Library.

1825 GIANNOTTI (Donato) de la Republica de Vinitiani. (*Senz' anno luogo e Stampatore.*)—Gasparo Contarino la republica e i Magistrati di Vinegia, nuovamenti fatti volgari, small 8vo. *old vellum*, 5*s* .. .. *Stampata in Vinegia*, 1545

Sir Christopher Hatton's copy, with C. H. impressed on the sides, unfortunately stained.

1826 GIBBON'S (Edward) History of the Decline and Fall of the Roman Empire, with variorum notes, 6 vols. post 8vo. *cloth*, £1 1*s* *H. G. Bohn*, 1853

1827 — the same abridged, 2 vols. 8vo. *calf, neat, scarce*, 8*s* 1789

An excellent abridgment, by the Rev. Charles Hereford of Bristol.

1828 — Miscellaneous Works, with Memoirs of his Life and Writings by himself and Lord Sheffield, *portrait*, 2 vols. 4to. *half russia*, 10*s* .. .. .. .. 1796

With the book-plates of Thomas Fowell Buxton and J. J. Gurney.

1829 — Life, with Selections from his Correspondence and Illustrations by H. H. Milman, *fine portrait*, 8vo. *cloth*, 7*s* 6*d* *Murray*, 1839

1830 GIBBON (John) Introductio ad Latinam Blasoniam; an Essay to a more correct Blason in Latine than formerly hath been used, *cuts of arms*, 8vo. *calf, very neat*, SCARCE, 9*s* *For the Author*, 1682

"A curious piece of heraldic pedantry."—*Lowndes*.
Many of the arms are emblazoned. This book is advertised at the bottom of the curious article, No. 1509.

1831 GIBSON'S (Rev. James, *of Worlington, Suffolk*) Sermons, thick 8vo. *cloth*, 5*s* 6*d* (*pub. at* 10*s* 6*d*) .. .. 1851

1832 GIFFORD'S (John) English Lawyer, a Summary of the Constitution of England, its Laws and Statutes, *portrait*, thick 8vo. *boards*, 3*s* 6*d* .. .. .. .. 1823

1833 GILBERT (Baron) History and Practice of the High Court of Chancery, 8vo. *old calf*, last edition, *scarce*, 5*s* 1758

Autograph of "W. Ward, Middle Temple."

1834 GILDON'S (C.) Deist's Manual; a rational Enquiry into the Christian Religion, 8vo. *old calf*, 2*s* 6*d* .. 1705

Considerations on Hobbs, Spinosa, and others, with a letter from Mr. Leslie.

1835 GILLIES (John) Historical Collections relating to remarkable periods of the success of the Gospel in England, Scotland, Germany, America, &c., vol. 1 only, 8vo. *original binding*, *scarce*, 8*s* .. .. *Glasgow, Foulis*, 1754

1836 GILLIES (Dr. John) History of Ancient Greece, including its Literature, Philosophy, and the Fine Arts, *portrait and map*, 4 vols. 8vo. *calf, very neat*, 10*s* 6*d* .. 1809

1837 GILPIN'S (William) Essay on Prints, with remarks on Picturesque Beauty, &c., 2nd Edition, 12mo. *old calf, gilt*, 3*s* 6*d* 1768

1838 — Essay on Prints, 3rd Edition, 12mo. *calf, neat*, 4*s* 1781

1839 — Observations on the Coasts of Hampshire, Sussex, and Kent, in 1774, relative chiefly to Picturesque Beauty, *plates in aquatint*, 8vo. *boards*, 4*s* .. .. .. 1804

1840 — Dialogues on Various Subjects, 8vo. *boards*, 3*s* 1807

1841 GIRDLESTONE'S (Charles) Commentary on the Old Test., Genesis to Esther, 4 parts, 8vo. (being 2 vols. of 4) *cloth*, 18*s* (*pub. at* 36*s*) .. .. .. 1836

1842 — Commentary on the New Testament, complete, 4 parts, 8vo. 18*s* (*pub. at* 36*s*) .. .. .. 1835

One of the best practical Commentaries extant.—See *Horne's Introduction.*

1843 GISBORNE'S (Tho.) Enquiry into the Duties of the Female Sex, 12mo. *half bound*, 1*s* 6*d* .. .. *Dublin*, 1798

1844 GIUSTINIANO (Bernardo) Historie Chronologiche della vera origine di tutti gl' ordini Equestri, e Religioni Cavalleresche, *numerous wood-cuts of arms*, 4to. *curious and rare, old foreign binding*, 12*s* .. .. *Venetia*, 1672

From Lord Orford's collection.

1845 GLADSTONE'S (Rt. Hon. W. E.) Church Principles considered in their Results, thick 8vo. *cloth*, 5*s* 6*d* (*pub. at* 12*s*) 1840

1846 GLAS'S (George) History of the Discovery and Conquest of the Canary Islands, *maps, and charts*, 4to. *calf, very neat*, 9*s* 1764

Includes Bethencourt's and Herrera's Discoveries and Adventures.

1847 GLASGOW, Picture of, with a Sketch of a Tour to Lochs Lomond and Ketturin, Inverary, and the Falls of Clyde, *plates*, 12mo. *half calf, neat*, 3*s* .. .. *Glasgow*, 1812

1848 GLASS.—Plate-Glass-Book, its value, &c., with the Complete Appraiser, for Valuing Household Furniture, &c. 8vo. *bound*, 2*s* 6*d* 1760

1849 GLASSII (Salomonis) Philologia Sacra, his temporibus accommodata a D. I. O. Dathe, 2 vols. 8vo. *half calf*, 10*s* *Lipsiæ*, 1776

"An inestimable and immortal work, than which none can be more useful for the interpretation of Scripture."—*Mosheim's Eccles. Hist.*

1850 GLEIG'S (Rev. G. R.) History of the British Empire in India, *portraits and plates*, vols. 1, 3, and 4, 18mo. *cloth, boards*, 7*s* 6*d* (*pub. at* 15*s*) .. .. *Fam. Lib.*, 1830

1851 — British Military Commanders, 3 vols. 12mo. *cloth*, 7*s* 6*d* *Lardner's Cyclopædia*, 1836

1852 GLOSSARY of Terms used in Grecian, Roman, Italian, and Gothic Architecture, 3 vols. 8vo. *whereof* 2 *are* 264 *well-engraved plates, cloth*, £1 14*s* (*pub. at* £2 8*s*) *Oxford, J. H. Parker*, 1850

5th and best edition, illustrated with 1700 wood-cuts. The most comprehensive work on this subject.

1853 GLOUCESTERSHIRE, Moreau's (Simeon) Tour to Cheltenham Spa, or, Gloucestershire Displayed, 12mo. *sewed*, 2*s* *Bath*, 1788

1854 — Collectanea Glocestriensia; a Catalogue of Books, Tracts, Prints, Coins, &c., relating to the County of Gloucester, in the possession of John Delafield Phelps, Esq., royal 8vo. *cloth*, 6*s* 1842

"Stephen Clissold, Esq., with Mr. Phelps's compts."

1855 GLOVER'S (Richard) Leonidas, a Poem, with Life, *plates by Bartolozzi*, 2 vols. post 8vo. *calf, neat*, 6*s* 1804

1856 GODEAU (Bp. of Grasse) Elevations to Jesus Christ, being Christian Meditations on St. Paul's Epist. to the Hebrews, Englished by Joshua Smith, 12mo. *old calf, neat*, 2*s* 6*d* 1715

1857 GODEFROY (Theodore) le Ceremonial de France; ou Description des Ceremonies, Rangs, et Seances Observées aux Couronnemens, Entrées et Enterremans des Roys et Roynes de France, et autres Actes et Assemblées solemneles, thick 4to. of 718 pages, *old calf, gilt,* 10*s* 6*d* .. .. *Paris,* 1619

These extend from 1467 to 1594, the crowning of Henry the Great. Lord Leicester's arms on the sides.

1858 GODFRIDUS—The Knowledge of Things Unknown, the effects of the Planets, with the Strange Events that befal Men, Women, and Children born under them, *very curious old wood cuts,* 12mo. *original sheep,* RARE, 12*s*
*Printed by J. Wilde, for H. Rhodes, in Fleet Street,* 1707

This is an edition not noted by Lowndes, or, after him, by Mr. Bohn. A 2nd part is called, "The Husbandman's Practice; or, Prognostication for Ever, as teacheth Albert, Alkind, and Ptolemy, with the Shepherd's Prognostication for the weather, and Pythagoras his Wheel of Fortune."

1859 GODMOND'S (Christ.) Memoir of Therrouanne, the ancient capital of the Morini, in Gaul, from its Invasion by Jul. Cæsar, with a Discourse of the Portus Itius of Cæsar, 2 *plates,* 12mo. *cloth,* 3*s* 1836

1860 GODWINUS de Præsulibus Angliæ Commentarius, curâ G. Richardson, *fine portrait, by Vertue,* folio, LARGE PAPER, *half russia, a very handsome and beautiful volume,* £1 18*s*
*Cantabrigiæ,* 1743

A fit companion to these Lives of the Bishops is Archbishop Parker's Lives of the Archbishops of Canterbury.—*See Parker.*

1861 GODWYN'S (Dr. Thomas) Hebrew and Roman Antiquities, with Rous's Attic Antiquities, small thick 4to. *good sound copy, in old calf, neat,* 5*s* 6*d* .. .. .. 1647

1862 — another edition, in 1 thick volume, small 4to. *old calf, neat,* 7*s* 6*d*
*Oxford,* 1658

Formerly one of our most popular school books.

1863 GODWIN'S (William) Lives of the Necromancers, 8vo. *half cloth,* 8*s* (*pub. at* 14*s*) .. .. .. 1834

1864 GOLDONI (Carlo, *Avvocato Veneto)* Commedie Scelte, 2 vols. of 3, 12mo. *bound,* 2*s* .. .. *Londra,* 1811

1865 GOLDSMITH'S (Dr. Oliver) Miscellaneous Works, with his Life, *portrait,* 4 vols. 8vo. *calf, neat,* 12*s* .. 1801

1866 — Works, Poetry, Prose, Dramas, Fictions, Essays, and Letters, *fine portrait and plates,* royal 8vo. *cloth,* 7*s* 6*d* 1858

A very cheap and complete edition of Dr. Goldsmith's works.

1867 — Miscellaneous Works, vols. 2, 3, 5, 6, 18mo. *boards,* 4*s*
*S. Richards,* 1823

1868 — Citizen of the World, 2 vols. 12mo. *old calf,* 4*s* 1762

These letters first appeared in a newspaper called the Ledger, this is the first separately published edition.

1869 — Essays, 12mo. *old calf, gilt,* 2*s* 6*d* .. 1766

1870 — Essays and Poems, 12mo. *calf,* 2*s* 6*d* .. 1782

1871 — Vicar of Wakefield, with Memoir of Goldsmith, 200 *plates,* 8vo. *cloth, gilt edges,* 3*s* 6*d* (*pub. at* 6*s*) .. 1841

1872 — Poetical Works, with Life, by Blanchard, *numerous engravings,* crown 8vo. *cloth, elegant, gilt edges,* 4*s* 6*d* 1859

1873 GOLDSMITH'S History of Rome to the destruction of the Western Empire, 2 vols. 8vo. *boards*, 6*s* 6*d* (*pub. at* 14*s*) 1821

1874 — History of Greece from the Earliest State to the Death of Alexander the Great, 2 vols. 8vo. *calf, very neat*, 7*s* 1817

1875 — Hist. of Greece, 12mo. *bound, neat*, 2*s* (see *Pinnock*) 1837

1876 — History of England, with continuation to the Death of George III., by Dr. Coote, 4 vols. 8vo. *boards*, 12*s* 1823

"Whatever he composed, he did it better than any other man could, and whether we regard him as a poet, as a comic writer, or as an historian, he was one of the first writers of his time, and will ever stand in the former class."—*Dr. Johnson.*

1877 GONZAGA—Lettere della molto Illustre Sig. la Sra donna Lucretia Gonzaga da Gazuolo, small 8vo. *old limp vellum, curious*, 12*s* *In. Vinegia, appresso Gualtero Scotto*, 1552

Sir Christopher Hatton's copy. "Sono di Ortensio Landi."—*Haym.*

1878 GOODE'S (William) Divine Rule of Faith and Practice, 3 vols. 8vo. *cloth*, 21*s* (*pub. at* 36*s*) .. .. 1853

Written against the "Authors of the Tracts for the Times and the Romanists."

1879 GOODISSON'S (Wm.) Historical Essay upon the Islands of Corfu, Leucadia, Cephalonia, Ithaca, and Zante, *maps and plates of antiquities*, 8vo. *boards*, 5*s* (*pub. at* 12*s*) .. 1822

1880 GOODMAN'S (Dr. J.) Penitent Pardoned, a Discourse of the Nature of Sin, and the efficacy of Repentance, *all the plates*, 4to. *good copy, in old calf*, 6*s* .. .. 1683

A copy of this book, with all the plates, some of which are usually missing, produced 27*s* at Mr. Williams's sale.

1881 GOODWIN'S (John) Redemption Redeemed, wherein the most glorious work of the Redemption of the World by Jesus Christ is Vindicated, with a Discussion of Election and Reprobation, small folio, *newly and neatly half bound*, SCARCE, 12*s* 1651

For another book in connection with this, see Dr. Twisse in this catalogue.

1882 GORE (T.) Nomenclator Geographicus, Latino-Anglicus et Anglico-Latinus, Alphabeticè digestus, complectens plerorumque omnium M. Brit. et Hiberniæ Regionum nomina et appellationes, small 8vo. *nice clean copy, old calf*, 6*s* .. *Oxoniæ*, 1667

A very useful work for finding the old names of Cities, Towns, Rivers, &c. in G. Britain and Ireland.

1883 GORGUOS (A.) Cours d'Arabe Vulgaire, Grammaire, Thèmes, Vocabulaire et Traduction des Themes en Arabe, 12mo, *sewed*, 4*s* 6*d* .. .. .. *Paris*, 1849

Ouvrage autorisé par le Conseil de l' Université.

1884 GOTTOFREDI (Iac.) Orationes Politicæ tres, 4to. *sewed*, 5*s* 1634

I. Ulpianus; seu, de majestate Principis Romani legibus soluta.—II. Julianus; seu de arcanis Juliani Imp. artibus, ad profligandam Relig. Christ.—III. Archaica; seu, de causis interitus Reipublicæ Achæorum. *No place or printer's name*, but has the *Aldine Anchor* on the title-page.

1885 GOTTSCHED (Professeur) Grammaire Allemande, avec Dialogues et Germanismes et Proverbes, small 8vo. *boards*, 3*s* *Brienne en Swisse*, 1782

1886 GOULART (Simon) Thresor des Histoires admirables et memorables de nostre temps, vols. 3 and 4 only, 8vo. *old vellum*, 10*s* *Cologny*, 1614

Contains the stories of "Measure for Measure," and the Induction to the "Taming of the Shrew," also, many of the Plots of the Early English Dramatists.

1887 GOVEANI (Antonii, *Jureconsulti)* Opera Varia, see *Balduinus.*

1888 GOVERNMENT of the Tongue, by the author of the Whole Duty of Man, 8vo. LARGE PAPER, *old calf, gilt leaves,* 5s *Oxford,* 1675

A nice specimen of old panelled calf binding.

1889 GOVETT (Rev. R., *Curate of St. Stephen's, Norwich)* Isaiah Unfulfilled, an Exposition of the Prophet, with New Version and Critical Notes, 8vo. *cloth,* 6s (*pub. at* 10s 6*d*) 1841

1890 GOZLISKI'S (Lawrence G.) Accomplished Senator, by Mr. Oldisworth, 4to. *fine copy, in panelled calf, gilt,* 9s *For the author,* 1733

Done into English from the Venice edition of 1568. Dedicated amongst others to "the Rt. Hon. and Noble Sir Robert Walpole." The author was Senator and Chancellor of Poland and Bishop of Pozen.

1891 GRABE (J. E.) Spicilegium S. S. Patrum et Hereticorum, sec. I. et II., Gr. et Lat., 2 vols. 8vo. *calf, very neat,* 10s *Oxoniæ,* 1714

"Excellent, and to be commended for its use."—*Dr. Routh, Reliquiæ Sacræ.*

1892 GRACIEN (Baltazar) Le Heros, traduit de l'Espagnol, avec des remarques de J. de Courbeville, small 8vo. *calf, neat,* 3s *Paris,* 1725

1893 GRAGLIA'S (C.) Italian-English and English-Italian Dictionary and Grammar, 2 vols. 12mo. *Italian vellum,* 6s 6*d* *Genoa,* 1815

This edition is increased with a Marine Vocabulary by J. Graberg, of Hemso. Autograph of *Charles Penrice.*

1894 — Italian and English Dictionary, 16mo. *bound,* 3s (*pub. at* 6s) 1822

1895 — Italian and English Dictionary, 16mo. *neat,* 3s 6*d* 1837

1896 GRAHAM'S (Dr. T.) Modern Domestic Medicine, thick 8vo. *boards,* 5s 6*d* (*pub. at* 15s) .. .. 1826

1897 GRAHAM, (Miss Mary Jane, of *Stoke Fleming, Devon*) Memoirs of, by the Rev. Charles Bridges, 12mo. *boards,* 3s (*pub. at* 7s) 1834

1898 GRAMMONT'S (Count) Memoirs of the Court of Charles the Second, with additions by Sir Walter Scott, and the Boscobel Tracts, *portrait of Nell Gwynn,* post 8vo. *cloth,* 3s .. 1846

"Perhaps the most witty and amusing of literary productions."—*Walpoliana.*

1899 GRAMMONT'S Memoirs, in French. See *Hamilton.*

1900 GRAMOUNDI (Gabr. Barth.) Historia Prostratæ a Ludovico XIII. sectariorum in Gallia Rebellionis, *engraved title and portrait of the King on horseback,* 4to. *rough calf,* 10s 6*d* *Tolosæ,* 1623

Gramont was President of the Parliament of Toulouse. This history "contains some curious and interesting facts."—See *Chalmers.* Some former possessor of this copy has greatly interpolated various portions of it in writing.

1901 GRANADA (Ludovico de) Concionum de Tempore, tom. 2, 8vo. *old calf, scarce,* 5s .. *Antwerpiæ, Plantin,* 1592

1902 GRANBY, a Novel, 3 vols. post 8vo. *half calf, very neat,* 7s 6*d* (*pub. at* £1 11s 6*d*) .. .. .. 1826

1903 GRANGER'S (Rev. James) Biographical History of England, from Egbert to the Revolution, 3rd edition, 4 vols. 8vo. *very fine tall copy in old russia, marbled leaves,* £1 11s 6*d* .. 1779

This is a catalogue of engraved British portraits, "interspersed with variety of anecdotes, and memoirs of a great number of persons, not to be found in any other biographical work." "A delightful and instructive book. It is surprising what he has done. His style is always clear, pointed, and lively."—*Dr. Dibdin.*

1904 — another edition, 6 vols. 8vo. *boards,* £1 1s .. 1824

For a continuation of this work, see *Noble.*

1905 GRANGER'S (Rev. James) Letters between him and some of the most eminent Literary Men of his Time, edited by J. P. Malcolm, *frontispiece*, 8vo. *boards*, 5*s* .. 1805

A copious history and illustration of his "Biographical Hist. of England."

1906 Grant Herbier, en Francoys, contenant les qualitez, vertus et proprietes des Herbes, extraict de Avicenne, Rasis, Ypocras, etc., *with numerous cuts in wood*, small 4to. *old calf, neat*, £2 2*s* *Paris, Denis Janot*, 1548

A very curious little book, with a great number of figures of plants rudely cut in wood. See *Dodonæus* and *Lyte* for similar books.

1907 GRANVILLE'S (Dr. A. B.) Journal of Travels to and from St. Petersburg, through Flanders, Germany, and France, *maps and plates*, 2 vols. 8vo. *cloth*, 12*s* (*pub. at* £2 5*s*) .. 1828

"Contains the most copious and detailed description of the gigantic edifices of this extraordinary city, which has hitherto been laid before the public."—*Quarterly Review.*

1908 GRATII (Orthuini) Fasciculus Rerum expetendarum ac fugiendarum de Concilio Basiliensi, &c. folio, *old stamped binding, rare*, 15*s* *Colonniæ*, 1535

"Libri præstantissimi et rari, editio originalis perrara."—*Bibl. Solgr.* and *Clement, Bibl. Curieuse*, v. 8, p. 238-241. Contains a variety of Tracts, amongst others Wilhelmus Widefordus adversus Johannem Wiclephum Anglum, 1396.—Articuli J. Wiclephi Angli in Concilio Constant. damnati.—Laurentii Vallæ in Donation. Constantini, declamatio.—Ænæi Sylvii de Gestis Basilien. Concilii liber, etc.

1909 GRAVES'S (George) Naturalist's Pocket Book; with Directions for Collecting and Preserving Insects, &c., 8vo. *boards*, 3*s* 1817

1910 GRAVES'S (John) History of Cleveland, in the North Riding of York, its Soil, Produce, and Natural Curiosities, with the Origin and Genealogy of the principal Families, *plates*, 4to. *boards, uncut*, 8*s* 6*d* .. .. .. *Carlisle*, 1808

With the folded pedigree of the family of Chaloner of Guisbrough.

1911 GRAY'S (Bp. Robert) Discourses on the Evidence, Influence, and Doctrines of Christianity, 8vo. *half calf, neat*, 4*s* 6*d* 1793

1912 — Connection between the Sacred Writings and the Literature of Jewish and Heathen Authors, 2 vols. 8vo. *boards*, BEST EDITION, 12*s* (*pub. at* £1 4*s*) .. .. .. 1819

"Indispensably necessary to the biblical student who cannot command access to *all* the classical authors."—*Horne.*

1913 — Key to the Old Testament and Apocrypha, 8vo. *boards*, 6*s* 6*d* (*pub. at* 14*s*) .. .. .. 1822

"A most valuable work, containing a great mass of information from authorities not easily accessible."—*Horne's Biblical Bibliography.*

1914 GRAY'S (Thomas) Poems and Letters, with Memoirs of his Life and Writings by W. Mason, *portrait*, 4 vols. crown 8vo. *calf, neat*, 8*s* .. .. .. *York*, 1778

"A favourite edition."—*Lowndes.* It contains his most interesting letters.

1915 — Works, with Memoirs of his Life and Writings, by Mason, *portrait*, 2 vols. 8vo. *calf, neat*, 7*s* .. 1807

1916 — another copy, *portrait*, 2 vols. 8vo. *boards*, 6*s* 6*d* 1807

Autograph of "*Rachel Gurney, Earlham, Oct.* 1814."

1917 — another edition, *portrait*, 18mo. *boards*, 2*s* 6*d* (*pub. at* 5*s*) 1821

1918 GRAY'S Works, containing his Poems and Correspondence, with Memoirs of his Life and Writings, *portrait*, 2 vols. crown 8vo. *boards, scarce*, 12*s* .. *Harding*, 1835

This is one of the prettiest editions of Gray ever published.

1919 — Bard, with Illustrations by the Hon. Mrs. J. Talbot, 8vo. *cloth*, 3*s* (*pub. at* 7*s*) .. .. *Van Voorst*, 1837

1920 — Observations on the Writings and Character of Mr. Gray, by Thomas James Mathias, small 8vo. *half calf, neat*, 3*s* 1815

Joseph John Gurney "from the author."

1921 — another copy, 8vo. *boards*, LARGE PAPER, 5*s* 1815

"From the author."—*Autograph.*

1922 GRAY'S (William) Historical Sketch of the Origin of English Prose Literature, till the reign of James I. 8vo. *boards*, 3*s* *Oxford, Talboys*, 1835

1923 GREAT Exhibition of London, Official Catalogue of the Great Exhibition of the Industry of all Nations, 4to. 320 pages, *sewed*, 2*s* .. .. .. 1851

1924 [GREEN (Thomas, *of Ipswich*,)] Extracts from the Diary of a Lover of Literature, 4to. *half calf, neat, scarce*, 10*s* *Ipswich*, 1810

Mr. W. Repton's copy. Clever remarks on a great variety of books. Published anonymously.

1925 — Memoir of him, with a Critique on his Writings, and an account of his Family and Connections, *fine portrait, by Worthington, on India Paper*, 4to. *boards*, 15*s* .. *Ipswich*, 1825

LARGE PAPER, VERY SCARCE, not in *Lowndes*. "To Robert Maundrell, Esq., from the guardians and executors under the will of the late Thomas Green, Esq."

1926 GREEN (Jonathan, M.D.) Practical Compendium of Diseases of the Skin, 8vo. *coloured plates*, 5*s* (*pub. at* 12*s* 6*d*) 1837

1927 GREGORY'S (G.) History of the Christian Church from the earliest periods, 2 vols. 12mo. *calf, neat*, 6*s* 1790

1928 GREGORY'S (Dr. John) Comparative View of the State and Faculties of Man, with those of the Animal World, 12mo. *old calf, gilt*, 2*s* 6*d* .. .. .. 1767

1929 GREGORY (Olinthus, LL.D.) Letters to a Friend, on the Evidences, Doctrines, and Duties of the Christian Religion, 2 vols. small 8vo. *boards*, 2*s* 6*d* .. .. 1822

1930 GRENADA—Narrative of the Insurrection and Rebellion in the Island of Grenada, by Henry Thornhill, Esq., with a Discourse on the Excellence of the British Constitution; 4to. *sewed*, £1 1*s* *Barbadoes, printed in the Bay between the two Bridges*, 1798

Extremely rare, the only production that I can find of the Barbados press; and Barbados not mentioned by Dr. Cotton at all. See the author's remarks at the end of the preface, in which he recounts the extreme difficulty he had in getting it printed; first he tried Grenada, then Barbados, then Bridgetown, where the printer "was pleased to undertake it."

1931 GRESHAM College, Dr. Grew's Catalogue and Description of the rarities in, *portrait and plates*, folio, *old calf*, 9*s* 1681

1932 GRESHAM (Sir Thomas) His Life and Times, including notices of many of his Contemporaries, by J. W. Burgon, *fine portrait*, 2 vols. 8vo. *boards*, 8*s* (*pub. at* £2 2*s*) .. 1839

Sir Thomas Gresham of a Norfolk family living at Holt, temp. Henry VIII.

1933 GRESHAM'S Life, by Knight, *portrait*, 18mo. *stiff cover*, 1*s* 1847

1934 GRESWELL'S (E.) View of the Early Parisian Greek Press; including the Lives of the Stephani, and other contemporary Greek Printers of Paris, 2 vols. 8vo. *cloth*, 10*s* 6*d* *Oxford*, 1833

1935 GREW'S (Dr. Nehemiah) Cosmologia Sacra; a Discourse on the Universe, demonstrating the Truth and Excellency of the Bible, *portrait*, folio, *old calf*, 4*s* .. .. 1701

1936 GREY (Lady Jane) and her Times, by George Howard, *portrait*, crown 8vo. *boards*, 4*s* 6*d* (*pub. at* 12*s*) .. 1822

1937 [GREY'S (Dr. Zach.)] Spirit of Infidelity Detected, an Answer to a Scandalous Pamphlet, by Barbeyrac, 8vo. *half calf*, 3*s* 1723

1938 GRIFFIN'S Book of Trades, square 18mo. *numerous engravings*, *cloth*, 4*s* .. .. .. 1850

1939 GRILLO (Luigi) Favole, 18mo. *neat*, 2*s* *Londra*, 1796

1940 GRIMM'S German Fairy Tales and Popular Stories, as told by Gammer Grethel, translated by Edgar Taylor, *plates by Cruikshank*, 12mo. *cloth*, *gilt*, 4*s* 6*d* *H. G. Bohn*, 1851

1941 GROOME'S (John) Dignity and Honour of the Clergy, showing how useful and serviceable they have been, 8vo. *old calf*, *neat*, *scarce*, 5*s* .. .. .. 1710

Biographies of many hundreds of learned men, with recommendation by Dr. Hickes.

1942 GROSIER'S (Abbe) General Description of China, *map and plates*, 2 vols. 8vo. *half calf*, *neat*, 6*s* 6*d* .. 1788

1943 GROTIUS (Hugonis) Annotationes in libros Evangeliorum, thick folio, *old calf*, 10*s* .. *Amst.*, *Blæu*, 1641

Mr. Conybeare in his Bampton Lectures, calls Grotius, "the illustrious and accomplished." At the end of this volume is some *old parchment*, dated, 1604, commencing "Andreæ dei gratia et auctoritate aplica: Patriarcha et Archiepiscopus Bituricensis," &c. with an *Autograph*.

1944 — de jure Belli ac Pacis, et Dissertatione de Mari Libero, cum notis Variorum et J. Barbeyrac, *portrait*, 2 vols. 8vo. *calf*, *neat*, 9*s* *Amst.*, 1735

"Grotius (De Groot) was a great lawyer, a great critic, a great divine, and a good man. His numerous writings have immortalized him, especially his *Truth of the Christian Religion* and his Treatise on *War and Peace*."—*Dr. Adam Clarke.*

1945 — de veritate Religionis Christianæ, 12mo. *calf*, *neat*, 3*s* 6*d* *Amst.*, *Elzevir*, 1680

1946 — idem, cum notulis Jo. Clerici, 12mo. *old calf*, *neat*, 2*s* 6*d* *Hagæ-Comitis*, 1734

1947 — idem, cum notulis Jo. Clerici, 12mo. *calf*, *neat*, 3*s* *Glasguæ*, *Urie*, 1745

1948 — alia editio, 12mo. *bound*, 1*s* 6*d* .. *Oxonii*, 1807

1949 — La Verité de la Religion Chrestienne, traduit du Latin, small thick 8vo. *old vellum*, 573 pages, *curious large script type*, 10*s* 6*d* *Paris*, *no date*

As this book is dedicated to M. Bignon, who was Councillor of State in 1640, we may assign it to its *probable* date. It is said to be printed in "*Nouveaux caracteres inventez par Pierre Moreau.*" It has a singular appearance, and is not noticed by *Brunet*.

1950 — On the Truth of the Christian Religion, Englished by Bp. Patrick, *plate*, small 8vo. *old calf*, *neat*, 3*s* .. .. 1707

1951 — another translation, by Spencer Madan, of Trin. Coll. Cambridge, small 8vo. *neat*, 2*s* .. .. .. 1782

1952 GROTIUS'S Life, the History of his Negociations, and a Critical Account of his Works, by De Burigney, 8vo. *calf*, 3*s* 1754

1953 — Life, with Brief Minutes of the Civil, Ecclesiastical, and Literary History of the Netherlands, by Charles Butler, 8vo. *calf, neat*, 5*s* 6*d* .. .. .. .. 1826

1954 — another copy, by Charles Butler, 8vo. *boards*, 4*s* 6*d* 1826

1955 GUALDO (Conte Galeazzo) Arte della Guerra, ó sia Maneggio dell' Armi Moderno, 18mo. *old calf*, 3*s* 6*d* .. *Vienna*, 1672

At the end of this treatise is another in Latin, by Theophilus Eulalius, entitled, "Aurea Monita Religiosissimæ Societatis Jesu."—*Placentiæ*, 1670.

1956 GUARDIAN, The, 2 vols. in 1, 12mo. *very fine copy in old purple morocco*, £1 1*s* .. .. *J. Tonson*, 1714

With the book-plate of Charles Cadogan, Esq. The first volume of the book is dedicated to Lieut. General Cadogan, and the second to Mr. Pulteney. This is the first collected edition. These papers, commenced by Sir Richard Steele and assisted by Addison, appeared, Mar. 12, 1713, to Oct. 1, 1713.

1957 GUARINI (Cavalier Giambatista) Il Pastor Fido, Tragi-Comedia Pastorale, 12mo. *bound*, 1*s* .. *Parigi*, 1759

1958 — Il Pastor Fido, *plates*, 12mo. *calf, neat*, 5*s* *Glasguæ, Foulis*, 1763

A very nicely printed edition by Foulis of Glasgow.

1959 — Il Pastor Fido, 12mo. *vellum*, 3*s* *Parigi, Prault*, 1766

1960 — Pastor Fido, 2 vols. 8vo. *calf, very neat*, 12*s* *Londra*, 1800

Of this elegant edition, dedicated to the Duchess of Rutland, by Leonardo Nardini, only 250 copies were printed.

1961 GUENYVEAU (A.) Principes Généraux de Métallurgie, *plates*, 8vo. *sewed*, 3*s* .. .. .. *Paris*, 1824

1962 GUEVARA, Marcus Aurelius's Diall of Princes, written by Don Antonio of Guevara, Lord Bishop of Guadix, and translated by Thomas North, folio, *old calf*, 8*s* .. .. 1619

1963 GUICCIARDINI (Francesco) I quattro ultimo libri dell' Historie d' Italia, nuovamenti ristampati di M. Papirio Picedi, small 4to. *old calf, gilt, scarce*, 7*s* 6*d* .. *Parma, Seth Viotti*, 1564

A very pretty volume, nicely printed and nicely bound.

1964 — Histoire des Guerres d'Italie, trad. en François, par H. Chomedey, avec les Observations Politiques, Militaires, et Morales du Sieur de la Nove, thick 8vo. *old vellum*, 5*s* 6*d* *Eustache Vignor*, 1593

Guicciardini's Hist. is from 1492 to 1512; with the autograph of A. de Lescale Longchamp; and a note by him.

1965 — Maxims, translated by Emma Martin, *portrait*, square 12mo. *antique boards*, 8*s* .. .. .. 1845

*From the translator.* "The breadth and depth of Bacon, the worldly wisdom and long experience of Lord Burleigh, the detail and temper of Rochefoucault combined."

1966 GUICCIARDIN (Louis, *Gentilhomme Florentin*,) Description de Touts les Pais-Bas, trad. en Françoise par F. De Belle Forest, *numerous maps, portrait of Francis I. and finely engraved title-page*, folio, *old calf*, 12*s* .. *Anvers, C. Plantin*, 1582

1967 GUIDES to Birmingham, no date.—Kenilworth Castle, *Warwick*, 1813, and Oxford, 1815, *maps and plates*, 3 vols in 1, 12mo. *half calf, neat*, 3*s* 6*d* .. .. .. V.Y.

1968 GUIDES to York, 1814.—Teesdale including Rokeby, *York*, 1813. —Durham, 1813.—Carlisle, 1810, *maps and plates*, 4 in 1, 12mo. *half calf, neat, 5s* .. .. .. V.Y.

1969 GUIDES to Northampton, 1815.—Gloucester, 1802.—Monastery of Gloucester and St. Peter's Cathedral, 1814.—Matlock, Buxton, and Castleton, Derbyshire, 1814.—Monumental Inscriptions in Ashbourne Church, Derbyshire, by Sir Brooke Boothby, 1813; 5 in 1 vol. 12mo. *half calf, neat 5s* .. .. V.Y.

1970 GUITONNIERE (Leon de la) Le Protestant pacifique, ou Traité de la paix de l'Elise, contre M. Jurieu, 12mo. *old calf, neat, 4s* *Amsterdam, G. Taxor*, 1684

With the autograph of the celebrated "*John Locke.*"

1971 GUIZOT.—Histoire Générale de la Civilisation en Europe, 12mo. *sewed, 2s* .. .. .. *Bruxelles*, 1846

1972 — Histoire de la Révolution d'Angleterre, depuis l'avénement de Cha. I., jusqùa sa mort, (1629-1649) 2 vols. 12mo. *half bound, 5s* *Bruxelles*, 1850

1973 — Democracy in France, Jan. 1849, 8vo. *boards, 2s 6d* 1849

1974 — Shakspeare and his Times, 8vo. *cloth, 7s (pub. at 10s 6d)* 1852

1975 — Memoirs to Illustrate the History of my Times, vol. 1, 8vo. *cloth, 8s (pub. at 14s)* .. .. .. 1858

1976 GURNEY'S (Hudson, Esq.) translation of Cupid and Psyche. See *Apuleius*

1977 GURNEY'S (Joseph John) Observations on the Religious Peculiarities of the Society of Friends, 8vo. *boards, 5s (pub. at 9s)* 1824

1978 — Essays on the Evidences, &c., of Christianity, 12mo. *boards, 3s 6d (pub. at 6s 6d)* .. .. 1827

1979 — Biblical Notes and Dissertations on the Deity of Christ, 8vo. 1st edition, *cloth, 5s* .. .. 1830

1980 — second edition, 8vo. *half cloth, 6s (pub. at 10s)* 1833

1981 — Letter to a Clerical Friend, on the Accordance of Geological Discovery with Natural and Revealed Religion, 18mo. *sewed, 1s* *Norwich*, 1836

1982 — Sabbatical Verses, 8vo. *cloth, scarce, 3s 6d* *Norwich*, 1837

Composed during a period of much affliction.

1983 — Winter in the West Indies, *view of Sligoville*, 8vo. *cloth, 5s* 1840

1984 — Gedanken uber Gewohnheit und Disciplin, 12mo. *cloth, 2s* 1852

1985 GUTHRIE'S (William) Geographical, Historical, and Commercial Grammar, *maps*, 8vo. *neat, 4s* .. .. 1812

1986 GUTHRIE'S (Rev. Will.) Christian's Great Interest, with an Introductory Essay, by Dr. T. Chalmers, post 8vo. *boards, 2s* *Glasgow*, 1825

1987 GUY'S (Joseph) Elements of Ancient History, 12mo. *neat, 2s* 1836

1988 — Elements of Modern History, France, Germany, America, &c., 12mo. *bound, neat, 2s* .. .. 1836

1989 — Elements of British History, 12mo. *bound, 1s 6d* 1836

1990 GUZMAN d'Alfarache, Histoire de, par Le Sage, 2 vols. 18mo. *sewed, 2s 6d* .. .. *Paris*, 1808

1991 GWILLIM (Henry) On Tithes, 4 vols. royal 8vo. *half calf, very neat, 10s* .. .. .. 1801

1992 GWILT'S (Joseph) Rudiments of Architecture, practical and theoretical, *plates*, royal 8vo. *boards*, 9*s* (*pub. at* 18*s*) 1826

1993 — Elements of Architectural Criticism, for the use of Students, &c., royal 8vo. *cloth*, 4*s* .. .. 1837

1994 GYLLII (P.) de Constantinopoleos Topographia lib. IV. 24mo. *old calf, neat, scarce*, 5*s* .. *L. Bat., Elzevir*, 1632

1995 HAGER'S (Dr. Joseph) Dissertation on the Newly Discovered Babylonian Inscriptions, *plates*, 4to. *boards*, 5*s* 1810

1996 HAGUE—Memorial delivered to the States General, by the Marquess of Castell Moncayo, Envoy of Spain to the Hague, 1684—a similar Memorial by the Count D'Avaux, Envoy from France, folio, *broadside*, 5*s* .. *Richard Morris*, 1684

1997 HAKLUYT'S (Richard) Principal Navigations, Voyages, and Discoveries made by the English Nation, folio, **Black Letter**, page 53 to 683, *half bound*, £3 13*s* 6*d* .. 1588

This volume, though imperfect, is valuable on account of "The famous Voyage of SIR FRANCIS DRAKE into the South Sea and there thence about the whole Globe of the Earth," begun 1577, ended 1580, on 6 unpaged leaves. GEORGE TURBERVILLE'S account of MUSCOVIA, written in 1568, describing the manners of the country and people to his friends in London, is in VERSE, as are the 1st and 2nd Voyages of ROBERT BAKER to GUINEA, in 1562-63, at pages 130 to 142.

1998 HALE'S (Sir Matthew, *Lord Chief Justice of the King's Bench*) Life and Death, by Bp. Burnett, *portrait*, 8vo. *calf, neat*, 3*s* 1682

1999 HALIBURTON (Judge) Bubbles of Canada, 12mo. *cloth*, 3*s* 6*d* *Philadelphia*, 1839

2000 HALIFAX (Charles, Earl of) Poetical Works, with his Life and Times, 8vo. *old calf, neat*, 3*s* 6*d* .. 1716

2001 HALL'S (Capt. Basil) Extracts from a Journal written on the Coasts of Chili, Peru, and Mexico, in 1820, to 1822, 2 vols. post 8vo. *boards*, 6*s* (*pub. at* £1 1*s*) .. *Edinburgh*, 1825

2002 HALL'S (Joseph, Bp. *of Norwich*) Works, thick folio, nearly 1400 pages, *old calf, neat*, 12*s* .. .. 1647

Contents; Meditations and Vows, Epistles, Sermons, Censure of Travel, Honour of the Married Clergy, Contemplations on the Old Testament, &c.

Dr. Ferriar, pointing out the plagiarisms of Sterne, says, "It has long been my opinion, that the manner, the style, and the selection of subjects for his sermons were derived from the excellent *Contemplations* of Bp. Hall."

2003 — Resolutions and Decisions of Divers Practical Cases of Conscience, *portrait*, 12mo. *MS. title page*, 2*s* 6*d* .. 1650

2004 — Shaking of the Olive Tree, with his Hard Measure, written by himself, *portrait*, 4to. *old calf, scarce, original edition*, 12*s* 1660

2005 — Satires, with the Illustrations and Notes of Warton and Singer, *portrait*, 12mo. *cloth, scarce*, 6*s* *Chiswick, Whittingham*, 1824

A valuable edition with "Some Specialities in his Life," and "Hard Measure" dealt to him by the Parliament, written by himself. "Full of spirit and poetry; as much of the first as Dr. Donne, and far more of the latter. Written in Q. Elizabeth's time, when he was 23."—*Gray to Dr. Wharton.*

2006 HALL'S (Robert) Works and Remains, a Memoir of his Life by Dr. Gregory, and Critical Estimate of his Writings by John Foster, *portrait*, post 8vo. *cloth*, 2*s* 6*d* .. .. 1846

2007 HALLAM'S (Henry) Introduction to the Literature of Europe, in the 15th, 16th, and 17th Centuries, 4 vols. post 8vo. *cloth, new*, £1 4*s* .. .. .. .. 1855

2008 HALLAM'S Constitutional History of England from the Accession of Henry VII. to the Death of George II. 3 vols. *cloth, new*, 18*s* 1857

"On a general survey, we do not scruple to pronounce the *Constitutional History* the most impartial book we ever read."—*Edinburgh Review.*

2009 — History of Europe during the Middle Ages, 3 vols. post 8vo. *cloth*, 18*s* .. .. .. .. 1858

2010 HALLER, Enumeratio Methodica Stirpium Helvetiæ Indigenarum, 24 *plates*, large folio, *half bound, uncut*, 18*s* *Gottingæ*, 1742

2011 HALLIWELL'S (James O.) Letters Illustrative of the Progress of Science in England from the Reign of Queen Elizabeth to that of Charles II., 8vo. *cloth, neat*, 3*s* 6*d* .. 1841

Printed for the Historical Society of Science.

2012 HAMBURG, Map of, *mounted on canvas in a case*, 1*s* 1813

2013 HAMILTON (Le Comte Antoine) Œuvres Complètes, *portraits*, 3 vols. 8vo. *calf, very neat*, £1 1*s* .. .. *Paris*, 1805

Contents: Notice sur la Vie et les ouvrages d'Hamilton, Memoires de Grammont, Contes, Relations de Différens Endroits d'Europe, Lettres et Epitres, Poesies Diverses, et Chansons.

2014 — Fairy Tales and Romances, Englished from the French, *fine portrait*, post 8vo. *cloth*, 3*s* .. *H. G. Bohn*, 1849

2015 HAMILTON'S (Dr. A.) Hand-book of Useful Medicine, 18mo. *stiff cover*, 1*s* 6*d* .. .. .. 1837

2016 HAMILTON'S (James) Sinai, the Hedjaz and Soudan, Wanderings around the Birth-place of the Prophet, &c. *maps*, post 8vo. *cloth*, 5*s* (*pub. at* 10*s* 6*d*) .. .. .. 1857

2017 HAMILTON (Sir Will., Bt.) Lectures on Metaphysics, edited by Mansel and Veitch, 2 vols. 8vo. *cloth, new*, £1 4*s* 1859

Sir W. Hamilton was Professor of Logic and Metaphysics in the University of Edinburgh. These are to be succeeded by 2 other volumes on Logic, £1 4*s*.

2018 — Autograph Note of Sir William Hamilton, from Huntfield House, Biggan, relative to his Edition of Reid's Works, 2*s*

2019 HAMPSON'S (Sir G. F.) Short Treatise on the Liabilities of Trustees, 8vo. *boards*, 3*s* 6*d* (*pub. at* 6*s*) .. 1830

2020 HAMPTON COURT.—Hand-Book of the Contents of Hampton Court, by Felix Summerly, *plates*, 18mo. *sewed*, 1*s* 1856

2021 HAMPTON COURT Conference, held Jan. 14, 1603; the Summe and Substance of it, done by Bp. Barlow, 8vo. *sewed*, 3*s* 6*d* *Re-printed*, 1807

2022 HANCARVILLE, Recherches sur l'origine des Arts de la Grèce, sur leur connexion avec les arts des plus anciens peuples connus, *numerous plates*, 3 vols. in 2, 4to. *remarkably fine copy in half morocco, extra*, £2 .. .. *Londres*, 1785

Lord Valentia's copy with his book-plate. A highly interesting and valuable book.

2023 HANDS'S (William) Law and Practice of Patents for Inventions, 8vo. *boards*, 2*s* .. .. .. 1808

2024 HAND-BOOK of American Literature, Historical, Biographical, and Critical, post 8vo. *cloth, gilt*, 3*s* 6*d* *Edinburgh, Chambers*, 1858

2025 — of French Literature, by Mrs. M. Foster, post 8vo. *cloth, gilt*, 3*s* 6*d* .. .. .. .. *ib.*, 1858

2026 HAND-BOOK of German Literature, by J. Gostick, post 8vo. *cloth, gilt,* 3*s* 6*d* .. .. *Edinb., Chambers,* 1849

2027 — of Italian Literature, by Mrs. Foster, post 8vo. *cloth, gilt,* 3*s* 6*d* *ib.,* 1858

2028 — of Spanish Literature, by Mr. A. F. Foster, post 8vo. *cloth, gilt,* 3*s* 6*d* .. .. .. .. *ib.,* 1858

2029 HANDEL'S (George Fred.) Esther, a Sacred Oratorio, in Score, composed in 1720, large folio, 185 pages, *uncut, scarce,* 15*s*

2030 — Songs, 12 of them, newly arranged by Charles Czerny, folio, *boards,* 6*s* (*pub. at* 12*s*) .. .. *No date*

2031 — Life, with a Catalogue of his Works, *portrait by Chambers,* 8vo. *calf, neat,* 3*s* 6*d* .. .. .. 1760

2032 HANDMAID to the Arts, Painting, Gilding, Silvering, Bronzing, &c., 2 vols. 8vo. *fine copy in old calf, gilt,* 10*s* .. 1764

It is not generally known that this work is the production of William Dossie, Esq.

2033 HANE (P. F.) Historia Sacrorum ab Luthero Emendatorum, 1517-1555, 4to. *old calf, gilt,* 6*s* .. *Lipsiæ,* 1729

From Lord Orford's Library.

2034 HANROTT (P. A., Esq.) Catalogue of his Splendid, Choice, and Curious Library sold by Mr. Evans, *some of the prices given,* 5 parts in 1 vol. 8vo. *half calf, neat,* 10*s* .. 1833-34

2035 — another copy, 5 parts, royal 8vo. LARGE AND THICK PAPER, *boards, uncut,* £1 5*s* .. .. .. 1833-34

*With prices and purchasers' names,* only 50 COPIES printed on this paper.

2036 HARDWICK'S Shilling Peerage, 1858.—Shilling Baronetage, 1858.—Shilling Knightage, 1857.—Shilling House of Commons, 4 vols. 24mo. *cloth,* 1*s each* .. .. 1858

2037 HARINGTON'S (Sir John) Brief View of the State of the Church of England, as it stood in Q. Elizabeth's and K. James his Reigne to 1608, 12mo. *old calf, scarce,* 7*s* 6*d* .. 1653

A continuation of Bp. Godwyn's Catalogue of Bishops.

2038 — NUGÆ ANTIQUÆ; a Miscellaneous Collection of Papers in Prose and Verse, temp. Hen. VIII., Q. Eliz., &c. 12mo. *half bound, neat,* 4*s* 6*d* .. .. .. 1769

2039 HARLEIAN LIBRARY.—Catalogus Bibliothecæ Harleianæ, in Locos Communes distributus, 5 vols. 8vo. *old calf, neat,* £1 1*s* *Londini, T. Osborne,* 1743-45

"This Catalogue (which was Philip Champion Crespigni's copy and has his book-plate) was made by Dr. Samuel Johnson, with the assistance of that industrious antiquary William Oldys and the learned Michael Maittaire. It is the best catalogue of a large library of which we can boast; it should be in every good collection."—*Nicholls's Lit. Anecd.,* v. 3, p. 403.

2040 HARMER'S (THOMAS) Observations on Divers Passages of Scripture, 4 vols. 8vo. *nice clean copy, in old calf,* 12*s* 1776

The Scriptures are here illustrated as to rites and customs, by the observations made by voyagers and travellers into the East. "Happily executed."—*Horne.*

2041 HARRIS'S (James) Works, *portrait by Bartolozzi, and plates,* 5 vols. 8vo. FINE AND LARGE PAPER COPY, *calf, grained,* £2 2*s* 1792

In writing, "from Lord Malmesbury to Viscountess Perceval," has also the Viscountess's book-plate. This copy is printed on WRITING PAPER.

2042 HARRIS'S Works; Three Treatises on Art, Music, Painting and Poetry and Happiness.–Hermes.–Philosophical Arrangements.–Philosophical Enquiries, with an Account of his Life by his son, Lord Malmesbury, *portrait and plates*, 2 vols. 4to. LARGE PAPER, *good copy in calf*, £1 10*s* .. .. 1801

The LARGE PAPER copies were printed for private distribution only.

2043 — Philosophical Arrangements, 8vo. *calf, neat*, 4*s* 1775

2044 HARRY MOWBRAY, by Captain Knox, *numerous plates*, 8vo. *cloth*, 6*s* 6*d* (*pub. at* 13*s*) .. .. .. 1843

2045 HARWOOD'S (Dr. Edward) Introduction to the Study and Knowledge of the New Testament, 2 vols. 8vo. *calf, very neat*, 7*s* 1773

2046 — View of the various Editions of the Greek and Roman Classics, with remarks, 1st edition, 12mo. *calf, neat*, 3*s* 6*d* 1775

2047 — 2nd edition, 12mo. *calf, neat*, 3*s* 6*d* .. 1778

2048 — 3rd edition, 12mo. *calf, gilt*, 3*s* 6*d* .. 1782

2049 — 4th and best edition, 12mo. *very fine copy, in old calf, gilt, scarce*, 6*s* .. .. .. 1790

These are all the editions.

2050 HASCIAC (Laurentii) de postrema Melitensi Lue, praxis historica, small 8vo. *limp vellum*, 3*s* 6*d* .. *Panormi*, 1677

2051 HATCHER'S (Henry, *author of the History of Salisbury*) Memoirs of the Life, Writings, and Character of, by John Britton, *portrait*, 8vo. *stiff covers*, 5*s* .. .. 1847

2052 HATTON (Sir Christopher, K.G.) Memoirs of his Life and Times, including his Correspondence with Queen Elizabeth and other distinguished persons, by Sir Harris Nicolas, *fine portrait*, 8vo. 600 pages, *cloth*, 7*s* 6*d* (*pub. at* 15*s*) .. 1847

"Of Sir Christ. Hatton, Gentleman Pensioner, Captain of the Guard, Vice-Chamberlain, and Lord Chancellor to Queen Elizabeth, and her distinguished personal favourite, less was known than of almost any other statesman of that period."—*Sir H. Nicolas.*

2053 HATTON (Edward) Index to Interest, with easy rules for valuation of 1, 2, or 3 lives, *very fine impression of the portrait, by Sherwin*, 8vo. *old calf, neat*, 3*s* 6*d* .. 1711

As to the Portrait, "one of the best specimens of Sherwin's manner."—*Noble.*

2054 HAVEMANNI (Michaelis) Gamologia Synoptica; istud est Tractatus de Jure Connubiorum, IV. libris, 4to. *old calf, neat*, 6*s* *Francofurti*, 1672

2055 HAWKER'S (Dr. Robert) Poor Man's Daily Portion, for every Morning and Evening throughout the Year, thick 8vo. *cloth*, 6*s* .. .. .. .. *No date*

2056 HAY (Joannis) de Rebus Japonicis. See *Japan*

2057 HAYM (Niccola Francesco) Notizia de' Libri rari nella Lingua Italiana, 1st edition, 8vo. *calf, neat*, 4*s* 6*d* *Londra, Tonson*, 1726

Baron Stuart de Rothesay's copy with his arms impressed on the sides.—See *Lodge's Peerage.*

2058 — Biblioteca Italiana ossia notizia de' Libri rari Italiani, 4 vols. 8vo. *calf, neat*, 16*s* .. .. *Milano*, 1808

2059 HAYNE (Thoma) Pax in Terra; seu Tractatus de Pace Ecclesiastica, small 8vo. *old calf, neat*, 4*s* 6*d* *Londini, J. Norton*, 1639

"Hayne, was a noted critic, an excellent linguist, and a solid divine, beloved of learned men, and particularly respected by Selden."—See *Wood's Athenæ.*

2060 HAYTER (Chas.) Introduction to Perspective, Practical Geometry, Drawing, and Painting, &c. 8vo. *half calf, neat, plates,* 4s *London,* 1832

2061 HAYWARD'S (Sir John) Lives of III. Norman Kings of England, William I. and II., Henrie I., *at London, by R. B.,* 1613.—Life and Reigne of King Henrie the IIII. *London, by John Wolfe,* 1599, in 1 vol. 4to. *old calf, neat,* £2 2s

Many pages of these treatises are torn out, but then the first has on the title-page the autograph of "BEN JONSON, TANQUAM EXPLORATOR," and the second has the dedication to the Earl of Essex, which gave such offence to Queen Elizabeth that she employed Bacon to see if he could not find treason in the book, for writing which he was imprisoned.

2062 — Annals of the four first years of the Reign of Q. Elizabeth, edited from a MS. by J. Bruce, Esq., 4to. *cloth,* 5s *Camden Soc.,* 1840

2063 HAZLITT'S (William) Lectures on the English Poets, 8vo. *boards,* 4s (*pub. at* 10s 6*d*) .. .. .. 1818

2064 — Lectures on the Dramatic Literature of the Age of Elizabeth, 8vo. *boards,* 4s 6*d* (*pub. at* 12s) .. .. 1821

2065 — Characters of Shakespear's Plays, 8vo. *boards,* 4s (*pub. at* 10s 6*d*) 1817

2066 — Lectures on the English Comic Writers, 8vo. *half cloth,* 4s 6*d* (*pub. at* 10s 6*d*) .. .. .. 1819

"All these volumes will be read with luxury on account of their brilliant execution, and with instruction on account of the many delicate remarks which are interspersed among the declamation."—*Monthly Review.*

2067 HEAD'S (Capt. F. B.) Rough Notes taken during some Rapid Journies across the Pampas and among the Andes, post 8vo. *boards,* 3s 6*d* (*pub. at* 9s 6*d*) .. .. 1826

2068 HEAD'S (H. E., *Rector of Feniton, Devon,*) Ultimate and Proximate Results of Redemption, 8vo. *cloth, new,* 4s (*pub. at* 12s) 1854

2069 HEARNE'S (Thomas) Collection of Curious Discourses written by eminent Antiquaries upon several heads in our English Antiquities, *plates,* 2 vols. 8vo. *fine clean copy in old calf,* 14s 1771

2070 — Liber Niger Scaccarii, nec non Wilhelmi Worcestrii Annales Rerum Anglicarum; accedunt Chartæ Antiquæ et Opusc. Varia Hist. et Antiquitat. Angliæ spectantia, 2 vols. 8vo. *fine clean copy in old calf, uniform with the above,* 18s *Londini,* 1771

2071 — Lives of John Leland, Thomas Hearne, and Anthony à Wood, with Memoirs of many of the Literati, *portraits and plates of Antiquities,* 2 vols. 8vo. *very fine clean copy in old calf, gilt,* 15s *Oxford,* 1772

Amongst a vast amount of very curious matter, these volumes contain, "The Laboryouse Journey and Serche of John Laylande for Englande's Antiquitees, geven of hym as a Newe Years gifte to Kynge Henry the VIII. in the XXXVII. yeare of his Reygne, with Declaratyons enlarged by Johan Bale." Reprinted from the edition of 1549.

2072 HEATH'S Picturesque Annual, 1832 to 1836, *numerous plates beautifully engraved,* 8vo. *morocco, gilt edges,* 9s *each,* (*pub. at* £1 1s *each*) .. .. .. 1832

These are of permanent value, as each delineates some continental tour.

2073 HEBENSTREIT (Dr. W.) Dictionarium Editionum tum selectarum tum Optimarum Auctorum Classicorum et Græcorum et Romanorum, 12mo. *boards,* 7s 6*d* .. *Vindobonæ,* 1828

2074 HEBER'S (Bp. Reginald) Journey through the Upper Provinces of India, 1824-25, with Notes on Ceylon, and a Journey to Madras, &c., 1826, *plates*, 3 vols. 8vo. *half morocco, neat*, £1 1*s* 1828

2075 HEBER—Bibliotheca Heberiana; a Catalogue of the Library of Richard Heber, Esq., sold by Messrs. Sotheby and Son, 1834, 35, 36, 37, 13 parts; also containing William Bentham's, 1836, Sir Francis Freeling's, 1836, George Wilkinson's, and 5 other Catalogues, in 5 vols. 8vo. *nicely half bound in calf, clean as new*, £1 10*s* .. .. .. V. Y.

2076 HEDERICI Lexicon Græco-Latinum, cura Ernesti et Morell, 4to. *calf, neat*, 6*s* .. .. *Londini*, 1810

2077 — alia Editio, cura Ernesti, Morell, Larcher, et Blomfield, 4to. *boards*, 10*s* (*pub. at* 34*s*) .. .. *ib.* 1825

2078 HEDGEHOG, Mole, and Owl, 8vo. *sewed*, 6*d* *Norwich, Muskett*, 1854

Re-published, by the late Rev. F. Bevan, from Mr. Jesse's book, to remove popular prejudices existing against these interesting animals.

2079 HEEREN (A. H. L.) Manuel Historique du Système politique des états de l'Europe et de leurs Colonies, depuis la découverte des deux Indes, 2 tom. en 1, 8vo. *half calf, very neat*, 7*s* 6*d* *Paris*, 1821

2080 — Historical Researches into the Politicks, Intercourse, and Trade of the Carthaginians, Ethiopians, and Egyptians, *maps*, 2 vols. 8vo. *boards*, 14*s* (*pub. at* 24*s*) .. *Oxford*, 1832

"We look upon Heeren as having breathed a new life into the dry bones of ancient history."—*Edinburgh Review.*

2081 — Historical Researches into the Politics, Trade, &c., of the principal Asiatic Nations of Antiquity, *maps*, 3 vols. 8vo. *cloth*, 18*s* (*pub. at* £1 16*s*) .. .. *Oxford*, 1833

Vol. I Persians.—II. Phœnicians, Babylonians, Scythians.—III. Indians.

2082 HEIDELBERG—Le Guide des Voyageurs à Heidelberg, Manheim, Schwezingen, &c. trad. par l'Abbé Henry, *large folded map*, 12mo. *half calf, neat*, 2*s* 6*d* *Heidelberg*, 1818

2083 HEINECII (Io. Gottl.) Antiquitatum Romanarum Jurisprudentiam illustrantium Syntagma, secundum ordinem Institutionum Justiniani digestum, 2 vols. 8vo. *law calf, neat*, 10*s* *Francofurti*, 1771

2084 — Elementa Juris Civilis secundum ordinem Institutionum, 8vo. *law calf, neat*, 5*s* .. .. *L. Bat.*, 1751

2085 HELMESII (Henrici) Homiliæ in Evangelia Dominicalia, 8vo. *old calf, scarce*, 6*s* *Parisiis, apud Andoenum Paruum*, 1552

2086 HENDERSON'S (E.) Biblical Researches and Travels in Russia, the Crimea, &c., *plates*, 8vo. *boards*, 7*s* 6*d* (*pub. at* 16*s*) 1826

Mr. Hartwell Horne acknowledges himself much indebted to the information contained in this "very interesting volume of Travels."

2087 — Journal of a residence in Iceland in 1814 and 15, an account of its History, Literature, and Antiquities, *maps and plates*, 2 vols. 8vo. *half calf*, 8*s* (*pub. at* 28*s*) *Edinburgh*, 1818

"The inquiry into the nature and characteristic features of Icelandic Poetry, evinces an acquaintance with the subject never attained before."—*Quarterly Review.*

2088 HENRY II.—The History of his Life, and of the Age in which he lived, by George, Lord Lyttleton, 6 vols. 8vo. *calf, gilt*, 15*s* 1769

With a History of the revolutions of England from the Death of Edward the Confessor to the birth of Henry II. "A most important and instructive work."—*Dr. Valpy.*

2089 HENRY VIII.—Life, with Biographical Sketches of eminent men in his Reign, by P. F. Tytler, *portrait*, 12mo. *cloth*, 3*s* *Edinburgh*, 1837

2090 HENRIE IV. OF FRANCE.—A very curious collection of Tracts chiefly in the French Language, viz.—

1.—De la Souveraintè des Roys, POEME EPIQUE, a la Reine, mere du Roy, Regente en France, par P. de Nancel, .. .. 1610

This is a very considerable poem extending to 83 pages, 32 lines to a page. *Not mentioned by Brunet*, but who does mention another work by this author, who was "Substitut du Procureur General."—See *Le Long.*

2.—Querimonia, super acerbo Henrici Magni funere, Elegiaco Carmine expressa, 8 leaves .. .. .. .. 1610

3.—La Doctrine de Jesus Christ et celle de Robert, Cardinal Bellarmin, Jesuiste, touchant les Roys et Princes, 14 leaves *No Place or Printer*, 1611

Dedicated "a la Royne," par C.D.S.C.

4.—Jesuites Establis et Restablis en France, et le fruict qui en est arrivé à la France .. .. .. .. 1611

Eight unpaged leaves of Poetry, one a Sonnet by Ronsard; another is entitled, "Sur la ruine de la Pyramide de Chastel, presage de l'assassinat Henry IV."

5.—La Paternostre des Iesuistes, Loyalistes, Marianistes, Bellarministes, 1611

Four more leaves of Poetry, written against Coton, Garnet, Chastel, Guignard, Ravaillac, Barriere, and other Jesuits.

6.—L'Ave Maria des Catholiques, avec sa Suitte, .. 1611

Four leaves of Poetry, after the ave a Sonnet, "a la Royne, mere du Roy."

7.—Salutation Angelique, ou advis, dediée a la Royne Regente par les François .. .. .. ... 1611

Four more leaves of Poetry.

8.—Le Credo des Jesuistes, dedié aux François, Poetry on 4 leaves 1611

9.—Le Confiteor de Henry le Grand, dedié au Roy Louys XIII., poetry, 4 leaves

10.—Considerations a la France, sur la Consolation envoyée de Rome, a la Royne mere du Roy, Regente, Prose, 8 leaves

11.—Lettre de Monsieur de Rosny, a le Royne Regente, 8 leaves 1611

in 1 vol. 8vo. *in old limp vellum*, EXCESSIVELY RARE, £2 12*s* 6*d*

Neither of these Tracts have any place where printed, or the printer's name attached to them. With the exception of the 1st Tract, I can find no account of any of the others in Le Long's "Bibliotheque Historique de la France," and there can be no doubt that all of them are exceedingly rare, curious, and valuable.

2091 — Henrici Navarrorum Regis Epistolæ, 1583-84, 12mo. *boards*, 3*s* 6*d* .. .. .. *Ultrajecti*, 1679

2092 — Henri IV. Roi de France, Les amours de, avec ses Lettres galantes à la Duchesse de Beaufort et à la Marquise de Verneuil, 2 vols. 24mo. *calf, gilt edges*, 4*s* .. *Londres*, 1781

2093 — Henry the Great, Memoirs of, and of the Court of France during his Reign, 1547-1610, *portraits*, 2 vols. 8vo. *half calf*, 8*s* (*pub. at* £1 8*s*) .. .. .. 1824

To be read with Miss Aikin's Histories of Q. Elizabeth and K. James I.

"That the present work is ably written, and exhibits a spirited narrative of facts, will be manifest from the extracts which follow. The account of the Massacre of St. Bartholomew is the fullest in our language."—*Monthly Magazine.*

2094 HENRY and Scott's Commentary upon the Holy Bible, Genesis to Deuteronomy, and Joshua to Esther, *maps*, 2 vols. 8vo. *cloth*, 5*s* .. .. .. .. 1832

2095 HENRY'S (Matthew) Select Works, Communicant's Companion, on Daily Communion, a Religious Life, Sober-mindedness, &c. by C. Bradley, 12mo. *boards*, 3*s* (*pub. at* 7*s*) .. 1829

2096 HENRY (Philip) Account of his Life and Death, 1631-1696, by his Son, Matthew Henry, with Funeral Sermon for his Mother, *portrait*, small 8vo. *bound*, 3s .. .. 1712

"A beautiful delineation of Primitive Christianity and of the power of godliness."—*Dr. Williams.*

2097 HENRY'S (Robert) History of Great Britain, from Cæsar to Henry VIII., *fine portrait*, 12 vols. 8vo. *good set in calf*, £1 10s 1805

A valuable work, divided into the Civil and Military History, the Religious History, and the History of the Constitution, Government, and Laws. "Too much cannot be said of its arrangement, nor for the great store of valuable materials which it contains." It occupied Dr. Henry 30 years.

2098 HEPHÆSTIO de Metris, Gr., cum notis Variorum, curante Th. Gaisford, accedit Procli Chrestomathia Grammatica, 8vo. *good copy in calf, scarce*, 10s .. .. *Oxonii*, 1810

2099 HERACLIDIS Pontici, qui Aristotelis Ætate vixit, Allegoriæ in Homeri fabulas de Diis, Gr. et Lat. à Conrado Gesnero interprete, small 8vo. *old calf*, 5s *Basiliæ, J. Oporinus*, 1544

2100 HERBERT of Cherbury—The Life of Edward, Lord Herbert, of Cherbury, written by himself, edited by Horace Walpole, *portrait*, 4to. *a fine copy, in calf*, 7s 6d .. 1770

"The whole relation throws singular light on the manners of the age."—*Horace Walpole.* It is as interesting as a novel; a most romantic life. Born 1581, died 1648.

2101 — another copy, *portrait*, 4to. *old calf, neat*, 9s 1770

One of the most amusing Auto-biographies in our language, chiefly relating to the time of Q. Elizabeth. Sir Walter Scott speaks rapturously of it.

2102 HERBERT'S (George) Temple, Sacred Poems, and Private Ejaculations, 4th edition, 12mo. *scarce, wants a leaf of Index*, 8s *Cambridge, Buck and Daniel*, 1635

2103 — another edition, with his Life, by Isaac Walton, 12mo. *old calf*, 6s .. .. .. .. 1679

2104 HERBSTER (Mad. F.) Les Soirées de Londres, *plate*, 12mo. *half calf, neat*, 2s .. .. *Londres, Dulau*, 1810

2105 HERESBACHII (Conradi) de laudibus Græcarum literarum oratio.—Joan. Sturmii de Educatione Principis.—Rogeri Aschami et Joannis Sturmii Epistolæ duæ, de Nobilitate Anglicana, small 8vo. *old vellum*, 6s *Argentorati, V. Rihelius*, 1551

2106 HERETIQUES—Moyens surs et honnêtes pour la Conversion de tous les Heretiques, 2 parts in 1 vol. 12mo. *neat, scarce*, 4s *Cologne, P. Marteau*, 1683

2107 HERODIAN of Alexandria, his History of Twenty Roman Cæsars and Emperors of his Time, small 4to. *neat, scarce*, 6s 1629

"This was the Duke of Sussex's copy,"—*J. G. C.(rosse).* It has the Duke's book-plate.

2108 HERODOTUS, Græcè, cum Vallæ interpretat. Lat., ab H. Stephano recognita, folio, *a fine copy, in old calf, gilt*, 15s *Excudebat H. Stephanus*, 1592

This is Henry Stephens's 2nd and best edition.

2109 — Græcè, cum notis Creuzeri et Baehr, 4 vols. 8vo. VELLUM PAPER, *sewed*, £1 12s (*pub. at* £2 12s 6d) *Lipsiæ*, 1830-35

One of the best library editions of Herodotus.

2110 HERON'S Robert) Letters on Literature, 8vo. *old calf, very neat,* 5*s* .. .. .. .. 1785

Generally attributed to John Pinkerton, the Antiquarian Scottish Tourist.

2111 HERTELIUS (Jac.) Vetustissimorum et Sapientiss. Comicorum L. Sentnetiæ quæ supersunt, Gr. et Lat., cum uniuscujusque Poetæ Vita, etc. thick 8vo. above 800 pages, *old calf, scarce,* 9*s* *Basileæ,* 1560

Out of the 50 authors mentioned here are a few, Anaxandrides, Antiphanes, Axionicus, Bathon, Crates, Diphilus, Epicharmus, Eubulus, Machon, Menander, Plato, Theognetus.

2112 HERTFORD—Assize Sermon at Hertford, Aug. 7, 1704, before Lord Ch. Justice Holt and Mr. Justice Gould, by John Savage, 4to. *sewed,* 1*s* .. .. *Cambridge,* 1704

2113 HERVEY'S (James) Meditations and Contemplations, 12mo. *bound,* 1*s* 6*d* .. .. .. .. 1774

2114 HESIODUS, Gr. et Lat., accedit insuper Pasoris Index, opera et studio C. Schrevelii, small 8vo. *old calf, gilt,* 4*s* *Lugd. Bat., Hackii,* 1653

A very neat pocket edition.

2115 — Gr. et Lat. cum notis Selectissimis, opera et studio C. Schrevelii, small 8vo. *calf, neat,* 6*s* .. .. *ib.,* 1658

A very pretty edition, very neatly printed, and has Barlæus's Notes extending to 259 pages; there is a large "Index Vocabulorum."

2116 HEURTLEY'S (Charles A.) Parochial Sermons, 1st series, 12mo. *cloth,* 3*s* 6*d (pub. at* 5*s* 6*d)* .. *Oxford,* 1851

2117 HEWLETT'S (Rev. John) Sermons on Different Subjects, 8vo. *boards,* 2*s* 6*d* .. .. .. 1788

2118 — Sermons, 3 vols. 8vo. *hf. cf.* 4*s* 6*d* .. *London,* 1805

2119 HEY'S (Dr. John) Lectures in Divinity, vol. 1 only, 8vo. *boards,* 3*s* .. .. .. *Cambridge,* 1796

2120 HEYLYN'S (Peter) Microcosmos; a Little Description of the Great World, thick 4to. *old calf,* 5*s* 6*d* *Oxford,* 1631

2121 — Help to English History, containing a succession of all the Kings, Dukes, Bishops, &c., of England, with notes, by Paul Wright, *wants the plates of arms,* 8vo. *neat,* 7*s* 6*d* 1786

2122 — another edition, by Paul Wright, *with the Coats of Arms of the Nobility, &c.,* 8vo. *old calf,* 10*s* .. 1772

This is the best edition of "a very useful work."—*Dr. Will. King.*

2123 HIBBERT—Catalogue of the Library of George Hibbert, Esq., of Portland Place, sold by Mr. Evans, March, 1829, *priced, portraits,* 8vo. *boards,* 10*s* .. .. .. 1829

2124 — another copy, *portraits,* 8vo. *half calf, very neat,* 10*s* 1829

Cost, £35,000; sold for, £21,560; loss, £13,440.—In MS. in the book.

2125 — another copy, *with prices and purchasers' names,* 8vo. *half russia, uncut, top edges gilt,* 14*s* .. .. 1829

2126 HIGGINS'S (Wm.) Mosaical and Mineral Geologies Illustrated and Compared, 8vo. *cloth,* 3*s* (*pub. at* 7*s*) 1832

Autographs of *Sam. Woodward* and *J. W. Draper, the gift of the Author.*

2127 HILDANUS (William Fabricius) Lithotomia Vesicæ; an accurate description of the Stone in the Bladder, Englished by Nicholas Culpeper, *plates*, small 8vo. *old binding*, 3*s* 6*d* 1640

"Therefore, I exhort all that have a desire to exercise themselves in this part of Surgerie, that they get this book, and make themselves exactly perfect in the same."—*Alexander Reid, M.D. and M.R.C.P.*

2128 HINDOOS—Sketches relating to their History, Religion, Learning, and Manners, 8vo. *calf, gilt*, 5*s* .. 1790

2129 HIND'S (John) Elements of Algebra, 8vo. *half calf, neat*, 5*s* *Cambridge*, 1837

2130 HINDS'S (Dr. Samuel, *Bp. of Norwich)* Scripture, and the Authorised Version of Scripture, with Notes, and a Glossary of obsolete words, 8vo. *sewed*, 3*s* .. .. 1845

2131 — Primary Charge to the Clergy of the Diocese of Norwich, June and July, 1852, 8vo. *sewed*, 1*s* .. 1852

2132 HIPPISLEY'S (J. H., Esq.) Chapters on Early English Literature, post 8vo. *half calf, very neat*, 7*s* .. 1837

Mr. Hippisley says, in his title page, "not for the lerid bot for the lewed," not so, it is a work commencing with Chaucer and ending with Shakspeare, exhibiting considerable reading.

2133 HIPPOCRATIS Aphorismi, Gr. et Lat., accurante Theodoro Janssonio ab Almeloveen, 24mo. *neat*, 3*s* *Amst., Wetstein*, 1685

2134 — Camilli Flavii Paraphrasis de Ære, Aquis, et Locis, 4to. *old boards*, 3*s* .. *Venetiis, apud R. Meiettum*, 1596

2135 HISTOIRE du Differend d'Entre le Pape Boniface VIII., et Philippes le Bel, Roy de France, (1296-1311) ensemble le proces criminel fait a Bernard Evesque de Pamiez l'an 1295, le tout justifié par les Actes et Memoires, folio, LARGE PAPER, *a very fine copy, in old calf, gilt*, £1 11*s* 6*d* *Paris, S. Cramoisy*, 1655

This HISTORY occupies 42 pages. It is also in Latin, occupying 38 pages, but the PROOFS occupy 620 pages. At the end is a Treatise, "de Potestate Papæ." *Le Long Bibliotheque Hist. de la France*, says, "L'Histoire de ce Demêlé, composée par Simon Vigor."

2136 HISTORI Van de Oost-Indische Zeeroovers, en in't byzonder Van den Vermaarden Angria,—Histori der Oorlogen tuschen den Grooten Mogol en Angria, small 8vo. *white vellum, neat, scarce*, 6*s* *Amsterdam, by J. Loveringh*, 1738

This book is signed at the end Klement Downing, and on the title-page are the names of Thomas Matthews and Jan Plantain.

2137 HISTORIÆ Apostolicæ, autore Abdia Babyloniæ Episcopo, et ipsorum Apostolorum discipulo, quam ex Hebraica lingua in Latinam Africanus vertit per Wolfgangium Lazium, small 8vo. *vellum, wants title*, 6*s* *The Preface dated Vienna*, 1551

2138 HISTORIÆ Augustæ Scriptores (Suetonius, Aurelius Victor, Eutropius, Paulus Diaconus) Annotationes etiam Erasmi in Suetonium, &c., thick 8vo. *original calf binding*, £1 1*s* *Venetiis, Aldus*, 1521

A very fine, clean, and large copy, seldom, according to Renouard, found in fine condition. This has the Autograph of C. Macro, who possessed a very curious collection of early printed books. Erasmus's Annotations occupy 28 leaves out of the 60 of introductory matter.

2139 HISTORY of England, from the Text of Hume and Smollett, and continued to the present Reign, by Tho. Gaspey, Esq., *numerous plates*, 20 vols. imp. 8vo. *scarlet cloth, gilt*, £3 (*pub. at* £7 10*s*) *Tallis*, 1856, *&c.*

This work is illustrated by above 240 portraits and historical plates; about 4 parts more complete it.

2140 HOADLEY (Bp.) Plain Account of the Sacrament of the Lord's Supper, 1735.—Anonymous Remarks on, 1735.—Letter to a Lord on, 1736.—Dr. Richard Warren's Answer to Hoadley, 2 parts, 1736.—Dr. Thos. Burnet's Nature, Use, and Efficacy of the Sacrament, 1731; in 1 vol. 8vo. *half bound*, 5*s* V. Y.

2141 HOARE'S (Clement) Treatise on the Cultivation of the Grape Vine on open walls, 8vo. *boards*, 3*s* (*pub. at* 7*s* 6*d*) 1835

2142 HOBART'S (Bp. J. H., *New York*) Sermons on the Principal Events and Truths of Redemption, 2 vols. 8vo. *boards*, 12*s* 1824

2143 HOBBES (Thomæ) Historia Ecclesiastica, *portrait inserted, Augustæ Trinobantum*, 1688.—Sanderson (Rob. Episc. Lincoln) Casus Conscientiæ, *Cantabrigiæ*, 1688.—Bp. Sanderson's Nine Cases of Conscience, in English, 1678; in 1 vol. small 8vo. *fine clean copies*, 7*s* 6*d* .. .. .. V. Y.

2144 HODGES (William) Travels in India in 1780 to 83, *large map and plates*, 4to. *calf, neat*, 10*s* 6*d* .. .. 1793

Nice original copy, Sir Lambert Blackwell's, with fine impressions of the plates.
"Its value as an acquisition to national information is far beyond its bulk."—*British Critic.*

2145 HODGSON'S (H. J.) Digest of the Statutes relating to the practice of Appeals against Orders of Removal, 12mo. *boards*, 3*s* (*pub. at* 5*s* 6*d*) .. .. .. 1845

2146 HODSON'S (G., *Birmingham*) XII. Sermons on the Leading Doctrines of the Gospel, 12mo. *boards*, 3*s* (*pub. at* 7*s*) 1825

2147 HOFFMAN (Benj.) Some considerations of present Use, in which the true notion of the Strong and Weak is stated, a Farewell Sermon at St. George's, Bottolph Lane, 4to. *sewed*, 1*s* 6*d* 1683

2148 HOGAN (William) on Auricular Confession and Popish Nunneries, 12mo. *sewed*, 1*s* .. .. .. 1848

2149 HOGARTH (William) Biographical Anecdotes of, with a List of his Works, chronologically arranged, by John Nichols, 8vo. *half bound, uncut*, 10*s* 6*d* .. .. 1785

3rd and best edition. In Edwards's sale, 15*s*; The Duke of Roxburgh's, £1 8*s*

2150 HOGG'S (James, *Ettrick Shepherd*) Queen's Wake, a Legendary Poem, 8vo. *half calf*, 3*s* 6*d* .. *Edinburgh*, 1814

2151 — Mountain Bard, consisting of Ballads and Songs, founded on Legendary Tales, 8vo. *half calf, neat*, 2*s* 6*d* *ib.* 1807

2152 HOGG'S (T.) Treatise on the Culture of the Carnation and other Flowers, *coloured plates*, 12mo. *boards*, 3*s* 6*d* (*pub. at* 8*s*) 1822

2153 — another edition, on the Culture of the Carnation, Pink, Tulip, Rose, and other Flowers, *many coloured plates*, 12mo. *half calf, neat*, 5*s* .. .. .. 1836

2154 HOGSKIN'S (Thomas) Travels in the North of Germany, 2 vols. 8vo. *boards*, 9*s* .. .. *Edinburgh*, 1820

"A work containing much information."—*Stevenson.*

2155 HOLDER'S (Rev. Mr., *of Barbadoes)* System of French Accidence and Syntax, with Notes, by G. Satis, 8vo. *boards,* 2*s* 6*d* 1791

A very elaborate Grammar, written in correction of Chambaud.

2156 HOLE'S (Matthew) Practical Exposition of the Church Catechism, 2 vols. in 1, 8vo. *old calf,* 4*s* .. .. 1715

2157 HOLLAND—Protest of the City of Amsterdam in opposition to the States of Holland, who pretend to raise 16,000 new levies, contrary to their privileges, folio, *broadside,* 2*s* 6*d* *T. Malthus,* 1684

2158 — Batavian Anthology; Specimens of the Dutch Poets, and their Poetical Literature, by Sir John Bowring, 12mo. *cloth,* 2*s* 6*d* 1824

2159 — Family Tour through South Holland, up the Rhine, and across the Netherlands to Ostend, *etchings by Col. Batty,* 18mo. *cloth,* 2*s* 6*d* (*cost* 5*s*) .. .. *Fam. Lib.*, 1831

2160 HOLLAR—Catalogue of the Capital Collection of Hollar's Prints, the property of John Townley, Esq., sold by Mr. King, in May, *priced,* 4to. *sewed,* 3*s* .. .. 1818

2161 HOLLES (Denzil Lord, *Baron of Ifield, Sussex)* Memoirs, from 1641 to 1648, *portrait, by R. White,* 8vo. *calf, neat,* 4*s* 6*d* 1699

2162 HOLLINGWORTH'S (Richard) Christian Principles no abettors of Popish Practices, a Sermon at Guildhall, London, Jan. 23, 1680, 4to. *sewed,* 1*s* 6*d* .. .. .. 1681

2163 HOLLOWAY'S (Benjamin) Letter and Spirit; Annotations on the Holy Scriptures, 8vo. *old calf, neat,* 4*s* 6*d* *Oxford,* 1753

2164 HOLMES (John, Esq., F.S.A., *of East Retford, Norfolk)* a Descriptive Catalogue of the Books in his Library, with notices of Authors and Printers, and all the SUPPLEMENTS, forming 5 vols. 8vo. *portraits and plates, boards, extremely scarce,* £3 3*s*
*Norwich, Matchett, Stevenson, and Matchett,* 1828-1840

PRIVATELY PRINTED. So complete a copy of this curious Catalogue, compiled by the author when he was between 70 and 80 years of age, could scarcely now be found. In addition, it has an AUTOGRAPH LETTER written by Mr. Holmes to *Mr. Bartlett, Master of the Classical School, Blandford, Dorsetshire,* thanking him for a copy of *Horace,* "Just received, 9 Sept, 1833;" also another dated, 2nd Oct., 1833. It has also, a Catalogue of the sale of his books by Mr. Sotheby, Oct. 1841.

2165 — another copy, 4 vols. 8vo. *calf extra, grained, scarce,* £2 2*s*
*Norwich,* 1828-34

"A curious and amusing Catalogue," *privately printed.* "Lieut. Colonel Harvey, with S. W. Stevenson's (the printer's,) respectful compliments."

2166 — part 2 of Supplement, page 93 to 171, 8vo. *sewed, scarce,* 3*s* 6*d*
*Norwich,* 1840

Dedicated to his "kind friend and liberal patroness, Frances Mary Richardson Currer, of Eshton Hall, Yorkshire."

2167 HOLT (Sir John) Life, 8vo. *calf, neat, scarce,* 4*s* 1764

Autograph of "*W. Oglander,* 1764." Contains Lord Chief Justice Holt's Arguments on the Rights and Liberties of the People, delivered with remarkable courage, temp. Will. III. and Q. Anne.

2168 HOME'S (Charles) Chronological abridgement of the History of England, from the earliest times to the Accession of the House of Hanover, with Lists of contemporary Sovereigns, 8vo. *half calf, neat,* 3*s* 6*d* .. .. .. 1791

"A judicious compilation."—*Lowndes.*

2169 HOME'S (Sir Everard) Lectures on Comparative Anatomy, with the Supplement complete, 6 vols. 4to. LARGE PAPER, *half cloth, lettered on leather*, £7 7*s* (*pub. at* £27 6*s*) 1814-28

"The Right Honble. The Earl of Orford, from the Author." This fine book, "in high estimation with the profession," is illustrated by 371 plates, finely engraved by James Basire, with a proof portrait of Sir Everard before the letters.

2170 HOME (Henry, *Lord Kaimes)* Elements of Criticism, 2 vols. 8vo. *old calf, gilt*, 7*s* 6*d* *(see Kaimes)* *Edinburgh*, 1769

2171 HOMERI Ilias, Græcè, 2 vols. small 4to. LARGE PAPER, *ruled throughout with red lines, old yellow morocco*, 15*s* *Glasguæ, Foulis*, 1747

"A very beautiful and correct edition."—*Dr. Harwood.* It is very scarce.

2172 — Iliad and Odyssey, translated into English verse, by Alexander Pope, *plates*, 11 vols. 12mo. *old calf, neat*, 11*s* 1750

2173 — Iliad, Englished by Alexander Pope, with notes by Gilbert Wakefield, 6 vols. 8vo. *stiff covers*, £1 1*s* 1796

2174 — Odyssey, translated by Pope, 12mo. *neat*, 2*s* *Edinburgh*, 1792

2175 — Iliad, truly translated by George Chapman, with Introduction and Notes, by the Rev. Richard Hooper, *portrait*, 2 vols. foolscap 8vo. *cloth*, 12*s* .. *J. R. Smith*, 1857

"The translation of Homer, published by George Chapman, is one of the greatest treasures the English language can boast."—*Godwin.*

2176 — Odyssey, truly translated by George Chapman, with Introduction and Notes, by the Rev. Richard Hooper, 2 vols. foolscap 8vo. *cloth*, 12*s* .. .. *J. R. Smith*, 1857

"Chapman's translation, with all its defects, is often exceedingly Homeric, an excellency to which Pope himself seldom attained."—*Hallam.*

2177 — Batrachomyomachia, Hymns and Epigrams, Hesiod, Musæus, and part of Juvenal, translated by George Chapman, with Introduction and Notes, by the Rev. Richard Hooper, *frontispiece*, foolscap 8vo. *cloth*, 6*s* .. *J. R. Smith*, 1857

"Chapman writes and feels as a poet,—as Homer might have written had he lived in England in the reign of Elizabeth."—*Coleridge.*

2178 — Blackwell's Enquiry into the Life and Writings of Homer, 8vo. *calf, neat*, 3*s* 6*d* .. .. .. 1736

"By Blackwell of Aberdeen, or rather by Bishop Berkley. A fine though sometimes fanciful effort of genius and learning."—*Gibbon.*

2179 HOMILIES of such matters as were promised and entitled in the former part, the 2nd tome, folio, **Black Letter**, *boards*, EXTREMELY RARE, £3 3*s* .. .. *John Bill*, 1623

As clean as when it first issued from the press. This 2nd tome consists of 21 Homilies, the former editions having only 20; the 21st is the Homily against "Disobedience and Wilfull Rebellion," "added to the after-printed editions of the Homilies *both parts*. The EARLIEST EDITION KNOWN is in *folio, Lond. J. Bill*, 1623."—*Lowndes.*

2180 HOMILIES, or Sermons used in the time of Q. Elizabeth, with the Articles of Religion, and the Constitutions and Canons Ecclesiastical, 8vo. *purple morocco, marbled leaves*, 5*s* 6*d* .. 1817

2181 HOMILIES, and the Articles of Religion, *cuts*, 12mo. *boards*, 2*s* 6*d* (*pub. at* 5*s*) .. .. .. 1824

2182 HOMILIES, with the Articles of Religion, and the Constitutions and Canons of the Church of England, 4to. *cloth*, 7*s* (*cost* 16*s*) 1833

2183 HOOD'S (Thomas) Poems of Wit and Humour, 12mo. *cloth, new,* 5*s* (not contained in the following) *Moxon,* 1858

2184 — Poems, *portrait,* 12mo. *cloth, new,* 7*s* .. *ib.,* 1859

2185 HOOGEVEEN (Henrici) Doctrina Particularum Linguæ Græcæ, in epitomen redegit C. G. Schütz, 8vo. *calf, neat,* 5*s* 6*d* *Glasguæ,* 1813

2186 HOOKER (Richard) of the Lawes of Ecclesiastical Politie, 8 books, (there are but 5 books) *engraved frontispiece containing portrait of K. James I., London, Will. Stansby,* 1617.—Certayne Divine Tractates and other Godly Sermons, *four title pages in elegant wood-cut compartments,* folio, *good clean copy, in old calf,* £1 1*s* *Henry Featherstone,* 1618

Early editions of this book are rare. I can find no mention of this. It is said the 5th edition appeared in 1597, the 6th 7th and 8th in 1648, 4to. What edition is this? Perhaps the 3rd.

2187 — Lawes of Ecclesiastical Politie, in 8 bookes, *engraved title,* folio, *good copy in calf,* 12*s* *London, by Will. Stansbye, no date*

Although the title page says there are 8, there are but 5 books. At the end are "Certain Divine Tractates, and other Godly Sermons," by Richard Hooker, dated, severally, 1635, 1636, and 1639. Printed by W. Stansby and R. Bishop.

2188 — of Divine Service, the Sacraments, &c., Selections by Keble, 18mo. *morocco, gilt leaves,* 3*s* 6*d (cost* 5*s* 6*d) Oxford, Parker,* 1845

"The adamantine and imperishable work of Hooker is his Ecclesiastical Polity. Bishop Lowth, in the Preface to his English Grammar, has bestowed the highest praise upon the purity of Hooker's style. Bishop Warburton, in his book on the Alliance between the Church and the State, often quotes him, and calls him 'the *excellent,* the *admirable,* the *best good man of our order.*' "—*Dr. Parr.*

2189 HOOKER (Sir William) Journal of a Tour to Iceland in the Summer of 1809, *maps and plates,* 8vo. *boards,* 10*s* *Yarmouth,* 1811

This was a privately printed edition, "not published."

2190 — second edition, *maps and plates,* 2 vols. 8vo. *boards,* 9*s* (*pub. at* £1 6*s*) .. .. .. .. 1813

"I trust that I am equally satisfying my own conscience and the good taste of the public when I give my unqualified recommendation of this work."—*Dr. Dibdin.* See *Henderson.*

2191 — British Flora, comprising the Flowering Plants and Ferns, *coloured plates,* vol. 1, 8vo. *cloth, new,* 14*s* (*pub. at* 24*s*) 1842

2192 HOOLE'S (Charles) Common Accidence examined and explained, the Rudiments of Latin Grammar used in Rotheram School, 12mo. *original binding, scarce,* 5*s* *T. Longman, at the Ship, in Paternoster Row,* 1730

2193 HOPE'S Historical Essay on Architecture, *numerous plates,* 2 vols. royal 8vo. *cloth,* 3rd edition, with index, £1 5*s* (*pub. at* £2) 1840

"The most comprehensive elucidation of the Architecture of the middle ages which has ever appeared in this country."—*Gentleman's Magazine.*

2194 HOPKINS'S (Ezekiel, *Bp. of London-Derry,*) Exposition on the Lord's Prayer, with Sermons on Providence, *portrait by Sturt,* 8vo. *old calf,* 3*s* 6*d* .. .. .. 1698

2195 — Doctrine of the Two Sacraments, the Way of Salvation, *portrait by Vdr Gucht,* 8vo. *old calf,* 3*s* 6*d* .. 1712

These two pieces are not contained in the Bishop's works in folio.

2196 HORATIUS, de Arte Poetica, Jacobi Grifoli interpretatione explicatus, small 8vo. *limp vellum,* (*wants some of the Index*) 2*s* 6*d* *Lutetiæ,* 1552

2197 HORATIUS, Animadversiones et Notæ Dan. Heinsii, 3 vols in 1, 18mo. *old calf, neat*, 9*s* .. *L. Bat., Elzevir*, 1629

2198 — Scholiis sive annotationibus instar Commentarii illustrata a Jo. Bond, 12mo. *fine copy, in original calf, gilt*, 4*s* 6*d* *Amst., Janson*, 1635

2199 — cum annotationibus Joan. Bond, 12mo. *MS. title, old calf*, 3*s* *Amst., Elzevir*, 1676

2200 — ex Antiquis Codd. et certis observat. emendavit, A. Cuningamius, 8vo. *old calf*, 3*s* .. .. *Hagæ Comitum*, 1721

2201 — Latin and English, with Notes by P. Francis, 4 vols. 12mo. *calf, neat*, 5*s* .. .. .. .. 1747

2202 — Latin and English, by D. Watson and Dr. S. Patrick, 2 vols. 8vo. *a fine copy in old calf, gilt*, 10*s* .. 1750

With a Catalogue of all the editions of Horace, from 1476 to 1738.

2203 — Latin and English, with Notes by Philip Francis, 4 vols. 12mo. *nice copy in old calf, gilt*, 8*s* .. .. 1756

2204 — Baxteri, Gesneri, et Zeunii, 8vo. *calf, very neat*, 6*s* *Londini*, 1809

2205 — Valpy, 18mo. *bound*, 1*s* 6*d* .. *ib.* 1814

2206 — ad fidem Editionis Gesneri, *engraved frontispiece and bust*, 12mo. *green morocco, gilt leaves*, 8*s* *Londini, Harding, Mavor et Lepard*, 1824

This is a delightfully printed little volume, and with the Terence and Virgil are highly esteemed.

2207 — another copy *in boards*, 5*s* .. .. *ib.*, 1824

2208 — cum novo Commentario ad modum Jo. Bond, 18mo. *cloth*, £1 15*s* *Parisiis, Didot*, 1855

This most elegant little edition is illustrated with photographic views of places mentioned by Horace; only a few copies printed.

2209 — Latin et François, avec des Remarques critiques et historiques, par M. Dacier, 10 vols. 12mo. *old calf, gilt*, 12*s* *Paris*, 1709

2210 — I dilettevoli Sermoni, altrimenti Satire e le Morali Epistole di Horatio, insieme con la Poetica, ridotte da M. L. Dolce, small 8vo. *old vellum, rare*, 12*s* *Vinegia, G. Giolito de' Ferrari*, 1559

"E' libro molto raro."—*Fontanini*. "Ce volume est très-difficile à trouver."—*Brunet*.

2211 — The Epodes, Satires, and Epistles of Horace, translated into English verse, by the late Rev. Francis Howes, M.A., Minor Canon of Norwich Cathadral, 12mo. *cloth, new*, 3*s* 6*d* (*pub. at* 6*s*) *W. Pickering*, 1845

Beautifully printed by W. Pickering. This elegant translation has received the warm encomiums of many excellent judges.

2212 HORN'S (Robert, *of Clonbury, Ludlow*) Shield of the Righteous, or the 91st Psalm expounded, small 4to. above 150 pages, *sewed*, 4*s* 6*d* .. .. .. 1625

Written on account of the Pestilence "raging so sore in London and other parts of this kingdom."

2213 HORNE'S (Thomas) Sermon at Whitehall, Feb. 8, 1684-5, the Sunday after the death of K. Cha. II., 4to. *sewed*, 1*s* 1685

2214 HORNE'S (Bp. G.) Commentary on the Book of Psalms, 2 vols. 8vo. *calf, very neat*, 8*s* .. .. *Oxford*, 1790

This is "his capital performance; the Preface is a masterpiece of composition and good sense."—*Orme*.

2215 — Selection from Bp. Horne's Commentary on the Psalms, 12mo. *bound*, 2*s* .. .. .. 1819

2216 HORNE'S Discourses on several Subjects and Occasions, 3 vols. 8vo. *boards*, 12*s* (*pub. at* £1 7*s*) .. 1812

"The good Bishop is a cheerful, pious, elegant companion. The openings of his sermons are often beautiful."—*Bp. Jebb.*

2217 — Considerations on the Life and Death of Abel, Enoch, Noah, &c., 12mo. *bound*, 1*s* .. .. 1822

2218 HORNE'S (Thomas H.) Introduction to the Study of Bibliography, with a Memoir of the Public Libraries of the Antients, *plates*, 2 vols. 8vo. *calf, gilt, newly bound, scarce*, 18*s* 1814

2219 — Manual of Biblical Bibliography, being a Catalogue, methodically arranged, of the principal Editions of the Holy Scriptures, with Philologers, Critics, &c. royal 8vo. *cloth*, 8*s* (*pub. at* 12*s*) 1839

200 of these published separately for the use of Biblical and Bibliographical Students.

2220 HORSLEY'S (Bishop Samuel) Speeches in Parliament, 8vo. *old calf, neat*, 7*s* 6*d* .. .. *Dundee*, 1813

2221 — Sermons, 3 vols. 8vo. *boards*, 10*s* 6*d* .. 1816

2222 — Sermons, vol. 3 only, 8vo. *boards*, 4*s* .. *Dundee*, 1813

"Fine specimens of commanding eloquence."—Appendix to *Williams's Christian Preacher*.

2223 HORSFIELD'S (Rev. T. W.) History and Antiquities of Lewes (Sussex) and its Vicinity, *numerous lithographic and copper-plate views, and pedigrees of the Families*, 2 vols. 4to. *boards*, £2 2*s* (*pub. at* £4 4*s*) .. .. *Lewes*, 1824-27

An appendix containing, "An Essay on the Natural History of the District by Gideon Mantell, F.L. and G.S." But this copy unfortunately wants 2 plates, "the Plan of the Borough, Cliffe, and Southover," and "Framfield Place, the seat of Mr. Donovan."

2224 HORT (Major) The Rock; various Legends and Original Songs and Music descriptive of Gibraltar, 12 *plates lithographed by Hullmandel*, 4to. *cloth*, £1 1*s* (*pub. at* £2 2*s*) .. 1839

Autograph of "E. Berners," Lord Berners.

2225 HORTICULTURAL Society of London, Transactions of the, *coloured plates*, 2nd series, vol 2, parts 5 and 6, 4to. *sewed*, 10*s* 1842

2226 — second series, vol. 3, parts 1, 2, and 3 complete, 4to. *sewed*, £1 1*s* .. .. .. .. 1848

Part 3 of this contains the GENERAL INDEX to the 1st and 2nd series of these transactions.

2227 — 2nd series, vol 3, part 2, *sewed*, 5*s*

2228 HORTICULTURAL Tour in Flanders, 8vo. *half calf*, 8*s* 6*d* (*sold at Mr. Hibbert's sale for* 20*s*) .. .. 1823

2229 HOUDANCOUR.—Les quatre Factum pour Messire Philippes de la Mothe Houdancour, Duc de Cardonne, & Mareschal de France, cy-devant Vice-Roy & Capitaine General de Catalogne, contre Monsieur de Procureur General du Roy au Parlement de Grenoble, 4to. *old calf*, RARE, £1 1*s* *No place or date, but* 1647

With the arms of the Marshal stamped outside the covers, and the initials of his name at each corner. For another book illustrative of this subject, see *Catalonia*.

2230 HOUSE of Commons; Catalogue of Books in the Library at the House of Commons, the preface signed J. R., folio, *sewed*, 10*s* *Ordered by the H. of Com. to be printed*, 27 *Feb.* 1830

This was the old library before the fire happened.

2231 HOUSSAIE (Amelot de la) Hist. du Governement de Venise, vol. 1 only, 18mo. *bound*, 1*s* .. .. *Paris*, 1676

2232 HOUTTEVILLE'S (Abbé) Discourse on the Method of the Principal Authors who wrote for and against Christianity, Englished with a Dissertation on the Life of Apollonius Tyanæus, 8vo. *old calf*, SCARCE, 4*s* .. .. .. 1739

2233 HOWARD (John, Philanthropist,) View of his Character and Public Services, by Dr. John Aikin, *portrait*, 8vo. *half calf*, 3*s* 1792

2234 HOWARD (Philip, Earl of Arundel,) his Life, with that of Anne Dacres, his Wife, edited from the original MS. by the Duke of Norfolk, Earl Marshall, post 8vo. *cloth, old style*, 6*s* (*pub. at* 10*s* 6*d*) .. .. .. .. 1857

2235 HOWARD'S (Sir Robert) Poems, with a Play, the Blind Lady, 8vo. *old calf, neat*, 9*s* .. .. 1696

Some copies are dated 1660. This has John Dryden's Poetical Epistle, signed "John Driden." In the Bibliotheca Ang. Poet. £1 10s.

2236 HOWE'S (John) Thoughtfulness for the Morrow, and on the Immoderate desire of Foreknowing things to Come, 1681, also his Redeemer's Tears wept over lost Souls, 1705, in 1 vol. small 8vo. *old calf, neat*, 3*s* 6*d* .. .. .. V.Y.

"A vast number of uncommon thoughts; one of the most valuable writers in our language."—*Dr. Doddridge.*

2237 H(OWELL) (James) Philanglus; some sober Inspections made into the Carriage and Consults of the late Long Parlement, 12mo. *old calf*, 4*s* 6*d* .. .. .. .. 1658

Dedicated "to His Highness the Lord Protector," Cromwell.

2238 — Dodona's Grove; or, the Vocall Forest, with Poetry by Sir Henry Wotton and others, folio, *fine impressions of the Trees by M. Merian, old calf*, 7*s* .. .. 1640

The Oak is representative of the King of England; the Vine, France; the Fir, Denmark; the Ash, Sweden; the Myrtle, the Turk; the Willowes, the Hollanders; the Cedar, the Emperor of Germany.

2239 HOWELL'S (Dr. W.) Medulla Historiæ Anglicanæ; Ancient and Modern History of England and its Monarchs to the time of Geo. III., *plates*, 8vo. *old calf, very good copy*, 8*s* 1766

Best edition of "a very concise and excellent epitome of our history."—*Lowndes.*

2240 HOWES (Rev. F., *Minor Canon of Norwich Cathedral*,) First Book of Horace's Satires, in English Verse, 8vo. *sewed*, 3*s* *Norwich, C. Muskett*, 1842

"100 copies printed for private distribution."—See *Horace, No.* 2211.

2241 HOWITT'S (Mary) Birds and Flowers and other Country Things, *plates*, 12mo. *cloth*, 3*s* (*pub. at* 6*s*) .. .. 1837

2242 — Picture Book for the Young, *with* 20 *pretty illustrations*, 4to. *cloth, gilt, gilt edges*, 4*s* .. .. 1858

2243 HUBERI (Ulrici) Dissertationes Jurid. pro Eunomia Romana, thick 4to. *vellum*, 7*s* 6*d* .. *Franequeræ*, 1692-5

The works of this learned lawyer are held in considerable estimation abroad.

2244 HUDSONI (Gulielmi) Flora Anglica, 2 vols. 8vo. *calf, gilt, very neat*, 9*s* .. .. .. *Londini*, 1778

2245 HUET (Bp. of Avranches) Memoirs of his own Life, translated with copious Biographical Notes by Dr. John Aikin, 2 vols. 8vo. *boards*, 6*s* .. .. .. .. 1810

A very amusing life, being a history of the literature and learned men of his period, 1630 to 1721.

2246 HUGENII (Constantini, *Equitis,*) Monumenta Desultoria, Poemata Epigrammata, cum Præfatione Casp. Barlæi, thick 12mo. of 498 pages, *old vellum, neat,* 6*s* *Hagæ Comitum, A. Vlacq,* 1665

A nicely printed volume, much like an Elzevir, with this writing, Nobilisso. Ampmo. doctissoq. Viro d. Guilielmo de Blytterswyck in suprema Geldriæ Curia quæ Rurmondæ est, Consiliario dignm. Aut. d. 1656."

2247 HUGHES'S (John) Itinerary of Provence and the Rhone in 1819, *numerous etchings by the Author,* 8vo. *half calf, neat,* 5*s* 1822

2248 HUGHES'S (Will.) Quæries; or, Choice Cases for Moots, 12mo. *old calf,* **Black Letter,** 4*s* 6*d* .. .. 1675

Containing several points of law not resolved in the books. Autograph of *Isaac Hawkins Browne.*

2249 HUMBOLDT (Alexandre de) Essai Géognostique sur le Gisement des Roches dans les deux Hémisphères, 2nd edit., 8vo. *sewed,* 5*s* *Paris,* 1826

2250 — Views of Nature; Contemplations on the Sublime Phenomena of Creation, Englished by Otté and H. G. Bohn, *coloured frontispiece,* post 8vo. *calf, gilt, very pretty copy,* 5*s* (*cost* 8*s* 6*d*) 1850

2251 — Aspects of Nature in different Lands and Climates, Englished by Mrs. Sabine, 2 vols. post 8vo. *cloth, neat,* 5*s* 1849

2252 — Cosmos; a Sketch of a Physical Description of the Universe, translated from the German, by E. C. Otté, 2 vols. post 8vo. *cloth,* 5*s* (*pub. at* 7*s*) .. *H. G. Bohn,* 1849

2253 — Personal Narrative of Travels to the Equinoctial Regions of America, in 1799-1804, Englished by Thomasina Ross, 3 vols. post 8vo. *cloth,* 12*s* 6*d* .. *H. G. Bohn,* 1852

"Humboldt, the most illustrious traveller of his day, nothing seems too vast, too varied, too wonderful, or too minute for the penetrating intellect of this extraordinary man."—*Dr. Dibdin.*

2254 HUME and Smollett's History of England to the end of George the 2nd's reign, 1760, 13 vols. 8vo. *a fine set in russia, illustrated with numerous plates from Thurston's designs, and a set of portraits,* £4 14*s* 6*d* .. .. .. 1808

2255 HUME'S (David) History of England to the Revolution in 1688, 10 vols. bound in 5, imperial folio, *a fine set in full russia, gilt edges,* £8 8*s* .. .. .. 1806

Bowyer's splendid edition cost, with the binding, £88 10*s*. Illustrated with numerous fine historical plates.

2256 — Towers's (J.) Observations on Hume's History of England, 8vo. *half calf,* 2*s* 6*d* .. .. .. 1778

2257 — Essays and Treatises, Moral, Political, and Literary, 2 vols. 8vo. *calf, neat,* 12*s* .. .. *Edinburgh,* 1793

2258 HUMPHREY'S (H. N.) Ocean and River Gardens, History of the Marine and Fresh Water Aquaria, *finely coloured plates,* small 4to. *cloth, new, gilt edges,* 8*s* 6*d* (*pub. at* 10*s* 6*d*) 1857

A very beautifully illustrated little work.

2259 HUNT'S (Leigh) Book for a Corner, 80 *wood cuts*, post 8vo. *cloth*, 5*s* .. .. .. *H. G. Bohn*, 1858

A selection of amusing extracts from Horace Walpole, De Foe, Le Sage, Mrs. Radcliffe: celebrated Travellers, as Marco Polo, Mungo Park, &c.; Essayists, as Steele, Goldsmith, Smollett, Fielding, &c.

2260 — Selections in Prose and Verse, from the best authors, *plates*, 2 vols. in 1, post 8vo. *cloth, new*, 5*s* .. 1856

2261 HUNT'S (Robert) Manual of Photography, *numerous engravings*, post 8vo. *cloth*, 6*s* .. .. .. 1857

2262 HUNTER'S (Dr. John) 34 Plates, with descriptions, of the Anatomy of the Human Gravid Uterus, atlas folio, *cloth*, £1 1*s* *Sydenham Society*, 1851

"No work on the same subject at all approaching to this in beauty and excellency has ever appeared. To provincial members (of the Sydenham Socieyt) such a work cannot fail to be considered an invaluable boon."—*Address.*

2263 HUNTERIAN Society, Catalogue of the Library of the, royal 8vo. 44 pages, *cloth*, 10*s* .. .. 1836

"Printed for the Hunterian Society, not published."—*Title page.* Not in Mr. Martin's Catalogue of privately printed books.

2264 HUNTINGDON Peerage; a Genealogical and Biographical History of the Illustrious House of Hastings, with a Memoir of the present Earl and Family, by Henry Nugent Bell, Esq., *portraits*, first edition, 4to. *boards*, 8*s* .. .. 1820

2265 — 2nd edition, *portraits*, 4to. *half calf, gilt*, 14*s* (*pub. at* £2 2*s*) 1821

This is illustrated with many additional portraits.

2266 HURD'S (Bp.) Moral and Political Dialogues, with Letters on Chivalry and Romance, 5th edit., 3 vols. small 8vo. *old calf, gilt, fine copy*, 8*s* .. .. .. 1776

2267 — another copy, 3 vols. *old calf*, 7*s* .. 1776

This edit. not in Lowndes. "One of the best scholars in the kingdom, and of parts and genius equal to his learning."—*Bp. Warburton.*

2268 HUSBANDRY—Bath Society, Letters and Papers on Agriculture, Planting, &c., in Somerset, Wilts, Glo'ster, and Dorset, *plates*, 8 vols. 8vo. *old calf, gilt*, £1 5*s* .. 1783-96

2269 — Blith's (Walter) English Improver Improved, or the Survey of Husbandry Surveyed, discovering the Improveableness of all Lands, *engraved title by T. Cross, and plates*, small 4to. *half calf, neat, scarce*, 7*s* 6*d* .. .. .. 1652

2270 — another edition, *curious frontispiece by T. Cross, and plates*, 4to. *old binding*, 7*s* 6*d* .. .. .. 1653

"A well known and very ingenious work."—*Quarterly Review.*

2271 — Certain Ancient Tracts concerning the management of Landed Property, reprinted, 8vo. *boards, scarce*, 6*s* 1767

Contents:—1. Xenophon's Treatise of Household out of the Greke, by Gentian Hervet.—2. Sir Anthony Fitzherbert's Boke of Husbandry.—3. His Boke of Surveying, originally printed by Thomas Berthelet, 1539.

2272 — Columella of Husbandry and Trees, Englished, with Illustrations from Ancient and Modern Authors, 4to. *boards*, 7*s* 6*d* (*See No.* 1176) .. .. .. .. 1745

2273 — De Re Rustica; the Repository for Select Papers on Agriculture, Arts, and Manufactures, 2 vols. 8vo. *calf, very neat*, 8*s* 1769

2274 HUSBANDRY—Duhamel du Monceau's Practical Treatise on Husbandry, 4to. *old calf, neat,* 5*s* .. 1759

For the character of Duhamel, see *Young's Travels in France*, p. 55.

2275 — Elkington's Mode of Draining Land, by authority of the Board of Agriculture, by Johnstone, *plates,* 8vo. *bds,* 3*s* 6*d* 1808

2276 — Epitome of the Art of Husbandry, with Directions for the use of the Angle, Ordering of Bees, and the Gentleman's Heroic Exercise, Discoursing of Horses, by J. B. Gent, 8vo. *old binding, scarce,* 5*s* 6*d* .. .. .. 1675

"Liber rarus et utilis," MS. To this edit. is added, "Directions for taking, ordering, and teaching SINGING BIRDS."

2277 — Harte's (Walter) Essays on Husbandry, *plates,* 8vo. *calf, very good copy,* 5*s* .. .. .. 1770

"An elegant, erudite, and valuable work."—*Lowndes.*

2278 — Hartlib (Samuel) Advice of W. P. to Mr. Samuel Hartlib, for the advancement of some particular parts of Learning, 1648.—His Legacie, or an enlargement of the Discourse of Husbandry used in Brabant, Flanders, *with the chart,* 4to. 1652.—An Interrogatory relating more particularly to the Husbandry and Natural History of Ireland, *Richard Wodenothe,* 1652.—Hartlib's Discoverie for Division or Setting out of Land, as to the best form for planters in the Fens and Waste places in Ireland, *with the chart,* 1653; 4 tracts, 1 vol. small 4to. *old calf, neat, scarce,* 9*s* .. .. .. .. V. Y.

The "advice to Mr. Hartlib for the advancement of learning" was written by Sir Will. Petty.

2279 — Hartlib (Samuel) his Legacie; an Enlargement of the Discourse of Husbandry used in Brabant and Flanders, 2nd edition, with annotations, 4to. *old binding, scarce,* 6*s* .. 1652

2280 — Hartlib (Samuel) his Legacie, 2nd edition, with annotations, and an interrogatory relating to the Husbandry and Natural History of Ireland (this part imperfect) 4to. *half bound,* 3*s* 1653

This, although called the 2nd edit., differs entirely from the following. This work was written by Robert Child, at Hartlib's request, who corrected, revised, and published it. Hartlib was the friend of Milton.

2281 — Hartlib's (Samuel) Discourse of Husbandrie, used in Brabant and Flanders, small 4to. *half russia, neat,* 6*s* *W. Du-Gard,* 1652

2282 — Heresbachius's (Conradus) Four Bookes of Husbandry, containing the whole Art, and of Gardening, Graffing and Planting, newly Englished and encreased by Barnaby Googe, 4to. *limp vellum, curious,* 10*s* 6*d* .. .. *Thomas Wight,* 1601

2283 — Home's (Dr. Francis) Principles of Agriculture and Vegetation, 8vo. *old calf, neat,* 3*s* 6*d* .. *Edinburgh,* 1759

Dr. Home was Fellow of the Roy. Coll. of Physicians in Edinburgh.

2284 — Horse-Houghing Husbandry; an Essay on the Principles of Tillage and Vegetation, Introducing Vineyard-Culture into the Corn Fields, &c. 4to. *old calf, neat,* 3*s* 6*d* *For the Author,* 1731

2285 — Hunter's (Dr. A.) Georgical Essays, *plates,* 8vo. *nice copy in calf,* 5*s* .. .. .. .. *York,* 1777

These Essays on Husbandry are highly esteemed. Dr. Hunter edited a valuable edition of the Sylva, see *Evelyn.*

2286 HUSBANDRY—Lawson's (William) New Orchard and Garden; with the Husbandry of Bees, 1676.—Gervase Markham's Farewell to Husbandry, 1676.—Markham's Cheap and Good Husbandry, 1676.—Markham's English Housewife, 1675.—Markham's Enrichment of the Weald of Kent, 1683.—Markham's Farewell to Husbandry, 1684, in one volume, small 4to. *half calf, neat,* 15*s* .. .. .. V.Y.

2287 — Markham's (Gervase) Country Contentments, or the Husbandman's Recreations in Hunting, Hawking, Coursing, Shooting, Bowling, Tennis, Angling, Fighting Cocks, &c., 1654.—Markham's Farewell to Husbandry, 1653.—Lawson's (George) New Orchard and Garden, with the Husbandry of Bees, 1653, in 1 volume, small 4to. *half bound,* 7*s* 6*d* .. 1653-4

2288 — Markham's (Gervase) Farewell to Husbandry; or, the Enriching of all sorts of Barren and Sterile Grounds in our Nation, small 4to. *half calf, very neat,* 5*s* 6*d* .. .. 1656

2289 — Mascall's (Leonard) Booke of the Arte and Manner how to Plant and Graffe all sorts of Trees, by one of the Abbey of S. Vincent in France, Englished, *wood-cuts,* 4to. **Black Letter,** *sewed,* 8*s* 6*d* *Imprinted at London,* 1596

2290 — Smith's (John) England's Improvement Reviv'd, in a Treatise of all manner of Husbandry and Trade, by Land and Sea, 4to. *old calf, neat,* 6*s* .. .. .. 1673

"I have perused your accurate Treatise, and find it so industriously performed that I cannot but cheerfully give it my approbation."—*John Evelyn, Saye's Court,* 1669.

2291 — Stillingfleet's (Benjamin) "Esteemed" Miscellaneous Tracts on Natural History, Husbandry, and Physic, with the Calendar of Flora, 8vo. *neat,* 3*s* .. .. .. 1762

2292 — Treatise on Fallowing Ground, Raising of Grass Seeds, and Training of Limp and Hemp, *plates,* small 8vo. *old calf, neat, scarce,* 5*s* .. *Edinburgh, Robert Fleming,* 1724

"Published by the Honble. Society for improving in the Knowlege of Agriculture."

2293 — Tusser's (Thomas) Five Hundred Points of Good Husbandry, 4to. **Black Letter,** *boards,* (wants 1 leaf near the end,) £1 1*s* *Rich. Yardley and Peter Short,* 1630

"An edition which does not often occur, and is not included in the list of editions prefixed to Dr. Mavor's excellent re-impression of our old agricultural Poet."—*Bibliotheca Ang-Poet.,* where it is priced 4 guineas.

2294 — 500 Points of Good Husbandry with Notes by Dr. William Mavor, 8vo. *boards,* 7*s* 6*d* .. .. 1812

The first edit. of this Poem exhibiting a Picture of the Agriculture, Customs and Manners of England in the XVI. Cent. was published in 1557.

2295 HUSENBETH'S (Dr. F. C.) Emblems of Saints by which they are Distinguished in Works of Art, 12mo. *cloth, gilt,* 5*s* 1850

Part I.—Saints with their Emblems. II.—Emblems with their Saints.

2296 HUSKISSON'S (Hon. Will.) Questions concerning the Depreciation of our Currency, 8vo. *sewed,* 1*s* 6*d* .. 1810

2297 — Biographical Memoirs of, *proof portrait by W. Finden,* 8vo. *cloth,* 9*s* .. .. *Privately printed,* 1831

2298 HUTCHINSON'S (Benjamin) Biographia Medica; Historical and Critical Memoirs of the Lives and Writings of Eminent Medical Characters, 2 vols. 8vo. *half calf, neat,* 7*s* .. 1799

2299 HYLLE'S (Thomas) Arte of Vulgar Arithmeticke both in Intigers and Fractions, 4to. Black Letter, *calf, neat,* 8s 6d . 1600

Dedicated to Sir Thos. Sackville, Baron Buckhurst, Lord Treasurer, with Introductory Complimentary Verses.

2300 HYMERS'S (J.) Theory of Algebraical Equations, 8vo. *calf, very neat,* 5s 6d (*pub. at* 9s 6d *in boards*) .. *Cambridge,* 1840

2301 IBBOT (Henry, Esq.) Catalogue of his fine Collection of Prints, chiefly British Portraits, sold by Mr. Sotheby, February, 1818, *with the prices at which they sold,* mounted on 4to. *writing paper, neatly half bound,* 18s .. .. .. 1818

*"This Sale Catalogue was given to my father by Miss Ibbot, sister and heiress of Henry Ibbot, Esq. A. Fountaine, Narford, April 8, 1825."*

2302 ICELAND, Hooker's Journal of a Tour in, in 1809, *etchings,* thick 8vo. *boards,* 8s .. *Yarmouth, Keymer,* 1811

This is the original *privately printed* edition of Sir W. J. Hooker's interesting work.

2303 ILLUSTRATED LONDON NEWS, a complete set from its commencement in 1843 to the end of 1855, *many thousands of woodcut illustrations, neatly and uniformly half bound, in* 20 vols. folio, £12 .. .. .. .. 1843-55

A very desirable set of what is to young persons a very entertaining and highly instructive work.

2304 — vols. 24, 25, 26, being for the year 1854, complete, and the first half of 55, *stamped cloth, the large plates nicely mounted on canvas,* £2 5s .. .. .. .. 1854-55

These volumes narrate the history of the Crimean War.

2305 — Jan. to Oct. 10, 1846, *large view of Dublin,* folio, *boards,* 6s

2306 IMP. LEONIS Augusti Constitutiones Novellæ, aut correctoriæ legum repurgationes Latinæ nunc primum ab Henrico Agylæo factæ, 8vo. *old binding, scarce,* 7s 6d .. *H. Stephanus,* 1560

Contents: Imp. Justiniani Edicta, Justini Constitut. Tiberii et Zenonis Constitutiones. Sir Christopher Hatton's copy.

2307 IMPEY (Sir Elijah) Memoirs of, with Anecdotes of Warren Hastings, Sir P. Francis, Halhed, and other Contemporaries, *fine portrait,* 8vo. *cloth,* 6s 6d (*pub. at* 15s) .. 1846

Written by his Son to confute the calumnies of Lord Macaulay. Sir Elijah was first Chief Justice of the Supreme Court of Judicature, Fort William, Bengal.

2308 INCIDENTS of the Apostolic Age in Great Britain, post 8vo. *cloth,* 4s 6d (*pub. at* 6s) .. .. *W. Pickering,* 1844

2309 INDIA—Diversi Avisi particolari dall' Indie di Portogallo ricevuti, dall' Anno 1551 fino al 1558 dalli Reverendi Padri della Compagnia di Giesu, tradotti dalla Lingua Spagnuola nella Italiana, small thick 8vo. *vellum,* 15s *Venezia, M. Tramezzino,* 1558

"Libro Raro."—*Haym.* With the license of Pope Julius III. for 15 years. It is a considerable volume of 294 leaves.

2310 — Historical and Descriptive Account of British India, by Hugh Murray and others, *map and pates,* 3 vols. 12mo. *cloth,* 7s 6d (*pub. at* 15s) .. .. *Edinb. Cab. Lib.,* 1832

2311 — The Three Presidences of, a History of the Rise and Progress of the British Indian Possessions by John Capper, *portrait and plates,* 8vo. *half calf, neat,* 5s (*cost* 9s) .. 1853

2312 INDIA—Indian Vocabulary, to which is prefixed the forms of Impeachments, 12mo. *half calf, neat*, 4*s* .. 1788

Got up to assist people to understand terms used at Warren Hastings's trial.

2313 INSECTS—5 Tracts on, in 1 vol. 8vo. *half calf, neat*, 6*s* 1770-75

Contents:—1. Forster's Catalogue of British Insects, *Warrington*, 1770.—2. Novæ Species Insectorum, Centuria I. auctore, J. R. Forster, *Londini*, 1771.—3. Moses Harris's English Lepidoptera; Catalogue of 400 Moths and Butterflies, *coloured plates*, 1775.—4. [Curtis's] Instructions for collecting and preserving Insects, *plate*, 1771.—5. [Dr. Lettsome's] Naturalist's and Traveller's Companion, *plates*, 1772.

2314 INTRIGUES Galantes de la Cour de France, 2 *plates*, 2 vols. 12mo. *neat*, 5*s* 6*d* .. .. .. *Cologne*, 1694

Commences with the amours of Pharamond to the death of Cardinal Mazarine, about 1660, temp. Louis XIV. Barbier attributes the work to Vannel, and dates the 1st edit. 1695.

2315 IRELAND—Two Petitions from the Kingdome of Ireland to the Commons, small 4to. *sewed, clean as new*, 5*s* *J. Reynor*, 1641

2316 — Copie of the Oath taken by the Papists as it was given to the Governour and Captaines by Fryer Darcy, lately Guardian of the Franciscans in Ireland, and employed by the rebels upon a Treaty, by N. B., small 4to. *sewed, clean as new, rare*, 7*s* 6*d* *W. Bladen*, 1642

2317 — Remarkable Propositions by the Council in Ireland to the Parliament in England, small 4to. *sewed*, 6*s* 1642

2318 — True and Credible relation of the barbarous crueltie and bloudy Massacre of the English Protestants in Ulster, in Ireland, 1641, by a Gentleman, who was forc'd to abandon his house, and arrived in London, Jan. 15, 1641, small 4to. *stiff cover, clean as new, rare*, 10*s* 6*d* .. .. *E. Griffin*, 1642

2319 — Irish Protestants, in London, Sermon to them, Oct. 23, 1690, by Richard, Bp. of Killala, 4to. *sewed*, 1*s* 6*d* .. 1691

Anniversary Thanksgiving Sermon for Deliverance of Protestants from Popish Massacre begun Oct. 23, 1641.

2320 — True List of the Parliament held in Dublin, Sept. 21, 1703, before James, Duke of Ormond, Lord Lieut., *a broadside, rare*, 5*s* *Dublin, by Andrew Crook, on the Blind Key*, 1703

2321 — Davies's (Sir John) Discoverie of the true causes why Ireland was never subdued until the beginning of H. Maiestie's happie raigne, 12mo. *calf, neat, scarce*, 6*s* .. 1747

A reprint of the edition of 1612. Sir John Davies was Attorney General of Ireland, temp. James I.

2322 — Gentleman and Citizen's Almanack, for 1747, by John Watson, bookseller, 12mo. *old morocco, elaborately gilt, gilt edges, curious*, £1 1*s* .. .. .. *Dublin*, 1747

A beautiful specimen of old morocco binding. This Almanack was published by authority and has the names of all the Officers of the Four Courts, Philip Earl of Chesterfield, Lord Lieutenant.

2323 — Bush's (J) Hibernia Curiosa; a general view of the Manners, Customs, &c., of the Inhabitants of Ireland, and Remarkable Natural Curiosities, *map and 5 large folded plates*, 8vo. *original edition, calf, neat*, 6*s* .. .. 1769

2324 — Irish Almanack, for 1772, containing the names of all the great officers of State, &c., small 8vo. *sewed, scarce*, 4*s* *Dublin, S. Watson*, 1772

2325 IRELAND—Holmes' (G.) Sketches of some of the Southern Counties of Ireland, in 1797, *plates*, 8vo. *half calf*, 4*s* 6*d* 1801
2326 — Post Chaise Companion; or, Traveller's Directory through Ireland, *maps and plates, by Martyn*, 8vo. *calf*, 3*s* *Dublin*, 1803
2327 — Excursions in Ireland, 100 *plates, proof impressions*, 2 vols. 8vo. LARGE PAPER, *half morocco, extra, top edges gilt, new*, 18*s* 1820
2328 — Irish History, Sketches of, its Antiquities, Religion, Customs, and Manners, with a Preface by Charlotte Elizabeth, *map and plates*, 12mo. *cloth*, 2*s* 6*d* .. *Dublin*, 1844
2329 IRVING'S (David) Lives of the Scottish Poets, with Dissertations on the Literary History of Scotland, and its early Drama, 2 vols. 8vo. *calf, very neat*, 10*s* .. *Edinburgh*, 1804

"A work displaying great research and critical ingenuity."—*T. Park.*

2330 IRVING'S (Washington) Salmagundi, by the author of the Sketch Book, crown 8vo. *boards*, 4*s* 6*d* (*pub. at* 7*s* 6*d*) *T. Davison*, 1824
2331 — Life and Voyages of Christopher Columbus, 4 vols. 8vo. *boards*, 16*s* (*pub. at* £2 2*s*) .. .. 1828
2332 — Astoria; Enterprize beyond the Rocky Mountains, 3 vols. post 8vo. *boards, large letter edition*, 6*s* (*pub. at* £1 11*s* 6*d*) 1836
2333 — Tales of the Alhambra, with Legends of the Conquest of Spain, 8vo. *half bound, neat*, 3*s* .. .. 1840
2334 — Tales of the Alhambra, *plate*, 12mo. *cloth*, 2*s* 6*d* *Bentley*, 1850
2335 — Chronicles of Wolfert's Roost, and other Papers, post 8vo. *cloth*, 3*s* .. .. *Edinburgh*, 1855
2336 IRWIN'S (Eyles) Adventures during a Voyage up the Red Sea, &c., in the years 1777, and Aleppo and Bagdad in 1780, and 1781, *portrait, plates, and maps*, 2 vols. 8vo. *half calf, neat*, 7*s* 1787

Valuable for the information given of the manners, &c., of the Arabs.

2337 ISLE of Man, Descriptive and Historical Account of, *map*, 12mo. *boards*, 2*s* .. .. *Newcastle*, 1809
2338 ISLE of Wight, New Picture of, *with* 36 *nicely engraved plates, by W. Cooke*, 8vo. *boards*, 5*s* (*pub. at* 21*s*) .. 1808
2339 — another copy, 36 *plates*, 8vo. *half morocco, neat*, 5*s* 6*d* 1808
2340 ISOCRATES, Orationes, Gr. et Lat., cum notis Hieron. Wolfii, thick 8vo. *half russia, good copy*, 9*s* *Basileæ, Jo. Oporini*, 1553

"The merits of Wolf are very considerable, his conjectures are frequently happy, and his corrections judicious. The Latin version is greatly amended in *this* edition."—See *Dibdin.*

2341 — Orationes et Epistolæ, Græcè, cum Lat. Interp. Wolfii, thick 8vo. *old calf*, 3*s* 6*d* .. *Colon. Allobrogum*, 1618
2342 ITALIAN—Nomenclature, English and Italian, 12mo. *old calf, scarce*, 6*s* .. .. .. 1726

"Let. Bacon, her Italian book, March ye 30th, 1727.
Let. Bacon is my name, and with a pen I wrote ye same,
And if my pen it had been better, I would have mended every letter.

It has also the autograph of Mary Bacon, sister to Sir Edmund.

"For God's sake learn Italian as fast as you can, if it be only to read Ariosto. There is more good poetry in Italian than in all other languages that I understand put together."—*Cha. James Fox to Mr. Fitz-Patrick. In Lord John Russell's Life and Times of C. J. Fox* See No. 243 in this Catalogue.

2343 ITALY—Journal of a Tour in Italy, in 1821, with a Description of Gibraltar, by an American, *plates*, 8vo. *bds*, 5*s* *New York*, 1824

2344 JACKSON'S (John) History of the City and Cathedral of Lichfield, *plates*, 8vo. *half calf, neat*, 4*s* 6*d* .. 1805

2345 JACKSON'S (William, *of Exeter*) Four Ages, with Essays on various subjects, 8vo. *calf, neat, scarce*, 6*s* 1798

2346 JACOB'S (Alexander) Complete English Peerage; *numerous finely engraved portraits, coats of arms, and genealogical tables*, vols. 1 and 2, in 3 vols. folio, *old calf, a fine copy*, £1 1*s* *For the author*, 1766-67

2347 JACOBS (Friedrick) Hellas; or, the Home, History, Literature, and Art of the Greeks, translated by John Oxenford, 12mo. *cloth*, 2*s* 6*d* (*pub. at* 4*s* 6*d*) .. .. 1855

2348 JACOMB (Samuel) of St. Mary, Woolnoth, Lombard Street, London, Funeral Sermon for him, 1659, see *Patrick*.

2349 JAFFRAY (Alexander) Diary, with particulars of his subsequent Life, being Memoirs of the Rise, Progress, &c. of the Quakers in the north of Scotland, by John Barclay, 8vo. *boards*, 6*s* (*pub. at* 10*s* 6*d*) .. .. .. 1834

Alexander Jaffray was Provost of Aberdeen, one of the Scottish Commissioners to K. Cha. II. and a Member of Cromwell's Parliament.

2350 JAMES I. King of Scotland, Poetical Remains, with his Life, and a Dissertation on the Scottish Music, by W. Tytler, 8vo. *calf, neat*, 6*s* .. .. .. *Edinb.*, 1783

Contents: the King's Quair, a Poem on his wife, Queen Jane, and Christ's Kirk of the Grene.

2351 JAMES II.—Account of what his Majesty said at his first coming to Council, folio, *broadside, rare*, 10*s* 6*d* *Henry Hills*, 1684

The date of this should be 1685. The substance is given in Howell's Medulla.

2352 — Exact List of both Houses of Parliament to meet at Westminster, May 19th, in the 1st year of K. James's reign, folio, *broadside*, £1 1*s* .. .. *J. Leake*, 1685

Members for Norfolk, Sir Thomas Hare and Sir Jacob Astley, Baronets,—for Norwich, Robert Paston, Esq. and Sir Nevill Catlyn, Kt.

2353 — another List of James II. first Parliament, folio, *broadside*, £1 1*s* *Printed by Tho. Newcomb*, 1685

2354 — Mr. Pen's Speech to the King, and the King's Answer to it, in MS., folio, *broadside*, 5*s* .. *No date, but* 1685

This Speech differs from that given by Hume.

2355 — An Act of Indempnity and Pardon of James Stuart, late King of England, folio, *broadside*, in MS., *nicely written, with a recommendatory letter accompanying it*, 10*s*

Done with the consent of K. William and Q. Mary, who was eldest daughter of K. James II.

2356 — King of France's Letter to the Earl of Tyrconnel, found in a ship laden with arms for Ireland, folio, *broadside*, 5*s* *For T. P.*, 1688

"We have sent you arms for 30,000," &c.—*Quotation.*

2357 — His Majesties reasons for withdrawing himself from Rochester, folio, *broadside, curious*, 10*s* *Rochester, Dec.* 22, 1688

2358 — King's Letter to the Great Council of Peers, folio, *broadside*, 5*s* *W. Thomson*, 1688

2359 JAMES II.—Full account of the Death and Character of the Princess Royal Louisa Maria Teresa Stuart, daughter of the late King James, born at St. Germains, 1692, died of the small pox, Ap. 18. 1712, folio, *broadside, rare,* 6*s* .. .. 1712

2360 — Tyranny detected, and the late Revolution justify'd, being a History of the late K. James's Reign, by Ric. Kingston, 8vo. *cloth, scarce,* 3*s* 6*d* .. .. .. 1699

Not in Lowndes, but who mentions another book by Kingston, dated 1698.

2361 JAMES'S (Charles) Military Dictionary, in English and French, 8vo. *calf, very neat,* 8*s* .. .. 1816

2362 JAMES'S (G. P. R.) Henry of Guise, or the States of Blois, *frontispiece,* 8vo. *cloth,* 4*s* 6*d* (*pub. at* 8*s*) 1845

2363 — One in a Thousand, or the days of Henry Quatre, *frontispiece,* 8vo. *cloth,* 4*s* 6*d* (*pub. at* 8*s*) .. .. 1847

2364 JAMES'S (Henry, *Queen's Coll., Camb.*) Sermon before K. Cha. II. at Newmarket, Oct. 11, 1674, 4to. *sewed,* 1*s* 6*d* 1674

2365 JAMES'S (Prebendary John) Comment on the Collects, 12mo. *purple morocco, gilt edges,* 8*s* .. *Rivington,* 1843

2366 JAMES'S (William) Account of the chief Naval Occurrences of the late War between Great Britain and the United States of America, 8vo. *half calf, neat,* 5*s* .. 1817

2367 — Naval History of Great Britain, *portraits, maps, and plates,* 7 vols. 8vo. *half calf, gilt, new,* £2 16*s* .. 1837

This is the best library edition, edited by Capt. Chamier. The folded Annual Abstracts are put into a volume by themselves.

2368 JAMESON'S (Mrs.) Memoirs of Celebrated Female Sovereigns, 2 vols. post 8vo. *boards,* 8*s* (*pub. at* £1 1*s*) 1834

2369 JAMIESON'S (Dr. John) Dictionary of the Scottish Language, abridged by J. Johnstone, *portrait,* thick 8vo. *cloth,* 10*s* (*pub. at* £1 1*s*) .. .. *Edinburgh,* 1846

2370 JANICON (F. M.) État présent de la Republique des Provinces-Unies, et des Pais qui en dependent, 2 vols. 12mo. *neat,* 4*s* *La Haye,* 1755

2371 JANNEY'S (Samuel M.) Conversations on Religious Subjects, 12mo. *boards,* 2*s* .. .. *Philadelphia,* 1835

"Presented to J. J. Gurney by his friend, S. M. J.," the author.

2372 JAPAN—De Rebus Japonicis, Indicis et Peruanis Epistolæ recentiores, a Joanne Hayo Dalgettiensi Scoto Societetis Jesu, thick 8vo. of 1000 pages, *fine clean copy, rare,* £1 *Antverpiæ,* 1605

These interesting letters were written from about 1577 to 1599, by Lewis Frois, Nicholas Pimenta, Jerome Xavier, Alexander Valignani, Anthony Dalmeid, Nicholas Longobard, Martin Perez, Francis Vaez, Emmanuel Pinner, Francis Pace, Francis de Castro, and others.

2373 JARVIS'S (George, *of Tuttington, Norfolk*) Sermons on Particular Occasions, 8vo. *cloth,* 3*s* 6*d* (*pub. at* 7*s* 6*d*) *Oxford,* 1851

2374 JEANES (Henry, *Rector of Chedzoy, Somersetshire*) Mixture of Scholastic Divinity with Practicall, 2 vols. 4to. *old calf, neat,* 14*s* *Oxford,* 1656

One of the Polemical Disputants with Bp. Jeremy Taylor, who is spoken of with respect by Bp. Heber in his Life of Bp. Taylor. See also Twisse's Riches of God's Love, folio, 1653 in this Catalogue.

2375 JEANS'S (Rev. George) Practical Astronomy, for the unlearned, post 8vo. *boards*, 8*s* 6*d* .. .. 1841

2376 JEANS'S (H. W., F.R.A.S., *Royal Naval College, Portsmouth)* Navigation and Nautical Astronomy, 12mo. *cloth*, 2*s* 1853

Rules for finding the latitude and longitude, and the variation of the compass. Author of many other valuable works on Navigation and Astronomy.

2377 JEANS'S (Rev. Thomas, *Rector of Witchingham, Norfolk, and Chaplain to the Bishop)* Sermon on Church Discipline, preached at Norwich Cathedral, June 17, 1791, at the Primary Visitation of Bishop Horne, 4to. *sewed*, 2*s* 6*d* *Norwich*, 1791

2378 JEANS (Mr. W. D., *Secretary to the late Rear Admiral Boxer)* Despatch containing the Correspondence relative to the state of the Harbour of Balaklava, August, 1855, *with view of the harbour*, folio, *sewed*, 5*s* .. .. . 1855

2379 JEBB'S (Bp. John) Life, by Charles Forster, *portrait*, 2 vols. 8vo. *half calf, very neat*, 15*s* (*pub. at* 28*s*) .. 1836

2380 JEFFERSON'S Tales—Tales of Old Mr. Jefferson, of Gray's Inn, collected by Young Mr. Jefferson, of Lyon's Inn, 2 vols. 12mo. *half bound in green morocco, uncut, top edges gilt*, 7*s* 6*d* 1823

2381 JENKIN'S (Dr. Robert) Reasonableness and Certainty of the Christian Religion, 2 vols. 8vo. *calf, neat*, 6*s* 1721

A valuable and learned work, recommended by the late Bishop of Oxford, Dr. Lloyd, to his clergy.

2382 JENNINGS'S (Dr. David) Jewish Antiquities; Lectures on the three first books of Godwin's Moses and Aaron, with a Dissertation on the Hebrew Language, 2 vols. 8vo. *boards*, 5*s* 1808

With *Mr. Joseph John Gurney's* book-plate. "This work has long held a distinguished character for accuracy and learning."—*Horne's Introduction.*

2383 JERRAM'S (Charles) Tribute of Paternal Affection to the Memory of a beloved and only Daughter and Son, 12mo. *half morocco, neat*, 3*s* .. .. .. 1824

2384 JERROLD'S (Douglas) Cakes and Ale, post 8vo. *half calf*, 3*s* 1852

2385 JERVIS'S Acts relating to the Duties of Justices of the Peace, 2nd Edit., by Archbold, 12mo. *cloth*, 3*s* 6*d* (*pub. at* 8*s*) 1849

2386 JESSE'S (Edward) Angler's Rambles, post 8vo. *cloth*, 6*s* 6*d* (*pub. at* 10*s* 6*d*) .. .. *Van Voorst*, 1836

2387 JESSOPP'S (John) Woman, in 8 chapters; Woman "an help meet for Man;" Woman in her domestic relations, the Christian Wife, Maiden, and Mother, &c., small 8vo. *antique cloth, gilt, new*, 3*s* 6*d* .. .. .. 1857

2388 JESUITES—The Legend of the Jesuites, Englished, small 4to. *sewed*, 5*s* 6*d* .. . .. 1623

The reasons for which the Citizens of Troyes, in France, being Roman Catholics, refuse to receive them.

2389 JEWEL'S (Bp. John) Apology of the Church of England, with an Epistle by him on the Council of Trent, and his Life, *portrait*, 8vo. *old calf, neat*, 4*s* 6*d* .. .. 1685

"No book, excepting the Common Prayer and the Homilies, has received a greater share of public sanction and authority in the English Church."—*Dr. Hook's Call to Union.*

2390 JEWISH Spy; Philosophical, Historical, and Critical Correspondence, by letters between Jews in Turkey, Italy, France, &c., 5 vols. 12mo. *calf, neat, scarce,* 15*s* .. 1766

2391 JEWS—The History of the Jews, by Milman, *maps,* 3 vols. 18mo. *cloth,* 7*s* 6*d* (*pub. at* 15*s*) .. .. 1829

2392 JEWSBURY'S (M. J.) Letters to the Young, 12mo. *cloth,* 2*s* 1837

2393 JOHNSON (Dr. James) Sketch of his Life and Writings, by his Son, Henry J. J., of St. George's Hospital, London, *fine portrait,* 8vo. *sewed,* 2*s* 6*d* .. .. .. 1846

2394 [JOHNSON'S (John)] Holy David and his old English Translators clear'd, 8vo. *old calf, neat, scarce,* 7*s* 6*d* .. 1706

Anonymous, but performed by the learned author of the Clergyman's Vade-Mecum. See *Masters's Hist. of C. C. C. Camb.* This is the PSALTER, *pointed* with large explanatory Notes, and a General Defence of the old Translation in the Great Bible.

2395 — Clergyman's Vade-Mecum; an account of the Ancient and Present Church of England, with the Canonical Codes of the Eastern and Western Church (translated at large from the Greek) down to A.D. 787, 2 vols. 12mo. *old calf, neat, scarce,* 9*s* 1714-15

2396 — vol. 1 of ditto, on the Duties and Rights of the Clergy, 12mo. *old calf, neat,* 3*s* .. .. .. 1723

2397 JOHNSON'S (John, *Printer,*) Typographia; or the Printer's Instructor, including an account of the Origin of Printing, with Biographical Notices of the Printers from Caxton to the close of the XVI. Century, 2 vols. 8vo. LARGEST PAPER, *boards, uncut,* £2 12*s* 6*d* (*pub. at* 4 *guineas*) .. .. 1824

Dedicated to Earl Spencer and the members of the Roxburghe Club, on which account this is called "the Roxburghe Copy." "An extremely useful book."—*Lowndes.* It is embellished with a series of ancient and modern alphabets, foreign as well as English, and Domesday characters.

2398 JOHNSON'S (J.) Voyage to India and China in 1803 to 1806, *map,* 8vo. *half morocco, neat,* 3*s* 6*d* .. .. 1807

2399 JOHNSON'S (Dr. Samuel) Works, with an Essay on his Life and Genius, by Murphy, *portrait,* 12 vols. 8vo. *boards,* £1 10*s* (*pub. at* £4 16*s*) .. .. .. 1810

2400 — Dictionary of the English Language, with the addition of several thousand words by Todd, *portrait,* 5 vols. 4to. *newly half bound, in calf,* £4 4*s* (*pub. at* £11 11*s*) .. 1818

2401 — Dictionary of the English Language abridged from H. J. Todd's enlarged edition, by A. Chalmers, 8vo. *boards,* 5*s* 6*d* (*pub. at* 10*s* 6*d*) .. .. .. .. 1824

2402 — another copy of Chalmers's abridgement, 8vo. *half cloth,* 6*s* (*pub. at* 12*s*) .. .. .. 1837

2403 — Lives of the most Eminent English Poets, *portrait,* 4 vols. 8vo. *calf, neat,* 10*s* .. .. .. 1783

2404 — another edition, 2 vols. 8vo. *calf, grained, neat,* 7*s* 1821

2405 — Cary's (Henry F.) Lives of the English Poets, from Johnson to Kirke White, 12mo. *cloth, new,* 3*s* 6*d* (*pub. at* 6*s*) 1846

Designed as a continuation of Dr. S. Johnson's Lives of the Poets.

2406 — Journey to the Western Islands of Scotland, 8vo. *calf, neat,* 4*s*

2407 — another edition, small 8vo. *boards,* 2*s* 6*d* *Edinburgh,* 1798

2408 — Debates in Parliament, 1740 to 43, 2 vols. 8vo. *calf, very nice copy,* 9*s* .. .. .. 1787

2409 JOHNSON'S (Dr. Samuel) Letters to and from him, by Hester Lynch Piozzi, 2 vols. 8vo. *calf, neat,* 6s .. .. 1788

2410 — Life, by Sir John Hawkins, 8vo. *calf, neat,* 5s 1787

2411 — second edition, 8vo. *fine copy, in old calf,* 6s 1787

2412 — Life, by Boswell, with Mr. Croker's Notes, *above* 40 *plates,* 10 vols. 12mo. *cloth,* £1 15s (*pub. at* £2 10s) .. 1844

2413 — Life, by Boswell, Notes by Croker, vol. 10 only, 12mo. *cloth,* 3s .. .. .. .. 1835

2414 — Life, by Boswell, Malone's Notes, complete in 1 vol. *portrait,* 12mo. *cloth,* 5s (*pub. at* 12s) *Chiswick, Whittingham,* 1831

2415 — Johnsoniana; a Collection of Anecdotes and Sayings of Dr. S. Johnson, *portrait and plate,* 12mo. *cloth, neat,* 3s 6d (*pub. at* 6s)

2416 JOHNSTONE'S (Chevalier de) Memoirs of the Rebellion of 1745 and 1746, with an Account of his Sufferings and Privations after the Battle of Culloden, *portraits of the Pretender and James Stuart, and plan,* 8vo. *boards,* 7s 6d (*pub. at* 15s) *Longmans,* 1822

"This work should be looked at, particularly the introduction, which is sensible and important."—*Professor Smyth.*

2417 JONES'S (D.) Secret Hist. of Whitehall from the Restoration (1660) to the Abdication of James II. (1688), 2 vols. 12mo. *old calf, very neat,* 9s .. .. .. 1717

"This is the best edition of this scandalous history."—*Lowndes.*

2418 JONES (Eliz.) Chronological Hist. of England, in English and French, 18mo. *sewed,* 1s 6d .. .. *Paris,* 1843

2419 JONES'S (John) Greek Grammar, 12mo. *boards,* 2s 1808

2420 JONES (John) Attempts in Verse, with some Account of the Writer, and an Essay on the Lives and Works of our uneducated Poets by Robert Southey, 8vo. *boards,* 4s 6d (*pub. at* 10s 6d) 1831

2421 JONES (Richard Roberts, *of Aberdaron, Carnarvon, N. Wales,*) Memoir of, exhibiting a remarkable instance of a partial power and Cultivation of Intellect, *fine portrait,* 8vo. *boards, original edition,* 3s .. .. .. 1822

2422 JONES'S (Thomas, *of Creaton*) Baskets of Fragments, notes from Sermons, 2 vols. 12mo. *cloth,* 4s .. 1834

2423 JONES'S (Sir William) Works, with Life, by Lord Teignmouth, *portrait,* 13 vols. 8vo. *boards,* £2 12s 6d (*pub. at* £6 16s 6d) 1807

One of the most elegant and accomplished scholars England ever produced.

2424 — Poems, consisting chiefly of Translations from the Asiatick Languages, with two Essays on the Poetry of the Eastern Nations, and on the Imitative Arts, 8vo. *calf, very neat,* 5s 1777

2425 — Grammar of the Persian Language, 4to. *curious ornamented oriental binding,* 8s .. .. 1771

At the end is a catalogue of the most valuable books in the Persian language.

2426 — another edition, 4to. *calf, neat,* 8s 6d .. 1809

2427 — Essay on the Law of Bailments, with Notes, &c., by John Balmanno, 8vo. *calf, neat,* 3s 6d .. .. 1798

"Know him, Sir?" said Parr, "Who did not know him? Who did not bend in devout respect at the variety and depth of his learning, the integrity of his principles, and the benevolence of his heart?"—*Parriana,* p. 322.

2428 JONES'S (Will.) Catholic Doctrine of the Trinity, with Reflections on Dr. S. Clarke and other Arians, 8vo. *calf, neat,* 2s 6d . 1767

2429 JONSON (Ben,) his Autograph, see *Hayward.*

2430 JONSTONI (Arturi) Psalmi Davidici, cum argumentis et notis, 12mo. *calf, very neat,* 3*s* *Londini, Bowyer,* 1741

2431 JORIO (Andrea de) Notizie su gli Scavi di Ercolano, 5 *plates,* 8vo. *sewed,* 3*s* 6*d* .. .. *Napoli,* 1827

2432 JORTIN'S (Dr. John) Remarks on Ecclesiastical History, 3 vols. 8vo. *old calf,* 12*s* .. .. 1751-54

2433 — Remarks on Ecclesiastical History, vols. 1 and 2, 8vo. *calf, neat,* 6*s*

"Dr. Jortin has, in a little compass, taken notice of so many facts and animadverted upon them with so much judgment, that his work will ever be held in deserved repute." —*Bp. Watson.*

2434 — Six Dissertations on different subjects, 8vo. *calf, very neat,* 4*s* 1755

"These dissertations are equally remarkable for taste, learning, originality, and ingenuity."—*Dr. Knox.*

2435 — Sermons, 7 vols. 8vo. *a very fine clean copy, in old calf,* £1 1*s* 1771

2436 — Sermons, published by his Son, with an account of his Life, *portrait, by J. Hall,* 7 vols. 8vo. *nice clean copy in the original calf,* £1 4*s* .. .. .. 1787

"In these sermons, good sense and sound morality appear; not, indeed, dressed out in the meretricious ornaments of a florid style, but in all the manly force and simple graces of natural eloquence. They will always be read with pleasure and edification." —*Knox's Essays.* Dr. Parr acknowledged himself much indebted to Dr. Jortin for affording him "rational entertainment and solid instruction."

2437 — Sermons, 4 vols. *half morocco,* 7*s* .. *London,* 1826

2438 JOSEPHUS'S (Flavius) Works, containing the Jewish Antiquities and Wars of the Jews, with 3 Dissertations by the translator, W. Whiston, *portrait,* 4 vols. 8vo. *half cloth,* 12*s* 1806

2439 — another edition, with Life, by Whiston, *portrait and plates,* thick 8vo. *cloth,* 5*s* 6*d* (*pub. at* 12*s*) .. 1849

"The fidelity, the veracity, and the probity of Josephus, are universally allowed; and Scaliger, in particular, declares, that not only in the affairs of the Jews, but even of foreign nations, he deserves more credit than all the Greek and Roman writers put together."—*Bp. Porteus.*

2440 JOURNAL of a Tour and Residence in Great Britain, in 1810 and 1811, by a French Traveller, *mezzotint plates,* 2 vols. 8vo. *half calf, neat,* 10*s* .. .. *Edinburgh,* 1815

2441 JOURNAL of a Naturalist, *plates,* post 8vo. *cloth,* 6*s* *Murray,* 1838

2442 JOURNAL of Design and Manufactures, *fabric patterns inserted and numerous engravings,* vol. 1 to 6, bound in 3, 8vo. *cloth,* 15*s* (*pub. at* 45*s*) .. .. .. 1849-52

2443 JOURNAL of a Horticultural Tour, through Flanders, Holland, and the North of France in 1817, by a deputation of the Caledonian Horticultural Society, *plates,* 8vo. *half calf, neat,* 5*s* *Edinburgh,* 1823

2444 JOURNAL of the Horticultural Society of London, vols. 2 and 3, in 4 parts each, complete, *coloured plates,* royal 8vo. *sewed,* £1 (*pub. at* £2) .. .. .. 1847-48

2445 JOURNAL of the Royal Agricultural Society of England, a complete set to vol. 19, part 1, 41 numbers, 8vo. *sewed,* £4 10*s* 1839-1858

2446 — other volumes and parts of volumes, vol. 2, parts 1, 2, 3.—vol. 3, parts 1, 2, 3.—vol. 4, parts 1, 2.—vol. 8, part 2.—vol. 10, parts 1, 2.—vol. 11, part 1.—vol. 12, part 2, 3*s* each part, (*pub. at* 10*s each part*)

2447 JOURNAL—vol. 3, parts 2 and 3.—vol. 11, part 1, 3*s* each part

2448 JOURNEY through England, in Letters from a Gentleman here to his Friend abroad, 2 vols. 8vo. *old calf*, 5*s* .. 1722

2449 JOUY, l'Hermite de la Chaussée d' Antin, edition dirigée par M. de Rouillon, 32mo. *calf, elegant, gilt leaves*, 3*s* 6*d* *Norwich*, 1838

2450 JOVII (Pauli) Historia sui Temporis, vol. 2 only, beginning at the 19th book, 4to. *bound*, 7*s* 6*d* *Venetiis, Matt. Bosellus*, 1553

As the 1st edition was printed in 1552, this is quite an early edition.

2451 — Elogia Virorum bellica virtute illustrium, 128 *portraits*, folio, *vellum*, 15*s* *Basiliæ, P. Pernæ, typog.* 1596

"The writings of Jovius cannot be wholly rejected without the loss of much important information, copiously narrated and elegantly expressed."—*Roscoe's Leo X.*

2452 JOWETT'S (Will.) Christian Researches in Syria and the Holy Land, in 1823-4, *plans*, 8vo. *half calf, neat*, 5*s* 6*d* (*pub. at* 12*s*) 1825

Contains, also, Mr. Greaves's Journal of his visit to the Regency of Tunis.

2453 JOYCE (George, *Cornet Joyce, Governor of the Isle of Wight, temp. Car. I.*) unique Tract about him. See *Charles I.*, No. 983.

2454 JOYCE'S (Rev. J.) Scientific Dialogues, in which the first principles of Natural and Experimental Philosophy are Explained, 7 vols. 18mo. *half bound*, 3*s* 6*d* .. .. 1812

2455 — Dialogues in Chemistry, 2 vols. 18mo. *half bound*, 1*s* 6*d* 1809

2456 JUDKIN'S (Rev. C.) Account of a Mission in Arabia and the Banks of the Euphrates, in 1824-5, to propagate Christian Knowledge, post 8vo. *cloth*, 4*s* (*pub. at* 9*s*) .. .. 1828

2457 JUNCKERI (Christ.) Schediasma Historum de Ephemeridibus sive Diariis Eruditorum et Centuria Fæminarum eruditione et Scriptis illustrium, 12mo. *scarce*, 6*s* .. *Lipsiæ*, 1692

"Historiographer to the Ernestine branch of the House of Saxony; had a great knowledge of the belles lettres and medals."—*Moreri.*

2458 JUNII (Adriani) Nomenclator Octolinguis omnium rerum propria nomina continens, accessit Nomenclator è duobus Vet. Glossariis H. Germbergii opera, 8vo. *old calf, scarce*, 6*s* *Jacobus Stœr*, 1602

2459 — Animadversiones et Observationes variæ, historicæ, criticæ, &c., ejusdemque Commentarium de Coma, *portrait*, 8vo. LARGE PAPER, *calf, neat*, 6*s* .. .. *Hagæ Comitum*, 1737

The treatise "de Coma," was first printed at Basle in 1556.

2460 JUNII (Francisci) Observationes in Willerami abbatis Franciscam Paraphrasin Cantici Canticorum, 8vo. *clean copy, in old calf, scarce*, 6*s* .. .. .. *Amstelodami*, 1655

White Kennett's copy, Bishop of Peterborough, with his book-plate.

2461 JUNIUS, 2 vols. 12mo. *calf, a fine copy*, £1 1*s* *H. S. Woodfall*, 1772

"Now, referring to Junius's own editions of his letters, namely, that published by Woodfall in 1772, *the only edition which should be referred to* when it contains the information of which we are in search—we find," &c.—*Notes and Queries*, August 6, 1859, p. 103, in reference to Henry Flood being the author of Junius.

A copy of this edition made, at Horne Tooke's sale, £1 13*s*. This copy has, in addition to the collation given by Mr. Lowndes, a table of contents, 8 pages, and an index, 19 leaves. See further in Mr. Bohn's edition of Lowndes, just published, Feb. 1, for much important information about Junius.

2462 — The authorship of the Letters of Junius elucidated; including a Biographical Memoir of Lieutenant Colonel Isaac Barré, M.P., by John Britton, F.S.A., *portraits of Lord Ashburton, Barré, and Lord Lansdowne*, royal 8vo. *cloth, new*, 9*s* .. 1847

2463 JUNIUS—another copy, *portraits*, royal 8vo. *cloth*, 6*s* 1848

2464 JUSTINIANI (Petri) Rerum Venetarum ab urbe condita Historia, folio, *a fine copy in old calf, gilt, rare*, £1 5*s* *Venetiis, apud Cominum de Tridino Montisferrati*, 1560

This is a finely printed volume, not mentioned by Brunet.

2465 JUSTINIANI Novellarum Constitutionum, G. Haloandro interprete, Canones Apostolici, Extravagantes, Edicta, &c. H. Agylæo interprete, 8vo. *old calf, neat*, 9*s* .. *Parisiis*, 1562

Sir Christopher Hatton's copy. "The edicts which Justinian promulgated, after the new edit. of the Codex, were collected into one volume in the last year of his reign, (A.D. 566) and published under the name of *Novellæ*."—*Butler's Horæ Jurid. Subsecivæ.*

2466 JUSTINI Martyris Apologia prima pro Christianis, Gr. et Lat., edita à J. E. Grabe, 8vo. *calf, neat*, 3*s* 6*d* *Oxoniæ*, 1700

The first edit. of the first Apology, with the latin version of Langius and Variorum notes.

2467 JUSTINUS, cum notis Variorum, 8vo. *calf, very neat*, 6*s* *Amst., apud Elzevirios*, 1659

"An elegant and correct book."—*Dibdin.*

2468 JUSTUS Researches on the Chemistry of Food; by W. Gregory, 8vo. *cloth, uncut*, 3*s* 6*d* (*pub. at* 5*s*)

2469 JUVENALIS Satyræ XVI., et in eas Commentarii I. Grangæi, B. Autumni et D. Calderini, thick 4to. *fine copy in old calf, gilt edges*, 10*s* 6*d* .. .. *Parisiis, R. Fouet*, 1614

An edition not mentioned by bibliographers, it has Lord Leicester's arms impressed on the sides.

2470 — Satires, translated into English Verse by Rev. W. H. Marsh, 8vo. *calf, elegant*, 4*s* .. .. .. 1804

2471 JUVENILE LIBRARY; containing Lives of Remarkable Youths.—Historic Anecdotes, France.—History of Africa, *portraits and plates*, 3 vols. 18mo. *cloth*, 6*s* 6*d* (*pub. at* 12*s*) 1830-32

2472 KALTSCHMIDT'S (Dr. J. H.) Dictionary of the English and German and German and English Languages, with two Sketches of Grammar, thick 8vo. *bound*, 8*s* .. *Leipzig*, 1837

2473 KAIMES'S (Lord) Essays on the Principles of Morality and Natural Religion, 12mo. *neat*, 2*s* 6*d* .. .. 1758

For another work by his lordship, see *Henry Home*, No. 2170.

2474 — Memoirs of his Life and Writings by Alex. F. Tytler, of Woodhouselee, *portrait*, 3 vols. 8vo. *cloth*, 7*s* 6*d* *Edinburgh*, 1814

2475 KEIGHTLEY'S (Thomas) Outlines of History, *vignette*, 12mo. *half morocco, very neat*, 4*s* (*cost* 9*s*) .. .. 1830

2476 — Fairy Mythology, Illustrative of the Romance and Superstition of various Countries, *plates*, 2 vols. 12mo. *cloth*, 7*s* 6*d* (*pub. at* 15*s*) .. .. .. .. 1833

2477 KEITH (Dr. A.) Evidence of the Truth of the Christian Religion, derived from the literal fulfilment of Prophecy, *plates*, 12mo. *cloth*, 5*s* (*pub. at* 7*s* 6*d*) .. *Edinburgh*, 1854

2478 KEITH (George) Sermon at Turner's Hall, May 5, 1700, giving an account of his joyning in communion with the Church of England, 4to. *sewed*, 1*s* 6*d* .. .. 1700

2479 — Two Sermons at St. George's, Botolph Lane, London, May 12, 1700, being his first preaching after ordination, 4to. *sewed*, 1*s* 6*d*

2480 KEITH'S (P., F.L.S.) System of Physiological Botany, *plates*, 2 vols. 8vo. *half calf, neat*, 7*s* .. .. 1816

2481 KEITH'S (Bp. Robert) Historical Catalogue of the Scottish Bishops to 1688, also an account of all the Religious Houses at the time of the Reformation, by J. Spottiswoode, *plate of arms*, 8vo. *boards*, 12*s* .. .. *Edinburgh*, 1824

This edition has a continuation of the Bishops, with a life of the author by Dr. M. Russel. A valuable book.

2482 KELLAND'S (Philip) Theory of Heat, 8vo. *calf, very neat*, 5*s* 6*d* (*cost* 12*s*) .. .. *Cambridge*, 1837

2483 KELLY'S (Walter K.) History of Russia to the present time, *portrait*, 2 vols. post 8vo. *cloth*, 5*s* *H. G. Bohn*, 1855

2484 KELSALL'S (Charles) Phantasm of an University, with Prolegomena, 21 *large folding plates*, imperial 4to. LARGE PAPER, *boards*, £1 1*s* .. .. .. 1814

Mr. Kelsall seems to have been the author of many *privately printed* books, and this would appear to be one of them. The cost of this University, which is designed upon a grand scale, is 5 millions.

2485 KEMP (Edward) Handbook of Gardening, 18mo. *cloth*, 1*s* 6*d* 1851

2486 KEMP (Rev. E. C.) on Calvinism, with reference to the Church's authority, and to Scott's reply to Bp. Tomline, 8vo. *cloth*, 4*s* (*pub. at* 8*s* 6*d*) .. .. .. 1843

2487 KEMPIS (Thomas à) Christian's Pattern; a Treatise of the Imitation of Christ, with Meditations and Prayers, by Dean Stanhope, *plate*, 8vo. *old calf, neat*, 3*s* .. .. 1721

2488 — another edition, by Dean Stanhope, 12mo. *calf*, 2*s* 1727

2489 — L'Imitation de Jésus Christ, traduction nouvelle de M. l'Abbé Dassance, 18mo. *purple morocco, gilt edges*, 10*s* 6*d* *Paris, L. Curmer*, 1843

With Bosses and Silver Clasp, illuminated title-page, plates, and coloured border round each page.

"The highest encomium which any work has yet received was pronounced on this little book by Fontenelle. 'C'est le livre le plus beau qui soit sorti de la main d'un homme, puisque l'évangile n'en vient pas.'"—*Butler's Reminiscences.*

Leibnitz says, "It is one of the most excellent Treatises that have been composed. Happy is he who puts its contents into practice, and is not satisfied with merely admiring them."

2490 KEN (Tho., *Bp. of Bath and Wells)* Life, 1640-1688, including some account of the Fortunes of Morley, Bp. of Winchester, his first patron, and the friend of Isaac Walton, by W. L. Bowles, *portrait and plates*, 2 vols. 8vo. *boards, scarce*, 16*s* 1830-31

Viewed in connection with the spirit of the times from 1660 to 1688, including the period of fanatical Puritanism from 1640 to the death of Cromwell.

2491 KENNEDY'S (Dr. James) Conversations on Religion, with Lord Byron and others, held in Cephalonia, 8vo. *cloth*, 5*s* 6*d* (*pub. at* 12*s*) .. .. .. .. 1830

2492 KENRICK'S (John) Introduction to Greek Prose Composition, part 1, 12mo. *cloth*, 2*s* (*pub. at* 4*s* 6*d*) .. 1839

2493 KENT—Fussell's (L.) Journey round the Coast of Kent, including Penshurst, Tunbridge-Wells, with Rye, Winchelsea, Hastings, and Battle, *map*, 8vo. *boards*, 3*s* 6*d* (*pub. at* 9*s*) 1818

2494 KENT—Authentic Memoirs of the Wicked Life and Dying Words of John Collington of Thornleigh in Kent, Executed Saturday, April 7th, 1750, also containing the Life and Dying Words of John Stone, John Clarke, and others executed at the same time, 4to. *wants a leaf at end*, 2s 6d .. .. 1750

2495 KENT'S (Samuel) Grammar of Heraldry, *numerous arms*, 8vo. *calf, neat*, 4s .. .. .. .. 1718

2496 KEPPEL (Augustus, Viscount, *Admiral of the White*,) Life, by the Hon. and Rev. Thomas Keppel, *fine full length portrait*, 2 vols. 8vo. *cloth*, 14s (*pub. at* £1 11s 6d) .. 1842

Fitting accompaniment to the lives of Anson, Rodney, and Howe.

2497 KEPPEL'S (Captn. Hon. George, now *Lord Albemarle*) Journey from India to England by Bussorah, Bagdad, Babylon, Persia, Astrakan, Moscow, and St. Petersburgh, 1824, *maps and coloured plates*, 2 vols. 8vo. *boards*, 9s .. .. 1827

2498 — another copy, 2 vols. 8vo. *boards*, 10s .. 1827

"We have not for a long while met with a more unaffected sensible and agreeable narrative."—*Literary Gazette.*

2499 KEPPEL'S (Capt. Hon. Henry, now *Admiral*,) Expedition to Borneo for the Suppression of Piracy, with Extracts from the Journal of Sir James Brooke, Rajah of Sarrawak, *maps and plates*, 2 vols. 8vo. *cloth*, 12s (*pub. at* 32s) .. .. 1846

2500 KER (John, Esq., *Kersland, N. Britain*,) Memoirs containing his Secret Transactions and Negotiations in Scotland, England, the Courts of Vienna, Hanover, &c., parts 1 and 2, 8vo. *old calf*, 3s 6d .. .. .. .. 1726

Dedicated to the Rt. Hon. Sir Robert Walpole. "We, fully sensible of the fidelity of John Ker, Esq., grant him our royal license to keep company with such as are disaffected to us, in such way as he shall judge most for our service, &c. Windsor, 7 July, 1707."—*Q. Anne.*

2501 KETT'S (Henry) History, the Interpreter of Prophecy, a View of Scriptural Prophecies and their Accomplishment, 2 vols. 8vo. *boards*, 5s .. .. .. 1801

2502 — Elements of General Knowledge, with Lists of the most approved Authors, including the best editions of the Classics, 2 vols. 8vo. *boards*, 8s (*pub. at* 24s) .. .. 1815

"A very useful work, designed chiefly for the junior students in the Universities and the higher classes in schools."—*Lowndes.*

2503 — Flowers of Wit; a choice collection of Bon Mots, 2 vols. 1814.—A Visit to Flanders in July, 1815, being an Account of the Field of Waterloo, &c., by J. Simpson, *map*, in 1 vol. 12mo. *calf, neat*, 6s .. .. *Edinburgh*, 1815

2504 KETT, (Robert) his Latin Translation and Epitome of the Alcoran, 1543. See *Mahomet.*

2505 KETTLEWELL'S (John) Measures of Christian Obedience, thick 4to. *calf, neat*, 5s .. .. .. 1681

2506 — Discourse Explaining the Nature of Edification, Visitat. Serm. at Coventry, May 7, 1684, 4to. *sewed*, 1s .. 1684

2507 — Help and Exhortation to Worthy Communicating, a Treatise on the Sacrament, *portrait by V. Gucht*, 8vo. *old calf, neat*, 2s 6d *E. Curll*, 1710

2508 KEY'S (Astley C.) Narrative of the Recovery of H.M.S. Gorgon, Stranded in the Bay of Monte Video, 1844, *plates*, 8vo. *cloth*, 3s 6d (*pub. at* 7s 6d) .. .. .. 1847

2509 KIEN-LONG (Empereur de la Chine) Éloge de la Ville de Moukden, Poeme, avec de Notes curieuses sur la Géographie, Hist. Naturelle, &c. de la Tartarie Orientale, traduit en François par le P. Amyot, Missionaire à Péking, 8vo. *old binding*, 5s *Paris*, 1770

There are 71 pages devoted to a treatise on the origin of the different sorts of Chinese characters in the Chinese edition. This book was published by M. Deguignes.

2510 KINDERSLEY'S (N. E., Esq., *of the Hon. E.I.C. Service*,) Specimens of Hindoo Literature, consisting of Translations from the Tamoul Language, 8vo. *calf, very neat, scarce*, 7s 6d *Bulmer*, 1794

At the Fonthill sale, 15s.

2511 KING'S (John, *of Bungay*,) Essay on Hot and Cold Bathing, *frontispiece*, post 8vo. *old calf, neat*, 2s 6d *For the Author*, 1737

2512 KING'S (Joseph, *Liverpool*,) Tables of Interest, calculated at 5 p. cent. from 1 to 10,000, from 1 day to 100, with Tables of Interest from 1 to 12 months, 8vo. *boards*, 5s *Liverpool*, 1811

2513 KING'S (Apb. W.) Sermon on Divine Predestination, 1709.—Anonymous Remarks on ditto, 1710.—Remarks on Basnage, Whiston, Locke, and Le Clerc, 1709.—Life of Bishop Edward Stillingfleet, *portrait*, 1735, together with 4 Sermons, by Conybeare, in 1 vol. 8vo. *half calf, clean and neat*, SCARCE, 6s 1709-35

2514 KING'S (Dr. Will.) Historical Account of the Heathen Gods and Heroes, *plates*, 12mo. *calf*, 2s 6d .. .. 1727

2515 KINGSLEY'S (Rev. C.) Heroes; Greek Fairy Tales, *plates*, 8vo. *cloth, new, gilt edges*, 4s (*pub. at* 7s 6d) *Cambridge*, 1856

2516 KIRBY'S (John) Suffolk Traveller, an actual Survey in 1732-4, 2nd edition, 8vo. *old calf*, 4s .. .. 1764

2517 KITCHENER'S (Dr. W.) Cook's Oracle, 12mo. *boards*, 4s (*pub. at* 7s 6d) .. .. .. .. 1829

2518 KITCHEN'S (Thomas) Post Chaise Companion through England and Wales, containing all the Ancient and New Roads, *engraved on* 103 *copper plates*, oblong 4to. SCARCE, 10s *For John Bowles*, 1767

2519 KITSON'S (Roger, *Writing-Master*,) Short Introduction to English Grammar, with Orthographical Exercises, 12mo. *bound*, 2s 6d *Norwich*, 1798

2520 KITZELIUS Synopsis Matrimonialis. See *Matrimony*.

2521 KLIMIUS (Nicholas) Journey to the World Underground, 12mo. *boards, uncut*, 6s .. .. .. 1742

"An amusing and interesting fiction; apparently formed on the model of Gulliver's Travels, and the satire is chiefly directed against the abuses of the Government."—*Lowndes*. A copy sold at Mr. Bindley's sale for 10s 6d

2522 KLOSS—Catalogue of the Library of Dr. Kloss, of Frankfort, sold by auction, by Mr. Sotheby and Son, May 1835, *fac-similies of writing, &c.* 8vo. *half cloth*, 5s .. .. 1835

2523 KNATCHBULL'S (Sir Norton) Annotations upon some difficult Texts in all the Books of the New Testament, 8vo. *very fine copy in old blue morocco extra, gilt leaves*, 8s *Cambridge*, 1693

"This learned man has rendered very considerable service to sacred literature."—See *Orme* and *Dr. Campbell*.

2524 KNIGHT'S Popular History of England, *numerous well-engraved portraits and plates*, 6 vols. 8vo. *cloth, new*, £2 14*s* 1859

Highly spoken of in the *Times* as the best History of England extant. Two other volumes will complete it.

2525 — Monthly Volumes—History of the Mammalia, *numerous plates*, 6 vols. 18mo. *stiff covers*, 6*s*.—Life of Sir Thomas Gresham, 1*s*.—Samuel Butler and his Hudibras, 1*s*.—The Horse, 1*s*.—Monkeys, 1*s*.—The Elephant, 1*s* .. .. 1849

2526 KNOX (John) Life, containing illustrations of the History of the Reformation in Scotland, by Dr. Thomas M'Crie, *portrait*, 2 vols. 8vo. *calf, very neat*, 16*s* .. *Edinburgh*, 1818

"A very valuable book."—*Professor Smyth*. With biographical notices of the principal reformers, and sketches of the progress of literature in Scotland in the XVIth century.

2527 KNOX'S (Dr. Vicesimus) Essays, Moral and Literary, 2 vols. 12mo. *nice copy, in old calf, gilt, yellow edges*, 4*s* 6*d* 1795

2528 KOLBEN'S (Peter) State of the Cape of Good Hope, an account of the Hottentots, their Religion, Laws, Customs, Language, &c., Englished by Mr. Medley, *numerous plates*, 2 vols. 8vo. *old calf, scarce*, 7*s* 6*d* .. .. .. 1738

2529 KOLLI (Baron de) Memoirs of, written by himself, with Memoirs of the Life of the Queen of Etruria, by herself, *portrait*, 8vo. *boards*, 4*s* 6*d* (*pub. at* 10*s* 6*d*) .. .. 1823

Relative to his secret mission in 1810, for liberating Ferdinand VII. King of Spain from captivity at Valencay. Autograph of "*Catherine Nassau*."

2530 KONIGSHOVEN (Jacob Von) Elsassische und Straszburgische Chronicke, nunc primum editum ex MSS., observationibus historicis illustratum à Io. Schiltero, *engraved title, plates, and view of Strasburgh in* 1680, very thick 4to. of 1392 pages, *fine clean copy, in vellum*, £1 5*s* .. *Straszburg*, 1698

Konigshoven was Presbyter at Strasburgh in 1386, and his Chronicle was in 1698 for the first time printed. The book is in GERMAN, at the end is another "Chronicke der Stadt Freyburg in Brisgaw, ex MS. Archivi Reip. Argentor." Of the editor, John Schilter, an eminent jurist, an account may be found in *Niceron*.

2531 KORNMANN (Hen.) de Miraculis Elementorum et de Virginum Statu ac Jure, 12mo. *neat*, 2*s* .. *No date*

2532 KOTZEBUE (Augustus Von) Almanach Dramatischer Spiele, *coloured plates*, 18mo. *boards*, 2*s* .. *Riga*, 1810

2533 — Historical, Literary, and Political Anecdotes and Miscellanies, *portrait*, 3 vols. 12mo. *boards*, 3*s* 6*d* .. 1807

2534 KUTUFFA (Giorgio, *Ateniese*) Compendio di Grammatica della Lingua Græca Moderna, 8vo. *sewed*, 2*s* 6*d* *Livorno*, 1834

2535 KYTELER—Proceedings against Dame Alice Kyteler, prosecuted for Sorcery in 1324, by Richard de Ledrede, Bp. of Ossory, edited by Tho. Wright, 4to. *cloth*, 6*s* *Camden Soc.*, 1843

A curious picture of the state of Ireland and forms an interesting chapter in the history of English Superstition.

2536 LABORDE (Léon de) Journey through Arabia Petræa to Mount Sinai, and the excavated city of Petra, the Edom of the prophecies, *numerous plates*, 8vo. *cloth*, 7*s* 6*d* (*pub. at* 18*s*) *Murray*, 1836

2537 LACROIX (S. F.) Élémens de Géométrie et Complément, *plates*, 2 vols. 8vo. *sewed*, 5*s* .. *Paris*, 1812-19

2538 LADIES Calling, in two parts, *frontispiece*, 12mo. *old calf, gilt, gilt edges*, 5*s* .. *Oxford, at the Theatre*, 1673

Nice specimen of old panelled binding, the back full gilt.

2539 LADIES Diary: or the Woman's Almanack for 1706 (being the 3rd Almanack ever published of that kind) to 1723, and from 1744 to 1754, *portraits of Queen Anne and Geo. II. on the title pages*, bound in 2 thick vols. 12mo. *old calf, neat*, VERY SCARCE, £2 2*s* .. 1706 to 1723 and 1744 to 1754

From Lord Orford's Library, at Woolterton, Norfolk. These very curious Almanacks have at the end of each, enigmas, charades, arithmetical and mathematical questions, (some of which were by Dr. C. Hutton thought worthy of republication in 1775,) and various other curious information, not elsewhere now easily procurable.

2540 LADIES Library, written by a Lady, and published by Sir Richard Steele, *plates*, 3 vols. 12mo. *calf, neat*, 7*s* 6*d* 1722

Dedicated by Sir Richard Steele to the Countess of Burlington.

2541 LADVOCAT'S (Abbé) Historical and Biographical Dictionary, from the French, by Mrs. C. Collignon, 4 vols. 8vo. *boards*, 10*s* *Cambridge*, 1799

2542 — another copy, 4 vols. 8vo. *half calf, very neat*, 12*s* *ib.* 1799

The best edition of a "work held in great esteem for the notices it contains of the works of authors and the best editions." See *Lowndes*.

2543 LADY'S New Year's Gift; or, Advice to a Daughter, 18mo. *neat*, 3*s*

With these autographs, *M. Harbord, G. De Grey, Ld. Halifax*, date 1688.

2544 LA FONTAINE, Fables Choisies, Mises en Vers, avec un Commentaire par M. Coste, et La Vie d'Esope, 2 vols. 12mo. *neat*, 4*s* *Paris*, 1745

2545 LAKE'S (Dr. Edw.) Reform'd Devotions: in Meditations, Hymns, and Petitions for every day in the week, with Holy Offices for the Sacrament, 5th edit., 12mo. *old binding*, 3*s* 6*d* 1700

2546 LAING'S (Major A. G.) Travels in the Timannee, Kooranko, and Soolima Countries in Western Africa, *map and plates*, 8vo. *boards*, 6*s* 6*d* (*pub. at* 18*s*) .. .. 1825

2547 LAING'S (Samuel) Residence in Norway, in 1834, 5, and 6, 2 parts, 12mo. *sewed*, 1*s* 6*d* .. .. 1851

2548 LAMB'S (Charles) Adventures of Ulysses, 12mo. *hf cf, neat*, 2*s* 1819

2549 LAMBARD'S (Will.) Archion; or, a Commentary upon the High Courts of Justice in England, 8vo. *limp vellum, neat*, 4*s* 1635

2550 — another copy, small 8vo. *old calf, neat*, 5*s* 1635

This Treatise, by the learned author of the Perambation of Kent, was written in 1591, and dedicated to Sir Robert Cecill.

2551 LAMBETH—Index of such English Books printed before 1600, as are in the Archiepiscopal Library, Lambeth, by the Rev. S. R. Maitland, librarian, 8vo. *cloth, new*, 5*s* *Rivington*, 1845

2552 LAMPRIDII (Benedicti) necnon Io. Bap. Amalthei Carmina, 8vo. *Venetiis, apud Gabrielem Iolitum de Ferrariis*, 1550

Edited by Ludovico Dolce. This is a very early edition of Amaltheus's Poems. Brunet does not give one earlier than 1627.—This volume has the following rare tracts in it:

1.—Pascalis (Ludovici) Julii Camilli, Molsæ, et aliorum illustrium Poetarum Carmina, 8vo. .. *Venetiis, ap. G. Iolitum, et Fratres*, 1551

Elegant specimens of the Gioliti Phœnix.

2.—Beatiani (Augustini) Lachrymæ in Funere Petri Cardinalis Bembi, 8vo. *Venetiis, apud G. Iolitum,* 1548

Some of these are in Italian.

3.— — ad Franciscum Donatum Electum Venetiarum Principem Carmen, 8vo. .. .. .. *Venetiis, apud G. Iolitum,* 1548

These are very early editions of Beatiano's works. See *Brunet.*

4.—Rosseti (Petri, *Poetæ Laureati,*) Christus, nunc primum in lucem æditus, 8vo. .. .. *Parisiis, apud G. Colinæum,* 1534

This is the 1st edition and very scarce.

5.—Cursii (Petri) in Urbis Romæ excidio deploratio, 8vo. *Parisiis, ex officina Rob. Stephani,* 1529

A latin Poem on 8 leaves, inclusive of title and dedication. Not in Brunet.

the above 6 rare Poetical Tracts in 1 vol. *in old vellum,* RARE, *from the Leicester Library,* £2 2*s* .. V. Y.

2553 LANCASHIRE WITCHES—The Arraignement and Triall of Witches at Lancaster, (Anne Whittle, alias Chattox, Eliz. Device, James Device, Anne Redferne, Alice Nutter, Kath. Hewet, and 4 others,) Aug. 19, 1612, at the Assizes at Lancaster, before Sir Edward Bromley, Knight, one of the Barons of H. M. Court of Exchequer.—The Triall of Jennet Preston, of Gisborne, in Craven, Yorkshire, July 27, 1612, before Sir James Altham, Knight, and Sir Edw. Bromley, Barons of the Exchequer, small 4to. 84 unpaged leaves, £1 11*s* 6*d* *London, W. Stansby,* 1612

Collates from B to Y, in fours, wants something at the beginning and end.

2554 LANCELLOTTI (P. D. S.) l'Hoggidi, overo il Mondo non peggiore ne più calamitoso del passato, e gl'Ingegni non inferiori à 'passati, 2 vols. small 8vo. 1300 pages, *old limp vellum,* 9*s* *Venetia,* 1630-36

"Lancellotti is a very copious and learned writer, his elaborate work, 'L'Hoggidi, To-Day,' is, throughout, a ridicule of those whom he calls Hoggidiani, perpetual declaimers against the present state of things." See *Hallam's Literature of Europe.*

2555 LANDER'S (Richard and John) Expedition to explore the source and termination of the river Niger, *portrait, maps, and plates,* 3 vols. 12mo. *original cloth,* 7*s* 6*d* (*pub. at* 15*s*) *Fam. Lib.,* 1832

A very entertaining narrative.

2556 LANGHORNE'S (Dr. John) Sermons, 2 vols. 12mo. *calf, very neat,* 4*s* 6*d* .. .. .. 1764

2557 LANGLEY'S (Thomas) History and Antiquities of the Hundred of Desborough, and Deanery of Wycombe, Buckinghamshire, *map,* 4to. *boards,* 9*s* .. .. .. 1797

With the 4 plates and the pedigrees of the Borlase and Goodwin Families.

2558 LANGUETI (Huberti) Epistolæ Secretæ ad Principem suum Augustum Saxoniæ ducem, *portrait,* thick 4to. *of* 1086 *pages, half calf, gilt,* 12*s* .. .. *Halæ,* 1699

One of the most learned men of his time, had many great employments, and enjoyed the friendship of Melancthon, Thuanus, the Sieur du Plessis Mornay, our Sir Philip Sydney, Gustavus Adolphus, and many other royal and noble personages. From Lord Orford's library.

2559 LANE'S (R. J.) Life at the Water Cure; or, a month at Malvern, *numerous plates,* post 8vo. *cloth,* 6*s* 6*d* (*pub. at* 14*s*) 1846

2560 LANZI'S History of Painting in Italy, translated by Thomas Roscoe, 3 vols. post 8vo. *cloth, 7s 6d* (*cost* 10*s* 6*d*) *H. G. Bohn*, 1847

2561 — also vol. 1, of ditto, 2*s* .. .. *ib.* 1847

2562 LARDNER'S Cyclopædia—Bell's Lives of British Poets, 2 vols. 5*s*.—Cooley's Maritime and Inland Discovery, 3 vols. 7*s* 6*d*.—Dunham's Europe during the Middle Ages, 4 vols. 10*s*.—British Dramatists, 2 vols. 5*s*.—Early Writers of Great Britain, 2*s* 6*d*.—Fosbroke's Greek and Roman Antiquities, 2 vols. 5*s*.—Gleig's British Military Commanders, 3 vols. 7*s* 6*d*.—Mackintosh's History of England, 10 vols. 25*s*.—Montgomery's Eminent Italian, Spanish, and Portuguese Authors, 3 vols. 7*s* 6*d*.—Moore's History of Ireland, 4 vols. 10*s*.—Roscoe's British Lawyers, 2*s* 6*d*.—Shelly's Eminent French Authors, 2 vols. 5*s*.—Southey's British Admirals, 5 vols. 12*s* 6*d* (*pub. at* 6*s each*) *all for* 2*s* 6*d each.*

2563 LASSELS (Richard, Gent.) Voyage of Italy, the second part, 12mo. *old calf*, 2*s* .. *Paris, by Vincent du Moutier*, 1670

The celebrated John Wilkes said this was the best account of the curious things of Italy ever printed.

2564 LATHBURY'S (Tho.) Guy Fawkes; a Complete History of the Gunpowder Treason of 1605, with notices of the Revolution of 1688, 12mo. *cloth*, 2*s* .. .. 1839

2565 LATIN Grammar, with a bibliographical preface, shewing whence it was compiled, signed John Ward, 12mo. *original binding, curious*, 7*s* 6*d* .. *S. Buckley and T. Longman*, 1765

The rare Grammars of Dr. John Colet, William Lilly, Dean Robertson, John Holt, John Stanbridge, Robert Whittington, Cardinal Woolsey, Thomas Hayne, and others, were made use of in the compilation of this Grammar.

2566 LATINII (Latini, *Viterbiensis*) Epistolæ, Conjecturæ et Observationes Sacra, profanaque eruditione ornatæ, 4to. *old calf, neat, rare*, 8*s* .. .. *Romæ, typis Tynassii*, 1659

One of the most learned critics of the XVI. Cent., born at Viterbo, 1513, died at Rome, 1593; in 1573 he was engaged to correct Gratian's Decretal.

2567 LATRO (Francesco Capece, *Napoletano*) Historia della Citta, e Regno di Napoli, detto di Cicilia, *arms in title page*, 4to. *limp vellum (some leaves mended)* 7*s* *Napoli, O. Beltrano*, 1640

2568 LATROBE'S (C. I.) South African Journal, in 1815-16—United Brethren's Mission, *coloured plates*, 4to. *half russia, neat, original edition*, 10*s* 6*d* .. .. .. 1818

Mr. J. J. Gurney's copy of an interesting Mission.

2569 — reprint, 8vo. *boards*, 3*s* 6*d* .. *New York*, 1818

Highly praised in the *Quarterly Review*. In describing the natural history, Mr. Latrobe was assisted by the African Traveller, J. W. Burchell, Esq.

2570 — Alpenstock; Sketches of Swiss Scenery and Manners, 1825-26, *plates*, 8vo. LARGE PAPER, *calf, gilt, neat, a nice volume*, 7*s* 6*d* 1829

Alpenstock is the name of the long iron-spiked pole in common use on the Alps. This is the 1st edition. The 2nd is a duodecimo.

2571 — Rambler in North America, in 1832-33, *map*, 2 vols. post 8vo. *cloth*, 5*s* 6*d* (*pub. at* £1 1*s*) .. .. 1836

2572 LA TROBE (J. A.) Scripture Illustrations, being a Series of Engravings on Steel and Wood, illustrative of the Geography and Topography of the Bible, 4to. *half bound morocco*, 10s 6d (*pub. at* 31s 6d) .. .. *London*, 1838

2573 LAUD'S (Abp. William) Seven Sermons, preached upon several occasions, 12mo. *original binding, nice clean copy*, 10s 6d 1651

2574 — Brief relation of the Death and Sufferings of the Most Revd. and renowned Prelate the L. Archbishop of Canterbury, his Speech on the scaffold, &c., small 4to. *stiff covers, scarce*, 15s *Oxford*, 1644

This scarce little tract, which is a very fine clean copy, is attributed to Dr. Peter Heylin; at the end is an "Elegie on the Archbishop, attached Dec. 18, 1640, beheaded Jan. 10, 1644," on six leaves. VERY RARE. Not in *Lowndes*, or the *Bibliotheca Anglo-Poetica.*

2575 — Remains, vol. 2 only, collected by the learned Henry Wharton, folio, *old binding*, 8s .. .. 1700

Contains his history of his Chancellorship of Oxford, 1630-1641;—his Answer to Lord Say's Speech against the Bishops, 1641;—his Speech in the Star Chamber, 1637, at the Censure of Bastwick, Burton, and Prinn.

2576 — Life, being the Ecclesiastical History of the Kingdom, from his first rising till his death, by Dr. Peter Heylin, folio, *old calf, neat*, 10s 6d .. .. 1668

2577 — Life and Times, by J. P. Lawson, *fine portrait by Dean*, 2 vols. 8vo. *half calf, very neat*, 12s .. .. 1829

2578 LAVATER'S (J. C.) Aphorisms on Man, 12mo. *bds. sc.* 3s 6d 1789

2579 LAW.—Russell and Ryan's Crown Cases reserved for consideration and decided by the 12 Judges, 8vo. 16s (*pub. at* 25s) 1799-1824

2580 — Moody's Continuation of ditto, 2 vols. 8vo. £1 10s (*pub. at* £2 4s) .. .. .. 1824-44

2581 — Dennison's Continuation of Moody, 5 parts, 8vo. being vol. 1 complete, £1 3s (*pub. at* £1 14s) .. 1844-50

2582 — Statutes at Large, from 2nd William IV. to 12th of Victoria, 17 vols. 1 in folio, the others royal 8vo. *neatly half bound*, £5 5s 1832-47

These belonged to a magistrate in this county and cost him ten guineas.

2583 — Carrow, Hamerton, and Allen's New Sessions Cases, vol. 1, 8vo. Hilary Term 1844 to Easter Vacation, 1845; *pub. at* £1 19s, for £1 6s; vol. 2, part 1, *sewed*, 3s, Trin. Term, 1845.

2584 — Hare's Reports of Cases in Chancery, vol. 4, part 3, royal 8vo. *sewed*, 3s (*pub. at* 9s) .. .. 1846

2585 LAWRENCE'S (John) Modern Land Steward, his Duties and Functions, 8vo. *boards*, 5s (*pub. at* 10s 6d) 1806

2586 LAWYERS—Strictures on the Lives and Characters of the most Eminent Lawyers of the present day, 8vo. *hf. cf. neat*, 2s 6d 1790

2587 LAZARILLO de Tormes, La Vida del, y de sus fortunas y a adversidades, 12mo. *old calf, neat, scarce*, 6s 6d *Paris*, 1670

In Spanish, with a French Translation by L. S. D. on opposite pages. A long account of this most amusing Spanish rogue will be found in the *Retrospective Review*, vol. 2, p. 133.

2588 LEAKE'S (Stephen Martin, *Clarenceux*) Historical account of English Money, from the Conquest to this time, 2nd Edition, 8vo. *old calf*, 6s .. .. .. 1745

2589 LEAKE—another copy, 8vo. *old calf, neat,* 7*s* 1745

**Includes those of Scotland from the Union. (James I.)**

2590 LE BRET (Car.) de la Souveraineté du Roy, thick 4to. of above 700 pages, *limp vellum,* 5*s* .. *Paris,* 1634

2591 LE CLERC de l'Incredulité et de la Verité de la Religion Chrétienne, 12mo. *calf, neat,* 2*s* 6*d* *Amst., Mortier,* 1714

2592 — Histoire des Provinces Unies des Pais-Bas, *numerous plates of medals, views, maps, &c.,* 3 vols. folio, *fine copy, in old calf, gilt,* £1 5*s* .. .. *Amsterdam,* 1737

2593 LECTII (Jac.) Poemata Varia, small 8vo. *old limp vellum,* 4*s* 6*d* *Genevæ, Chouet,* 1609

**With Aldine Anchor on the title-page. Contents; Sylvæ, Elegiæ, Epigrammata, Epicedia, Ecclesiastes, Jonah.**

2594 LEGES Suecorum Gothorumque per Dr. Ragualdum Ingemundi, Archidiaconum Ubsalensis MCDLXXXI. latinitate primùm donatæ nunc autem Zelo Patriæ illustrandæ Iohannis Messenii, 4to. *old vellum,* RARE, £1 11*s* 6*d* *Stockholmiæ,* 1614

2595 LEGH'S (Edward) Treatise of the Divine Promises, small 4to. *calf, neat,* 3*s* 6*d* .. .. .. 1633

2596 LEGUAT—Voyage et Aventures de Francois Leguat, et de ses compagnons au deux Isles desertes des Indes orientales, *charts and plates of Natural History, &c.,* 2 vols. 12mo. *old binding, scarce,* 9*s* .. .. .. *Londres,* 1708

2597 LEIGHE (Gerarde) An Extract of Gerarde Leighe, his Accidence of Armorye, in *Manuscript,* small 4to. *emblazoned, old vellum wrapper, uncut,* 15*s* .. .. 1642

2598 LEIGHTON'S (Abp. Robert) Practical Commentary on the First Epistle of St. Peter, by Bradley, 12mo. *boards,* 3*s* 6*d* (*pub. at* 7*s* 6*d*) .. .. .. .. 1831

2599 LE KEUX'S Memorials of Cambridge, a Series of Views of the Colleges and other Public Buildings, 2 vols. 8vo. *with numerous engravings, cloth,* £1 4*s* .. .. 1858

2600 LELAND (John) Lives of Leland, Hearne and Wood, *portraits and plates,* 2 vols. 8vo. *very fine copy, in old calf, gilt,* 15*s* 1772

2601 — his laboryouse Journey and Serche for Englande's Antiquities, geven of hym as a newe year's gyfte to Kynge Henry the VIII., by Johan Bale, 15*s* .. .. *Reprint of* 1549

**In the Lives of Leland, Hearne, and Wood. 2 vols. 8vo, 1772.**

2602 LELAND'S (Dr. John) Divine Authority of the Old and New Testament Asserted, (in Answer to Morgan's Moral Philosopher) 2 vols. 8vo. *old calf, very neat,* 5*s* .. 1739

2603 — Remarks, in 2 Letters, on Collins's Pamphlet, "Christianity not founded on Argument," 8vo. *old calf, neat,* 2*s* 6*d* 1744

2604 — Divine Authority of the Old and New Testament Asserted, 8vo. *cloth, uncut,* 2*s* 6*d* .. .. *London,* 1837

2605 — View of the Principal Deistical Writers, 8vo. *cloth, uncut,* 3*s* (*pub. at* 14*s*) .. .. *London,* 1837

2606 LE LONG (Jacobi) Bibliotheca Sacra; seu, Syllabus omnium fermè Sacræ Scripturæ editionum ac Versionum, notis historicis et criticis illustratus, 2 vols. 8vo. *old calf, gilt,* 12*s* *Parisiis,* 1709

**The 1st editon of a very laborious work.**

2607 LE LONG, Bibliotheque Historique de la France, contenant le Catalogue de tous les ouvrages tant imprimez que MSS. qui traitent de l'Histoire de ce Royaume, huge folio, LARGE PAPER, *old calf, neat,* £1 4*s* .. .. *Paris,* 1719

"A work of vast labour and research." With critical and historical notes. Le Long was Librarian to the Fathers of the Oratory.

2608 LEMOINE (Henry) Typographical Antiquities, Origin and History of the Art of Printing, foreign and domestic, Chronological Lists of Eminent Printers in England, Scotland, and Ireland, &c., 12mo. *cloth, scarce,* 6*s* .. .. 1813

Second edition, by T. A. Esq. of the Inner Temple. Much curious information.

2609 LE MOYNE (Le Pere) Le Gallerie des Femmes Fortes, *full length portrait of Mary Queen of Scots, and many others,* 2 parts in 1 vol. 12mo. *old binding,* 5*s* .. *Paris,* 1663

2610 LEMPRIERE'S (Dr. John) Classical Dictionary of all the proper names in Ancient Authors, with Greek and Roman Coins, Weights, and Measures, and a Chronology, 8vo. *half vellum, neat,* 6*s* .. .. .. .. 1812

2611 — another edition, revised by the Rev. Tho. Smith, 8vo. *half cloth,* 5*s* 6*d* .. .. .. .. 1828

2612 — Collection of Supplements to all the editions of Lempriere's Classical Dictionary, including the large one by Professor Anthon, 8vo. *cloth, as good as new,* 6*s* (*pub. at* 15*s*) 1837

Contents; I. Sillig's Dictionary of the Artists of Antiquity.—II. Payne Knight's Inquiry into the Symbolical Language of Ancient Art and Mythology.—III. Barker's 15 Supplements and Indexes.

2613 LENGLET du FRESNOY, Methode pour Etudier l'Histoire, avec le Supplement, 6 vols. 4to. *old calf, neat,* £1 1*s* *Paris,* 1735-39

Has a very valuable catalogue of the principal Historians, with remarks on the goodness of their works, and on the choice of the best editions.

2614 — Chronological Tables of Universal History, with a Catalogue of Books necessary for Studying History, Englished, 2 vols. in 1, 8vo. *calf, neat,* 6*s* .. .. 1752

2615 — another copy, in 2 vols. 8vo. *neat,* 6*s* .. 1762

2616 LE NOBLE, Contes et Fables, avec le sens Moral, *numerous plates,* 2 vols. 12mo. *old binding,* 7*s* 6*d* *Paris, M. Brunet,* 1700

Viscountess Howe's Book-plate, and autograph of "Henr. White of Lichfield, Oct. 6, 1806."

2617 LEO X.—His Life and Pontificate, by William Roscoe, *portraits,* 2 vols. post 8vo. *cloth,* 5*s* .. .. 1846

Edited by William Hazlitt with additions.

2618 LEOPOLD'S (Emperor of Germany) Proclamation; being his Act of Oblivion to the Hungarian Rebels, folio, *broadside, curious,* 5*s* *James Partridge,* 1684

2619 LEPSIUS (Dr. Richard) Letters from Egypt, Ethiopia, and the Peninsula of Sinai, translated by L. and J. B. Horner, *plates,* post 8vo. *cloth,* 3*s* (*cost* 5*s*) .. *H. G. Bohn,* 1853

2620 LERMITE (Pierre) Grammaire Françoise et Allemagne, thick 12mo. *vellum,* 2*s* 6*d* .. .. *Hanover,* 1718

2621 LESAGE—Histoire de Gil Blas de Santillane, 4 vols. 12mo. *nice copy, in old calf, gilt,* 10*s* .. *Paris,* 1768

2622 LESAGE—Hist. de Gil Blas, *plates*, 4 vols. 18mo. *bound*, 4*s* *Paris*, 1771

2623 — une autre edition, avec d'une notice historique et Littérarie par M. Patin, 4 vols. 32mo. *sewed*, 7*s* 6*d* (*pub. at* 14*s*) *Paris*, 1829

2624 — Gil Blas, translated into Spanish, by Don Felipe Fernandez, 4 vols. 12mo. *boards*, 10*s* .. *Londres*, 1808

2625 — Adventures of Gil Blas, of Santillane, Englished by Dr. T. Smollett, *plates*, 3 vols. 8vo. *half calf, gilt, a very nice copy*, £1 4*s* .. .. .. .. 1802

"A translation of great merit."—*Lowndes.* Tytler also speaks very well of it.

2626 LESLIE'S (Charles) Short and Easy Method with the Deists and Jews, showing the certainty of the Christian Religion, 8vo. *old calf, neat*, 3*s* 6*d* .. .. .. 1726

2627 LESLIE'S (John) Geometrical Analysis and Geometry of Curve Lines, 24 *plates*, 8vo. *boards*, 8*s* (*pub. at* 16*s*) *Edinburgh*, 1821

2628 LESLIE (John) Catalogue of English and Foreign Theology, 8vo. *boards*, 2*s* 6*d* .. . .. 1844

2629 LETTERE Volgari di diversi nobilissimi Huomini, et excellentissimi insegni, scritte in diverse materie, Libro primo (*raccolto da Paolo Manuzio*), *In Vinegia*, 1544.—Libro secondo (*raccolto da Antonio Manuzio*) 2 vols. in 1, 8vo. *vellum*, £1 1*s* *In Vinegia, Figliuoli di Aldo*, 1545

The edition of 1544 of the 1st vol. not cited by Haym. This is the 1st edition of the 2nd volume.

2630 — another copy, in 2 vols. *old stamped calf*, £1 4*s* *In Vinegia, in casa de' Figliuola di Aldo*, 1544-45

2631 — another edition, 2 vols. in 1, 8vo. *newly bound in parchment*, 16*s* *In Vinegia, Aldus*, 1549-50

Neither of these editions cited by Haym, and the Aldine Anchors differ from the former editions. Highly interesting letters written by some of the most eminent men from about 1525 to 1540.

2632 LETTERE della molto illustre Sig. la Sra. donna Lucretia Gonzaga da Gazuolo, small 8vo. *old limp vellum*, 15*s* *In Vinegia appresso Gualtero Scotto*, 1552

This curious little volume belonged to Sir Christopher Hatton, of Elizabethan memory.

2633 LETTERE di Monsignor Guidicione, Annibale Caro, Giacomo Bonfadio, Baldassar Castiglione, Francesco della Torre, Michel Agnolo Buonaroti, Lorenzo de Med., B. Tasso., Speron Sperone, etc., small 8vo. *old vellum*, 9*s* *In Vinegia, Gabriel Giolito*, 1559

Commences at p. 7, and wants title.

2634 LETTERE di Principi, le quali, o si scrivono da Principi, o' à Principi, o' ragionan di Principi, libro (Tomo) primo, 4to. *old vellum, limp*, 8*s* 6*d* .. .. *Vinezia, Ziletti*, 1562

This is the 1st edition of this valuable collection of Letters written by many illustrious persons, Popes, Cardinals, the Medici, Bembo, Strozzi, Macchiavelli, &c. and edited by Girolamo Ruscelli. Sir Christopher Hatton's copy.

2635 LETTERE di diversi Nobilisimi Huomini, et eccellentissimi ingegni, di M. Bernardino Pino, libro quarto, 8vo. *vellum, much stained*, 3*s* 6*d* .. .. .. *In Venetia*, 1574

Sir C. Hatton's copy with his initials on the sides. These letters are dated 1537 to 1573.

2636 LETTERE di diversi Nobilisimi Huomini, con un discorso della commodita dello scrivere di M. Bernardino Pino, 2 vols. in 1, *vellum, rare,* 15*s* .. .. *Venetia,* 1582

The letters here written are by all the most illustrious men of that great age. This copy belonged to Sir Christopher Hatton and has his initials impressed on the sides.

2637 LETTERS from a Tutor to his Pupils, small 8vo. *cf. nt.* 2*s* 6*d* 1780

2638 LETTERS from the Virgin Islands, Illustrating Life and Manners in the West Indies, *map,* post 8vo. *cloth,* 4*s* (*pub. at* 9*s* 6*d*) 1843

2639 LETTERS writen by Eminent Persons in the 17th and 18th Centuries, with Hearne's Journeys to Reading and Whaddon Hall; and Lives of Eminent Men, by John Aubrey, 3 vols. 8vo. *half cloth,* 10*s* 6*d* (*pub. at* £1 11*s* 6*d*) .. .. 1813

A very interesting collection of Letters, from the originals in the Bodleian Library and Ashmolæan Museum.

2640 LETTER-WRITER, every Man his own, by Wallace and Townshend, *plate by Heath,* 12mo. *neat,* 2*s* *Cooke, about* 1780

2641 LETTICE'S (Dr. John) Fables for the Sea-side, 12mo. *cloth,* 2*s* 1813

2642 LEUNCLAVIUS (Joannes) Annales Sultanorum Othmanidarum, a Turcis sua lingua scripti, 4to. *nice copy, in old calf, gilt,* 10*s* 6*d* *Francofurdi, And. Wechel,* 1588

"During his stay in Turkey he collected such excellent materials for an Ottoman History that the public are indebted to him for their best information respecting that empire."—*Chalmers's Biog. Dict.*

2643 LEUSDEN (Joh.) Novi Testamenti Clavis Græca, 12mo. *old calf, neat,* 5*s* .. .. .. *Ultrajecti,* 1672

"As a critic this eminent oriental scholar is entitled to high commendation for skill and accuracy."—*Saxii Onomasticon.*

2644 LEVI'S (David) Succinct Account of the Rites and Ceremonies of the Jews, with a Chronological Summary, &c. 8vo. *neat,* 5*s* 1782

With an account of the Mischna and its teachers.

2645 LEWIS'S (John) Complete History of the several Translations of the Bible and New Testament into English, both in MS. and in Print, with Bishop Newcome's List continued, *plate,* 8vo. *old boards,* 7*s* 6*d* .. .. .. 1818

2646 [LEWIS'S (Thomas)] Scourge; in Vindication of the Church of England, 5 *portraits of James I. to Q. Anne, by Vdr Gucht,* 8vo. *old calf, scarce,* 5*s* .. .. .. 1720

In 2 parts.—I. The Danger of the Establishment from the Insolence of the Protestant Dissenters.—II. The Anatomy of the Heretical Synod at Salter's Hall.

2647 LEYCESTER—Copie of a Letter to the Rt. Hon. the Earle of Leycester, Lieut. Gen. of all Her Maiesties Forces in the Lowe Countreys, with a Report of Certaine Petitions and Declarations made to the Queen, and H. M. Answeres, the Royal Arms on a separate leaf, small 4to. *sewed, scarce,* 8*s* *Christ. Barker,* 1586

2648 LIBANII Opera, Gr. et Lat., edidit Morellii, adjectæ sunt Notæ et variæ Lectiones, 2 vols. folio, *fine copy in russia, with Lord Leicester's arms on the sides,* £1 1*s* *Parisiis, C. Morelli,* 1606

The binding of these handsome volumes must have cost 2 guineas at least. This celebrated sophist flourished under Constantius and the following Emperors till the time of Theodosius the Great, his works contain many fine passages, and instructive traits of the manners and spirit of the times under the first Byzantine Emperors. See *Dr. Adam Clarke.*

2649 LIBANII Opera—vol. 1 only, folio, *rough calf*, 7s 6d *Parisiis*, 1606

This volume contains the "Declamationes XLV," and the "Dissertationes Morales."

2650 LIBERTÉ, Essai sur la Liberté de produire ses Sentimens, dedicated "a la Nation Angloise," small 8vo. *old calf, neat*, 5s *Au Pays libre, pour le Bien Public*, 1749

Has besides, these tracts; I. Principes Phisiques de la Raison et des Passions des Hommes, par Dr. Maubec, *Paris*, 1709.—II. Venus Metaphysique, ou Essai sur l'Origine de l'ame Humaine, par M.L. (la Mettrie), *Berlin*, 1752.—III. La Folle Sensée, ou Histoire de Mlle. F.—dediée a Mad. la Marquise de V.—par le Chevalier D.L., 2 parts, *Londres*, 1752

2651 LIBRARIES—Plans for Gentlemen's Libraries, with Remarks on their Formation and Arrangement, 12mo. *cloth*, 2s *Saunders & Otley*, 1858

2652 LIBURNIO (Nicolo) Occorrenze Humane, 8vo. *old binding*, 16s *In Vigenia, in Casa de' Figliuoli di Aldo*, 1546

"Ce volume est devenu assez rare."—*Renouard*. This little gossiping volume was formerly held in great esteem, and not unjustly, as it contains much curious information connected with the revival of letters.

2653 — Le Tre Fontane, sopra la Grammatica et Eloquenza di Dante, Petrarcha et Boccaccio, 8vo. *old binding*, RARE, 15s *In Vinegia, per Merchio Sessa*, 1534

With the curious device of Sessa, of the Cat and Mouse, which has been engraved by Dr. Dibdin in his *Bibliographical Decameron*.

The late lamented Bishop of Ely used to say, "whenever you see a book with a cat and mouse in the frontispiece, seize upon it, for the chances are as three to four that it will be found both curious and valuable."—*Dibdin's Bibliog. Decameron*, v. 2, p. 232.

2654 — Elegantissime, Sentenze et aurei Detti de Diversi Excellentissimi Antiqui, Greci comme Latini in Volgar tradotti da M. Marco Cadamosto da Lodi, 8vo. *curious*, 10s *In Venetia, Gab. Gioli di Ferrarii*, 1543

With the elegant devices on the title-page and at the end of the Gioliti, engraved also by Dr. Dibdin in the *Decameron*.

2655 LICETI (Fortunii) Encyclopædia ad Syringam Publilianam, small 4to. *old parchment*, 3s 6d .. .. *Patavii*, 1635

2656 — Encyclopædia ad aram Pythiam Publilii Optatiani Porphyrii, 4to. *vellum*, 3s 6d .. .. .. *ib.*, 1630

2657 — idem, 4to. *old calf*, 3s 6d .. .. *ib.*, 1630

2658 — de Quæsitis per Epistolas a Claris Viris responsa, vols. 1, 2, 4, and 6, 4to. *neat*, RARE, 12s *Bononiæ et Utini*, 1640-48

Vol. 1 contains a remarkably fine characteristic wood-cut portrait of Licetus, who was an eminent Physician at Rapalo, born in 1577, died 1656. He was author of many works, which are all on curious and uncommon subjects. The 4th volume is entitled, "De Motu Sanguinis, origine Nervorum," &c

2659 LIDDELL'S (H. G.) Greek-English Lexicon, by Dr. Scott, last edition, thick 4to. *cloth*, £1 12s *Oxford University Press*, 1855

2660 — the same abridged, for School Boy's use, in 1 vol. square 12mo. *bound*, 7s .. .. .. .. 1855

2661 LIFE and Character of Gerhard Tersteegen; with Selections from his Letters and Writings, 1s 6d (*pub. at* 5s 6d)

2662 LIGHT, its Nature, Sources, Effects, and Applications, *photograph of the Prince of Wales, and cuts*, 12mo. *cloth*, 2s 1857

2663 LIGHTFOOT'S (John) Flora Scotica; an arrangement in the Linnæan Method of the Native Plants of Scotland and the Hebrides, *plates*, 2 vols. 8vo. *calf, very nice clean copy*, 10s 1777

"A valuable work, with 35 plates."—*Lowndes*.

2664 LIGUE, Memoires de la, small 8vo. *half bound, neat,* 5*s* 1598

This is the 5th volume only. Period embraced 1592, 1593.

2665 LIGUORO (Ottavio) Ristretto Istorico dell' origine degli abitanti della Campagna di Roma de suoi Re consoli dittatori, e delle Medaglie, Gemme, &c. con la Rarita, e col vero modo di conoscere le vere dalle false, 12mo. *old parchment, scarce,* 5*s* *Genova, A. Casamara,* 1718

In this work is a Catalogue of books on ancient medals.

2666 LILLY'S (John, *the Euphuist,*) Dramatic Works, with a Life and Notes by F. W. Fairholt, 2 vols. fcap. 8vo. *cloth,* 10*s* *J. R. Smith,* 1858

2667 LILLY'S (William, *Student in Astrology,*) Christian Astrology, *remarkably fine impression of his portrait by W. Marshall,* thick 4to. of 876 pages, *very fine clean copy, in sound old calf,* RARE, £3 13*s* 6*d* .. .. *Tho. Brudenell,* 1647

With introductory complimentary Verses by John Booker and others, dedicated to Bolstrod Whitlock, Esq., M.P. At the end is a very curious and complete catalogue, occupying 6 entire leaves of "most astrological authors now extant." "These I mention," he says, "are all his own." This is the most considerable work ever published on this once popular subject, firmly believed in now by many. State policy, in the time of Elizabeth, rendered it fascinating and fashionable, and the great Lord Burleigh consulted Dr. John Dee.

2668 — History of his Life and Times from 1602 to 1681, written by himself; 12 *portraits,* 8vo. *boards,* 7*s* 6*d* (*pub. at* 12*s* 6*d*) *Charles Baldwyn,* 1822

A notice of this curious book, "certainly one of the most entertaining narratives in our language," containing anecdotes of K. Charles I. Dr. John Dee, Doctor Forman, and all the Great Astrologers of that time, will be found in the *Retrospective Review,* vol. 2.

2669 LIMBORCH (Philippi) Theologia Christiana, thick 4to. nearly 1000 pages, *vellum, nice copy,* 6*s* .. *Amstlelodami,* 1686

"This was the first system of Divinity, according to the doctrine of the remonstrants that had appeared in print, undertaken at their request, and received with eagerness by them."—*Chalmers,* from *Moreri.*

2670 LINCOLNE—The Petition of Sir Ralph Verney, Nath. Hobart, W. Denton, and H. Chester, Esqres. and other Adventurers, for the Dreyning of Deeping Fenns, folio, *broadside, curious,* 5*s* 1651

Francis Earle of Bedford, and Sir Will. Russell, mentioned at the back in writing "For Sur Ralph Varny. Send me word if this be —— and, if so, how to be uesed."

2671 — Articles of Visitation and Enquiry concerning matters Ecclesiastical in Lincoln Diocese, in the first Episcopal Visitation of Bishop Sanderson, *Autograph of Roger L'Estrange,* small 4to. *sewed,* 3*s* 6*d* .. .. .. 1662

2672 — Stanley (Dr. Will.) Sermon, at Lambeth, Jan. 10, 1691-2, at the Consecration of Thomas Tenison, Lord Bp. of Lincoln, 4to. *sewed,* 1*s* 6*d* .. .. .. 1692

2673 [LIND'S (John)] Letters on the Present State of Poland with the Manifestoes of the Courts of Vienna, Petersburgh, and Berlin, 8vo. *half calf, uncut,* 4*s* 6*d* (*sold at W. Heath's sale for* 9*s*) 1773

"This book was written by the sagacious and benevolent Mr. Lind, the friend of the profoundly philosophical Dr. N. Forster of Colchester, and the celebrated Jeremy Bentham, and tutor to the worthy and enlightened King of Poland."—*Dr. Parr.*

2674 LINDSEY'S (Theophilus) Memoirs, with a brief Analysis of his Works and Anecdotes and Letters of Eminent Persons, his Friends and Correspondents, by Thos. Belsham, *portrait,* 8vo. *boards, scarce,* 5*s* .. .. .. .. 1812

2675 LINNÆI (Caroli) Systema Naturæ, editio duodecima, reformata, —Mantissa Plantorum, *plates,* 5 vols. 8vo. *clean copy in rough calf,* 15*s* .. .. *Holmiæ,* 1766-71

2676 — Species Plantarum, Edit. 2nda, aucta, 2 vols. 8vo. *rough calf, uniform,* 10*s* .. .. .. *ib.,* 1762

2677 — Genera Plantarum, 8vo. *old calf, gilt,* 6*s* *ib.,* 1764

2678 — Flora Suecica, Edit. 2da, 8vo. *old calf, gilt,* 6*s* *Stockholmiæ,* 1755

2679 — Families of Plants, with their Natural Characters, by a Botanical Society at Lichfield, 2 vols. 8vo. *calf, neat,* 8*s* *Lichfield,* 1787

2680 — Institutes of Botany, a description of all the known Genera of Plants, &c., Englished by Colin Milne, 4to. *calf, neat,* 10*s* 1771

At the end is Richard Steele's Essay on Gardening, with a Catalogue of Exotic Plants for British Green Houses, Plates, *York,* 1793.

2681 — Lachesis Lapponica, a Tour in Lapland, now first published by Dr. James Edw. Smith, *plates,* 2 vols. 8vo. *boards,* 6*s* 6*d* (*pub. at* £1 1*s*) .. .. .. 1811

2682 — General View of the Writings of Linnæus, by Dr. Richard Pulteney, 8vo. *calf, neat,* 4*s* .. .. 1781

2683 — Life, with a List of his Works, and a Biographical Sketch of the Life of his Son, by D. H. Stoever, Englished by Joseph Trapp, *portrait,* 4to. *calf, neat,* 6*s* .. 1794

2684 LINNÆAN Society's Transactions, *coloured and plain plates,* vols. 1, 2, 3, and 4, bound in 2, 4to. *nice clean copies, in old calf,* £2 2*s* .. .. .. 1791-98

2685 LITERARY Gazette, from its commencement in 1817 to 1853 inclusive, 37 vols. 4to. *neatly half bound,* £5 5*s* 1817-53

The first 15 volumes of this set originally cost £12 10*s*. It is a very desirable set of books for a public library.

2686 LITERARY History, Introduction to the, of the XIV. and XV. Centuries, 8vo. *calf, neat, scarce,* 6*s* .. 1798

"Replete with interesting information relative to the state of Literature during the dark ages."—*Lowndes.*

2687 LITERATURE—The Importance of Literature to men of Business, 12mo. *cloth,* 3*s* 6*d* .. .. .. 1852

Addresses delivered publicly by Sir W. Herschel, Rt. Hon. B. D'Israeli, Talfourd, Professor Phillips, the Earl of Carlisle, Lord Mahon, Sir David Brewster, Alison, and other eminent men.

2688 LITHGOW'S (William) Nineteen Years Travels, from Scotland through Europe, Asia, and Africa, 10th Edition, *curious cuts,* 8vo. *old binding, scarce,* 12*s* .. .. 1692

"It is surprising that this most extraordinary narrative (of his sufferings in the Inquisition) has not been made better known. It bears every mark of truth, as does, indeed the whole volume."—*Retrospective Review,* vol. xi. Lithgow started from Paris in 1609.

2689 LITTLE Warbler—English, Irish, Naval, and Jacobite Songs, 4 vols. 64mo. *sewed,* 2*s* .. *Edinburgh, no date.*

2690 LITURGIA, Græcè, 24mo. *purple morocco, gilt leaves,* 5*s* 6*d* (*cost* 10*s*) *Londini, Bagster,* 1823

2691 LITURGIA—in Ecclesia Anglicana receptus, *plate by Sturt*, 12mo. *old calf, gilt*, 3*s* 6*d* .. .. *Londini*, 1713

2692 — Liber precum publicarum, ordo administrandæ cœnæ domini, Catechismus, Ecclesiæ Anglicanæ, Psalterium, 18mo. *antique calf, new*, 7*s* 6*d* .. *Londini, J. G. Parker*, 1848

2693 — selon l'usage de l'Eglise Anglicane, 8vo. large type, *bound, neat*, 2*s* 6*d* .. .. *Londres*, 1706

2694 — une autre edition, 12mo. *very fine copy, in old purple morocco, gilt, gilt edges*, 5*s* .. .. *Londres*, 1729

Added are "Les Pseaumes de David, mis en Rime Françoise, par Clement Marot et Theod. de Beze, Amst. Wetstein, 1710." Set to music.

2695 — 12mo. *nice copy, in purple morocco, extra, gilt leaves*, 6*s* *ib.* 1764

2696 — 12mo. *old morocco, gilt, gilt leaves*, 3*s* 6*d* *ib.* 1780

2697 — 18mo. *bound*, 1*s* 6*d* .. .. *ib.* 1828

2698 LIVERPOOL—Catalogue of the Library of the Athenæum, Liverpool, by G. Burrell, principal Librarian, 8vo. *boards, scarce*, 10*s* 6*d* .. .. .. *Liverpool*, 1820

To S. W. Stevenson, Esq., from his faithful friend the author. Mr. Roscoe is considered the original designer of this Catalogue.

2699 LIVES of British Physicians, *portraits*, 18mo. *cloth*, 2*s* 6*d* (*cost* 5*s*) *Fam. Lib.*, 1830

2700 — of Eminent Christians, Abp. Usher, Dr. Hammond, Bp. Wilson, John Evelyn, Esq., by R. B. Hone, *portraits*, 12mo. *cloth*, 3*s* 1833

2701 — of Philip Howard, Earl of Arundel, and of Anne Dacres, his wife, Edited by the Duke of Norfolk, E. M., small 8vo. *cloth*, 6*s* (*pub. at* 10*s* 6*d*) .. .. .. 1857

2702 LIVIUS, Decas prima, small 8vo. *large margin copy, Aldine Anchor at beginning and end*, 15*s* *Venetiis, in Ædibus Aldi*, 1518

2703 — Decas Tertia, small 8vo. *ample margins*, 2 *anchors*, 15*s* *Venetiis, Aldus*, 1519

This is the 2nd volume of the Aldine Livy, the 2nd Decade being lost, it of course was not printed, although it was afterwards pretended to be found.

2704 — Decadum Epitomæ—Lucius Florus, small 8vo. *a fine clean copy, in old calf*, 10*s* 6*d* *Aldine Anchor on title, no date.*

This forms part of the Aldine Livy, collates by Renouard who dates it Venetiis, 1521

2705 — Decades III. IV. et V., 3 vols. small 8vo. *in a nice clean state, in old stamped calf, large margins*, 15*s* *Basileæ, apud Nicolaum Episcopium*, 1554

This is an early impression, not noticed by Bibliographers.—It wants the 1st Decade, but the last volume has Florus's Epitome of the XIV. Decades, a fullChronology, and an ample "Index Rerum ac Verborum."

2706 — vol. 2 only, 18mo. *bound*, 4*s* *L. Bat., Elzevir*, 1634

2707 — ex recensione J. F. Gronovii, 2 vols. 12mo. *fine copy, with very large margin, old calf, very neat*, 15*s* *L. Bat., Elzevir*, 1678

"This is the *Editio Optima*, it may be pronounced a masterpiece of printing. Livy had never before appeared in so small a space."—*Dr. Dibdin.*

2708 — 4 vols. 18mo. *cloth*, 6*s* .. *Oxonii, Parker*, 1859

2709 LIVIO.—Discorsi di M. Vincentio Dini, sopra il primo libro de le Terza Deca di T. Livio, parte 2nda, 4to. 147 *leaves, old limp vellum*, 15*s* *Roma, per Antonio Blado*, 1563

VINCENTIO DINI's name is *not to be found* in HAYM, which is *remarkable*, nor can I find him elsewhere mentioned, at the end of the volume are some Orations, one by "Carlo V. Imp. in Germania," and a very considerable Treatise, title'd, "Parlamento di Carlo V. Imperatore al Rè Filippo suo figliuolo ne la consegnatione del Governo del suoi Stati p. 1, del tempo de la pace, p. 2, del tempo de la Guerra." See Charles Vth's abdication in favour of his son, in a rare Treatise in this Catalogue, under Valerio Faenzi.

2710 — Machiavelli (Nicolo) Discorsi, sopra la prima Deca di Tito Livio, small 8vo. *vellum*, 9*s* *Palermo, Antonielli*, 1584

At the end is Machiavelli's celebrated Treatises, "Il Prencipe, Vita di Castruccio, Del Duca Valentino, Ritratti di Francia, and Ritratti al Alamagna." *Palermo*, 1584, with a new pagination.

2711 — Ciccarelli (Dottore Antonio, *da Foligno*) Discorsi sopra Tito Livio, 4to. *old calf, gilt*, 7*s* 6*d* *Roma, Stefano Paolini*, 1598

2712 — Gronovii (Jo. Fred.) Observationum liber novus, 12mo. *old calf, neat*, 6*s* .. .. *Daventriæ*, 1652

Harles says this little volume should be added to Gronovius's Livy, of 1679— but it would be more appropriate to that of 1645, 3 vols. 12mo.

2713 — A Bridge of Roman Histories to passe the nearest way from Titus Livius to Cornelius Tacitus, see *Fulbeck*.

2714 LLOYD'S (David) Modern Policy Compleated, the Publick Actions and Councels of his Excellency the Lord Generall Monck, 1639-1660, 12mo. *old binding, very clean copy, scarce*, 6*s* 1660

2715 — State Worthies; the Statesmen and favourites of England, from the Reformation to the Revolution, by C. Whitworth, 2 vols. small 8vo. *old calf, gilt*, 12*s* .. .. 1766

This is from the *Reformation* to the Revolution, not from the *Restoration* as is somewhere said. It is a useful book, and this is the best edition.

2716 LLOYD'S (Rev. David, *of Llanbister*) Horæ Theologicæ, Essays on Physics, Morals, and Theology, 8vo. *boards*, 3*s* 6*d* (*pub. at* 10*s* 6*d*) .. .. .. 1823

Written under the patronage of Dr. Burgess, Bp. of St. David's.

2717 LOCKE'S (John) Works, with an account of his Life, 10 vols. 8vo. *calf, very good set*, £2 5*s* .. .. 1812

2718 — Essay on Human Understanding, *portrait*, 2 vols. 8vo. *old calf, gilt*, 6*s* .. .. .. 1741

2719 — another edition, *portrait*, 2 vols. 8vo. *calf, neat*, 6*s* 1748

2720 — Letter to a Deist, in answer to Objections against the Truth and Authority of the Scriptures, small 8vo. *bound*, 2*s* 1677

2721 — Life, with Extracts from his Correspondence, Journals, and Common-place Books, by Lord King, *portrait*, 4to. *half calf, neat*, 10*s* 6*d* (*pub. at* £2 2*s*) .. .. 1829

"This is a work which must ever remain a standard book in English libraries."—*Literary Gazette.*

2722 LOCKHART'S Memoirs of Scotland, from Queen Anne's Accession to the Union of Scotland and England, in 1707, 8vo. *calf, neat*, 3*s* 6*d* .. .. .. 1714

With an account of the intended French Invasion in March, 1708.
"A staunch Jacobite, and a strenuous opponent of the Union."—*Sir Walter Scott.*

2723 LOCKHART'S Life of Sir W Scott, see *Scott;* and of Burns, see *Burns.*

2724 LOCKMAN'S (John) Entertaining Instructor, being Judicious Sayings, Smart Repartees, &c., in French and English, 12mo. *bound,* 3*s* .. .. .. 1765

2725 LODGE'S (Edmund) 240 Portraits of Illustrious Personages of Great Britain, with Biographical and Historical Memoirs of their Lives and Actions, 8 vols. post 8vo. *cloth,* £2 *H. G. Bohn,* 1849

2726 — Parts 1 to 5, *containing* 15 *portraits,* imp. 8vo. *sewed,* 12*s* 6*d* (*pub. at* £1 17*s* 6*d*) .. .. 1832

2727 — Peerage of the British Empire, with the Baronetage of the three Kingdoms, 8vo. *cloth,* 5*s* .. .. 1833

2728 — Peerage of the British Empire, with the Baronetage, *arms,* royal 8vo. *cloth,* 10*s* .. .. 1837

2729 — new edition, royal 8vo. *cloth, gilt edges, new,* £1 11*s* 6*d* 1860

2730 — The Genealogical Volume, shewing the Peerage and Baronetage from the Earliest Times, royal 8vo., uniform with the above, 1860

This is an important adjunct to the yearly Peerage, and of permanent value.

2731 LOMEIERI (Johannis, *Ecclesiastæ Zutphaniensis)* de Bibliothecis liber singularis, Editio 2nda, small 8vo. *old calf, neat,* 7*s* 6*d* *Ultrajecti,* 1680

Mr. Horne on the Study of Bibliography, says, there are copies of this scarce little book in the London Institution, and in Dr. Williams's library, but he quotes the 1st Edition of 1669.

2732 LONDON.—THE FATAL VESPER; or, a true and punctuall relation of that lamentable and fearfull accident, hapening on Sunday in the afternoon the 26 of October last, by the *fall of a roome in the* BLACKFRIARS, at a Sermon to be preached by FATHER DRURIE, a *Jesuit,* small 4to. *on* 26 *unpaged leaves, sewed, very rare,* £2 2*s* .. *London, John Haviland,* 1623

Has "the names and number of such persons as therein unhappily perished, or were miraculously preserved." It seems there were above 300 persons, English, Scotch, Welsh, and Irish, and the sermon was to have been preached by "Father Drurie, a Jesuite by profession, and by birth a gentleman, being extracted out of the house of the Norfolcian Druries, and sonne unto Doctor Drurie, late professor of the Civil Law in the Court of Arches here in London."

2733 — Great Fire, Account of the several sums paid for Tythes in the City of London, when the Churches were demolished by the late FIRE, folio, *broadside, curious,* 7*s* 6*d* .. 1670

2734 — Great Fire; a Common Council of the Lord Mayor and Aldermen of London, held at Gresham House, 21 March, 1666, declaring according to the Act for Re-building the City, which be Streets or Lanes of Note, with an enumeration of them on 2 folio *broadsides, city arms, curious and rare,* 10*s* 6*d*
*Printed by James Flesher, printer to the Honourable City of London*

2735 — Great Fire; Proclamation against Incendiaries, and Suspicions as to the late Fire, given at the Court of Whitehall, Aug. 19, 1670, on a folio *broadside, with the royal and city arms,* 6*s*

2736 — Some Memoirs of the Life of Mr. Thos. Tryon, late of London, Merchant, written by himself, 12mo. *old calf, neat,* 2*s* 6*d* 1705

2737 LONDON—Strange and Wonderful News from the Man in Chains, near Little Chelsea, shewing how four Gentlemen took Coach, and told the Coachman, Thomas Jarvis, to cut down the Man in Chains, which he not performing, they tied Jarvis to the Man in Chains and left him there all night, folio, *broadside, extremely rare,* £1 1*s* *For S. Johnson, near Tower Hill,* 1707

This is a most curious narration, and no doubt unique.

2738 — Account of the Barbarous Murder committed by Captain Rogers, of Westminster, on the body of Lieut. Beckworth of the Marines, near the Bear, in Bow Street, Covent Garden, on the 20 instant, *broadside, rare,* 5*s* .. .. *W. Wise,* 1710

2739 — Jones's Secret History of Whitehall, from the Restoration of K. Cha. 2nd, 1660 to 1696, with the Tragical History of the Stuarts, from 1068, 2 vols. 12mo. *very neat,* 12*s* 1717

2740 — Continuation of the Secret Hist. from 1688 to 1696, with the Tragical Hist. of the Stuarts from 1068, 8vo. *old cf, nt.* 5*s* 1697

2741 — View of the Old Exchange, print by Sutton Nicholls, 1*s* 1729

2742 — View of London Bridge before the late Alteration in 1760, (Houses on the Bridge) *oblong,* by P. C. Canot, *good impression,* 2*s* .. .. .. .. 1761

2743 — Herbert's (W.) Antiquities of the Inns of the Court and Chancery, with a Concise History of the English Law, 24 *plates,* royal 8vo. *half calf, neat,* 7*s* 6*d* .. .. 1804

2744 — Wilson's (J. J.) History of Christ's Hospital from its foundation, with Memoirs of Eminent Men educated there, *plates,* 8vo. *half calf, very neat,* 6*s* .. .. .. 1821

2745 — Post Office London Directory, the full one; royal 8vo. *cloth,* 10*s* (*pub. at* 24*s*) .. .. .. 1842

2746 — for 1847, complete, royal 8vo. *calf, gilt edges,* 15*s* (*cost* 35*s*) 1847

2747 — for 1855, *map,* royal 8vo. *cloth,* 7*s* 6*d* (*pub. at* 15*s*) 1855

2748 — Post Office London Directory, and Nine Counties, Cambridgeshire, Norfolk and Suffolk, Essex, Hertfordshire, Kent, Middlesex, Surrey and Sussex, *maps,* 2 vols. royal 8vo. *cloth,* £1 10*s* 1846

2749 LONDON and Paris; or Comparative Sketches, by the Marquis De Vermont and Sir Charles Darnley, 8vo. *boards,* 3*s* 6*d* (*pub. at* 9*s*) *Longman,* 1823

2750 LONDONDERRY'S (Marquess of) Narrative of the Peninsular War from 1808 to 1813, 2 vols. 8vo. *half cloth,* 10*s* (*pub. at* £1 11*s* 6*d*) .. .. .. 1829

"We have read nothing descriptive of any portion of the Peninsular War at all to be compared, in point of interest and important information, with the volumes now before us."—*Blackwood.*

2751 LONGFELLOW'S (Henry Wadsworth) Poetical Works, including Evangeline, Voices of the Night, Seaside and Fireside, and other Poems, *Illustrated with above* 100 *elegant wood engravings, by Birket Foster and others,* crown 8vo. *printed on toned paper, extra antique cloth, gilt edges,* 12*s* (*pub. at* £1 1*s*) .. 1858

2752 — Hyperion, a Romance, *above* 70 *engravings after Birket Foster,* crown 8vo. *cloth, elegant, gilt edges,* 12*s* (*pub. at* 21*s*) 1853

2753 — Kavanagh, a Tale, *profusely illustrated,* crown 8vo. *cloth, elegant, gilt edges,* 6*s* 6*d* (*pub. at* 10*s* 6*d*) .. .. 1858

2754 LONGFELLOW—Evangeline, a Tale of Acadie, 45 *elegant engravings*, crown 8vo. *cloth, elegant, gilt edges,* 7*s* 6*d* (*pub. at* 10*s* 6*d*) 1854

2755 — Golden Legend, 50 *engravings on wood*, crown 8vo. *cloth, elegant, gilt edges,* 8*s* (*pub. at* 12*s*) .. .. 1854

All these elegant editions of Longfellow's various works are printed on toned paper. "In respect of melody, feeling, pathos, and that exquisite simplicity of expression which is the criterion of a genuine poet, Mr. Longfellow need not shun comparison with any living writer."—*Blackwood's Magazine.*

2756 LONGIANO (Fausto da) Duello regolato a le leggi de l'Honore, con tutti li cartelli missivi, e risponsivi ec, e con due risposte, small 8vo. *old vellum, scarce,* 9*s* *Vinegia, Rutilio Borgominerio,* 1559

An edition not mentioned by *Haym.* For another book on this subject see *Mutio.*

2757 LONGINI (Dionsii) de Sublimi dicendi genere liber, à Petro Pagano, latinitate donatus, small 4to. *old calf, neat,* £1 1*s* *Venetiis, apud V. Valgrisium,* 1572

A latin translation which I can find no where mentioned, it would appear to be the earliest and unknown. In mentioning the Genevan edit. of 1612, Dr. Dibdin says, "This is the first edition in which a latin translation appears."

2758 — de Sublimitate, Gr. et Lat. 8vo. *calf, neat,* 1*s* *Lond.* 1794

2759 LONGUS—Les Amours Pastorales de Daphnis et de Chloé, *fine impressions of the* 28 *engravings by B. Audran, after the designs of Philip of Orleans,* small 8vo. LARGE PAPER, *old red morocco, extra, marbled and gilt leaves,* RARE, £2 12*s* 6*d* *Paris,* 1718

A sumptuously bound copy, with broad borders of gold on the sides, and lined with silk.

2760 LORENZO de Medici, called the Magnificent, his Life by William Roscoe, *portrait,* post 8vo. *cloth,* 3*s* *H. G. Bohn,* 1847

"I recommend it to our country as a work of unquestionable genius, and uncommon merit. It adds the name of Roscoe to the very first rank of English classical historians." —*Matthias's Pursuits of Literature.*

2761 LORRAINE (Le Duc de) Catalogue des Livres, Estampes, et Planches Graveés, disposé par Jos. Ermens, 1781, *priced,* 8vo. *half bound, uncut,* 5*s* .. .. .. *Bruxelles,* 1781

2762 LOTTINI (Giovanfrancesco) Avvedimenti Civili, small 8vo. *old vellum, wormed,* 5*s* .. *In Venetia, Zopini,* 1582

Sir Christopher Hatton's copy, stamped C. H. An edition not mentioned by *Haym.*

2763 LOUDON'S (Mrs.) Facts from the World of Nature, Animate and Inanimate, *numerous plates,* 12mo. *cloth, gilt edges, new,* 4*s* 1848

2764 LOUDON'S (John) Treatise on Forming, Improving, and Managing Country Residences, with Remarks on Mr. Repton's Practice of Landscape Gardening, *plates,* 2 vols. 4to. *boards, scarce,* 25*s* 1806

2765 LOUDON'S (J. C.) Self-Instruction for Young Gardeners, Foresters, Bailiffs, Land-Stewards, and Farmers in Arithmetic and Book-keeping, Geometry, Trigonometry, &c., &c., with Memoir of him, *portrait,* 8vo. *boards,* 7*s* 6*d* .. .. 1847

2766 LOUIS XIV. Ordonnance d'Aout 1681, touchant la Marine, 24mo. *old binding,* 2*s* .. .. .. 1691

2767 — Le Siecle de Louis XIV. (1661-1714) publié par M. de Francheville, 2 vols. 12mo. *old calf, very neat,* 6*s* *Londres, Dodsley,* 1752

The 2nd volume consists of Anecdotes, Government, the History of Calvinism, Jansenism and Quietism, Writers, Artists, &c.

2768 LOUIS XIV.—The Age of Louis XIV. by Voltaire, *portrait*, 2 vols. 12mo. *neat*, 4*s* .. .. .. 1753

2769 — Life and Times of Louis XIV. by G. P. R. James, 2 vols. post 8vo. *cloth*, 5*s* (*cost* 7*s*) .. *H. G. Bohn*, 1851

2770 LOUIS XVI.—Private Memoirs relative to the Last Year of the Reign of Lewis XVI., late King of France, by A. F. Bertrand de Moleville, 6 *well-engraved portraits by Agar*, 3 vols. 8vo. *half calf, neat*, 9*s* .. .. .. 1797

2771 LOVAT (Lord) Memoirs of the Life of, 1746.—Foster's Account of the Behaviour of the late Earl of Kilmarnock on the Day of his Execution, 1746.—Summus Anglicæ Seneschallus, a Survey of the Office, Dignity, &c. of the Lord High Steward of England, on the Manner of Arraigning a Peer indicted of Treason, 1746. —Account of the Behaviour of Simon, Lord Lovat, from the Time of his Death Warrant, 1747.—Popery always the same, 1746.—The Reasonableness of Mending and Executing the Laws against Papists, 1746.—The Lords' Protest on a Motion for Keeping our Forces at Home until the Dutch declare War against France, 1746.—Britain's Remembrancer, 1747.—Turnbull on Fiefs or Tenures, *no date*, in 1 vol. 8vo. VERY CURIOUS, *all very clean and neat*, 10*s* 6*d* .. .. 1746-47

•2772 LOVER'S (Samuel) Lyrics of Ireland, *portraits and plates*, post 8vo. *cloth, gilt, new*, 5*s* .. .. .. 1858

2773 — Songs and Ballads, *portrait*, 12mo. *cloth, gilt, new*, 2*s* 6*d* 1858

2774 LOWMAN'S (Moses) Dissertation on the Civil Government of the Hebrews, &c. 8vo. *old calf, neat*, 6*s* .. 1745

"Lowman had a great knowledge of Jewish affairs."—*Orme*. It contains a vindication of the Mosaical Constitutions against the misrepresentations of Morgan's Moral Philosopher.

2775 LOWNDES'S (William T.) Bibliographer's Manual of English Literature, 4 vols. thick 8vo. LARGE AND THICK PAPER, *half bound in russia, uncut, top edges gilt*, .. .. 1834

In a most desirable state, on LARGE PAPER, of which there were only 50 copies printed, and with large additions in MS.

2776 — Bibliographer's Manual of English Literature, with Additions by Mr. H. G. Bohn, 5 parts, post 8vo. *cloth*, 3*s* 6*d each part*, 1857-9

Three other parts are intended to complete this valuable work, to which we are promised a supplement by Mr. Bohn, which will be looked forward to with much interest by all interested in bibliographical pursuits.

2777 — British Librarian, or Book Collector's Guide to the Formation of a Library, arranged in Classes, parts I to XI, in parts, all published, 8vo. *sewed*, 12*s* (*pub. at* £1 7*s* 6*d*) 1839-42

2778 — part I of ditto, 8vo. *sewed*, 2*s* .. .. 1839

2779 LOWTH'S (Geo. T.) Wanderer in Arabia; or Western Footsteps in Eastern Tracks, *plates*, 2 vols. post 8vo. *cloth*, 9*s* 6*d* (*pub. at* £1 1*s*) .. .. .. .. 1855

2780 LOWTH'S (Bishop Robert) Isaiah, a New Translation with a Dissertation and Notes, Critical, Philological, and Explanatory, 2nd edition, 4to. *boards, uncut*, 21*s* .. .. 1779

"*From the Author*" to "*J. Duncan*." Two autographs. At the back of the title is a highly complimentary letter in the hand-writing of Bishop Lowth, to Dr. Duncan, written from *London House, May* 1, 1779, signed, "*R. London.*"

2781 LOWTH'S Short Introduction to English Grammar, with Critical Notes, 12mo. *calf,* 2s 6d .. .. 1793

2782 LOYSEAU (Charles) Traité des Seigneuries, 4to. above 400 pages, *limp vellum,* 5s .. .. .. *Paris,* 1608

2783 LUBBOCK'S (Rev. Richard, *Eccles,*) Observations on the Fauna of Norfolk, more particularly on the District of the Broads, *map and plate,* 8vo. *cloth,* 3s 6d (*pub. at* 6s) *Norwich, C. Muskett,* 1845

A beautiful specimen of Typography. The book worthy to take a place with White's Natural Hist. of Selborne.

2784 LUCANI Pharsalia, small 8vo. *old stamped binding,* 2s 6d *Parisiis, apud S. Colinæum,* 1528

2785 — Pharsalia, Autograph of "John Bridges," 8vo. *old calf, neat,* 3s *Antwerpiæ, Jo. Loeus,* 1556

2786 — Pharsalia, J. Micylli Annotationes, small 8vo. *old calf,* £1 1s *Lipsiæ,* 1589

With the autographs of "Gulielmus Hatton," and of "Ann Swale," "George Swale," and "Edward Swale." The biographer of Sir Christopher Hatton, who was brother to this William Hatton says, that Sir Christopher, who was Lord Chancellor in 1587, used in all matters of great moment to consult Dr. Swale, a civilian, &c., see *Nicolas's Life of him.*

2787 — Pharsalia; sive de Bello Civili Cæsaris et Pompeii lib. X., ex Emendat. H. Grotii, 18mo. *vellum,* 3s *Amst., Elz.,* 1651

2788 — Pharsalia, Englished by N. Rowe, *map and frontispiece,* 2 vols. 12mo. *calf, neat,* 4s .. .. .. 1722

Book-plate of George Venables Vernon, Baron of Kinderton.

2789 LUCAS'S (Dr. Richard) Enquiry after Happiness, 2 vols. 8vo. *old calf, neat,* 6s .. .. .. 1717

"I am sure that time will be well spent which you bestow on Lucas's Enquiry after Happiness."—*Dean Stanhope.*

2790 LUCIANI Timon, Gr. et Lat., a Lamb. Barlæo, 8vo. *half bound,* 3s *Lugd. Bat.,* 1652

2791 — La Pharsale de Lucain, en Vers François par Mr. de Breboeuf, 12mo. *vellum, neat,* 5s .. *Leide, Jean Elzevier,* 1658

2792 — Sämtliche Werke, aus den Griechischen übersetz, mit Anmerkungen und Erläuterungen von C. M. Wieland, vols. 1, 2, 3, (out of 6) 8vo. *hf. bd.* 7s 6d .. *Leipzig,* 1788

2793 LUCRETIUS, de Rerum Natura, 12mo. *nice copy in calf, gilt,* 10s 6d *Birminghamiæ, J. Baskerville,* 1773

Autograph of PETER ELMSLEY to whom this book was presented by Dr. VINCENT, Master of Westminster School, on his having gone through the Iliad. In the hand writing of Dr. Vincent is "*Petro Elmsly Iliade* bene perlectâ hic Liber. συνσοφεῖν τοῖς σοφοῖς."

2794 — cum notis variorum et G. Wakefield, vols. 2, 3, 4, 8vo. *boards,* 6s *Glasguæ,* 1813

2795 — 18mo. *cloth,* 2s .. .. *Oxonii, Parker,* 1855

2796 LUDLOW'S (Edmund) Memoirs, with the Case of Charles I. *portrait,* folio, LARGE PAPER, *fine copy in calf,* £1 5s .. 1751

Ludlow was Lieut. General of Horse, and M.P. in 1640.
"Highly deserving a careful perusal by all such persons as are desirous of rightly understanding the history of the reign of King Charles I. and the true grounds of the great civil war."—*Baron Maseres.*

2797 LUDOLPHUS'S (Job) History of Ethiopia, *plates*, folio, *old calf, neat*, 9*s* .. .. .. .. 1684

"A work full of recondite and important information on the origin of the Abyssinians, the climate, soil, productions, &c."—*Lowndes*.

2798 LUIGI di Granata, trattato Secondo dell' Aggiunta del Memoriale della Vita Christiana, tradotto dalla lingua Spagnuola per Camillo Camilli, *wood cuts*, 12mo. *limp vellum*, 3*s* 6*d* *Vinegia, Giorgio Angelieri*, 1581

2799 — del Memoriale della Vita Christiana, parte Seconda, tradotta dalla lingua Spagnuola dal Timotheo da Bagno, *cuts*, 12mo. *limp vellum*, 3*s* 6*d* (see No. 1901) .. .. *ib.*, 1581

2800 LUISINI (Aloysii) Aphrodisiacus, sive de Lue Venerea vel Morbo Gallico opus, cum præfat. Herm. Boerhaave, vol. 1 only, folio, *neat*, 8*s* .. .. .. *L. Bat.*, 1728

This volume contains a collection of 53 ancient treatises on this disease.

2801 LUMLEY'S (W. G.) Poor Law Acts, with Notes, 12mo. *boards*, 2*s* .. .. .. .. 1849

2802 LUPANI (Vincentii) Annotationes in Ælium Spartianum, Julium Capitolinum, Ælium Lapridium, Vulcatum Gallicanum, Trebellium Pollionem, &c. small 8vo. *boards*, 3*s* *Parisiis, A. Wechel*, 1560

2803 LUSHINGTON'S (Mrs. Charles) Narrative of a Journey from Calcutta to Europe by way of Egypt in 1827, post 8vo. *half cloth*, 3*s* 6*d* (*pub. at* 8*s* 6*d*) .. .. *Murray*, 1829

2804 LUTTRELL'S (Henry) Letters to Julia, in Rhyme, with Lines written at Ampthill Park, 3rd edition, 12mo. *morocco, extra, gilt edges, scarce*, 9*s* .. .. .. 1822

2805 LYELL'S (Charles) Principles of Geology, *frontispiece*, 4 vols. 12mo. *boards*, 12*s* (*pub. at* 24*s*) .. .. 1835

2806 — another copy, 3 vols. 12mo. 14*s* (*pub. at* 24*s*) *London*, 1840

2807 LYNDE (Humfrey, Knight) Via Devia; the By-Way, misleading the Weake and Unstable into Dangerous Paths of Error, thick 12mo. of 754 pages, *old calf, neat*, SCARCE, 6*s* *For R. Milbourne*, 1630

Dedicated to the ingenuous and moderate Romanists of this kingdom. He was also author of Via Tuta and Via Recta, not in Lowndes. Book-plate of Rev. W. T. Spurdens of North Walsham, Norfolk.

2808 LYON'S (Capt. G. F.) Journal of a Residence and Tour in the Republic of Mexico, in 1826, with some account of the Mines, 2 vols. post 8vo. *boards*, 6*s* (*pub. at* 16*s*) .. 1828

2809* LYRE (La) Protestante, Consacrée aux Partisans de la Bonne Cause, 12mo. *calf, neat*, 3*s* 6*d* *No place, date, or printer's name, but about* 1760

2810 LYRE (The) Fugitive Poetry of the 19th Century, by Professor Wilson, Moore, Byron, Miss Hemans, &c., 18mo. *morocco, gilt edges*, 3*s* (*cost* 6*s*) .. .. 1841

2811 LYSIÆ Opera Omnia, Græcè et Latinè, cum versione nova, etc. edidit A. Auger, 2 vols. 8vo. *calf, very neat*, 10*s* 6*d* *Parisiis, Didot*, 1783

Nice copy bound by Kalthœber, formerly priced 24s.

2812 LYSIAS—Eratosthenes, hoc est, brevis et luculenta defensio Lysiæ pro cæde Eratosthenis, Gr. et Lat., prælectionibus illustrata Andreæ Dunæi, small 8vo. *old calf, neat,* 3*s* 6*d*
*Cantabrigiæ, John Legatt,* 1593

A. Dunæus, was Regius Professor of Greek in Cambridge. "*E. Libris Tho. Bennet.*"

2813 LYTE (Henry, Esquyer) Niewe Herball, or Historie of Plantes, first set foorth in the Doutche or Almaigne, by that learned Physition to the Emperour, D. Rembert Dodoens, now first translated into English, *hundreds of wood cuts,* thick folio of 814 pages, **Black Letter,** *old calf, neat,* £2 2*s*
*At London, by me Gerard Dewes, Dwelling in Pawles Churchyarde,* 1578

Dedicated to "The renowned Princesse, Queen Elizabeth, from my poore house at Lytescarie, within your Maiesties Countie of Somerset, the first day of Januarie, 1578." At the back of the title are Lyte's arms, further on a very nice *wood cut portrait* of Dodonæus, the author; several commendatory verses by Thomas Newton, W. Clowes, and others, both in Latin and English; on the title-page the *autograph* of *Xtofer Halleley,* or *Hasseley,* and, at the end, that of "*Tho. Macro,*" a Norfolk gentleman, who says, that he "*est Verus possessor huius libri Anno Do.* 1641." On all these accounts a very interesting old volume.

2814 LYTTLETON'S (George Lord) History of the Life of King Henry the Second, 6 vols., with his Miscellaneous Works, 3 vols. together 9 vols. 8vo. *calf, neat,* £1 11*s* 6*d* .. 1769

2815 — Works, Observations on the Life of Cicero; Observations on St. Paul; Dialogues of the Dead; Poems, &c., *portrait,* 4to. *a very fine copy, in old calf, gilt,* 12*s* .. .. 1774

"The works of the great Lord Lyttleton are most important and instructive. Among his lighter pieces is found the most beautiful song in the English language, '*The Heavy Hours.*'"—*Dr. Valpy.*

2816 — History of England in Letters from a Nobleman to his Son, with two letters on the study and Biography of the Ancient and Modern British Historians, 2 vols. 12mo. *calf, gilt, neat,* 6*s* 1827

Sir Walter Scott says, this work is "attributed to Lord Lyttleton, but really written by Oliver Goldsmith."

2817 LYTTON'S (Sir E. Bulwer) Confessions of a Water Patient, 12mo. *sewed,* 1*s.* (see Bulwer, No. 737) .. 1847

2818 — Caxtons, a family picture, *plate,* post 8vo. *cloth,* 4*s* 1854

2819 MABLY'S (Abbé de) Observations on the Romans, small 8vo. *calf, neat,* 2*s* 6*d* .. .. .. 1751

"A proper companion to Montesquieu's declension of the Roman Empire."—*Clement.*

2820 MACARTNEY'S (Earl) Account of his Embassy to China, drawn up by Sir George Staunton, 2 vols. 4to. *half bound, neat, with the large folio volume of plates,* £1 11*s* 6*d* 1798

2821 MACAULAY'S (Lord) History of England, 7 vols. post 8vo. *cloth,* £2 2*s* .. .. *Longmans,* 1858-9

2822 — Critical and Historical Essays, contributed to the Edinburgh Review, 2 vols. post 8vo. *cloth,* 8*s* .. 1859

On Milton, Machiavelli, Hallam's Constitutional History, Southey's Colloquies, Boswell's Life of Johnson, Lord Nugent's Hampden, Burleigh, Lord Bacon, Pitt, Mackintosh's Revolution, Sir W. Temple, Warren Hastings, Addison, &c., &c.

2823 — Essays, 3 vols. post 8vo. *cloth,* £1 1*s* .. 1858

2824 — another edition in 3 vols. 8vo. *cloth,* £1 16*s* 1858

2825 MACAULAY'S Lays of Ancient Rome, with Ivry and the Armada, post 8vo. *cloth*, 4*s* 6*d* .. .. 1860

2826 — another edition, *classically illustrated*, 4to. *antique cloth*, £1 1*s* 1859

2827 — Essay on the Life and Writings of Addison, and Horace Walpole, 16mo. *stiff cover*, 1*s* .. .. 1852

2828 — Essay on Hallam's Constitutional History of England, 16mo. *sewed*, 1*s* .. .. *Longmans*, 1856

2829 — Speeches, corrected by himself, 8vo. *cloth*, 12*s* *Longmans*, 1854

2830 — Biographies contributed to the Encyclopædia Britannica, small 8vo. *cloth*, 6*s* .. .. .. 1860

2831 MACDIARMID (John) Lives of British Statesmen, *portraits*, 2 vols. 8vo. *half cloth*, 10*s* (*pub. at* 21*s*) 1820

Contains the Lives of Sir Thomas More, Lord Burleigh, Lord Strafford, and Lord Clarendon, elegantly written. "A work full of great promise, luckily and wisely reprinted."—*Dr. Dibdin's Lib. Comp.*

2832 MACHIAVELLI (Nicolo, *Cittadino et Secretario Fiorentino)* Tutte le Opere di, divise in V. parti, *portrait on title page*, thick 4to. *old calf, neat, and very clean*, £1 11*s* 6*d* .. 1650

No place or printer's name, cannot find this edition mentioned anywhere. Contains, History of Florence; the Prince, Lives of Castruccio Castracani, Vitellozo, Vitelli, and others; Discourses on Livy; the Art of War; Poems, Comedies, &c., and consists of 1044 pages collectively, but each of the 5 parts is separately paged, parts 2 to 5 are dated 1550, but the 1st is dated a century later.

2833 — Opere, small 8vo. see *Livius*.

2834 — Il Prencipe, small 8vo. *a very fine copy, in old calf, gilt*, 12*s* *Palermo, Antonielli*, 1584

At the end is Machiavelli Vita di Castruccio Castracani da Lucca, Del Duca Valentino, Ritratti di Francia, and Ritratti al Allamagna.

"His book, 'Il Prencipe,' was quite a Text Book with Sovereigns who wished to govern tyrannically."—*Mills's Theodore Ducas.*

2835 — Works, translated into English, folio, *good copy, in calf*, 12*s* 1695

Contains his history of Florence, The Prince, Life of Castruccio Castracani, of the States of France and Germany, Discourses on Livy, and the Art of War.

"The style of Machiavel, is eminent for simplicity, strength, and clearness. It would not be too much to place him at the head of the prose writers of Italy."—*Hallam.*

2836 MACINTOSH'S (Charles) Practical Gardener, and Modern Horticulturist, *portrait and coloured plates*, thick 8vo. *half calf, very neat*, 12*s* (*pub. at* 26*s*) .. .. .. 1839

2837 MACKAY'S (Dr. Charles) Book of English Songs, *plates*, post 8vo. *cloth, gilt, new*, 2*s* 6*d* .. .. 1858

2838 — Songs of Scotland, from the 16th to the 19th Century, *plates numerous, cloth, gilt, new*, 2*s* 6*d* .. 1858

2839 MACKENZIE'S (Henry) Works, Man of Feeling, Man of the World, &c., with his Life, *frontispiece*, 24mo. *boards*, 2*s* 6*d* 1816

2840 — another edition, *plates*, 18mo. *half calf, neat*, 3*s* 1826

2841 — Man of the World, original edition, 2 vols. 12mo. *old calf, neat*, 3*s* 6*d* .. .. .. *T. Cadell*, 1773

2842 MACKGREGORY'S (John) Account of the Sepulchres of the Antients, with a description of their Monuments, to the destruction of Jerusalem, sm. 8vo. *old cf., neat*, 5*s* *For the Author*, 1712

A copy sold at the Roxburghe sale for 9*s*.

2843 MACKINTOSH'S (Sir James) History of England, to 1760, 10 vols. 12mo. *cloth*, £1 5*s* (*pub. at* £3) .. 1850

2844 MACKNIGHT'S Harmony of the Four Gospels, 2 vols. 8vo. *cloth, uncut*, 6*s* .. .. .. *London*, 1819

2845 MACLAINE'S (Dr. Archibald) Discourses delivered in the English Church at the Hague, 8vo. *boards*, 2*s* 6*d* 1799

2846 MACLAURIN'S (Rev. John, *Glasgow)* Sermons and Essays, edited by Dr. John Gillies, 12mo. *boards*, 2*s* 6*d* 1815

2847 MACLAURIN'S (Professor) Treatise of Algebra, with a Treatise on the general properties of Geometrical Lines, *plates*, 8vo. *bound*, 3*s* 6*d* .. .. .. 1788

2848 M'CLURE (Capt. Sir Rob.) Discovery of the N. W. Passage by H. M. S. Investigator, edited by Capt. Sherard Osborn, *portrait and plates*, 8vo. *cloth*, 14*s* .. *Longmans*, 1859

2849 MACRAY'S (Will. Dunn *of the Bodleian Library, Oxford*,) Manual of British Historians, to A.D. 1600, containing a Chronological Account of the Early Chroniclers and Monkish Writers, their printed Works and unpublished MSS. 8vo. *half morocco*, 8*s* 1845

2850 MADDEN'S (R. R.) Travels in Turkey, Egypt, Nubia, and Palestine, 1824-27, *coloured portrait*, 2 vols. 8vo. *boards*, 8*s* (*pub. at* £1 8*s*) .. .. .. 1827

2851 MADDOCK'S (James) Florist's Directory; a Treatise on the Culture of Flowers, on Soils, Manures, &c., improved by Samuel Curtis, *plates*, 8vo. *half calf, neat*, 5*s* .. .. 1810

2852 MADOX'S (Thomas) Baronia Anglica; an History of Land-honors and Baronies, and of Tenure in Capite, verified by Records, folio, *old calf, neat*, 15*s* .. .. .. 1741

2853 — History and Antiquities of the Exchequer of the Kings of England, 2 vols. 4to. *a very fine copy, in old calf*, £1 16*s* 1769

Best edition of what Bp. Nicholson characterizes as "a most valuable and accurate work."

2854 MAESTRECHT—Recueil des Recés emanez de la part des deux Seigneurs et Princes de Maestrecht, l'an 1665, 4to. *old binding*, 4*s* .. .. .. *Maestrecht*, 1716

Has also a copy of "La Veille carte de la Ville de Maestrecht, de l'an, 1283," and a "Copie de l'ordonnance publiée devant la Maison de Ville, 1580," the "Capitulation de l'année, 1632," &c., &c.

2855 MAFFEI (Marchese Scipione) Merope, Tragedia, 4to. *sewed*, 3*s* *Modena*, 1714

"Terza editione assai bella, con un discorso del Marchese Orsi."—*Haym.* This trajedy was acted with the most brilliant success, it is esteemed a masterpiece.

2856 MAGRI (Carlo, *della Valleta)* Il Valore Maltese, contro le Calunnie di Girolamo Brusoni, 8vo. *old vellum*, 5*s* *Roma*, 1667

2857 MAHOMETIS Abdallæ Filii Theologia dialogo explicata, Hermanno Nellingaunense intertrete,—Alcorani Epitome Roberto Ketenense Anglo interprete—J. A. Vuidmestadii notationes et Vita Mahometis, *no place or printer's name, date*, 1543.—Muhammedis Testamentum, sive Pacta cum Christianis in Oriente inita, accessit T. Bibliandri Apologia pro editione Alcorani, ed. Joh. Fabricio, *Rostochii*, 1638.—Programma de Angelis Mahometis Turcarum psuedo-Prophetæ Christique Simiæ in defungenda legatione ministris festo Michaelis Archangeli in Academia Julia, 1716, *Helmstadii, H. D. Hammii*, 1716; 3 RARE Tracts in 1 vol. small 4to. *half calf, clean and neat*, 18*s* .. V. Y.

2858 MAHON'S (Lord) History of England from the peace of Utrecht to that of Aix-la-Chapelle, vol. 1 only, (1713 to 1719) 8vo. *half cloth,* 6*s* (*pub. at* 12*s*) .. .. 1836

2859 MAITLAND'S (Rev. S. R.) Index of English Books printed before 1600, in the Archiepisc. Library at Lambeth, 8vo. *cloth,* 6*s* 1845

2860 MAITTAIRE (Mich.) Annales Typographici ab Artis inventæ origine ad annum 1536, *portraits of John Guttenburg, John Faust, Lawrence Coster, Aldus Manucius, John Froben, and Henry Stephens,* 3 vols. 4to. *nice clean copy, in old calf,* £1 1*s* *Hagæ Comitum,* 1719-22

"These annals will ever be considered a lasting monument of this sound scholar's diligence and zeal, and are indispensable in every bibliographical library."—*Lowndes.*

2861 MALCOLM'S (Lt. Col.) Sketch of the Sikhs, a singular nation, who inhabit the Provinces of the Penjab, royal 8vo. *boards,* 5*s* (*pub. at* 8*s* 6*d*) .. .. .. 1812

"This interesting Sketch originally appeared in the Asiatick Researches."—*Lowndes.*

2862 MALHERBE, Poesies de, avec la Vie de l'Auteur et de courtes Notes par A. G. M. Q. (Meunier de Querlon) *fine portrait,* 12mo. LARGE PAPER, *old calf, gilt edges,* 6*s* *Paris, Barbou,* 1776

An elegant edition, has Malherbe's Letter to Louis XIII., on the death of his son, who was killed in a duel.

2863 MALINGRE (Claude) Historie Generale de le Rebellion de Boheme, 1617-1623, *fine portrait of the Count de Buquoy,* thick 8vo. of 998 pages, *vellum,* 15*s* *Paris, Jean Petit,* 1623

The 5 parts, very scarce, Contenant la Vie et Exploicts de Guerre du Comte de Buquoy, la Reduction de la Boheme, Lusatie, Silesie, Moravie, Hongrie et Austriche à l'obeissance de l'Empereur et tout ce qui s'est passé en Allemagne depuis l'an 1617, jusques à present.

2864 MALKIN'S (Benj. H., F.A.S.) Father's Memoirs of his Child, *plates and portrait by W. Blake,* royal 8vo. *bds,* 6*s* *T. Bensley,* 1806

Printed for private distribution only.

2865 MALLETT'S (P. H.) Northern Antiquities; a description of the Manners, Customs, Religion, and Laws of the Ancient Danes, and our Saxon Ancestors, with a translation of the Edda and Notes, by Bp. Percy, 2 vols. post 8vo. *boards,* 6*s* *Edinburgh, Stewart,* 1809

"A highly valuable work."—*Lowndes.* Who does not mention this edition.

2866 MALLING'S (Ove) Great and good deeds of Danes, Norwegians, and Holsteinians, Englished, 4to. LARGE PAPER, *boards,* 8*s* 1807

2867 MALONE'S Early English Poetry.—A Catalogue of Early English Poetry, and other Miscellaneous Works, illustrating the British Drama, collected by Edmond Malone, Esq., and now preserved in the Bodleian Library, folio, *sewed,* 10*s* *Oxford University Press,* 1836

2868 MALORY'S (Sir Thomas) History of King Arthur, and the Knights of the Round Table, with Notes, by Thomas Wright, Esq., 3 vols. foolscap 8vo. *cloth, new,* 15*s* *J. R. Smith,* 1858

This is a reprint of the famous old romance "La Mort d'Arthure," 1636, a book of great rarity, for reproducing which the public ought to be very grateful to its learned Editor.

2869 MANBY'S (Charles W.) Tom Racquet and his three Maiden Aunts, *plates,* 8vo. *cloth,* 4*s* 6*d* (*pub. at* 9*s*) .. 1848

2870 MANCHESTER al Mondo; Contemplatio Mortis et immortalitatis, *engraved title page*, 12mo. *vellum*, 3*s* *London, Rich. Thral, no date.*

An English book with a Latin title, by Henry Ley, Earl of Manchester. Date about 1640.

2871 MANNING'S (Robert) Moral Entertainments on the most important Practical Truths of the Christian Religion, 3 vols. 12mo. *old calf, very neat*, 7*s* 6*d* .. *Tho. Meighan*, 1742

Dedicated "to the Rt. Hon. the Lord Petre, Baron of Writtle."

2872 MANNING'S (Thomas) Introduction to Arithmetic and Algebra, 8vo. *old boards*, 3*s* .. .. *Cambridge*, 1796

2873 MANSTEIN'S (General) Memoirs of Russia, Historical, Political, and Military, from 1727 to 1744, in her Wars with Turkey and Sweden, *maps and plans*, 4to. *half bound, neat*, 7*s* 6*d* 1770

As this work was deemed to be authentic, David Hume gave it his sanction, and wrote the Preface. This copy has the book-plate of Lord Walpole, and the autograph of *Thomas Pownall, Governor of British America.*

"His memoirs describe the internal history of Russia, and her wars with the Porte, during the time in which he served, with the spirit of an eye-witness."—*Lord John Russell.*

2874 MANT'S (Bishop) Order for the Visitation of the Sick, 12mo. *half bound*, 1*s* .. .. .. .. 1806

2875 — British Months, a Poem, 2 vols. 12mo. *cloth*, 5*s* (*pub. at* 9*s*) *J. W. Parker*, 1835

For fine copies of Bp. Mant's Bible and Common Prayer Book, see Nos. 1195 and 1480.

2876 MANT'S (Rev. F. W.) Ballads and Lays, 12mo. *cloth*, 3*s* (*pub. at* 5*s*) .. .. .. *Bell & Daldy*, 1857

A very prettily printed book on tinted paper. These ballads are illustrative of events in early English History.

2877 MANTELL'S (Dr. G. A.) Thoughts on Animalcules, or a Glimpse of the Invisible World revealed by the Microscope, small 4to. *cloth*, 7*s* 6*d* .. .. .. *Murray*, 1846

This edition, with beautifully coloured plates, is out of print.

2878 — Geological Excursions round the Isle of Wight, and adjacent Coast of Dorsetshire, *plates*, post 8vo. *cloth, gilt*, 6*s* 6*d* (*pub. at* 12*s*) .. .. .. .. 1847

2879 — Wonders of Geology, a familiar Exposition of Geological Phenomena, *plates*, 2 vols. post 8vo. *cloth*, 12*s* (*pub. at* 18*s*) 1848

2880 MANUAL for the Aged, *large type*, 12mo. *bound*, 1*s*

2881 MANUSCRIPT Book, thick 4to. *half russia*, 5*s*

2882 MS. Sermons, 5 of them, in a fine bold hand, by Charles Tucke, July 26, 1746, 8vo. *black calf*, 3*s* 6*d*

2883 MS. Sermons, 12 on IX. Isaiah, 6, For unto us a Child is born; a Funeral Sermon on VII. Acts, v. 59; and 3 on V. Ephesians, 8, in 1 vol. 8vo. written about 150 years ago, *in a plain old hand*, 10*s*

2884 MANUTII (Pauli) Commentarius in Epistolas Ciceronis ad Atticum, 8vo. 808 pages, besides an "Index rerum et Verborum," *old calf*, 10*s* 6*d* .. .. .. *Venetiis*, 1572

2885 — Catalogue of Books printed by the Manutii from 1494 to 1597, by John Bohn, Henrietta Street, Covent Garden, London, royal 8vo. *sewed*, 3*s*

2886 MAPS—Collins's Map of Russia and Turkey, shewing the Baltic, North, Black, and Mediterranean Seas, folded into 12mo. *stiff covers*, 1*s*.—Sardinia, by Churchley, *coloured*, folded into 12mo. *cover*, 1*s*.—France, in Provinces, *coloured*, 1*s*.—Prussia, *coloured*, 1*s*.—Collins's Map of the World, folded 1*s*.—Philips's Map of Australia, ditto of New Zealand, 6*d* each.—Seat of War in North Italy, by Johnston, *coloured*, folded into 8vo. 1*s* 6*d* 1859.—Oxford, 1808, 1*s*.—Cambridge, 1804, 1*s*

2887 MARCA (Peter de) S. Baluzii Epistola de Vita, rebus gestis, moribus et Scriptis illustrissimi Viri Petri de Marca Archiepiscopi Parisiensis, 8vo. *old calf, neat, scarce*, 6*s* *Parisiis*, 1663

This is the volume from which Mr. Chalmers got his account of the life of this most learned man, inserted in his Biographical Dictionary.

2888 MARCELLO (Pietro) Vite de' Prencipi di Vinegia, tradotte in Volgare de L. Domenichi, small 8vo. *old calf, gilt*, (*much wormed*) 6*s* .. .. *In Venetia, per F. Marcolini*, 1558

"Libro assai raro."—*Haym*.

2889 MARCET'S (Mrs.) Conversations on Vegetable Physiology, comprehending the Elements of Botany, with their Application to Agriculture, 2 vols. 12mo. *cloth*, 6*s* (*pub. at* 14*s*) 1829

2890 — Conversations on Chemistry, 2 vols. 12mo. *cth*, 6*s* (*pub. at* 14*s*)

2891 MARCHAND (Prospere) Histoire de l'origine et des prémiers progrès de l'Imprimerie, 4to. *boards, both parts*, 10*s* *La Haye*, 1740

"A treatise remarkable for various interesting and curious information."—*Bibliographical Miscellany*.

2892 MARIANÆ (Joannis, *Hispani, e Soc. Jesu*) de Ponderibus et Mensuris, 8vo. *half vellum*, 4*s* *Francofurti, Wechel*, 1611

2893 MARIDAT (Petro de) Tractatus de Pileo, cæterisque capitis tegminibus tam Sacris quam Profanis, *fine portrait by L. Spiriux*, 4to. *sewed*, 3*s* 6*d* .. .. *Lugduni*, 1655

2894 MARIN (Pieter) Methode pour apprendre les Principes et l'usage des Langues Françoise et Hollandoise, 12mo. *parchment*, 2*s* *Deventer*, 1751

2895 MARINE Society, Incorporated 1772, Bye-Laws, Regulations and Historical Account of, *plate*, 12mo. *bound*, 2*s* .. 1787

2896 MARINE Views and Ships and Shipping, collected by the Rev. ALFRED SUCKLING, of Barsham, with an immense quantity of Newspaper cuttings about Regattas, Naval Actions, Biographies of Eminent Seamen, Shipwrecks, &c. *all neatly inlaid*, 84 *illustrations, many of them drawings*, 2 vols. 4to. *half bound in russia, neat*, £2 2*s* .. .. .. V. Y.

2897 MARINER'S (Will.) Account of the Natives of the Tonga Islands in the S. Pacific Ocean, by Dr. John Martin, *plates*, 2 vols. 8vo. *boards*, 9*s* .. .. *For the Author*, 1817

"One of the most interesting narratives which we have ever perused."—*Quarterly Review*. Its value is enhanced by a LARGE VOCABULARY and GRAMMAR of their language.

2898 MARINO, La Murtoleide Fischiati del Cavalier Marino con la Marineide risate del Murtola, aggiontovi le Strigliate a Tomaso Stigliani, e l' Innamoramento di Pupolo et la Pupola, &c. 12mo. *old calf, scarce*, 10*s* 6*d* .. *Norinbergh*, 1619

*Haym* says, the later editions have not *Le Strigliate*. "Nor did Dante, Petrarch, or Tasso, or perhaps any of the eminent poets obtain in their lives so much applause as Giovanni Battista Marini; he is, more than any other poet, the counterpart of Ovid." See *Hallam*.

2899 MARKHAM'S (Gervase) Maison Rustique; or Countrey Farme; translated out of French, Italian, and Spanish, and made to agree with ours here in England, folio, above 700 pages, *good copy in old calf*, 12*s* .. .. .. 1616

2900 — Maister-Peece; containing all Knowledge belonging to Smith, Farrier, or Horse-leech, touching the Curing of all Diseases in Horses, *frontispiece by R. Elstrak*, 5th edition, 4to. 600 pages, *half calf, neat*, 6*s* 6*d* .. *Nicolas Okes*, 1636

For many other works by this author, see list of books on Husbandry in this Catalogue, commencing No. 2268.

2901 MARKHAM'S (Mrs.) History of England from the First Invasion by the Romans to the end of the Reign of George IV. *plates*, 2 vols. 12mo. *half cloth*, 5*s* (*pub. at* 12*s*) .. 1840

This large letter edition out of print.

2902 — History of France, with Conversations at the end of each chapter, *numerous cuts*, 2 vols. 12mo. *half cloth*, 6*s* 1830

2903 MARKS (Henry John, a Jew, now a follower of the Lord Jesus Christ) Narrative, written by himself, with Preface by Rev. C. B. Tayler, 12mo. *cloth*, 2*s* .. .. 1842

2904 MARLBOROUGH—Private Correspondence of Sarah Duchess of Marlborough, Illustrative of the Court and Times of Queen Anne, with her Opinions of her Contemporaries and the Select Correspondence of her Husband, John Duke of M., *portraits*, 2 vols. 8vo. *boards*, 12*s* (*pub. at* 28*s*) .. 1838

"This is a very delightful work. We have closed the volumes with a confirmed impression that the Duchess was the most remarkable woman of her own or any other day."—*Examiner.*

2905 MARLBOROUGH (John Churchill, Duke of) Memoirs of, with his Original Correspondence, by Archdeacon Coxe, revised by Wade, *portraits*, 3 vols. post 8vo. *cloth*, 10*s* 6*d* *H. G. Bohn*, 1847

2906 — Life, by Charles Bucke, *portrait*, 12mo. *cloth*, 2*s* 6*d* (*pub. at* 5*s*) *Fam. Lib.*, 1839

For a remarkably curious collection of broadsides relating to the great Duke of Marlborough, see Queen Anne in this Catalogue, No. 130, *et Seq.*

2907 MARMONTEL'S Belisarius, a Tale, Englished, 18mo. *neat*, 1*s* *Whittingham*, 1814

2908 — Belisarius, with Numa Pompilius by Florian, 24mo. *morocco, gilt edges*, 3*s* (*cost* 5*s*) .. .. .. 1824

2909 MAROLLES. Specimen of Papal and French Persecution, exhibited in the Cruel Sufferings of Lewis de Marolles, &c. 8vo. *bd*, 2*s* 6*d*

Marolles was condemned to the galleys in 1686, and died in a dungeon in 1692

2910 MARRIAGE, some Reflections upon, 4th edition, 8vo. *elegantly bound in old red morocco, gilt edges*, 7*s* 6*d* .. 1730

With this writing, "When this you see, dearest Jenney, think of me. E. G."

2911 MARRIED for Love, a Novel, by the Author of Cousin Geoffrey, 3 vols. post 8vo. *cloth*, 6*s* 6*d* (*pub. at* £1 11*s* 6*d*) 1857

2912 MARRYAT (Captain) Jacob Faithful, Peter Simple, Midshipman Easy, Frank Mildmay, Newton Forster, Pacha of many Tales, Dog Fiend, Poacher, Rattlin the Reefer, King's Own, Phantom Ship, Japhet in Search of a Father, and Percival Keene, 13 vols. 12mo. *cloth*, £1 19*s* (*cost* £3 18*s*) .. 1838, &c.

Out of print and not now to be had. These are all Capt. Marryat's novels republished in Bentley's Standard Novels.

2913 MARSEILLES—Les Antiquitez de la Ville de Marseille, par N. Jules Raymond, trad. en François par C. A. Fabroy, small 8vo. *old vellum*, 4*s* .. .. .. *Lyon*, 1632

2914 MARSH'S (Bishop Herbert) Course of Lectures on the several Branches of Divinity, with an Account of the Principal Authors, &c. 2 vols. 8vo. *calf, very neat*, 18*s* *Cambridge*, 1810-16

All the parts containing 32 Lectures, Scarce. "An important work, indispensably necessary in every Theological library. It embraces almost every topic of biblical criticism and interpretation, &c." See *Horne's Introduction to the Scriptures.*

2915 — Lectures on Divinity, parts 1, 2, 3, and 4, 8vo. *sd.* 6*s* *ib.*, 1810-16

2916 — Lectures, parts 1, 2, and 3, containing 18 Lectures, 8vo. *russia, neat*, 5*s* 6*d* .. .. .. *ib.*, 1810

2917 — Lectures on the Criticism and Interpretation of the Bible, 8vo. *boards*, 8*s* (*pub. at* 14*s*) .. .. *ib.*, 1828

Interspersed with opinions on books. "This is an enlarged edition of the first four parts of the preceding course of Lectures."—*Horne.*

2918 — Lectures on the Authenticity and Credibility of the New Testament, 8vo. *cloth*, 5*s* (*pub. at* 8*s*) .. .. 1840

2919 — Reply to the Strictures of Dean Milner, 8vo. *sewed*, 2*s* 6*d* *Cambridge*, 1813

2920 MARSTON'S (John) Dramatic and Poetical Works, now first collected by J. O. Halliwell, 3 vols. foolscap 8vo. *cloth, new*, 15*s* *J. R. Smith*, 1857

"A poet of distinguished celebrity in his own day, no less admired for the versatility of his genius in tragedy and comedy than dreaded for the poignancy of his satire."—*Rev. P. Hall.*

2921 MARTIALIS Epigrammata, cum D. Calderini ac G. Merulæ Commentariis, folio, *limp vellum*, 12*s* *Venetiis, P. Ravani*, 1552

2922 — Epigrammata, cum notis Variorum et Schrevelii, 8vo. *a very good copy in old calf*, 7*s* 6*d* .. .. *Lugd. Bat.*, 1670

Dr. Harwood says, he read through this edition of Martial and found it a very good one. It is considered the Editio optima.

2923 MARTII (Galeotti, *Narniensis*) de Doctrina promiscua liber, 8vo. 461 pages, *old vellum*, 6*s* *Florentiæ, apud L. Torrentinum*, 1548

Paulus Jovius gives a highly laudatory account of the learning and abilities of Galeottus Martius.

2924 MARTIN'S (John, F.S.A., *Librarian, Woburn Abbey*) Bibliographical Catalogue of Privately printed Books, *plates*, thick 8vo. 2nd Edition, *good as new*, £1 8*s* *Van Voorst*, 1854

This excellent Catalogue, as well as the Books it records, is *privately printed.*

2925 MARTIN'S (R. M.) History of Upper and Lower Canada, *map and frontispiece*, 12mo. *cloth*, 3*s* (*pub. at* 6*s*) .. 1856

2926 — History of the West Indies, *map and frontispiece*, 2 vols. 12mo. *cloth*, 6*s* (*pub. at* 12*s*) .. .. 1836

2927 MARTINEAU'S (Harriet) Sketches from Life, *plates*, post 8vo. *antique cloth, gilt edges*, 3*s* 6*d* (*sells* 5*s*) .. 1856

2928 — British Rule in India, a Historical Sketch, 8vo. *cloth*, 2*s* 6*d* 1857

2929 MARTINELLI (Vincenzio) Istoria Critica della Vita Civile, 4to. *good copy, in calf, gilt*, 6*s* *Londra, G. Woodfall*, 1752

Lord Walpole of Woolterton's copy, with the Book-plate.

2930 — Istoria d'Inghilterra, dedicata all' Illmo. Sigr. Tommaso Walpole, *portrait by Bartolozzi*, 3 vols. 4to. *a very fine copy, in old calf, gilt*, £1 1*s* .. *Londra, P. Molini*, 1770

Book-plate and AUTOGRAPH of Lord Walpole of Woolterton.

2931 MARTINII (Petri) Grammatica Hebræa, notis illustrata, à G. Coddæo, item Grammatica Chaldæa, et commentariolus de recta Lectione Linguæ Ebrææ, Sixti Amama, 8vo. *old calf*, 3s 6d *Amstelodami*, 1621

2932 MARTYN'S (Henry, *Missionary to the East Indies)* Memoir of, 12mo. *half calf, neat*, 3s 6d .. .. 1821

2933 MARTYROLOGY—Historia Martyrum Angliæ, small 4to. (wants the title page) *but a very fine clean copy, in calf extra, edges gilt*, RARE, £2 2s *(valued by Mr. Lowndes at 4 Guineas)* *Moguntiæ, apud S. Victorem*, 1550

The author of this very rare and highly interesting historical little volume was Maurice Channey, or Chauncy, a Carthusian.—It contains, 1. The Epitaph of Sir Thomas More. 2. The Captivity and Martyrdom of John Fisher, Bp. of Rochester. 3. The Captivity and Martyrdom of the said Sir Thomas More, Lord Chancellor to Henry VIII. 4. The Martyrdom of Reginald Brigitt, a pious Divine, and of others. 5. The Passion of XVIII. Carthusians of London. *All of the time of Henry VIII.*

2934 — Van Geluwe (Arnoudt) ontledinghe Van dry Verscheyden Nieuw-Ghereformeerde Martelaers Boecken, ofte Reden-Kamp-Strydt Tusschen de Lutheriaenen, Calvinisten, ende Weder-doopers, *many plates of Saints, Martyrs, and Tortures*, 4to. **Black Letter**, *a fine clean copy, in vellum*, RARE, £1 11s 6d *T' Antwerpen, Jan Cnobbaert*, 1656

2935 — History of those who suffered death for opposing the Romish Religion, from 1400 to 1558, the end of Mary's reign, 8vo. *calf, neat, scarce*, 7s 6d .. .. .. 1720

2936 MARVELL (Andrew) Gregory Father-Greybeard, with his Vizard off; or, News from the Cabal, in some reflexions on the Rehearsal transpos'd, small 8vo. *old binding, rare*, 6s *London, printed by Robin Hood, at the sign of the He-Cow, I. O., if it be not a Bull*, 1673

The author of this is Edmund Hickeringill, against Andrew Marvell's very witty Satire, the Rehearsal Transpos'd. See also *Parker*.

2937 MARY, Princess, daughter of K. Henry VIII., afterwards Queen, her Privy Purse Expenses, with a Memoir and Notes, by Sir Fred. Madden, 8vo. *cloth*, 9s (*pub. at* £1 1s) 1831

This is a very curious archæological volume, extending from 1536 to 1546, elegantly printed by W. Pickering.

2938 MARY, Queen of Scots, Memoirs of her Life, with Anecdotes of the Court of Henry II., during her residence in France, by Miss Benger, *portrait*, 2 vols. post 8vo. *half calf, very neat*, 9s (*pub. at* 18s) .. .. .. 1823

"Excellently fitted to supply the defects in history, where a leading personage may not have his or her proper share of distinction."—*Gent's Mag.*

2939 — Mary, Queen of Scots Vindicated, by John Whitaker, 3 thick vols. 8vo. *nice clean copy, in old boards, uncut*, 9s 1790

This the second, and best edition, enlarged and corrected.

2940 MASENII (Jac.) Anima Historiæ hujus temporis in juncto Caroli V., et Ferdinandi I., fratrum imperio, repræsentata, *portraits*, 4to. *good copy in vellum*, 10s *Coloniæ Agrippinæ*, 1672

An uncommon book, not in *Brunet*. Period embraced 1516-1558.

2941 MASON (John) Essays on Poetical and Prosaic Numbers and Elocution, 8vo. 2nd Edit., *neat, scarce*, 6*s* 1761

These are very ingenious Essays by the excellent author of "Self-knowledge, the way to attain it."

2942 MASON'S (William) Poems, English Garden, with Commentary and Notes, by Dr. Burgh, 3 vols. small 8vo. *calf, gilt, neat*, 7*s* 6*d* *York*, 1779-83-97

John Hunter's copy, with his Book-plate.
"The strains of Musæus and the Druid Minstrels have still their charms, and he must have cold feelings who cannot be moved by the simplicity of Elfrida. The English Garden, likewise, deserves the thanks of every admirer of our national taste."—*Pursuits of Literature.*

2943 MASSANIELLO, account of him, in MS., extracted from Lady Morgan's Life of Salvator Rosa, 4to. *sewed*, 2*s*

2944 MASSILLON (Evêque de Clermont) Petit Carême de, 8vo. *bound, stained*, 1*s* 6*d* .. .. *Paris*, 1827

2945 MASSINGER'S (Philip) Plays; namely, The Bondman, 1624.—The Renegado, 1630.—The Emperour of the East, 1632.—The Roman Actor, 1629.—The Picture, 1630.—The Fatal Dowry, 1632.—The Maid of Honour, 1632.—The Duke of Millaine, 1623.—8 Plays in 1 vol. small 4to. *fine clean copies in old calf*, £3 3*s* .. .. .. V. Y.

It is not often now-a-days we meet with original editions of Massinger's Plays, this is a very interesting old volume.

2946 — Beauties of, 12mo. *boards*, 3*s* 6*d* (*pub. at* 8*s*) 1817

2947 MASSONII (Papirii) Annalium libri IV.; quibus res gestæ Francorum explicantur, 4to. *nice copy, in old calf*, 7*s* 6*d* *Lutetiæ, apud M. Chesneau*, 1578

This is esteemed a "good work." Period from Clodius to Francis I. De Thou (Thuanus) was his friend, and has eulogized him. He was a very learned man.

2948 MASTERS'S (Mary) Poems on Several Occasions, 8vo. *old cf., gilt*, 3*s* *For the Author*, 1733

2949 MATHER'S (Increase) Remarkable Providences illustrative of the Earlier Days of American Colonisation, with a Preface by George Offor, foolscap 8vo. *portrait, cloth*, 5*s* *J. R. Smith*, 1856

This is an extremely curious book, very difficult to get in the original.

2950 MATHIAS'S (B. W.) Twenty-one Sermons at Bethesda Chapel, *portrait*, 8vo. *half cloth*, 4*s* 6*d* (*pub. at* 12*s*) *Dublin*, 1838

2951 [MATHIAS'S (T. J.)] Pursuits of Literature, a Satirical Poem, with Notes, the citations translated, and an Index of names, 14th edition, 8vo. *boards*, 6*s* .. .. 1808

"This satirical publication created a great sensation and considerable controversy." See *Lowndes*.

2952 — another copy, 8vo. *calf, gilt*, 7*s* 6*d* .. 1808

2953 — Poesie Liriche Toscane, *Napoli, Agnello Nobile*, 1818.—Alle Najadi inno alla Greca dall' Inglese di Marco Akenside, M.D., recato in Verso Italiano da T. J. Mathias, small 8vo THICK PAPER, *nice copy, in Italian vellum*, 10*s* 6*d* *Napoli, Marotta*, 1821

Presentation copy, privately printed, with this writing "Dall' Autore," and a note from Mathias. "*I hope you received a little parcel, which contained two small volumes, which I designed as a mark of friendly attention to you, &c., T. J. Mathias.*"

2954 MATON'S (William G.) Observations on the Natural History, Picturesque Scenery, and Antiquities of the Western Counties of England, 1794 and 1796, *map and plates, in aquatinta, by Alken*, 2 vols. 8vo. *half bound*, 10*s* .. *Salisbury*, 1796

2955 MATRIMONY—Kitzelii (Johannis) Synopsis Matrimonialis theorico-practica, jura constituendorum et dissolvendorum matrimoniorum, &c., 4to. *old calf, neat*, 6*s* *Francof. ad Mænum*, 1669

2956 MATTEI (Loreto) Teorica del Verso Volgare e prattica di retta pronuntia con un Problema delle Lingua Latina, e Toscana in Bilancia osservationi, *portrait*, 12mo. *vellum*, 4*s* 6*d* *Venetia*, 1695

2957 MATTHEW (Patrick) on Naval Timber, and Arboriculture, with Critical notes on Authors who have lately treated on Planting, 8vo. *boards*, 5*s* 6*d* (*cost* 10*s*) *Edinburgh, A. Black*, 1831

2958 MATTHIÆ'S Greek Grammar, by Bp. Blomfield and Edwards, 12mo. *cloth*, 2*s* .. .. 1835

2959 MATTHIOLI Opera Omnia, ed. C. Bauhini, *portrait, and thousands of wood cuts, principally of Plants*, very thick folio of above 1400 pages, *half bound, uncut*, £1 5*s* *Basiliæ*, 1674

Contains his Commentaries on Dioscorides, as well as his Apology, Epistles, &c.

2960 MAUND'S (B., F.L.S.) Botanic Garden; representations of hardy ornamental Flowering Plants cultivated in Great Britain, with the Floral Register and Auctarium to each volume, 192 *coloured figures*, vols. 8, 9, and 16 and 17, small 4to. LARGE PAPER, *half bound neat*, £1 12*s* .. .. 1830

2961 — Floral Register, part 1, and Auctarium, part 1, with Indexes, figures of 1133 Plants, small 4to. *half morocco*, 16*s* 1824, &c.

These are Supplemental to the 1st 8 volumes of Maund's Botanic Garden.

2962 — Floral Register, immediately in continuation of the above, figure 1150 to 2298,—Auctarium, page 185 to 280, and page 1 to 48, all on separate leaves, 7*s* 6*d*

2963 MAUNDER'S (Samuel) Biographical Treasury, thick 12mo. 6th Edition, *cloth*, 6*s* 6*d* (*pub. at* 10*s*) .. 1847

2964 — Treasury of Knowledge; an English Dictionary and Grammar; a Gazetteer; a Classical Dictionary; Scripture Proper Names; a Chronology; a Law Dict., &c., in 1 vol. thick 12mo. *cloth*, 6*s* 6*d* (*pub. at* 10*s*) .. .. .. 1853

2965 MAUNDRELL'S (Hen.) Journey from Aleppo to Jerusalem in 1697, *plates*, 8vo. *old calf, neat*, 4*s* *Oxford*, 1749

"This is doubtless a most curious and interesting book."—*Dibdin.*

2966 — another copy, *plates*, 8vo. *calf, very neat*, 4*s* 6*d* 1749

This 7th Edition, contains the author's journey to the Banks of the Euphrates at Beer, and to the country of Mesopotamia.

2967 MAURICE'S Poem to the Memory of Sir William Jones, 1795.—Peter Pindar's Epistle to John Nichols, printer, 1790.—His Rights of Kings, 1791, and his Pathetic Odes, 1794.—Ann Yearsley's (Clifton Milkwoman) Poems, 1787; in 1 vol. 4to. *half russia, neat*, 5*s* .. .. V.Y.

With Mrs. Hannah More's Letter to Mrs. Montagu, in commendation of Ann Yearsley, and Ann Yearsley's Explanation of the quarrel between them.

2968 MAURICE'S (Rev. Tho.) Grove Hill, Camberwell, a descriptive Poem, with an ode to Mithra, 15 *wood engravings by Anderson*, royal 4to. *boards*, 6*s* .. .. 1799

A fine specimen of printing by Bensley.

2969 — Dissertation on the Oriental Trinities, *plates*, 8vo. *hf. cf.*, 4*s* 6*d*

2970 — Modern History of Hindostan, comprehending that of the Greek Empire of Bactria, 2 vols. 4to. *a good copy, in calf*, £1 11*s* 6*d* (*pub. at* £5 5*s*) .. .. .. 1802

From Mr. J. J. Gurney's library.—It is elegantly printed by Bulmer.
"I *recommend*," says Bp. Tomline, "in the most earnest manner, both the Dissertations and the History of this writer, to the attention of all those who are desirous of seeing additional light thrown upon some of the most important doctrines of the Holy Scriptures."

2971 MAW'S (Lieut. H. L.) Journal of a Passage from the Pacific to the Atlantic, crossing the Andes and descending the Amazon, *map*, 8vo. *boards* 5*s* (*pub. at* 12*s*) .. .. 1829

2972 MAWE'S (John) Catalogue of Minerals, their Classification and Arrangement, 12mo. *bound*, 2*s* 6*d* .. .. 1829

2973 MAXIMI Tyrii Dissertationes, Gr. et Lat., cum notis Variorum et Marklandi, curavit Reiske, 2 vols. 8vo. *good copy in calf*, 7*s* *Lipsiæ*, 1774-5

"An excellent edition."—*Bibliog. Dict.* "Maximus Tyrius is one of the most eloquent and pleasing of the Platonic Philosophers."—*Bibliog. Dict.*

2974 MAXWELL'S (W. H.) Wanderings in the Highlands and Islands, with Sketches taken on the Scottish Border, *portrait*, 2 vols. 8vo. *cloth*, 10*s* (*pub. at* £1 4*s*) .. .. 1844

Exceedingly amusing, full of fun and merriment.

2975 MAYHEW'S Letters left at the Pastrycook's, *plates*, 12mo. *sewed*, 1*s* . .. .. 1853

2976 MAZZUCHELLI (Conte Giammaria) Gli Scrittori d' Italia, cioé Notizie Storiche, e Critiche intorno alle Vite, e agli scritti dei Letterati Italiani, vol. 1, parts 1 and 2, (Abano-Azzone) in 2 vols. folio, *old calf, gilt*, 16*s* .. .. *Brescia*, 1753

"Excellent ouvrage."—*Brunet.* But 6 vols. of this work were ever printed, to the letter B.

2977 MEAD (Rich.) Oratio Anniversia Harveiana, Oct. 18, 1723.—Adjecta est dissertatio de Nummis Smyrneis, 4to. *hf. bd.* 3*s* 6*d* *Londini*, 1724

There is also, in this volume another Harveian Oration, by Dr. John Freind, delivered in 1720.

2978 — Medica Sacra; a Commentary on the most remarkable Diseases mentioned in the Scriptures, Englished by Dr. Thomas Stack, with his Life and Writings, 8vo. *calf, neat*, 4*s* .. 1755

2979 MEDALS—Prontuario delle Medaglie degli Uomini, e Donne illustri con i loro ritratti, e Vite in compendio, *numerous engravings of medals*, 2 parts in 1 vol. 4to. *a good clean copy, scarce*, 12*s* *Lione, Guil. Rouillio*, 1553

The first part is from Adam to the time of Christ, and is, in some sort, imaginative; the 2nd part dates from Christ to Hen. 2nd of France. The medals better authenticated.

2980 MEDICAL TRACTS—Chiocci (Andræi) Questionum Philosophicarum et Medicarum libri III., above 200 pages, small 4to. *old calf, neat*, RARE, 21*s* .. *Veronæ, apud H. Discipulum*, 1593

This volume contains also the following curious tracts.—I. Academia Monspeliensis à JACOBO PRIMIROSIO *Oxoniensi* Doctore descripta, ejusdem Laurus Monspeliaca, *Oxoniæ*, 1631.—II. De Rabie Contagiosa, cui Epistola de Plantarum ex Seminibus generatione præposita est aucto e JOSEPHO DE AROMATARIIS, *Francofurti*, 1626.—III. Discursus de Melancholia Hypochondriaca potissimum, auctore JOHANNE HAWKINS, M.D. Anglo, *Heidelbergæ*, 1633.—IV. De Vera Ratione curandi Bubonis atque Carbunculi Pestilentis commentarius, authore Io. BAPT. GEMMA, *Veneto, Dantisci, Jacobus Rhodus*, 1599.—V. De Febribus, per ARNOLDUM GEULINCX, *Lugd. Bat., apud Johan. Elzevirium*, 1658.

The Tract above printed 'at *Dantzic* is a very early one, its author was physician to Sigismund III. King of Poland.

2981 MEDICI—Vita di COSIMO MEDICI, Primo Gran Duca di Toscana, Discritta da M. BACCIO BALDINI, suo Protomedico, small folio, *fine clean copy in limp vellum*, RARE, £1 1*s* *Firenze, Bart. Sermartelli*, 1578

Cosmo de Medici, who died in 1464, was a great patron of learning and the arts, —during his rule printing was commenced.

2982 — Vita del S. Signor Cosimo de' Medici, Primo Gran Duca di Toscana, scritta da Giouambatista Cini, 4to. *limp vellum*, 15*s* *Firenze, Giunti*, 1611

Autograph of Sir Thomas Bowlby. This is the only edition of this book that was ever published; it is a very considerable volume of 528 pages.

2983 — Lettere del Cardinale Gio. de Medici, figlio di Cosimo I. Gran Duca di Toscana, thick 4to. of 570 pages, *clean copy, old vellum, scarce*, 12*s* .. .. *In Roma, A. De Rossi*, 1752

These letters "Non piu Stampate estratte da un Codice MS. de G. B. Catena," are chiefly dated 1560-61. There are 36 pages of "Rime di Benedetto Varchi in Morte del Card. de Medici."

Autograph complimentary note from "Lady and Mr. T. Bowlby to the Prince and Princess Giustiniani."

2984 — Life of Lorenzo de Medici, by William Roscoe, *portrait*, 12mo. *cloth*, 3*s* .. .. .. *Bohn*, 1847

See also in this Catalogue, *Leo.* X. and *Lorenzo.*

2985 — The Girlhood of Catherine de' Medici, by T. A. Trollope, *portrait*, post 8vo. *cloth, antique style*, 5*s* 6*d* (*pub. at* 10*s* 6*d*) 1856

2986 MEGISERI (Hieron.) Anthologia; seu, Florilegium Græco latinum; hoc est, Veterum Græcorum Epigrammata, 2 vols. in 1, thick 8vo. above 1100 pages, *old calf, scarce*, 9*s* *Francofurti*, 1602

"Edition peu commune."—*Brunet.*

2987 MEIERN, Acta Pacis Westphalicæ Publica, 1643-1649, in German and Latin, *fine portrait and plates*, 6 vols. folio, *a fine copy in old foreign calf, gilt*, £3 3*s* .. *Hanover*, 1734-36

Belonged to the famous minister, Sir Robert Walpole, with a MS. dedication to him in these highly laudatory terms, "Illustrissimo Walpolio omnium qui hodie sunt Europæ Pacificatorum moderatori et arbitro prudentissimo, sagacissimo felicissimo hæc antecessorum suorum orbis Christiani pacificatorum Acta in pietatis et devotionis symbolum C. Auctor." &c. dated Hanover, 10th Dec., 1736, to which Court he was accredited Plenipotentiary.

2988 MEJER (Joan.) Atlas Hispania, Gallia, Helvetia, Germania, Belgium, Britannia, Scandinavia, 361 *maps, fine engraved*, in 4 huge folio volumes, *in a fine clean state in old calf, gilt*, £2 2*s* *Amstelodami, apud Joannem Jansonium*, 1651-59

From the Library at Woolterton, with Lord Walpole's book-plate. There are portraits of Tycho Brahe and the author, and the arms and costumes of the various countries are given.

2989 MELVILLE'S (Andrew) Life, containing Illustrations of the Ecclesiastical and Literary History of Scotland during the 16th and 17th Centuries, by Dr. Thos. M'Crie, 2 vols. 8vo. *half cloth,* 12*s* (*pub. at* £1 1*s*) .. .. *Edinburgh,* 1824

Dr. Mc Crie's works are highly and deservedly valued. This is a very interesting period of Scottish history; the book full of literary information.

2990 MENAGIANA; ou, Bons Mots, rencontres agreables, pensées judicieuses et observations curieuses de M. Menage, de l' Acad. Françoise, *frontispiece,* 12mo. *vellum,* 3*s* 6*d* *Amsterdam,* 1693

A very amusing collection by the Varro of his times, so called from his great learning.

2991 MENASSEH Ben-Israel de Resurrectione Mortuorum libri III., *Amstelodami,* 1636.—Menasseh Ben-Israel Dissertatio de Fragilitate Humana, ex lapsu Adami, in 1 vol. 12mo. *old calf, neat, scarce,* 6*s* *Typis et Sumptibus Auctoris, Amst.,* 1642

2992 MENDHAM'S Prohibitory Indexes, see *Cotton.*

2993 MENZELL'S (Wolfgang) History of Germany, translated by Mrs. George Horrocks, *portraits,* 3 vols. post 8vo. *cloth,* 6*s* (*cost* 10*s* 6*d*) .. .. .. *H. G. Bohn,* 1848

2994 — also vol. 1, 2*s*; and vols. 1 and 2, 4*s* .. *ib.,* 1848

2995 MERLINI Cocaii (*i.e.* Theophili Folengi) Pocta Mantuani Macaronicorum Poemata, nunc recens accurate recognita *cum figuris* locis suis appositis, thick 12mo. of 252 pages, besides 19 introductory leaves, entitled "Amor Tonelli," *old parchment, clean as new,* VERY RARE, £2 2*s*
*Venetiis, cum privilegio Illustris. Senatus Venetorum,* and at the end, *Venetiis, apud hæredes Petri Ravani, et Socios,* 1554

This EXTREMELY RARE edition is not mentioned by Brunet, De Bure, or any other bibliographer to whose works I have access.

2996 MERRYWEATHER'S (F. Somner) Bibliomania in the Middle Ages, from the Anglo-Saxon and Norman periods to the Introduction of Printing into England, post 8vo. *cloth,* 4*s* 1849

2997 MERSENNE (F. Marin) L'Impieté des Deistes, 2nde Partie, small 8vo. *old vellum,* 4*s* .. .. *Paris,* 1624

Written to refute the Dialogues of Jordano Bruno.

2998 MESMERISM; True or False, a Critical Examination of the Facts, Claims, and Pretensions of Animal Magnetism, by Dr. John Forbes, 8vo. *sewed,* 2*s* 6*d* .. .. 1845

2999 MESSE, La Sainte, ou sont representés par les actions du Prêtre les Misteres de la Passion de N. S. Jesus Christ, avec les Oraisons applique a chacun Mistere, 12mo. *old red morocco, neat,* 7*s* 6*d*
*Paris, François Jouenne, no date*

The whole engraved on 35 plates by St. Landry, with a Prayer to each engraving on a separate leaf opposite. On the backs of several leaves are other prayers in the Portuguese language in MS.

3000 MESSIA (Pietro) Selva di Varia Lettione, et Varii Discorsi appartenenti, cosi alle Scientie, come alle Historie de gli Huomini, et de gli animali, thick 8vo. *fine clean copy in vellum,* 10*s* 6*d*
*In Venetia, Alessandro Griffio,* 1582

In Brunet, under Mexia, it is a translation from the Spanish by Francesco Sansovino; a book much in vogue in the middle of the 17th Century. Has the 5 parts.

3001 METAMORPHOSIS Anglorum; sive Mutationes Variæ Regum, Regni, rerumque Angliæ, opus Historicum et Politicum, 24mo. *calf, neat,* 3*s* 6*d* : *No place or Printer's name,* 1653

"Ex bibliot. P. Bruyere, S. T. P."—The author *Boxhorn.* At page 163, Joannis Seldeni Janus Anglorum, with autograph of "*Bruyere.*"

3002 METAXA (Professore Luigi) Monografia de' Serpenti di Roma e suoi contorni, *coloured plate,* 4to. *stiff cover,* 6*s* *Roma,* 1823

3003 METROPOLITAN Magazine, vol. 32 only, 8vo. *half calf, neat,* 3*s* 1841

3004 MEURSII (Joannis) Creta, Rhodus, Cyprus; sive de Nobilissimarum harum insularum rebus et antiquitatibus Commentarii, 4to. *very fine copy in white vellum,* 9*s* *Amst., Ab. Wolfgang,* 1675

"Of this learned Dutchman, John Imperialis said that he had published more Greek authors with Latin versions than all the learned together for the last 100 years."—*Moreri.*

3005 MEXICO—Istoria della Conquista del Messico, scritta in Castigliano da Don Antonio de Solis, tradotta in Toscano da un' Accademico Della Crusca, thick 4to. of 763 pages, *a fine copy in old calf,* £1 1*s* .. .. .. *Firenze,* 1699

Lord Leicester's copy, a finely printed book, with three portraits, of the author, Cortes, and Montezuma.

3006 MEYER'S (H. L.) Illustrations of British Birds and their Eggs, 422 *beautifully coloured plates,* 7 vols. 8vo. *handsome copy, half bound in calf, gilt,* £6 16*s* 6*d* (*cost* £19 19*s*) 1853-57

This is the only complete history of British Birds and their Eggs with coloured plates. It is a very attractive set of books.

3007 MICHELET'S (T.) History of the Roman Republic, translated by William Hazlitt, *portrait,* post 8vo. *cloth,* 2*s* (*cost* 3*s* 6*d*) 1847

3008 MIDDLETON'S (Dr. Conyers) History of the Life of Cicero, 3 vols. 8vo. *old calf, very neat,* 9*s* .. 1755

"An elaborate, learned, and admirably written performance."—*Dr. Dibdin.* Mr. Fox, no mean arbiter in literary taste, always spoke warmly of this biography, for its style as well as its matter.

3009 MIDOSI (L. F.) Portuguese English and English Portuguese Grammar, 8vo. *bound, neat,* 3*s* (*sells* 5*s*) .. 1840

3010 MIDWIFERY, Introduction to the Practice of, by Dr. Tho. Denman, with Memoir of him, *and Smellie's anatomical plates reduced,* 8vo. *half calf, neat,* 6*s* .. .. 1824

3011 MILESI (Bianca) Vita di Saffo.—Vita di Maria Gaetana Agnesi, 12mo. *sewed,* 5*s* .. .. *Chantilly,* 1824

Privately printed. "From the authoress."

3012 MILITARY and other Poems, by an Officer of the Army, with Socrates Triumphant, a Play, 8vo. *old calf,* 3*s* .. 1716

3013 MILL'S (James) Essays on Government, Jurisprudence, Liberty of the Press, &c. 8vo. *half calf, neat,* 3*s* 6*d* *Privately printed, no date*

3014 MILL'S (Dr. W. H.) Sermons on the Nature of Christianity, preached before the University of Cambridge, in 1846, 8vo. *cloth,* 5*s* (From the Author) .. *Cambridge,* 1848

3015 MILLS'S (Charles) Travels of Theodore Ducas at the revival of Letters and Art, 2 vols. in 1, 8vo. *half calf, extra,* 10*s* 6*d* (*pub. at* 24*s*) .. .. .. 1822

Imaginary Travels, but full of information respecting the Scholars, Poets, Painters, and Literature of Italy, from 1514 to 1554.

3016 MILLAR'S (Professor John) Observations on the distinctions of Ranks in Society, 2nd edit. 8vo. *old calf, neat,* 4*s* 6*d* 1773

3017 — Historical View of the English Government, from the settlement of the Saxons in Britain to the Revolution in 1688, 4 vols. 8vo. *boards,* 21*s* .. .. .. 1812

"Very excellent."—*Bibliotheca Parriana.*

3018 MILLER'S (Dr. George) History philosophically Illustrated, from the Fall of the Roman Empire to the French Revolution, *portrait,* 4 vols. post 8vo. *cloth,* 8*s* (*cost* 14*s*) *H. G. Bohn,* 1848

3019 MILLER'S (Hugh) Labour and Triumph; the Life and Times of, by Tho. N. Brown, 12mo. *cloth, new,* 5*s* 1858

3020 MILLER'S (Philip) Gardener's Dictionary, with Supplement, 2nd edition, 2 vols. folio, *good copy in calf,* 10*s* 1733-39

3021 — new edition, newly arranged, with large additions, by Professor Tho. Martin, 21 *plates,* 2 vols. folio, vol. 1 in *boards,* vol. 2 in parts, £2 .. .. .. 1797-1807

There are title pages for 4 vols. dated 1807, in which number it is intended it should be bound, this is a genuine subscriber's copy published at 11 Guineas.

"We cannot expect often to see a work of such magnitude, executed in so complete and masterly a style as this edition of Miller's *Gardener's Dictionary.* It includes a complete and accurate translation of the *Genera Plantarum* of Linnæus; the exact enumeration of the several species belonging to each genus, with their respective specific characters, accompanied by their various synonymes, as well as by the particular history or account of each individual species; with its medicinal, and other qualities." *British Critic.*

3022 MILLER'S (W. H., *Tutor of St. John's, Camb.)* Elements of Hydrostatics and Hydrodynamics, 8vo. *bds,* 3*s* 6*d* *Camb.,* 1831

3023 MILLOT (l'Abbé) Élémens d'Histoire Ancienne et Moderne, 9 vols. 8vo. *French calf, gilt,* 18*s* .. *Paris,* 1800

"Millot is one of the most correct and pleasing of the French writers of the XVIII. Century." "The most elegant and at the same time the most comprehensive view of Ancient and Modern History which has yet appeared."—*Edinburgh Review.*

3024 MILMAN'S (Dean) History of the Jews, *maps and plates,* 3 vols. 18mo. *cloth,* 7*s* 6*d* (*cost* 15*s*) .. *Fam. Lib.,* 1829

3025 — Fall of Jerusalem, a Dramatic Poem, 8vo. *boards,* 4*s* 6*d (pub. at* 8*s* 6*d*) .. .. .. *Murray,* 1820

3026 — another copy, 8vo. *calf, elegant,* 5*s* 6*d* .. *ib.* 1820

3027 — Martyr of Antioch, a Dramatic Poem, 8vo. *boards,* 4*s* 6*d* (*pub. at* 8*s* 6*d*) .. .. .. *ib.,* 1822

3028 MILNER'S (Joseph) Church History, by Dean Milner, with continuation by Scott, to 1560, 8 vols. 8vo. *boards,* £2 2*s* (*pub. at* £4 16*s*) .. .. .. 1827-28

"The best account I know of the more intellectual part of the History of the Reformation."—*Professor Smyth.*

3029 — Church History, (for 5 centuries) vols. 1 and 2 only, 8vo. *boards,* 5*s* .. .. .. 1810

3030 — Church History, with Dr. Haweis's continuation, thick 8vo. *cloth,* 5*s* 6*d* (*pub. at* 12*s*) .. *Edinburgh,* 1837

3031 MILTON'S Poetical Works, with Notes of various authors and Bp. Newton, *fine portrait by Vertue, and plates by Grignon,* 3 vols. 4to. *old calf, very neat, best edition,* £1 11*s* 6*d* 1754

This is a remarkably fine and handsomely printed Library Edition of Milton. "The best edited English Classic up to the date of its publication."—*Dibdin.*

3032 MILTON'S Poetical Works, with his Life and large Verbal Index, by Todd, *portrait*, 7 vols. 8vo. *good copy, half bound, russia*, £1 16s 1809

3033 — Poetical Works, with a Memoir, and Critical Remarks on his Genius and Writings, by James Montgomery, 120 *engravings after Harvey*, 2 vols. cr. 8vo. *cloth, new*, 18s (*pub. at* 24s) 1859

3034 — Paradise Lost and Regained, Comus, a Masque, and Minor Poems, with a Tractate on Education, *portrait and plates*, 4 vols. 24mo. *old calf, neat*, 8s .. *Tonson*, 1746

"An edition by Tonson, printed with great correctness."—*Lowndes.*

3035 — Paradise Regained, Samson Agonistes, Minor Poems, and a Tractate of Education, thick 12mo. *calf, neat*, 3s 6d *ib.*, 1747

3036 — Poems upon several occasions, English, Italian, and Latin, with Notes, by Thomas Warton, 8vo. *calf, neat*, 7s 6d 1785

This is the best edition of Milton's Minor Poems, and contains Lycidas, l'Allegro, Il Penseroso, Arcades, Comus, Odes, Sonnets, &c., and is the best edited Classic in our language.

3037 — Paraphrasis Poetica in tria J. Miltoni Poemata, Paradisum Amissum et Recuperatum, et Samsonem Agonisten, autore G. Hogæo, 8vo. *old calf*, 5s .. *Londini*, 1690

Book-plate of "*Edward Astley, Armig. of Melton Constable*, with his autograph.

3038 — L'Allegro and Il Penseroso illustrated, (Art Union of London,) 30 *plates, nicely engraved*, 4to. *boards*, 10s 6d 1848

3039 — Remarks on Johnson's Life of Milton, with Milton's Tractate of Education and Areopagitica, 12mo. *boards, scarce*, 4s 6d 1780

Privately printed at the expense of Archdeacon Blackburne, without his name.

3040 — Familiar Explanation of the Poetical Works of Milton, alphabetically digested, with Addison's Criticism on the Paradise Lost, and a Preface by Dr. Dodd, 12mo. *nice copy, in old calf, gilt*, 3s 6d .. .. .. 1762

3041 — History of England to the Norman Conquest, *very fine impression of Faithorne's portrait of him*, 4to. *old calf, neat*, 10s 6d 1671

"Vertue looked upon this head as the finest representation of Milton."—*Granger.*
"This History is written with great simplicity—but, he sometimes rises to a surprising grandeur both in the sentiment and the expression."—*Bp. Warburton.*

3042 — another edition, *portrait*, royal 8vo. *boards, scarce*, 9s 1818

To this edition, edited by Baron Maseres, are added several Tracts relating to Civil Government, and the advantages of a Commonwealth, with a Life of Milton, by his nephew, E. Philips.

3043 MINUCII Felicis Octavius et Cæcilii Cypriani de Idolor. Vanitate, N. Rigaltii Observationes, 4to. *vellum*, 6s *Lutetiæ*, 1643

An edition of Minucius Felix, not noticed by Bibliographers, it is very beautifully printed. Its editor was esteemed a most erudite man.

3044 — Octavius, cum notis Variorum, 8vo. *remarkably fine copy in russia, gilt leaves, ruled throughout with red lines*, 18s *L. Bat.*, *Hackii*, 1672

Ouzelius's best edition of this eloquent defence of the Christian religion greatly admired for the purity and sweetness of its style, beautifully and accurately printed by Hackius.

3045 — Octavius, cum notis Variorum et Gronovii, 8vo. *good sound copy, in old calf*, 7s 6d .. .. *Lugd. Bat.*, 1709

Emphatically and justly called the Editio Optima of this "most excellent Christian writer." With it are printed C. Cyprianus *de Idolorum Vanitate* and Julius Firmicus Maternus *de Errore Profanarum Religionum.—Drs. Dibdin and Harwood.*

3046 MIRABEAU'S (Count) Secret History of the Court of Berlin, with Anecdotes of the King, his Ministers, Courtiers, Favourites, &c. 2 vols. 8vo. *half calf, neat,* 8*s* .. .. 1789

Very amusing, not in *Lowndes.*

3047 MISERIES of Human Life, *coloured plates,* 12mo. *hf cf, neat,* 3*s* 1806

3048 MITCHELL'S (James) Conversations on General Knowledge, or Cathechisms of all the Arts and Sciences, *plates,* 12mo. *bound, neat,* 3*s* 6*d* (*pub. at* 7*s*) .. .. 1845

3049 MITCHELL'S (Joseph) Jonah, a Poem, *pl.* 8vo. *old cf, neat,* 6*s* 1720

With the Earl of Nottingham's Answer to Whiston on the Eternity of the Son of God, 1721.—List of the Lords and Commons, 1715 to 1722.—with a blank margin for new Members which are filled in, 1722.—Earbery's Review of the Bp. of Bangor's Sermon, and his Answer to the representation of the Committee of the Lower House of Convocation, both parts, 1718.

3050 MITFORD'S (William) History of Greece, with his Life by his brother, Lord Redesdale, *portrait,* 10 vols. 12mo. *cloth,* 21*s* (*pub. at* £2 10*s*) .. .. .. 1835

3051 MODENA (Leon, *Rabi Hebræo di Venetia)* Historia de Gli Riti Hebraici, 12mo. *limp vellum,* 4*s* .. *Parigi,* 1637

A valuable little book on the Rites, Ceremonies, and Customs of the Jews at that time.—"*Ex Bibl. Petr. de Cardonnel,* 1645."

3052 MODERN Literature, *portraits and plates,* 8vo. *half calf, neat,* 4*s* *No date*

An amusing selection from various modern authors, of Anecdotes, &c.

3053 MOJON (G.) Corso analitico di Chimica, 2 vols. small 8vo. *half bound in Italian vellum,* 6*s* .. *Genova,* 1825

3054 MOLIERE, Œuvres de, et Memoires sur la Vie et les Ouvrages, *fine portrait and plates by J. Punt,* 4 vols. 18mo. *old calf, neat,* 8*s* .. .. .. *Amsterdam,* 1750

In Dulau at 16*s*, the plates are very nicely engraved.

3055 MONK (Duke of Albemarle) his Life, by Dr. Thomas Skinner, with a Vindication of the General's Conduct, by W. Webster, 8vo. *calf, neat,* 3*s* 6*d.* *W. Bowyer, for the Editor,* 1723

For another account of the General, see *Lloyd, No.* 2714.

3056 MONNARD (Charles) Caroline Perthès, ou l'Epouse et la Mère Chrétienne, 12mo. *sewed,* 1*s* .. *Paris,* 1856

3057 MONOD, Les adieux d'Adolphe Monod, 12mo. *sewed,* 1*s* *Paris,* 1857

3058 MONRO'S (Rev. Edward) Vast Army, an Allegory, 12mo. *sewed,* 1*s*

3059 MONTAGU (Basil) Selections from the Works of Taylor, Hooker, Milton, Hall, Barrow, and Bacon, with an analysis of the advancement of Learning, 2 vols. 12mo. *half calf, neat,* 6*s* 1807

Mr. Joseph John Gurney's copy.

3060 — Essays and Selections, 12mo. *morocco extra, gilt leaves,* 9*s* *W. Pickering,* 1837

"I have been steadily occupied in the completion of a work on the conduct of the understanding, on which I have been engaged for many years. In times of recreation I have collected these trifles."—*Preface.* There are Essays on the Death of Q. Elizabeth and Lord Bacon.

3061 MONTAIGNE (Michel) Les Essais, Livre second, *engraved title containing portrait by N. de Larmessin,* 12mo. *old binding,* 9*s* *Paris, C. Journal,* 1659

With this autograph "Perlegi L. B. De La Coste," who edited an edition in 1724. The portrait is very scarce.

3062 MONTAIGNE (Michel) ses Essais, avec les Notes de M. Coste et Memoire sur sa Vie et ses Ouvrages, 10 vols. 12mo. *calf, very neat,* £1 1*s* .. .. .. *Londres,* 1769

The 10th volume is occupied by a "Preface sur les Essais par Ma demoiselle de Gournay," and "Jugemens et Critiques sur les Essais." This is a very good edition.

3063 — Essayes, done into English, by John Florio, with all the dedications, folio, *original binding, very scarce, in a most pristine state,* 21*s* .. .. *Valentine Sims,* 1603

A copy of this first English translation, with Shakspeare's autograph, sold for above £100. "Montaigne's immortal history of his own mind, for such are his Essays, have assumed, perhaps, too modest a title, and not sufficiently discriminative."—*D'Israeli's Curios. of Literature.*

3064 MONTALBANI (Ovidio) Le Antichità più antiche di Bologna, *Bologna, per C. Zenero,* 1651.—Diologogia, overo delle cagioni, e della naturelezza del parlare, e spetialmente del più antico, e più vero di Bologna, *Bologna, per C. Zenero,* 1652.—Cronopostasi Felsinea, overo le Saturnali Vindicie del Parlar Bolognese, e Lombardo, 3 vols. in 1, 4to. *old limp vellum,* RARE, 15*s* *Bologna, per G. Monti,* 1653

3 Treatises by Ovidio Mont'albani, Professor of Philosophy and Doctor of Law. At the end is a very curious large folded map of Bologna Antica, giving a bird's eye view of the place.

3065 MONTALEMBERT, Procès de M. le Comte de, avec les discours de M. Berryer et Dufaure, précédé de sa Vie, 8vo. *sewed,* 1*s* 1858

3066 MONT BLANC—Extracts from my Journal, 1852, *plates,* 8vo. *cloth,* RARE, 6*s* .. .. *Norwich, C. Muskett,* 1853

"PRINTED FOR PRIVATE CIRCULATION ONLY," and only 100 COPIES so printed. This is an account of Mr Bulwer's Ascent of Mont Blanc—the passage of the Col de St. Theodule and of the Weiss Thor.

3067 — another copy, Mr. W. Repton's, with his Autograph, 7*s* 6*d* 1853

3068 — the 4 plates with which the above is illustrated, worked off on 4to. paper for illustration, 5*s*

3069 — ditto on tinted paper, (believed to be unique) 10*s*

3070 MONTEATH'S (Robert, *of Stirling,*) Forester's Guide and Profitable Planter, 15 *plates,* 8vo. *boards,* 9*s* (*pub. at* 14*s*) *Edinburgh,* 1824

This is a practical treatise on planting, moss, rocky, waste, and other lands; on transplanting large trees; on valuing growing wood; the cure of the dry rot, &c.

3071 MONTGOMERY'S (James) Christian Correspondent; Letters by Eminent Persons of both Sexes, 3 vols. 12mo. *cloth,* 9*s* (*pub. at* 18*s*) .. .. .. .. 1837

Exemplifying the fruits of holy living and the blessedness of holy dying.

3072 MONTGOMERY'S (Robert) Omnipresence of the Deity, a Poem, 8vo. *calf extra, gilt,* 4*s* 6*d* .. .. 1828

3073 MONTGOMERY'S and Shelley's Lives of Eminent Italian, Spanish, and Portuguese Authors, 3 vols. 12mo. *cloth,* 7*s* 6*d* *Lardner's Cab. Cyclopædia,* 1840

3074 MONTHLY Packet, complete for 1856, 57, and 58, being vols. 11 to 16 in numbers, 8*s* (*pub. at* 24*s*) .. 1856-8

3075 MONTI (Abate Vincenzo) Aristodemo, tragedia, 4to. *calf, very neat,* £1 1*s* .. .. .. *Parma,* 1786

An elegant volume, printed by Bodoni, of Parma, ranking with our Baskerville.

3076 MONTICELLI e Covelli prodromo della Mineralogia Vesuviana, 19 *plates*, 2 vols. 8vo. *interleaved, hf. bound, neat*, 8*s* *Napoli*, 1825

3077 MOON, Boys, and Graves's Catalogue of Engravings, *priced*, 8vo. *boards*, 3*s* .. .. .. .. 1829

3078 MOORE'S (Edward) Poems, Fables, and Plays, 4to, *old calf*, 2*s* 6*d* .. .. .. .. 1756

3079 MOORE'S (Dr. John) View of Society and Manners in France, Switzerland, and Germany, with Anecdotes of eminent Characters, 2 vols. 12mo. *boards*, 3*s* .. .. 1810

3080 MOORE'S (Thomas) Epistles, Odes, and other Poems, 2 vols. 12mo. *old boards*, 6*s* .. .. .. 1814

3081 — Poetical Works of Thomas Little, Esq., 12mo. *boards*, 4*s* 1817

3082 — another edition 12mo. *boards*, 4*s* 6*d* .. 1833

3083 — Lalla Rookh, an Oriental Romance, *plates after Westall*, 12mo. *calf, gilt*, 5*s* .. .. .. 1832

3084 — Irish Melodies, *portrait*, 32mo. *cloth, gilt*, 2*s* *Longmans*, 1854

3085 — Memoirs of Captain Rock, the celebrated Irish Chieftain, with some Account of his Ancestors, 12mo. *boards, scarce*, 5*s* 6*d* 1824

3086 — Epicurean, a Tale, with Alciphron, a Poem, *plates, after Turner*, 12mo. *cloth*, 3*s* 6*d* .. .. .. 1839

3087 — another copy, 12mo. *cloth, gilt*, 4*s* .. 1839

3088 — History of Ireland, 4 vols. 12mo. *cloth*, 10*s* (*pub. at* £1 4*s*) 1835

3089 MORABITI (Caroli) Annalium Prothometropolitanæ Messanensis Ecclesiæ, vol. 1, folio, *a fine copy in vellum*, 7*s* 6*d* *Messanæ*, 1669

3090 MORBI Gallici curandi ratio exquisitissima conscripta, 8vo. *old binding, neat*, 6*s* .. .. *Lugduni*, 1536

Contains reprints of 6 rare old tracts on this disease, by Peter A. Matthiolus, John Almenar, Nicholas Massa, Nicholas Poll, Benedict Victor, with 2 Treatises by Angelus Bolognini, "de ulcerum exteriorum" and "de unguentis."

3091 MORE'S (Hannah) Strictures on the Modern System of Female Education, 2 vols. post 8vo. *half calf, neat*, 4*s* 6*d* 1799

3092 — Sacred Dramas, small 8vo. *bound*, 2*s* .. 1800

3093 — Cœlebs in Search of a Wife, 2 vols. post 8vo. *half calf, neat*, 5*s* .. .. .. .. 1817

3094 MORE'S (Henry) Divine Dialogues, the fourth and fifth, with a Discourse of the True Grounds of Faith, and Divine Hymns, small 8vo. *neat*, 4*s* .. .. .. 1668

3095 — Exposition of the Seven Epistles to the Seven Churches, with a Discourse of Idolatry, *Autograph of Elizabeth Bacon*, small 8vo. *old calf, scarce*, 5*s* .. .. .. 1669

3096 — Enchiridion Ethicum, 18mo. *old calf*, 2*s* *Amst.*, 1695

"Dr. Henry More," says Headley, "was one of the first men of this or any other country;" and Kippis observes, "that he was a great adept in the Platonic philosophy."

3097 MORE (Sir Thomas) Il moro d' Heliseo Heivodo Inglese, all' illustrissimo Cardinal Reginaldo Polo, small 8vo. *old vellum, rare*, £1 11*s* 6*d* .. *In Fiorenza, Lorenzo Torrentino*, 1556

With autograph of "*J. Donne.*" "This small Treatise of 180 pages in Italian, is styled, Il Moro, from Sir Thomas More, at whose house in Chelsea the author supposes Sir Thomas to have frequent conversations with learned men of his time."—*Lowndes.* For an account of the author, Ellis Heywood, son of the famous Epigrammatist, John Heywood, see *Wood's Athenæ Oxon.*

3098 MORE (Sir Thomas) Utopia; or the Happy Republic, Englished by Bp. Burnet, *portrait in mezzotint*, 8vo. *calf, neat*, 4s 6d *Glasgow, Foulis*, 1743

Autograph of "William Nasmith, Glasgow, Nov. 28, 1754."

3099 — Life, with his History of Utopia, describing the most perfect state of a Commonwealth, with Notes by Dr. Ferdinando Warner, 8vo. *nice copy in old calf*, 6s .. .. 1758

Lord High Chancellor, temp. Henry VIII., born 1480, beheaded, for what? 1535.

3100 MORGAN'S (J.) Phœnix Britannicus, being a Collection of Scarce and Curious Tracts, No. 2, 4to. *sewed*, 3s 6d .. 1731

Contains reprints of 12 rare tracts, many of them about Oliver Cromwell.

3101 MORGAN'S (Lady) France in 1829-30, *portrait*, 2 vols. 8vo. *2nd edition, half cloth*, 15s (*pub. at* £1 11s 6d) .. 1831

3102 MORINUS'S (J.) Atheist Silenced; the Existence of a Deity demonstrated from Reason, 12mo. *bound*, 2s .. 1672

3103 MORIER'S (James) Second Journey through Persia, Armenia, and Asia Minor, to Constantinople, 1810-16, *maps and coloured plates*, 4to. *calf gilt, a fine copy*, £1 1s (*pub. at* £3 13s 6d) 1818

"The opportunities which Mr. Morier possessed from his residence in Persia (as Minister Plenipotentiary) being much superior to those of a mere traveller, his work is justly regarded as one of authority."—*Stevenson.*

3104 MORLEY'S (John, *of Halsted, Essex*,) Essay on the Nature and Cure of Scrophulous Disorders, vulgarly called King's Evil, *coloured plate*, 8vo. *half calf*, 2s .. .. 1769

3105 MORLAND'S (George) Life with Critical Observations on his Works by J. Hassell, *portrait and plates*, 4to. *boards*, 9s (*pub. at* £1 1s) .. .. .. .. 1806

3106 MORNING Meditations; or, Reflections on Passages of the Holy Scripture, and Scriptural Poetry for every day in the Year, 12mo. *calf, extra*, 3s 6d .. .. .. 1825

3107 MORNING Thoughts, in Prose and Verse, on St. Mark, 12mo. *boards*, 3s 6d .. .. .. 1827

3108 MORNINGS with Mamma; Dialogues on Scripture, 1*st series*, 18mo. *neat*, 2s .. .. *Edinb.*, 1835

3109 MOROCCO—Barbarian Cruelty; a Narrative of the Unparalleled Sufferings of the British Captives belonging to the Inspector Privateer, Capt. Veale, in 1745 to 50, *plates*, 12mo. *bound*, 3s 6d .. .. .. .. 1751

3110 MORRIS, (Drake, *Merchant in London*,) his Travels, containing his Sufferings and Distresses in several Voyages at Sea, written by himself, 12mo. *half bound, uncut*, 4s *For the Author*, 1755

Scarce. Not in *Lowndes*. He travelled to Tortuga, Fernando Po, Abyssinia, &c.

3111 MORRIS (B. R.) British Game Birds and Wildfowl, 60 *beautifully coloured plates*, royal 4to. *a very handsome volume, half bound in calf extra, marbled leaves*, £1 15s (*cost* £2 15s) 1855

3112 — Naturalist, No. 23 to 36, *numerous plates*, 14 Nos. royal 8vo. *sewed*, 3s 6d (*pub. at* 7s) .. .. 1853-4

3113 MORSO (Salvadore, *R. Professiore di Lingua Arabica*,) Descrizione de Palermo Antico, ricavata sugli autori Sincroni e i Monumenti de' tempi, *portrait, and numerous plates*, 8vo. *sewed*, 12s *Palermo*, 1827

3114 MORTIER'S (Pierre) Atlas, Views of Fortified Cities in Flanders, Belgium, Holland, &c. atlas folio, *half bound, neat,* 15*s* *Amsterdam,* 1734

One shews the source and course of the Po by Placide, 1703, on a map 8 feet long.

3115 MOSHEIM'S (Dr. John L.) Ecclesiastical History, Ancient and Modern, Englished, with Notes, &c. by Dr. A. Maclaine, C. Coote, and Bp. Gleig, 6 vols. 8vo. *calf, neat,* 12*s* .. 1811

3116 MOSS'S (Joseph W.) Manual of Classical Bibliography, with an Account of the principal Translations, new edition to 1836, 2 vols. 8vo. *cloth,* 12*s* .. *H. G. Bohn,* 1837

3117 — another copy, 2 vols. 8vo. *half morocco, uncut, top edges gilt,* 16*s* .. .. .. .. 1837

Very useful as containing not only a list of the Greek and Latin Classics, but, in addition, lists at the end of each author's works, of CRITICAL and PHILOGICAL works, published in illustration of them; as well as the principal TRANSLATIONS of them into English, French, Italian, Spanish, German, &c. with Critiques upon them.

3118 MOTHS and Butterflies—British Moths and Butterflies, with their Transformations, by Humphreys and Westwood, *many hundred figures beautifully coloured,* 3 vols. 4to. *gilt, cloth,* £4 4*s* (*pub. at* £5 15*s* 6*d*) .. .. .. 1848-51

3119 MOUNTAIN'S (Jacob H. B.) Twenty One Sermons, 12mo. *boards,* 3*s* 6*d* (*pub. at* 7*s* 6*d*) .. .. *Rivington,* 1835

3120 MUDGE'S (Z., *Prebendary of Exeter,*) Sermons, 8vo. *old calf, neat,* 3*s* 6*d* .. .. .. .. 1739

Mudge was a learned man, very much conversant in the Platonic philosophy. An intimate friend of Sir Joshua Reynolds .. *Burke to Malone.*

3121 MULL—A Scotch Mull, Silver mounted, with Silver Chain, 15*s*

3122 MULLER'S (K. O.) History of the Literature of Ancient Greece, vol. 1, and parts 1 and 2 of vol. 2, 8vo. *cloth,* 3*s* 6*d* 1840

3123 — another copy, to the period of Isocrates, Englished by George C. Lewis and John W. Donaldson, 8vo. *cloth new,* 7*s* 6*d* 1850

3124 MUNDY (Anthony) Briefe Chronicle of the Successe of Times, from the Creation of the World to this instant, thick small 8vo. **Black Letter,** *old binding,* (wants title and 2 leaves at the end) 6*s* .. .. .. *London,* 1611

The list of Lord Mayors of London, from 1189 comes down to 1610.

3125 MUNICH GALLERIES, by Payne, *numerous fine plates after paintings by the old masters,* 3 vols. 4to. *half calf, very neat,* £3 3*s* (*cost* £5) 1840

3126 MURAT (Achille) Sketch of the United States of America, with a Note on Negro Slavery, *map,* post 8vo. *boards,* 4*s* (*pub. at* 10*s* 6*d*) .. .. .. .. 1833

3127 MURATORI (Lod. Antonio) Della Perfetta Poesia Italiana spiegata, e dimostrata con varie osservazioni, 2 vols. 4to. *fine clean copy in old calf,* 12*s* .. .. .. *Modena,* 1706

The 1st edition of this "esteemed work."

3128 MURCHISON (Sir R. J.) Geological Map of England and Wales, mounted on canvas for the pocket, *coloured, cloth,* 3*s* (*pub. at* 5*s*) .. .. .. .. 1843

3129 MURRAY'S (Hugh) and others, Historical and Descriptive Account of China, *map and plate by Jackson,* 3 vols. 12mo. *cloth,* 7*s* 6*d* (*pub. at* 15*s*) *Edinburgh,* 1843

3130 MURRAY'S (Lindley) English Grammar, with Exercises and Key, 2 vols. 8vo. *boards*, 9*s* (*pub. at* £1 1*s*) .. *York*, 1824

3131 MUSCI SCOTICI; Dried Specimens of the MOSSES which have been discovered in Scotland, by Thomas Drummond, Forfar, 2 vols. 4to. *boards*, £3 3*s*

These specimens are very nicely laid on, some very rare, belonged to the late Mr. Wigham, of Norwich.

3132 MUSCOVY and SPAIN — Rerum Moscoviticarum Commentarii, Sigismundo Libero Barone in Herberstain authore Russiæ brevissima descriptio, et de Religione eorum varia inserta sunt, *Antverpiæ, I. Steelsii*, 1557.—Francisci Taraphæ de origine ac rebus gestis Regum Hispaniæ liber, *portrait in title and arms on reverse*, in 1 vol. sm. 8vo. *vellum*, £5 5*s Antverpiæ, I. Steelsii*, 1535

Two rare tracts on Russia and Spain. At the end of the first is "De Admirandis Hungariæ aquis Hypomnemation, G. Vuernhero authore," and Pauli Jovii de legatione Moscovitarum liber. A copy of the first under HERBERSTAIN sold for above £20 at the recent sale of M. Libri's books.

3133 MUSCULORUM—De Ratione Motus Musculorum, *plate*, 4to. *sewed*, 2*s* .. .. .. *Londini, J. Hayes*, 1664

3134 MUSÆ—Examen Poeticum duplex; sive Musarum Anglicanarum Delectus alter; cui subjcitur Epigrammatum seu Pomatum minorum specimen novum, small 8vo. *old calf, neat*, 5*s* *Londini, R. Wellington*, 1698

The names of Jo. Addison, Gul. Shippen, Dr. Tho. Burnet, Dr. Robert Creyghton, G. Stephney, C. Dryden, Jo. Wallis, Rob. Friend, and John Milton, occur in this collection.

3135 MUSGRAVE (Sir William) Catalogue of his fine Collection of British Portraits, sold by Mr. Richardson, Feb. *partially priced*, 8vo. *half calf, uncut*, 6*s* .. .. 1800

3136 MUSIC—Dr. ARNE's Comus, a Masque.—Eliza, an Opera.—Alfred, a Masque.—Thomas and Sally, a Pastoral.—Lyric Harmony, 2 parts, composed for the Voice, Harpsichord, and Violin, oblong, *bound*, ORIGINAL EDITIONS, *very scarce*, £2 12*s* 6*d Harrison, no date*

3137 — BACH's (John Christian) 3rd Sett of Six Concertos, for the Harpsichord or Pianoforte, with Accompaniments for Violins, a Bass, Hautboys, and French Horns, (Opera 13) 4to. *half bound*, 7*s* 6*d*

3138 — Dr. BOYCE's Chaplet, a Musical Entertainment.—Solomon, a Serenata, by Dr. BOYCE.—The Beggar's Opera, by Dr. PEPUSCH.—Polly, being the 2nd part.—Two to One, an Opera, by Dr. ARNOLD.—Spenser's Amoretti, by Dr. GREENE, all composed for the Voice, Harpsichord, and Violin, oblong, *bound*, ORIGINAL EDITIONS, VERY SCARCE, £2 12*s* 6*d* .. *Harrison*, 1784

3139 — Brock (Michael) Collection of Church Music for the Use of his Scholars, oblong, 90 *leaves, scarce*, 6*s* .. *No date*

3140 — Busby's (Dr. Thomas) Dictionary of Music, Theoretical and Practical, 12mo. *half calf, gilt*, 3*s* 6*d* .. 1813

3141 — Cahusac's Annual Collection of 24 favourite Country Dances, as performed at Court, Bath, &c., 1800.—Bland and Weller's 24 ditto, for 1800.—Thompson's 24 ditto, for 1800.—Gray's 24 ditto, for 1800.—Preston's 24 ditto, for 1800.—Preston's 24 more for 1801.—24 more, anonymous.—Cahusac's 24 more, for 1802.—Thompson's 24, for 1802.—Bland and Weller's 24 more, for 1802.—in all 240, in 1 vol. oblong, *sewed*, 8*s*

3142 MUSIC—Dr. WILLIAM CHILD'S Te Deum, Jubilate Deo, Kyrie Eleeson, Nicene Creed, Magnificat and Nunc Dimittis, in D, with the greater Third.—The same in E, with the lesser Third.—Anthem, "Praise the Lord, O my Soul," for 4 voices, in F, with the greater Third.—Anthem, "O Lord Grant the King a long Life," for 4 voices, in F, with the greater Third.—Anthem, "Sing we merrily unto God," for 7 voices, in F, with the greater Third.—Hallelujah Sanctus.—all in 1 vol. folio, *half bound, neat*, SCARCE, £1 15*s* .. .. .. *No date*

3143 — Clementi's (Muzio) 6 Progressive Sonatinas, for the Piano.—32 Songs, 15 Hymns, and 21 Psalms.—Non Nobis Domine.—Martin Luther's Hymn.—Pleyel's celebrated German Hymn, and several others, folio, *sewed*, 6*s*

3144 — Coglan's Essay on the Church Plain Chant, containing Anthems, Litanies, Proses, and Hymns, 3 parts, 8vo. *bound*, 3*s* 6*d* *With Approbation*, 1782-3

3145 — Corfe's (Joseph) Thorough Bass Simplified, extracted from Handel, Corelli, Geminiani, and others, oblong, *sewed*, 6*s*

3146 — De Beriot's (C.) 7 Airs with Variations, for the Violin with Pianoforte Accompaniments.—Praeger's Musical Recreations, 12 Popular Melodies, for Violin and Piano.—3 others by Mayseder, Rode and Ghys.—in 1 vol. 4to. *half calf, neat*, £1 5*s* (*pub. at* £3 5*s*)

3147 — Dyke's (Rev. Will., *Curate of Oxwick, Norfolk*,) Original Sacred Music, consisting of 46 Hymns, Anthems, Communion Services and Chants, folio, *sewed*, 12*s* (*pub. at* 25*s*) *For the author, no date*

3148 — Forde's (Will.) Essay on the Discrimination of the Key in Music, 8vo. *sewed*, 2*s* .. : .. 1841

3149 — Hagart's (W. H.) Selection of 24 Scotch and Irish Airs, set for the Violoncello, oblong, *sewed*, 2*s*

3150 — Loder's (J. D.) Instruction Book for the Violin, upwards of 100 Progressive Exercises, 4to. *half bound*, 6*s* (*pub. at* 10*s* 6*d*)

3151 — Longman and Broderip's Favourite Duettos, arranged for 2 German Flutes, Violins, or Hautboys, vols 1 and 2, oblong, *bound* 6*s*

From Cambini, Pleyel, Storace, Hook, Shield, Mancinelli, and other esteemed masters.

3152 — Magdalen and Female Orphan Asylums; the Hymns, Anthems, and Tunes, and Psalms and Hymns sung at these Asylums set for the Organ, Harpsichord, &c, *portraits of the Magdalen and Orphan*, 2 vols. in 1, 4to. *hf. bd., neat*, 5*s*

3153 — MS. The Norfolk Quick and Slow Marches.—Ashly's Flag, and various other Hornpipes by Thomas Brightwell of Binham, oblong, *bound*, 3*s* .. .. .. 1803

3154 — Marsh's (J.) Select Movements from the Works of Corelli, Handel, Haydn, Pleyel, Mozart, Arne, Bach, &c. arranged for the Organ and Piano, 6 vols. oblong, *sewed, scarce*, 16*s* (*pub. at* £2 5*s*)

3155 — Miller's (Edward, *Organist at Doncaster*,) Institutes of Music, Instructions for the Harpsichord, 4to. *hf. bd.* 5*s*

3156 — Musical Mason; a Collection of Songs used in all Lodges, with the Free Mason's March, and Ode, 8vo. *half bound*, 3*s* 6*d*

3157 MUSIC—North's (Honble. Roger, *Attorney General to James II.*) Memoirs of Musick, now first printed from the original MS. with copious Notes by Dr. Edward Rimbault, *portrait*, 4to. *half morocco*, 15*s* .. .. .. .. 1846

"An exceedingly lucid and well drawn sketch of the progress of the art, from the period of the ancient Greeks down to the commencement of the 18th Cent."—*Dr. Rimbault.*

3158 — Peck's Miscellaneous Collection of Sacred Music, 12 Nos., some leaves missing, with some MS. pieces at the end, oblong, 4*s* 6*d*

3159 — Psalmist's New Companion, 43 Psalm Tunes and 25 Anthems composed after the Cathedral Manner, in 3 and 4 parts by Abraham Adams, at Shoreham in Kent, oblong, *scarce*, 7*s* 6*d*

3160 — Ravenscroft's (Thomas) Harmonia Perfecta; a complete Collection of Psalm Tunes, in 4 parts, 8vo. *old calf, neat*, VERY SCARCE, 18*s* .. .. .. .. 1730

Undertaken by Nathaniel Gawthorn, who says, it is "the *first of this kind* ever yet extant." For an account of Ravenscroft, see *Burney's* and *Hawkins's* Hist. of *Music.*

3161 — Romberg. Trois, Duos, Concertans, pour Deux Violons.—Pleyell's 6 Duetts, Op. 15, for 2 violins.—Pleyell's 6 Duett's, Op. 18, for 2 violins.—Luigi Borghi, 6 Divertimentos, for 2 violins.—12 Opera Overtures, Figaro, Masaniello, Lodoiska, Don Juan, Semiramide, &c. from Rossini, Mozart, &c. for 2 violins, by Muller, in 2 vols. 4to. *half bound, very neat*, £1 5*s* (*cost above* £3)

3162 — Rossini's Air di tanti palpiti, for Flute and Piano, by Monzani.—Kohler's 12 favorite Ariettes, with Variations for the German Flute.—Kohler's 2nd Set of 12 Ariettes.—Kreith's 3rd Set of Airs for the Flute, in 1 vol. 4to. *stiff cover*, 8*s*

3163 — Songs in the Opera called PYRRHUS and DEMETRIUS, by Alexander SCARLATTI and Sig. Nicolino HAYM.—Songs in the Opera of CALYPSO and TELEMACHUS, composed by M. GALLIARD, the Words by Mr. Hughes.—THREE CANTATAS composed, by Mr. G. HAYDEN. with several SONGS, by G. BICKHAM, *nicely engraved*, in 1 vol. folio, *old binding*, £2 2*s* .. .. 1710 to 1723

3164 — Tans'ur's (William) Introduction to the Grounds and Theory of Musick, with the Compleat Melody or Harmony of Zion, oblong (wants title) 3*s* 6*d* .. .. .. 1738

3165 — Vivaldi's (Antonia) Concertos in all their parts for Violins and other Instruments, with a Thorough Bass for the Harpsichord, folio, *stiff cover*, 6*s* .. .. *Walsh, no date*

This contains Violino Primo, 2 parts, 12 Concertos.

3166 — — Violino Quarto, 2 parts, 12 Concertos, folio, *stiff cover*, 6*s* *Walsh, no date*

3167 — The Usefulness of Church Musick, a Sermon at Christ Church, Oxford, Nov. 27, 1696, upon the Anniversary Meeting of the Lovers of Musick on St. Cæcilia's Day, 4to. *sewed*, 2*s* 6*d* 1696

3168 — Its Nature and Influence, a Lecture at Hurdsfield, by Rev. Will. Pearson, 8vo. *sewed*, 1*s* .. .. 1846

3169 — a Quantity of Music both printed and in MS.

3170 MUTINY of the Bounty; the Eventful History of the Mutiny and Piratical Seizure of H. M. S. Bounty, its Cause and Consequences, *plates*, 18mo. *cloth*, 2*s* 6*d* .. .. 1831

3171 MUTIO (Hieronimo *Justinopolitano*) Il Duello, con le risposte Cavalleresche, small 8vo. *vellum*, 9*s* *In Venetia, Domenico Farri*, 1576

An edition not mentioned by *Haym* or *Brunet*.

3172 MYTHOLOGY—Histoire Mythologique des Dieux et des Heros de l' antiquité, *numerous plates*, 12mo. *old binding*, 2*s* *Amsterdam*, 1715

3173 — Heathen Mythology, *illustrated by* 200 *engravings*, 8vo. *cloth*, 3*s* (*cost* 5*s*) .. .. .. .. 1854

3174 NALSON'S (Dr. John) Common Interest of King and People, shewing the Original, Antiquity, and Excellency of Monarchy, *fine portrait of Charles II. by Van Hove*, 8vo. *good copy in calf*, 3*s* 6*d* .. .. .. .. 1678

3175 NAPLES—Historia della Citta, e Regno di Napoli, di D. Francesco Capece Latro, *arms on title page*, 4to. *fine tall copy, in limp vellum*, 10*s* 6*d* .. .. *Napoli, O. Beltrano*, 1640

3176 NAPOLEON—Les Six Codes, accompagnés du Texte annoté, thick 8vo. *calf, very neat*, 6*s* .. .. *Paris*, 1828

3177 — History of Napoleon Buonaparte, *portraits and plates*, 2 vols. 18mo. *cloth*, 5*s* (*cost* 10*s*) .. *Fam. Lib.*, 1829

3178 — Court and Camp of Buonaparte, 12mo. *cloth*, 2*s* 6*d* (*cost* 5*s*) *Fam. Lib.*, 1829

3179 — Napoleon and other Essays, by Dr. W. E. Channing, 2 vols. 32mo. *cloth*, 3*s* .. .. .. 1837

3180 NARDI (Jacopo) Historie della Citta di Fiorenza, 1494-1531, 4to. *fine copy, in old parchment*, 15*s* *Lione, Theobaldo Ancelin*, 1582

"Cette édition, qui est l'originale, cité par La Crusca, contient, 'il Catalogo de' Gonfalonieri di Giustizia' et 'il discorso sopra lo stato della magnifica Città di LIONE,' de Fr. Giuntini."—*Brunet*.

"The birth of Nardi, who derived his origin from a noble family at Florence, is placed in 1476. His History of Florence, which bears the marks of great accuracy, is not without some share of elegance. Nardi, being an implacable enemy of the Medici, was banished, he with Nerli, who espoused the opposite interest, must be read with caution." See *Roscoe's Leo X*.

3181 NASH'S (Thomas) Pierce Penniless's Supplication to the Devil, from the edition of 1592, with Introduction and Notes, by J. P. Collier, 8vo. *boards*, 5*s* *Shakspeare Soc.*, 1842

3182 NASMITH (Jacobi) Catalogus Librorum MSS. quos Collegio Corporis Christi in Academia Cantabrigiensi legavit M. Parker, Archiepisc. Cantuariensis, *fine portrait of the Abp., by M. Tyson*, 4to. *very fine copy, in old calf, scarce*, 15*s* *Cantabrigiæ*, 1777

"An excellent Catalogue."—*Lowndes*.

3183 — Charge to the Grand Jury of the Isle of Ely, Ap. 2, 1799, with Remarks on Mr. Saunder's Observations on the Poor Laws.—Nasmith's Sermon at Wisbech Assizes, July 28, 1796.—Dr. Priestley's Letters to the Swedenborgians, *Birmingham*, 1791, in 1 vol. thick 8vo. *half calf, neat*, 7*s* 6*d* V. Y.

With 1. Historical Account of the Antiquities in Lincoln Cathedral, 1771.—2. Dean Smith's IX. Discourses on the Beautitudes, 1782.—3. Garrick's Manner of Reading the Liturgy, 1797.—4. Dr. John Trusler's Sublime Reader, and Sermons.

3184 NASSAU'S Triumphs; the heroic Acts of his Excellencie Prince Maurice of Nassau, Englished by W. Shute, Gent., folio, *a fine copy, in old calf*, 9*s* .. .. 1613

Prince Maurice was Generalissimo of the Netherland Forces, this recounts his victories by land and sea. Autograph of "*John Coke*," of the Leicester family.

3185 NAUCLERI (Johannis) Chronica, ab initio Mundi usque ad A. C. 1500, very thick folio, of above 1200 pp., *old calf, neat,* 18*s* *Coloniæ, ap. G. Calenium,* 1579

An edition, not mentioned by Brunet.

3186 NAUDÉ (G.) Apologie pour tous les Grands Personnages qui ont esté faussement soupçonnez de Magie, thick 8vo. above 600 pages, *limp parchment,* 9*s* *La Haye, Adrian Vlac,* 1653

This *original* Edition is not mentioned by Brunet, he gives that of 1712.

3187 — Apologie pour tous les Grands Hommes qui ont esté accusez de Magie, 12mo. *old calf, neat,* 6*s* .. *Paris,* 1669

3188 NAVAL Histories of Great Britain. See Brenton, Campbell, Charnock, James, and Southey.

3189 NAVY List, published with Sanction of the Admiralty, July, 1848, 2*s*.—April, July, and Oct., 1854, 2*s* each. April, 1857, 2*s*

3190 NEALE'S (Dr. Adam) Travels in Germany, Poland, Moldavia, and Turkey, *coloured plates, on tinted paper,* 4to. *boards,* 9*s* (*pub. at* £2 2*s*) .. .. .. .. 1818

3191 NEILL'S (Patrick) Tour in the Islands of Orkney and Shetland, with a view chiefly to their Natural History, 8vo. *boards,* 3*s* 6*d* *Edinburgh,* 1806

3192 NELSON (Horatio, Lord) Memoirs of his Professional Life, by Joshua White, *portrait,* 12mo. *boards,* 4*s* 1806

3193 — Life, by T. O. Churchill, *portrait, and fine proof plates by Worthington,* royal 4to. LARGE PAPER, 2nd Edition, *half calf, very neat,* 14*s* (*pub. at* £2 12*s* 6*d*) .. .. 1810

Inserted is a fac-simile Letter of Lord Nelson's to Thos. Lloyd, Esq., written from Bath, Jan. 29, 1798.

3194 NELSON'S (Robert) Great Duty of frequenting the Christian Sacrifice, partly collected from the Ancient Liturgies, 12mo. *old calf, neat,* 2*s* .. .. .. 1723

3195 NEUMAN and Barretti's Dictionary of the English and Spanish Languages, vol. 2 only, 8vo. *calf, neat,* 6*s* 6*d* 1823

3196 NEWBERRY'S (J.) Art of Poetry, *plates,* 2 vols. 12mo. *calf, neat,* 4*s* .. .. .. 1762

3197 NEW Brunswick, B. N. A., Historical and Statistical Account of, with Advice to Emigrants, by Rev. W. C. Atkinson, *map,* small 8vo. *bound, neat, gilt egdes,* 2*s* 6*d* .. *Edinb.,* 1844

3198 NEWCOME'S (Bp. William) Historical View of the English Biblical Translations, the expediency of revising our present Translation, &c., 8vo. *half russia, neat,* 6*s* *Dublin,* 1792

3199 NEWMAN'S (Samuel) Complete Concordance to the Bible in English, with Daniel Featley's and W. Gouge's Prefaces, thick folio, *old calf, neat,* 7*s* .. .. 1643

This is a most laborious work.

3200 NEW Monthly Magazine, vol. 4, 5, 6, 8vo. *half calf, very neat,* 9*s* *H. Colburn,* 1822

3201 NEWSPAPER Press Directory, by Charles Mitchell, a very useful work, 12mo. *cloth,* 3*s* 6*d* .. .. 1847

3202 NEW Testaments, in English, Latin, Greek, and other Languages, see *Testament.*

3203 NEWTON (Sir Isaac) His Life, by Sir David Brewster, *portrait,* 18mo. *cloth,* 2*s* 6*d* (*cost* 5*s*) .. *Fam. Lib.*, 1831

3204 NEWTON'S (Dr. James) Complete Herbal, containing the Prints only, and the English names of SEVERAL THOUSAND Trees, Plants, Shrubs, Flowers, &c., *engraved on about* 200 *plates, with portrait,* 2 vols. small 8vo. *half bound, scarce,* 12*s* .. 1769

Published by James Newton, Rector of Neunham, Oxfordshire.

3205 NEWTON'S (James William) Hebrew Grammar, small 8vo. *sewed,* 2*s* .. .. .. .. 1809

3206 NEWTON'S (John) Cardiphonia; the Utterance of the Heart, in Letters, 2 vols. 12mo. *grained calf, neat,* 5*s* *Edinburgh,* 1821

3207 — 41 Letters on Religious Subjects, 12mo. uniform with the above, 2*s* 6*d* .. .. .. .. 1810

3208 NEW Whole Duty of Man, 12mo. *boards,* 1*s* 6*d* 1819

3209 NEY, Mémoires du Maréchal Ney, Duc d'Elchingen, Prince de la Moskowa, publiés par sa famille, 2 vols. 8vo. *boards,* 6*s* *Londres,* 1833

3210 NICEPHORUS, (*Archiepiscopo Constantinopolis,*) Chronologia secundum Græcorum rationem temporibus expositis, Camerarii, folio, *good copy, in old calf,* 15*s* *Basileæ, J. Oporini,* 1561

At the end are two Treatises. 1. De Historia Synodi Nicenæ. 2. De Synodis Œcumenicis.

3211 NICHOL'S (Dr. J. P.) Contemplations on the Solar System, *plates,* post 8vo. 2nd Edition, *cloth,* 6*s* (*pub. at* 10*s* 6*d*) *Edinburgh,* 1844

3212 — Views of the Architecture of the Heavens, *plates,* post 8vo. 4th Edition, *cloth,* 6*s* (*pub. at* 10*s* 6*d*) .. *ib.*, 1843

3213 NICHOLLS'S (Dr. William) Book of Common Prayer, with the Psalms of David paraphrased, and the Lives of the Apostles, 8vo. *old calf, neat,* 5*s* .. .. .. 1734

3214 NICHOLS'S (John) Literary Anecdotes of the 18th Century, comprising Memoirs of William Bowyer, printer, and many of his learned friends, with the Index, *portraits,* 9 vols. 8vo. *half cloth,* £5 5*s* .. .. .. .. 1812

A view of the progress and advancement of Literature in this kingdom during the last century, with bibliographical anecdotes.

3215 — Illustrations of the Literary History of the 18th Century, a Sequel to the Literary Anecdotes, *portraits,* vols. 1 and 2 only, 8vo. *boards,* 16*s* .. .. .. 1817

Consists of authentic Memoirs and original Letters of eminent persons.

3216 — another copy, *portraits,* 2 vols. 8vo. *half calf, neat,* 18*s* (*pub. at* 20*s per volume*) .. .. .. 1817

3217 NICHOLS'S (J. B.) Collectanea Topographica et Genealogica, parts 17 to 20, being vol. 5, complete, and part 21, or part 1, of vol. 6, royal 8vo. *sewed,* 15*s* (*pub. at* 25*s*) 1837-38

3218 NICOL'S (James) Guide to the Geology of Scotland, *a Geological map and plates,* 12mo. *cloth, new,* 3*s* (*pub. at* 6*s*) *Edinb.* 1844

3219 NICOLAS'S (Sir N. H.) Synopsis of the English Peerage, 2 vols. 12mo. *half cloth, scarce,* 9*s* .. .. 1825

Entirely out of print, a valuable work, inasmuch as it contains "*every Title* of Peerage which has existed in this country since the Conquest."

3220 NICOLSON'S (Bp. Will.) English, Irish, and Scotch Historical Libraries, giving a short view and character of most of our Historians, either in print or MS., 4to. *best edition, old calf, neat,* £1 4*s* .. .. .. : 1776

"A valuable work, indispensably necessary in the study of English History."—*Lowndes.*

3221 — English Historical Library only, 2 vols. 8vo. *old cf, neat,* 7*s* 1697

3222 NIEUHOFF'S (John) Relation of the Dutch East India Company's Embassies to the Emperor of China, describing the Cities, Towns, Villages, &c., from Canton to Peking, Englished by John Ogilby, Esq., *numerous fine plates by Hollar,* folio, *old calf, neat,* 15*s* .. .. .. .. 1673

3223 NOBILII (Flaminii) de Hominis Felicitate libri III., de vera et falsa Voluptate, et de Honore, 4to. *unbound, scarce,* 4*s* *Lucæ, apud Vincentium Busdracum,* 1563

3224 NOBLE'S (Mark) Genealogical History of the present Royal Families of Europe, *plate of arms,* 12mo. *calf, neat,* 2*s* 6*d* 1781

3225 — Memoirs of the Protectoral House of Cromwell from an early period, collected from original Papers and Records, *portraits and plates of arms,* &c., 2 vols. 8vo. *calf, neat,* 10*s* *Birmingham,* 1787

3226 — Continuation of Granger's Biographical History of England to the end of Geo. I.'s reign, 3 vols. 8vo. *boards,* 9*s* 1806

3227 NOEHDEN'S (Geo. H.) Grammar of the German Language, 12mo. *half vellum, very neat,* 3*s* 6*d* .. .. 1816

3228 — another edition, with reading lessons, 12mo. *boards,* 3*s* 6*d* (*pub. at* 7*s*) .. .. .. .. 1826

3229 NOEL et Chapsal, Grammaire Française, 12mo. *sd.* 1*s* 6*d* *Paris,* 1849

3230 — Corrigé des Exercices Français, 12mo. *sewed,* 1*s* 6*d* *ib.,* 1849

3231 — Exercises to their French Grammar, by Sienrac, 12mo. *bound, neat,* 2*s* .. .. .. 1834

3232 — et de Laplace, Leçons Françaises de Littérature et de Morale, tirés de La Harpe, Marmontel, Maury, &c., royal 8vo. *hf. bound, neat,* 5*s* .. .. .. *Bruxelles,* 1847

3233 NORDEN'S (Capt. F. L.) Travels in Egypt and Nubia, Englished by Dr. Peter Templeman, *plates,* 8vo. *calf, very neat,* 6*s* 1757

"Every subsequent traveller has borne evidence to the accuracy and fidelity of his researches and descriptions."—*Lowndes.*

3234 NORDEN'S (John) Progress of Piety, printed for the Parker Society, 12mo. *cloth, gilt,* 3*s* 6*d* *Cambridge,* 1847

3235 NORFOLK—Abstract of the Minutes of Evidence, before a Committee of the H. of Commons, 1826, on the bill for making a Navigable Communication between Norwich and Lowestoft, *coloured map,* 8vo. *sewed,* 2*s* *Norwich, Wilkin,* 1826

3236 — Capt. Geo. Nicholls's Report on Ditto, July 30, 1825, *sewed,* 1*s* *Norwich, Matchett,* 1825

3237 — Act for making a Navigable Communication between Norwich and Lowestoft, folio, *sewed,* 2*s* 6*d* .. 1827

3238 — Adams *v.* Farrow, a Detail of the circumstances in connexion with the Trusteeship of J. Farrow, Esq., under the Will of Mr. Joseph Adams, of Hardley, by his Son, 8vo. *sewed,* 2*s* *Privately printed,* 1850

3239 NORFOLK—Architectural Notes of the Churches and other Ancient Buildings of the city and neighbourhood of Norwich, by a member of the Architectural section, (Mr. J. H. Parker, of Oxford,) 4to. *sewed*, 5*s* .. .. .. .. 1847

Only 3 copies in this size privately printed.

3240 — — one copy, only, on Large Paper, 4to. *sewed*, 7*s* 6*d* 1847

3241 — Attleborough Church, Architectural Notes on, by Mr. Wm. Patton, Architect, Fulford, York, 8vo. *sewed*, 6*d* 1847

3242 — another, printed on one side of a very thin paper only, 8vo. *sewed*, 1*s* .. .. .. 1847

Only 3 copies so printed.

3243 — another, in 4to. (10 copies only so printed) *sewed*, 3*s* 1847

3244 — one on Large Paper, unique, 4*s* .. .. 1847

3245 — Bacton—Green's (Charles) History, Antiquities, and Geology of, *plate*, 8vo. *cloth*, 3*s* 6*d* .. *Norwich*, 1842

3246 — Bayfield and Glandford Minute Book, beginning 14 Oct., 1757, ending 22 April, 1767.—Alborow Hall, rental, 1780 and 1781. Anthony Norris, Esq., Lord, Thomas Emerson, Steward.—Framingham Piggott Manor, Minute Book, beginning Feb. 26, 1778, to Feb. 16, 1779.—*with the signatures of the attestors*, folio, *a Manuscript*, *sewed*, 12*s*

3247 — Beccles Exhibition of Paintings, Prints, Articles of Vertu, &c., 8vo. *sewed*, 1*s* .. .. *Beccles*, 1839

3248 — Blomefield and Parkyns's Topographical History of the County of Norfolk, *portraits*, *plates*, *genealogies*, *&c.*, 11 vols. royal 8vo. *very nice set*, *half bound in calf*, £5 15*s* 6*d* 1806-10

3249 — Britton and Brayley's Topographical and Historical Description of Norfolk, *map and plates*, 8vo. *half cloth*, 9*s* (*pub. at* 15*s*) 1816

3250 — Browne's (Sir Thomas) Hydriotaphia, Urn-Buriale, a Discourse of the Sepulchral Urnes lately found in Norfolk, *plate*, small 8vo. *calf*, *neat*, *scarce*, 6*s* .. .. 1658

"One of the most beautiful works of this admirable author."—*Quarterly Review.*

3251 — — Miscellanies, containing his Life, his Treatise on Urns found at Brampton Field, Norfolk, 1667.—Letters between him and Sir W. Dugdale, in 1658, his Account of Iceland, 1662.—Antiquitates Scholæ Regiæ Norvicensis.—Catalogue of Bishops, Priors, &c. of Norwich, 8vo. *sewed*, 2*s* 6*d* 1712

This is a portion only of this work, but it may do to complete another.

3252 — Bryant's Map of Norfolk, from Actual Survey, coloured, mounted on canvas, in a case like a book, 4to. *cf*, *nt*, £1 1*s* 1826

3253 — Cary's Map of Norfolk, divided into Hundreds, with a list of the Stations of the Constabulary Force, *mounted on canvas*, folded into small 4to. *coloured*, *boards*, 4*s* .. 1840

3254 — Cromer—Bartell's (Edmund) Observations upon the Town of Cromer, as a Watering place, and the picturesque scenery in its neighbourhood, *plate*, 8vo. *boards*, 3*s* *Holt*, *Parslee*, 1800

3255 — — second edition, *map and plates*, royal 8vo. *boards*, 4*s* 6*d* 1806

Book-plate of Sir Tho. Gery Cullum, Bart., F.R.S., and autograph of *Mary Cullum.*

3256 — Drurie (Father, a Norfolk Gentleman,) Fatal Accident to his Congregation in Blackfriars, Oct., 1623.—see *London.*

3257 NORFOLK—Elizabeth's (Queen) Entertaynemente in Suffolk and Norfolk, by Tho. Churchyarde, Gent., *vignette on title*, small 8vo. *sewed*, 2*s* 6*d* .. .. .. 1851

Reprint of Bynneman's Edition of 1579.

3258 — Excursions in the County of Norfolk, *map and* 100 *plates*, proof impressions, 2 vols. 8vo. LARGE PAPER, *half morocco, extra, top edges, gilt, new*, £1 1*s* .. .. 1818

3259 — — small paper edition, *map and plates*, 2 vols. 12mo. *calf, neat*, 10*s* .. .. .. .. 1819

3260 — — The Plates to Excursions through Norfolk, Suffolk, and Essex, 103 *of them, fine impressions*, 12mo. *half calf, very neat*, 10*s* .. .. .. .. 1819

3261 — Forby's (Rev. Robert, *of Fincham, Norfolk)* MS. Note Book, various extracts of his Reading, 4to. *half bound*, 10*s* 6*d* 1768, &c.

3262 — — MS. History of England, from Julius Cæsar to the Reign of Queen Anne, 1701, with many curious extracts on a variety of subjects, during his Reading, thick 4to. *vellum*, £1 1*s*

3263 — Forncett—Preston's (Rev. H. E.) Funeral Sermon for the late Rev. J. D. Lane, of Forncett St. Peter, 8vo. *sd.* 1*s* *Norwich*, 1847

3264 — General History of the County of Norfolk, *map*, 2 vols. thick post 8vo. *bds*, 10*s* (*pub. at* £1 11*s* 6*d*) *Norwich, J. Stacy*, 1829

3265 — H. (J., M.A.) Divine Physician; prescribing Rules for the prevention and cure of most Diseases, as well of the Body as the Soul, 12mo. *very fine clean copy, in the original binding, gilt edges*, VERY RARE, £1 1*s* *Printed for George Rose, Bookseller in Norwich*, 1676

This is a very early book, printed in Norwich, and exceedingly rare. It is dedicated to the Rt. Worshipful Robert Coke, Esq., M.P., and the author says in his Dedication that "he received his first breath, and part of his education within the sensible horizon of Hill-Hall, in Holkham."—Not mentioned by *Lowndes*.

3266 — Hagger.—Indenture between Mrs. Constance Hagger or Haggard and Mr. George Gay, sen., *on parchment, a nice old specimen of Caligraphy*, 21*s* .. *Dated* 10*th Dec.*, 1677

With the autographs of Constance Haggard, Roger Gay, George Gay, and Tho. Weld.

3267 — Harrod's (Henry, F.S.A.) Gleanings among the Castles and Convents of Norfolk, 69 *illustrations*, 8vo. *cloth*, 17*s* 6*d* *Norwich, C. Muskett*, 1857

3268 — another copy, on LARGE PAPER, *cloth*, £1 10*s* 1857

The LARGE PAPER COPIES of this desirable and handsomely printed book, which was published by subscription, are now quite out of print, and difficult to procure.

3269 — Hart's (Rev. Richard) Lecture on the Antiquities of Norfolk, delivered at the Museum, Mar. 14, 1844, 2 *plates*, 8vo. *sewed*, 3*s* 6*d* .. .. *Norwich, C. Muskett*, 1844

3270 — Hewitt's (W.) Essay on the Encroachments of the German Ocean along the Norfolk Coast, with a design to arrest its depredations, *plates*, 8vo. *cloth*, 3*s* 6*d* *Norwich, for the Author*, 1844

3271 — Hingham—Bailey's (Rev. Henry) Fast Sermon at Hingham, Mar. 24, 1847, 8vo. *sewed*, 1*s* .. *Norwich*, 1847

3272 — [Howes (Rev. George, *Spixworth*)] The Ephesian Matron, a Poem, 8vo. *sewed*, 2*s* 6*d* *Norwich, C. Muskett, no date*

100 copies anonymously and privately printed for presents.

3273 NORFOLK—Ives's (John) Remarks upon the Garianonum of the Romans, the Site and Remains fixed, *portrait and plates*, 8vo. *half calf, neat, scarce*, 5*s* .. .. .. 1774

3274 — — second edition, *portrait and plates*, 8vo. *hf. russia, neat*, 6*s* 1803

This Edition contains "some account of the Author."

3275 — Jerningham (Sir William) Autograph Letter from him to his Bookseller, Mr. Budd, of Pall Mall, written from "Cossey, near Norwich, April ye 22d., 1805," 10*s* 6*d*

3276 — Jones (Sir Willoughby) Address at Downham Market, Norfolk, Dec. 5, 1855, on Public Libraries, 8vo. *sewed*, 1*s* 1855

3277 — Ketteringham.—Hunter's (Joseph, F.S.A.) History and Topography of Ketteringham, the Seat of Sir J. P. Boileau, Bart., 7 *plates*, 1 *in gold and colours, and Genealogy of the Heveninghams*, 8vo. *sewed*, 7*s* 6*d* *Norwich, C. Muskett*, 1851

Privately Printed. "A few copies only are printed in this separate form, and to these only this Preface is prefixed." Extract from Mr. Joseph Hunter's Preface of 7 pages.

3278 — — another edition, in 4to. *sewed*, 12*s* .. *ib.*, 1851

Excessively rare, only two copies printed on this large paper.

3279 — — Plates, Interior of the Hall, Ketteringham, 6*d*.—Heveningham Tomb, Ketteringham Church, 6*d*.—Genealogy of the Heveninghams, from 1499 to 1702, 6*d*

3280 — List of the Towns, Villages, &c. in Norfolk, 18mo. *sewed*, 1*s* *Berry, Dove Lane*, 1811

3281 — Loddon.—Buchanan's (Cha., *of Ditchingham)* Sermon at Loddon, Ap. 26, 1710, at Dr. Cannon's Archidiaconal Visitation, 4to. *sewed*, 2*s* .. .. *Norwich, Cockey Lane*, 1710

3282 — Lubbock's (Rev. Richard, *Eccles)* Observations on the Fauna of Norfolk, more particularly on the district of the Broads, *map and plates*, 8vo. *cloth, new*, 3*s* 6*d (pub. at* 6*s)* *Norwich, C. Muskett*, 1845

3283 — Lynn.—Mackerell's (B.) History and Antiquities of the Corporation of King's Lynn, in Norfolk, *plates*, 8vo. *calf, very neat, scarce*, 15*s* .. .. .. 1738

3284 — — Richards's (William) History of Lynn from the earliest to the present time, *map and plates*, 2 vols. 8vo. *half calf, neat*, 12*s* *Lynn*, 1812

3285 — Manning's (Rev. C. R.) Remarks on some Churches in the neighbourhood of North Walsham, visited in 1854, 4to. *sewed*, 5*s* *Norwich*, 1854

Only 20 copies printed on this size paper.

3286 — Matchett's Norfolk and Norwich Remembrancer, being a Chronological retrospect of Remarkable Events, from 1701 to 1821, with an Index Villaris, *map*, 12mo. *bds*, 3*s* 6*d* *Norwich*, 1822

3287 — Munford (Rev. Geo.) List of the Flowering Plants found growing wild in Western Norfolk, 8vo. *sewed*, 2*s* 1841

3288 — Nevilli (Alexandri) Kettus, sive de furoribus Norfolciensium Ketto Duce liber, small 8vo. *old calf, neat*, 10*s* 6*d* *Londini, R. Newberie*, 1582

This is an elaborate account of Kett's Rebellion in 1549, it is attached to Ocland's Anglorum Prælia and his Elizabetha, two Latin Poems ordered by the Privy Council to be read in all Grammar schools.

3289 NORFOLK—Norfolcia, Antiqua et Nova; The Ancient and Modern History of the County of Norfolk and City of Norwich, *map by Robt. Morden,* 4to. *old calf,* 10s 6d *In the Savoy, by E. & R. Nutt,* 1723

3290 — Norfolk and Norwich Archæological Society's Original Papers, for the encouragement of research into the early Arts and Monuments of the County, 5 vols. 8vo. (all published) *very scarce, half morocco, top edges gilt,* £5 15s 6d .. 1846-59

Several parts of sets and volumes to complete.

3291 — Norfolk Benefices, List of, with the Names of their Respective Incumbents and Patrons, by the late Mr. Dawson Turner, royal 8vo. *sewed,* 2s (*pub. at* 5s) *Norwich, C. Muskett,* 1847

"Continued from Blomefield's History of Norfolk to this time." Only 200 copies printed.

3292 — another edition in 4to. to bind with the 4to. edition of Blomefield, 3s 6d (*pub. at* 7s 6d) .. .. *ib.,* 1847

Only 50 copies printed in this size.

3293 — Norfolk Poetical Miscellany, with some Select Essays and Letters in Prose, 2 vols. 8vo. *calf, neat,* 8s *For the author,* 1744

3294 — Norfolk Tour; the Traveller's Pocket Companion through Norfolk, with an Index Villaris, and a Short Account of the Chief Towns in Suffolk, 12mo. *old calf,* 3s *Norwich, Beatniffe,* 1795

3295 — Observations and Advices Œconomical, 12mo. *original calf,* VERY SCARCE, £1 1s
*Printed by T. R. for John Martyn, Printer to the Royal Society,* 1669

This is most probably the production of a Norfolk man, Sir Edward Coke being mentioned at p. 87. The author was evidently a person of quality. He says, in his preface, that he passed (or rather lost) some few years at Cambridge; then he lived with his parents at their London habitation; then he went to Italy, France, and Spain, "being present at Madrid and Paris, when the several marriages for our then Prince of Wales, (Charles I.) were treated of in those Courts;" then a soldier in Holland—came home and served under a Scotch Colonel; then married; was then M.P. in 4 successive Parliaments; then retired to the country being disgusted with the town; then he entertained himself by turning over old books, whereof he says, he had "good store in several languages," &c. &c. It is a most sensible little book, consisting of 85 maxims, or aphorisms, not to be found in *Lowndes.*

3296 — OXBURGH HALL—M'Gill's (Rev. G. H.) Account of Oxburgh Hall, with the Pedigree of Sir Henry Paston Bedingfield, royal 8vo. *sewed,* 2s 6d .. .. .. 1855

Only 6 copies printed on royal 8vo.

3297 — Peerage, Primogeniture, and Aristocracy of England; a Plan to Dispose of these Subjects by Omero Franc-coes, 12mo. *calf, extra, scarce,* 6s .. .. .. .. 1835

This rare little brochure dedicated to "T. W. Coke, Esq., the true friend of Reform," consists of 48 leaves printed on one side only on scarlet paper.

3298 — Phillips's (John) Plan for making a Navigable Canal from London to Norwich and Lynn, through Essex, Suffolk, and Norfolk, and from Bishop Stortford to Cambridge, *coloured map and plate,* 4to. *sewed,* 4s 6d .. .. .. 1785

3299 — Poll Book, taken at Norwich, May 22, 1734, 4to. *rough calf,* 10s 6d .. .. .. .. 1734

Candidates, Sir Edmund Bacon, Bart., William Wodehouse, Esq., Hon. Robert Coke, William Morden, Esq.

3300 NORFOLK—Poll for the County, taken at Norwich, Mar. 23, 1768, Candidates, Sirs A. Wodehouse and Edward Astley, and Tho. de Grey and Wenman Coke, Esqrs, 4to. *swd.* 5*s* *Norwich, J. Crouse,* 1768

3301 — Poll, Nov. 1806, with Narrative of the Proceedings previous to and after the Election, 8vo. *sewed,* 5*s* .. *Norwich,* 1806

**Sheriff, Henry Lee Warner, Esq.; Candidates, Windham, Coke, Wodehouse, Sir J. H. Astley, retired. This is a very interesting account, and contains a list of the Knights of the Shire since the reformation, 264 years.**

3302 — Poll, Eastern Division, Dec. 1832, 8vo. *sewed,* 2*s* 6*d* *Norwich,* 1833

**Mr. Windham and Major Keppel returned. W. L. W. Chute, of S. Pickenham, Sheriff.**

3303 — Poll Book, Western Division, January 1835, 8vo. *sewed,* 2*s* 6*d* 1835

**Sir W. Ffolkes and Sir Jacob Astley returned, Robert Marsham, Esq. Sheriff.**

3304 — Poll Book (Norfolk, both Divisions, and Norwich,) for 1835, 3 parts, 8vo. *half calf, neat,* 6*s* .. *Norwich,* 1835

3305 — Poll (Eastern Division) and Register, E. Wodehouse and H. N. Burroughs, Esq. returned, 8vo. *sewed,* 2*s* 6*d* *Norwich,* 1837

3306 — Poll for West Norfolk, August, 1847, 8vo. *sewed,* 1*s* *Norwich,* 1847

**Hon. E. K. Coke and Mr. Bagge returned, Sir J. H. Preston, Sheriff.**

3307 — Poor, Proposal for the more Comfortable Maintenance of, 4to. *sewed,* 1*s* 6*d* .. .. *Norwich, W. Case,* 1765

3308 — — Heads of a General Bill for the Better Relief of the Poor in the County of Norfolk, folio, *sewed,* 2*s* *Norwich, Crouse,* 1771

3309 — — A Proposal for the Relief and more Comfortable Maintenance of the Poor of the County of Norfolk, with Notes, MS. folio, 5*s* *about* 1780

3310 — RANDALL—COMMISSION, PRINTED on Parchment, (the names written in) signed by Lord Viscount TOWNSHEND, of Raynham and Baron of Lynn Regis, Lord Lieut. of Norfolk, appointing Thomas Randall, Gent., Lieutenant in Capt. Wm. Jubbs's Company in the Purple Regiment of Militia Foot, whereof Edmund Wodehouse, Esq. is Colonel, *in a very good state of preservation; with the Lord Lieutenant's seal,* £1 5*s* *Signed,* 13 *June,* 1707

**Viscount Townshend was conjunct Plenipotentiary with the Great Duke of Marlborough at the Hague in 1709; had to do with the Barrier Treaty in 1712, and held several high appointments in the reign of Q. Anne. See *Bp. Burnet's History of his own Times.***

3311 — — COMMISSION, Printed on Parchment (the names written in) signed by the Lord Viscount TOWNSHEND, appointing Thomas Randall, Gent., Lieutenant in Capt. Henry Davy's Company called the Purple Regiment, £1 1*s* *Signed, 4th Oct.* 1711

3312 — — COMMISSION, WRITTEN on Parchment, signed by James, Duke of ORMONDE, Lord Lieutenant and Custos Rotulorum of the County of Norfolk, appointing Thomas Randall, Gent., Lieutenant to that Company in the Militia Regiment of Foot, (whereof Robert Seaborne, Esq., is Captaine) called the Purple Regiment, commanded by Sir John Woodhouse, *with the Duke's Seals, all complete and in a very perfect and desirable state,* £2 2*s* *Signed, "By his Grace's Command,* D. KENNEDY."

**Temp. Queen Anne. On the outside is written, "Nov. 13, 1713. Delivered then this Commission to Tho. Randall, Gent., by me, *Robt. Seaborne.*" This Commission therefore, has three autographs—the Duke of ORMONDE'S (who held very high offices, was a Knight of the Garter, Lord Lt. of Ireland, &c.) his Secretary's, and Captn. Seaborne's.**

3313 NORFOLK—RAYNHAM—Phayre (Rev. Richard) Sermon at Raynham St. Mary, on the Sinfulness of Astrology, 12mo. *sewed*, 1*s* *Norwich*, 1849

3314 — Robberds's (J. W., Jun.) Geological and Historical Observations on the Eastern Vallies of Norfolk, *plan*, 8vo. *half bound, uncut, scarce*, 6*s* .. .. *Norwich, Bacon & K.*, 1826

3315 — — another copy, *plan*, 8vo. *half bound, uncut, scarce*, 8*s* *ib.*, 1826

"This copy is printed on WRITING PAPER. Presented (no doubt) by the printer to James Parsons, Bookseller of Norwich." *In MS.* inside.

3316 — Rush; Trial of J. B. Rush, for the Murder of Mr. Jermy and his Son, at Stanfield Hall, *portrait*, 8vo. *sewed*, 1*s* 1849

3317 — SAHAM-TONY; Will of Elizabeth Allen, of Saham-tony, one of the Daughters of Thomas Cullier of Wymondham, *on parchment, very legibly written and in a very good state of preservation, with her signature and seal*, 10*s* 6*d* .. *Dated, 4th June*, 1659

Witnesses, Thomas Cullyer, Joseph Bragy, John Westhorpe, and Cuthbert Brereton. This will has reference to a will made by Thomas Cullyer in 1634.

3318 — SPARHAM—Sketches for an Ecclesiology of the Deaneries of Sparham and Taverham, Nos. 1, 2, 3, 12mo. *sewed*, 1*s* 6*d* *Norwich*, 1845

3319 — Stafford (Baroness) Funeral Sermon for, Nov. 27, 1856, by Dr. F. C. Husenbeth, V. G., 8vo. *sewed*, 1*s* .. 1856

3320 — STANFIELD HALL; Catalogue of the Furniture, &c. at Stanfield Hall, sold by Mr. Butcher, in June, 1849.—View of the Hall, and the Rev. R. H. Tripp's Sermon on Rush, 8vo. *sd. gt. leaves*, 2*s* 1849

3321 — STRATTON HALL, alias LONG STRATTON, a MS. on 40 leaves, dated 1666 to 1672, shewing the Homage rendered by various persons whose names are all signed, folio, *parchment wrapper*, £2 2*s* .. .. .. 1672

3322 — Stratton Hall—MS. a Rentall received at the Court holden for the Manor in 1684, shewing the Acres and the value of the Lands for one Year, with all the Tenants alphabetically arranged, and shewing who were the Owners of the Lands in James 1st's time, Queen Elizabeth's, and so backwards, folio, *a valuable document*, £1 1*s* .. .. .. .. 1684

3323 — Taylor (Rich. C., F.G.S.) On the Geology of East Norfolk, with Remarks on Mr. Robberds's Hypothesis respecting the former Level of the German Ocean, *coloured plates*, 8vo. *boards*, 6*s* 1827

*"J. W. Robberds, Esq., from the Author." MS.*

3324 — THETFORD—Blomefield's (Francis, *Rector of Fersfield, Norfolk;*) History of the Ancient City and Burgh of Thetford, Norfolk, 4to. *half bound, uncut, scarce*, 9*s* *Printed at Fersfield*, 1739

3325 — — Burrell's (Geo.) Account of Gifts and Legacies that have been bequeathed in Thetford, with a Chronology of Remarkable Events, 8vo. *boards*, 3*s* 6*d* .. .. *Thetford*, 1809

3326 — Tompson (Rev. F. C.) On Establishing Adult Schools in Agricultural Districts, 8vo. *sewed*, 1*s* .. *Norwich*, 1850

3327 — Trimmer (Joshua, F.G.S.) on the Geology of Norfolk, as illustrating the Laws of the Distribution of Soils, *sectional plate*, 8vo. *sewed*, 2*s* 6*d* .. .. .. 1847

3328 — Walker's Map of Norfolk, *cloth, mounted on canvas*, 1*s* 6*d*

3329 NORFOLK—White's (Will.) History, Gazetteer, and Directory of Norfolk, small 8vo. *half bound in green morocco, uncut, top edges, gilt,* 1st edition, 10*s* .. .. *Sheffield,* 1836

3330 — — 2nd and best edition, *hf. morocco, uncut, top edges, gt.* 15*s* 1845

3331 — — another, fine copy in *half morocco, elegant, top edges gilt, scarce,* BEST EDITION, 20*s* .. .. .. 1845

3332 — Woodward's (Sam.) Outline of the Geology of Norfolk, *map and plates,* 8vo. *cloth,* 3*s* 6*d* (*pub. at* 5*s*) .. 1833

3333 — Worship's (Francis, *of Yarmouth,* Esq.) Account of a MS. Genealogy of the Paston Family, in the possession of his Grace the Duke of Newcastle, *with plates of arms and pedigree,* 8vo. LARGE PAPER, *sewed,* 6*s* .. .. *Norwich,* 1852

6 copies only struck off, on LARGE PAPER. Private.

3334 — WYMONDHAM—Nicholas Baxter of Wymondham, his last Will and Testament, on 6 folios, on paper, *in a very good legible hand,* £1 1*s* .. .. *Dated* 10*th Jan.* 1588

This will was proved at Wymondham, before Mr. William Thorowgood, Clarke, Mr. of Arts, in and for the whole Archdeaconry of Norfolk, the 11th day of Aprill.

3335 — — Nicholas Baxter's Will, of Wymondham, *on parchment,* 10*s* *Dated,* 31*st Elizabeth,* 1588

The time of the descent of the Spanish Armada.

3336 — — LIBER COMPTORIUM—MS., *on* 102 *leaves, very nicely written,* folio, *old parchment,* £10 10*s* .. 1594

This is an account of the Abbey and Manor of Wymondham, taken in the 36th year of Q. Elizabeth's reign. All the Proprietors and Tenants are named. It is in two hands, one Elizabethan, the other about 1632 to 1646. The names of Norton, Hobbes, Woodhowse, the Ketts, Symondes, Bale, Clere, Raynoldes, and many others occur in it.

3337 — — Will of Thomas Cullyer of Wymondham, 1663, (in Latin) with reference to that of Thomas Cullyer the elder of 1634, *on parchment in a very good state,* 10*s* 6*d* *Dated,* 9 *Ap.,* 1663

Examined by *Norton* and *Aug. Reve.*

3338 — YARMOUTH—Catalogue of Daniel Boulter's Museum of Yarmouth, Natural and Artificial Curiosities, and Books and Prints, 8vo. *sewed,* 2*s* 6*d,* autograph of Dr. " *C. Sutton.*" *No date*

3339 — — Cannell's (Dr. Robert, *of Bradwell, Suffolk,*) Three Sermons Preached in St. Nicholas's Church and St. George's Chapel, Great Yarmouth, in 1724 and 25, 8vo. *old calf, neat,* 5*s* *Sold by the booksellers of Norwich,* 1726

Has also 3 Sermons by Dr. Thomas Macro, Minister of Yarmouth, preached at the same Church in 1731-33.

3340 — — Catalogue of the Library of Rob. Cory, Jun., Esq., of Yarmouth, sold Oct., 1840, by Mr. B. Rix, 4to. *hf. cf. neat,* 2*s* 6*d* 1840

3341 — — Harrod' (Henry) Notes on the Records of the Corporation of Great Yarmouth, 8vo. LARGE PAPER, *sewed,* 3*s* 6*d*

Six copies only struck off on large and thick paper.

3342 — — King (Tho. Will., Esq., F.S.A., *Rouge Dragon*) Remarks on some Ancient Shields in the ceiling of St. Nicholas Church, Great Yarmouth, 4to. *sewed,* 5*s* .. 1848

Only 3 copies struck off on this 4to. paper, privately printed.

3342*NORFOLK— — Narrative of the Grand Festival at Yarmouth, on Tuesday, Ap. 19, 1814, on the fall of Buonaparte, 3 *plates by T. S. Cotman*, 8vo. *boards*, 5*s* *Yarmouth, J. Keymer*, 1814

3343 — — Paget's (C. J. and James) Sketch of the Natural History of Yarmouth and its Neighbourhood, 8vo. *boards, very scarce*, 12*s* *Yarmouth*, 1834

3344 — — Poll Book, June, 1818, 8vo. *sewed*, 1*s* 6*d* *Yarmouth*, 1818

Hon. T. W. Anson and Mr. Rumbold returned. Sam. Paget, Esq. Mayor.

3345 — — Poll Book, March, 1820, 8vo. *sewed*, 1*s* 6*d* *Yarmouth*, 1820

Anson and Rumbold returned. Dr. Bateman, Mayor.

3346 — — Poll Book, June, 1826, with list of Members since 1297, 8vo. *sewed*, 1*s* 6*d* .. .. *Yarmouth*, 1826

Hon. G. Anson and C. E. Rumbold, Esq., returned. C. Costerton, Esq., Mayor.

3347 — — Poll Book, July, 1830, with all the Addresses, Squibs, Songs, &c., 8vo. *sewed*, 2*s* 6*d* .. *Yarmouth*, 1830

Colonel Anson and Mr. Rumbold returned.

3348 — — Repertory of Deeds and Documents relating to Great Yarmouth, in the County of Norfolk, 4to. *half vellum*, RARE, £1 1*s* 1855

Only 100 copies printed by order of the Town Council.

3349 — Young's General View of Agriculture of the County of Norfolk, drawn up for the Board of Agriculture, *map and plates*, 8vo. *calf, neat*, 4*s* 6*d* .. .. .. 1804

3350 NORRIS'S (John, *of Bemerton*) Collection of Miscellanies: consisting of Poems, Essays, Discourses, and Letters, 12mo. *old calf, neat*, 3*s* .. .. .. 1717

3351 — another edition, 12mo. *calf, neat*, 2*s* 6*d* .. 1722

3352 NORTHAMPTONSHIRE—History or Description, general and circumstantial, of Burghley House, the seat of the Rt. Hon. the Earl of Exeter, 8vo. 250 pages, *boards, uncut*, 4*s* 6*d* *Shrewsbury, Eddowes*, 1797

3353 — another edition, *view and plan*, 12mo. *boards*, 2*s* *Stamford*, 1818

3354 NORTH Briton (The) 2 vols. 12mo. *old calf, neat*, 7*s* 6*d* *Dublin, (no printer's name)* 1764

With the famous Number 45 at the end.—"This seditious publication was the source of Wilkes's celebrity and misfortunes, and the cause of his ultimate independence."—*Lowndes*.

3355 NORTHUMBERLAND — Metrical Legends of Northumberland, with notes and illustrations by James Service, *cuts by Bewick*, 12mo. *half cloth*, 2*s* 6*d* .. *Alnwick*, 1834

3356 NORWICH—Act for Paving, Lighting, Cleansing, and Watching Norwich, June 13, 1806, folio, *sewed*, 1*s* 1806

3357 — Act for Lighting Norwich with Gas, 1820, folio, *sewed*, 1*s*

3358 — Act for Building Duke's Palace Bridge, Norwich, folio, *sewed*, 1*s* 6*d* .. .. .. .. 1820

3359 — Bill for Building a Bridge over the Wensum, at or near the Duke's Palace, folio, *sewed*, 2*s* .. 1819-20

3360 — Act for a Bridge over the Wensum, in St. Clement's Parish, folio, *sewed*, 2*s* .. .. .. 1830

3361 NORWICH—Architectural Notes of the Churches and other Ancient Buildings of the City and Neighbourhood of Norwich, (by Mr. J. H. Parker, of Oxford,) 8vo. *sewed*, 2*s* .. 1847

3362 — another, printed on one side of the paper only, and but 3 copies so struck off, 2*s* 6*d* .. .. .. 1846

3363 — another, 8vo. LARGE PAPER, *sewed*, 4*s* .. 1847

Only 2 copies struck off on LARGE and THICK Paper.

3364 — Beatniffe's (R., *Bookseller, Norwich)* Catalogue of his Extensive Collection of Books, 8vo. *half bound, neat, scarce*, 5*s* *Norwich, Bacon, Cockey Lane*, 1803

3365 — Beaumont's (G., *Ebenezer Chapel, Ber Street, Norwich)* Catalogue containing a great variety of old and modern Books, 12mo. 209 pages, *sewed*, 2*s* 6*d* .. .. 1819

3366 — Bentley's (Elizabeth) Genuine Poetical Compositions, *portrait*, 12mo. *calf, very neat*, 4*s* 6*d* *Norwich, Crouse & Stevenson*, 1791

At the end is "Elmira, a Dramatick Poem, with Thoughts on Tragedy, by Edward Stanley, B.A.," *Norwich*, 1790. ? were these the "first productions" (see advertisement) of the late Bp. of Norwich?

3367 — Berney and Bedingfield—Joab's Bloody Complement to Abner, set forth in a Sermon occasioned by the much lamented death and cruell murther of Thomas Bedingfield, of Darsham Hall, Esq., by Thomas Berney, Gent., in the City of Norwich, July 20, 1684, preached at Carlton Colvile, in Suffolk, by John Browne, Rector there, 4to. *in MS., sewed*, £2 2*s*

Dedicated "To the ever honoured ladies the Lady Bedingfield and the Lady Knivett, of Darsham Hall, in Suffolk," signed Carlton Colvile, Aug. 1684. In the Norwich Chronology, we read, "1684, Thomas Berney, Esq., executed in the Town Close, for the murder of Mr. Bedingfield." This rencontre seems to have been caused by some religious dispute.

3368 — Berry's (C., *of Dove Lane)* Catalogue of his Books for Sale, 8vo. 306 pages, *sewed*, 3*s* *Crouse & Stevenson*, 1794

3369 — Blind Hospital, an account of, with the proceedings of the General Meeting, March, 1854, and the Committee's Report, 8vo. *sewed*, 2*s* 6*d* .. *Norwich, Muskett*, 1854

Only 2 copies printed on this thick paper.

3370 — Blyth's (G. K.) Norwich Guide and Directory, with an account of the Public Charities, *view of the Cathedral*, post 8vo. *cloth*, 3*s* 6*d* .. .. .. .. 1842

3371 — Boulter's (C. S., *Surgeon)* Address on the Construction put upon the Rules of the Dispensary, 8vo. *sewed*, 1*s* 1847

3372 — Britton's (John, F.S.A.) Essay on the Ancient Gate Houses in Norwich, *plates, with* 6 *original drawings*, 8vo. *sewed*, 5*s* 1847

"25 *printed, from the author*." In Mr. Britton's *hand-writing*.

3373 — Catalogue of the Books belonging to the Norfolk and Norwich Medical Book Society, 3 parts, 8vo. *boards*, 3*s* 6*d* *Norwich*, 1826-45

3374 — Catalogue of the Library of the Clerical Society, established 1828, interleaved, 8vo. *boards*, 2*s* 6*d* *C. Muskett*, 1838

3375 — Catalogue of the Library of the Dean and Chapter, 8vo. *cloth*, 3*s* *Norwich*, 1836

3376 NORWICH—Catalogue of the 1st Exhibition of the Norfolk and Norwich Art Union, at their Gallery, St. Andrew's, 1839, royal 8vo. *sewed,* 1*s* 6*d* .. .. *Norwich,* 1839

With a very pretty etching on the title page.

3377 — Charles II.—Narrative of the King's Visit to Norwich, September, 1671, drawn up by the late Mr. Dawson Turner, 8vo. *sewed, scarce,* 3*s* .. .. *Yarmouth,* 1846

3378 — Clayton's (Tho., *Rector of St. Michael at Plea, Norwich)* Unity of Worship earnestly recommended, Sermon at the Cathedral, Jan. 9, 1703, 4to. *sewed,* 1*s* 6*d* *For F. Oliver, Norwich,* 1704

Dedicated to "the Rt. Worshipful, John Freeman, Esq., Mayor of Norwich."

3379 — Coke, (The Lord) his Speech and Charge, (given at Norwich Assizes, August 4, 1606,) with a Discoverie of the Abuses and Corruption of Officers, small 4to. *scarce, sewed,* 7*s* 6*d* *London, Nathaniel Butter,* 1607

3380 — Copeman's (Dr. Edward) Brief History of the Norfolk and Norwich Hospital, with a few Biographical Observations on the late W. Dalrymple and J. G. Crosse, Esqrs., royal 8vo. *sewed;* 7*s* 6*d* .. .. *Norwich, C. Muskett,* 1856

Only one copy privately printed on large and thick paper.

3381 — Correspondence between Colonel Smyth (16th Lancers) and Capt. Coster, respecting Canon Wodehouse's Charge against Capt. Coster, 8vo. *sewed,* 1*s* .. *Norwich,* 1849

3382 — Essay on the Antiquity of the Castel of Norwich, its Founder and Governors, from the Kings of the East-Angles down to Modern Times, 8vo. 40 pages, *sewed, very scarce,* 10*s* 6*d* *Norwich, Henry Crossgrove,* 1728

3383 — — the same reprinted, 8vo. *sewed,* 5*s* *Matchett,* 1834

This Pamphlet, published anonymously in 1728, was written by Thornhaugh Gurdon, of Letton, Esquire. He was an active magistrate and Receiver-General for Norfolk, temp. Q. Anne. He died at Letton, in 1733, aged 70.

3384 — Fletcher's Norwich Hand-Book, compiled by Mrs. Madders, *plates,* 12mo. *sewed,* 1*s, or with map, in cloth,* 2*s* 1857

3385 — Gleed's (Jonathan, *Bookseller, in Norwich)* Catalogue of his Books, 8vo. *boards,* 2*s* 6*d* .. .. 1759

3386 — Gurney (Hudson, Esq.) Letter to Dawson Turner, Esq., with the Proofs that Norwich and not Caistor was the venta Icenorum, *map,* 8vo. *sewed,* 1*s* 6*d* *Norwich, privately printed,* 1847

3387 — — another, 8vo. *sewed,* 2*s* .. .. 1847

3 copies only struck off, on a thin paper printed only on one side.

3388 — the same Letter, on LARGE PAPER, (2 copies only printed) 3*s*

3389 — the same Letter, on 4to. paper, (10 copies only printed) 4*s* 1847

3390 — the same Letter, on 4to. LARGE PAPER, (1 copy only printed) 5*s*

3391 — Hancock's (Blith) Doctrine of Eclipses, with Astronomical Tables, from a MS. copy of the Tabulæ Dunelmenses, *plates,* 8vo. *cloth, scarce,* 6*s* *Norwich, J. Crouse, for the Author,* 1782

3392 — Harbord (Honble. E. V.) Speech to the Electors of Norwich, Dec. 23, 8vo. *sewed,* 1*s* .. .. 1834

3393 — Harrod (Henry, F.S.A.) Goods and Ornaments of Norwich Churches in the XIVth Century, royal 8vo. LARGE PAPER, *stiff cover,* 3*s* 6*d*

SIX COPIES only printed on a large thick writing paper.

3394 NORWICH—Hinds (Bp. Samuel) The Clergy Address on the Romish Movement, presented to the Lord Bishop of Norwich, on Saturday, Dec. 7, and his Lordship's Reply, 12mo. *sewed*, 5*s* *Norwich, C. Muskett*, 1850

With an autograph note of the Bishop's, dated Palace, Dec. 11, 1850.

3395 — History of the City and County of Norwich, from the earliest Accounts to the present time, *maps and plates*, 8vo. *both parts, scarce*, 10*s* 6*d* .. *Norwich, John Crouse*, 1768

3396 — Kemp's Nine Daies Wonder; performed in a Daunce from London to Norwich, Edited with Notes, by A. Dyce, 4to. *cloth*, 5*s* .. .. .. *Camden Soc.*, 1840

3397 — Kett's Rebellion in Norwich, History of, June to August, 1549, with a Chronology of Remarkable Events to 1843, 8vo. *half calf*, 3*s* .. .. .. .. 1844

3398 — Kirkpatrick's (John) Notes concerning Norwich Castle, 8vo. *cloth*, 6*s* .. .. .. 1847

3399 — Literary Institution, Catalogue of the Library of the Norfolk and Norwich Literary Institution, 8vo. *cloth, neat*, with all the Appendices, 15*s* .. *Norwich*, 1842-1859

3400 — Madders, (Mrs.) Rambles in an Old City, 8vo. *cloth*, 10*s* 6*d* 1855

3401 — Map of the City, 4to. 6*d*, and with Views of Buildings round the margins, 1*s*

3402 — Mason's (Francis) Sermon in the Greenyard at Norwich, in 1605, 4to. *sewed*, 2*s* 6*d* .. .. *Reprinted*, 1705

On "the authority of the Church in making Canons and Constitutions concerning things indifferent, and the obedience thereto required." "I thought I might do an acceptable piece of service to the church, and I hope to the Dissenters too, by reprinting this short and succinct discourse; the author was an eminent and learned divine."—*Editor*.

3403 — Memoirs Illustrative of the History and Antiquities of Norfolk, and the City of Norwich, *numerous plates*, 8vo. *cloth*, 12*s*, (*pub. at* £1 1*s*) .. .. .. 1851

The proceedings of the Archæological Institute held in Norwich, in July, 1847.

3404 — Merchants' Marks of the City, Notices of, by Mr. W. C. Ewing, 12 *plates*, imperial 8vo. *sewed*, 7*s* 6*d* *Norwich, C. Muskett*, 1850

3405 — another copy, 12 *plates*, folio, *half morocco*, £1 1*s* *ib.*, 1850

Only 10 copies struck off on this sized paper, and but 2 left.

3406 — Moral and Religious Aphorisms, (1000 of them) small 8vo. *old binding, scarce*, 10*s* 6*d* *Norwich, for Thomas Goddard*, 1703

This is a very early book printed in Norwich; the earliest known is dated 1701, unless we reckon those by Anthony de Solempne in 1570.

3407 — New District Schools, St. Augustine's Gates, Norwich, Statements respecting, 8vo. *sewed*, 1*s* .. *Norwich*, 1838

3408 — New Synagogue, Order of Service used for its Consecration, Sept. 6, A. M. 5609, Dr. Adler, Chief Rabbi, and Simon Asher, Officiated, 8vo. *sewed*, 1*s* 6*d*

3409 — Norwich Chronology from 1700 to 1801, with large Additions of Cuttings from Newspapers; Particulars of the Trial of Hadfield for Shooting at King George III. in Drury Lane Theatre, 1800, also of Lord Nelson's Nile Victory, &c. with MS. Remarks, 8vo. *stiff cover, curious*, £1 1*s* .. 1700 to 1801

3410 NORWICH Mercury, 1839, 1840, and 1841, in 1 vol. atlas folio, *neatly half bound,* 10s

3411 — Norwich Pageants, The Grocer's Play, from a MS. in possession of Robert Fitch, Esq., F.G.S., royal 8vo. LARGE PAPER, *embossed cover,* 7s 6d .. .. *Norwich, C. Muskett,* 1856

10 copies only printed of this most curious document on this sized paper.

3412 — Observations on the Controversy about the Mode of Assessment for the Poor's Rate in Norwich, *Norwich,* 1785.—Gardiner's Letter to Sir H. Harbord, on the Conduct of Thomas W. Coke, Esq. of Holkham, 1778.—Edward Rigby's Reports of the Special Provision Committee, in Court of Guardians, Norwich, 1788.—Mascall's Tables of the Net Duties payable on Imports and Exports, &c. 1787, in 1 vol. 8vo. *hf. cf.* 4s .. V.Y.

3413 — Peck's (Tho.) Norwich Directory, with a Concise History of the City, *map,* 8vo. *bds.* 2s 6d .. .. 1801

3414 — another edition, with Addenda, by Thomas Peck, *map,* 8vo. *boards, scarce,* 3s .. *Norwich, J. Payne,* 1802

3415 — Public Library, New Catalogue of the Books in the Public Library of the City of Norwich, with an Account of Mr. John Kirkpatrick's Roman and other Coins, 4to. *half morocco, uncut,* VERY SCARCE, 15s

*Norwich, printed by William Chase in the Cockey Lane,* 1732

3416 — — Catalogue of the Books in the Norwich Public and City Library, methodically arranged, with 5 Appendices, 8vo. *boards,* 6s .. .. .. *Norwich,* 1825

3417 — — new edition, with the Appendix, 8vo. *cloth,* 8s *Norwich,* 1847-56

3418 — Norwich Poll, taken Feb. 2, 1714, Robert Bene and Richard Berney, Esqrs., Candidates, small 8vo. (wants title) *newly bound in calf, very scarce,* 10s 6d *Norwich, Tho. Goddard,* 1716

3419 — Poll Book for 1734, 4to. *old calf, neat,* 10s 6d

*Norwich, T. Goddard,* 1735

Very scarce. Candidates, Sir Edward Ward and Miles Branthwayt, Horatio Walpole, Waller Bacon, and Thomas Vere, Esqrs.

3420 — Poll Book, July, 1830, 8vo. *sewed,* 2s *Norwich,* 1830

R. H. Gurney, Esq. and Rob. Grant, Esq. returned.

3421 — Poll Book, Dec. 1832, 8vo. *sewed,* 2s *Norwich,* 1832

Lord Stormont and Sir James Scarlet returned.

3422 — Poll Book, at Norwich, Candidates, Sir S. Bignold, A. Hamond, Esq., 8vo. *sewed,* 1s .. .. *Norwich,* 1854

3423 — Prints—Norwich Cathedral, from Cowgate Street, 4to. *coloured,* 2s, *Ninham.*—Fish Market, (now taken down) 4to. *coloured,* 3s.—South View of Norwich, rainbow, 4to. *coloured,* 2s.—Castle, oblong 4to. *coloured,* 2s.—Valley of Thorpe, from Butter Hills, oblong 4to. *coloured,* 2s .. .. 1842

3424 — REMNANTS of ANTIQUITY in Norwich, large folio, *half morocco, gilt top,* £2 2s

*Privately printed by the late Mr. C. Muskett, Norwich,* 1845

As but 10 copies of this now very rare work were printed on this size (and but this remains for sale), it will be next to impossible to procure one in a very short time. It consists of 40 plates, lithographed by Mr. Henry Ninham. The stones are destroyed. Subjects, Spandrills, Doorways, &c. &c.

3425 NORWICH—Smith's (Rev. Theyre T.) Ordination Sermon, Nov. 23, 1851, in Norwich Cathedral, 8vo. *sewed*, 1*s* 1852

3426 — Stanley (Rev. Edward) Address to the Parishioners of Alderley, Jan. 1, 1828.—His Address to his Parishioners after 25 years Residence among them, 1831.—Farewell Address to his Parishioners, June 4, 1837, *not published*, *Macclesfield*, 1837.—3 Tracts, 8vo. *sewed*, 2*s* 6*d* .. .. .. V.Y.

The Rev. Edward Stanley was inducted to the Rectory of Alderley, Nov. 16, 1805; and elected Bp. of Norwich, Ap. 29, 1837.

3427 — — Funeral Sermon, for Bp. Stanley, Sep. 23, 1849, by Dean Pellew, 8vo. *sewed*, 1*s* .. .. *Norwich*, 1849

3428 — Topographical and Historical Account of the City and County of Norwich, its Antiquities, &c., *map and view of the Cathedral*, 12mo. *boards*, 3*s* .. .. *Norwich, Stacy*, 1819

3429 — — another edition, *plan*, 8vo. *boards*, 4*s* 6*d* .. 1819

3430 — Wodehouse (Canon) Letter to the Bishop of Norwich, July, 1850, with his Lordship's Reply, 8vo. *sewed*, 1*s* *Norwich, C. Muskett*, 1851

3431 — Woodward's (Samuel, F.G.S.) History and Antiquities of Norwich Castle, *coloured maps and plates*, 4to. *cloth*, 12*s* (*pub. at* 21*s*) *Norwich, C. Muskett*, 1847

3432 NOSTRODAMO (Gio.) Vite delli piu Celebri et Antichi primi poeti Provenzali, trad. in Italiana per Gio. Giudici, small 8vo. *old vellum wrapper*, 10*s* 6*d* .. *Lione, A. Marsilii*, 1575

"Raro."—*Haym.* In this scarce little volume are 76 lives.

3433 NOTHING NEW, Tales by the Author of John Halifax, Gentleman, 2 vols. small 8vo. *cloth*, 10*s* 6*d* (*pub. at* 21*s*) 1857

3434 NOTICES to Correspondents, consisting of 10,000 Editorial Answers to Questions, supplying Information which cannot otherwise be obtained, small 8vo. *cloth, new, gilt*, 2*s* 6*d* .. 1859

3435 NOTTI Romane (Le) al Sepolcro de' Scipioni, 2 vols. 12mo. *foreign binding, neat*, 3*s* 6*d* .. .. *Milano*, 1816

3436 NOUVEAU Dictionnaire Historique-Portatif, de tous les Hommes qui se sont fait un Nom par des Talens, des Vertus, &c. depuis le commencement du monde jusqu' à nos jours, par une Société de Gens de Lettres, 4 vols. 8vo. *hf. cf. neat*, 12*s* *Amsterdam*, 1770

3437 NOVISSIMA Tuba, libellus, in VI. Dialogos apprimè Christianos, digestus, 18mo. *old calf, neat*, 2*s* 6*d* *Londini, F. Kyngston*, 1632

3438 NOVUM Testamentum, see *Testament* in various Languages

3439 NUGENT'S (Lord) Lands, Classical and Sacred, *map*, 2 vols. post 8vo. *cloth*, 8*s* (*pub. at* 18*s*) .. .. 1845

3440 NUGENT'S French and English Dictionary, sq. 12mo. *neat*, 4*s* 1793

3441 NUOVA Raccolta d' opus coli Scientifici, e Filologici, vol. 10 only, 12mo. *sewed, uncut*, 2*s* .. .. *Venezia*, 1763

3442 NURSEY'S (Rev. Perry) Evening, with other Poems, post 8vo. *boards*, 3*s* (*pub. at* 7*s* 6*d*) .. *Norwich*, 1829

3443 NUTT'S (Thomas) Humanity to Honey Bees, Practical Directions for their Management, *plates*, post 8vo. *cloth*, 4*s* 6*d* (*pub. at* 10*s*) *Wisbech*, 1834

3444 OCEAN (The) Spiritually Reviewed and Compared to Passing Scenes on Land, with Anecdotes, by the Author of the Retrospect, &c. *frontispiece*, 12mo. *calf, elegant*, 3*s* 6*d* (*cost* 9*s*) .. 1824

3445 OCKLEY'S (Simon) Translation from the Arabic of Abu Jaafar Ebn Tophail's Life of Hai Ebn Yokdhan, written above 500 years ago, *plates*, 8vo. *calf, neat*, 4*s* 6*d* .. .. 1708

"A very faithful translation," With an appendix "on the possibility of man's attaining the true knowledge of God."

3446 — Account of South-West Barbary, written by a person who had been a Slave there, *map*, 8vo. *old calf, neat*, 4*s* .. 1713

Also, two letters, one from the present King of Morocco (in Arabic) to Colonel Kirk, the other to Sir Cloudesley Shovel.

3447 OCLANDUS (Christ.) Anglorum Prælia, 1327-1558, Carmine perstricta. Item, de pacatissimo Angliæ Statu, imperante Elizabetha Narratio. Hiis Alexandri Nevilli Kettum adjunximus, sm. 8vo. *old calf, neat*, 10*s* 6*d* .. *Londini, R. Nuberie*, 1582

"Rare, Dawson Turner, 1820. This book belonged to the collection of the late James Bindley, Esq. in whose handwriting is the note upon the fly leaf at the end." Queen Elizabeth ordered this book to be received and publicly read and taught in all Grammar and Free Schools in the Kingdom.

3448 OFFICES of Our Church, for the Communion, Baptism, Matrimony, &c. 8vo. *black calf*, 5*s* *Oxford, the Clarendon*, 1855

3449 OFFICIUM Diurnum, ex decreto S. S. Concilii Tridentini restitutum, *nicely engraved plates*, 8vo. *old calf, scarce*, 7*s* 6*d* *Antverpiæ, C. Plantini*, 1594

This is printed in red and black. Cum privilegiis.

3450 OFFICIUM Hominis et Preces privatæ, 12mo. *old calf, neat*, 3*s* *Londini*, 1693

3451 OGDEN'S (Dr. S.) Sermons, 3 vols. small 8vo. *old calf, neat*, 6*s* *Cambridge*, 1780

"Ogden holds the highest rank amongst the most eminent preachers."—*Dr. Beardmore's Specimens of Literary Resemblance.* Presentation copy from Mr. W. Mason, of Necton, to Mrs. Pyle, 1781

3452 — another very fine copy, *in old calf*, 7*s* .. *ib.*, 1780

3453 OGILVY'S (Geo., Esq., *of Cove*,) Popular Objections to the Premillenial Advent and to the Study of the Prophetic Scriptures considered, 12mo. *cloth*, 2*s* (*pub. at* 4*s*) *Edinburgh*, 1842

3454 OLD ENGLAND; a Pictorial Museum of Regal, Ecclesiastical, Baronial, Municipal, and Popular Antiquities, *hundreds of plates*, 2 vols. folio, *nicely half bound in calf*, £1 15*s* (*cost* £3) *Charles Knight*, 1845

3455 OLD ENGLISH Baron, by Clara Reeve, and Castle of Otranto, by Horace Walpole, *plates*, 18mo. *boards*, 2*s* .. 1826

3456 OLDFIELD'S (H. G.) Anecdotes of Archery, Ancient and Modern, *plates*, 12mo. *calf, gilt, gilt edges*, 3*s* 6*d* .. 1791

"Traces the practice from the earliest nations."

3457 OLD PLAYS.—Cleomenes, the Spartan Hero, trag. by Dryden, with the Life of Cleomenes, 1692.—Dutchess of Malfey, trag. (Webster's Play adapted to the Theatre), 1678.—Heroic Love, trag. by Hon. Geo. Granville, 1698.—Iphigenia, trag. by Dennis, 1700.—Island Queens, or the Death of Mary Queen of Scotland, trag. by Jo. Banks, 1684, dedicated to the illustrious Princess Mary, Dutchess of Norfolk.—The Ingratitude of a Commonwealth, by N. Tate, 1682, (this is an adaptation of Shakspeare's CORIOLANUS).—History of KING LEAR, from Shakspeare, by N.

Tate, 1699.—History of King RICHARD the SECOND, from Shakspere, by N. Tate, 1681, (with the Prefatory Vindicatory Epistle to Geo. Raynsford, Esq., occasioned by the Prohibition of this Play on the stage)—Sophonisba, trag. by Nath. Lee, 1697.—TITUS ANDRONICUS; or, the Rape of Lavinia, trag. altered from Shakspeare by Edw. Ravenscroft, 1687.—Venice Preserved, trag. by Tho. Otway, 1696.—Vertue Betrayed; or, Anna Bullen, trag. by John Banks, 1692.—The Villain, trag. by T. Porter, Esq., 1694.—in 1 vol. 4to. *half bound, neat,* £2 2*s* .. V.Y.

Here are 13 Plays, most of them original editions, including 4 of Shakspeare's.

3458 OLD PLAY.—The Rover; or, the Banish't Cavaliers, original edition, small 4to. *half bound,* 4*s* 6*d* .. 1677

"By Mrs. Aphra Behn; very entertaining, much business, bustle and intrigue."—*Baker's Biog. Dramat.* Autograph of "*Wm. West,* 1727." Marginal MS. Notes and alterations.

3459 OLD POETRY.—ANTHOLOGIA; seu, Selecta quædam Poemata Italorum qui Latine scripserunt, 12mo. *old calf,* 5*s* *Londini,* 1684

3460 — D'Avenant (Sir William) Gondibert, an Heroick Poem, with the Author's Preface to Mr. Hobs and Mr. Hobs's Answer, also Commendatory Poems by Waller and Cowley, sm. 8vo. *stained,* 3*s* 6*d* .. .. .. *John Holden,* 1651

3461 — [Donne's (John, *Deane of St. Paul's*)] Poems, by J. D., with Elegies on the Author's Death, small 8vo. *old calf, neat,* 12*s* *For John Marriot,* 1639

For an account of Dr. Donne's Poems see *Retrospective Review,* vol. 8

3462 — Douza (Jan.) Poemata pleraque Selecta; Petr. Scriverius descripsit, collegit, ac junctim edidit, small 8vo. 700 pages, *a fine clean copy in old vellum wrapper,* 9*s* *Lugd. Bat., Tho. Basson,* 1609

Consists of Epigrams, Odes, Epodes, Satires, Love and other Songs.

3463 — Dunbar (John) Epigrammaton Joannis Dunbari Megalo-Britanni Centuriæ Sex, Decades totidem, small 8vo. *in the original vellum wrapper, a fine clean copy* £15 *Londini, ex typographeo Thomæ Purfootij,* 1616

"It is said there is a copy of this EXTREMELY RARE Book in the British Museum, and a copy sold at Mr. Bright's sale for the above sum. Lowndes says there should be 236 pages, but there are in this 238 pages, there being after page 91 in this copy an unpaged leaf dedicated to Prince Charles, which was probably not in that Mr. Lowndes collated. The book itself is dedicated to King James the First, and there is a long Panegyric on him occupying four entire leaves. The little volume is very curious as containing remarks on a great number of eminent persons, the author's contemporaries, on whom the Epigrammes are written. Besides the six hundred Epigrams, there is, at the end, an addenda of 10 Epigrams to each century, making 660 in all. It is extremely difficult to find anything about this book, but reference is made to it in *Mr. David Irving's Lives of the Scottish Poets,* vol. 2, p. 257

3464 — Fasciculus Florum; or, a Nosegay of Flowers, translated out of the Gardens of severall Poets, and other authors, 12mo. *old binding,* 12*s* .. .. *London, by A.M.,* 1636

Sold at Sir Mark Sykes's auction for 19*s*—at Mr. Heber's for 16*s*.

3465 — Florilegium Epigrammatum, Gr. et Lat., authore Tho. Farnabio, 12mo. *old binding,* 4*s* .. .. *Londini,* 1671

3466 — Haddon—Poematum Gualteri Haddoni, Legum Doctoris, sparsim collectorum, Libri duo, small 8vo. *unbound,* 10*s* *Londini, apud Guil. Seresium,* 1576

Collates from A. to K. in eights. Something wanting at the end. See *Beloe's Anecdotes,* v. 5, p. 217-23

3467 OLD POETRY—Howell's (James, Esq.) Poems upon divers emergent Occasions, 8vo. *old binding*, £1 10*s* (in the *Bib. Ang. Poet.* £3 6*s*) *Ja. Cotterel*, 1664

With the Dedication "to the innately noble Dr. Will. King, Bp. of Chichester," by Payne Fisher, the editor, with his long Poem of 8 pages, in Latin Hexameters, in which he eulogizes Howell's various works. The last 8 leaves are unfortunately injured by rats.

3468 — Oldham's (John) Works, with his Remains, *portrait by Vdr. Gucht*, 8vo. *old calf*, 4*s* 6*d* .. .. 1704

Contents.—Satires on the Jesuits, written in 1679, occasioned by the Popish Plot of 1678. The Passion of Byblis, out of Ovid. Translations of Horace, Juvenal, &c.—"*E. Libris Caroli Trelawny.*"

3469 — Overbury, (Sir Thomas) his Wife, with additions of new characters, and many other witty Conceits never before printed, small 8vo. *original state*, 15*s* *John Haviland*, 1638

This is the 16th impression of this little volume, of which Mr. *Neve* says, "The nice distinctions of moral character, and the pattern of female excellence here drawn, contrasted as they were with the heinous and flagrant enormities of the Countess of Essex, rendered this poem extremely popular, when its ingenious author was no more." See also the *Retrospective Review*, vol. 2.

3470 — Ovid's Heroycall Epistles, in English Verse, set out and translated by George Turbervile, Gent., small 8vo. **Black Letter**, 1st edition, and *original vellum wrapper*, £2 2*s* *John Charlewood, no date.*

This is sadly deficient. It wants the title. But has the Dedication to "Lorde Thomas Howard, Viscount Byndon," and other introductory matter occupying 4 leaves. It then collates from B. to T. in eights, V. has only the 4 first leaves. Q. wants the last leaf. The fore-edges are otherwise much dilapidated by damp. It may do to perfect another copy. A perfect copy of 168 leaves (for it is not paged) is priced in the Bib. Ang. Poet. £12, there are here 151 leaves.

3471 — [Pordage (Samuel)] Poems upon several Occasions, by S. P., Gent., small 8vo. *stained*, 12*s* *By W. G., for Henry Marsh*, 1660

For an account of this author see *Censura Literaria*, v. 8, p. 247.

3472 — — Troades Englished, small 8vo. imperfect, page 33 to the end, 4*s* .. .. .. .. *ib.*, 1660

3473 — Ripley's (George) Compound of Alchymy; conteining the right and perfectest meanes to make the Philosopher's Stone, Aurum potabile, &c., set foorth by Raph Rabbards, Gentleman, small 4to. *old calf, neat, rare*, £5 5*s* *Thomas Orwin*, 1591

In the Bibliotheca Anglo Poetica at £10. This singular book is dedicated by Raph Rabbards, to Queen Elizabeth, of whom there is a wood-cut portrait, there are also complimentary verses by Thomas Newton, P. Bales, Sir Edward Kelly, and others. And the value of this copy is enhanced by various marginal MS. "*Corrections conforme to the Latin coppie, done by Sr. Ed. Kelly, printed Cassellis*, 1649," and signed "*Thomas Houissime Naturæ Curiosus.*" It has also at the end a leaf, not contained in that described in the Bib. Ang. Poet., in which is a notice, that "but a small number of these bookes were imprinted."

3474 — Sandys's (George, *7th son of the Abp. of York*) Christ's Passion, a Tragedy, with annotations, small 8vo. *calf, very neat*, 12*s* 1640

Dedicated to K. Charles I., with 5 pages of Commendatory verses, by Lord Falkland. Dr. Warton thinks that Sandys did more to polish and tune the English versification than Denham or Waller, and Dryden has pronounced him the best versifier of his age.

3475 — Vaughan's (William, *Knight*) Church Militant, historically continued from the yeare of our Saviour's Incarnation, 33, untill this present 1640, small 8vo. 378 pages, *a very fine clean copy in its original binding*, RARE, £2 2*s* *For Tho. Paine*, 1640

Preceding this Poem is a metrical Preface on 10 unpaged leaves, inscribed to "The Right Hon. Richard, Earle of Carbery." Vaughan and Carbery are both Welsh names.

3476 OLD POETRY—Wallace—The Life and Acts of the most famous and valiant Champion Sir William Wallace, Knight of Ellerslie, maintainer of the Liberty of Scotland, thick 12mo. of 330 pages, **Black Letter**, *original binding*, RARE, £1 1*s*
*Glasgow, by Robert Sanders, one of his Majesties printers*, 1685

To this edition, (which is not noticed by Lowndes,) is prefixed, a large Preface of 27 pages, by the Printer, "containing a short sum of the History of that time."

3477 — Watson (James) Choise Collection of Comic and Serious Scots Poems, both Ancient and Modern, 3 parts in 1 vol. (all published,) 8vo. *original Scotch binding*, RARE, £1 5*s* *Edinburgh*, 1713

Part 1, is the 2nd edit. 1713.—Part 2, is dated, 1709.—Part 3, 1711.

3478 OLD Roads and New Roads, 12mo. *stiff covers*, 1*s* 1852

3479 OLD Religion, a Brief Survey of the, a Guide to all passengers to keep the Old-good-way to Heaven, small 8vo. *old calf*, 3*s* 6*d*
*No place*, 1672

Privately printed (apparently at Amsterdam) in the Jeer, 1672.

3480 OLDYS'S (W.) British Librarian; an abstract of our most scarce, useful, and valuable Books, 8vo. *nice copy, in hf. cf*, 10*s* 6*d* 1738

"A work of no common occurrence, or mean value, it is rigidly correct in bibliographical information."—*MS.*

3481 OLLENDORFF Méthode pour l'Etude de la Langue Allemande, per Rosenberg, 12mo. *half bound*, 2*s* 6*d* *Geneve*, 1847

3482 — Grammaire Italienne, par Simler, 12mo. *cloth*, 2*s* 6*d*
*Francfort*, 1851

3483 OMNIUM Gentium Mores, Leges, et Ritus, ex multis Scriptoribus à Jo. Boëmo collecti, 12mo. *old vellum*, CURIOUS, 6*s*
*Antverpiæ, Jo. Stelsii*, 1562

America is not here described.

3484 OPERAS—Stradella, Robert the Devil, Maid of Artois, Tancredi, Italian and English, Bohemian Girl, La Semiramide, Italian and English, La Sonnambula, in English, 1*s* each.

3485 ORATIO Dominica, nimirum, plus CENTUM Linguis, Versionibus, aut characteribus redditus et expressa, 4to. *old calf, neat*, 9*s*
*Londini*, 1713

3486 ORATIO de Studiis liberalium Artium habita Lucæ ad decemviros, Senatumque Lucensem.—Epigrammata diversorum Auctorum, —Jacobi Sadoleti Cardinalis oratio de Pace, small 8vo. *sewed*, 4*s*
*Lucæ, apud V. Busdragum*, 1549

3487 ORDERICUS Vitalis, Ecclesiastical History of England and Normandy, translated with Notes, by T. Forester, vol. 1, post 8vo. *cloth*, 3*s* (*cost* 5*s*) .. .. *H. G. Bohn*, 1853

3488 ORDINANCE of the Lords and Commons for calling an Assembly of Divines to settle the Government and Liturgy of the Church of England, 4to. *half bound, neat*, 6*s* .. 1658

Subjoined is the humble advice of the Assembly of Divines to the Parliament concerning a Confession of Faith; the preface is signed Tho. Manton.

3489 ORDINATIONS of the Church of England, Vindication of, by Gilbert Burnet, afterwards Bp. of Salisbury, 8vo. *old calf neat*, 4*s* 6*d* .. .. .. .. 1677

Has another Treatise in the same volume Englished by him, a "Letter writ by the last Assembly General of the Clergy of France to the Protestants, inviting them to return to their Communion, with the methods proposed by them for their conviction, examined."—1683.

3490 ORFORD'S (Lord) Reminiscences written in 1788 for the amusement of Miss Mary and Miss Agnes B(err)y, 12mo. *boards*, 5*s* *Sharpe*, 1818

"In these miscellanies are to be found many keen and correct remarks on Society, and on Men and Manners of the age in which Walpole lived."—*Gent's Mag., Jan.* 1853

3491 ORIENTAL Field Sports, exhibiting the Natural History of the Elephant, Rhinoceros, Tiger, Leopard, Bear, Wolf, &c., &c. from Capt. Williamson's designs, by E. Orme, 40 *spirited plates, by Howett*, 2 vols. 4to. *fine copy, in russia, gilt*, £1 16*s* *Bulmer*, 1808

3492 ORIENTAL Manuscript, written on the Bark of a Tree, 22 feet long by 7 inches wide, written on both sides, with singularly rude drawings of various animals, as Elephants, Scorpions, Crocodiles, Insects, Human Figures, Boats, &c., folded into the form of a book, about 7 by 6 inches square, 100 *Guineas*.

In Mr. Horne's *Introduction to the Study of Bibliography*, vol. 1, p. 43, I read, "The Books of the Battas (one of the nations inhabiting the Island of Sumatra) are composed of the inner bark of a certain tree, cut into long strips, and folded in squares, leaving part of the wood at each extremity to serve for the outer covering. For this purpose, the bark is shaved smooth and thin, and afterwards rubbed over with rice-water; the pen employed is a twig or the fibre of a leaf, and their ink is made of the soot of *dammar* (a species of resin or turpentine) mixed with the juice of the sugar-cane. One of these books in the *Batta* character is in the Slonian Library, (No. 4726,) written in perpendicular columns on a long piece of bark folded up so as to represent a book. The Sumatran Manuscripts of any bulk and importance are written on the inner bark of a tree, cut into slips of several feet in length, and folded together in squares; each square or fold answering to a page or leaf."

The book above described answers in every particular to this account, excepting only that it is not written perpendicularly, but from left to right, which proves it to be Birman or some language allied to that family of languages. The character of which it is composed is not given either in Mr. Bagster's most interesting Book the "Bible of every Land;" in Mr. Bernard's Table of Alphabets of nearly 200 languages, improved by Mr. Morton, Librarian of the British Museum in 1776; in the Oratio Dominica, plus centum Linguis, or in Mr. Astle's Origin of Writing.

3493 ORLANDI (Fr. P. Antonio) Notizie degli Scrittori Bolognesi, e dell' opere loro Stampate e Manoscritte, 4to. *good copy, in calf, scarce*, 8*s* .. .. .. *Bologna*, 1714

3494 ORME'S (Robert) Historical Fragments of the Mogul Empire of the Morattoes, and of the English concerns in Industan from the year 1659, with the Life and Writings of the Author, *portrait & maps*, 4to, *boards*, 12*s* .. .. 1805

3495 ORME'S (William) Bibliotheca Biblica; a select List of Books on Sacred Literature, with Notices biographical, critical, and bibliographical, 8vo. *half cloth, scarce*, 10*s* 6*d* *Edinburgh*, 1824

3496 ORMOND—Memoirs of the Life of his Grace, James, late Duke of Ormond, *portrait* 8vo. *neat, scarce*, 6*s* .. 1738

This is the History of his Amours, &c., extracted from his own private Memoirs, printed at the Hague. Not mentioned in *Lowndes*.

3497 — His Life, with an Historical Account of his Grace's Family, *portrait*, 8vo. *old calf, neat*, 5*s* .. .. 1747

3498 ORMEROD (Archdeacon) Visitation Sermon, 8vo. *sewed*, 1*s* *Norwich, Muskett*, 1845

3499 OROSIUS—Anglo-Saxon Version from that Historian, by Alfred the Great, with an English translation, by Daines Barrington, 8vo. *fine copy, in old calf, gilt*, 12*s* 6*d* .. 1773

3500 OROSII (Pauli, *Presbyteri Hispani)* adversus Paganos Historiarum libri VII., et Apologeticus contra Pelagium, cum Notis, F. F. Marcodurano, thick 8vo. *old calf, neat,* 8*s* *Coloniæ,* 1582

In 414 Orosius went to Hippo and studied a year under St. Augustine. In 415 to Jerusalem to consult St. Jerom, on his return, by St. Agustine's advice, he wrote this History which extends to A.D. 416. See *Dr. Adam Clarke.*

3501 ORPHANS, a Chapter in Life, by the author of Margaret Maitland, (Mrs. Oliphant) post 8vo. *cloth,* 5*s* 6*d* (*pub. at* 10*s* 6*d*) 1858

3502 ORR'S Circle of the Sciences—Practical Astronomy, Navigation, Nautical Astronomy, and Meteorology, by Young, Breen, Scoffern, and Lowe, *plates,* 8vo. *cloth, gilt, new,* 5*s* 1856

3503 ORRERY (John Boyle, Earle of Corke and Orrery) Letters from Italy, in 1754-55, with Notes, &c., by John Duncombe, *frontispiece,* 12mo. *old calf, gilt,* 3*s* 6*d* .. 1773

The Preface contains a Life of the Earl, and the notes are very instructive.

3504 ORTELII (Abrahami, *Antverpiani*) Synonymia Geographica, 4to. *old vellum,* 7*s* 6*d* .. *Antverpiæ, C. Plantini,* 1578

Sir Christopher Hatton's copy, with this writing on the title-page. "*Generoso ac erudito Dno. Danieli Rogersio cognato suo cariss. Auctor D.D.*"

3505 OSBECK'S (Peter) Voyage to China and the East Indies, Englished by J. Reinhold Forster, *plates,* 2 vols. 8vo. *calf, neat,* 7*s* 1771

Contains also Olof Toreen's Voyage to Suratte, Captn. Eckeberg's Chinese Husbandry and a Faunula and Flora Sinensis.

3506 OSSIAN'S Poems, translated by James Macpherson, *plates,* 2 vols. 12mo. *old calf,* 6*s* .. *Perth, Morrison,* 1795

"The genius of the Scots has, in every age, shone conspicious in Poetry and Music. Of the first the Poems of Ossian, composed in an age of rude antiquity, are sufficient proof. The peevish doubt entertained, by some, of their authenticity, appears to be the utmost refinement of scepticism. As genuine remains of *Celtic* poetry, the Poems of Ossian will continue to be admired as long as there shall remain a taste for the *sublime and beautiful.*" *Tytler's Dissertation* on Scottish Music, appended to *James the First's Poetical Remains,* (which see No. 2350.) *Edinb.,* 1783, 8vo.

3507 OSTERVALD Catechisme; ou Instruction dans la Religion Chrétienne, 12mo. *bound,* 2*s* .. *Amsterdam,* 1707

3508 OTTONIS (Everardi) de Ædilibus Coloniarum et Municiporum liber singularis, small 8vo. *old calf, neat,* 5*s* *Francofurti,* 1719

An account of the dignity, privileges, &c of these roman magistrates, involving much curious and learned antiquarian research.

3509 OUGHTON (Thomæ) Ordo Judiciorum; sive, Methodus Procedendi in Negotiis et Litibus in Foro Ecclesiastico-Civili Britannico et Hibernico juxta *Norman Ordinis Judiciarii,* exhibentur, 2 vols. 4to. *old calf, neat,* 18*s* .. *Londini, impensis Authoris,* 1738

"A useful work."—*Lowndes.* With autograph of Capel Lofft.

3510 OVERBURY'S (Sir Thomas) Miscellaneous Works in Prose and Verse, now first collected, with a Life and Notes by E. F. Rimbault, *portrait after Pass,* fcap. 8vo. *cloth,* 5*s* *J. R. Smith,* 1857

3511 OVIDII Opera, Heinsii, 3 vols. in 1, 12mo. *vellum, very neat,* 8*s* *Amst., Elzevir,* 1676

This is a pocket edition of Ovid. Heinsius's text only, and not mentioned by bibliographers.

3512 — Opera, vol. 2, (Continens Metamorphoseon) 18mo. *vellum, neat,* 2*s* .. .. .. *L. Bat., Elzevir,* 1629

3513 OVIDII—Opera, recognovit, et argumentis distinxit J. A. Amar, 5 vols. 18mo. *hf. calf, neat,* 12*s* 6*d* *Parisiis, Lefevre,* 1822

3514 — Epistolæ, Joannis Scoppæ Expositiones, small folio, *old vellum,* 9*s* *Venetiis, apud J. M. Bonellum,* 1558

3515 — Fasti, Tristia, et de Ponto, small 8vo. *old calf, clean,* 3*s* 6*d* *Parisiis, S. Colinæus,* 1536

3516 — Fasti, with English Notes and an Introduction by Thomas Keightley, 8vo. *cloth,* 4*s* (*pub. at* 7*s* 6*d*) *Dublin,* 1833

3517 — Metamorphoseon lib. XV., R. R. Volaterrani luculentissima explanatio, cum novis J. Micylli additionibus, folio, *numerous cuts, old calf, neat, scarce,* 15*s* *Venetiis, apud I. Gryphium,* 1565

An uncommon edition with Annotations by Rhodiginus, Egnatius, Glareanus, Longolius, and other learned men.

3518 — Metamorphoses, 12mo. *bound,* 2*s* .. *Cantabrigiæ,* 1704

3519 — Metamorphoses, ad usum Delphini, 8vo. *bound,* 5*s* (*cost* 10*s* 6*d*) *Londini,* 1820

3520 — Metamorphoses Englished by George Sandys, *engraved title by Cecill, mounted,* folio, *old calf, neat,* 12*s* .. 1626

*Head of Ovid by W. Marshall.* "The best versifyer of the last age."—*Dryden of Sandys.* "English poetry owes much of its present beauty to Sandys' translations."—*Pope's Iliad.*

3521 — Metamorphoses, translated by Sandys, 12mo. a portion of the work, pages 49 to 72, 97 to 146, 193 to 374, 401 to 412, may complete another copy, *sewed,* 2*s* 6*d* .. 1690

3522 — Metamorphoses, made English by several hands, with Mr. Sewell's Improvements, 2 vols. 12mo. *old calf,* 4*s* .. 1724

3523 — Metamorfosi di, ridotte da Gio Andrea dell' Anguillara in ottava Rima, con le Annotationi di M. Gio. Horologgi et Gli Argomenti et Postille di M. F. Turchi, *fine plates by Giacomo Franco,* 4to. *old calf, neat,* RARE, 18*s* *In Vinegia, presso Bern. Giunti,* 1584

The plates are much after the style of those illustrating Sir John Harington's Orlando Furioso, 1591.

3524 — il medesimo, *plates* 8vo. *russia, neat,* 12*s* *Venetia, Marc'Antonio Zaltieri,* 1610

"The Italian version of Ovid in Ottavo Rima, by Anguillara, is a work of great poetical merit."—*Tytler on Translation.*

3525 — Ciofani (Hercules) in Ovidii Observationes, 8vo. *old calf, wants title,* 2*s* 6*d* .. *Antwerpiæ, C. Plantini,* 1581

3526 OWEN'S (Ashford) Lost Love, post 8vo. *cloth, neat,* 4*s* 6*d* (*pub. at* 10*s* 6*d*) .. .. .. .. 1855

3527 OWEN (Dr. John) On the Nature, Power, Deceit and Prevalency of the Remainders of Indwelling Sin in Believers, small 8vo. *hf. cf. neat,* 2*s* 6*d* .. .. .. 1668

3528 — new edition, with an Essay by Dr. T. Chalmers, 12mo. *calf, elegant,* 3*s* 6*d* (*cost* 7*s* 6*d*) .. *Glasgow, Collins,* 1825

3529 — Brief Instruction in the Worship of God, and Discipline of the Churches of the New Test., 12mo. *bound,* 2*s* 6*d* 1688

3530 OXENHAM'S (W.) English Notes for Latin Elegiacs, 12mo. *cloth,* 2*s* (*pub. at* 4*s*) .. .. .. 1849

3531 OXENSTIERN'S (Count, *Swedish Ambassador,*) Memorial to the Emperor of Austria, stating the Case of the Oppressed Protestants of Germany and Hungary, folio, 4 *leaves, scarce,* 5*s* *Tho. Newcomb,* 1674

3532 OXFORD—Theatri Oxoniensis Encænia Jul. 11, an. 1679, celebrata, *broadside*, 4*s* .. .. *E Theatro Sheldon.* 1679
3533 — Quæstiones in Sacræ Theologiæ, Jure Civili et Medicina, discutiendæ Oxonii, Julii 12, 1679, *broadside*, 4*s* *Oxonii*, 1679
3534 — Nowell's (Dr. Thomas, *Principal of St. Mary's Hall,*) Answer to 'Pietas Oxoniensis' wherein the Grounds of the Expulsion of Six Members from St. Edmund's Hall are set forth, 8vo. *calf, neat,* 3*s* 6*d* .. .. *Oxford, Clarendon*, 1769
3535 — Oxford University and City Guide, also of Blenheim, Nuneham, &c. *map and plates*, 12mo. *stiff covers*, 2*s* *Oxford*, 1828
3536 — Oxford University Calendar, 12mo. *boards*, 4*s* .. 1858
3537 — Oxford, Cambridge, Southampton, and Isle of Wight Guides, 4 vols. in 1, 12mo. *maps and plates, calf, neat*, 5*s* *Oxford*, 1759-91
3538 — Oxford Latin Prize Poems, Translations of by Nicholas Lee Torre, new series, part 1, 12mo. *cloth*, 2*s* 6*d* *(pub. at 5s)* 1848
3539 PADUA—Historia di Padova, di Sertorio Orsato, parte prima, dalla sua fondazione sino l' anno 1173, (all published) *many plates*, folio, *fine copy in calf*, 10*s* 6*d* .. *Padova*, 1678
3540 — Pitture, Sculture, Architetture, ed altre cose Notabili di Padova descritte da Pietro Brandolese, *Plan of the City*, 12mo. *half calf, very neat*, 2*s* 6*d* .. .. *Padova*, 1795
3541 PAGE (John) Jus Fratrum, the Law of Brethren, touching the Power of Parents, and the Customes in several Counties, 12mo. *bound*, 3*s* .. .. .. .. 1658
3542 PAGET'S (C. J. and James) Sketch of the Natural History of Yarmouth and its Neighbourhood, 8vo. *bds, scarce*, 12*s*, *Yarmouth*, 1834
3543 PAGET'S (F. E.) Tales of the Village, 18mo, *cloth*, 2*s* 1840
3544 PAINE'S (Thomas) Life, with a Review of his Rights of Man, by Francis Oldys, of Philadelphia, added is The Rights of Man, parts 1 and 2, in 1 vol. 8vo. *calf, neat, scarce*, 6*s* 1792

The Rights of Man is an Answer to Mr. Burke's attack on the French Revolution, see *Burke* and *Bp. Watson.*

3545 PAINTERS, Sculptors, Architects, and Engravers, Dictionary of, containing Biographical Sketches of Celebrated Artists; with an Appendix comprising the Substance of Walpole's Anecdotes of Painting in England, thick 12mo. *boards*, 4*s* 6*d* (*pub. at* 10*s* 6*d*) .. .. .. .. 1810
3546 PAINTING—The Art of Painting in Miniature, with the Method of Mixing Colours, 2 *plates*, 12mo. *scarce*, 2*s* .. 1752
3547 — Lectures on Painting by the Royal Academicians, Barry, Opie, Fuseli, with Critical Notes by R. H. Wornum, post 8vo. *cloth*, 3*s* 6*d* (*cost* 5*s*) .. .. *H. G. Bohn*, 1848
3548 PAINTINGS in OIL of the celebrated NELL GWYNN, and Louise de Querouille, DUCHESS of PORTSMOUTH, see Charles II. No. 1027.
3549 — Two other Portraits of MARY, QUEEN of Scots, and THOMAS HOWARD, 4th Duke of Norfolk, to whom she was affianced, 10 in. by 9 in., *Painter unknown, but well executed*, £10 10*s*

These are oval, and are striking resemblances to those portraits of these distinguished personages found in Houbraken and Vertue's Heads by Dr. Birch.

3550 PALÆONTOGRAPHICAL SOCIETY; Wood's (Searles V.) Monograph of the Crag Mollusca, part 1, Univalves, 21 *plates*, 4to. *sewed*, 18*s* .. .. .. 1848

Shells from the Middle and Upper Tertiaries of the East of England.

3551 PALÆPHATI de Incredibilibus, Gr. et. Lat., edidit, notasque adjecit M. Brunnerus, small 8vo. *old calf, neat*, 6*s* *Upsaliæ*, 1663

Some suppose Palæphatus lived before Homer, others that he was contemporary with Alexander the Great. His name is wholly omitted in Mr. Rosse's "Index of Dates."

3552 PALERMO—Caii (Pauli) Jura Municipalia; seu, Consuetudines Foelicis Urbis Panhormi, 4to. *limp vellum, wormed*, 6*s* *Venetiis, Pauli Peguli, Panhormi Bibliopolæ*, 1575

3553 — Capitoli del Governo ed Amministratione della Tavola di questa felice Citta di Palermo, 4to. *limp vellum, scarce*, 5*s* *Palermo, per Decio Cirillo*, 1634

3554 PALERMO'S (Evangelist) Grammar of the Italian Language, 8vo. *old calf*, 2*s* 6*d* .. .. .. 1768

3555 PALESTINE—Early Travels in Palestine, Edited, with Notes, by Thomas Wright, Esq., *map*, post 8vo. *cloth*, 3*s* (*cost* 5*s*) *H. G. Bohn*, 1848

Arculf, Willibald, Bernard, Sæwulf, Sigurd, Benjamin of Tudela, Maundeville, La Brocquière, and Maundrell.

3556 — The Holy Land, Sketches of the Jews and the Land of Palestine, *map*, 12mo. *cloth*, 3*s* .. .. .. 1844

3557 PALEY'S (Edmund) Sermons, vol. 1 only, 8vo. *boards*, 2*s* 1825

3558 PALEY'S (Archdeacon) Works, with an Account of his Life and Writings, 6 vols. 8vo. best Edition, *fine copy, in brown russia*, £3 3*s* .. .. .. .. 1830

3559 — Principles of Moral and Political Philosophy, 2 vols. 8vo. *calf, very neat*, 6*s* .. .. .. 1787

3560 — Horæ Paulinæ; the Truth of the Scripture History of St Paul evinced by Comparison with the Acts of the Apostles, 8vo. *old calf, neat*, 4*s* .. .. .. 1794

3561 — Joyce's (Jeremiah) Analysis of Dr. Paley's Natural Theology, *Camb.*, 1804.—Le Grice's Analysis of Paley's Moral Philosophy, in 1 vol. 8vo. *half, calf, neat*, 3*s* 6*d* .. *Harlow*, 1807

3562 PALGRAVE'S (Sir F.) Merchant and the Friar, *frontispiece*, 12mo. *calf, very neat*, 5*s* 6*d* .. .. .. 1837

3563 PALINGENII (Marcelli) Zodaicus Vitæ, 12mo. *old binding*, 6*s* *Parisiis*, 1566

"This Poem, on which Palingenius had employed several years, brought him into trouble, as it contains many sarcastic remarks on Monks and Church Abuses." See *General Dict.* the 1st edit., was printed in 1536, at which time he was living.

3564 PALLAS (P.S.) Flora Rossica; (i.e. Russica) seu, Stirpium Imperii Rossici per Europam et Asiam indigenarum descriptiones et Icones, 101 *beautifully coloured plates*, parts 1 and 2, large folio, *half bound in russia, uncut*, £4 4*s* (*formerly priced* 10 *guineas*) *Petropoli*, (*St. Petersburgh*) *e typog. Imperiali*, 1784-88

This is all that was done of this "splendid work executed at the Empress Catharine's expense." The Rev. F. Bevan, late of Carlton Rode, to whom this copy belonged, has added a MS. Index to each part, this book is rarely procurable in this country. See *Coxe's and Clarke's Travels.*

3565 PALMER'S (Charles, *Deputy Serjeant of the H. of Commons)* Collection of Select Aphorisms and Maxims, 4to. *old calf, neat,* 7*s* 6*d* .. .. .. *E. Cave,* 1748

Scarce, not in Lowndes. Mr. Joseph John Gurney's copy, and this autograph, "*John Gurney, Earlham.*"

3566 PALMER'S (Samuel) Moral Essays on some of the most Curious and Significant English, Scotch, and Foreign Proverbs, 8vo. *old calf, neat,* 6*s* .. .. .. 1710

3567 PALMERIN of England, by Francisco de Moraes, from the original Portuguese, by Robert Southey, 4 vols. 12mo. *half russia, neat,* £1 4*s* .. .. .. .. 1807

3568 PALMYRENE Inscriptions taken from Wood's Ruins of Palmyra and Balbec, transcribed into the Ancient Hebrew Characters, and Englished by S. Salome, 8vo. *cloth,* 3*s* 6*d* 1830

3569 PANIZZI'S (Antonio) Extracts from Italian Prose Writers, for the use of Students in the London University, 12mo. *cloth,* 6*s* (*pub. at* 10*s* 6*d*) .. .. .. 1828

3570 — another copy, 12mo. *morocco, gilt leaves, by Hayday,* 10*s* 1828

These "Extracts are taken" as Mr. Panizzi says, "from the works of some of the most distinguished prose writers of Italy. Prose compositions are usually altogether disregarded; and yet Prose is the only means by which familiarity with a language can be acquired." See his *interesting Preface.*

3571 PANVINII (Onuphrii) Romanorum Principum libri IV., ejusdem de Comitiis Imperatoriis liber, folio, *fine copy, in old calf, gilt,* 12*s* .. .. .. *Basiliæ,* 1558

3572 — Fastorum libri V. a Romulo Rege usque ad Carolum V. Austrium Aug., ejusdem in Fastorum libros Commentarii, folio, *old vellum,* 12*s* .. .. *Venetiis, Vincentii Valgrisii,* 1558

At the end is the Appendix containing the Fasti Consulares, which contains Cassiodorus's, Prosper of Aquitaine's, and Marcèllinus's Chronicles, and a Treatise "De Ludus Sæcularibus."

3573 — Antiquitates Veronenses, *many fine plates,* large folio, *vellum,* 10*s* 6*d* .. .. .. *Petavii,* 1648

"Onofrio Panvinio edited Fasti Consulares—also on the Annals and Antiquities of Verona. Mazzochius, a printer at Rome, published in 1522, the first book of Inscriptions. There was a generous emulation between him and Carlo Sigonio—both very learned men. The first died in 1568, Sigonio in 1584." See *Mills's Theod. Ducas,* p. 379, v. 2.

3574 PARABOSCO (Girolamo) La Progne, tragedia nova, in Verso, 12mo. *sewed,* 3*s* .. *In Vinegia, per Comin da Trino,* 1548

3575 PARADINI (Gulielmi) Memoriæ Nostræ, libri IV., folio, *old binding,* 6*s* .. .. .. *Lugduni,* 1548

3576 — Histoire de notre Tems, thick 18mo. of above 900 pages, *old calf,* 5*s* .. .. *Lion, per Jan de Tournes,* 1558

3577 — une autre edit., faite en Latin et par lui mise en François, thick 12mo. *parchment, neat,* 5*s* *Lyon, P. Michel,* 1558

3578 PARENT'S High Commission, 12mo. *cloth,* 2*s* 1843

3579 PARIS—Galignani's New Paris Guide, *map and* 59 *plates,* thick 12mo. *bound, neat,* 4*s* (*pub. at* 7*s* 6*d*) *Paris,* 1841

3580 PARK'S (Mungo) Travels in the Interior of Africa, *plates,* square 12mo. *cloth, new, gilt, gilt edges,* 3*s* 6*d* *Edinburgh,* 1858

3581 PARKER (Archiepisc.) de Antiquitate Britannicæ Ecclesiæ, cum Archiepiscopis ejusdem LXX. Historia, edidit S. Drake, *fine portrait, by Vertue, and numerous plates*, royal folio, *a remarkably fine copy, in half russia, uncut*, £2 2*s* *Londini*, 1729

This magnificent volume (reprinted from the excessively rare edition of 1572,) with Godwin's Lives of the Bishops described earlier in this list, are fit companions—for the 1st and 2nd editions of the Archbishop's Bible. See *Bible*, Nos. 476-477.

3582 PARKER Society—Two Liturgies of the Reign of King Edward VI., with the Primer, Catechism, and Articles, 8vo. *cloth*, 8*s* *Cambridge*, 1844

3583 — Zurich Letters, in the Reign of Queen Elizabeth, 1558-1579, 8vo. *cloth, gilt*, 6*s* .. .. *Cambridge*, 1842

3584 — Zurich Letters, 1558-1602, second series, 8vo. *cloth, gilt*, 6*s* *Cambridge*, 1845

3585 — Letters from the Archives of Zurich, 8vo. *cloth, gilt*, 7*s* *Cambridge*, 1846

This is the second edition of the second series.

3586 — Abp. Parker's MSS. in C. C. C. Library, Cambridge, see *Nasmith*.

3587 PARKER (Samuel, *Master of Arts, lately of the Society of Trinitie College, Oxford)* Naturall Theologicall Essayes of God; or, the Divinitie of the Scholastickes fitted to the Rule of the New and Reformed Philosophy, and comprehended in two bookes, folio, *old binding*, IN MANUSCRIPT, £2 2*s* .. *Date about* 1663

Dedicated to Archbishop Sheldon, by Parker, who was made afterwards Bishop of Oxford. This seems to be the English of a book he published in Latin, in 1665, with this title, "Tentamina Physico-Theologica de Deo," answered by Dr. N. Fairfax, in his "Bulk and Selvedge of the World."

3588 — Demonstration of the Divine Authority of the Law of Nature, and of the Christian Religion, 4to. *old calf, neat*, 7*s* 6*d* 1681

This volume likewise contains "Dr. Joseph Glanvill's VII. Essays on several important subjects in Philosophy and Religion, 1676," one of which treats of "Modern Sadducism in the matter of Witches and Apparitions."

3589 PARKES'S (Samuel) Chemical Catechism, with Notes, &c., 8vo. *half calf, neat*, 4*s* 6*d* .. .. 1812

3590 PARKHURST'S (John) Hebrew and English Lexicon, without points, *portrait*, royal 8vo. *half bound, uncut*, 9*s* 1813

3591 — Greek and English Lexicon to the New Testament, *portrait*, royal 8vo. *half calf, very neat*, 10*s* .. 1822

3592 PARKINSON'S (James) Outlines of Oryctology, an Introduction to the Study of Fossil Organic Remains, 10 *plates*, post 8vo. *cloth*, 7*s* 6*d* (*pub. at* 12*s*) .. .. 1830

3593 — Organic Remains of a Former World, 54 *coloured plates*, 3 vols. 4to. *boards*, £3 3*s* (*pub. at* £5 5*s*) .. 1833

3594 PARKINSON'S (Sydney) Journal of a Voyage to the South Seas, with Remarks by Dr. John Fothergill, and an account of Byron's, Cook's and other Voyages, *portrait, maps, and plates*, 4to. *old calf, neat*, 12*s* .. .. 1784

"Parkinson was draughtsman to Sir Joseph Banks, the engravings from his drawings are a valuable addition to the Journal."—*Dr. Lettsome.*

3595 PARLEY'S (Peter) Tales of Animals, 280 *plates*, 12mo. *cloth*, 2*s* 6*d* (*pub. at* 5*s*) .. *Chiswick, Whittingham*, 1835

3596 — Penny Library, *plates*, 8 vols. 18mo. *cloth*, 8*s*

3597 PARNELL'S (Dr. Thomas, *Archdeacon of Clogher)* Poems, published by Mr. Pope, 8vo. *old calf*, 2*s* 6*d* *B. Lintot*, 1722

3598 — another edition, with the Life of Zoilus, 12mo. *old cf*, 2*s* 6*d* 1760

3599 PAROCHIAL Tales, 12mo. *cloth, new*, 2*s* *Oxford, Parker*, 1852

3600 PARR'S (Samuel) Spital Sermon, 4to. *hf. cf, neat, scarce*, 5*s* 1801

This is the famous Spital Sermon, preached at Christ Church, Ap. 15, 1800, with a profusion of learned Notes, unsparingly severe on Godwin, author of "Political Justice."

3601 — Bibliotheca Parriana; a Catalogue of his Library, with bibliographical notices, *portrait*, thick 8vo. *cloth*, 8*s* (*pub. at* 16*s*) 1827

"The Catalogue itself, which is, as might be expected, extremely curious and interesting, illustrates in a remarkable manner most of the leading features of Dr. Parr's political and literary character."—*Times.*

3602 — Parriana; Notices of the Rev. Dr. Parr, by E. H. Barker, Esq., of Thetford, Norfolk, &c., 2 vols. 8vo. *boards*, 12*s* 1828

"From the author, August 2nd, 1828." "Francis Howes, Norwich." 2 autographs.

3603 — Memoirs of his Life, Writings, and Opinions, with Biographical Notices of many of his Friends, Pupils, and Contemporaries, by the Rev. William Field, *portrait*, 2 vols. 8vo. *boards*, 10*s* 1828

"From the writer, with his best thanks and respects to the Rev. F. Howes."

3604 PARRY'S (Capt. W. E.) Journal of a Voyage for the discovery of a North-West Passage from the Atlantic to the Pacific, in 1819 and 1820, with the North Georgia Gazette and Winter Chronicle, *map*, 8vo. *boards*, 6*s* .. *Philadelphia*, 1821

3605 — Journal of a Second Voyage in 1821-22-23, in the Fury and Hecla, *frontispiece*, royal 8vo. *boards*, 5*s* 6*d* *New York*, 1824

3606 — another edition, 5 vols. 18mo. *boards*, 7*s* 6*d* (*pub. at* 20*s*) 1830

3607 PARSON'S Vade-Mecum; of Moveable Feasts, Ember-Weeks, Primitive Fathers, Bishopricks, Archdeaconries, &c., 12mo. *bound, curious*, 3*s* .. .. .. 1693

3608 PARSONS his Christian Directory, a Treatise of Holy Resolution, Englished by Dean Stanhope, 8vo. *good copy, in calf*, 3*s* 6*d* 1742

3609 PARTRIDGE'S (Samuel) Sermons adapted to an English Pulpit, from French writers, 8vo. *boards*, 2*s* 6*d* 1805

3610 PARUTA (Paolo, *Nobile Venetiano*) Discorsi Politici, aggiontovi nel fine un suo Soliloquio della sua Vita, *portrait in title*, thick 4to. *old parchment*, 8*s* *Venetia, Domenico Nicolini*, 1599

"Such was his character for wisdom, integrity, and zeal for the public welfare, that he was called the Cato of Venice."—*Chalmers.* This book was published by his sons—not to be found in *Haym.*

3611 PASORIS (Georgii) Lexicon Græco-Latinum in Novum Testamentum, 8vo. *old calf*, 5*s* .. *Genevæ*, 1637

3612 PASSIONS Personified, in Familiar Fables, *plates by S. Miller*, royal 8vo. *neat*, 3*s* .. *J. Whiston, no date.*

3613 PASQUALIGO (Messer Aloise) Lettere Amorose, thick 8vo. 671 pages, *old calf, very neat*, £1 1*s*
*In Vinegia, appresso G. B. Somascho*, 1572

Not in Haym, rare, dedicated to Il Sig. Francesco Emo, by Egidio Regazzola.

3614 PASQUIER (Estienne) Recherches de le France, plus, un pour parler du Prince, 2 vols. in 1, 12mo. *vellum, scarce*, 4*s*
*Orleans, P. Trepperel*, 1567

3615 PATERNO (Ignazio, *Principe di Biscari*) Viaggio per tutte le Antichita' della Sicilia, *map and plates*, 12mo. *sewed*, 2*s* 6*d* *Palermo*, 1817

3616 PATERSON'S (William) Four Journeys into the Country of the Hottentots and Caffraria, 1777-78-79, *map and* 19 *plates, chiefly on Natural History*, 4to. *half calf*, 4*s* 6*d* .. 1789

3617 — another copy, 2nd edition, 4to. *old calf, neat*, 7*s* 6*d* 1790

3618 PATERSON'S Road Book of England and Wales, *map*, small 8vo. 2*s* .. .. .. .. 1781

3619 PATIN (Charles) Relations Historiques et curieuses de Voyages en Allemagne, Angleterre, &c. *portrait and plates*, 12mo. *old calf*, 3*s* *Amsterdam*, 1695

3620 PATRES Apostolici, Gr. et Lat., textum recognovit, annotationibusque illustravit C. J. Hefele, 8vo. *neatly half bound and interleaved*, 7*s* 6*d* .. .. .. *Tubingæ*, 1842

Barnabas, Clemens Romanus, Ignatius, Polycarpus et Hermes.

3621 PATRICK (Bp. Simon) Friendly Debate between a Conformist and a Non-Conformist, 8vo. *old calf, neat*, 3*s* 6*d* *R. Royston*, 1669

3622 — Christian Sacrifice, shewing the Necessity, End, and Manner of Receiving the Holy Communion, with Prayers and Meditations, *frontispiece*, 12*mo. old calf, neat*, 3*s* .. 1675

3623 — Mensa Mystica; a Discourse concerning the Sacrament of the Lord's Supper, 8vo. *old calf, neat*, 4*s* 6*d* .. 1676

3624 — Witnesses to Christianity, or the Certainty of our Faith and Hope, part 2 only, 8vo. *old red morocco, gilt leaves*, £1 5*s* 1677

This is a particularly choice specimen of elaborately tooled old morocco binding. A good price would be given for the other volume if uniform.

3625 — Divine Arithmetick; or the Right Art of Numbring our Dayes, a Sermon Preached June 17, 1659, at the Funeral of Mr. Samuel Jacomb, Minister of St. Mary Woolnoth, Lumbard St., London, 3rd Edit., small 8vo. *old calf, neat*, SCARCE, 4*s* 6*d* 1677

Contains also at the end an account of his life. This is a piece of Bp. Patrick's seldom now seen.

3626 — Search the Scriptures, Directions to Christians to Read the Holy Books, 12mo. *old binding*, 2*s* .. .. 1693

3627 — Discourse concerning Prayer and the frequenting Daily Public Prayers, by F. E. Paget, 18mo. *morocco, elegant, stamped gilt edges*, 5*s* (*cost* 8*s*) .. : *Oxford, J. H. Parker*, 1840

3628 — Advice to a Friend, 18mo. *morocco gilt edges*, 3*s* (*cost* 5*s* 6*d*) *Oxford, Parker*, 1840

"Do good unto thy friend before thou die."—*Ecclesiast.* 14, 13.

3629 — his Translation of Grotius de Veritate, see *Grotius*

3630 PATRITII (Francisci) Discussionum Peripateticarum Tomi Primi, libri XIII., 4to. *parchment, neat*, 3*s* 6*d* *Venetiis*, 1571

"This learned, perspicuous, and elegant work fully explains the reason on which his disapprobation of the Peripatetic (Aristotelian) philosophy was founded."—*Brucker*.

3631 PAUL (Father) Letters of the Renowned Father Paul, Englished by Edward Brown, *fine portrait by Sturt*, 8vo. *old calf, nt*, 5*s* 1693

Father Paul (Sarpi) Counsellor of State to the most Serene Republick of Venice and author of the excellent History of the Council of Trent.

3632 PAUL (Father) Vita del Padre Paolo, 12mo. *vellum*, RARE, 10*s* *In Leida*, 1646

This little Life of Father Paul Sarpi is rare, it appears to have been printed by an Elzevir.

3633 PAUL'S Letters to his Kinsfolk, 8vo. *boards*, 6*s* 6*d* *Edinburgh*, 1816

These letters were written by Sir Walter Scott.

3634 PAUSANIAS'S Description of Greece, translated from the Greek into English, *maps*, 3 vols. 8vo. *half calf, neat, reduced from* £2 8*s* to 15*s* .. .. .. 1824

3635 PAUW (Cornelius de) Philosophical Dissertations on the Egyptians and Chinese, by Capt. J. Thompson, *large maps of Egypt and China*, 2 vols. 8vo. *half bound, very neat*, 8*s* 1795

"A work of extraordinary merit."—*Quarterly Review.*

3636 PAVILLON (Estienne, *de l'Acad. Francoise,*) Œuvres, small 8vo. THICK PAPER, *old calf, neat*, 5*s* *La Haye, H. du Sauzet*, 1715

These Poems were written from 1680 to 1696. There is also an Eulogium on M. Pavillon, his Discourse before the Academy, Dec. 17, 1691; and M. Charpentier's Response.

3637 PAXTON'S (Sir Joseph) Pocket Botanical Dictionary, by Professor Lindley, 12mo. *cloth*, 7*s* 6*d* *(pub. at* 16*s)* .. 1840

3638 PAYNE (Mr., *Bookseller,*) Anonymous Poems by him, see *Poems.*

3639 PAYS-BAS—Guide des Voyageurs dans les Pays-Bas et le Grand-Duché du Rhin, 12mo. *neatly half bound*, 2*s* *Bruxelles*, 1826

3640 — Le Voyageur dans le Royaume des Pays-Bas par J. Gautier, *map*, 12mo. *half calf, neat*, 2*s* .. *Bruxelles*, 1827

3641 PEACOCK'S (Reynold) Life, being a Sequel to the Life of Dr. J. Wiclif, by John Lewis, 8vo. *cloth*, 5*s* *Oxford, the Clarendon Press*, 1820

Reynold Peacock was Bishop of St. Asaph and Chichester temp. Henry VI., and this book is an Introduction to the History of the English Reformation.

3642 PEARSON (Joannes, *Episc. Cestriensis,*) Vindiciæ Epistolarum S. Ignatii; accesserunt Is. Vossii Epistolæ duæ adversus D. Blondellum, 4to. *calf, neat, but stained by damp*, 10*s* *Cantabrigiæ*, 1672

At the end of this volume is "Is. Vossii de Septuaginta Interpretibus, eorumque translatione et Chronologia dissertationes. *Hagæ-Comitum*, 1661."

3643 — — Opera Posthuma; viz., de Serie et Successione primorum Romæ Episc. quibus præfiguntur Annales Paulini et Lectiones in Acta Apost. cum notis H. Dodwell, &c. 4to. *old calf, stained at end*, 6*s* .. .. .. *Londini*, 1688

"These Dissertations are written with that accuracy and judgment, that they have been admired and quoted by the most curious and learned of foreign countries."—*Biographia Britannica.*

3644 — Exposition of the Creed, *portrait by W. Elder*, folio, *half bound*, 4*s* 6*d* .. .. .. .. 1692

3645 — another edition, *fine portrait by W. Elder*, folio, *old calf, neat*, 4*s* 6*d* .. .. .. .. 1701

3646 — Funeral Sermon for him, Dec. 12, 1672, by Dr. W. Lloyd, Dean of Bangor, 4to. *sewed*, 2*s* .. .. 1672

3647 PEERAGE, Primogeniture, and Aristocracy of England, a Plan to Dispose of these Subjects, 12mo. *calf, elegant*, 6*s* 1835

This book, which appears to be privately printed, dedicated to "Thomas William Coke, Esq., (of Holkham) the true friend of reform," is printed on scarlet paper, the reverse of each page blank.

3648 PELEGROMIUS (Simon) Synonymorum Sylva in Anglicanum transfusa, &c. per H. F.; Accesserunt Synonyma quædam poetica, small 8vo. *old binding*, 6*s* .. *Londini*, 1619

3649 PELLICO (Silvio) Mie Prigioni, con addizioni di Pietro Maroncelli 12mo. *cloth*, 2*s* 6*d* (*pub. at* 4*s* 6*d*) *Londra, Rolandi*, 1850

3650 — Memoirs of his Imprisonments, in English, 18mo. *morocco, gilt, gilt leaves*, 2*s* 6*d* (*cost* 4*s* 6*d*) .. .. 1845

3651 PELLOUTIER (Simon) Histoire des Celtes, et particulierement des Gaulois et des Germains, vols 1 and 2, 12mo. *calf, neat*, 4*s* *La Haye*, 1750

3652 PENN (Guil.) Point de Croix, point de Couronne, trad. en François par C. Gay, 12mo. *old calf*, 3*s* *Bristol, S. Farley*, 1746

3653 PENNANT'S (Thomas) Tour in Scotland and Voyage to the Hebrides in 1772, *plates*, 4to. *boards*, 9*s* .. *Chester*, 1774

Original edition, with fine impressions of the numerous plates.

3654 — another copy, *fine original impressions of the plates*, 4to. *old calf, neat*, 10*s* 6*d* .. .. .. *ib.*, 1774

"Pennant is the best traveller I ever read; he observes more things than any one else does."—*Dr. S. Johnson.*

3655 PENNINGTON'S (Thomas) Journey into Various Parts of Europe, with Notes, Historical and Classical, 2 vols. thick 8vo. *boards*, 12*s* (*pub. at* 30*s*) .. .. .. 1825

Contains also, Memoirs of the Grand Dukes of the house of Medici; of the Dynasties of the Kings of Naples; and of the Dukes of Milan. Two very entertaining volumes.

3656 PENNY CYCLOPÆDIA, by Charles Knight, vols. 1 to 10, 14 to 17, 21 to 25, in all 19 vols. *cloth*, 38*s* .. 1833-43

3657 — another copy, vols. 1 to 17, (A. to Per.) *cloth, new*, £2 2*s* 1833-40

3658 — parts 1 to 19, 28 to 40, 45 to 48, small folio, in all 36 parts, *sewed*, 10*s* (*pub. at* 29*s* 9*d*) .. 1833 to 1836

3659 PEN OWEN, 3 vols. post 8vo. *boards*, 6*s* *Edinburgh*, 1822

By the Dean of Worcester, Dr. Arthur James Hook, father of Theodore Edward Hook.

"If wit and eloquence combined
With playful satire flowing,
Can give applause, or charm the mind,
It is to thy *pen owing*."—*in MS. in the Book.*

3660 PENTAMERONE (Il); del Cavalier Giovan Battista Basile, overo lo Cunto de li Cunte, trattenemiento de li Peccerille di G. A. Abbattutis, thick 12mo. 648 pages, *in the original parchment*, RARE, £1 11*s* 6*d* .. *In Napoli, Antonio Bulifon*, 1674

"Edition rare de ces Nouvelles en patois Napolitain."—*Brunet.*

3661 PERCY of Northumberland—The Humble Petition of James Percy, Esq., Right Heir-male unto, and lawfully claiming the Earldom of Northumberland, *with the pedigree and arms*, 2 *broadsides*, RARE, 10*s* .. .. *Printed 23rd March*, 1688-9

3662 PERCY'S (Bishop) Reliques of Ancient English Poetry, *portrait*, 3 vols. 8vo. *cloth*, 18*s* .. .. .. 1855

"I esteem this the most elegant compilation of the early poetry of a nation that has ever appeared in any age or country. Every page evinces the fine taste, the genius and learning of the editor."—*Evans's Old Ballads.*

3663 PERCY ANECDOTES—Instinct and Fidelity, 2 *portraits*, 2 vols. in 1, 2*s* 6*d*.—Hospitality and Humanity, 2 *portraits*, 2 vols. in 1, 2*s* 6*d*.—Heroism and Shipwreck, 2 *portraits*, 2 vols. in 1, 2*s* 6*d*. —Enterprise and Captivity, 2 *portraits*, 2 vols. in 1, 2*s* 6*d*.—4 vols. *neatly half bound* .. .. 1821

3664 — Honour, 18mo. *sewed*, 1*s* 6*d*, 1822.—Enterprise, 18mo. *hf. bd. neat*, 1*s* 6*d*, 1820.—Hospitality, *portrait of T. W. Coke, Esq.*, *boards*, 2*s* .. .. .. 1821

3665 PERIZONII (Jac.) Origines Babylonicæ et Ægytiacæ, 12mo. *old calf, neat*, 3*s* .. .. *Lugd. Bat.*, 1711

This is vol. 1 only, containing Babylonian Antiquities, written principally to confute Sir John Marsham's Chronological system.

3666 PÉROUSE'S Voyage Round the World, 1785 to 88, with a Voyage from Manilla to St. Blaise, and M. de Lessep's Travels over the Continent from Kamtschatka, with Perouse's Despatches, Englished, *portrait, maps, and* 51 *plates*, 2 vols. 8vo. *boards*, 8*s* 1798

3667 PERSE; Histoire de la derniere Revolution de Perse, *map*, 2 vols. 12mo. *calf, very neat*, 5*s* .. .. *La Haye*, 1728

This history is preceded by a "Histoire des Sophy," from 1499

3668 PERSIA; Sketches of Persia, from the Journal of a Traveller in the East, 2 vols. post 8vo. *hf. russia, very nt.* 6*s* (*pub. at* 16*s*) 1828

3669 PERTH (James, Earl of,) Letters to his Sister the Countess of Errol, 1688-96, Edited by Will. Jerdan, 4to. *cloth*, 4*s* 1845

3670 PERUVIAN TALES, Translated into English by Samuel Humphreys, *plates*, thick 24mo. *boards*, 3*s* 6*d* (*pub. at* 6*s*) 1817

3671 PETER, a Tale in Verse, 4to. 27 pages, *sewed*, 3*s*
*Privately printed*, 1744

Norwich beer then celebrated, thus:
"He lives amongst us in good cheer,
Grows fat and sleek on Norwich beer."

3672 PETR-ADOLPHI (Ivari, *Norvegi*,) Medulla Oratoria, 18mo. *vellum, neat*, 5*s* .. .. *Amst., Elzevirii*, 1656

3673 PETITI (Sam.) Eclogæ Chronologicæ, 4to. *old calf, neat*, 7*s* 6*d*
*Parisiis, C. Morelli*, 1632

This profoundly learned man was at a very early age made Professor of Theology and of Greek and Hebrew at Geneva. With Dr. Geo. Stanhope's, Dean of Canterbury, book-plate.

3674 PETRARCA, (Francesco) con l'Espositione di M. Gio. Andrea Gesualdo, thick 4to. 884 pages, *fine tall copy in limp vellum*, £1 1*s*
*Venetia, appresso Alessandro Griffio*, 1581-2

This edition, illustrated with wood cuts, has Lives of Petrarch and Laura, with their portraits. "Edizione assai apprezzata."—*Haym*. It is the *last* of Gesualdo's editions. "Edition la plus estimée de ce Commentaire."—*Brunet.*

3675 — le medesime, *ornato di Figure*, 4to. *nice clean copy, in old calf*, 16*s*
*In Venetia, Alessandro Griffio*, 1581

This copy belonged to the late Joseph John Gurney, Esq., and has his book-plate.

3676 — Le Rime del, brevemente sposte per Lodovico Castelvetro, 4to. *very fine copy, in old vellum, rare*, £1 11*s* 6*d*
*Basilea, Pietro de Sedabonis*, 1582

"Edizione stimatissima, e rara."—*Haym.*

3677 PETRARCA Sonetti, Canzoni e Trionfi, con Vita, 32mo. *old red morocco*, 5*s* .. .. *Venetia*, 1596

3678 — Le Rime, memorie della Vita, 2 vols. 8vo. *sewed*, 10*s* *Milano, per Bettoni*, 1824

3679 — Life, from De Sacy, by Mrs. Dobson, 2 vols. 8vo. *cf, nt*, 6*s* 1775

3680 — another edition, by Mrs. Dobson, *plates by Ridley*, 2 vols. 8vo. *old calf, neat*, 6*s* 6*d* .. .. 1797

3681 PETRE of Stapleton, Catalogue of the Library of the Honble. E. Petre, at Stapleton Park, in MS., 4to. *bound, gilt edges*, £1 1*s*

3682 PETRONII Arbitrii, Equitis Romani, Satyricon, cum Petroniorum Fragmentis, accesserunt notæ et Observationes variorum, thick 12mo. *limp vellum*, 6*s* .. *Lugduni*, 1615

3683 PETRONJ and Davenport's Italian-English and French, and English-Italian and French Dictionary, 2 vols. 8vo. *very good copy, in new substantial calf*, £1 5*s* (*pub. at* £2 2*s*) *Treuttel and Wurtz*, 1824

3684 PETTY'S (Sir Will.) Several Essays in Political Arithmetic, 8vo. *old calf*, 6*s* .. .. *Robert Clavel*, 1699

On the Growth of the City of London,—On the Dublin Bills of Mortality, 1681.—Comparison between London and Paris.—London and Rome.—Of London, Paris, Amsterdam, Venice, Bristol, &c., in French and English.—On the extent and value of Lands, &c.

3685 PETZHOLDT'S (A.) Lectures to Farmers on Agricultural Chemistry, post 8vo. *cloth*, 2*s* 6*d* (*pub. at* 5*s*) .. 1844

3686 [PEZRON (Le P. Paul)] L'Antiquité des Tems retablie et defenduë contre les Juifs et les nouveaux Chronologistes, 12mo. *vellum, neat*, 4*s* .. .. *Amsterdam*, 1687

3687 PHÆDRI Fabulæ, et Publii Syri Sententiæ, 24mo. LARGE PAPER, *neat*, 3*s* 6*d* (*formerly priced* 9*s*) *Parisiis, Typog. Regia*, 1729

"An elegant little edition."—*Dibdin*. The type most minute and clear, uniform with the Horace of 1733.

3688 — Fables, Latin and English, with an ordo and notes, 8vo. *bound*, 2*s* 6*d* .. .. .. .. 1745

3689 PHILIDOR'S (A. D.) Studies of Chess; containing Caissa, a Poem, by Sir William Jones, and the whole Analysis of Chess, 2 vols. 8vo. *neat*, 6*s* .. .. .. 1804

3690 PHILIP (King of Macedon, Father of Alexander) History of his Life and Reign, by Dr. Thomas Leland, 2 vols. 8vo. *old calf, gilt*, 7*s* 6*d* .. .. .. 1775

"The Life of Philip contains many curious researches into the principles of government established among the leading States of Greece; many sagacious remarks on their intestine discords, &c."—*Dr. Parr.*

3691 PHILIPS'S (John) Poems, with his Life, *port.*, 12mo. *neat*, 1*s* 1728

3692 PHILIPPS'S (H.) Grandeur of the Law; an exact Collection of the Nobility and Gentry of this Kingdom, whose ancestors were Lawyers, 8vo. *old calf, scarce*, 5*s* .. 1684

3693 PHILLIPI (Jacobi *Bergomensis*) Opus de Claris Mulieribus et D. Catharinæ Senensis Vita per Jo. Pinum, folio, *a fine copy, in old calf, gilt*, £1 11*s* 6*d* *Parisiis, S. Colinæi*, 1521

At the end of this Treatise is reprinted another by Varanius, "De gestis Joanne Virginis Franciæ, Anglorum expultricis,"—and another Book of Theodoret's, Bisho of Cyricus in Syria, "De curatione affectionum libri XII. Zenobio Acciaolo interprete." *Parisiis, H. Stephani*, 1519.

3694 PHILLIPS'S (Henry) Purchaser's Pattern, the true Value of Land or Houses, the Measuring of Land, Gauging, &c., 18mo. *bd*, 2*s* 1721

3695 PHILLIPS'S (Henry) Pomarium Britannicum; an Historical and Botanical Account of Fruits known in Great Britain, *coloured plates*, royal 8vo. *half morocco, neat*, 8*s* 6*d* 1820

3696 — another copy, *coloured plates*, 8vo. 2nd edition, *boards*, 6*s* (*pub. at* 10*s* 6*d*) .. .. .. 1822

3697 PHILLIPS'S (Will.) Outlines of Mineralogy and Geology, *plate*, 12mo. *boards*, 2*s* 6*d* .. .. 1816

3698 — Elementary Introduction to the Knowledge of Mineralogy, post 8vo. *boards*, 3*s* 6*d* (*pub. at* 12*s*) .. 1819

3699 PHILLIPPS'S (S. M.) Treatise on the Law of Evidence, 3rd Edition, royal 8vo. *boards*, 7*s* 6*d* .. 1817

3700 — eighth edition, by A. Amos, Esq., royal 8vo. *bound to lap over, a Magistrate's book*, 12*s* .. .. 1838

3701 PHILOSOPHY in Sport made Science in Earnest, *numerous woodcuts*, post 8vo. *cloth*, 9*s* .. .. 1857

An attempt to implant into the young mind the first principles of Natural Philosophy, by the aid of the popular Toys and Sports of Youth.

3702 PHOTII Lexicon, Græcè, e Codice Galeano descripsit R. Porson, 2 vols. 8vo. *boards*, 10*s* (*pub. at* 30*s*) *Cantabrigiæ*, 1822

3703 PHOTOGRAPHY, Guide to the Art of, *plates*, 8vo. *cloth*, 2*s*

3704 PHRENOLOGY, Observations on Combe on the Constitution of Man, principally in reference to Phrenology, 12mo. *sd*, 1*s* 1847

3705 PHYSICAL Dictionary: an Interpretation of such crabbed words and Terms of Arts, as are deriv'd from the Greek and Latin, and used in Physick, Anatomy, Chirurgery, and Chemistry, 12mo. *old calf, curious*, 5*s* .. *John Garfield*, 1657

"This Dictionary will be as useful and sufficient as any Dictionary of Ten Shillings price."—*Quotation.*

3706 PICKERING'S (Dr. Charles) Races of Men, and their Geographical Distribution, with an Analytical Synopsis of the Natural History of Man, by Dr. Hall, *coloured plates*, post 8vo. *cloth*, 5*s* 6*d* (*pub. at* 7*s* 6*d*) .. .. .. 1851

3707 PICKERING'S (William) Christian Classics, 17 vols. 18mo. *sewed*, £1 1*s* .. .. *J. Whittingham*, 1853

Reprints in antique style, of old Authors, or separately.—Dr. Doddridge's Rise and Progress of Religion in the Soul, 1*s* 6*d*.—Dr. J. Goodman's Old Religion, 1*s* 6*d*.—Bp. Hall's No Peace with Rome, 1*s* 6*d*.—Bp. Hall's Meditations and Vows, 1*s* 6*d*.—Bp. Hall's Mystery of Godliness and Invisible World, 1*s* 6*d*.—Dr. R. Hill's Pathway of Piety, 2 vols. 3*s*.—John Mason on Self Knowledge, 1*s* 6*d*.—Bp. Patrick's Heart's Ease, 1*s* 6*d*.—Bp. Patrick's Discourse concerning Prayer, 1*s* 6*d*.—Bp. Patrick's Advice to a Friend, 1*s* 6*d*.—The Penitent Pilgrim, anonymous, 1*s* 6*d*.—Saltmarsh's Sparkles of Glory, 1*s* 6*d*.—Dr. C. Sutton's Godly Meditations, 1*s* 6*d*.—Sutton's Learn to Live, 1*s* 6*d*.—Sutton's Learn to Die, 1*s* 6*d*.—Bp. J. Taylor's Contemplations of the State of Man, 1*s* 6*d*.

3708 PICTET (Benedict.) de Præstantia et Divinitate Religionis Christianæ, cum Oratione de Crucis Trophæis ab Christi Triumphis, 8vo. *old calf, neat*, 5*s* .. .. *Genevæ*, 1719

3709 — Theologie Chrétienne, et la Science du Salut, *fine portrait*, 3 vols. 4to. *old foreign binding, gilt*, £1 1*s* *ib.*, 1721

Lord Walpole of Woolterton's copy, as was the following. All have the book-plate.

3710 PICTET Morale Chrétienne; ou l'Art de bien Vivre, 2 vols. 4to. *uniform with No.* 3709, 15*s* .. *Genevæ,* 1710

These works are highly spoken of by *Walchius* and *Senebier.*

3711 PICTORII (Georgii) Sermones Conviviales, omnibus historica, poetica, sales, jocos, facetias, &c.; quibus accedunt Ebrietatis in exilium relegatæ Threnodia, et ejusdem resurgentis τροπαιων, small 8vo. *old vellum,* 16*s* *Basileæ, per H. Petri,* 1559

At the end of this volume is a Treatise by Theodore Ulsenius "de Pharmacandi comprobata ratione," and a Latin Poem by Q. Serenus "de curatione morborum," both edited by the above George Pictorius, and printed at Basle, by the same printer, in 1559.

3712 PICTURE of Greece in 1825, as exhibited in the Personal Narratives of James Emerson, Count Pecchio and W. H. Humphreys, *portrait of the Greek Admiral,* 2 vols. post 8vo. *boards,* 4*s* 6*d* (*pub. at* 16*s*) .. .. .. 1826

3713 PIECES Curieuses, thick 4to. *(no title page) old parchment, scarce,* 6*s* .. .. .. .. 1647

Here are 35 curious Tracts reprinted from the originals which are dated 1631 to 1643, they consist of Treaties of Peace, Remonstrances, Letters, &c., from Cardinal Richelieu and other eminent persons of that time.

3714 PIERCE (Dr. Thomas) Primitive Rule of Reformation, a Sermon before Cha. II., in Vindication of our Church against the Novelties of Rome, 4to. *sewed,* 2*s* .. 1663

"This Sermon sate the Popish Priests all on Fire to answer it."

3715 PIERS Ploughman's Vision and Creed, edited by Thomas Wright, new edition, with additions to the Notes and Glossary, 2 vols. foolscap 8vo. *cloth,* 10*s* .. *J. R. Smith,* 1857

The author of these poems (supposed to be Robert Langland) was contemporary with Chaucer; and the learned Tyrwhitt states them to be "very curious and masterly productions."

3716 PIGNÆ (Jo. Baptistæ) Carminum libri IV.; His adjunximus Cælii Calcagnini Carminum libri III.; Ludovici Areosti Carminum libri II., small 8vo. *a fine copy in vellum, ruled with red lines, gilt leaves, rare,* 15*s*
*Venetiis, ex officina Erasmiana, Vincentii Valgrisii,* 1553

"Ce recuil se recommande surtout par le nom du célèbre Lod. Ariosto, auteur des poésies qui le terminent."—*Brunet.*

3717 — Historia de Principi di Este, thick folio of 635 pages, besides a large Table, and Genealogies, *arms on title emblazoned,* old folio, £2 12*s* 6*d* .. *In Ferrara, Francesco Rossi,* 1570

This rare book is dedicated "a Donno Alfonso Secondo, Duca di Ferrara," to whom Pigna was first Secretary. See *Black's Life of Tasso,* who says "The family of Este was the most ancient and illustrious in Italy, and the historian who would trace it, is lost amidst the mazes of genealogy. It is the parent stock of the House of Brunswick, consequently of the family which is seated on the throne of the British Empire."—v. 1, p. 121.

3718 PIGNORIA (Lorenzo) Le Origini di Padova, con Annotationi, *numerous curious wood-cuts,* 4to. *old calf, neat,* 7*s* 6*d*
*Padova, Pietro P. Tozzi,* 1625

Pignorius distinguished himself by deep researches into antiquity, and published many curious works, two of which are here enumerated. See *Tiraboschi.*

3719 — de Servis, et eorum apud Veteres ministeriis, Commentarius, in qua Familia, tum Urbana, tum Rustica ordine producitur et illustratur, *fine portrait and curious cuts,* 4to. *old calf, neat,* 6*s*
*Patavii, P. Frambotti,* 1656

3720 PIGOTT'S (Grenville) Manual of Scandinavian Mythology, containing a popular account of the two Eddas, and of the Religion of Odin, post 8vo. *cloth*, 8*s* (*pub. at* 12*s*) *W. Pickering*, 1839

3721 PINDARI Olympia, Pythia, Nemea, Isthmia cæterorum VIII. Lyricorum Carmina, Alcæi, Sapphus, Stesichori, Ibyci, Anacreontis, Bacchylidis, Simonidis, Alcmanis nonnulla etiam aliorum, Editio II., Græco Latina H. Steph. recognitione, thick 18mo. *old vellum, gilt edges*, 5*s* *Parisiis, H. Stephanus*, 1566

A very pretty volume ruled throughout with red ink.

3722 PINELLI (Bartolomeo) Nuova Raccolta di cinquanta costumi de' Contorni di Roma, *fine impressions of the* 50 *plates*, large oblong 4to. *sewed*, 15*s* .. .. *Roma*, 1823

"Pinelli is one of the most esteemed of the Italian artists. His etchings are remarkable for their fidelity and force."—*Bohn.*

3723 PINELLI—Catalogue of the magnificent Library of Maffei Pinelli, late of Vienna, sold by auction, in London, March, 1789, 8vo. *half bound, uncut*, 5*s* .. .. 1789

With Morelli's Latin preface explaining its contents.

3724 PINKERTON'S (John) Essay on Medals, small 8vo. 1st Edition, *calf, very nice old copy*, 3*s* 6*d* .. .. 1784

With a review of all previous works on this subject.

3725 — Modern Geography, *numerous maps*, 2 vols. thick 4to. *boards*, 10*s* (*pub. at* £5 5*s*) .. .. .. 1802

"The best work of Geography is by Pinkerton."—*Major Rennell.*

3726 — Literary Correspondence, Edited by Mr. Dawson Turner, *portrait*, 2 vols. 8vo. *boards*, 12*s* (*pub. at* £1 12*s*) .. 1830

"They include, among others from personages known to fame, epistles by Lord Buchan, Gibbon the historian, and Horace Walpole, besides a copious store of curious anecdotes, exhibiting the history of a literary man from the beginning to the end of his career."—*Dawson Turner.*

3727 PINNOCK'S Goldsmith's History of Greece for the Use of Schools, by Dr. Taylor, *plates*, 12mo. *bound, new*, 3*s* 6*d* (*pub. at* 5*s* 6*d*) 1847

3728 — History of Rome, by Dr. Taylor, *plates*, 12mo. *bound, new*, 3*s* 6*d* (*pub. at* 5*s* 6*d*) .. .. .. 1848

3729 — Catechisms of Chronology and Astronomy, *plates*, 24mo. *stiff covers*, 9*d each*

3730 PINTO (Fernando Mendez) Les Voyages Advantureux de, trad. de Portuguais par Barnard Figuier, thick 4to. of above 1200 pages, *vellum*, (wants title page) RARE, £1 1*s* .. *Paris*, 1628

"Volume recherché et peu commun."—*Brunet.* The value of this volume is greatly enhanced by the *autograph*, at page 1193, of "CHARLES COTTON," the friend of the celebrated IZAAC WALTON, *Piscator.* Ferdinand Mendez Pinto for the space of 21 years travelled, from 1537, in Ethiopia, China, Tartary, Siam, Pegu, Japan, and a great part of the East Indies; there is an excellent account of him in the *Retrospective Review*, vol. 8, in which ample justice is done him against Cervantes who called him 'the Prince of Liars.'

3731 PIOZZI'S (Hester L.) British Synonymy; an Attempt at Regulating the Choice of Words in General Conversation, 2 vols. 8vo. *boards*, 6*s* .. .. .. .. 1794

3732 PIOZZIANA—Recollections of the late Mrs. Piozzi, with Remarks, by a Friend, post 8vo. *boards*, 3*s* 6*d* (*pub. at* 7*s*) *Moxon*, 1833

3733 PITMAN'S (J. H.) Course of Sermons for the Year, for the Use of Families and Schools, 2 vols. 8vo. *boards*, 10*s* (*pub. at* 18*s*) 1825

3734 PITT (Right Hon. William) Memoirs of the Life of, by Bp. Tomlins, 3 vols. 8vo. *boards*, 15*s* (*pub. at* 36*s*) .. 1821

3735 PLACETE (Jean la) Essais de Morale, 4 vols. *Amst.*, 1716.—Nouveaux Essais, 2 vols. *La Haye*, 1715.—Eclaircissemens sur la Liberté, *Amst.*, 1709.—Traité de la Justification, *Amst.*, 1733.—Traité de l'Aumone, *Amst.*, 1699.—together 9 vols. 12mo. *old calf, neat*, £1 2*s* 6*d* .. .. .. V.Y.

Placete, a Protestant Minister of great eminence, born 1639, died 1718. "He was the author of many works upon piety and morality, which are reckoned excellent in their kind."—*Niceron.*

3736 PLANTING and Ornamental Gardening, a Practical Treatise, thick 8vo. 638 pages, *calf, neat*, 5*s* .. .. 1785

Evelyn, Miller, Hanbury, Wheatley, Mason, and Dr. Hunter's books used in its compilation, it is alphabetically arranged.

3737 PLAT'S (Sir Hugh) Garden of Eden; an Accurate Description of all Flowers and Fruits now Growing in England, parts 1 and 2, 2 vols. 12mo. *old calf, neat, curious*, 6*s* .. 1653-1660

3738 PLATINA'S (Baptista) Lives of the Popes, from the Time of Christ to the Reign of Sixtus IV., Translated and Continued to this Time by Sir Paul Rycaut, *many plates of Popes inserted*, folio, *fine copy in calf*, 15*s* .. .. .. 1685

3739 PLATO, Opera Omnia, Gr. et Lat., annotationes, Indicesque adjecit Astius, 11 vols. 8vo. *sewed*, £1 16*s* (*pub. at* £4 16*s*) *Lipsiæ*, 1819-32

One of the best library editions of Plato.

3740 PLATON'S (*Metropolitan of Moscow*) Present State of the Greek Church in Russia, with an Account of the different Sects of Russian Dissenters, by Robert Pinkerton, 8vo. *half calf, neat*, 4*s* 6*d* *Edinburgh*, 1814

Book-plate of *Mr. Joseph John Gurney*, and Autographs of "*C. and R. Gurney, Earlham.*"

3741 PLATT'S Universal Biography, Chronologically arranged, in Periods, to the 16th Century, with an Alphabetical Index, 5 vols. 8vo. *boards*, 12*s* (*pub. at* £4) .. .. 1825

3742 PLATUS'S (Fa. Hierome, *of the Societie of Jesus*,) Happiness of a Religious State, Englished, thick 4to. 627 pages, *calf, neat*, 7*s* 6*d* *Permissu Superiorum*, 1632

3743 PLAUTI Comœdiæ, Charpentarii, small 8vo. *old stamped binding*, 10*s* 6*d* .. .. *Denis Roce, (absque anno)*

A portion of the title page and of the first two leaves of this rare edition, are eaten off.

3744 — alia editio, 12mo. *vellum*, 3*s* 6*d* *Amst., Elzevir*, 1652

With the autograph of "Joan. Veenhuysen, ao. 1671."

3745 — alia editio, cum Notis Variorum et J. F. Grovonii, 8vo. *fine copy, in calf, gilt*, 10*s* 6*d* .. .. *Lugd. Bat.*, 1664

"Gronovius, by the assistance of six ancient MSS. and his own sagacious conjectures, has improved the text in many places."—See *Dibdin.*

3746 — Jani Dousæ Centurionatus sive Plautinarum explanationum libri IV., 12mo. 3*s* .. .. *Francofurti*, 1602

3747 PLAYFORD'S (John) Whole Book of Psalms, *with all the ancient and proper Tunes, Cantus, Medius, and Bassus,* 18th edition, 8vo. *half bound, neat,* SCARCE, 8*s* .. *W. Pearson,* 1729

Dr. Cotton says there was "no edition" of the Psalms printed in 1729; he instances the 17th and 19th editions of Playford's Psalms (both in the British Museum) but not this, the 18th, clearly, therefore, it is not there, and it had not come to Dr. Cotton's knowledge.

3748 PLAYS—The Devil of a Duke, a Farcical Ballad Opera, 21 Songs, *with the Music,* 8vo. *scarce,* 2*s* 6*d* .. .. 1732

Not in Baker's Biographia Dramatica.

3749 — Cibber's Damon and Phillida, 15 Songs, *with the Music, scarce,* 8vo. 2*s* 6*d* .. .. .. .. 1765

"This entertainment was extremely applauded."—*Baker's Biog. Dramat.*

3750 — Gay's Achilles, an Opera, *with the Music to all the* 54 *Songs,* 8vo. *scarce,* 2*s* 6*d* .. .. .. 1733

"This Play was acted at Covent Garden in 1733, 18 nights."—*Baker's Biog. Dramat.*

3751 — 5, Mahomet, Tancred and Sigismunda, Suspicious Husband, Love for Love, and Mourning Bride, with Remarks by Mrs. Inchbald, 12mo. *calf, neat,* 2*s* 6*d* .. .. V.Y.

3752 — 6, Mountaineers, by Colman, Speed the Plough, Wheel of Fortune, Lover's Vows, Isabella, Venice Preserved, with Mrs. Inchbald's Remarks, 12mo. *half morocco, neat,* 3*s* V.Y.

3753 — 6, Careless Husband, by Cibber; Love in a Village; Busy Body, Mrs. Centlivre; Plain Dealer, Wycherley; Recruiting Officer; Miser, Fielding; in 1 vol. 12mo. *calf, neat,* 3*s* *Edinburgh,* 1768

3754 — Poor Gentleman, by George Colman, 18mo. *hf. bd.* 1*s*

3755 PLINII Secundi, Historia Naturalis, cum Notis Turnebi, Lipsii, etc., 3 very thick vols. in 12mo. *old stamped vellum,* 12*s* *Genevæ,* 1593

3756 — Historia Naturalis, 3 vols. 18mo. *very fine copy in white vellum,* £1 5*s* .. .. *L. Bat., Elzevir,* 1635

This is the only 12mo. edition of the elder Pliny ever published by the Elzevir family, and its beauty is a theme of extraordinary commendation by the French bibliographers. The editor was De Laet, the text Salmasius's, and is considered to be very correct.

3757 — Natural History, Translated, with Notes by Bostock and Riley, 4 vols. post 8vo. *cloth,* 16*s* .. *H. G. Bohn,* 1855

3758 — Epistolæ et Panegyricus, M. Z. Boxhornius recensuit, 12mo. *old calf, gilt,* 6*s* .. .. *L. Bat., Elzevir,* 1653

3759 — Epistolæ, cum Notis Variorum et Veenhusii, 8vo. *old vellum,* 7*s* 6*d* (*usually sells for* 16*s*) .. *Lugd. Bat.,* 1669

"This is one of the scarcest and most valuable of the Octavo Variorum Classics, the select notes of Veenhuysen do great credit to his learning and judgment."—*Dr Harwood.*

3760 — Panegericke; a Speech in Senate wherein Public Thanks are Presented to the Emperour Traian, Englished by Robert Stapylton Knight, 4to. *stiff cover,* 6*s* .. *Oxford,* 1644

With Life of Pliny and Dediction to Prince Charles.

3761 PLOWDEN'S (John) Law of Landlord and Tenant, 8vo. *boards,* 2*s* 6*d* (*pub. at* 6*s* 6*d*) .. .. *No date*

3762 PLUTARCHO, Vite di, de gli Huomini Illustri Græci et Romani, tradotte per Lodovico Domenichi et altri, 2 vols. 4to. *fine copy in vellum*, £1 11*s* 6*d* *In Vinegia, Gabriel Giolito de Ferrari*, 1567

"I own myself an arrant enthusiast in these Gioliti publications, and, among them of those which came from the press of Gabriel, perhaps the most distinguished of those who bore the name."—*Dibdin's Bibliographical Decameron*, v. 2, pp. 239-41. There are fine specimens at the beginning and end of each volume of Giolito's wood-cut devices. "Questa è l' impressione, che si pone nella Collana."—*Haym.*

3763 PLUTARQUE, Les Vies des Hommes Illustres, translatées de Grec en François, par M. I. Amyot, 2 vols. *Paris*, 1587.—Les Œuvres Morales de Plutarque, translatées par le meme, 2 vols. *Paris*, 1612.—together 4 thick vols. 8vo. *fine old morocco*, £1 11*s* 6*d*

A remarkably fine copy in old red morocco, gilt leaves. "The French generally date the beginning of an easy and natural style in their own language from the publication, of James Amyot's translation of Plutarch, in 1559. It is well known how popular, more perhaps than any other ancient, this historian and moralist has been in France, but it is through Amyot that he has been read."—*Hallam.*

3764 — Lives, Translated by several hands, *plates*, 5 vols. 12mo. *calf, neat*, 6*s* .. .. .. .. 1716

3765 — Lives, Translated from the Greek, with Notes, Critical and Historical, by J. and W. Langhorne, *plates*, 6 vols. 8vo. *fine copy in old calf, very clean and neat*, £1 1*s* .. 1770

3766 — Lives, Translated by the Langhornes, with Archdeacon Wrangham's additions, 8 vols. 12mo. *nice copy in half green morocco, uncut, top edges gilt*, 18*s* .. .. 1810

3767 — Morals, Translated by Dr. Philemon Holland, thick folio, *old calf, neat*, 16*s* .. .. .. 1659

Dr. Zachary Grey considered this "a most accurate translation."

3768 POE'S (Edgar Allen, *American*,) Poetical Works with Life, by Hannay, *nicely illustrated by engravings*, crown 8vo. *cloth, elegant, gilt edges*, 4*s* .. .. .. 1859

3769 POEMS—The Fair Circassian, by Dr. Croxall, 1732.—Boileau's Art of Poetry, 1715.—Savage's Collection of Pieces in Verse and Prose, occasioned by the Dunciad, 1732.—Akenside's Pleasures of Imagination, 1754.—Deity, a Poem, 1749.—James Thomson's Castle of Indolence, 2nd edition, 1748.—James Burgh's Hymn to the Creator, 1750.—W. Somerville's Chace, and Hobbinol, 1749.—Poems, Amicis Candidisque Legenda, (*by Mr. Payne the Bookseller*) 1742-45, in 1 vol. 8vo. *hf. bd.* 6*s*

3770 — by a Father and Daughter, containing Memorials of Eminent Characters and Events, 12mo. *cloth*, 3*s* 6*d* (*pub. at* 8*s* 6*d*) 1845

3771 POESIS Philosophica; vel Saltem Reliquiæ Poesis Philosophicæ; Græcè, small 8vo. *a fine copy in old vellum*, 8*s*
*Parisiis, H. Stephanus*, 1573

Contents: Empidocles, Xenophanes, Timon, Parmenides, Cleanthes, Epicharmas, Orpheus, Heraclitus, Democritus. "This collection is highly interesting, and the typography is beautiful."—*Greswell's Early Parisian Gr. Press*, v. 2, p. 315.

3772 POETICAL Epitome, or Elegant Extracts abridged, by W. Enfield, square 12mo. 2*s* .. .. .. 1789

3773 POETRIARUM Octo (Erinnæ, Myrus, Myrtidis, Corinnæ, Telesillæ, Praxillæ, Nossidis, Anytæ) Fragmenta et Elogia, Gr. et Lat., cum Vir. doct. Notis, accedit G. Olearii Dissertatio de Poetriis Græcis, Cura et Studio J. C. Wolfii, 4to. *old calf, gilt*, 7*s* 6*d*
*Hamburgi*, 1734

3774 POHLMAN'S (J. G.) Complete Time Tables, royal 8vo. *calf, neat,* SCARCE, 20*s* .. .. .. 1815

Most useful Tables "exhibiting at one view the number of days from any particular date, exclusively, to every subsequent date, inclusively, throughout the year."

3775 POLAND—The Utmost Fury of Antichrist against the Protestants of the Bohemian Confession in Poland, this Narrative signed, A. S. Hartman, Pastor of the Church of Lesna, 4 leaves, folio, *sewed,* 5*s* *Hills & Field, printers to his Highness,* (*Cromwell,*) 1658

3776 POLE—Vita Reginaldi Poli Cardinalis ac Cantuariensis Archiepiscopi, small 8vo. *old calf, neat,* 4*s* .. *Londini,* 1690

At the end "Nobilissima Disceptatio super dignitate et Magnitudine regnorum Britannici et Gallici, habita ab utriusque Oratoribus et Legatis in Concilio Constantiensi, Lovanii, An. 1517." The learned Henry Wharton the author of the Life.

3777 — Ridley's (Dr. Glocester) Review of Phillips's Life of Cardinal Reginald Pole, 8vo. *calf, neat,* 4*s* 6*d*,—*boards,* 3*s* 6*d* 1766

3778 POLEHAMPTON'S Gallery of Nature and Art, edited by J. Mason Good, 93 *plates,* 6 vols. 8vo. *bds,* £1 11*s* 6*d* (*pub. at* £7 4*s*) 1819

This is a very amusing book for young persons; it contains a great deal of useful information.

3779 POLLOK'S (Robert) Course of Time, a Poem, 2 vols. 12mo. *boards,* 3*s* 6*d* .. .. *Edinb., Blackwood,* 1827

3780 POLWHELE'S (Rev. Richard) Biographical Sketches in Cornwall, 3 vols. 12mo. *old boards,* £1 1*s* .. *Truro,* 1831

Very scarce, not mentioned by *Lowndes,* illustrated with many portraits of the author, Lord Exmouth, Sir H. Davy, Davies Gilbert, Attorney Gen. Noye, John Opie, &c., &c Presentation copy to "*Mr. Higman, with the author's respectful compliments.*"

3781 POLYBII Historia, Gr. et Lat., Casauboni, folio, LARGE PAPER, *a fine copy, in russia,* £1 11*s* 6*d* .. *Parisiis,* 1609

"A most excellent edition, the merits of which have long been known to the literary world. The *Preface* to Henry IV. of France, in the opinion of the late Dr. Joseph Warton, is one of the finest ever written. The large paper copies are exceedingly rare and valuable." See *Dr. Dibdin.*

3782 — Historia, Græcè, ad opt. lib. fidem accurata edita, 4 vols. 18mo. *sewed,* 6*s* .. .. *Lipsiæ, Tauchnitz,* 1836

3783 — Diodori Siculi, Nicolai Damasceni, Dionysii Halicarnassei, Appiani Alexandrini, Dionis, et Joannis Antiocheni, excerpta ex Collectaneis Constantini Augusti Porphyrogenetæ, Gr. et Lat., opera et studio Henrici Valesii, 4to. LARGE PAPER, *a fine copy, in red morocco, gilt edges,* £1 1*s* *Parisiis, Du Puys,* 1634

"Ouvrage très reserché, et dont on trouve difficilement des exemplaires. Il y en a eu quelques-uns des tirés sur *Grand Papier,* mais ils sont rares."—*De Bure, Bibliog. Instructive.*

3784 — Selecta de Legationibus et alia, a Fulvio Ursino, 4to. *old calf, neat,* 6*s* .. .. *Antverpiæ, Plantini,* 1582

Fulvius Ursinus first published the 'Excerpta Legationum' in 1582. Harles calls it a "rare work."

3785 — Historico Greco, tradotti per Lodovico Domenichi, 4to. *very fine clean copy, in white parchment,* 15*s* *Vinetia, Gabriel Giolito,* 1563

Dedicated by Donenichi to Cosmo de Medici, and by Thomaso Porcacchi to Filippo Pini. This edition, which is a very desirable one, has 17 Books, some of the others have only 11. With 2 of Giolito's elegant wood-cut devices. This book forms, as the title page expresses, "Il quinto Anello della nostra Collana Historica."

3786 POMET'S History of Drugs, Vegetables, Animals, Minerals, translated by Sir John Hill, 400 *copper cuts*, 4to, *old calf, very neat*, 7*s* 6*d* .. .. .. .. 1748

"A work of very great use and curiosity." Pomet was chief Druggist to Louis XIV. of France.

3787 POMPONIUS Mela, Julius Solinus, Itinerarium Antonini Aug., Vibius Sequester, P. Victor, Dionysius Afer de Situ orbis, Prisciano interprete, small 8vo. *old stamped binding, rare*, £1 1*s* *Venetiis, in Ædibus Aldi*, 1518

With the autograph of SOCINUS on the title page.

3788 PONTANI (Jacobi, *e Soc. Jesu)* Progymnasmatum Latinitatis, thick 8vo. of 1334 pages, *old calf, neat*, 9*s* *Francofurti*, 1643

3789 PONTANI (Joannis Joviani) Opera; sc. de Fortitudine; de Principe; Charon; Antonius; de Liberalitate; de Beneficientia; de Magnificentia; de Splendore; de Conviventia; de Obedientia, et de Prudentia, 8vo. *tall copy, in limp vellum*, £1 5*s* *Lugduni, expensis Barth. Troth*, 1514

See an account of this very rare Lyonese counterfeit in *Annales des Alde*. Sold in Renouard's sale for £6 8*s* 6*d*. This copy unfortunately wants sheets H. to L.

3790 POOLE'S (Matthew) Annotations upon the Bible, *portrait by White*, 2 vols. thick folio, *good sound copy, in half russia*, £1 18*s* 1683-5

Best edition, usually marked £3 3s. These annotations are allowed to be "very judicious." See *Horne's Introduction*.

3791 POPE'S (Alexander) Works, with Notes, by Warburton, *plates*, 9 vols. small 8vo. *old Cambridge pannelled calf, very neat*, 18*s* 1751

3792 — Works, with his Life and Notes, selected by William Roscoe, *portrait*, 10 vols. 8vo. *full bd. in cf, gilt*, £3 3*s* (*cost* £6 6*s*) 1824

This, which is the best edition of Pope, by Roscoe, is entirely out of print and difficult to procure.

3793 — Works, with Life, by W. L. Bowles, vol. 3, only, *portraits of Pope and Addison*, royal 8vo. *boards*, 5*s* 1806

3794 — Poetical Works, with Notes, by Bp. Warburton, and Life, *portrait and plates*, 12mo. *cloth, new, gilt*, 5*s* 1858

3795 — Letters of Mr. Pope, and several Eminent Persons, from 1705 to 1735, *portrait*, 12mo. *half calf*, 3*s* 6*d* .. 1735

At the end, Pope's Letters to a Lady, never before published, *Dodsley*, 1769.

3796 — Rape of the Lock, *with plates by Bartolozzi and others, after Stothard*, 8vo. *fine copy, half bound in red morocco, top edges gilt*, 6*s* .. .. .. .. 1798

Dr. Roveray's fine edition, printed by T. Bensley.

3797 — Essay on Man, *plate*, 12mo. *boards*, 1*s* .. 1815

"Neither time, nor distance, nor grief, nor age, can ever diminish my veneration for him, who is the great moral poet of all times, of all climes, of all feelings, and of all stages of existence. The delight of my boyhood, the study of my manhood, perhaps,—if allowed me to attain it—he may be the consolation of my age. His poetry is the Book of Life."—*Byron*.

3798 — Life, with Critical Essay on his Writings and Genius, by Owen Ruffhead, 8vo. *calf, neat*, 4*s* .. .. 1769

3799 POPERY—The 7th and 8th Controversial Letters, or Grand Controversie, concerning the pretended Temporal Authority of Popes over the whole Earth, 4to. *sewed*, 2*s* .. 1673

3800 POPERY—A Reasonable Defence of the Seasonable Discourse: shewing the necessity of maintaining the Established Religion in opposition to Popery, 4to. *sewed*, 2*s* .. 1674

3801 — Protestants Remonstrance against Pope and Presbyter, in an Essay on the Times, by Philangus, small 4to. *sewed*, 2*s* 1681

3802 — Wake's (Abp.) Examination of the Doctrine of the Church of England, against the Bp. of Meaux, 1686.—His Defence of the Exposition, 1686.—His Second Defence, 1st part, 1687.—His Second Defence, 2nd part, 1687.—First part of Claude's Answer to Bp. of Meaux, 1687.—Second part of ditto, 1687.—A Vindication of A. Cressener, schoolmaster, of Long Acre, against Pulton, 1687, in 1 vol. thick 4to. *fine clean copies, old calf, neat*, 12*s* .. .. .. .. 1686-7

These tracts form a portion of Bp. Gibson's Preservative against Popery.

3803 PORCACCHI (Thomaso) Il primo volume (*solamente, Haym*) delle cagioni delle Guerre antiche, 4to. *fine copy, in limp vellum*, 10*s* 6d *Venegia, Gab. Giolito*, 1575

This is the 1st volume of the Italian's "Collana Greca," very scarce, two of Giolito's devices.

3804 — L'Isole piu famose del Mondo, *e intagliate da Girolamo Porro*, folio, *old vellum, a fine copy*, £2 2*s* *In Venetia appresso Simon Galignani, et Girolamo Porro*, 1576

This is the Original Edition, with the Initials of Sir Christopher Hatton's name stamped outside. The maps of the islands and the views of the cities are finely engraved by Porro.

3805 PORQUET'S Tresor de l'Ecolier Français, the Art of Translating English into French, 12mo. *cloth*, 2*s* (*pub. at* 4*s* 6*d*) 1835

3806 PORRÉE (Jonas) Traité des Anciennes Ceremonies, leur Naissance et Accroissement, leur entrée en l'Eglise et par quels degrez elles ont passé jusques à la superstition, 12mo. *old binding*, 3*s* *Quevilly*, 1673

Dedicated to our K. Charles II., and has the autograph of "*Blomefield, Caii*, 1727." the Norfolk Historian.

3807 — une autre edition, 12mo. *old binding*, 3*s* *ib.*, 1677

Dedicated to Charles I. and II. The Ceremonies date from A. D. 110 to 1470.

3808 PORSONI (Ricardi) Adversaria: Notæ et Emendationes in Poetas Græcos, curaverunt J. H. Monk et C. J. Blomfield, *portrait*, 8vo. *calf, grained, very neat*, 6*s* 6*d* (*pub. at* 25*s*) *Cantab.*, 1812

3809 PORTEUS'S (Bp. Beilby) Works, with his Life, by Robert Hodgson, *portrait*, 6 vols. 8vo. *boards*, 12*s* 6*d* 1811

3810 — Porteusian Index; or, Family Guide to the Holy Scriptures, 8vo. *bound*, 1*s* .. .. .. 1828

3811 PORTLAND Museum, a Catalogue of, with the Prices and Purchasers' Names at the end, *frontispiece by Grignion*, 4to. *half calf, neat*, 7*s* 6*d* .. .. .. 1786

The amount of the 39 days' sale of this splendid collection of articles of Vertu, was above £11,000. A copy of this Catalogue sold at the Fonthill sale for 20*s*.

3812 PORTRAIT Gallery: by the Society for the diffusion of Useful Knowledge, more than 150 *portraits*, 3 vols. imperial 8vo. 42*s* (*pub. at* 63*s*) .. .. *London*, 1853

3813 PORTRAIT of the "Father of the Turf," Tregonwell Frampton, Esq., of Moreton, Dorsetshire, by John Jones, *mezzotint*, large folio, 5*s*

Mr. Frampton was born in the reign of K. Cha. I., when racing first commenced at Newmarket, he died in 1727, at the age of 86. There is a most extraordinary story told here of his cruelty to his horse Dragon, see Dr. Hawkesworth's Adventurer, No. 37.

3814 — Sir Julius Cæsar, 1557-1636, 4to. *print*, 1*s* 1810

3815 — of Sir Robert Stapleton, *by P. Lombart, most brilliant impression*, taken out of Stapleton's Translation of Juvenal, 15*s* 1660

3816 — Michael Angelo Buonarotti, Florentine Painter, *by W. Sherwin*, folio, 2*s*

3817 — Giacomo Barozzio de Vignola, *by W. Sherwin*, folio, 1*s* 6*d*

3818 — of Sir Michael Foster, Judge, 6*d*.—Judge Blackstone, 6*d*.—Sir Matthew Hale, 6*d*.—Lord Chief Justice Holt, 6*d*.—Sir Edw. Coke, 6*d*.—Sir Thomas Littleton, 6*d*.—Lord Chief Justice Raymond, 6*d*.—Sir Will. Webb Follett, 6*d*

3819 — 32 from Lodge, imperial 8vo. clean, 1*s* each 1829

*A List of* 500 PORTRAITS *will be found at the end of this Catalogue*

3820 POSSEVINI (Doct. Antonii) Belli Montferratensis Historia ab 1612 ad 1618, folio, *old cf, nt*, 12*s* *Genevæ, Petri Chouet*, 1637

3821 POSSEVINI (Gio. Battista) Dialogo dell' HONORE, nel quale si tratta à pieno del DUELLO, 4to. *limp vellum, rare*, 10*s* 6*d*
*In Vinegia, appresso Gab. Giolito de Ferrari*, 1553

With the beautiful devices of Gioliti on the title page, and, on a separate leaf, at the end—this is an edition not mentioned by Haym or Brunet, and is a very early one.

3822 — le medesime, 4to. *vellum, stained*, RARE, 12*s*
*Vinegia, Gabriel Giolito*, 1559

A fine specimen of the device used by Sir Christopher Hatton for stamping his books outside. This edition has a Treatise by Antonio Possevinus, "dell' Honore," and three splendid specimens of the devices used by the Gioliti, copied by Dr. Dibdin into his Decameron.

3823 POSTELLI (Guil.) de Universitate lib. II., in quibus Astronomiæ, doctrinæ ve Cælestis compendium, *portrait*, 24mo. *vellum*, 3*s*
*L. Bat.*, 1635

3824 POST Office Directory of Cambridgeshire, Norfolk, Suffolk, Essex, Hertfordshire, Kent, Middlesex, Surrey, and Sussex, *maps*, very thick 8vo. *cloth*, 15*s*

3825 POTTER (Abp. John) Discourse on Church Government, Vindicating the Rights of the Church, 8vo. *old calf, neat*, 5*s* 1707

3826 — another, the Third Edition, 8vo. *old calf, neat*, 6*s* 1724

"An excellent Discourse."—*Dr. J. Seed.*

3827 POTTS'S (Tho.) Law Dictionary, 12mo. *law calf*, 3*s* 6*d* 1803

3828 POZZUOLO—Sito et Antichita della Cita di, con le figure de gli Edificii, e con gli Epitafi che vi sono del Signor Scip. Mazella.—Opusculum de Balneis Puteolorum, Baiarum et Pithecusarum.—Apparato delle Statue, nuovamente trovate nella distrutta Cuma, dal Sig. Antonia Ferro, small 8vo. *old vellum*, RARE, 12*s*
*Napoli*, 1606

Pozzuoli, anciently Puteoli, was the chief sea-port and mart of the inhabitants of Cumæ, and a rendezvous for merchants from Italy, Sicily, and Greece, whilst the attraction of the town and its baths allured the more opulent Romans to its vicinity.

3829 PRATT (Rev. Jermyn, *Rector of Campsey Ash, Suffolk,*) Record of the College of Christ Church, Brecon, *plate*, royal 8vo. *sewed*, 3*s* 6*d* .. .. .. .. 1846

3830 — another copy, *with a MS. Note from the Author*, 4*s* 6*d* 1846

"I send you 2 copies of the Record. It's not published and the copies are nearly all gone."—*MS. Note from Author.*

3831 PRATT'S (John Tidd) Summary of the Office and Authority of a Justice of the Peace out of Sessions, 12mo. *law calf, neat*, 5*s* (*cost* 10*s*) .. .. .. .. 1828

There has been no more recent edition.

3832 PRESTON'S (Dr. John) Saints Qualification, a Treatise of Humiliation and Sanctification and the Sacrament, XXII. Sermons, 4to. *half calf, gilt*, 7*s* 6*d* .. .. .. 1634

3833 — Breast-Plate of Faith and Love, XVIII. Sermons, 4to. *half calf, gilt*, 5*s* 6*d* .. .. .. 1634

3834 — Golden Sceptre; with the Churches Marriage and the Churches Carriage, three Treatises, *engraved frontispiece by G. Glover*, in 1 vol. 4to. *half calf, gilt*, 5*s* 6*d* .. .. 1638

3835 — Saints Daily Exercise; V. Sermons, 1629.—V. Sermons Preached before H. Majesty, 1637.—Doctrine of Saint's Infirmities, 1638. —in 1 vol. 4to. *half, calf, very neat*, 5*s* 6*d* .. V.Y.

3836 — New Covenant; or, The Saint's Portion in XVIII. Sermons, 4to. *old calf, neat*, 6*s* .. .. .. 1639

3837 — New Covenant; or, the Saint's Portion, 1630.—Saint's Daily Exercise, the Whole Dutie of Prayer, 1631.—Sermons Preached before his Majestie, 1631.—in 1 vol. thick 4to. *in very fine condition, old calf*, 10*s* 6*d* .. .. 1630-31

Mr. Bickersteth says, Preston is "a holy, evangelical and lively writer."

3838 PRETENDER (The) Memorie del Cavalier di San Giorgio, e le promesse del Re' di Francia al Pretendente, con le Quistioni proposte a Londra nel mese di Luglio, 1712, in favore dello stesso, trad. dal Dottor P. Alberizzi, *portrait*, 12mo. *sewed, scarce*, 3*s* 6*d* *Milano*, 1714

Autograph of *T. Hobart*, an old Norfolk name.

3839 PRICE'S (John) History of the City of Hereford, with Remarks on the River Wye, *maps and plates*, 8vo. *half calf, neat*, 3*s* 6*d* *Hereford*, 1796

3840 PRICE'S (Dr. Richard) Observations on Reversionary Payments, Annuities, Life Assurances, The National Debt, &c. 2 vols. 8vo. *boards*, 4*s* .. .. .. .. 1783

3841 PRIDEAUX'S (Humphrey, *Dean of Norwich,*) Life of Mahomet, with his Letter to the Deists, vindicating Christianity from the Charge of Imposture, 8vo. *old calf, gilt, a fine copy on* THICK PAPER, 5*s* .. .. .. 1708

"*N. L'Estrange ex dono Autoris.*" L'Estrange an old Norfolk name.

3842 — Old and New Testament Connected in the History of the Jews, &c. to the Time of Christ, *maps and plates*, 4 vols. 8vo. *old calf, neat*, 12*s* .. .. .. .. 1725

3843 — another copy, vol. 4 only, *old calf*, 2*s* 6*d* .. 1725

"Contains a large mass of erudition and accurate information on every topic of Jewish history and antiquities."—*Orme.*

3844 PRIDEAUX'S Original and Right of Tythes, with the Draught of a Bill for Restraining Pluralities, 8vo. *good copy in cf.* 3s 6d *Knaplock,* 1736

3845 PRIMERS—Three Primers put forth in the Reign of Henry VIII., 8vo. *cloth,* 5s .. *Oxford, the Clarendon,* 1848

Contents; 1. A Goodly Primer, 1535.—II. The Manual of Prayers, or the Prymer in English, 1539.—III. King Henry's Primer, 1545.

3846 PRINT—"William Penn's Treaty with the Indians, in 1681," engraved by John Hall, after Benjamin West, framed and glazed, £2 12s 6d .. .. .. 1775

A remarkably fine impression of a very scarce print.

3847 — Mill, by Woollett, fine impression, framed and glazed, 12s

3848 — Queen Philippa Pleading for the Burgesses of Calais, *gilt frame and glazed,* £1 1s .. .. *Art Union,* 1853

3849 — Christ Led to Crucifixion, *gilt frame and glazed,* 15s *Art Union,* 1853

3850 — The Clemency of Cœur de Lion and the Piper, two prints, 10s (*pub at* £1 1s) .. .. *Art Union,* 1857

3851 PRIOLI (Benj.) ab excessu Ludovici, XIII. de Rebus Gallicis Historiarum libri XII., 4to. *old boards,* 6s .. *Parisiis,* 1665

"A very impartial history from 1642 to 1664."—*Chalmers.*

3852 — alia editio, 12mo. *old calf, gilt,* 6s *Ultrajecti, Elzevirii,* 1669

3853 PRIOR (Matthew) Poems, *frontispiece by Baron and plates,* royal folio, LARGEST PAPER, *old calf, gilt,* 10s *Jacob Tonson,* 1717

This edition is celebrated as containing the reprint of the "Nut Brown Maid, written 300 years since," and "Henry and Emma," by himself, a Poem founded upon that beautiful ballad. The original of which is in Arnold's Chronicle, see No. 257.

3854 — another edition, *portrait,* 2 vols. 12mo. *calf,* 4s .. 1741

3855 — another copy, *portrait,* 12mo. *old calf, neat,* 3s 6d 1741

"Prior's seems to me amongst the earliest, the richest, the most charmingly humorous of English lyrical poems."—*Thackeray's English Humourists,* p. 175.

3856 PRISCIANI Opera Grammatica, recensuit, lectionum Varietatem notavit et Indices locupletissimos adjecit A. Krehl, Editio Optima, 2 vols. 8vo. *half calf, neat,* 10s. .. *Lipsiæ,* 1819-20

3857 PRIVATE Devotions in the Practice of the Ancient Church, called the Hours of Prayer, afterwards pub. by Q. Elizabeth's Authority in 1560, 12mo. *old calf,* 3s .. *Royston,* 1672

3858 PROLOGUES and EPILOGUES; a Collection and Selection of English, commencing with Shakespeare and concluding with Garrick, *portraits of celebrated Actors dressed in character,* vols. 1, 2, and 3, (vol. 4 missing) 12mo. *clean and neat,* 9s 1779

The Prologues are all here, it is the 2nd vol. of Epilogues that is missing.

3859 PROPHECIES of Christopher Kotterus, Christiana Poniatovia, Nicholas Drabicius, being Three Famous and Eminent Prophets in Germany, Foretelling this present Invasion of the Turks into the Empire of Germany, Englished by R. Codrington, 12mo. *bound, curious,* 5s .. .. .. 1664

3860 PROPHECY concerning the Seventh Millenium, *on a broadside,* CURIOUS, 5s .. .. *No date, about* 1680

3861 PROVERBI Italiani, da Orlando Pescetti, e Proverbi Italiani e Latini, thick 12mo. *old vellum, injured by damp,* 4s *In Vinetia, S. Combi,* 1611

An edition not mentioned by Haym; this is edited by Tobia Scoltetti, Poet Laureat.

3862 PROVERBS—Walker (Will.) Phraseologia Anglo-Latina; English and Latin Phrases, with a Collection of English and Latin Proverbs and Proverbial Sayings Match'd together, 8vo. *old binding*, 5*s* .. .. .. *R. Royston*, 1672

Mr. Walker was Master of the Public School at Grantham.

3863 PRUDENTIUS (Aurelius) Carmina, a Sicardo et Erasmo, small 8vo, *good copy in old calf*, 8*s* *Basiliæ, per H. Petrum*, 1540

Born at Saragossa, in Spain in 348. Highly esteemed by the Emperor Honorius. Some of his Poems are allowed to possess the true poetic spirit. See *Dr. Clarke's Bib. Dict.*

3864 PRYNNE'S (Will.) Histrio-Mastix, the Player's Scourge, or Actor's Tragædie, showing that Stage Playes (the very Pompes of the Divell) are Sinfull, Heathenish, Lewde, Ungodly Spectacles, thick 4to. of above 1100 pages, *wants title and a leaf or two of Index, also stained by water*, 18*s* .. .. 1633

For writing this book, Prynne was tried in the Star Chamber and sentenced "to have his book burnt by the common hangman, to be put from the bar, to be for ever incapable of his profession, to be degraded at Oxford, to stand in the Pillory, to lose both his ears, to pay a fine of £5000, and to suffer perpetual imprisonment." Sharp work this my masters.

3865 PSALTERIUM, Hebræum, Græcum, Arabicum et Chaldeum, cum tribus latinis interpretationibus et Glossis, folio, *old vellum*, £2 2*s* *Genoæ, Petrus Paulus Porrus Mediolanensis, Taurini degens*, 1516

This early Polyglott Psalter was executed at Genoa, its editor was Agostino Giustiniani Bishop of Nebo. The Arabic in it is the first that ever was printed. "Justinianus in his curious edition of the Polyglott Psalter, 1516, has introduced by way of commentary on Ps. XIX, 4, a very curious sketch of the Life of Columbus, (who was born at Genoa) an account of his discovery of America, and also a description of the inhabitants, particularly of the female native Americans."—*Chalmers' Biog. Dict.* As Columbus died in 1506, this is probably the first printed account of him now existing.

3866 — Hebraicè, 12mo. *calf, neat*, 3*s* *L. Bat., J. Maire*, 1637

3867 — 1 to 41, in Hebrew, (the Radicals black, the Serviles hollow) with Interlineary Greek and English Translations, 4to. *hf. bd. neat*, 10*s* 6*d* .. .. .. 1846

Printed at the private press of Dr. Bialloblotsky, at Winchmore Hill, and not mentioned in Mr. Martin's list of privately printed books.

3868 — Græcè, 18mo. *old cf. neat*, 3*s* 6*d* *Parisiis, apud C. Morellum*, 1618

At the end, Sternhold and Hopkins's Psalms in English, 1672, and "a paraphrase on the 148 Psalm by the Lord Roscommon," in MS.

3869 — Metaphrasis Libri Psalmorum Græcis Versibus contexta, cum Versione Lat., per Jac. Duportum, sm. 8vo. *old binding*, 4*s* *Londini*, 1674

Dr. Duport was Regius Professor of Greek in Cambridge. This book is very honourably mentioned by Fabricius and Dr. Birch in his Life of Abp. Tillotson.

3870 — The Whole Booke of Psalmes, with the Note, by Sternhold and Hopkins, 8vo. £1 1*s* .. *London, by J. Daye*, 1581

Dr. Cotton says there is a copy of this rare book in Brasen Nose College Library, Oxford. This is bound up at the end of an old volume of MS. Sermons of the time of Charles I.

3871 — by Sternhold and Hopkins, *Stationer's Companie*, 1647.—The Psalter with Titles and Collects fitted to each Psalme, 1647.—Devotions for the Help and Assistance of all Christian People, *R. Royston*, 1647, *engraved frontispiece*, 12mo. (Psalter wants title) *scarce*, 10*s* .. .. .. 1647

3872 PSALMS; a New Translation from the Original Hebrew, with Explanatory Notes by Dr. French, Master of Jesus Coll. Camb., and Rev. Geo. Skinner, 8vo. *cloth*, 8*s* (*pub. at* 12*s*) *Cambridge*, 1842

3873 — Nouvelle Version des Psaumes, faite sur le Texte Hébreu; avec des Argumens et des Notes, qui en développent le double sens Literal, et le sens Moral, par les Auteurs des Principes discutés, 12mo. *french calf, gilt*, 4*s* 6*d* .. *Paris*, 1762

3874 PSELLI (Michaelis) de Operatione Dæmonum Dialogus, Gr. et Lat., Notis illustravit Gilb. Gaulminus, small 8vo. *old vellum wrapper*, 10*s* 6*d* .. .. .. *Lut. Par.*, 1615

Michael Psellus was preceptor to and friend of Michael Ducas, Emperor of Constantinople. He flourished in 1070.

3875 PUBLISHER'S CIRCULAR (Lowe's) vol. 1, Sept. 1837 to Dec. 1838—then from 1844 to 1859, complete, being vol. 7 to 22, the last 3 vols have the 5*s* Indexes, £5

3876 PUFENDORF (Le Baron) Devoirs de l'Homme et du Citoien, traduits du Latin par Jean Barbeyrac, *portrait*, thick 12mo. *calf, neat*, 3*s* .. .. .. *Amsterdam*, 1715

3877 PUFFENDORF (Sam.) Elementorum Jurisprudentiæ Universalis librii II., cum Appendice de Sphæra Morali, small 8vo. *old calf, neat*, 3*s* .. .. *Cantabrigiæ, Hayes*, 1672

3878 PULPIT—Index to 50 volumes of the Pulpit, an Index of Authors and a Textual Index, 8vo. *cloth*, 2*s* 6*d*

3879 PUNCH—Vols. 10, 11, 12, 13, 16, 17, 18, 19, 8 vols. bound in 4, *half calf*, 25*s* .. .. .. 1846-50

3880 PUNCH'S Almanack for 1848, Illustrated by John Leech and Richard Doyle, *coloured plates*, imperial 4to. *stiff covers, gilt edges*, 4*s* .. .. .. .. 1848

3881 PUNCH and Judy, with an account of the Puppet Show, and of its Origin in Italy and England, 24 *coloured plates by George Cruikshank*, post 8vo. *bds*, SCARCE, 6*s* (*pub. at* 12*s*) *Prowett*, 1828

3882 PURCHAS (Samuel) Theatre of Political Flying Insects, 4to. (wants title) 5*s* .. .. .. 1657

"An amusing book on the Natural History of Bees."—*Lowndes.*

3883 PURGATORY—The Vision of Purgatory, Anno 1680, in which the errors and practices of the Church and Court of Rome are discover'd, by Heraclito Democritus, *frontispiece*, small 8vo. *half calf, gilt*, 3*s* 6*d* .. .. .. 1680

3884 PURNELL'S (Robert) Little Cabinet richly stored with all sorts of Heavenly Varieties, and Soul-reviving influences, small 8vo. *half calf, neat*, 7*s* 6*d* .. .. .. 1657

Not in Darling, Stewart, Straker, Rivington, or Lowndes.

3885 PURSUITS of Literature, a Satirical Poem, with Notes, and the citations translated, attributed to T. J. Mathias, 4to. *boards*, 12*s* (*pub. at* £3 3*s*) .. .. .. 1812

Handsomely printed by Bulmer, and this Quarto edition intended for illustration.

3886 PYCROFT'S (James) Course of English Reading, with Anecdotes of Men of Genius, 12mo. *cloth, neat*, 3*s* 6*d* (*pub. at* 5*s*) 1844

3887 — another edition, 12mo. *cloth, new*, 5*s* *Longmans*, 1854

3888 PYE'S (H. J.) Summary of the Duties of a Justice of the Peace out of Sessions, 4th and last edition, 12mo. *law calf*, 4*s* 1827

3889 QUAIN'S (Dr. Jones) Muscles of the Human Body, with Physiological Comments, 51 *plates*, in royal folio, *hf. cf, neat*, £2 2*s* 1836

This is a very fine Work, and the most elaborate on this subject, in addition it has a fine figure by Michael Angelo from the Sistine Chapel.

3890 QUAKERS—Barclay's (Robt.) Apology for the True Christian Divinity, a Vindication of the Principles and Doctrines of the Quakers, thick 8vo. *calf, neat*, 5*s* .. 1765

3891 — Barton (Bernard) Devotional Verses, 12mo. *boards*, 3*s* 6*d* (*pub. at* 6*s* 6*d*) .. .. .. 1826

"Jos. John Gurney, from his affectionate friend, the author."

3892 — Bates (Elisha, *of Mount Pleasant, Ohio*) Doctrines of Friends, as held by them, 12mo. *calf, neat*, 2*s* 6*d* *Leeds*, 1829

3893 — Bayly's (William) Collection of the several Wrightings of that true prophet and sufferer who finished his testimony, 1675, small 4to. *old calf, neat, scarce*, 7*s* 6*d* .. 1676

3894 — Besse's (Joseph) Defence of Quakerism, in answer to Patrick Smith's Preservative against Quakerism, 8vo. *old cf, nt*, 3*s* 6*d* 1732

3895 — Collection of Acts of Parliament and Clauses of Acts relative to the Quakers, from 1688, 4to. *bound*, 3*s* 6*d* *Luke Hinde*, 1757

3896 — Collection of Memorials concerning divers deceased Ministers and other Quakers in Pennsylvania, New Jersey, from nearly the first settlement thereof, 8vo. *neat*, 5*s* *Philadelphia*, 1787

3897 — Gratton's (John) Journal of his Life, 1641 to 1711, with his Treatises on Baptism, the Lord's Supper, Tithes, and some Poetry, 8vo. 5*s* .. .. *J. Sowle*, 1720

3898 — Hancock's (John) Reasons for withdrawing from the Quakers, 1802.—Joseph Gurney Bevan's Refutation of some of the more modern misrepresentations of the Quakers, with a Life of James Naylor, 1800.—Joseph Phipps's Dissertations on Christian Baptism, 1796.—Josiah Forster's People called Quakers Defended, and the Baptists Confuted, 1740.—W. Savery and G. Dillwyn, of N. America, 3 Sermons at the Meeting House, Houndsditch, July 19, 1796, in 1 vol. 8vo. *half bound*, 5*s*

3899 — Holland's (Rich.) Sermon at St. Magnus the Martyr, by London Bridge, Feb. 11, 1699, at the baptizing some Quakers now conform'd to the Church of England, 4to. *sewed*, 1*s* 6*d* 1700

3900 — Keith's (George) Way to the City of God described, and the way to discern the motions of the Spirit of God, small 8vo. *old binding, scarce*, 5*s* 6*d* .. .. *No place*, 1678

This is apparently privately printed either in Aberdeen or Edinburgh, he says he wrote the 1st Treatise in 1669, when he was a close prisoner in the Tolbooth, in Edinburgh: the 2nd was written in 1676, during the time of his confinement in Aberdeen.

3901 — Penn's (Will.) Quakerism a new Nick-name for Old Christianity, in answer to Faldo's Quakerism no Christianity, small 8vo. *bound*, 3*s* 6*d* .. *No place nor Printer's name*, 1672

In this book the Rise, Doctrine, and Practice of the abused Quakers are truly declared.

3902 — — Brief account of the Rise and Progress of the Quakers, 12mo. *bound*, 2*s* .. .. .. 1748

3903 QUAKERS Martyrology—The Spirit of the Martyrs Revived, in a brief Compendious collection of faithful Martyrs in all ages, thick 8vo. *old calf*, SCARCE, 6*s* .. *J. Sowle*, 1719

One portion of this contains an abridgement of Fox.

3904 — Obituary for 1857, 18mo. *cloth*, 1*s* .. 1857

3905 — Rules of Discipline of the Religious Society of Friends, with Advices, 3rd Edition, 4to. *calf, neat*, 10*s* .. 1834

Mr. Joseph John Gurney's copy.

3906 — Sewell's (Will.) History of the Rise, Increase, and Progress of the Quakers, 2 vols. 8vo. *nice copy, in calf*, 10*s* 6*d* 1795

3907 — Stirredge's Strength in Weakness manifest: in the Life of Elizabeth Stirredge, who died at Hempsted in Hertfordshire, the 7 of 9 mo. 1706, written by her own hand, 12mo. *old calf, neat*, 4*s* .. .. .. 1711

With the autograph of Richd. Elliott, her great grandson, and of Frances Cressey, who bought it of the widow Elliott in 1794.

3908 — The Perfect Pharisee under Monkish Holines, published by Thomas Weld, Rich. Prideaux, Sam. Hammond, W. Cole, W. Durant, Ministers in Newcastle, 4to. *sewed*, 3*s* 6*d* *London, R. Tomlins*, 1654

3909 — Thompson's (Thomas) The Glorious Truth of Universal Grace and Atonement exalted, 8vo. *calf, neat*, 3*s* 6*d* 1749

3910 QUARLES'S (Francis) Judgment and Mercy for afflicted Souls, Meditations, Soliloquies, and Prayers, with a biographical and Critical Introduction by Reginalde Wolfe, (i.e. Thomas Frognall Dibdin,) *portrait after Marshall*, 8vo. *boards, scarce*, 5*s* 1807

3911 — Enchiridion; containing Institutions, Divine, Contemplative, Practical, Moral, &c., *portrait*, foolscap 8vo. *cloth*, 3*s* *J. R. Smith*, 1857

"Had this book been written at Athens or Rome, its author would have been classed with the wise men of his country."—*Headley*.

3912 QUARTERLY Review, 96 to 101, 104 to 116, 121, 123 to 129, 132, 3, 4, 136, 138 to 144, 146 to 158, 161, 163 to 167, 169 to 172, 185 to 188, 197, 198, 201 to 206, 1*s* 6*d* *each* (*pub. at* 6*s*)

3913 QUEEN'S Closet opened; Incomparable Secrets in Physick, Chyrurgery, Preserving, Candying, &c., *portrait of Queen Henrietta Maria*, 18mo. *old binding, curious*, 5*s* .. 1679

The 2nd part is called "The Queen's Delight." See Lord *Ruthven's* Ladies Cabinet Opened.

3914 QUERARD—Notice Bibliographique des Ouvrages de M. De La Mennais de leurs réfutations de leurs apologies et des biographies de cet Ecrivain, 8vo. *sewed*, 3*s* 6*d* *Paris*, 1849

3915 QUINCY (Le Marquis de) L'Art de la Guerre; ou Maximes et Instructions sur l'Art Militaire, *plates and tables*, 2 vols. 12mo. *old calf, gilt*, 4*s* .. .. *La Haye*, 1728

3916 QUINTILIANI Institutionum Oratoriarum lib. XII., diligentius recogniti, 1522, 8vo. *old vellum, title and* 1 *leaf mended*, 16*s* *Venetiis in Ædibus Aldi*, 1521

This impression was edited by Ramusius, it contains Naugerius's Preface, with the Table of Chapters and Greek Words, "quas ipse author in latinum non transtulit."

3917 QUINTILIANUS, alia editio, juxta Edit. Gottingensem J. M. Gesneri; accedunt Præfatio et Indices copiosissimi, 2 vols. 8vo. *calf, very neat,* 7*s* 6*d* .. .. *Oxonii,* 1806

3918 — alia editio, juxta Edit. Gottingensem J. M. Gesneri, 2 vols. 18mo. *half vellum, very neat,* 5*s* .. *Edinburgi,* 1810

3919 QUINTUS CALABER (sive Quintus Smyrnæus) Gr. et Lat., a Laurentio Rhodomano, thick 8vo. *old cf, nt,* 8*s* *Hanoviæ,* 1604

"This edition is a very respectable one."—*Dr. Clarke.* Cardinal Bessarion discovered this ancient poem, which is a sort of supplement to the Iliad of Homer, in Calabria, Q. Smyrneus lived A.D. 500.

3920 QUINTUS CURTIUS, small 8vo. *old binding,* 10*s* 6*d* *Venetiis, in Ædibus Aldi,* 1520

"Ce volume est rare."—*Renouard.*

3921 — alia editio, 2 vols. 18mo. *purple morocco, gilt leaves,* 8*s* *Londini, typis J. Brindley,* 1746

Very beautiful little pocket volumes. Brindley's type is extremely clear though diminutive.

3922 QUIQUERAN (Pierre, *Evéque de Senés*) La Provence, donné en Français par F. Nyny de Claret, archid. d'Arles, *arms,* 8vo. 640 pages, (wants title,) *scarce,* 6*s* *Lyon, Rob. Raynaud,* 1614

This curious work has many introductory laudatory Sonnets by Nostradamus and others.

3923 RABELAIS (Francois) Œuvres, contenant cinq. livres de la Vie, Faits et ditt Heroiques de Gargantua & de son fils Pantagruel, thick 12mo. *neat, rare,* £1 1*s* *Anvers, par Jean Fuet,* 1605

This curious edition of Rabelais, is printed in the very year that Cuesta, of Madrid, put forth his First Edition of Don Quixote.

3924 — his Works, translated from the French, by Sir Thomas Urquhart and Motteux, with explanatory Notes, and Life, *portrait,* 2 vols. post 8vo. *cloth,* 6*s* .. *H. G. Bohn,* 1849

3925 RABENHORST'S Pocket Dictionary of the German and English Languages, by Noehden and Lloyd, thick 24mo. *bound,* 5*s* 1829

3926 RABUTIN (Roger, *Comte de Bussy, Lt. Gen. des Armées du Roy)* Memoires, 1635-1666, 3 vols. 12mo. *old French calf, gilt,* 6*s* *Paris,* 1712

Details the adventures at Court and in the Army, of this distinguished French officer and wit.

3927 RADCLIFFE'S (Mrs.) Mysteries of Udolpho, a Romance, *plates,* 2 vols. 24mo. *boards,* 5*s (pub. at* 9*s*) .. 1826

3928 RADCLIFFE (Dr. John) Memoirs of the Life of, with several original Letters, and a Copy of his Will, 8vo. *sewed,* 4*s* 1715

There is a notice of this scarce Tract in the *Retrospective Review.*

3929 RAFFLES (Sir Thomas Stamford) Memoir of his Life and Public Services, with his Correspondence, by his Widow, *bust, maps, and plates,* 4to. *half calf, gilt,* £1 5*s* (*pub. at* £2 12*s* 6*d*) 1830

Governor of Java 1811-1816, and of Bencoolen and its dependencies 1817-1824.

3930 RAII (Joannis) Synopsis Methodica Avium et Piscium, *plates,* 8vo. *old calf, neat, scarce,* 6*s* 6*d* .. *Londini,* 1713

3931 — Synopsis Methodica Stirpium Britannicarum, 24 *plates, coloured,* 8vo. *calf, neat,* 6*s* .. .. *ib.,* 1724

3932 RAILWAY CHRONICLE, Travelling Charts, London, Wolverton, Birmingham, 140 *cuts*, 1*s*

3933 RALEGH (Sir Walter) III. Discourses, 1. of a War with Spain, written by Command of K. James I. in 1602.—II. of Civil War.—III. of Ecclesiastical Power, *portrait by Van Hove*, 8vo. *half bound neat*, 2*s* 6*d* .. .. .. 1702

3934 RAMBLES in the United States and Canada in 1845, with an Account of Oregon, by Rubio, *plate*, post 8vo. *cloth, gilt leaves*, 3*s* .. .. .. .. 1846

3935 RAMI (Petri, *Regii Eloquentiæ Philos. Professoris*) Oratio, Sept. 8, 1551, sm. 8vo. *sewed*, 3*s* .. *Parisiis, M. Davidis*, 1551

3936 — Grammatica Latina, *Londini, Tho. Orwin*, 1589.—Grammatica Græca, præcipué quatenus à Latina differt, in 1 vol. small 8vo. *old calf*, 7*s* 6*d* .. *Francofurdi, A. Wechel*, 1586

This is a rare little volume. Its author, who suffered much persecution for opinions he entertained, was cruelly massacred in Paris on St. Bartholomew's day in 1572.

3937 RAMSEY'S (Allan) Ever Green; a Collection of Scots Poems, wrote by the Ingenious before 1600, vol. 2 only, 12mo. first edition, *old calf*, 5*s* .. .. *Edinburgh*, 1724

Contains New Year's Gift to Queen Mary, 1562.—Flyting of Dunbar to Kennedy—Dunbar's 2nd to Kennedy.—Kennedy's 2nd to Dunbar.—The Cherry and the Slae.—Johnie Armstrang.—Hardyknute and others, with a Glossary.

3938 RAMSGATE—81 Poems on single leaves, in 1 volume, 4to. *half bound, neat*, 7*s* 6*d*
*Privately printed by Burgess, Ramsgate*, 1785 to 1807

To dear Grandmamma Gostling, signed, James and George Townley, Doctor's Commons, May 28, 1789.—To Capt. and Mrs. Neville, with a goose, Shooter's Hill, Aug. 11, 1789.—Mrs. Townley's Address to the Ramsgate Volunteers, Sept. 22, 1797.—Rules to be observed at the Little Sherwood Ball, Oct. 26, 1799.—On the Degree of A.B. taken by my son Charles at Merton Coll., Oxford, 1803.—May serve to identify the author.

3939 RANDOLPH (Bishop, *of London*,) Catalogue of his Library, sold by Mr. Evans in April, *priced*, 8vo. *hf. cf. neat*, 2*s* 6*d* 1814

3940 RANDOLPH'S (Dr. Tho.) Prophecies and other Texts, Cited in the New Testament, compared with the Hebrew Original and Septuagint Version, in Hebrew and Greek, with Notes, 4to. *sewed, scarce*, 6*s* .. .. .. .. 1782

"This valuable and beautifully printed tract is now rarely to be met with."—*Prebendary Horne.* This "excellent critic" was President of C. C. C. Oxford, and Lady Margaret's Professor there.

3941 RANKE'S (Leopold) History of Servia, the Insurrection in Bosnia, and the Slave Provinces of Turkey, translated by Mrs. Alexander Kerr, post 8vo. *cloth*, 2*s* (*cost* 3*s* 6*d*) *H. G. Bohn*, 1853

3942 RANTZOV—Genealogia Nobilis ac Vetustæ Familiæ Ranzoviorum, nunc primum publicata, *wood cut portraits*, small 4to. 13 *leaves, sewed, clean as new*, 12*s* .. .. 1585

This curious and rare little tract is illustrated with 6 portraits and with arms cut in wood of this ancient Danish family.

3943 RAPHAEL—History of the Family of Medici, 14 *plates finely engraved by Bartoli and J. de Rubeis, after designs by Raphael*, oblong 4to. *boards*, 10*s* 6*d* .. .. *Romæ*, 1685

3944 RASTAL (William) Collection of Statutes from Magna Charta to the 28 Elizabeth, thick folio, **Black Letter**, above 1200 pages, *old binding*, £1 1*s* .. .. *Christ. Barker*, 1588

"Old Acts of Parliament are, as far as they go, the very best materials for an English History, and they are likewise strongly descriptive of the manners of the times."—*Barrington on the Statutes.*

3945 RATHBORNE'S (Aaron) Surveyor, in foure bookes, folio, *good copy in old calf*, RARE, £1 1*s* .. *London, W. Stansby*, 1616

With a PORTRAIT of the author, the only one there is of him, by Simon Pass; an engraved title-page by W. H., probably William Hole, not mentioned by Lowndes; and another portrait of Prince Charles, (afterwards King Charles I) engraved by Francis Delaram. The book is dedicated to the Prince. The engravings are all fine impressions.

3946 RAUMER (Fred. Von) Contributions to Modern History from the British Museum and State Paper Office, Queen Elizabeth and Mary Queen of Scots, *portrait*, post 8vo. *cloth*, 5*s* 6*d* (*pub. at* 10*s* 6*d*) .. .. .. .. 1836

3947 — Frederick II. and his Times, *portrait*, post 8vo. *cloth*, 5*s* 6*d* (*pub. at* 10*s* 6*d*) .. .. .. 1837

3948 RAY—Philosophical Letters between the Learned Mr. Ray and Several of his Ingenious Correspondents, with those of Francis Willoughby, Esq., published by W. Derham, 8vo. *calf, neat*, 3*s* 6*d* (see *Raii*) .. .. .. 1718

3949 READ (D. C. *of Salisbury*,) Catalogue of his Etchings, "*To my friend Miss Riseborough, D. C. Read*, 1832." 12mo. *boards*, 2*s* *Salisbury*, 1832

3950 READER'S (Thomas) Remarks on the Prophetic Part of the Revelation of St. John, 8vo. *calf, neat*, 4*s* .. 1778

3951 READING'S (Will.) Hist. of the Life of Christ, also of the Apostles and Evangelists, with Meditations and Prayers, *plates by Du Guernier*, 12mo. *calf, neat*, 3*s* 6*d* .. .. 1716

3952 REASONS WHY?—Housewife's Reason Why, 2*s* 6*d*—On General Science, 2*s* 6*d*—Biblical Reason Why, 2*s* 6*d*—Historical Reason Why, English History, 2*s* 6*d* .. .. 1859

3953 RECUEIL de quelques discours Politiques, escrits sur diverses occurrences des affaires et Guerres Estrangers depuis quinze ans en ça, 4to. 410 pages, *old limp vellum*, 6*s* .. 1632

No place or printer's name. Privately printed.

3954 REDDING'S (Cyrus) History and Description of Modern Wines, *plates*, 2nd edition, 8vo. *cloth*, 7*s* (*pub. at* 16*s*) .. 1836

3955 REDI (Francisci) Experimenta circa Generationem Insectorum, *numerous plates*, 12mo. *calf, very neat*, 4*s* *Amst.*, 1671

Autograph of "T. Fuller, Octob. 15, 1684."

3956 REECE'S (Dr. Richard) Medical Guide, 8vo. *calf, gilt*, 3*s* 1810

3957 — Popular Catalogue of Drugs, their Properties, Doses to Adults and Children of Different Ages, &c., royal 8vo. *cloth*, 2*s* 6*d* 1836

3958 REED (Isaac, Esq., *Editor of the last edition of Shakspere*,) Catalogue of his Curious Library, sold by King and Lochée, in November, 8vo. *boards, uncut*, 5*s* .. .. .. 1807

"*The Prices of several of the most valuable lots are affixed.*"—*Wm. Stevenson.*

3959 REEK'S (Richard) Sermon at the Spittle, London, Faith and Good Workes United, small 4to. *sewed*, 2*s* *Tho. Harper*, 1630

3960 [REEVE'S (Clara)] Progress of Romance, with Remarks on the Good and Bad Effects of It, 2 vols. in 1, small 8vo. *calf, neat*, 5s *Colchester, for the Author*, 1785

A most entertaining book, by the author of the "Old English Baron."

3961 REEVE (Dr. Henry) Essay on the Torpidity of Animals, 8vo. *boards*, 2s 6d .. .. .. 1809

3962 REFLEXIONS sur les Grands Hommes qui sont Morts en Plaisantant, augmentée d'Epitaphes et autres Pieces Curieuses (par Deslandes) *frontispiece*, 16mo. *sewed, uncut*, 3s *Amst. Wetstring*, 1732

3963 REFORMATION in the Catholic Church of Germany, and the Downfall of Papal Authority, Englished, 8vo. *boards*, 2s (*pub. at* 5s 6d) .. .. .. .. 1819

3964 REGIMEN Contra Pestilentiam, sive Epidimiam Reverendissimi Domini Kaminti Episcopi Arusiensis Civitatis regni dacie artis Medicine expertissimi professoris.—Regimen sanitatis per Circulum anni valde utile, 6 leaves, **Black Letter**, 4to. *white vellum*, RARE, £1 11s 6d .. *No place, date, or printer's name*

The latter treatise in verse on three pages. The date of this curiosity is not easy to find, but it was certainly printed in the latter part of the XVth Century.

3965 REGIMEN Sanitatis Salerni; the Schoole of Salernes, most learned and Juditious Directorie for the Governing the Health of Man, Latin and English Verse, with the Comment, 4to. **Black Letter**, *old vellum, very neat*, 15s *London, Barnard Alsop*, 1617

"This celebrated poem was written by the learned Doctors of Salerno about the end of the XIth Century, and was composed for the use of Robert of Normandy, son of William the Conqueror. No poem was more popular in the middle ages, and many of its precepts are quoted even to this day."—*Sir A. Croke on Rhyming Latin Verse.*

3966 REID'S (Dr. D. B.) Rudiments of Chemistry, *cuts*, 12mo. *cloth*, 2s .. .. .. .. 1851

3967 REID'S (Eliza P.) Historical and Literary Botany; the Superstitions, &c. Relative to Trees, Plants, &c., and Proverbs deriving their Origin from Vegetables, 3 vols. 12mo. *boards*, 5s 1826

3968 RELIGIO Stoici, with a Friendly Address to the Phanaticks of all Sects and Sorts, 12mo. *old calf, scarce*, 3s 6d *Edenburgh, R. Brown*, 1665

By Sir George Mackenzie of Rosehaugh, born at Dundee 1636, died 1691.

3969 RELPH'S (Josiah, *of Sebergham, Cumberland*,) Miscellany of Poems, consisting of Pastorals in the Cumberland Dialect, Glossary, &c., 8vo. *old calf, scarce*, 5s .. *Glasgow, R. Foulis*, 1747

3970 REMARKS Addressed to the Common People, by a calm Observer, (the late Professor Smyth) 8vo. *sewed*, 6d *Norwich, C. Muskett*, 1848

3971 REMBRANDT Van Rhyn, a Catalogue and Description of the Etchings of, with Some Account of his Life, and a List of his best Pieces, by M. Gersaint, Englished, *etched portrait*, 12mo. *bound, scarce*, 9s .. .. .. 1752

Sold at Mr. Brockett's sale for 14s.

3972 RENNIE'S (James) Hand-Book of Plain Botany, *cuts*, 18mo. *cloth*, 1s .. .. .. .. 1839

3973 RENOUARD (Ant. Aug.) Annales de l'Imprimerie des Alde; où Histoire des trois Manuce et de leurs Editions, avec le Supplement, *portraits and plates*, 3 vols. in 2, 8vo. *good copy in calf, gilt leaves*, 14*s* .. .. .. 1803-12

"A very able work, and quite a sine quâ non on this subject."—*Classical Collector's Vade-Mecum*, 1822.

3974 — third edition, *portrait and devices*, 8vo. *newly half bound in green morocco, uncut, top edges gilt*, 18*s* .. *Paris*, 1834

3975 — Catalogue de la Bibliothéque d'un Amateur, avec Notes Bibliographiques, critiques et littéraries, 4 vols. 8vo. *sewed*, 12*s* *Paris*, 1819

This is a Catalogue of his own Library, and contains much curious and interesting bibliographical information. See *Preface to Dibdin's 4th edition of his Introduction to the Classics*.

3976 REPORTERS (OLD) Atkyns's (John Tracy) Chancery, in the Time of Lord Hardwicke, 1736 to 1754, 3 vols. folio, *law calf, neat*, £1 16*s* .. .. .. .. 1765-68

3977 — Burrow's (James) King's Bench, since the Death of Lord Raymond, 1756 to 1761, 2 vols. folio, *law calf, neat*, £1 4*s* 1766

3978 — Coke's (Lord Chief Justice) Reports, 11 parts, in English, with 2 Tables, and Lord Chancellor Egerton's Observations on, folio, *law calf, neat*, 12*s* .. .. .. 1680

3979 — Strange's (Sir John, *Master of the Rolls*,) Adjudged Cases in Chancery, K. Bench, Com. Pleas, and Exchequer, 2 Geo. 1 to 21, Geo. 2., 1715 to 1748, 2 vols. folio, *law calf, neat*, £1 4*s* 1755

Has a remarkably fine impression of the portrait by Houbraken.

3980 — Williams's (Will. Peere) Chancery and King's Bench, 1695 to 1734, 2 vols. folio, *law calf, neat*, £1 4*s* .. 1740

Very fine impression of the portrait, by George Vertue, after Sir Godfrey Kneller.

3981 — Harrison's Analytical Digest of all the Reports, from 1756 to 1843, vol. 4 only, being the Alphabetical Index of the Names of Cases, royal 8vo. *boards*, 21*s* .. .. 1844

3982 RESPUBLICA, sive Status Regni Scotiæ et Hiberniæ diversorum autorum, 18mo. *neat*, 3*s* .. *L. Bat., Elzevir*, 1627

Extracted out of Buchanan, Camden, Hector Boethius, and others.

3983 RESPUBLICA, sive Status Regni Poloniæ, Lituaniæ, Prussiæ, Livoniæ, etc. diversorum autorum, 24mo. *vellum, neat*, 4*s* *L. Bat., Elzeviriis*, 1627

The authors Stanislaus Krzistanovvic, Martin Cromer, Alexander Guagninus, Philip Honorius, John Boterus.

3984 RESPUBLICA Romana, 18mo. *old cf. nt.* 3*s* 6*d* *L. Bat., Elz.*, 1629

Consists of reprints of many rare Tracts on the Roman Laws, the Magistracy, &c.

3985 RETOFORTIS (Sam. *Theol. Professoris in Acad. Andreapolitanâ)* Disputatio Scholastica de Divina Providentia, variis Prælectionibus adversus Jesuitas, Arminianos, Socinianos, etc., thick 4to. of 620 pages, *old cf, nt*, 10*s* *Edinburgi, Georgii Andersoni*, 1650

This very scarce book is by Samuel Rutherford, author of "Religious Letters," once very popular. It is singular that there is no account of him in *Chalmers's Biog. Dict.*

3986 RETROSPECTIVE REVIEW, vols. 1 to 12, bound in 6, 8vo. *half calf, very neat,* vols. 13 and 14, p. 1, in parts, 2nd Series, vol. 1, in 3 parts, and parts 2 and 3 of vol. 2, £5 5*s* 1820-28

Wanting, therefore, part 2, of vol. 14, and part 1, vol. 2, of Second Series, for which 15*s* is offered.

3987 RETZ (Cardinal de) Memoirs of his Life, by himself, containing the most secret transactions of the French Court and the Civil Wars, *portrait,* 4 vols. 12mo. *calf, neat,* 10*s* 1774

"A valuable historical work," *Lowndes,*—and amazingly entertaining.

3988 RETZSCH'S (Moritz) Outlines to Schiller's Song of the Bell, with the Song in German and English, oblong, *sewed,* 10*s* *Stuttgart,* 1837

3989 — Outlines to Goethe's Faust, oblong, *sewed,* 12*s* *ib.,* 1836

3990 REUCHLIN (Jean) Dissertation Critique sur la nouvelle Bibliotheque des auteurs Ecclesiastiques, 24mo. *old binding, wormed,* 3*s* *Francfort,* 1688

Not in Brunet, it seems to be a critique on Dupin.

3991 REYNER'S (Edward, *Lincoln)* Rules for the Government of the Tongue, the Thoughts, and Affections, small 8vo. *calf, very neat,* 5*s* .. .. .. 1656

3992 REYNOLDS'S (Dr. George) Historical Essay on the Government of the Church of England, from the Earliest to the Present Times, 8vo. *newly bound in calf, very neat, very scarce,* 18*s* 1743

This is a very scarce book, "Vindicating the measures of Henry VIII. Edward VI. and Elizabeth," against DOD'S CHURCH HISTORY.

3993 REYNOLDS'S (Sir Joshua) Works, with Life, by Edmond Malone, *portrait,* 3 vols. 8vo. *good copy, in calf,* 12*s* 1809

Containing his Discourses to the Royal Academy, Idlers, Journey to Flanders and Holland, and his Commentary on Du Fresnoy's Art of Painting.

3994 — Seven Discourses delivered in the Royal Academy, 8vo. *calf, a nice clean copy,* 5*s* .. .. .. 1778

"Sir Joshua's profound knowledge in the art he professed, his classical attainments and polished mind, all appear conspicuous in his literary works."—*Monthly Review.*

3995 RHIN—Manuel des Voyageurs sur le Rhin, par Schreiber et Henry, *maps,* 12mo. *half bound, neat,* 2*s* *Francfort,* 1817

3996 — Slight Reminiscences of the Rhine, Switzerland, and a corner of Italy, *etchings,* 2 vols. post 8vo. *cloth,* 6*s* (*pub. at* £1 1*s*) *Longmans,* 1834

"Mrs. Opie, with kindest wishes, from her old friend."

3997 RHIND'S (Will.) History of the Vegetable Kingdom; embracing the Physiology of Plants, with their uses to man and the lower animals, *numerous engravings and wood-cuts,* royal 8vo. *nicely half bound, in calf, gilt,* 18*s* (*cost* 30*s*) .. 1855

3998 RHODOMANI (Laurentii) Palestinæ, seu Historiæ Sacræ, libri IX., Gr. et Lat., 4to. *old calf, neat,* 12*s* *Francofurdi, A. Wechel,* 1589

This learned German was especially skilled in Greek, he was Professor of History in the University of Wittemberg, where he died in 1606. An intimate of Scaliger and Henry Stephens.

3999 RHYTHMUS—Introductory Essay on the Study of English Rhythmus, 8vo. *half russia, neat,* 2*s* *No date*

4000 RIBELLES (Bartolomé) Compendio Historico de Todas las Epidemias padecidas en Valencia antes del anno 1647, *En Valencia, Joseph de Orga*, 1804.—Memoria de los sucesos particulares de Valencia y su Reyno en los annos de 1647 y 1648, tiempo de Peste escrita por Francisco Gavalda, 2 Tracts in 1 vol. 4to. *Spanish parchment binding, very clean and neat*, 10*s* *Valencia, Josef Estevan*, 1804

4001 RICAUT (Paul) Present State of the Greek and Armenian Churches, 8vo. *old calf, neat, scarce*, 6*s* .. 1679

4002 RICH (Claudius James) Second Memoir on Babylon, an inquiry into the Correspondence between the ancient descriptions of Babylon, and the remains still visible on the site, royal 8vo. *boards*, 3*s* .. .. .. 1818

"With the author's compliments." With 3 plates, shewing 3 forms of Babylonian cuneiform writing. Mr. Rich was resident for the Hon. E. I. Comp. at the Court of Bagdad.

4003 RICHARDI (Barth. Christ.) Historia Bibliothecæ Cæsareæ Vindobonensis ad nostra Tempora deducta, small 8vo. *old calf*, VERY SCARCE, 6*s* .. *Jenæ, ap. I. F. Bielckium*, 1712

4004 RICHARDSON'S (Jonathan) Works, by his Son, Mr. J. Richardson, 8vo. *calf, neat*, 6*s* .. .. 1773

1. Theory of Painting. II. Art of Criticism in Painting. III. The Science of a Connoisseur. "Sir Joshua Reynolds had the first fondness for his art excited by the perusal of Richardson's works."—*Lowndes.*

4005 RICHARDSON'S (Professor, *Glasgow*) Poems, chiefly Rural, small 8vo. *calf, gilt*, 2*s* 6*d* .. .. 1775

4006 RICHARDSON'S (Samuel) History of Sir Charles Grandison, in a Series of Letters, 7 vols. 12mo. *old calf*, 10*s* 1754

"Mr. Gray was much pleased with an answer which Dr. Samuel Johnson once gave to a person on the different and comparative merits of *Fielding* and of *Richardson*—"Why, Sir, Fielding could tell you what o'clock it was; but, as for Richardson, he could make a clock or a watch."—*Mathias's Observations on Gray's Writings*, p. 50.

4007 — another copy, *portrait*, 7 vols. 12mo. *calf, neat*, 6*s* 1766

"The power of Richardson's painting, in his deeper scenes of tragedy, never has been, and probably never will be excelled."—*Sir Walter Scott.*

4008 RICHELIEU—Testament Politique du Cardinal Duc de, avec des Observations Politiques de M. l'Abbé de S. Pierré, 2 vols. in 1, 12mo. *old calf, gilt*, 3*s* 6*d* .. *Amsterdam*, 1738

Autograph of "John Gurney, Earlham," and book-plate of "Joseph John Gurney, Earlham." Cardinal Richelieu was first Minister of France during the reign of Louis XIII.

4009 RIDDLE'S (J. E.) Progressive Latin-English Vocabulary, 12mo. *cloth*, 1*s* 6*d* .. .. .. 1847

4010 RIDDOCH'S (James, *of Aberdeen*) Sermons, 2 vols. 8vo. *boards*, 8*s* (*pub. at* 18*s*) .. .. .. 1831

4011 RIDLEY (Bp. Nicholas, *Martyr*) Life, shewing the plan and progress of the Reformation, by Dr. Glocester Ridley, *portrait*, 4to. *half vellum, uncut*, 7*s* 6*d* .. .. 1763

"In this, which is the most useful of all his works, he proved himself worthy of the name he bore, a thorough master of the Popish Controversy, and an able advocate of the Reformation."—*Chalmers's Biog. Dict.*

4012 RIDPATH'S (George) Border History of England and Scotland, from the Earliest Times to the Union of the two Crowns, in 1603, 4to. *half rough calf,* 16*s* .. .. 1776

This book is scarce, and has always obtained good prices at auctions. "Read Mr. Ridpath's Border History as a good introduction to this subject."—*Dibdin.* See also Scott's Minstrelsy of the Scottish Border.

4013 RILEY and Bohn's Dictionary of Latin and Greek Quotations, post 8vo. *cloth,* 4*s* 6*d* .. *H. G. Bohn,* 1856

4014 RIME di diversi Nobilissimi et Excellentissime autori, *Venezia, Bartholomeo Cesano,* 1550.—Rime di diversi autori nella Lingua Volgare, (raccolte da Ercole Bottrigaro) 2 vols. in 1, small thick 8vo. *old vellum,* SCARCE, 12*s* *Bologna, Anselmo Giaccarello,* 1551

These are the 3rd and 4th volumes of this collection, of the 3rd, Haym says, "Le raccolse lo stesso Domenichi." It is dedicated to the "Illust. Signor Luca Grimaldo," by Andrea Arrivabene.

4015 — Scelte di diversi Autori, 12mo. 624 pages, *old vellum, impressed gilt edges,* 10*s* *In Vinegia, appresso Gabriel Giolito,* 1564

With the beautiful device of G. Giolito on the title page, which has been re-engraved by Dr. Dibdin, dedicated to the "Eccellente Dottore, M. Vincenzo Ritio, Secretario della Illust. Sig. di Vinegia," by Lodovico Dolce.

4016 — Scelte di diversi Autori, 12mo. 624 pages, *old vellum,* SCARCE, 6*s* *In Venetia, appresso i Gioliti,* 1586

Dedicated by Giovanni Giolito de' Ferrari, to "Il Signor Diomede Borghesi Gentilhuomo Sanese." It has a different device of the Gioliti to the last article.

4017 RIPPERDA (Duke de) Memoirs of, 1715 to 1736, 8vo. *old calf, neat,* 3*s* 6*d* .. .. .. 1740

Ambassador from the States-General to the Court of Spain, afterwards Prime Minister to the Emperor of Morocco. Curious particulars of Alberoni, Cardinal Giudice, Prince Cellamere, &c.

4018 RITSON'S Robin Hood, with Notes and Illustrations, 8vo. *sewed,* 1*s* .. .. .. .. *No date.*

4019 RIVERII (Lazari) Observationum Medicarum et curationum insignium Centuria IV., small 4to. *sewed,* 2*s* 6*d* *Hagæ-Comitum, Ad. Vlacq,* 1659

4020 RIVINGTON'S and Cochran's Catalogue of Books in various Languages, 8vo. *half russia, gilt, a nice copy,* 9*s* 1824

4021 ROBERTS (James) on the Culture of the Vine under Glass, 12mo. *cloth,* 2*s* 6*d* (*cost* 5*s* 6*d*) .. .. 1842

4022 ROBERTS (Lewes, *Merchant*) Merchant's Map of Commerce, shewing the Standard and Current Coins, Weights and Measures used in various Countries, with descriptions of those Countries, *and a set of Vischer's maps inserted,* folio, *old calf, neat,* 10*s* 6*d* 1671

"This work gained Roberts a great reputation, as he was the first systematic writer upon Trade in the English language."—*Lowndes.*

4023 ROBERTS (Mary) Progress of Creation, considered with reference to the present condition of the Earth, *plates,* 12mo. *cloth, gilt edges,* 2*s* (*cost* 4*s* 6*d*) .. .. 1837

4024 ROBERTS'S Holy Land, Syria, Idumea, Arabia, Egypt, and Nubia, with historical descriptions by Dr. Croly, 6 vols. in 3, imperial 8vo. *nice copy, new, in halfmorocco, edges gilt,* £5 15*s* 6*d* (*pub. at* £9 9*s*) .. .. .. 1855

Illustrated by about 250 plates in double tinted lithography by Day and Son, a most beautiful book, every page illustrative of Scripture story.

4025 ROBERTSON (Jac.) Clavis Pentateuchi, Hebraicè, una cum Versione Latina et Anglica, thick 8vo. *old cf, gilt,* 12*s* *Edinb.,* 1770

"A very useful manual."—*Horne.* It has also two Dissertations. I. De Antiquitate Linguæ Arabicæ. II. De Genuina Punctorum Vocalium Antiquitate, contra Capellum, Waltonum, Masclefum aliosque.

4026 ROBERTSON'S (Dr. William) Works, History of Scotland, America, India, &c., with his Life, by Dugald Stuart, *portrait,* 8 vols. 8vo. *boards,* £1 10*s* (*pub. at* £3 4*s*) 1827

4027 — History of the Reign of the Emperor Charles V., *portrait,* 4 vols. 8vo. *calf, gilt,* 8*s* 6*d* .. .. 1777

4028 — History of Scotland during the Reigns of Queen Mary, and King James the 6th, till his Accession to the Crown of England in 1603, 2 vols. 8vo. *calf, gilt, nice copy,* 7*s* 1776

4029 ROBINSON'S (Dr.) Magistrate's Pocket Book, or the Duties and Practice of a Justice of Peace, by Archbold, 8vo. *cf, nt,* 8*s* 1837

4030 ROBINSON'S (Rear-Admiral H.) Sea Drift, *portrait,* 8vo. *cloth,* 3*s* (*cost* 5*s* 6*d*) .. .. *Portsea,* 1858

4031 ROBINSON'S (Thomas) Scripture Characters, *portrait,* 2 vols. 8vo. *cloth,* 9*s* (*pub. at* 24*s*) .. .. .. 1827

4032 ROBINSON CRUSOE; The Life and Strange Surprizing Adventures of, *full length portrait by Clarke and Pine,* 5th edition, 1720.—The Farther Adventures of R. Crusoe, 6 *well engraved plates,* 3rd edition, 2 vols. 8vo. *old binding,* RARE
*Printed for W. Taylor, at the Ship in Pater-Noster Row,* 1722

These editions are not noticed by bibliographers, or, indeed, they are so very rare, that they do not appear to have fallen into the hands of Mr. Lowndes, or, more recently, into those of Mr. Bohn, his new editor, than which there cannot well be a greater proof of their excessive rarity. They seem to fill up the gaps recorded by the latter gentleman, as he mentions the fourth and the sixth editions of the 1st volume, and the second and the fourth of the 2nd.

4033 — another edition, *with* 300 *illustrations by Grandville,* 8vo. *cloth, gilt edges,* 6*s* .. .. .. 1850

4034 — another, with a Life of Defoe, small 8vo. *calf, extra, marbled leaves,* 10*s* .. .. .. 1856

An elegant edition illustrated with 70 wood engravings after Harvey, and 12 steel engravings after Stothard's designs.

4035 — Robinson Crusoëus, Latinè scripsit F. J. Goffaux, 12mo. *bound,* 2*s* .. .. .. *Londini,* 1820

4036 ROCCA (Bernardino, *Piacentino,*) La Seconda e Terza parte del Governo della Militia, *remarkably fine portrait of a Cavalier on horseback, probably the Author,* 2 vols. in 1, 4to. *old vellum, very fine copy,* £1 1*s* .. *In Vinetia, Gabriel Giolito,* 1570

Collates by the description given in Haym, vol. 1, p. 20, n. 1. Sir Christopher Hatton's copy with his initials and device in gold on the sides. This volume is elegantly printed by Gabriel Giolito.

4037 ROCHEFORT (Count de) Memoirs of, containing an Account of what Passed most Memorable under the Ministry of Cardinals Richelieu and Mazarin, 8vo. *old calf,* 4*s* .. 1696

4038 ROCHEFOUCAULT (Duke of) Moral Maxims and Reflections, *frontispiece,* 18mo. *old binding,* 3*s* .. .. 1694

4039 — another edition, 24mo. *calf, neat,* 2*s* *Edinburgh,* 1783

4040 ROCHESTER (John, Earl of,) Some Passages of his Life and Death, by Bishop Gilbert Burnet, *portrait*, small 8vo. *old calf, neat*, 2*s* 6*d* .. .. .. .. 1700

This celebrated Nobleman died July 26, 1680. Of this life Dr. Johnson says, "The critic ought to read it for its elegance, the philosopher for its arguments, and the saint for its piety."

4041 ROCHESTER; History and Antiquities of, and its Environs, 2nd edition, *map and plates*, 8vo. *half vellum*, SCARCE, 7*s* 6*d* 1817

4042 RŒMER (Jo. Jac.) Genera Insectorum Linnæi et Fabricii iconibus illustrata, 37 *plates beautifully coloured*, 4to. *red morocco, extra, gilt leaves*, £3 3*s* *Vitoduri Helvetorum*, (*Winterthour*,) 1789

This is a most elegant volume, appropriately bound with insects on the back; 1789, according to Dr. Cotton, (Typog. Antiq.) is the first date of a book printed at Winterthour in Switzerland. "The authorities of Zurich claimed the right of preventing the erection of a printing press there, lest it should interfere with the interests of their own city." The printers of this beautiful volume were Henry Stainer and Co., as a specimen of Typography it is an honor to the place.

4043 ROGERS (Dr. John) 56 Sermons, with his Life, by Dr. J. Burton, 2 vols. 8vo. *boards*, 8*s* .. .. *Oxford*, 1819

"An excellent writer."—*Chalmers*. Recommended by Bps. Randolph and Coleridge as well as by Professor Burton.

4044 — XIX. Sermons, with the Author's Life, by John Burton, 8vo. *old calf, neat*, 2*s* 6*d* .. .. .. 1735

4045 ROGERS'S (Samuel) Poems, *plates from Stothard's elegant designs*, 12mo. *calf, extra*, 7*s* 6*d* .. .. *Bensley*, 1812

4046 — Poems, *portrait after Sir T. Lawrence, and plates after Stothard*, 12mo. *purple morocco, gilt edges*, 9*s* *Chiswick, Whittingham*, 1849

4047 — Poetical Works, 18mo. *cloth, new*, 5*s* .. *Moxon*, 1856

4048 — Pleasures of Memory, with other Poems, 12mo. *boards*, 2*s* 1793

4049 — Italy, a Poem, *with elegant illustrations by Goodall after Turner*, 8vo. *boards*, RARE, *free from spot*, £1 11*s* 6*d* .. 1830

4050 ROGERS'S (Thomas) Treatise upon Sundry Matters contained in the XXXIX. Articles of Religion which are Professed in the Church of England, sm. 4to. *original edition, neat, scarce*, 6*s* 1639

4051 ROGERS'S (Timothy) Discourse on Trouble of Mind and the Disease of Melancholy, with an Account of his Life, 12mo. *calf, very neat*, 3*s* 6*d* .. .. .. 1808

This "most excellent performance" was first printed in 1691. It details the author's own experience in a great affliction.

4052 ROGET'S (Dr. P. M.) Thesaurus of English Words and Phrases, post 8vo. *cloth, new*, 10*s* 6*d* .. .. 1858

Classified to facilitate the expression of ideas and assist in literary composition.

4053 ROHAN; Les Memoires du Duc de Rohan,—Veritable Discours, de ce qui s'est passé en l'Assemblée politique des Eglises Reformés de France, l'an 1611, 18mo. *old calf, very neat*, RARE, 10*s* 6*d* 1644

Without date, place, or printer's name, but printed by an Elzevir.

4054 ROLLIN, Histoire Ancienne des Egyptiennes, Carthaginois, Assyriens, Babyloniens, Medes, Perses, Macedoniens et Grecs, 13 vols. in 14, 12mo. *french calf, gilt*, £1 1*s* *Paris*, 1769

4055 — Histoire Romaine, depuis la fondation de Rome jusqu' à la bataille d'Actium, 12 vols. 12mo. *neat set in calf*, 18*s* *Paris*, 1803

4056 ROMANELLI (Abate Domenico) Antica Topografia Istorica del Regno di Napoli, *portrait, maps and plates,* 3 vols. 4to. *boards, scarce,* £2 2*s* .. .. *Napoli,* 1815-19

4057 ROMANTIC TALES, by the Author of John Halifax, Gentleman, 12mo. *cloth,* 2*s* .. .. .. 1859

4058 ROME—Brocchi (G.) dello stato Fisico del Suolo di Roma, memoria per servire d'illustrazione alla Carta Geognostica di questa Citta, *coloured charts,* 8vo. *half bound in Italian vellum,* 7*s* 6*d* *Roma,* 1820

4059 — Donati (Alex.) Roma, Vetus ac Recens, utriusque Ædificiis ad eruditam cognitionem expositis, 4to. *plates, good copy, old vellum,* 6*s* .. .. *Romæ, Manelphi Manelphii,* 1639

4060 — Falda (Gio. Bat.) Nuovo Teatro della Fabrichi et Edificii di Roma Moderna, 85 *fine plates,* oblong folio, *old Italian vellum,* £1 1*s* .. .. .. *Roma, Rossi,* 1665

4061 — Historiæ Romanæ Epitome, thick 18mo. of 525 pages, *neat,* 4*s* *Amst., Janson,* 1625

Contents: Florus, V. Paterculus, Aur. Victor, Festus, Corvinus, Eutropius, P. Diaconus, Cassiodorus, Jornandis and Julius Exuperantius, added is a Treatise de Mensuris et Ponderibus.

4062 — Li Tesori della Corte Romana, in varie Relationi fatte in Pregadi d'Alcuni Ambasciatori Veneti, residenti in Roma, 12mo. *old vellum, scarce,* 6*s* .. .. *Bruxelles,* 1672

Relations of 4 Ambassadors to Rome.—1. Paolo Tiepolo from Venice during the Pontificates of Pius IV. and V.—2. Almaden, French to Urban VIII.—Corraro from Venice to Alexander VII.—4. Grimani from Venice to Clement IX.

4063 — Nardini (Famiano) Roma Antica, *maps, plans, and numerous plates,* thick 4to. *old vellum,* 7*s* 6*d* .. *Roma,* 1704

4064 — Santi (Padre Fra) Le Cose Maravigliose dell' alma Citta di Roma, —Antichita di Roma di M. Andrea Palladio.—Stationi delle Chiese di Roma, con la Vita di tutti Santi et Sante, *numerous views of Antiquities, Churches, &c.* in 1 vol. small thick 8vo. *fine copy in russia,* £1 11*s* 6*d* .. *Venetia, per G. Francino,* 1588

A copy of this very scarce little volume sold at Christie's for £2 12*s* 6*d*. Autograph of "Alaric Alexander Watts, 1815."

4065 — Vasi e Nibby, Itinerario di Roma, e delle sue Vicinanze, *plan and numerous views of public buildings,* 2 vols. 12mo. *stiff covers,* 6*s* *Roma,* 1844

With Autograph of the late Lord Orford on each volume.

4066 ROMILLY (Sir Samuel) his Life, written by himself, with a Selection from his Correspondence, edited by his Sons, *portrait and fac-similies,* 2 vols. f.cap. 8vo. *cl. new,* 6*s* 6*d* (*pub. at* 12*s*) 1842

4067 RONDEAULX, translated from the Black Letter, French Edition of 1527, by J. R. Best, Esq., crown 8vo. 90 pages, *boards,* RARE, 12*s* .. .. .. *Southampton,* 1838

"Nor can I forget the curiosity with which I looked into the little black letter volume which at my last visit (to Cornborough House, near Bideford,) you presented to me. I well remember remarking what a valuable acquisition the book would be to a writer of historical romances of the middle ages." Mr. Best's dedication to his cousin *R. S. Vidal, Esq.*, translator of *Mosheim's Commentaries.* "Francis Thirkill, Esq., with the author's compts.," and Mr. Thirkill's book-plate.

4068 ROPER (R. S. Donnison) on the Law of Real Property arising from the Relation between Husband and Wife, 2 vols. royal 8vo. 2nd edition, by Edward Jacob, Esq., Barrister, *boards,* £1 5*s* (*pub. at* £2 12*s* 6*d*) .. .. .. 1826

4069 ROQUELAURE; Aventures divertissantes du Duc de, *curious portrait*, 18mo. *neat*, 2*s* 6*d* .. .. *Versailles*, 1789

4070 ROSCOE'S (Henry) Digest of the Law of Evidence in Criminal Cases, by T. C. Granger, 2nd Edit., thick 12mo. *law calf, very neat*, 8*s* (*cost* 28*s*) .. .. .. 1840

4071 — British Lawyers, 12mo. *cloth*, 2*s* 6*d* *Lardner's Cab. Cyclopædia*

4072 ROSCOE'S (Thomas) Novelist's Library, *portraits and illustrations by Cruikshank*, 12 vols. 12mo. *cloth, gilt*, £1 15*s* (*pub. at* £3) .. .. .. .. 1831-32

Contents: Smollett's Humphrey Clinker, Roderick Random, Peregrine Pickle, and Sir Launcelot Greaves; Fielding's Tom Jones, Joseph Andrews, and Amelia; Goldsmith's Vicar of Wakefield; Sterne's Tristram Shandy.

4073 ROSCOE'S (William) Lives of Lorenzo de Medici and Leo. X. See *Leo. X.* and *Medici.*

4074 — Catalogue of his very Select Library, sold by Mr. Winstanley, in Liverpool, August, 1816, 8vo. *boards*, 5*s* .. 1816

4075 — Life, by his Son, *portrait*, 2 vols. 8vo. *half cloth*, 10*s* 6*d* (*pub. at* 30*s*) .. .. .. .. 1833

4076 — another copy, 2 vols. 8vo. *full cloth*, 12*s* .. 1833

This is a very pleasing addition to the literature of our country.

4077 ROSINI (Giovanni) Luisa Strozzi, Storia del Secolo XVI., *fine portraits*, 4 vols. 8vo. *sewed*, £1 1*s* .. *Pisa*, 1833

Large Letter Edition, out of print. Very fine portraits of Antonio Carafulla, Michael Angelo, Benvenuto Cellini, and Guicciardini, and plates after Michael Angelo, Leonardo da Vinci, Raffael, Andrea del Sarto, and other portraits in outline.

4078 ROSS (Alex.) Virgilii Evangelisantis Christiados lib. XIII., small 8vo. *old calf*, 4*s* .. .. *Londini, I. Legate*, 1638

4079 — View of all Religions in the World, and all known Heresies, *fine portrait by Lombart, and engraved title*, 12mo. 1st edition, *neat*, 5*s* .. .. .. .. 1653

4080 ROSS (Sir John) 2nd Voyage in Search of a N. W. Passage, and of a Residence in the Arctic Regions in 1829 to 1833, royal 4to. LARGE PAPER, *boards*, £1 1*s* (*pub. at* £2 12*s* 6*d*) 1835

Illustrated with 30 fine plates, many of them coloured. Includes also the Reports of Capt. J. C. Ross, and the Discovery of the Northern Magnetic Pole.

4081 — another copy, with the Appendix containing a Sketch of the Boothians, also the Zoological, Botanical, and Scientific Portions of the Voyage, Esquimeaux Vocabulary and Dialogues, &c., 20 *fine plates*, 2 vols. 4to. LARGE PAPER, *cloth*, £1 16*s* (*pub. at* £4 7*s* 6*d*)

4082 ROSSI (Bartolomeo, *da Verona, comico*) Fiammella, Pastorale, 4to. 110 pages, *limp vel. rare*, 15*s* *Pariggi, per Abell Angeliero*, 1584

Not to be found in Haym, Brunet, or De Bure, there is a page of complimentary verses by Francois de Beroalde, and the book is dedicated to the "Duca di Gioiosa," by Oratio Rossi.

4083 ROSSINI (Pietro) il Mercurio Errante delle Grandezze di Roma, 12mo. *parchment*, 2*s* .. .. *Roma*, 1704

4084 ROUILLON (M. de) Principes de la Versification Françoise, 18mo. *half bound*, 1*s* 6*d* .. .. *Norwich*, 1817

4085 — Tourist's French Companion, French and English Conversations, 18mo. 3rd edition, *half bound*, 2*s* .. *Norwich*, 1820

4086 — another edition, 18mo. *hf. bound, neat*, 2*s* 6*d* (*pub. at* 4*s* 6*d*) 1832

The true pronunciation given, all the silent letters being marked.

4087 ROUILLON (M. de) another edition, 18mo. *half bound, neat,* 3*s* 1854

4088 — Cours Élémentaire de Littérature Générale, 12mo. *half bound, neat,* 3*s* .. .. .. *Norwich,* 1821

4089 — Grammatical Institutes of the French Language, 12mo. 2nd Edition, *half calf, very neat,* 3*s* .. .. 1823

4090 — another edition, 12mo. *half bound,* 3*s* 6*d* .. 1845

4091 — Mythologie des Demoiselles, *plates,* thick 18mo. *half calf, very neat,* 5*s* .. .. .. *Norwich,* 1827

4092 — Introduction to the Exercises on French Conversation, 32mo. *boards,* 2*s* .. *Norwich, Fletcher, no date.*

4093 — Exercises on French Conversation, 3rd Edition, 18mo. *half calf, neat,* 3*s* 6*d* .. .. *Norwich, Wilkin,* 1827

4094 — Choix de Fables, Contes et Histoires de Fenelon, 32mo. *boards,* 2*s* *Norwich,* 1829

4095 — Phraseology, or Key to the Exercises on French Conversation, adapted to the 4th Edition, 18mo. *cloth,* 2*s* 1830

4096 — Abrégé de l'Histoire ancienne de la Grèce, 2nd edit., 18mo. *boards,* 3*s* 6*d* .. .. *Norwich,* 1834

4097 — Tasso's Jerusalem Delivered, the four first Cantos, with an Interlineary and a literal Translation, 18mo. *sewed,* 4*s* 6*d* *ib.,* 1836

For the use of those who have not the advantage of masters.

4098 ROUSE'S (Rolla) Practical Man; a Pocket Companion for Solicitors, Valuers, and Owners of Property, oblong 12mo. *bound,* 4*s* (*cost* 8*s* 6*d*) .. .. .. .. 1837

4099 ROUSSEAU (J. J.) Letters on the Elements of Botany, Englished by Thomas Martyn, 38 *coloured plates,* 2 vols. 8vo. *half morocco,* SCARCE, 12*s* .. .. .. 1794

4100 ROUTH Reliquiæ Sacræ; sive, Auctorum fere jam perditorum secundi, tertiique Sæculi post Christum natum quæ supersunt; accedunt Synodi, et Epistolæ Canonicæ Nicæno Concilio Antiquiores, 5 vols. 8vo. *cloth,* £2 10*s* *Oxonii, e typog. Acad.,* 1846

This valuable work, the production of the late learned President of Magdalen Coll., Oxford, having become exceedingly scarce, is here reprinted for the first time since its original issuing from the press in 1814.

4101 ROXBURGHE—Catalogue of the Library of John, Duke of Roxburghe, sold by Auction, by Mr. Evans, in May, 1812, 8vo. *half calf, very neat, uncut,* 10*s* .. *Bulmer,* 1812

This Catalogue, arranged by Messrs. Nicol, is quite perfect, with the Supplement, the *prices printed* at the end, and the celebrated Preface, which is wanting in many copies.

4102 ROYAL INSTITUTION—Catalogue of the Library of the Royal Institution of Great Britain, with a List of all the Greek Writers methodically arranged, by Dr. Charles Burney, and an Index of Authors, by William Harris, 2nd Edition, royal 8vo. *half russia, uncut, top edges gilt,* 9*s* .. .. 1821

4103 — Classified Catalogue of the Library, with Indexes of Authors and Subjects, by Mr. B. Vincent, thick 8vo. *half bound, neat, new,* 15*s* .. .. .. 1857

Mr. Vincent is Assistant Secretary and Keeper of the Library, this is a well arranged Catalogue of a valuable collection of books.

4104 ROYAL Society, Natural History of Animals, containing the Anatomical Description of several Creatures dissected by the Royal Acad. of Sciences of Paris, Englished by A. P. Fellow of the Royal Society, and published by an order of its Council, *numerous plates,* folio, *fine old copy in calf, gilt,* 7*s* 6*d* 1702

At the end is a separate Treatise on 40 pages, with plates of "the Measure of the Earth."

4105 — Catalogue of the Library of the Royal Society, 4to. *boards,* 10*s* *Nicol,* 1825

4106 RUCHAT (A.) Abregé de l'Histoire Ecclesiastique du Pays de Vaud, small 8vo. *sewed, uncut,* 5*s* .. *Berne,* 1707

This curious little piece, is accompanied by I. Dissertat. sur l'origine des noms des principaux lieux de la Suisse. II. Liste des Baillifs de Vaud 1270-1536. III. Généalogie des Anciens Comtes de Gnuyere 1080-1535.

4107 RUDDIMAN (Thomas) Life, containing new Anecdotes of Buchanan, by George Chalmers, *a fine portrait by Bartolozzi,* 8vo. *half calf, uncut,* 6*s* .. .. .. 1794

"In this volume will be found, among much interesting matter, a very curious Chronological List of Newspapers."—*Lowndes.*

4108 RUSCELLI (Girolamo) Commentarii della Lingua Italiana, 4to. *half calf, title and few leaves injured by damp,* 4*s* *Venetia, Damian Zenaro,* 1581

4109 RUSHWORTH'S (John) Historical Collections, 1618 to 1629, being vol. 1 only, folio, *old calf, neat,* 7*s* .. 1659

4110 RUSSELL'S (Lord William) Life and Times, by Lord John Russell, 2 vols. 1820.—Life of his wife the Lady Rachael Wriothesley Russell, being her Letters from 1672 to 1682, together 3 vols. 8vo. *portraits, half bound, in calf, neat,* 16*s* (*pub. at* £1 13*s*) 1819

4111 RUSSELL'S (John) Tour in Germany and some of the Southern Provinces of the Austrian Empire, 2 vols. 12mo. *boards,* 6*s* 6*d* (*pub. at* 16*s*) .. .. *Edinburgh,* 1827

4112 RUSSELL'S History of Modern Europe, to 1825, 6 vols. 8vo. *boards,* £1 8*s* (*pub. at* £3 3*s*) .. 1827

4113 — History of Ancient and Modern Europe, by Coote and Russell, 9 vols. 8vo. *very neat set, half calf,* £2 2*s* 1814-15

4114 RUSSIA Self-condemned: Secret and Inedited Documents connected with Russian History and Diplomacy, translated by John Reynell Morell, 8vo. *cloth, uncut,* 2*s* (*cost* 9*s*) *Lond.* 1854

4115 RUSSIAN—A Manual of an English and Russian Grammar, by W. H. M. D., 8vo. *sewed,* 2*s* 6*d* *St. Petersburg,* 1822

4116 RUTHERFORD'S (Samuel, *Professor of Divinity at St. Andrew's)* Religious Letters, 18mo. *calf, very neat,* 5*s* *Reprint,* 1839

Greatly distinguished for his conduct and sufferings during the reign of Charles I. These letters are dated from 1628 to 1660, they are addressed to some of the most eminent persons in Scotland.

4117 — Disputatio, see *Retofortis.*

4118 RUTHVEN'S (Lord) Ladies Cabinet Enlarged and Opened, 18mo. *old boards,* 4*s* .. .. .. 1658

Containing many rare secrets in Candying, Preserving, Physick, and Chirurgery, Cookery, and Housewifery, this 3rd edition not in *Lowndes.*

4119 RUTLAND Papers; illustrative of the Courts and Times of King Henry VII. and VIII. edited by Mr. Jerdan, 4to. *cloth*, 4*s* *Camden Soc.*, 1842

4120 RUTTER'S (John) Delineations of the North Western Division of the County of Somerset, and of its Antediluvian Bone Caverns, with a Geological Sketch of the District, *plates*, 8vo. *half cloth*, 7*s* 6*d* (*pub. at* 15*s*) .. .. .. 1829

4121 RYCAUT (Paul) Present State of the Ottoman Empire, containing the Maxims of the Turkish Politie, their Religion, Military Discipline, &c., *plates*, folio, *a very fine copy in calf*, 10*s* 1670

Sir Paul Rycaut was Secretary to his Excellency the Earl of Winchilsea, Ambassador to Turkey, and gives an account of the Seraglio, and other then inaccessible matters, which his position enabled him to do.

4122 — History of the Turkish Empire, from 1623 to 1677, *portraits by R. White and Van Hove*, folio, *old calf, neat*, 7*s* 6*d* 1680

For another book by Sir Paul Rycaut, see *Platini*, No. 3738, and *Ricaut*, 4001.

4123 SAAVADRA-Faxardo (Don Diego) Royal Politician represented in *one hundred emblems*, Englished by Sir Ja. Astry, 2 vols. 8vo. *old calf, neat*, 8*s* .. .. .. 1700

4124 SACCI (Bernardi, *Patritii Papiensis*) de Italicarum Rerum Varietate et Elegantia libri X., small 4to. *old calf, neat, Holkham arms on the sides*, 12*s* *Papiæ, Hieron Bartholus*, 1565

The running title of this book is "Ticinensis Historiæ libri X.," in fact, "Papia or Ticinum, Pavia, an ancient city of Austrian Italy, in the Duchy of Milan. It is a Bishop's See." See *Cotton's Typog. Gazetteer*. At the end of the book we read, "Ego Hippolitus Rubeus Episcopus Papiensis, visa D. Inquisitoris subscriptione, subscripsi."

4125 SACRAMENT—Plain account of the Institution, Nature, and end of the Lord's Supper, 12mo. *old calf, scarce*, 3*s* 6*d* 1713

4126 SACRED History, Outlines of, from the Creation to the Destruction of Jerusalem, *plates*, 18mo. *cloth*, 2*s* *J. W. Parker*, 1833

4127 ST. GEORGE'S (Dr. Arthur) Archdeacon's Examination of Candidates for holy orders, with thoughts on the proper manner of studying Divinity, by Dr. W. Wotton, 12mo. *bound*, 2*s* 6*d* 1757

4128 ST. JOHN'S (J. A.) Lives of Celebrated Travellers, vols. 1 and 3, 12mo. *cloth*, 4*s* .. *National Library*, 1831

4129 ST. PALAYE, Memoirs of Ancient Chivalry, with Anecdotes of the Times from the Romance Writers, Englished by Mrs. Dobson, 8vo. *boards*, 6*s* .. .. .. 1784

"St. Palaye is an extremely pleasing and ingenious writer, and his style has a fine relish of antiquity, his whole life was spent in making these researches, the essence of which is here."—See *Retrospective Review*, v. 8, p. 315.

4130 — Literary History of the Troubadours, containing many particulars of the Customs, &c., of the XII. and XIII. Centuries, by Mrs. Dobson, 12mo. *calf, neat*, 3*s* .. 1807

4131 ST. VINCENT de Paul, Vie de, par B. Capefigue, 8vo. *half calf, very neat*, 4*s* 6*d* .. .. *Paris*, 1827

4132 SALDENI (Guil.) Concionator Sacer; accedit de Jure Zelotarum dissertatio, 12mo. *boards, edges rough*, 3*s* *Hagæ Comitis*, 1678

4133 — Otia Theologica; sive Exercitationes subsecivæ varii argumenti, thick 4to. of 900 pages, *old calf*, 5*s* *Amst.*, 1684

4134 SALISBURY—Child's (Miss) Spinster at Home in the Close of Salisbury. No Fable, with Tales and Ballads, *plates*, 4to. *cloth*, 15*s* .. .. *Salisbury, Brodie*, 1844

4135 SALLUSTIUS, e scriptoribus antiquis ab Aldo Manutio, Paulli F. collecta, Scholiæ Aldi Manutii, small 8vo. *old vellum*, 9*s* *Venetiis, ex Bibliotheca Aldina*, 1588

4136 — cum Veterum Historicorum fragmentis, 12mo. *very fine tall copy, in vellum*, 12*s* .. .. *Amst., Elzevir*, 1658

4137 — 12mo. *calf, neat*, 3*s* 6*d* .. *Parisiis, Barbou*, 1761

4138 SALMAGUNDI; a Miscellaneous combination of Original Poetry, consisting of Illusions of Fancy, *engraved title by Heath*, 4to. *boards*, 5*s* .. .. .. 1791

Handsomely printed by T. Bensley, not in Lowndes.

4139 SALMASIUS (Claudius) de Re Militari Romanorum, 4to. *vellum, neat*, 6*s* .. *L. Batavorum, ap. J. Elzevirium*, 1657

4140 — Defensio Regia, 1649.—I. Miltonii defensio contra Salmasii Defensionem Regiam, in 1 vol. 12mo. *neat*, 6*s* *Londini*, 1650

A proclamation was issued in 1660 for suppressing Milton's seditious answer to Salmasius, and ordering all the copies that could be found to be burnt by the common hangman.—*Davis's Olio*, p. 67.

4141 — ad Johannem Miltonum responsio, sm. 8vo. *old binding*, 2*s* 6*d* *Londini*, 1660

4142 SALOMONII (Jacobi, *Ord. Prædicator.*) Urbis Patavinæ Inscriptiones, Sacræ et Prophanæ, Collectæ, *plates*, thick 4to. 631 pages, *old boards, uncut*, 7*s* 6*d* .. .. *Patavii*, 1701

4143 SALT'S (Henry, *Consul General in Egypt*,) Life and Correspondence by J. J. Halls, *portraits*, 2 vols. 8vo. *boards*, 12*s* (*pub. at* 30*s*) 1834

4144 SALTZBURG—Account of the Sufferings of the Persecuted Protestants in the Archbishopric of Saltzburg, with their Confession of Faith, small 8vo. *sewed*, 2*s* .. .. 1732

20,678 Protestants were driven out the Archbishopric by the decree of the Archbishop, Christmas, 1731.

4145 SANCHEZ—Discurso del Doctor Francisco Sanchez de Oropesa, para Averiguar, q. mal de Urina sea, el q. padece Diego ANTIGUEZ LEON su amigo i conpadre, small 4to. *fine copy in old vellum with ties*, 12*s* .. .. *Sevilla, Juan de Leon*, 1594

Spanish books of this date are rare. Not in *Brunet*.

4146 SANCROFT (Abp. of Canterbury) Occasional Sermons, with Remarks on his Life in a Letter to a Friend, *very fine impression of portrait by W. Elder*, 8vo. *nice copy in old purple morocco, gilt edges*, 7*s* 6*d* .. .. .. .. 1694

4147 — Life, also that of the learned Henry Wharton by Dr. George D'Oyley, *portrait*, 2 vols. 8vo. *calf, very neat*, 12*s* 1821

The appendix contains a reprint of Fur Prædestinatus, and other tracts by the Archbishop. For the original edition of Fur Prædestinatus see No. 262 in this Catalogue, and an answer to it by *Kendall* in the Appendix.

4148 SANCTII (Franc.) Minerva; seu de Causis Linguæ Latinæ Commentarius, cum Notis G. Schoppii et J. Perizonii, 8vo. *calf, neat*, 5*s* .. .. .. .. *Amst.*, 1714

4149 SANDBACH'S (Mrs. Henry R.) Giuliano de' Medici, a Drama, with other Poems, post 8vo. *cloth*, 3*s* 6*d* (*pub. at* 8*s*) *W. Pickering*, 1842

4150 SANDERSON'S (Rob. *Bp. of Lincoln,*) Two Cases of Conscience Resolved, 18mo. 1*s* 6*d* .. .. 1668

4151 — Visitation Sermon, ad Clerum, at Grantham, Lincolnshire, Oct. 8, 1641, *sewed,* 1*s* 6*d* .. .. *Oxford,* 1670

4152 — Casus Conscientiæ, *Cantabrigiæ,* 1688.—De Obligatione Conscientiæ, *Londini,* 1686.—De Juramenti Promissorii Obligatione, *ib.,* 1686.—Judicium Univers. Oxon. (1647) de Solenni Liga et Fœdere, de Ordinationibus Parliamenti circa Disciplinam et Cultum, &c. *ib.,* 1682.—4 tracts in 1 vol. small 8vo. *old cf,* 6*s* V.Y.

4153 — Life, by Izaak Walton, small 8vo. *old calf, neat, scarce,* 7*s* 6*d* 1678

Added are several cases of Conscience by Bp. Sanderson, and a Sermon by Hooker.

4154 SANDFORD'S (Sir D. K.) Introduction to the Writing of Greek, 12mo. *bound,* 2*s* .. .. *Edinburgh,* 1831

4155 — Extracts from Greek Authors, Lucian, Herodotus, Homer, Xenophon, &c. 12mo. *half calf, neat,* 3*s* (*pub. at* 6*s*) 1837

4156 SANDFORD'S (Bishop Daniel) Remains, including Extracts from his Diary, Correspondence, &c. with a Memoir by John Sandford, 2 vols. 8vo. *calf, neat,* 8*s* .. *Edinburgh,* 1830

4157 SANDII (C.C.) Interpretationes Paradoxæ IV. Evangeliorum, quibus affixa est dissertatio de Verba, sm. 8vo. *old calf, very neat,* 4*s* 6*d* .. .. .. *Amst.,* 1669

4158 — Tractatus de Origine Animæ, small 8vo. (wants title) *old calf, neat,* 2*s* 6*d* .. .. .. *Cosmopoli,* 1671

4159 — Bibliotheca Anti-Trinitariorum; sive Catalogus Scriptorum, et Succincta Narratio de vita eorum Auctorum, small 8vo. *old calf, neat,* 8*s* .. .. .. *Friestadii,* 1684

At the end is a "Compendium Historiæ Ecclesiasticæ Unitariorum;" and a distinct work "Historia Reformationis Polonicæ, authore Stanislao Lubieniecio, *Friestadii,* 1685." Of the latter work Voght says, "Liber perrarus."

4160 SANDWICH (Earl of) Memoriæ Sacrum, Edvardi Comitis Sandovici Baronis Mountacuti de S. Neoto, Angliæ Vice-Admiralli, qui Mai 28, 1672, in illa fatali Naumachia sublatus est, folio, *broadside, curious,* 5*s* .. *Londini, J. Redmayne,* 1672

4161 SANDYS'S (George) Christ's Passion, a Tragedy, with Annotations, *and plates by W. Elder,* 2nd Edit. 8vo. *old calf,* 5*s* 1687

4162 SANFORD'S (John Langton) Studies and Illustrations of the Great Rebellion, thick 8vo. *boards,* 8*s* 6*d* (*pub. at* 16*s*) *Parker,* 1858

4163 SANGSCRIT—Sounds given by the Hindoo Pundits to the Letters of the Sangscrit Alphabet by W. Fox, MS. 4to. 2*s*

4164 SANNAZARO (Giacomo) Arcadia di Messer Iacomo Sannazaro Gentilhuomo Napolitano, small 8vo. 89 *leaves, with the anchor on a separate leaf at the end,* £1 1*s* *In Vinegia, Aldo Romano,* 1514

"The Arcadia of Sannazaro is justly esteemed one of the most elegant compositions in the Italian language."—*Tiraboschi.*

4165 — Arcadia, nuovamente corretta, ed ornata di Annotazioni da Giuseppe Serafini, small 8vo. *neat,* 5*s* *Londra, S. Hooper,* 1768

To this edition is added a Life of Sannazaro, and a vocabulary of obscure words explained in English and French.

4166 — Opera, cura Brouckhusii; accedunt Altilii, Cereti et Fratrum Amaltheorum Carmina, cum Notis P. Vlamingii, *portraits,* 8vo. *fine copy in old calf,* 10*s* 6*d* .. *Amst.,* 1728

"Bonne édition, qu'on annexe à la collection *Variorum.*"—*Brunet.*

4167 SANSOVINO (Francesco) Ordine de Cavalieri del Tosone, *elegant vignette in title page,* 4to. *sewed,* £1 1*s* *Nell' Acad. Venet.,* 1558

From the Aldine Press, and extremely rare. It has the dedication to "Don Francesco de Medici, Prencipe de Fiorenza." Remarkably fine clean copy, clean as new.

4168 — l'Historia di Casa Orsina, con quattro Libri de gli Huomini illustri della famiglia, *portraits,* folio, *old calf, a good copy,* £3 3*s* *In Venetia,* 1565

A copy of this rare volume produced six guineas at the sale of Mr. Roscoe's library. At page 69 of vol. 2, occur the celebrated lines of Pietro Bartoli, commencing—
Vivi immortali o gran Napoleone,
Poi che l'opere tue sono immortali.

4169 — Cronica Universale del Mondo, 1555 al 1581, 2 vols. 4to. *original vellum,* RARE, £1 11*s* 6*d* *Vinegia, Altobello Salicato,* 1581

Sir Christopher Hatton's copy, with the autograph of his Nephew and Heir Sir "William Hatton" both on the title page and at the end of the last volume; it has also, MS. remarks by him on the margins. At the end of the 2nd vol. is "Alessandro PICCOLOMINI la Sfera del Mondo." *Vinegia, G. Varisco et Compagni,* 1579; and his Treatise "De la Stelle Fisse libro uno," *with* 48 *plates of the Stars, printed by the same Company,* 1579. See *Bergamo,* No. 439.

4170 SARRATT'S (J. H.) Treatise on the Game of Chess, Revised, with Notes by Lewis, 8vo. *best edition, boards,* 6*s* 6*d* *(pub. at* 12*s)* 1822

"An excellent work."—*Lowndes.*

4171 SASSONIA (Landolfo di) Vita di Gieusu Christo nostro Redentore, et fatta Volgare da M. Francesco Sansovino, thick folio, of nearly 1000 pages, *badly stained, vellum,* 12*s* *Venetia, Altobello Salicato,* 1581

Sir Christopher Hatton's copy, with the initials of his name on the sides.

4172 SAURIN (Jacques) Sermons sur divers Textes de l'Ecriture Sainte, 7 vols. 8vo. *old foreign binding, gilt,* 15*s* *La Haye,* 1721-32

4173 — Nouveaux Sermons sur l'Histoire de la Passion de notre Seigneur Jesus Christ, 2 vols. 8vo. *old calf, gilt,* 6*s* *Rotterdam,* 1732

"Lord Walpole's, of Woolterton," copy, with his book-plate.

4174 — Sermons sur divers Textes, vol. 1 only, 8vo. *old binding,* 2*s* *La Haye,* 1715

4175 SAUSSURE (H. B. de) Voyages dans les Alpes, précédés d'un Essai sur l'Histoire Naturelle des Environs de Geneve, *numerous plates,* 2 vols. 4to. *foreign binding, gilt,* 18*s* *Neuchatel,* 1779

"Les deux premiers volumes de cet excellent ouvrage se trouvent quelquefois séparément."—*Brunet.*

4176 SAVAGE'S (Mrs.) Poems, 2 vols. 12mo. *neat,* 2*s* 6*d* 1777

4177 SAVAGE'S (John) Account of New Zealand, particularly the Bay of Islands, *portrait of Tiarrah,* 8vo. *boards,* 2*s* 6*d* 1807

4178 SAVOIE—l'Histoire d'Emanuel Philibert Duc de Savoie, Gouverneur General de la Belgique, [1526-1580] 12mo. *sewed, uncut,* 3*s* 6*d* .. .. .. *Amsterdam,* 1693

4179 SAYER'S (Dr. F., *of Norwich,*) Poems, containing Sketches of Northern Mythology, &c. 1803.—Nugæ Poeticæ, 1803.—Miscellanies, Antiquarian and Historical, 1805.—2 vols. 8vo. LARGE AND THICK PAPER, *a fine copy in half red morocco,* 10*s* 6*d* *Norwich, Stevenson & Matchett,* 1803-5

Containing Treatises on St. George of England, on the Rise and Progress of English Poetry, on Architecture, on Saxon Literature, Lives of Edgar Atheling and Edmund Mortimer, &c. This copy is illustrated by *a fine portrait of Dr. Sayer, by Edwards, after Opie.*

4180 SAYER (Frank) Poetical Works, with Life by William Taylor, 8vo. *portrait*, 3*s* *(pub. at* 10*s* 6*d)* .. *Norwich*, 1830

4181 SCACCHI (Fortunati) Sacrorum Elæochrismaton Myrothecia tria, in quibus exponuntur olea atque unguenta divinos in Codices relata, *numerous plates*, large folio, *old calf, neat*, 12*s* *Amst., Franciscus Halma*, 1702

"Opus hoc erudite ac diligenter conscriptum."—*Walch.*

4182 SCALIGERI Epistolæ et Orationes, accessere I. T. Freigii Orationes, 12mo. *old calf, neat*, 2*s* 6*d* .. *Hanoviæ*, 1612

4183 SCANDALI (Petra) de Ortu Schismatis inter Ecclesias Orientalem et Occidentalem, in Lingua Arabica, 8vo. *half bound, uncut*, 6*s* *Haleb*, 1721

With the autograph of "H. Townsend," and the book-plate of Mr. "Joseph John Gurney." "Studio patris Venerabilis Athanasii Patriarchæ Alexandrini anno 1721 Christi."—*Schnurrer Bibliotheca Arabica*, p. 275.

4184 SCANDERBEG, De Vita Moribus ac Rebus præcipue adversus Turcas, Gestis, Georgii Castrioti, Clarissimi Epirotarum Principis, per Marinum Barletium conscripti, folio, *old vellum*, RARE, 12*s* *Argentorati*, 1537

4185 SCAPULÆ Lexicon Græco-Latinum, folio, *strongly bound*, 7*s* *Basileæ, no date*

4186 SCATTERGOOD (Antonii) Annotationes in Vetus Testamentum, et in Epistolam ad Ephesios, incerto Auctore, 8vo. *old calf, neat*, 5*s* .. .. .. *Cantabrigiæ*, 1653

Scattergood, who found these notes in the Library of the Abp. of York, says of them, "Breves utique sunt, nec obscuræ, utiles simul et dulces, piae non minus quam eruditae."

4187 SCHADE'S (C. B.) German Grammar, 12mo. *sewed*, 2*s* *Leipsic*, 1828

4188 SCHEFFER (John) History of Lapland, *engraved title*, folio, *map and plates, old calf, neat*, 6*s* .. *Oxford*, 1674

"A curious and entertaining work," highly praised by Dr. E. D. Clarke.

4189 SCHERZER (Dr. Carl) Travels in the Free States of Central America, Nicaragua, Honduras, and San Salvador, *map*, 2 vols. post 8vo. *cloth*, 7*s* 6*d* *(pub. at* 16*s)* .. *Longmans*, 1857

4190 SCHEUCHZERI (Joh. Jac.) Herbarium Diluvianum, *portrait, engraved title and* 14 *plates*, folio, *neat*, 15*s* *L. Bat., P. Vander Aa*, 1723

Best edition; in Wood's Natural History Catalogue at 25*s*

4191 SCHIAPPAL'ARIA (Sig. Stefano Ambrogio) Osservationi Politiche et Discorsi pertinenti a' governi di Stato, con la Vita di Caio Giulio Cesare, 4to. *very clean, old boards*, 8*s* *Verona, appresso la Compagnia de gli Aspiranti*, 1600

An author not to be found mentioned in Haym, the dedication is signed, Orlando Pescetti.

4192 SCHIKARD (Wilhelm) Tarich, h. e. Series REGUM PERSIÆ, ab Ardschir-Babekan, usq. ad Iazdigerdem à Chaliphis expulsum per annos fere 400, small 4to. *old binding*, 10*s* *Tubingæ*, 1628

CURIOUS. "Omnia ex fide Manuscripti Voluminis authentici apud Musulmanos."

4193 SCHILLER'S Sammtliche Werke, 10 vols. 8vo. *sewed*, £1 8*s* 1844

The best octavo edition of Schiller, and a very cheap book, printed on very nice paper at Stuttgart.

4194 SCHILLER'S Song of the Bell, Fridolin, a ballad, &c., Englished by Grenville Pigott, Esq. 12mo. *cloth*, 1*s* *Whittingham*, 1838

4195 SCHLEGEL'S (A. W.) Course of Lectures on Dramatic Art and Literature, translated by J. Black, *portrait*, post 8vo. *cloth*, 2*s* 6*d* (*cost* 3*s* 6*d*) .. .. *H. G. Bohn*, 1846

"A work of extraordinary merit."—*Quarterly Review*.

4196 SCHLEGEL'S (F. Von.) Philosophy of Life, and Philosophy of Language, translated from the German, by Rev. A. J. W. Morrison, post 8vo. *cloth*, 2*s* 6*d* (*cost* 3*s* 6*d*) *ib.*, 1847

4197 — Philosophy of History, translated, with a Memoir of the Author, by J. B. Robertson, *portrait*, post 8vo. *cloth*, 2*s* 6*d* (*cost* 3*s* 6*d*)

4198 — Æsthetic and Miscellaneous Works, translated by E. J. Millington, post 8vo. *cloth*, 2*s* 6*d* (*cost* 3*s* 6*d*) *ib.*, 1849

4199 — Lectures on the History of Literature, Ancient and Modern, revised, with, for the first time, an Index by Mr. H. G. Bohn, post 8vo. *cloth*, 3*s* 6*d* .. .. 1859

4200 SCHMITZ'S (Dr. L.) History of Rome from the Earliest time to the death of Commodus, A.D., 192, thick 12mo. *cloth*, 4*s* (*pub. at* 7*s* 6*d*) .. .. .. 1849

4201 SCHOLA SALERNITANA, sive de conservandâ Valetudine præcepta metrica, autore Joanne de Mediolano hactenus ignoti, thick 12mo. *calf*, *neat*, 8*s* .. .. *Roterodami*, 1657

"The celebrated Poem, the Schola Salerni, is to be referred to the end of the XIth Century. Composed for the use of Robert of Normandy, son of William the Conqueror. No poem was more popular in the middle ages."—*Sir A. Croke on rhyming Latin Verse*, p. 82. See *Regimen*, No. 3965.

4202 SCHOLEFIELD (Professor) Hints for an Improved Translation of the New Testament, 8vo. *boards*, 3*s* *Cambridge*, 1836

4203 SCHOMBERG'S (Alexander C.) Historical and Chronological View of the Roman Laws, with notes and illustrations, 8vo. *cf*, *neat*, 5*s* *Oxford*, 1785

At the end is a "Treatise on the Maritime Laws of Rhodes."

4204 SCHOMBERG'S (Capt. Isaac) Naval Chronology from the time of the Romans to the Treaty of Peace, 1802, 5 vols. 8vo. *calf*, *neat*, 12*s* .. .. .. 1802

4205 SCHREVELII Lexicon Græco-Latinum et Latino-Græcum, accurante C. Taylor, 8vo. *bound*, 3*s* 6*d* *Londini*, 1821

4206 SCHULZE (Ernst) Enchanted Rose, a Romaunt in three Cantos, from the German, by Caroline de Crespigny, square 12mo. *cloth*, 3*s* 6*d* (*pub. at* 7*s*) .. .. *Heidelberg*, 1844

4207 SCHUSTER Dictionnaire Allemand-Français et Français-Allemand, revu pour le Français par Regnier, 2 vols. in 1, very thick 8vo. *strong calf*, *very neat*, 12*s* (*cost* 25*s*) .. *Paris*, 1844

4208 SCHVALENBERG (Henrici) Aphorismi Hieroglyphici, 12mo. *nice copy in old stamped calf*, 7*s* 6*d* .. *Lipsiæ*, 1606

With the autograph of one of the old Suffolk Knyvett's thus written, "*Thomas Knyvett*, 27 *Junii*, 1608." I have seen an old folio Shakspere with the same name on it, and I would I had it now.

4209 SCOFFERN, Oxland, Truran, Fairbairn, Clay, Aitkin, and Pickett's Useful Metals, and their Alloys, with their applications to the Industrial Arts, *numerous plates*, thick 8vo. *cloth*, *new*, 7*s* 6*d* 1857

4210 SCOTLAND—Barclay's (Robert) and George Keith's account of a dispute betwixt some students of Divinity, of the University of Aberdeen, and the Quakers, 14th day, 2nd month, 1675, thick 8vo. *old calf, neat, scarce,* 5*s* .. *J. Sowle,* 1717

4211 — Marchant's (John) History of the present (1745) Rebellion, a particular description of the several actions at Preston Pans, Cliefton, and Falkirk, the Sieges and Defence of the Castles of Edinburgh and Stirling, &c., &c., 8vo. *old binding, scarce,* 7*s* 6*d* *For the Author,* 1746

A copy of this uncommon book sold for 10*s* 6*d* at Mr. Bindley's sale.

4212 — Scotch Loyalty Exemplify'd, in the behaviour of the Dean of Faculty, and his brethren, at Edinburgh, in relation to the reception of a Medal of the Pretender, presented to them by the Dutchess of Gourdon, *broadside, curious,* 5*s*

"Mr. Duncomb Forbes said, it was time enough to receive the Medal when the Pretender was hang'd," &c.

4213 — Scots Chronicles—The Abridgement or Summarie of the Scots Chronicles, from the comming of Gathelus, their first Progenitour, out of Græcia into Egypt, &c., with all the most rare and wonderfull things in Scotland, and the Isles, small 8vo. *old binding,* 12*s* .. .. *Edinburgh, for John Wood,* 1633

It is very annoying to say that some of the later leaves in this rare little volume are gnawed by rats. This edition is not paged the next is.

4214 — An Abridgement of the Chronicles of Scotland.—A Table of all the Kings of Scotland, Fergus to James 6.—A briefe description of Scotland.—Description of the Western Isles, and Wonderful Things, 12mo. 239 pages, *bound,* RARE, £1 1*s*

As this wants the title, there is no date to this curious little volume, dedicated to King James the 6th of Scotland, and 1st of England, and signed I. M. At page 175 we read, "He is now presently King of Scotland, and this year 1597 is the 31 year of his reign."

4215 — Scottish Lakes, 9 Views of, 4to. *india proofs,* 4*s* 6*d* 1838

4216 — The Demands and Behaviour of the Rebels of Scotland, small 4to. *four leaves, sewed,* 4*s* .. *R. Young,* 1640

4217 — Warnings of the Eternal Spirit to Guy Nutt, Thomas Dutton, and others, 1709. (wants title.)—Warnings of ditto to the City of EDENBURGH, by the mouths of Margaret Mackenzie and James Cuninghame, 1710. (wants last leaf.)—Warnings of ditto to the City of GLASGOW, by the same mouths, 1711, in 1 vol. 12mo. *scarce,* 4*s* .. .. .. 1709-11

4218 — View of Edinburgh, *from illustrated London News,* 1*s* 1848

4219 — Wood's (John) Account of the Edinburgh Sessional School, &c., 1812, with Strictures on Education in general, 12mo. *cloth,* 2*s* 6*d* (*cost* 5*s*) .. .. *Edinburgh,* 1833

4220 SCOTT'S (Rev. Benj.) Sermons, 8vo. *hf. cl,* 2*s* 6*d* *Buckingham,* 1831

4221 SCOTT'S (Jonathan) Ferishta's History of the Dekkan, and of Bengal, to 1780, 2 vols. 4to. *half calf, neat,* 15*s* *Shrewsbury,* 1794

Mr. Joseph John Gurney's copy, with his Book Label.

4222 SCOTT'S (Rev. Thomas, *Rector of Aston Sandford)* Works, edited by the Rev. John Scott, 10 vols. 8vo. *bds,* £2 2*s* (*pub. at* £6) 1823

Contains Force of Truth, Essays, Sermons, Bunyan's Pilgrim's Progress, with notes, Answers to Tom Paine, Reply to Bp. Tomline on Calvinism, &c.

4223 SCOTT'S (Rev. Thomas) Essays on the most Important Subjects in Religion, thick 18mo. *boards*, 2*s* (*pub. at* 3*s* 6*d*) 1825

"A divine possessed of sound discriminating judgment, strong sense, and a reflecting mind, with a clear display of evangelical truth."—*Rev. H. Bickersteth.*

4224 — Bible, with Explanatory Notes, practical observations, and copious Marginal References, 9th edition, 6 vols. 4to. *good sound copy, substantially bound in calf, gilt and grained*, £4 14*s* 6*d* (*cost* £9 9*s*) .. .. .. 1825

"Held in high and deserved estimation."—*Prebendary Horne.*

4225 SCOTT'S (W.) Twelve Sermons on the Wisdom and Goodness of God, 8vo. *old calf*, 2*s* .. *For the Author*, 1702

4226 SCOTT'S (Sir Walter) Sir Tristrem, a Metrical Romance of the Thirteenth Century, by Thomas of Erceldoune, called the Rhymer, 8vo. *half vellum*, 7*s* 6*d* *Edinburgh*, 1806

A very curious specimen of the old Scottish Language, from the Auchinlech MS. in the Library of the Faculty of Advocates, Edinburgh.

4227 — Marmion, a Tale of Flodden-Field, *plates by Heath*, 2 vols. post 8vo. *half calf, neat*, 7*s* 6*d* .. *Edinburgh*, 1810

4228 — Minstrelsy of the Scottish Border, historical and romantic Ballads, with illustrative Notes, 3 vols. 8vo. *boards*, 10*s* 6*d* *Edinburgh, Ballantyne*, 1812

"I consider these notes as a most admirable and hitherto unrivalled style of historical illustration."—*Dibdin's Lib. Comp.*

4229 — Guy Mannering; or, the Astrologer, 3 vols. post 8vo. *boards*, 5*s* *Edinburgh*, 1815

4230 — Letters on Demonology and Witchcraft, *plate*, 18mo. *cloth*, 2*s* 6*d* (*cost* 5*s*) .. .. .. *Fam. Lib.* 1830

4231 — History of Scotland, written for Dr. Lardner's Cabinet Cyclopædia, 2 vols. 12mo. *cloth*, 6*s* .. .. 1830

4232 — Bridal of Triermain, Harold the Dauntless, Field of Waterloo, and other Poems, 18mo. *morocco, gilt edges*, 3*s* (*cost* 5*s*) 1836

4233 — Novels, complete, *portrait, and wood-cut titles*, 5 vols. royal 8vo. *cloth*, £2 2*s* .. .. .. 1857

4234 — Novels, a new edition, *plates*, to be published in 48 vols. 18mo. 22 of which are ready, *cloth, new*, 4*s* 6*d per vol.* 1859-60

2 volumes a month will be published of this nice Edition, printed uniformly in size with Sir Walter's own favourite Edition in 48 vols.

"His highest praise is that in all the volumes which he has written, there is not a single line which in dying he would have wished to put out."—*Sir Robert Peel.*

4235 — Memoirs of his Life, by J. G. Lockhart, Esq., Sir Walter's son-in-law, *portrait*, 7 vols. post 8vo. *cloth*, £1 11*s* 6*d* (*pub. at* £3 15*s*) .. .. .. 1837-8

This is the original and the best of all the Editions in large letter, now entirely out of print.

4236 — Refutation of the Misstatements and Calumnies contained in Mr. Lockhart's Life of Sir W. Scott, respecting the Messrs. Ballantyne, by the Trustees and Son of the late Mr. James Ballantyne, 2nd Edition, post 8vo. *sewed*, 3*s* .. 1838

4237 — The Ballantyne Humbug Handled, in a Letter to Sir Adam Fergusson, by the author of the Memoirs of Sir Walter Scott, (J. G. Lockhart,) post 8vo. *sewed, scarce*, 4*s* *Edinb.* 1839

4238 — Life, by J. G. Lockhart, Esq., *portraits*, royal 8vo. *cloth*, 12*s* (*pub. at* 21*s*) .. .. .. *ib.*, 1844

4239 SCOUGAL'S Life of God in the Soul of Man, with an account of a Spiritual Life, and Preface by Bp. Burnet, 12mo. *bd.* 2*s* 1749

4240 SCRIBBLEOMANIA; or, the Printer's Devil's Polichronicon, a Sublime Poem, edited by Anser Pen-drag-on, Esq., (who was this Goose? )8vo. *newly half bound, neat,* 5*s* .. 1815

4241 SCRIBE, Choix des Meilleures Pièces, edit. dirigée par M. de Rouillon, 32mo. *calf, elegant, gilt leaves,* 3*s* 6*d* *Norwich,* 1838

4242 SCRIPTORES Rei Rusticæ Veteres Latini. (Cato, Varro, Columella, Palladius, Vegetius et Gargilius Martialis) cum Notis Variorum et Lexico Rei Rusticæ, curante Gesnero, cum præfatione Ernesti, 2 vols. 4to. *editio 2nda et optima, old calf,* £1 1*s* *Lipsiæ,* 1773

"This is the celebrated edition of Matthew Gesner. Far superior to every preceding one for variety and importance of materials. It has an excellent lexicon." See *Dibdin.*

4243 SCUDERY'S Artamenes; or, the Grand Cyrus, that excellent Romance, written by that Famous Wit of France, Monsieur de Scudery, Governour of Notre-Dame, Englished by F. G. Esquier, vols. 3 to 10, *frontispiece to each volume,* 12mo. *old binding,* 8*s* 1690

With the autograph and book-plate of "Cary Coke, wife of Edward Coke of Norfolk, Esq., 1701." "The greatest work of its kind."—*Granger.*

4244 SCULTETI (Abr.) Exercitationes Evangelicæ, both parts, small 4to. *old calf, neat,* 6*s* .. .. *Amst.,* 1624

"These exercitations illustrate successfully some obscure passages in the Evangelists." —*Orme.* *Calmet* gives a good account of him.

4245 — Secular Sermon concerning the Doctrine of the Gospell Restored in the 15th age from the birth of Christ, Englished from the High Dutch, small 4to. *sewed, curious,* 3*s* 6*d* *W. Jones,* 1618

4246 SECRET History of the Lives and Reigns of all the Kings and Queens of England from William the Conqueror to the End of the Reign of Queen Anne, by a Person of Honour, 2 vols. 8vo. *neat,* 6*s* .. .. .. .. 1725

4247 SECRETARY'S Assistant for Addressing the Nobility, Clergy, &c. 18mo. *cloth,* 2*s* 6*d* .. .. .. 1832

4248 SECUNDUS (Joannes) Kisses; being a Poetical Translation of the Basia, with the Latin, and an Essay on his Life and Writings, *portrait,* 12mo. *calf, neat, scarce,* 6*s* .. 1803

A nice little edition, not in Lowndes. It has the Epithalamium; some from Bonefonius and translations from the Italian and French.

4249 SEDGWICK'S (Rev. Professor Adam) Discourse on the Studies of the University, post 8vo. 3rd edit. *cloth,* 2*s* *Cambridge,* 1834

4250 SEGERI (Georgii) Dissertatio Anatomica, de usu communium corporis humani integumentorum, sm. 4to. *sewed,* 2*s* 6*d* *Francof.* 1656

4251 SEGUINI (Petri) Selecta Numismata Antiqua, ex Musio, P.S., ejusdem observationibus illustrata, *numerous plates of Coins,* 4to. *old calf, neat,* 10*s* 6*d* .. *Lutetiæ Parisiorum,* 1684

Added are 8 Treatises by Du Fresne, Falconerius, Spanheim, and others, on various monies.

4252 SEGUR, (M. le Comte de) Memoires, Souvenirs, et Anecdotes, 3 vols. 8vo. *hf. cf. extra,* 10*s* 6*d* .. *Paris,* 1827

4253 — ses Œuvres, completès, *portraits, maps, &c.* 33 vols. 8vo. and 1 4to. *old boards,* £3 3*s* (*pub. at* £9 9*s*) *Paris, Eymery,* 1824

Contents—Mêmoires, ou Souvenirs et Anecdotes, 3 vols.—Décade Historique, 3 vols.—Politique de Cabinets de l'Europe, 3 vols.—Hist. Ancienne, 3 vols.—Hist. Romaine, 4 vols.—Hist. du Bas-Empire, 4 vols.—Hist. de France, 9 vols.—Galerie Morale et Politique, 3 vols.—Melanges, 1 vol.

4254 SELDENI (Joannis) Existimationis suæ per Convitium Mendacissimum læsæ, Vindiciæ, adversus P. B. Burgum, small 4to. *sewed,* 3s 6*d* .. .. *Londini, Corn. Bee,* 1653

This is a defence, with rather a harsh title, of his "Mare Clausum," written to prove our dominion over the sea, against Grotius's "Mare liberum."

4255 — de Quatuor Monarchiis, cum Notis Meibomii et Hornii, 24mo. *old calf,* 2s 6*d* .. .. *Lugd. Bat.,* 1669

4256 — Jani Anglorum facies altera, memoria nempe a primula Henrici II., 12mo. *bound,* 3s .. .. *Londini,* 1681

4257 — Table-Talk, his Discourses on Religion and State, 18mo, *bound,* 2s .. .. .. .. 1716

4258 — Table-Talk, with Notes by Dr. David Irving, small 8vo. *cloth,* 5s .. .. .. .. 1854

4259 — Table-Talk, new edition by S. W. Singer, *portrait,* foolscap 8vo. *cloth,* 5s .. .. .. *J. R. Smith,* 1857

Coleridge thus emphatically expresses himself, "There is more weighty bullion sense in this book than I ever found in the same number of pages in any uninspired writer."

4260 — Memoirs of, and Notices of the Political Contest during his time, by George W. Johnson, *fine portrait,* 8vo. *boards,* 4s 6*d (pub at 12s)* .. .. .. .. 1835

4261 SELWYN (Will. *Canon of Ely Cath.*) Notes on the proposed Amendment of the Authorized Version of the Scriptures, 8vo. *sewed,* 1s .. .. .. *Cambridge,* 1856

4262 SEMEDO (P. Alvaro) Relatione della Grande Monarchia della Cina, *fine portrait, and engraved title page,* 4to. *old binding,* RARE, 10s 6*d* *Romæ, Hermanni Scheus,* 1643

Dedicated to Cardinal Barberini. Father Semedo was a Portuguese Jesuit, and this account of his Mission to China is very curious.

4263 SENECÆ TRAGÆDIÆ, 8vo. *old vellum,* 8s *Venetiis, in Ædibus Aldi,* 1517

"This edition is by no means of common occurrence."—*Moss.*

4264 — Tragedies, with the Rape of Helen out of the Greek of Coluthus, translated, with a Life of Seneca by Sir Edward Sherburne, *portrait and plates,* 8vo. *old calf, neat,* 12s .. 1702

With the autograph of "*Sam. Johnson.*" "Sherburne was a man of classical learning and a critic, and frequently conveys the sense of his author with considerable spirit."—*Chalmers's Biog. Dict.*

4265 — Opera Omnia, et Senecæ Rhetoris quæ extant, cum Notis Lipsii et Schotti, 3 vols. 12mo. *fine clean copy in vellum,* £1 5s *Lugd. Bat., Elzevir,* 1640

"This is the best 12mo. Elzevir edition."—*Dibdin.*

4266 — Epistolæ, ex recensione J. Lipsii, 18mo. *old calf, gilt,* 6s *L. Bat., Elzevir,* 1639

4267 — Flores, ex Operibus illius selecti, 18mo. *old binding,* 2s 6*d* *Col. Agrip.,* 1604

4268 — Workes, both Morall and Naturall, newly inlarged and corrected by Thomas Lodge, *frontispiece by R. Elstracke,* thick folio of 980 pages, *half bound, neat,* £1 1s *William Stansby,* 1620

This is Lodge's 2nd edition, dedicated to Thomas Earle of Suffolke. It is the only complete translation of the works of Seneca, "which are exceedingly valuable on account of the great number of just and beautiful moral sentiments which they contain, the extensive erudition which they discover, and the happy mixture of freedom and urbanity with which they censure vice, and inculcate good morals." See *Chalmers's Biog. Dict.*

4269 SENECA'S Morals, Englished by Sir Roger L'Estrange, 8vo. (wants first title) *old calf, neat,* 2*s* .. .. 1688

4270 SENNERTI (Andrea) Grammaticæ Chaldææ et Syriacæ Lib. II., accessit Lexici utriusque Linguæ compendium, sm. 4to. *old binding, scarce,* 6*s* .. .. *Wittebergæ,* 1651

At the end are five public Disputations on learned subjects, delivered at Wittemberg before the Greek Professor Ostermann, in 1648 and 9.

4271 SEPP'S (Christian) Insects of the Netherlands, (the descriptions in Dutch) 30 *highly finished coloured plates,* 4to. *hf. bd., very neat, scarce,* £1 10*s* .. *Amsterdam, for the Author,* 1762

Moths and Butterflies, each plate is accompanied by a MS. description in Dutch, in addition to the printed account.

4272 — Insects of the Netherlands, (the descriptions in German) 24 *coloured plates,* 4to. *foreign binding, gilt, clean and neat,* £1 4*s* *Leipsig,* 1783

4273 SERMONS, 12 to the Aged, by the author of Village Sermons, 12mo. *large type, neat,* 1*s* 6*d*

4274 — Cottage Sermons, 12 Short Discourses for Reading in Families, vol. 3, 12mo. *bound neat,* 1*s* 6*d*

4275 — XII. Preached at the Special Services for the Working Classes in Exeter Hall, 1857, with a Preface by the Bishop of Carlisle, 12mo. *cloth, neat,* 2*s*

4276 — for the Christian Seasons, 4 vols. 12mo. *boards,* 16*s* 1856

4277 — *a Collection of above* 100 *Various, in* 4to. *sewed,* 1*s each* 1680-1820

4278 SERVII (Petri) Dissertatio Philologica de ODORIBUS, small 8vo. *old calf, scarce,* 6*s* .. *Romæ, apud F. Caballum,* 1641

With a very curious printer's device in the title-page such as I never saw in any other book.

4279 SEVARAMBES, Histoire des, peuples qui habitent la Terre Australe, *numerous plates,* 2 vols. in 1, 12mo. *old calf, neat,* 6*s* *Amst.,* 1716

This curious book is a fiction, similar to Gulliver's Travels, written by Denis Varaisse d'Allais, see *Brunet* and *Barbier*. Has the autographs of William Nasmith, London, May 22, 1749, and of R. Tyrwhitt.

4280 SEWARD'S (Wm.) Anecdotes of some Distinguished Persons, chiefly of the present and two preceding Centuries, *portraits and plates,* 3 vols. crown 8vo. *half calf,* 7*s* 6*d* .. 1796

4281 — another copy, with Supplement, *portraits and plates,* 5 vols. crown 8vo. *calf, neat,* 12*s* .. .. 1796-7

A very amusing anecdotical work.

4282 SEYMER'S (John Gunning, *of St. Alban's Hall, Oxford,*) Fall of Saul, a Sacred Epic Poem, post 8vo. *cloth,* 3*s* (*pub. at* 8*s* 6*d*) 1839

4283 SHAFTESBURY'S (Anthony, Earl of,) Characteristicks of Men, Manners, Opinions, Times, *arms and vignette by Ravenet,* 3 vols. 18mo. *sewed, uncut,* 6*s,—bound,* 4*s* 6*d* .. 1749

Book-plate of Thomas Beecroft.

4284 SHAKESPEAR'S (John) Grammar of the Hindustani Language, 4to. *boards,* 9*s* (*pub. at* £1 1*s*) .. .. 1826

4285 SHAKSPEARE'S (William) Works with his Life, a Glossary, copious Indexes, and various Readings, Index, &c. 8 vols. 12mo. *old calf, neat,* 16*s* .. .. *Edinburgh,* 1753

4286 SHAKSPEARE'S Plays, Notes by Johnson, Steevens, and Read, 15 vols. 8vo. *old calf, very neat, fine paper*, £4 14*s* 6*d* 1793

Usually sells for £6 10*s*. This edition is preferred by many as containing the best selection of notes on Shakspeare.

4287 — Plays, accurately printed from the Text of Mr. Steevens's last edition, 8 vols. 12mo. *half russia, very neat, contents lettered*, £1 4*s* .. .. .. .. 1797

This is a much esteemed edition, with a judicious selection of Notes by Mr. J. Nichols, with these autographs, "Fredk. Bevan, (late of Carlton Rode) Emanuel Coll. Cambridge," and "Anne Eliza Bevan, the gift of her affectionate husband, Aug. 24, 1811."

4288 — Plays with Life, from Steevens's Text, with Notes, 8 vols. (vol. 8 missing) 24mo, *boards*, 7*s* .. *Trade Edit.*, 1811

4289 — Dramatic Works with a Glossary, 12mo. *morocco, extra, gilt edges*, 12*s* .. .. *Chiswick, Whittingham*, 1823

A beautifully printed edition, complete in 1 volume, in a diamond type.

4290 — another edition, with Introductory Essay and Notes, *portrait*, thick 8vo. *cloth*, 6*s* .. .. .. 1856

4291 — Dramatic and Poetical Works, with an Account of his Life and Writings, (Knight's Cabinet Edition) with Additional Notes, *portraits*, 12 vols. 18mo. *cloth*, 18*s* .. 1856

4292 — Supplement to the edition published in 1778 by Johnson and Steevens, with his Genuine Poems and seven Plays ascribed to him, *plate*, 2 vols. 8vo. *half calf, scarce*, 12*s* 1780

4293 — Collection of Poems, 8vo. *old calf, scarce*, 18*s* *London, Bernard Lintot, no date.*

Venus and Adonis from the edition of 1630. Rape of Lucrece from that of 1632. The Passionate Pilgrim, from that of 1599, and Sonnets to sundry notes of Musicke from the 1599 edition.

4294 — Play of the Winter's Tale, arranged for representation at the Princess's Theatre, with historical and explanatory notes, by Charles Kean, 2nd Edit. 8vo. *sewed*, 2*s* 6*d* 1856

The Notes at the end of each Act are extremely instructive and amusing.

4295 — Play of King Richard the 2nd, with notes, by Charles Kean, 8vo. *sewed*, 2*s* 6*d* .. .. .. 1857

4296 — Most Excellent Historie of the Merchant of Venice, *beautifully illustrated*, 4to. *ornamental covers, and printed on toned paper*, 10*s* 6*d* *S. Low*, 1860

Intended as a Christmas Present, it is very handsomely printed.

4297 — *AUTOGRAPH of WILLIAM SHAKSPEARE*, thus written, "*WILL. SPERRE, HIS BOOK, GIVEN HIM BY MR. WA——*," the rest is illegible. The S has a mark over it thus ◡ shewing it to be an abridgement of the first syllable.

This autograph is written on a leaf of "The Table" to Bp. Gervase Babington's "Comfortable Notes upon every Chapter of Genesis," published by Dr. Miles Smith, afterwards Bp. of Gloucester. This book, which is a small 4to., is dated 1596, at which time Shaksperre was 32 years of age, but of course it may have been written any time between then and his death, which happened 20 years later. The autograph as here written is wonderfully like a *Fac-Simile* of the immortal author's signature given in Steevens's Edition of his Works, vol. 1, page 101, in the 15 vol. 8vo. of 1793. Should it be so, that this is Shaksperre's writing, there is more of it here than is elsewhere known to be in existence. Query, what is become of all the MSS. of Shaksperre's Plays? Surely some of them exist somewhere, unless PRYNNE met with them and destroyed them, which it seems likely he would have done. See his Histrio-Mastix, No. 3864.

4298 SHAKSPEAR'S Fools and Jesters: with Robert Armin's Nest of Ninnies, 1608, and an introduction and notes, by J. P. Collier, 8vo. *cloth*, 2s 6d .. .. *Shakspeare Soc.*, 1842

4299 — Oberon's Vision in the Midsummer Night's Dream, illustrated by a comparison with Lylie's Endymion, by the Rev. N. J. Halpin, 8vo. *cloth*, 3s .. .. *ib.*, 1843

4300 — Marriage of Wit and Wisdom, an ancient interlude, with illustrations of Shakspeare and the early English Drama, by J. O. Halliwell, 8vo. *boards*, 6s .. .. *ib.*, 1846

4301 — Revisal of Shakespear's Text, wherein the alterations of more modern Critics are considered, 8vo. *old calf, neat*, 5s 1765

Anonymous, but done by Mr. Benjamin Heath, a very good scholar and critic. Warburton's Shakspeare is particularly aimed at.

4302 — Fragment on Shakspeare, extracted from Advice to a Young Poet, by Rev. M. Sherlock, 8vo. *sewed*, 1s 1786

4303 — Drake's (Dr.) Shakspeare and his Times, *fine portrait*, 2 vols. 4to. LARGE PAPER, *half morocco, uncut*, £2 12s 6d 1817

"Every person who is curious on the subject of our literature, manners, customs, and their history, must resort to this masterly production for information."—*Gentleman's Magazine.* These handsome volumes were published at 7 Guineas.

4304 — Shakspeare and his Times, by M. Guizot, 8vo. *cloth*, 7s (*pub. at* 10s 6d) .. .. .. *Bentley*, 1852

4305 — Shaksperiana; Catalogue of all the Books, Pamphlets, &c. relating to Shakspeare, 8vo. LARGE PAPER, *bds*, 5s *John Wilson*, 1827

4306 SHARP'S (Granville) Inquiry, whether the Description of Babylon in Revelations agrees with Rome as a City? 12mo. *bds.* 2s 6d 1805

"From the author," to "J. Duncan." 2 autographs.

4307 SHARP (Archdeacon) on the Rubric in the Common Prayer and the Canons of the Church of England, 8vo. *cloth*, 3s *Oxford*, 1853

4308 SHARP'S Diamond Dictionary, *plate after Harvey*, thick 48mo. *morocco, gilt edges*, 3s 6d .. .. 1835

4309 SHARPE'S (Samuel) History of Egypt under the Ptolemies, 4to. *half cloth*, 7s 6d .. .. *Moxon*, 1838

4310 SHARPIN'S (E. C.) Death Scenes: extracted from Biographical and other Works, 8vo. *cloth*, 5s *Yarmouth*, 1842

"For Private Circulation." "*From the Compiler.*" "There is nothing in History that is so improving to the reader as those accounts which we meet with of the death of eminent persons."—*Addison.*

4311 SHARROCK (Rob., L.L.D.) Judicia (seu Legum censuræ) de Adulterio, Polygamia et Concubinatu, Fornicatione, etc., 8vo. *old binding*, 3s .. .. *Oxoniæ*, 1662

4312 — Provinciale Vetus Provinciæ Cantuariensis cum Selectioribus Lindwodi Annotationibus; cum Constitutionibus Othonis et Othoboni, thick small 8vo. above 700 pages, *old binding*, 5s 1664

For an account of this good Divine, Civilian, and Lawyer, see *Wood's Athenæ Oxonienses.*

4313 SHAW'S (Dr. Thomas) Travels in Barbary and the Levant, *maps and plates*, folio, *half bound*, 7s 6d *Oxford*, 1738

4314 — Travels in Barbary, &c., *maps and plates*, 2nd and best edition, 4to. *old calf, very neat*, 14s .. .. 1757

4315 SHAW'S Travels in Barbary, &c., *plates*, 4to. *old calf*, 18*s* 1757

"These Travels are universally esteemed for the extent of their information, and their scrupulous fidelity."—*Murray*. "This valuable work, besides some observations on Egypt, Syria, and Arabia Petræa, contains the best information on Algiers and Tunis."—*Pinkerton*.

4316 SHAW'S (Thomas B.) Outlines of English Literature, post 8vo. *half morocco, new*, 8*s* (*pub. at* 12*s*) .. 1849

Contains much information, very agreeably told.

4317 SHAW and Nodder's Naturalist's Miscellany, containing accurate *coloured* figures of the most curious productions of nature, 984 *plates*, 22 vols. and 3 nos. of vol. 23, royal 8vo. *fine clean set, boards, uncut*, £5 5*s* (*pub. at above* £30) 1790-1811

4318 SHELLS. 59 DRAWINGS, exhibiting 112 SHELLS, *exquisitely painted*, royal 4to. *half bound, very neat*, £1 11*s* 6*d*

4319 SHELLY'S Lives of Eminent French Authors, 2 vols. 12mo. *cloth*, 5*s* .. .. *Lardner's Cab. Cyc.*, 1848

4320 SHENSTONE'S (Will.) Works in Prose and Verse, with R. Dodsley's description of his seat the Leasowes, *portrait and plan*, 2 vols. 8vo. *old calf*, 4*s* .. .. 1764

4321 — another edition, *portrait and plates*, 3 vols. 12mo. *good copy in old calf*, 7*s* 6*d* .. .. .. 1765

4322 — another, with Essays on Men and Manners, and his Letters from 1739 to 1763, *portrait and plates*, 3 vols. sm. 8vo. *cf. nt.* 8*s* 1777

"Many of his works are distinguished by elegance and simplicity. His Letters to his friends are entertaining." See *Dr. Johnson's Life of him*.

4323 SHEPHERD'S (Dr. Wm.) Life of Poggio Bracciolini, 8vo. *cloth, neat*, 6*s* .. .. .. *Liverpool*, 1837

Mr. Shepherd has here done that for Bracciolini which Mr. Roscoe did for Lorenzo de Medici. "Very interesting."—*Dr. Parr*. "This volume offers a rich and varied entertainment to the scholar, and considerable amusement to the miscellaneous cursory reader."—*Annual Review*.

4324 SHEPPARD'S (John) Thoughts preparative to private Devotion, 12mo. *boards*, 2*s* (*pub. at* 6*s*) .. .. 1826

4325 — Critical and Practical Elucidation of the Book of Common Prayer, 2 vols. 8vo. 6*s* (*pub. at* 21*s*) .. *Lond.* 1828

4326 SHERIDAN'S (Thomas) Lectures on the Art of Reading Prose and Verse, 8vo. *bound*, 2*s* 6*d* .. .. 1781

4327 — Pronouncing Dictionary of the English Language, with a Prosodial Grammar, 2 vols. 8vo. *calf, neat*, 7*s* .. 1797

4328 SHERLOCK (Dr. Will.) Second part of the Preservative against Popery, 4to. *sewed*, 2*s* .. .. 1688

4329 — Answer to Dr. Sherlock's Preservative against Popery, shewing that Protestancy cannot be defended, &c., 4to. *sewed*, 1*s* 6*d* *Henry Hills*, 1688

4330 — Discourse concerning the Happiness of Good Men, and the Punishment of the Wicked in the next World, 8vo. *old calf, neat*, 3*s* .. .. .. 1726

4331 — Practical Discourse concerning a Future Judgment, 8vo. *calf, neat*, 3*s* .. .. .. 1731

4332 — Practical Discourse concerning Death, 8vo. *old cf. nt.* 2*s* 6*d* 1731

4333 — another edition, 8vo. *old calf, neat*, 3*s* .. 1743

"He who has not perused this excellent piece, has not read one of the strongest persuasions to a religious life that ever was written in any language."—*Addison*.

4334 SHERLOCK (Dr. Will.) Practical Christian; or devout Penitent, 2 vols. 18mo. *morocco, gilt edges*, 9*s* (*cost* 15*s*) *Oxford, Parker*, 1844

4335 — Traité sur la Providence, traduit de l'Anglois, *portrait*, 8vo. *neat*, 2*s* .. .. .. *La Haye*, 1721

Dr. Sherlock was Dean of St. Paul's in 1691, a man of considerable learning and abilities, and father of the Bishop whose works follow.

4336 SHERLOCK'S (Bp. Thomas) Discourses, preached at the Temple Church, 4 vols. 8vo. *good clean copy, in old calf, gilt*, 12*s* 1756

4337 — another edition, with his Life, and Letter to the people of his Diocese, *portrait*, 3 vols. 12mo. *half russia, uncut*, 9*s* 1775

4338 — Six Discourses on the Use and intent of Prophecy, with Four Dissertations, 8vo. *calf, neat*, 3*s* .. 1749

"Bp. Sherlock was a man of the most acute parts I ever knew, and from 1749 to 1759 I had frequent and unreserved conversations with him."—*Isaac Reed's MS. Diary.*

4339 SHIP—History of a Ship, from her Cradle to her Grave, *plates*, square 12mo. *cloth*, 2*s* .. .. 1850

4340 SHOPKEEPER'S Guide, instructing him how to place his business upon a secure foundation, post 8vo. *cloth*, 2*s* 6*d* 1853

4341 SHOREY'S (William) Fourteen Discourses, 8vo. *old calf*, 2*s* *W. & J. Innys*, 1725

4342 SHUCKFORD'S (Dr. Samuel) Sacred and Prophane History of the World connected, *maps*, 4 vols. 8vo. *old calf, gilt, the 4th vol. in old red morocco, gilt edges*, £1 4*s* .. 1731-53

"This work has long been a standard book in its class, it was designed to complete the work of Prideaux, which begins where that of Shuckford ends."—*Orme.*

4343 SHUTTLEWORTH'S (Dr. Philip N.) Paraphrastic translation of the Apostolical Epistles, with notes, 8vo. *newly half bound in calf*, 12*s* .. .. .. *Oxford*, 1831

"An admirably executed work."—*Horne.*

4344 — Sermons on the Leading Principles and Practical Duties of Christianity, 2 vols. 8vo. *cloth*, 12*s* (*pub. at* 24*s*) 1829-34

4345 SIBYLLINA Oracula, Gr. et Lat., cum annotationib. Xysti Betuleii et Sebast. Castalionis, small 8vo. (wants pages 97 to 112) 8 blank pages are inserted, *sewed*, 3*s* *Basiliæ, Jo. Oporinus*, 1555

4346 — Marckii (Johan.) de Sibyllinis Carminibus Disputationes XII., small 8vo. *old calf*, 3*s* .. .. *Franekeræ*, 1682

4347 SICILIÆ Inventrice, overo le invenzioni lodevoli nate in Sicilia opera del Dottor Vincenzo Auria, *Palermitano*,—Divertimenti Geniali Osservazioni e giunte di Ant. Mongitore, alla Sicilia Inventrice, 4to. *limp vellum*, 5*s* *Palermo, F. Marino*, 1704

4348 SICILIÆ et objacentium Insularum Veterum Inscriptionum Illustrata, per Castellum, *plates of coins*, folio, *boards*, £1 5*s* *Panormi*, 1784

A desirable adjunct to Græevius and Gronovius's Thesaurus.

4349 SIDNEY'S (Sir Philip) Countesse of Pembroke's Arcadia, 8th edition, folio, *a nice copy in old calf*, £1 11*s* 6*d* *London, Simon Waterson*, 1633

Contains the Arcadia, Certaine Sonnets, Defence of Poesie, and Astrophel and Stella, the Arcadia has Sir William Alexander's Continuation of the third part and Richard Beling's sixth Booke. "A curious and copious account of this romance is given in Zouch's Life of Sir Philip, and a good analysis of the story is in Dunlop's History of Fiction." —*Lowndes.*

4350 SIDNEY (Sir Philip) The Correspondence of Sir P. Sidney and Hubert Languet, 1574-80, 8vo. *cloth*, SCARCE, 8*s* *Pickering*, 1845

A very interesting volume "now first collected and translated from the Latin with Notes, and a Memoir of the Life and Times of Sir P. Sidney, by S. A. Pears, Fellow of C. C. C. Oxford."

4351 — Memoirs of his Life and Writings by Dr. Thomas Zouch, Prebendary of Durham, *portrait*, 4to. *boards*, 7*s* 6*d* *York*, 1809

4352 SIDONIUS Apollinaris, Epistolæ et Carmina, small 8vo. *sewed*, a fragment of, from page 17 to the end p. 360, 2*s* *Lugd.*, *Tornesius*, 1552

4353 SIGONII (Caroli) Fasti Consulares et Comment. in Fastos et Triumphos Romanos,—de Nominibus Romanorum—Velleii Paterculi Historiæ Romanæ libri II., in 1 vol. thick 8vo. *old calf, gilt, a fine copy*, 9*s* .. *Parisiis, H. Stephanus*, 1568

4354 — de Republica Hebræorum, small 8vo. *old binding*, 2*s* 6*d* *Hanoviæ*, 1608

4355 SILIUS Italicus de Secundo Bello Punico, opera D. Heinsii, 18mo. *old calf, neat*, 4*s* .. .. *Ex off. Platiniana*, 1600

Contains notes under the title of *Crepundia Siliana*, it is said to have been taken from an Ancient MS.

4356 SIMEON'S Works, arranged by Prebendary Horne, vols. 1, 15, 17, and 21, only, 8vo. *cloth* £1 1*s* .. 1836

4357 SIMLER (Josia) Responsio ad Maledicum Francisci Stancari Mantuani librum adversus Tigurinæ Ecclesiæ Ministros de Trinitate et Mediatore Dom. nostro J. Christo, 12mo. *sewed*, 3*s* *Tiguri, Christ. Froschoverus*, 1563

4358 SIMON'S (Father) Critical Enquiries into the Various Editions of the Bible, with Animadversions on Vossius's Treatise on the Oracles of the Sibylls, 4to. *good copy in calf*, 6*s* 1684

4359 — Critical History of the Religions and Customs of the Eastern Nations, Englished by A. Lovell, sm. 8vo. *old binding*, 2*s* 6*d* 1685

4360 — Critical History of the Text of the New Testament, 4to. *old calf, neat*, 5*s* 6*d* .. .. .. 1689

With the pretty book-plate of Lucius Henry Hibbins, of Gray's Inne, Esqre.
"It would be worth your while to peruse 'Simon's Critical History of the Old and New Testament.'"—*Warburton.*

4361 SIMPSON'S (Rev. David) Plea for Religion and the Sacred Writings, addressed to the Disciples of Thomas Paine, 8vo. *bds.* 2*s* 6*d* 1810

4362 SIMPSON'S (L. F.) Literature of Italy, from the Origin of the Italian Language (1218) to the Death of Boccaccio, (1375) post 8vo. *cloth, new*, 5*s* (*pub. at* 10*s* 6*d*) .. 1851

4363 SIMPSON'S (William) Private Journal kept during the Niger Expedition, 1841-2, 8vo. *cloth*, 2*s* 6*d* .. .. 1843

4364 SINCERI (Jodoci) Itinerarium Galliæ; cum appendice de Burdigala, thick 18mo. of above 800 pages, *old parchment*, 3*s* *Argentorati*, 1617

4365 SIRI (Vittorio) Il Mercurio overo Historia de' Correnti Tempi, 4to. *Italian vellum, clean and neat*, 5*s* *In Casale, per C. della Casa*, 1644

The engraved title contains a portrait of "Gastone di Borbone, duca d'Orliens."

4366 SISMONDI'S Historical View of the Literature of the South of Europe, Englished, with Notes and Life by Thomas Roscoe, *portrait*, 2 vols. 12mo. *cloth*, 6*s* .. *Bohn*, 1846

"A work written in that flowing and graceful style which distinguishes the author, and succeeding in all that it seeks to give, a pleasing and popular, yet not superficial or unsatisfactory, account of the best authors in the southern languages."—*Hallam.*

4367 SKEELER'S (Thomas) XIV. Sermons as Preached before the University in Oxford, 8vo. *calf, neat*, 3*s* 6*d* *Oxford*, 1740

4368 SKELTON (Philip) Ophiomaches; Deism Revealed, in Answer to Lord's Herbert and Shaftesbury, Hobbes, Toland, &c. *vignette*, 2 vols. 8vo. *old calf, neat*, 5*s* 6*d* .. .. 1749

4369 — another edition, 2 vols. 12mo. *neat*, 4*s* .. 1751

"Skelton's learning is almost universal and his language is uncommonly fluent and vigorous."—*Philosophical Survey of Ireland.*

4370 SKINNER'S (Captain Tho.) Excursions in India, including a Walk over the Himalaya Mountains to the Sources of the Jumna and Ganges, *plates*, 2 vols. 8vo. *cloth*, 8*s* (*pub. at* £1 1*s*) 1832

"Replete throughout with admirable sketches of native scenes and native portraits, picturesque, amusing, and impressive."—*Lit. Gazette.*

4371 [SKIPPER (William, Esq., *of Thorpe*,)] Some Thoughts on Mental Culture, 12mo. *sewed*, 6*d* .. .. 1851

4372 — Chapters on Habit, by the same, square 12mo. *gilt edges*, 6*d* 1850

Both published anonymously, and both excellent little works inculcating the best possible precepts.

4373 SLADE'S (Rev. James) Annotations on the Epistles, 2 vols. 8vo. *boards*, 7*s* (*pub. at* 16*s*) .. *Cambridge*, 1816

This is a continuation of Elsley on the Gospels.

4374 — Explanation of the Psalms, 12mo. *cloth*, 2*s* .. *No date*

4375 SLEIDAN'S (Dr. John) General History of the Reformation of the Church, begun in Germany by Martin Luther, 1517 to 1562, Englished by Edmund Bohun, *fine portrait by Faithorne*, folio, *nice copy in calf, gilt*, £1 5*s* .. .. 1689

A very learned work and the best history of the Reformation.

4376 SMEE'S (Alfred) Elements of Electro-Metallurgy, *cuts*, 8vo. *cloth*, 6*s* (*pub. at* 10*s* 6*d*) .. .. .. 1843

4377 SMELLIE'S (Will.) Lives of Dr. John Gregory, Lord Kames, Hume, and Dr. Adam Smith, with a Dissertation on Public Spirit, 8vo. *boards, uncut*, 4*s* 6*d* .. *Edinburgh*, 1800

4378 SMETII (Henrici) Prosodia; quæ syllabarum positione et Dipthongis carentium quantitates, demonstrat, 8vo. *old vellum*, 5*s* *Francofurti*, 1691

4379 SMITH'S (Dr. Adam) Theory of Moral Sentiments, with a Dissertation on the Origin of Languages and Biography of him by Dugald Stewart, post 8vo. *cloth*, 2*s* (*cost* 3*s* 6*d*) *H. G. Bohn*, 1853

4380 — Inquiry into the Nature and Causes of the Wealth of Nations, 3 vols. 8vo. *nice copy in old calf*, 7*s* 6*d* .. 1786

"Dr. Smith has left us a work which contains a greater number of useful truths than have ever been given to the world by any other individual."—*Macculloch's Polit. Economy.*

4381 SMITH'S (Albert) Month at Constantinople, *portrait and cuts*, 12mo. *cloth, new*, 3*s* 6*d* (*pub. at* 5*s*) .. .. 1851

4382 SMITH'S (Lt. Col., C. H.) Natural History of the Human Species, *portrait and* 34 *coloured plates shewing the various tribes,* 12mo. *cloth, gilt, new,* 4*s* (*pub. at* 7*s* 6*d*) .. *Edinburgh,* 1848

4383 SMITH'S (C. Roach) COLLECTANEA ANTIQUA; Ancient Remains, 5 vols. 8vo. *cloth,* £8 .. *J. R. Smith,* 1843-60

4384 — Antiquities of RICHBOROUGH, RECULVER, and LYMNE, *with numerous etchings and wood cuts by Fairholt,* small 4to. *boards,* 21*s* *ib.*

4385 — On the Excavations of the ROMAN CASTRA at LYMNE and at PEVENSEY, *illustrated,* 10*s* 6*d each*

4386 — INVENTORIUM SEPULCHRALE, by Bryan Faussett, a Detailed Account of his Excavations in KENT, of upwards of 500 Saxon Tumuli, with Introduction and Notes by C. R. Smith, *richly illustrated by coloured plates and wood cuts,* 4to. *boards,* £3 3*s*

4387 — CATALOGUE of the Museum of LONDON ANTIQUITIES, collected by and the Property of C. Roach Smith, *copiously illustrated,* large 8vo. £1 1*s* .. .. .. 1854

4388 — Illustrations of ROMAN LONDON, *numerous plates, some coloured,* 4to. *stiff covers,* £3 3*s* .. .. .. 1859

Printed for the subscribers and not published. "Mr. Roach Smith has brought to his task a thorough and familiar acquaintance with the writings of Roman and Greek authors, which enables him to interpret at a glance the significance of isolated and otherwise inscrutable facts and allusions. But besides these acquirements he possesses an enthusiastic spirit which has neither been daunted by opposition, nor chilled by indifference; and to this we owe the results recorded in his splendid volume. How many thanks are due from all historical and antiquarian enquirers to Mr. Roach Smith for his public-spirited labours! Fortunately, he needs no other memorial than this his greatest work, to attest his labours and his services."—*Leicester Chronicle.*

4389 SMITH'S (H. and J.) Rejected Addresses, 7th edit., 1812—Theorie du Systeme Animal, *Leide,* 1767.—Ditto, En Essais de Poësie, *Norwich, Stevenson, no date,*—Sir Will. Jones's Principles of Government, 1796.—Poetical Translations from the Ancients, by Gilb. Wakefield, 1795.—in 1 vol. 12mo. *half calf, neat,* 3*s* 6*d* V.Y.

Collected by the late Rev. F. Howes, of Norwich.

4390 SMITH'S (Dr. Robert, *Master of Trin. Coll. Cambridge,*) Harmonics; or, the Philosophy of Musical Sounds, 2nd and best edition, 28 *plates,* 8vo. *boards, uncut,* SCARCE, 12*s* .. 1759

"Mathematicians have also applied their art to the theory of sounds and music. Dr. Smith's Harmonics is the principal book of the kind."—*Gibbon.*

4391 SMITH (Sidney) Peter Plymley's Letters on the Subject of the Catholics to his brother Abraham, 12mo. *half morocco, gilt edges,* 2*s* 6*d* .. .. .. *Wakefield,* 1808

4392 SMITH'S (Sidney) Settlers' New Home; or, Whether to Go, and Whither? a Guide to Emigrants, 12mo. *cloth, gilt,* 2*s* 1850

4393 SMITHI (Thomæ Angli) de Republica Anglorum, lib. III., 18mo. *old calf, neat,* 5*s* .. .. *L. Bat., Elzevir,* 1641

4394 — Commonwealth of England, the Manner and Government thereof, *engraved frontispiece by Marshall containing portrait of K. Chas. I.* 12mo. *old calf, neat,* 5*s* .. .. 1640

4395 — Life, by J. Strype, discovering many Singular Matters relating to the State of Learning, the Reformation of Religion, &c. *fine portrait,* 8vo. *old calf, neat,* 5*s* .. .. 1698

Sir Thomas Smith was a Doctor of both Laws, and principal Secretary of State to K. Edward VI. and Queen Elizabeth.

4396 SMITH (T.) Epistolæ duæ; quarum altera de Moribus ac institutis Turcarum agit: altera Septem Asiæ Ecclesiarum notitiam continet, small 8vo. *old calf, neat,* 4*s* .. *Oxonii,* 1672

4397 — Remarks on the Manners, Religion, and Government of the Turks, the VII. Churches of Asia and Constantinople, small 8vo. *old calf, neat,* 3*s* 6*d* .. .. 1678

Autograph of Mr. John Gurney, Earlham, Book-plate of Mr. Joseph John Gurney.

4398 — Miscellanea; Responsio ad nuperas D. Simonii cavillationes,—Vindiciæ 1 S. Joan. c. V, v. 7,—Comment. in 2 Epist. Petri cap. 2 and 3, 8vo. *old calf, neat,* 4*s* .. *Londini,* 1690

4399 — idem, 8vo. *old calf,* 2*s* 6*d* .. .. *ib.,* 1690

"Thomas Smith was so much noted for his great skill in the Oriental tongues, that he was commoly called Rabbi Smith, and by some Tograi Smith."—*Wood's Athenæ Oxon.* His works on the Greek Church are highly esteemed.

4400 SMOLLETT'S (Dr. T.) History of England from Julius Cæsar to the Treaty of Aix, 1748, *map, portraits, and plates,* 16 vols. (vol. 8 missing) 8vo. *calf,* 12*s* .. .. 1758

"It is written with uncommon spirit and correctness of language."—*Sir Walter Scott.*

4401 — Travels through France and Italy, 2 vols. 8vo. *calf, neat,* 5*s* 1766

4402 SMYTH (James) MISCELLANEOUS MANUSCRIPT, small 8vo. *old calf, neat,* 10*s* 6*d* .. .. .. 1735

The first part of this MS. consists of 128 Maxims, then Dissertations on several subjects, 1736-7; then Translations of some of the mottoes of the Tatlers, Spectators, &c., the Latin and English opposite. Epitaph on Charteris. A receipt to make Maw Wallop, very choice. The Inscription on the stone first laid of Sir Robt. Walpole's Hall at Houghton in Norfolk, &c.

4403 SMYTH'S (Professor W.) Lectures on Modern History, 2 vols. 12mo. *cloth,* 6*s* .. .. *H. G. Bohn,* 1854

4404 — List of Books recommended and referred to in the Lectures on Modern History, 8vo. *sewed, interleaved,* 2*s* *Camb. Deighton,* 1828

4405 SNOW'S (W. P.) Two Years' Cruise off Terra del Fuego, the Falkland Islands, Patagonia, and other places in the South Seas, *charts and coloured plates,* 2 vols. post 8vo. *cloth,* 8*s* (*cost* 24*s*) 1857

4406 SOAMES'S (Henry) Elizabethan Religious History, thick 8vo. *cloth, new,* 10*s* (*pub. at* 16*s*) .. .. 1839

4407 SOLINI (C. Julii) Polyhistor, et Solini Vita per Io. Camertem, small 8vo. *old binding,* 4*s* 6*d* *Lugduni, Gryphii,* 1538

This Latin Grammarian flourished about the end of the first century. This work is full of most marvellous matter.

4408 SOLIS Istoria della Conquista del Messico, see *Mexico.*

4409 SOLOMON'S SONGS in GERMAN VERSE, small folio, *half morocco, neat,* RARE, £1 11*s* 6*d*
*Franckfurt, durch Jacob von der Heyden Chalcographi,* 1622

On 67 leaves; on 64 of which are beautifully engraved emblems by Jacob von der Heyden, of whom we can find no account either in *Bryan* or *Pinkerton.*

4410 SOMERS (Lord John) Essay on his Life and Character, and that of Philip, Earl of Hardwick, by Richard Cooksey, 4to. *boards,* 6*s* 6*d*
*Worcester,* 1791

"An esteemed work."—*Lowndes.* A copy at Sir M. M. Sykes's sale sold for £1 11*s* 6*d*.

4411 SOMERVILE'S (William) Chace, a Poem, 1st edition, 4to. *sewed,* 3*s* .. .. .. .. 1735

4412 SOMERVILE'S Chase, a Poem, with a Critical Essay, by J. Aikin, *plates after Stothard*, 12mo. *half morocco, top edges gilt*, 3*s* 6*d* 1796

4413 SOMNER'S (William) Antiquities of Canterbury, 2nd Edition, enlarged by Battely, *plates by Hollar and Kip*, folio, *a fine copy, in russia, gilt, gilt edges*, £1 15*s (formerly priced* £3 3*s*) 1703

Bishop Nicolson says, "This is an excellent work."

4414 — Vocabularium Anglo-Saxonicum, Lexico Gul. Somneri Magna parte auctius, operâ Thomæ Benson, royal 8vo. *old calf, neat*, 10*s* 6*d* .. .. .. *Oxoniæ*, 1701

4415 SONNETS Chrêtiens, sur divers sujets, en IV. Livres, 4to. *old calf, neat*, 8*s* .. .. *Berlin, Robert Roger*, 1696

Here are 160 Sonnets sur la nature et sur son auteur, sur diverses Histoires du Vieux et Nouveau Testament, et sur diverses Graces et divers Etats.

4416 SONGS. 1. Sweet Robin; or, the Children in the Wood, 1794.—2. Harmonious Volunteer, *Wrexham, no date*.—3. Scottish Ballads and Songs, *Manchester*, 1796.—4. & 5. Neil's Pocket Melodist, Nos. 27 & 29, *no dates*.—6. Syren of Peace, *Ipswich*, 1802.—7. Songster's Museum, 1807, in 1 vol. 18mo. *half bound, neat*, 5*s* .. .. .. V. Y.

4417 — The Convivial Songster, Humerous, Satirical, Bacchanalian, &c., *with the Music to each Song*, 12mo. *scarce*, 10*s* 6*d* *Fielding, P. N. Row, no date.*

4418 — Ladies Polite Songster, *plate by M. Rennoldson, after Wale*, 12mo. *bound*, 3*s* 6*d* .. *For T. Shepherd, Minories, no date.*

4419 SONG-WRITING, Essays on, with a Collection of English Songs most eminent for poetical merit, with some original pieces, by [Dr. John Aikin,] small 8vo. *old calf, neat*, 4*s* *No date.*

First edition published anonymously, of "a much esteemed and elegant collection."—*Lowndes.*

4420 SOPHOCLIS Tragœdiæ Septem, Græcè, cum interpretationibus Vetustis et valde utilibus, 4to. *remarkably fine clean copy, in russia, extra, with joints and gilt leaves*, £2 2*s* *Florentiæ, per hæredes Philippi Juntæ*, MDXXII

The first edition of Sophocles was printed by Aldus in 1502.—This is the 2nd, and the 1st edition with the GREEK SCHOLIA, united to the Text, which was omitted by Aldus. This rare and important edition was edited by FRANCINUS. The book, with the exception of the dedication to Egnatius is entirely in Greek.

4421 SOPHOCLIS Tragœdiæ Septem, Græcè, 8vo. *old stamped calf*, 15*s* *Lut. Par., Colinæus*, 1528

This is a very rare book, in any state, it has the four leaves of errata at the end, usually missing. See *Brunet*. It is formed on the first Aldine of 1502, and is the 3rd edition of Sophocles ever published.

4422 — Brunck et Erfurdt, vol. 3 only, containing the Latin Version and Greek Scholia, *boards*, 3*s* .. *Londini*, 1824

4423 — Græcè, 18mo. *cloth*, 3*s* .. *Oxonii, Parker*, 1859

4424 SORBA (Laurentio Lomellino) Annali della CITTA di GENOA, folio, *fine copy in calf*, VERY RARE, £2 12*s* 6*d* *Genoa, per Antonio Bellono*, 1537

This author is not mentioned either by Haym, Brunet, or De Bure. The history extends from A.D. 87 to 1528. Christopher Columbus is mentioned under 1493, folio 249. The book consists of 282 leaves.

4425 SORBIERE'S Voyage to England, an Account of the State of Learning, Religion, &c. with Life, *plan*, 8vo. *bound*, 2*s* 6*d* 1709

4426 SOUTERI (Danielis) Palamedes; sive de Tabula Lusoria, Alea, et Variis Ludis libri III., 8vo. *old calf, scarce*, 7*s* 6*d* *L. Bat., Is. Elzevir*, 1622

4427 SOUTHAMPTON Guide, with the Isle of Wight, Lymington, &c. and Southampton Rooms, a Satyrical Poem, 12mo. *half calf, neat*, 1*s* 6*d* .. .. .. 1781

4428 — another edition, 12mo. *calf, extra, ornamental binding*, 2*s* 6*d* *Southampton, no date*

4429 SOUTHEY'S (Robert) Letters written during a Short Residence in Spain and Portugal, 8vo. *calf, neat*, 6*s* *Bristol*, 1797

With some account of Spanish and Portuguese Poetry. A very amusing and instructive book.

4430 — Joan of Arc, *portrait*, 2 vols. 12mo. *calf, neat*, 4*s* 1806

4431 — Palmerin of England, translated from the Portuguese by Robert Southey, 4 vols. 12mo. *half russia, neat*, SCARCE, £1 4*s* 1807

"Let Palmerin of England," says the Licentiate, "be preserved, and kept as a singular piece; and let such another case be made for it, as that which Alexander found among the spoils of Darius and appropriated to preserve the works of the poet Homer." —*Don Quixote*.

4432 — Lives of the British Admirals, 5 vols. 12mo. *cloth*, 12*s* 6*d* 1847

4433 — Life and Correspondence, edited by his Son, *portrait and plates*, 6 vols. 8vo. *cloth*, £1 12*s* (*pub. at* £3 3*s*) .. 1849

4434 — Catalogue of his Library, sold by Messrs. Sotheby, *partially priced*, 8vo. *half calf, neat*, 5*s* .. .. .. 1844

4435 SOUTH SEA SCHEME—All for the Better; or, the World Turn'd Upside Down, being the History of Head-longs and the Long-heads, with the Woolfe stripp'd of his Sheep's Clothing, by Charles Gildon, Gent., 8vo. *old calf*, 3*s* .. 1720

4436 SOUTHWELL'S (Rev. Robert) Poetical Works, edited by W. B. Turnbull, f.cap, 8vo. *cloth*, 4*s* .. *J. R. Smith*, 1857

"In sweetness, in classical purity of language, in melodious rhythm, these poems will not suffer by comparison with the contemporaneous works even of Edmund Spenser or Sir Philip Sidney."—*Northern Times*.

4437 SOWERBY'S General Indexes to the 36 vols. of English Botany, with an Alphabetical Index to English Fungi, royal 8vo. *sewed*, 3*s* .. .. .. .. 1814

4438 — Mineral Conchology, plate 504 to 609 the end of vol. 6, *coloured*, royal 8vo. *in sheets*, £2 .. .. 1830

4439 — Genera of Recent and Fossil Shells, number 42, 7 *coloured plates*, 8vo. *sewed*, 5*s*

4440 — Conchological Manual, *numerous plates representing above* 500 *figures*, 8vo. *cloth*, 15*s* (*pub. at* 25*s*) .. 1839

"This is the only work which in a moderate compass gives a comprehensive view of Conchology, according to the present advanced state of the science."

4441 SPALATINI (Georgii) Historia Vitæ ac Epistolæ, auctore Christ. Schlegelio, *curious portrait and plate*, 4to. *old calf, neat*, 8*s* *Jenæ*, 1693

No notice is found of this eminent man in Chalmers's Biog. Dict. He was known to Luther, born 1482, died at Altenburgh in 1545. It is somewhat singular that Luther was born in 1483, and died in 1546.

4442 SPALDING (Saml.) The Philosophy of Christian Morals, 8vo. *cloth, uncut,* 4*s* (*pub. at* 10*s* 6*d*)

4443 SPANHEMII (Frid.) Historia Imaginum restituta, præcipuè adversus L. Maimburg et N. Alexandrum, sm. thick 8vo. *old calf,* 4*s* 6*d* *Lugd. Bat.*, 1686

4444 — Elenchus Controversiarum de Religione cum Dissidentibus hodie Christianis et cum Judæis, small thick 8vo. *old calf,* 5*s* *Amst.*, 1701

"A writer of great acuteness and learning."—*Dowling.*

4445 SPANISH without a Master, 8vo. *sewed,* 1*s* 6*d* .. 1843

4446 — Spanish Grammar, by Don F. Fernandez, with Extracts in Prose and Verese from Cervantes, De Solis, Yriante, &c. 8vo. *bound,* 3*s* .. .. .. .. 1822

4447 — Ollendorf's Spanish Grammar, by Velazquez and Simonné, thick 12mo. *half bound, neat,* 4*s* 6*d* .. *New York*, 1850

4448 SPARRMAN'S (Dr. Andrew) Voyage to the Cape of Good Hope, and into the Country of the Hottentots and Caffres, *plates,* 2 vols. 4to. *nice clean copy in calf,* 12*s* .. .. 1786

"A most excellent work on that part of Africa."—*Pinkerton.* Sparrman was one of Linnæus's travelling pupils.

4449 [SPEARMAN'S (R.)] Enquiry after Philosophy and Theology, 8vo. *old calf, scarce,* 5*s* .. .. *Edinburgh*, 1755

Tending to show when and whence mankind came at the knowledge of these two important points. Parkhurst frequently refers to this ingenious Hutchinsonian with respect. See *Orme.*

4450 SPECTACLE de la Nature, or Nature Display'd, being Discourses on Natural History for Youth, *numerous plates,* 4 vols. 12mo. *old calf, neat,* 8*s* .. .. .. 1750

From the French of the Abbé Le Pluche by Mr. Humphreys.

4451 SPEED'S (Ad.) Adam out of Eden; an Abstract of Divers excellent Experiments touching the Advancement of Husbandry, 12mo. *old calf, neat, scarce,* 3*s* 6*d* .. .. 1659

Curious; not in Lowndes.

4452 SPELMAN'S (Sir Henry) Larger Treatise concerning Tithes, by Jer. Stephens, small 4to. *old calf,* 6*s* .. 1647

At the end, his Apology of the Treatise De non temerandis Ecclesiis, with his Epistle to *Richard Carew, Esq.*, of *Anthony* in *Cornwall*, on Tithes, and copy of a Letter of John Knox's on the same subject in 1571.

4453 SPELMAN'S (Sir John) Life of Alfred the Great, with Additions and Historical Remarks by Thomas Hearne, *portrait,* 8vo. *old calf, neat, scarce,* 12*s* .. .. *Oxford*, 1709

4454 SPELMAN and Lemon's History of the Civil Wars between York and Lancaster, 1450-1485, thick 8vo. *boards, scarce,* 5*s* 6*d* *Lynn, for the Author*, 1792

Mr. Lemon was rector of Gayton Thorpe, Norfolk. This is the History of Edward IV. and his brother Richard III.

4455 SPENCE'S (Joseph) Anecdotes, Observations, and Characters of Books and Men, collected from the Conversation of Mr. Pope, and other Eminent Persons of his Time, with Notes and a Life of Spence by S. W. Singer, *portrait on India paper,* folio, LARGE PAPER, £2 2*s* (*pub. at* £5 5*s*) .. .. 1820

Only 50 copies printed on this sized paper for illustration. "One of the most entertaining volumes of literary anecdote imaginable."—*Dr. Dibdin.*

4456 SPENCE'S Anecdotes, new edition, with Life, by Singer, *portrait*, f.cap 8vo. *cloth, new*, 6*s* .. *J. R. Smith*, 1858

4457 SPENSER'S (Edmund) Shepherd's Calendar, with a Latin translation, by Theodore Bathurst, an Account of his Life and a Glossary, *plates by Fourdrinier*, 8vo. *good copy in calf*, 6*s* *W. Bowyer*, 1732

"It is a work which has conferred upon him the title of the Father of the English Pastoral, and has almost indissolubly associated his name with those of Theocritus and Virgil."—*Drake's Shakspeare and his Times.*

4458 — Faerie Queene, with a Glossary and Notes, by Prebendary Upton, 2 vols. 4to. *calf, neat*, £1 8*s* .. .. 1758

4459 — Faery Queene, with his Life and a Glossary, 2 vols. 24mo. *boards*, 5*s* 6*d* (*pub. at* 10*s*) .. .. 1819

"The merits of Spencer are of so decided and exalted a nature as to place him, in spite of every deduction, in the same class with Homer, Dante, Shakspeare, and Milton."—*Dr. Drake.*

4460 SPERONI, Canace, Tragedia di Messer Sperone Speroni, *Nobile Padovano*, 8vo. *sewed*, RARE, 10*s* *In Fiorenza (si crede Venezia) per Francesco Doni*, 1546

This is the 1st Edition, "Tragedia di molto merito."—*Haym.*

4461 SPIERS Dictionnaire Français-Anglais et Anglais-Français, 2 large vols. 8vo. *cloth*, £1 1*s* .. *Paris*, 1858-9

Ouvrage autorisé par le conseil de l'instruction publique, rédigé d'après Johnson, Webster, Richardson, les Dict. de l'Académie, Laveaux, Boiste, etc.

4462 — Etude raisonnée de la langue Anglaise, 12mo. *half bound, neat*, 2*s* *Paris*, 1839

4463 [SPINOZÆ (B. de)] Tractatus Theologico-Politicus, cum adjunctus est Philosophia S. Scripturæ interpres, *ab Authore longe emendatior*, 8vo. *old calf*, RARE, 9*s* .. .. 1674

Published without the author's or printer's names, or the name of the place where printed at, during Spinosa's life time, he died in 1677. Dr. Ralph Cudworth's Intellectual System is a refutation of this celebrated atheistical work.

4464 SPRATT (Dr. Tho., *Bp. of Rochester)* Two Letters to the Earl of Dorset, concerning his sitting in the late Ecclesiastical Commission, small 4to. *sewed*, 3*s* .. .. 1688-89

4465 SPRENGEL'S (Dr. Kurt) Introduction to the Study of Cryptogamous Plants, translated from the German, 8vo. *boards, scarce*, 12*s* .. .. .. .. 1807

With 10 coloured plates representing 106 specimens.

4466 STACKHOUSE'S (Thomas) Defence of the Christian Religion from the objections of Modern Antiscripturists, 8vo. *neat*, 2*s* 6*d* 1731

4467 STACKHOUSE (T.) Two Lectures on the Remains of Ancient Pagan Britain, 40 *lithographic drawings*, 4to. *half cloth*, 10*s* 6*d* 1833

Only 75 copies printed for PRIVATE distribution, see Mr. Martin's Catalogue of Privately Printed Books. In this copy are two leaves in addition to those described by Mr. Martin.

4468 STAEL Holstein (Mme. la Baronne) de L'Allemagne, *portrait*, 3 vols. 8vo. *half calf, very neat*, 7*s* 6*d* .. *Paris*, 1818

4469 — de l'Allemagne, vol. 2 only, 8vo. *sewed*, 2*s* *Paris*, 1820

4470 STAGE—Witherspoon's (John, *of Beith)* Serious Enquiry into the Nature and Effects of the Stage, 12mo. *sd*, 1*s* 6*d* *Glasgow*, 1757

4471 STAMP DUTIES; Table of Commercial, the Duties on Probates, of Wills and Administrations, with forms of Wills, and of the distribution of Property under Intestacies, 8vo. *stiff covers*, 2*s* 6*d* *Huddersfield*, 1853

4472 STANDARD Library Cyclopædia of Political, Constitutional, Statistical, and Forensic Knowledge, vols. 1 and 2, post 8vo. *cloth*, 4*s* (*cost* 7*s*) .. .. *H. G. Bohn*, 1848

4473 STANDARD LIBRARY, a great number of the volumes, at 2*s* *each* (*pub. at* 3*s* 6*d*) .. *H. G. Bohn*, 1856

4474 STANDARD NOVELS—Self-Control, by Mary Brunton.—Corinne, by Mad. de Stael.—Schiller's Ghost-Seer concluded, and Edgar Huntly, in 1 vol.—Country Curate, by Gleig.—Hunchback of Notre-Dame.—Hungarian Brothers.—Discipline.—Thaddeus of Warsaw.—Vathek, Castle of Otranto and Bravo of Venice, in 1 vol.—St. Leon, by Godwin, all in *cloth, original editions*, 2*s* 6*d* *each* .. .. .. *Bentley*, 1831

4475 STANHOPE (Hon. Col. Leicester) Greece in 1823-24 and 25, Letters on the Greek Revolution, 8vo. *bds*, 5*s* (*pub. at* 15*s*) 1825

Contains Reminiscences of Lord Byron, with Memoirs of Mustapha Ali, wants the plates.

4476 STANISLAS I., Roi de Pologne, Duc de Lorraine, &c., Histoire de, 5 *portraits and plates of medals*, 2 vols. in 1, 12mo. *half bound*, 2*s* .. .. .. *Londres*, 1741

4477 STANLEY'S (Edward, *Bp. of Norwich*) Addresses and Charges, with a Memoir, by his Son, 8vo. *cloth*, 8*s* 6*d* (*pub. at* 12*s*) 1851

4478 STANLEY'S (Thomas) History of Philosophy, *fine impressions of the plates*, small folio, 1st Edition, *old calf*, 7*s* 6*d* 1655

4479 — third edition, *portraits*, folio, *old calf, much wormed*, 7*s* 6*d* 1701

4480 — History of Philosophy and Philosophers of every Sect, with the Life of the Author, 4to. 4th and best edition, *good copy in old calf*, £1 1*s* .. .. .. 1743

"This very elaborate and useful work has gone through four editions, and to which Mr. Stanley deservedly owed his high reputation as a scholar." See *Chalmers's Biog. Dict.*

4481 STANSBURY (Howard) Expedition to the Valley of the Great Salt Lake of Utah, royal 8vo. *profusely illustrated, and with separate volume of maps mounted on canvas*, 7*s* 6*d* (*pub. at* 25*s*)

4482 STARKE'S (Mariana) Travels on the Continent, written for the Information of Travellers, 8vo. *boards*, 9*s* (*pub. at* 25*s*) 1820

4483 STATE TRIALS; complete Collection of State Trials and Proceedings for High Treason from Richard II. to the end of the Reign of K. Geo. I., 6 vols. folio, (wanting vol. 4) *old cf, neat*, 15*s* 1730

4484 STATII Opera, ex recensione et cum notis I. F. Gronovii, 24mo. *old calf*, 6*s* .. .. *Amst., Elz.*, 1653

"The accurate notes of Gronovius please me exceedingly, from their being neither too long nor too short."—*Reinesius.* Dr. Harwood calls this "a very scarce edition of Statius."

4485 — cum notis Variorum et Veenhusen, 8vo. *good copy in vellum*, £1 1*s* .. *Lugd. Bat., ex off. Hackiana*, 1671

"There are few of the octavo Variorum Classics which exceed the present, either in rarity or intrinsic worth."—*Dibdin.*

4486 STATUES. 48 Engravings of celebrated Statues in Marble, small oblong 4to. *sewed*, 7*s* 6*d* .. .. *No date*

4487 STATUTES at LARGE, from MAGNA CARTA to 2 & 3 WILL. IV., 50 vols. 8vo. *boards*, £5 .. .. 1811-1832

The 1st 20 volumes are by Tomlins and Raithby, the rest are Pickering's and Butterworth's editions.

4488 — Continuation of Ditto, 3 & 4 WILL. IV. to 11 & 12 VICTORIA, 16 vols. royal 8vo. *half calf, neat*, (the 2 last vols. are in *boards*) £5 *Eyre & Spottiswoode*, 1833-1848

These are the "Public General Statutes" only, taking no notice of the Local, Personal or Private Acts passed each Session.

4489 STATUTI dell' Ordine de' Cavalieri di Sto. Stefano, ristampati con aggiunte in tempo del Sermo. Cosimo II. Gran Duca di Toscana e Gran Maestro, *engraved title*, 4to. *fine copy in vellum*, 10*s* 6*d* *Firenze, Pietro Cecconcelli*, 1620

The engraved title is by the celebrated *Jac. Callot*, and a very fine impression. These Statutes, dated 1561, and augmented in 1590, are in Latin and Italian.

4490 STEBBING'S (Dr. Henry) Essay on Civil Government, as to Religion 8vo. *old calf, neat*, 2*s* 6*d* .. .. 1724

4491 — Polemical Tracts; a Collection of Papers written in Defence of the Doctrines and Discipline of the Church of England, folio, *old calf, neat*, 7*s* 6*d* .. .. *Cambridge*, 1727

4492 — Brief Account of Prayer, the Sacrament and other Religious Duties, with a Discourse on Speech and the Abuse of it, 8vo. *old calf, neat*, 2*s* 6*d* .. .. .. 1739

4493 — Christianity Justified upon the Scripture Foundation, a Summary View of the Controversy between Christians and Deists, 8vo. *calf, neat*, 3*s* 6*d* .. .. .. 1750

4494 — Sermons on Practical Christianity, 2 vols. 8vo. *old calf*, 6*s* 1759-60

4495 — Sermons, with an Account of his Character by his Son, 2 vols. 8vo. *boards*, 4*s* .. .. .. 1788

"Of Garboldisham, Norfolk, a learned divine, distinguished himself in the Bangorian Controversy, for which Bp. Sherlock made him Chancellor of Salisbury."—*Gent's Mag.*

4496 STEELE'S (Sir Richard) Political Writings, including the Crisis, 12mo. *half calf, neat*, RARE, 12*s* .. .. 1715

In March, 1715, "The Crisis" fell under the cognizance of the House of Commons, and it was resolved by a large majority that "it is a scandalous and malicious libel, and that Sir Richard Steele, the author, be expelled the House." Sir Richard afterwards wrote "an Apology," which is here also. This volume is not mentioned in any bibliographical book to which I have reference, *Lowndes* included.

4497 — Ladies' Library, *plates*, 3 vols. 12mo. *calf, neat*, 7*s* 6*d* 1722

"The reader is to understand that the papers which compose the following volumes came into my hands upon frequent mention in the Spectator of a Ladies' Library."—*Sir R. Steele.*

4498 STEINSCHNEIDER'S (M.) Jewish Literature from the 8th to the 18th Century, with an Introduction on Talmud and Midrash, an Historical Essay, 8vo. *cloth, new*, 12*s* *Longmans*, 1857

4499 STEPHANI (Caroli) de re Hortensi libellus, et de Cultu Hortorum, sm. 8vo. *limp vellum*, 4*s* *Lutetiæ, Rob. Stephani*, 1545

4500 — Prædium Rusticum, 648 pages besides a large "Index Plantarum," 8vo. *old calf, neat*, 8*s* .. *Lutetiæ, Car. Stephani*, 1554

The 1st edition of a very popular book translated into many languages. Paul Manutius speaks of Charles Stephanus in very honourable terms and as a very learned man.

4501 STEPHENS—Estienne (Henri) Traicté de la Conformité du Langage François avec le Grec, small 8vo. *old calf, gilt, scarce,* 12*s* *Paris, I. du Puis,* 1569

Mr. Gresswell when he published his "View of the early Parisian Greek Press," seems not to have seen this volume, as he could not determine its date; nor could Maittarie before him. See *Greswell,* vol. 2, p. 211.

4502 STEPHENS'S (J. F.) Manual of British Coleoptera, or Beetles, post 8vo. *cloth,* 9*s* (*cost* 14*s*) .. *Longmans,* 1839

4503 STEPHENS (John L.) Incidents of Travel in Central America, Chiapas, and Yucatan, revised by F. Catherwood, *numerous plates,* 8vo. *cloth,* 7*s* (*pub. at* 12*s*) .. 1854

4504 STEPHANUS (Byzantinus) de Urbibus, Græcè, a Guil. Xylandro, folio, *old calf, neat,* 12*s* .. *Basiliæ, Oporini,* 1568

On the title page of this volume is this writing, "Ex Bibliotheca Doctissimi Charissimiq. Dni. Thomæ Stanleii Armigeri," then "Ab. Selleri Sum et Amicorum;" then there are numerous MS. notes on the Margins, and this notice, "Notæ MSS. sunt melioris notæ, et plerumq. omissæ in nupâ editione Berkelii." Berkelius's edit. was published at Leyden in 1694.

4505 STERNE'S (Lawrence) Works, with his Life, *portrait,* 7 vols. 12mo. *calf, neat,* 14*s* .. .. 1802

4506 — Works, with a Life of the Author, *portrait,* vols. 1, 2, and 4, 8vo. *boards,* 8*s* .. .. .. 1819

4507 — Letters supposed to have been written by Yorick and Eliza, 2 vols. 12mo. *boards,* 2*s* .. .. 1779

4508 — Beauties of, 12mo. *half bound,* 1*s* .. 1783

"The style of Sterne, though fancifully ornamental, is vigorous and masculine, and full of that animation and force which can only be derived by an intimate acquaintance with the early English prose writers."—*Sir Walter Scott.*

4509 STETIN, a Poem on the most renowned and undaunted Courage of the Burgers and Soldiers at the Siege of Stetin in Pomerania, folio, *broadside, curious,* 5*s* .. *No date, about* 1658

4510 STEVENS'S (Mrs.) Nature and Grace, 12mo. *boards,* 2*s* 6*d*—*calf, very neat,* 3*s* 6*d* .. .. .. 1827

4511 STEVENS'S (Geo. Alex.) Lecture on Heads and Songs, with Life, by C. Tolly, 18mo. *calf, gilt,* 3*s* 6*d* .. 1823

4512 STEVENSON'S (R.) Treatise on the Nature and Properties of Algebriac Equations, 8vo. *half cloth,* 2*s* 6*d* (*pub. at* 6*s* 6*d*) *Cambridge, Deighton,* 1835

4513 STEVENSON'S (S. W.) Journal of a Tour through part of France, Flanders, and Holland, including a visit to Paris, and a walk over the field of Waterloo, 8vo. *boards,* 3*s* 6*d* *Norwich,* 1817

4514 — another copy, 8vo. *boards,* 4*s* .. *ib.,* 1817

"Mr. Francis, with the author's respects."

4515 — Tour in France, Savoy, Northern Italy, Switzerland, Germany, and the Netherlands, in 1825, 2 vols. 8vo. *half cloth,* 8*s* (*pub. at* £1 1*s*) .. .. .. *ib.,* 1827

4516 STIGLIANI (Tomaso) his Strigliate, see *Marino.*

4517 STILLINGFLEET'S (Bp. Edw.) Sermons, with a Discourse on the True Reason of the Sufferings of Christ, Crellius's Ans. to Grotius is here considered, folio, *old calf, neat,* 5*s* 1673

4518 STILLINGFLEET'S (Bp. Edw.) Origines Sacræ; on the Truth and Divine Authority of the Scriptures, 4to. *old cf. nt.* 3*s* 6*d*—5*s* 1680

"One of the ablest defences of revealed religion that had then appeared."—*Chalmers.* This book has often been reprinted at the Clarendon Press, Oxford, consequently is of the first authority.

4519 — Origines Britannicæ; the Antiquities of the British Churches, 8vo. *cloth,* 6*s* (*pub. at* 9*s* 6*d*) .. .. 1837

"Learned and valuable."—*Bickersteth.*

4520 STIRLING; History of, with a Sketch of a Tour to Callander and the Trosachs, *plates,* 12mo. *half calf, neat,* 3*s* *Stirling,* 1812

4521 STOW'S Survey of London, continued to 1633, by Anthony Mundy, folio, *a very fine copy, in old calf, gilt,* by OLD JOHNSON, £2 12*s* 6*d* .. .. .. 1633

"We now come to Stow, a laborious and honest man; content to state simple facts, without any enlarged views, and in a style the most unpretending imaginable. But there are those who rank him even above Holinshed and the contemporaneous chroniclers."—*Dibdin.*

4522 STREINNII (Richardi) de Gentibus et Familiis Romanorum, *Venetiis, Aldus Junior,* 1571.—Serdonati (Francesco) de' fatti d'arme de' Romani, raccolti da Tito Livio, Plutarco, Dione, &c., 2 vols. in 1, 4to. *nice clean copies, in old vellum,* £1 1*s* *Venetia, Christoforo Zanetti,* 1572

In *Renouard* is a very long note attached to his description of Streinnius's book de Gentibus; and by *Haym* it would appear that there was never more than this edition of F. Serdonati.

4523 STRETCH'S Beauties of History; pictures of Virtue and Vice for the Instruction of Youth, 12mo. *bound,* 2*s* 1807

4524 STRUTT'S (Eliz.) Triumphs of Genius and Perseverance, *portraits,* 12mo. *boards,* 3*s* 6*d* (*pub. at* 7*s*) .. 1827

Lives of Bp. Prideaux, Linnæus, Ferguson, Saunders, the Milners, Lindley Murray, and others.

4525 STRYPE'S (John) Life of Abp. Cranmer, *portrait,* 1694; Bishop Grindal, *portrait,* 1710; Abp. Parker, *portrait,* 1711; Abp. Whitgift, *portrait,* 1718; Ecclesiastical Memorials, relating to the Reformation, *portrait of Strype,* 3 vols. 1721; Annals of the Reformation, 3 vols. 1735-37, together 10 vols. folio, *a remarkably fine set, re-bound in calf,* £10 10*s* .. V.Y.

4526 — Memorials of Abp. Cranmer, 2 vols. 12mo. *cloth, new,* 7*s* 6*d* *London,* 1853

"His fidelity and industry will always give a value to his numerous writings."—*Birch.* "Of Strype it would be impossible to speak too highly. His labours have supplied us with 'some of the most necessary as well as instructive portions of Church History. He is a fine, solid, instructive fellow for a large arm chair in a gothic study and *must* be consulted."—*Dibdin.*

4527 STUBBES (Philip, *Gent.*) Christall Glasse for Christian Women, a most excellent Discourse of the Godly Life and Christian Death of Mrs. Katherine Stubbes, his wife, at Burton upon Trent, Staffordshire, with her Confession of Faith, 4to. 12 *leaves,* Black Letter, (last leaf MS.) 10*s* 6*d* *For Sara White,* 1615

4528 STUART'S (Dr. Gilbert) Historical Dissertation on the Antiquity of the English Constitution, 8vo. *calf, neat,* 6*s* *Edinb.,* 1768

Of the ancient inhabitants of Germany and Britain, the State of the Land in the German and Gothic Kingdoms, of the Orders of men, Great Councils, &c.

4529 STUART'S (Dr. Gilbert) Observations concerning the Public Law and the Constitutional History of Scotland, with Remarks on English Antiquity, 8vo. *old calf, neat,* 5*s* *Edinb.*, 1779

"In this work he critically examined the preliminary book to Dr. Robertson's History of Scotland."—*Chalmers.*

4530 STUART'S (Moses) Commentary on the Epistle to the Romans, 8vo. *half calf, neat,* 7*s* 6*d* (*pub. at* 14*s*) 1836

"The Commentary is a work of great labour."—*American Mo. Review.*

4531 STURM'S (C. C.) Reflections on the Works of God and his Providence, for Every day, 3 vols. 12mo. *calf,* 5*s* .. 1791

4532 SUCHET (Maréchal, *Duc d'Albufera*) Mémoires sur ses campagnes en Espagne, depuis 1808 jusqu' a 1814, ecrits par lui-même, *portrait,* 2 vols. 8vo. *with large atlas, half russia, very neat,* 15*s* (*pub. at* £1 16*s*) .. .. *Paris,* 1828

4533 SUCKLING'S (Sir John) Fragmenta Aurea; Poems, Letters, Plays, *fine portrait by W. Marshall,* 8vo. *half calf, neat,* 8*s* 1648

This, the 3rd edition, is priced 18*s* in *Biblioth. Ang. Poetica.* "This darling of the Muses was worthy to be crowned with a wreath of stars."—*Winstanley.* See also *Retrospective Review,* vol. 9.

4534 — Works; containing his Poems, Letters, and Plays, 8vo. *old calf, neat, scarce,* 7*s* 6*d* .. .. 1709

4535 — another edition, *pretty port. by Vdr Gucht,* 18mo. *scarce,* 6*s* 1719

"For a perfect specimen of those 'men of wit and pleasure' who were 'about town' during the first Charles's time, commend us to Sir John Suckling, the gay, the graceful, the accomplished, the witty, the valiant, the wise, the scholar, the courtier, the soldier, and the gentleman."—*Retrospective Review.*

4536 SUCKLING'S (Rev. Alfred, *of Barsham, Suffolk*) Marine Views, Ships, and Shipping, see *Marine Views,* also *Suffolk.*

4537 SUETONII XII. Cæsares, Theod. Pulmani opera et studio emendati, 8vo. *good copy, in old calf,* 6*s* *Antverpiæ, Plantini,* 1574

4538 — le Vite de' Suetonio Tranquillo dodici Cesari, tradot. in Volgare Fiorentino da Paolo del Rosso, small 8vo. of 580 pages, *fine copy in old calf, gilt,* 7*s* 6*d* *Vinegia, per Giovan. Griffio,* 1554

"Traduction estimée."—*Brunet.* This copy unfortunately wants the title-page.

4539 SUFFOLK—Bradstreet (John, *Farrier, in Wingfield*) Farmer's Request; a Treatise of the Particular Distempers of Horses and Cows, 8vo. 2*s* .. *Norwich, W. Chase,* 1730

4540 — Description of the Ancient and Present State of the Town and Abbey of Bury St. Edmund's, 12mo. *sewed,* 2*s* *Bury St. Edmund's, W. Green,* 1782

4541 — Davy's (H.) Views of the Seats of the Noblemen and Gentlemen in Suffolk, 20 *plates by Lambert, after Mr. Henry Davy's Drawings,* 4to. *sewed,* 15*s* (*pub. at* 30*s*) *Southwold,* 1827

4542 — Estey's (Geo., *Preacher at St. Edmund's Burie*) Certaine Godly and learned Expositions upon divers parts of Scripture, sm. 4to. *old calf, neat,* SCARCE, 10*s* 6*d* *London, for R. Banckworth,* 1603

Dedicated "to the Right Vertuous Lady Anne Drurie," for a rare Treatise by *Father Drurie,* see No. 2732.

4543 — Excursions through Suffolk, *map and* 100 *engravings,* 2 vols. 12mo. *calf, neat,* 10*s* .. .. .. 1818

4544 — Fitch, Catalogue of a Collection of printed Books and MSS. collected by W. S. Fitch, Esq., of Ipswich, royal 8vo. *sewed,* 2*s* 6*d* .. .. .. .. 1855

4545 SUFFOLK—Halsted's (Rev. W.) Protestation, June 5, in St. Mary's Ch., Bury St. Edmund's, 1705, against the Rev. Dr. F. Hutchinson's being Lecturer of St. James's, Bury, with Dr. Hutchinson's Answer, Sept. 28, 1710, 4to. *sewed*, 2*s* 6*d* .. 1710

4546 — Harrod's (Henry, F.S.A.) Excavations at the Roman Station, Burgh Castle, Suffolk, in 1850 and 1855, 3 *plates*, 4to. *sewed*, 6*s* *Norwich, C. Muskett*, 1856

But 2 copies privately printed on this sized paper.

4547 — Herbert; the Sorrows of Herbert, or the Changes of Life and Friendships Consolation in Distress, small 8vo. 214 pages, *stiff covers*, 2*s* 6*d* *Frostenden, for the Author, by W. Harper, Halesworth*, 1821

4548 — Kirby's (John) Suffolk Traveller, *maps*, 8vo. *very clean*, 6*s* 1764

This is an actual survey made in 1732-34.

4549 — Kirby—Historical Account of 12 Prints of Monasteries, Castles, &c. in Suffolk, drawn by Joshua Kirby, Painter in Ipswich, 5 *plates*, *Ipswich, W. Craighton*, 1748.—Testimonies respecting the Colossal Statue of Ceres, in the Vestibule of the Public Library in Cambridge, 1803.—Dalton's Remarks on Prints to be published Relative to the Manners and Customs of the Egyptians, 1781.—Plan of a Catalogue of the European Museum, King St., St. James's Square, London, 1802.—in 1 vol. 8vo. *boards*, 5*s* V.Y.

4550 — Lowestoft — Gillingwater's (Edmund) Historical Account of Lowestoft, Suffolk, with an Account of the Island of Lothingland, 4to. *half calf, new, and very neat*, SCARCE, £1 1*s* 1790

4551 — Poetical Sketch of the Norwich and Lowestoft Navigation Works, by William Cole, Clerk of the Works; the Harbour Opened Aug. 10, 1831, *map*, cr. 8vo. *boards*, 2*s* *Norwich*, 1833

4552 — MS. Memorandum Book.—Mr. Benton of Watchfield (Whatfield) died Aug. 1675.—I looked up Tho. Benton's Bookes in a Presse, Mr. Wyncop hath the Bookes and other Things of Thomas Benton's in keeping till he comes of Age.—There is then a List of 743 very curious Books, enumerated, in a small 8vo. *in parchment, curious*, 15*s* .. .. 1675-1698

"Thos. Benton was borne the 10 of May, 1657, he is registered in Stratton St. Michael." Then there are various payments made to the Vynne's, Elders, and various others, up to 1698. There is a later account of Christopher Vynne's from 1714 to 1718, when he was entered at Bennet Coll. Cambridge.

4553 — MS.—The Royal Standard; a Treatise tending to ease the grieved hearts of the People for the most deplorable Loss of their late Sovereign Lord King Charles the Second, a Sermon preached at Carlton Colvil, Feb. 7, 1684, by John Browne, dedicated to Francis Gardiner, Esq., Mayor of the Citty of Norwich, 4to. *old calf*, £1 1*s* .. .. .. 1684-85

Besides the above, which is in manuscript, is another Thanksgiving Sermon, preached at Carlton, July 26, 1685, for "the Overthrow of the late Rebells," and another "at the Funeral of Mistris Reve, of Olton in Suffolk, with an account of her Life and Character, dedicated to his renowned friend Christopher Reve, Gent." And also, "Excerpta ex Historia Nicolai Harpsfeldii Archiepisc. Cantuariensis." For another Sermon by Browne, see No. 3367.

4554 SUFFOLK—Rastrick (John, M.A., *vicar of Kirkton, near Boston*) Account of his Nonconformity, with the occasions of his secession from that place, 1705—Sermon at the Ordination of Mr. Samuel Savage, at St. Edmund's Bury, Suffolk, Apr. 22, 1714, by John Rastrick, now of King's Lynn, Norfolk, with Savage's Confession of Faith, in 1 vol. 8vo. *bound*, 4*s* .. .. 1705-14

4555 — Shelton (Maurice, *of Barningham Hall, Esq.*) Charge to the Grand Jury, St. Edmund's Bury, 11th Oct., 1725, 4to. *sewed*, 2*s* 1726

4556 — Suckling's History and Antiquities of the County of, *numerous plates*, 2 vols. 4to. *nicely half bound in russia*, £2 12*s* 6*d* (*pub. at* £4 4*s*) .. .. .. 1846-48

4557 — the same on LARGE PAPER, 2 vols. imperial 4to. *half bound in russia* .. .. .. 1846-48

But 25 copies printed on LARGE PAPER, and no more than 6 left for sale.

4558 — — parts 1, 5, and 8, *plates*, demy 4to. in parts, 4*s* 6*d each*, (*pub. at* 10*s each*

4559 — Suffolk Garland; a Collection of Poems, Songs, Tales, Ballads, &c., Legendary, Romantic, Historical, and Descriptive, relative to that County, 8vo. *boards*, 9*s*—*cf, nt, scarce*, 12*s* *Ipswich*, 1818

4560 — Warren (Erasmus, *Worlington, Suffolk*) Rule for Shewing Mercy, 8vo. *old binding*, 2*s* 6*d* .. *Norwich, F. Burges*, 1706

With the autograph of "*Mary Brooke.*"

4561 — White's (William) History, Gazetteer, and Directory of Suffolk, 12mo. *half calf, neat, scarce*, 15*s* *Sheffield*, 1844

4562 — Wodderspoon's (J.) Guide to Ipswich, its Ancient and Modern History, Antiquities, &c. *plates*, 12mo. *red cloth*, 2*s* *Ipswich*, 1842

4563 SUIZERI (I. C.) Novi Testamenti Dictionum Sylloge Græco-Latina, 12mo. *old calf*, 4*s* .. .. *Tiguri*, 1648

Suicer, Professor of Greek and Hebrew at Zurich, the author of "Thesaurus Ecclesiasticus Patrum Græcorum."

4564 SULLY (Duc de, Principal Ministre de Henri-le-Grand) Memoires de, *portrait*, vols. 1 et 2, 8vo. *French calf, very neat*, 6*s* *Paris*, 1814

4565 — Memoirs, with the Trial of Ravaillac, 5 vols. 8vo. *old calf*, 7*s* 6*d* *Edinburgh*, 1770

4566 — Memoirs, vol. 1 to 4, (5 missing) 12mo. *bound*, 4*s* *Edinburgh*, 1760

"The example of Sully, that master of written portraits, shows that the study of History is practically useful to a statesman."—*Horace Walpole.*

4567 SULPITIUS SEVERUS, 12mo. *a beautiful copy in red morocco, extra gilt leaves by De Rome*, 18*s* *Lugd. Bat., Elzevir*, 1643

"His *Sacred History* includes a concise account of the remarkable occurrences of each century, from the Creation to the Consulate of *Stilicon*, A. D. 400. Severus has been termed the Christian *Sallust*, because of his close and often successful imitation of that historian. *Sleiden* has given us a continuation of this work, written with considerable elegance."—*Dr. Adam Clarke.* See *Sleidan.*

4568 SUMNER'S (Abp. of Canterbury) Apostolical Preaching considered in an Examination of St. Paul's Epistles, 8vo. *boards* 3*s* 6*d* (*pub. at* 9*s*) .. .. .. .. 1820

4569 — Sermons on the Christian Faith and Character, 8vo. 4*s* 6*d* 1823

4570 — another copy, 8vo. *boards*, 5*s* (*pub. at* 10*s* 6*d*) .. 1829

4571 — Sermons on the Principal Festivals of the Christian Church, with Three on Good Friday, 8vo. *calf, neat*, 5*s* 6*d* .. 1827

4572 SUMNER on the Festivals, 8vo. *boards*, 5*s* (*pub. at* 10*s* 6*d*) 1828

4573 — Practical Exposition of St. Matthew and St. Mark, 8vo. *boards*, 5*s* (*pub. at* 9*s*) .. .. .. 1831

4574 — 3rd Edition, 8vo. *boards*, 6*s* .. .. 1831

4575 SURREY'S (Henry Howard, Earl of) Poems, with a Memoir of him, *portrait*, 12mo. *morocco, gilt, gilt edges*, 8*s* *Pickering*, 1831

Son to Thomas, Duke of Norfolk, about 1543 he was at Kenninghall, in this county, and also at his beautiful seat Mount Surrey, Norwich.

4576 SUSSEX (Duke of) BIBLIOTHECA SUSSEXIANA, a Descriptive Catalogue, accompanied by historical and biographical notices of the MSS. and printed Books in the Library of H. R. H. at Kensington Palace, by Dr. T. J. Pettigrew, *portrait of the Duke, and plates*, 2 vols. in 3, imperial 8vo. *boards*, £2 16*s* 1827-39

"A magnificent work."—*Lowndes*. The 1st portion of vol. 1 is devoted to MSS. of the Scriptures, the 2nd part treats of printed editions, Polyglott and Hebrew, Greek and Latin Bibles. Vol. 2. of English, French, German, and other Bibles and Testaments. "In the Bibliotheca Sussexiana, Mr. Pettigrew has displayed his accurate and extensive knowledge as a bibliographer."—*Field's Life of Parr.*

4577 SUSSEX—The Unnatural Tragedy, a True Account of the Lady Treganey, near Rye, who miserably burnt her own child, a boy 8 years old, through jealousy, folio, *very curious broadside*, 6*s* *T. Wheymouth*, 1712

At the back is "Prince Eugene's Welcome to England, a Dialogue between two great Generals, (Eugene and Marlborough,) about the Peace."—*J. Jones*, 1711.

4578 SUTCLIFF'S (Robert) Travels in some parts of North America, in 1804-6, *plates*, 12mo. *half calf, neat*, 2*s* 6*d* *York*, 1815

4579 SUTHERLAND'S (Captain) Tour up the Straits from Gibraltar to Constantinople, 8vo. *hf. cf. neat*, 3*s* 6*d* .. 1790

Details the leading events in the war between the Austrians, Russians, and Turks.

4580 SUTTON'S (Dr. Christopher) Godly Meditations upon the Sacrament of the Lord's Supper, 12mo. 1st edition, *old calf*, 5*s* 1630

4581 — Disce Vivere; Learn to Live, 18mo. *purple morocco, gilt edges*, 4*s* (*cost* 7*s*) .. .. *Oxford, Parker*, 1841

4582 SWAINSON'S (W.) Preliminary Discourse on the Study of Natural History, 12mo. *cloth*, 3*s* 6*d* (*pub. at* 6*s*) .. 1834

4583 — Fishes, Amphibians, and Reptiles, *plates*, 2 vols. 12mo. *cloth*, 6*s* .. .. .. .. 1838

4584 — Natural History and Classification of Quadrupeds, *plates*, 2 vols. 12mo. *cloth*, 6*s* .. .. .. 1845

4585 SWEDISH—Konung Gustaf III. s Historia af Ernst L. Posselt, (in Swedish) 12mo. *sewed*, 2*s* 6*d* .. *Stockholm*, 1819

4586 SWEET'S (Robert) Hothouse and Greenhouse Manual, or Botanical Cultivator, 6th edition, thick 8vo. of 762 pages, *boards*, 12*s* (*pub. at* 16*s*) .. .. .. .. 1839

4587 SWIFT'S (Dean) Tale of a Tub, with the Battel of the Books in St. James's Library, and a Discourse of the Mechanical Operation of the Spirit, 12mo. *old binding*, 3*s* 6*d* .. 1711

Sir William Temple, Swift's friend and patron, is the hero of the Battle of the Books.

4588 — another edition, *plates*, 12mo. *old calf, neat*, 4*s* .. 1724

4589 — Essay on his Life, Writings, and Character, by Deane Swift, Esq., 8vo. *calf, neat*, 4*s* .. .. 1755

4590 SWIFT. Remarks on his Life and Writings, by John, Earl of Orrery, *portrait*, 8vo. *old calf*, 2*s* 6*d* .. 1752

4591 SWINBURNE'S (Henry) Treatise of Spousals or Matrimonial Contracts, 4to. *old calf, neat*, 5*s* .. *S. Roycroft*, 1686

1st Edition, the 2nd, containing the same, published in 1711, never done since.

4592 SWINBURNE (Henry) Travels through Spain 1775 and 76, *map and plates*, 4to. *half calf, neat*, 7*s* 6*d* .. 1779

"With regard to the kingdom of Granada, and particularly Catalonia, which has been visited by few travellers, this work is superior to most others."—*Pinkerton.*

4593 — another copy, *map and plates*, 4to. *calf, neat*, 10*s* 6*d* 1779

The Palace of the Alhambra, and several monuments of Roman and Moorish architecture are here illustrated.—See *Pinkerton.* "He was the first who brought us intimately acquainted with Spain, and the arts, and monuments of its ancient inhabitants."—*Chalmers.*

4594 SWINDEN'S (Tobias) Enquiry into the Nature and Place of Hell, 8vo. *old calf, neat*, 4*s* .. .. .. 1714

4595 SWITZERLAND—Etat et Delices de la Suisse, par plusieurs Auteurs Célèbres, *maps and plates by Wachsmucht*, 4 vols. 12mo. *half calf, neat*, 8*s* .. .. *Basle*, 1776

"Tiré des ouvrages de Ruchat, Stanyan, &c. par Altmann."—*Brunet.*

4596 SYLVA; or the Wood, being a Collection of Anecdotes, Characters, Apophthegms, Bon Mots, Original Letters, &c. 8vo. *cf. nt.* 6*s* 1788

4597 SYLVESTER'S (Joshua) rare Translation of Du Bartas's Divine Weekes and Workes, see *Bartas.*

4598 SYMES (Michael) Embassy to the Kingdom of Ava, in 1795, *maps and* 26 *fine plates*, royal 4to. *fine copy in calf, gilt*, £1 1*s* (*pub. at* £3 3*s*) .. .. .. 1800

"This is the only satisfactory account of the country which we possess."—*Pinkerton.* The book is handsomely printed by Bulmer.

4599 SYMONDS'S (W. S.) Stones of the Valley, *etchings*, post 8vo. *cloth, new*, 3*s* 6*d* (*pub. at* 5*s*) .. .. 1857

4600 SYR REGINALDE, or the Black Tower, a Romance of the XII. Century, with Tales and other Poems, by Brayley and Herbert, *plates*, 12mo. *half calf*, 3*s* 6*d* .. .. 1803

At the end, Anna Stone's Features of the Youthful Mind, *Margate*, 1802.

4601 TACHARD (Guy) Voyage de Siam, des Peres Jesuites, envoyés par le Roy, aux Indes et à la Chine, *numerous plates*, sm. 8vo. *old calf, scarce*, 6*s* .. .. *Amst.*, 1687

4602 TACITUS, *Amst.*, *Elzevir*, 1665.—Henrici Savillii Notæ in Tacitum, *Amst.*, *Elz.*, 1649.—Christ. Forstneri ad Tacitum Notarum Politicarum continuatio, *L. Bat.*, *F. Moyardum*, 1652.—together 3 vols. 18mo. *vellum, very neat and scarce*, £1 1*s* V.Y.

4603 — cum Notis Variorum et Gronovii, 2 vols. thick 8vo. *editio optima*, *old calf, neat*, 14*s* .. .. *Amst.*, *Blæu*, 1685

"Tacitus, the first of Historians who applied the science of philosophy to the study of facts."—*Gibbon.*

4604 — The Ende of Nero and beginning of Galba, fower bookes of the Histories of C. Tacitus, the Life of Agricola, Englished by Sir Henry Saville, folio, *fine copy in old calf, gilt*, 7*s* 6*d*
*Oxford, by Joseph Barnes*, 1591

Dedicated to Queen Elizabeth, unfortunately wormed and stained. The Agricola is "a most admirable translation, with learned notes."—*Bp. Nicolson.*

4605 TACITUS—Forstneri (Christopheri) Notæ Politicæ in Taciti Annales, 12mo. *vellum, neat, scarce,* 6*s* .. *Lugd. Bat.*, 1652

4606 TALÆI (Audomari) Rhetorica, 4to. *fine large copy, ruled throughout with red lines, and interleaved with writing paper,* 7*s* 6*d* *Parisiis, M. Davidis,* 1549

Scarce, not in Watt, although it is called the 3rd Edition, dedicated, "ad Carolum Lotharingum Cardinalem Guisianum."

4607 TALES from Blackwood, vols. 1 to 4, 12mo. *cloth,* 6*s* 1859

4608 TALES Illustrative of the Five Senses, their Mechanism, Uses and Government, post 8vo. *boards,* 3*s* 6*d* (*pub. at* 10*s* 6*d*) 1830

4609 TALES of the Genii, Englished by Sir Charles Morell, *fine plates by Heath, Landseer, and others,* 2 vols. 8vo. *calf, very neat,* 8*s* 1805

4610 — another edition, with Morell's Life, *plates,* 24mo. *boards,* 2*s* 6*d* (*pub. at* 4*s* 6*d*) .. .. .. 1824

4611 TALES of the Wars of our Times, 2 vols. post 8vo. *boards,* 3*s* 6*d* (*pub at* 16*s*) .. .. *Longmans,* 1829

4612 TALFOURD, Blomfield, and others History of Greek Literature, post 8vo. *cloth,* 6*s* 6*d* .. *Ency. Metropolitana,* 1850

4613 TANNER'S (Tho. *of Winchfield, Hampshire,*) Primordia; the Rise and Growth of the First Church of God described, 8vo. *old calf, scarce,* 6*s* .. .. .. .. 1683

With 2 Letters by Mr. Rudyerd. 1. About the multiplying of mankind until the Flood. 2. On the multiplying of the Children of Israel in Egypt.

4614 TARCAGNOTA (Giovanni) delle Historie del Mondo, con la continuatione di Mambrino Roseo, 5 vols. 4to. *original limp vellum, a fine clean copy,* £2 12*s* 6*d* *In Venetia, per F. & M. Tramezini,* 1562-1580

This is the 1st edition, and a very rare book.

4615 TARGUM Hierosolymitanum, in V. libros Legis è Lingua Chaldaica in Latinam conversum opera Fr. Tayleri, Angli, cum notis, small 4to. *old calf, scarce,* 6*s* *Londini,* 1649

4616 TARTAGLIA (Nicolo) Quesiti et Inventioni diverse, *curious woodcuts of artillery, &c., and a very fine portrait of the author on the title page,* 4to. *fine copy in vellum,* 15*s* *Venetia, per Nicolo de Bascarini,* 1554

Sir Christopher Hatton's copy, with impress of his initials on the sides, this is an EARLY PRIVATELY PRINTED book. "Appresso de l'auttore." "In this book will be found those celebrated letters and communications between Tartaglia and Cardan about cubic equations, the rules for which our author put the latter in possession of." See *Hutton's Dictionary.* At the end is another Treatise by Tartaglia "Fondata Nave e Navilii."—*Vinegia, per Curtio Troiano,* 1552, *with drawings of ancient ships, &c.* Neither of these editions are cited by *Haym.*

4617 TARVER (J. C., Eton) Le Caméléon; Recueil Mensuel de Morceaux de Littérature, Beaux Arts, Histoire, Géographie, Voyages, &c., 3 vols. 8vo. *cloth,* 12*s* .. .. *Londres,* 1837

4618 TASSO (Bernardo) delle Lettere, con la Vita dell' autore, scritta dal Sig. A. F. Seghezzi, *portrait,* 2 vols. 8vo. *Italian vellum, nice copy,* 10*s* .. .. .. *Padova,* 1733

4619 — la Gerusalemme Liberata, 2 vols. 12mo. *foreign binding,* 3*s* *In Nizza,* 1784

Has a Life of Tasso from the Eulogium of the Signor Lorenzo Crasso.

4620 — Gerusalemme Liberata, con note Gio. Deagostini, *portrait,* 2 vols. 12mo. *half calf, neat,* 5*s* .. *Londra, Dulau,* 1812

4621 TASSO—Gerusalemme Liberata, con note da R. Zotti, 2 vols. 12mo. *half calf, neat,* 6*s* .. .. *Londra,* 1820

4622 — Gerusalemme Liberata, *portrait,* 2 vols. 64mo. *purple morocco, gilt edges,* 10*s* .. .. *W. Pickering,* 1822

Intended for those who have microscopic eyes, printed in Diamond type, by C. Corrall, for W. Pickering. Certainly a chef d'œuvre of Typography.

4623 — Gerusalemme Liberata, publicata da A. Buttura, *portrait,* 4 vols. 32mo. *green morocco, gilt leaves, nice copy,* 10*s* 6*d* (*cost* 16*s*) *Parigi,* 1828

4624 — Life, with an Historical and Critical Account of his Writings, by John Black, *portrait,* 2 vols. 4to. *boards,* 12*s* (*pub. at* £3 3*s*) *Edinburgh,* 1810

"A very valuable and elaborate work."—*Lowndes.*

4625 — another copy, *portrait,* 2 vols. 4to. *boards,* 14*s* *ib.,* 1810

Presentation copy in his autograph from Mr. William to Mr. Seth Stevenson, of Norwich.

4626 — another copy, *portrait,* 2 vols. *half russia, neat,* 18*s* (*pub. at* £3 3*s*) .. .. .. *ib.,* 1810

"English Literature is much enriched by this very valuable and elaborate account of the Life of Tasso. The reader will here receive ample satisfaction as to the disputed parts of Tasso's eventful history, and many illustrations of the times in which he lived, and of the lives of his contemporaries, the relative state of literary history, and, indeed, will find an assemblage of every kind of evidence that can be expected to throw light on the genius of this truly great poet."—*Chalmers.*

4627 TATE (N.) Panacea; a Poem upon Tea, in two Cantos, 8vo. *large and thick paper, old panelled morocco, gilt leaves, scarce,* 7*s* 6*d* *London, J. Roberts,* 1700

Dedicated to the Rt. Hon. Charles Montague, Esq., a Privy Counsellor; not in *Lowndes.*

4628 TATE (Thomas) Experimental Chemistry for the use of beginners, *plates,* 24mo. *stiff cover,* 1*s* .. .. 1855

4629 TAYLER'S (Thomas) Law Glossary of the Latin, Greek, Norman, and French Terms used by Blackstone and other Lawyers, 8vo. *boards,* 6*s* .. .. .. 1823

4630 TAYLOR'S (G. N.) Oratorical Treatise on Plane Astronomy and Natural Philosophy, 8vo. *cloth,* 1*s* 6*d* *Norwich,* 1839

4631 TAYLOR'S (Henry) Answer to a View of the Internal Evidence of the Christian Religion, post 8vo. *half cloth,* 2*s* 1777

With a Sermon by Dr. Duncan, on the Moral and Religious Character of the Times, 1788.

4632 TAYLOR'S (Isaac) History of the Transmission of Ancient Books to Modern Times, 8vo. *cloth, scarce,* 6*s* .. 1827

4633 — Physical Theory of another Life, 8vo. *cloth,* 5*s* 6*d* *Pickering,* 1836

4634 TAYLOR'S (Bp. Jeremy) Life of Christ, with Dr. Cave's Lives of the Apostles, *plates,* folio, *old calf, neat,* £1 1*s* 1678

With autograph of "C. Gurney, Earlham, 1801;" also of "Mary Barnwell, 1726."

4635 — Rule and Exercises of Holy Living, *portrait,* 12mo. *cloth,* 3*s* 6*d* 1840

4636 — Holy Dying, *portrait,* 12mo. *cloth,* 3*s* 6*d* .. 1840

4637 — Holy Dying, in which are described the Means of Preparing Ourselves for a Blessed Death, *plates,* 8vo. *calf, gilt, very nice copy,* 5*s* 6*d* .. .. .. *Yarmouth,* 1814

"Often has my mind hung with fondness and admiration over the crowded yet clear and luminous galaxies of imagery diffused through the works of Bp. Taylor."—*Bishop Warburton.*

4638 TAYLOR'S Ductor Dubitantium, the Rule of Conscience in all her General Measures, *portrait by Lombart*, thick folio, *old cf., neat*, 10*s* 6*d*.. .. .. .. 1676

"Resembles those ancient inlaid cabinets whose multifarious contents perplex our choice, but whose ebony drawers and perfumed recesses, contain specimens of every thing that is precious or uncommon, and many things for which a modern museum might be searched in vain."—*Bp. Heber.*

4639 TAYLOR'S (John) Thesaurarium Mathematicæ; the Treasury of the Mathematicks, *portrait by F. H. Van Hove, and plates*, 8vo. *old calf, neat*, 6*s* .. .. .. 1687

On both covers is stamped "*Sr. Rog., Norwich.*"

4640 TAYLOR'S (John, *of Norwich*) Paraphrase, with Notes on the Epistle to the Romans, 4to. *old calf, neat*, 5*s* 1747

"A celebrated and learned work."—*Horne.*

4641 TAYLOR'S (John E.) Michael Angelo considered as a Philosophical Poet, with Translations, 12mo. *boards*, 4*s* .. 1840

4642 TAYLOR'S (W. Cooke) Memoirs of the House of Orleans, 3 vols. 8vo. *portraits, cloth*, 6*s* .. .. *Lond.*, 1849

4643 — Revolutions, Insurrections, and Conspiracies of Europe, 2 vols. 8vo. *cloth, uncut*, 6*s* .. .. *Lond.*, 1843

4644 TEGG'S (Thomas) Book of Utility, with many Notable Things in the Arts, Sciences, and History, 12mo. *half calf, neat*, 2*s* 6*d* 1822

Contains much useful information for householders.

4645 TELEMACHUS, The Adventures of, translated from the French of Abp. Fenelon by Mr. Ozell, *plates*, 2 vols. 12mo. *neat*, 4*s* 1740

4646 TELESCOPE, by Dollond, *a very good one*, £1 1*s*

4647 TENNANT'S (Dr. Will.) Indian Recreations; Strictures on the Domestic and Rural Economy of the Mahomedans and Hindoos, *portrait and plates*, 2 vols. 8vo. *calf, neat*, 7*s* 6*d* 1804

"These entertaining and valuable Letters, contain much amusement for the general reader, and much instruction worthy of the practical attention both of the subject and the ruler, they mix the useful with the agreeable, and will add to the information of the merchant, the farmer, the geographer, and the statist."

4648 TENNEMANN'S Manual of the History of Philosophy, Englished by A. Johnson, 8vo. *cloth*, 7*s* (*pub. at* 14*s*) *Oxford*, 1832

4649 TENNYSON'S (Dr. Alfred, *Poet Laureate*,) Maud, and other Poems, 12mo. *cloth, new*, 5*s* .. .. *Moxon*, 1859

4650 — Princess, a Medley, 12mo. *cloth, new*, 5*s* .. *ib.*, 1858

4651 — In Memoriam, 12mo. *cloth, new*, 6*s* .. *ib.*, 1859

4652 — Idylls of the King, 12mo. *cloth, new*, 7*s* .. *ib.*, 1859

4653 TERENTII Comœdiæ Sex, ab Antonio Goveano integritati suæ restitutæ, 4to. *old binding*, 12*s* *Lugduni, Gryphii*, 1541

This volume, which has the book-plate at the back of the title, of "Edward Coke of Norfolk, Esq., 1701," is covered over with a profusion of Fleurs-de-Lis, with this in the centre, "Lilium inter Spinas," and "Collegium Grassinæum," perhaps, Gratz, an Episcopal town of Germany.

4654 — Alia editio, 12mo. *old parchment*, 2*s* .. *ib.*, 1547

4655 — in quem triplex edita est P. Antesignani Rapistagnensis Commentatio, 4to. *old calf, neat*, 6*s* .. *Lugduni*, 1560

4656 — cum absolutis Commentariis, Ælii Donati, Calphurnii, etc., folio, *vellum, a good copy, an uncommon edition*, 16*s* *Venetiis, J. M. Bonelli*, 1573

4657 — ex Heinsii recensione, 24mo. *vellum, nt.*, 3*s* *Amst., Janson*, 1626

4658 TERENTIUS, ex recensione Heinsiana, GENUINE EDITION, 12mo. *fine copy in the original vellum*, 15*s* *L. Bat., Elzevir*, 1635

"The Edition of 1635 is very rare. If page 104 be numbered 108 it is the *Genuine* edition."—*Dr. Adam Clarke.* A copy sold for £3 at the Maccarthay sale.

4659 — a M. Antonio Mureto emendatus, small 8vo. 2*s* *Cantabrigiæ, ex Acad. Typog.*, 1636

4660 — large folio, *finely engraved title page, old calf*, 7*s* *Parisiis, e Typographia Regia*, 1642

"A very beautiful edition, executed in a very fine type."—See *Moss.* Autographs of Lord "*Rockingham*" and "*S. Parkins.*"

4661 — cum Notis Variorum et Schrevelii, 8vo. *prize vellum, neat*, 8*s* *L. Bat., ex off. Hackiana*, 1669

4662 — alia editio, 2 vols. 8vo. *calf, neat*, 10*s* 6*d* *Amst.*, 1686

"Of these Variorum Editions, the *last* of 1686 is the more enlarged and esteemed Edition."—*Dibdin.*

4663 — ex editione Westerhovii, 8vo. LARGE PAPER, *old calf, gilt*, 3*s* 6*d* *Glasguæ, Foulis*, 1742

4664 — Interpretatione et Notis, in usum Delphini, 8vo. *old calf, neat*, 3*s* 6*d* .. .. .. *Londini*, 1749

4665 — with English Prose Translation, an Ordo, and Annotations by Dr. S. Patrick, 2 vols. 8vo. *fine copy in old calf gilt*, 10*s* 1750

"An excellent work, as honourable to the learned editor as it is pleasing and satisfactory to the student."—*Dr. Clarke.*

4666 — cum Var. Lect. cura Sandby, *plates*, 2 vols. 12mo. *calf, very neat* 5*s* .. .. .. *Londini*, 1751

4667 — Latin and English, with Explanatory and Critical Notes by Cooke, 2 vols. 12mo. *bound*, 4*s* .. .. 1755

4668 — in usum Delphini, 8vo. *bound*, 3*s* .. *Londini*, 1811

4669 — ad fidem Editionis Zeunianæ accurate recensitæ, 2 *plates*, 12mo. *boards*, 6*s* *Londini, Harding, Triphook, et Lepard*, 1825

Beautifully printed, and highly esteemed. See also *Horace* and *Virgil* by the same publishers.

"The elegance of his dialogue, and the purity of his diction are acknowledged by all; by Cæsar, Cicero, and Quintilian, among the ancients, and by all the moderns." Erasmus says; "The purity of the Roman language cannot be learned from any ancient author so well as Terence;" and the great Scaliger maintains "that the Latin tongue cannot be lost, while the Comedies of Terence remain."

4670 TERENTII Comœdiæ, Phædri Fabulæ Æsopiæ, Publii Syri et aliorum Veterum Sententiæ, ex recensione et cum Notis R. Bentleii, *fine portrait by Vertue of Frederic Prince of Wales*, 4to. *nice copy in old calf, gilt*, 7*s* 6*d* .. *Cantabrigiæ*, 1726

This is a very handsomely printed Edition, and is a nice old library book.

4671 TESTAMENTUM NOVUM, Græcè, 12mo. *old calf, neat*, RARE, 10*s* 6*d* .. .. *Lutetiæ, Rob. Stephani*, 1549

"The 2nd '*O Mirificam*' Edition, preferred to the first of 1546 as being more correct and rare."—*Masch and Dibdin.*

4672 — Gr., 12mo. *fine copy in old morocco*, 12*s* *Lutetiæ, R. Stephani*, 1568-9

"Editio nitidissima et emendatissima."—*Masch.* An elegant little and much esteemed Edition. See *Dibdin.*

4673 — Gr. et Lat., Beza, folio, *half calf, neat*, 15*s* .. 1582

"Beza's 3rd Edition of 1582 is the most complete of those printed under his own eye. It has the Vulgate Latin Version and a new one of his own, together with philological, doctrinal and practical notes."—*Ho. ne's Introduction.*

4674 TESTAMENTUM NOVUM, Gr., ad Edit. H. Steph. impressum, et nunc cum ultima Th. Bezæ edit. diligenter collatum, thick 12mo. *original binding*, 10*s* *Londini, Vautrollier*, 1587

"A very scarce publication. A copy is in the Cracherode Collection, but not in that of the Duke of Sussex. What renders it an interesting book with the curious is, its being *the first Greek Testament printed in this country.*"—*Dibdin.*

4675 — Græcè et Latinè, Theodoro Beza interprete, cum duplici Interpretatione, thick 8vo. *calf, neat*, 8*s* *Apud Sam. Crispinum*, 1611

This has at the beginning the Common Prayer in English, *Norton and Bill*, 1629, and, at the end, Sternhold and Hopkins's Psalms. *For the Companie*, 1629.

4676 — Gr., ex Regiis aliisque opt. edit. cum curâ expressum, 2 vols. 18mo. *old purple morocco extra, gilt leaves*, 16*s* *L. Bat., Elz.*, 1624

The 1st (Elzevir) Fdition of 1624, besides being beautifully printed, and extremely scarce, has acquired the title of *Editio recepta.*—*Dr. Dibdin.*

4677 — Gr., cum interpretat. duæ; una, Vetus; altera, Theodori Bezæ, ejusdem Bezæ Annotationes, large folio, *a fine copy, in calf*, 16*s* *Cantabrigiæ*, 1642

"The reprint of Beza's Testament at Cambridge in 1642, with the addition of Joachim Camerarius's Notes, is considered as the Editio optima."—*Prebendary Horne.*

4678 — Gr., 12mo. *old calf, neat*, 7*s* 6*d* *Amstelodami, Elzevir*, 1656

This is the fourth Elzevir Edition, with the autograph of *J. Sandby.*

4679 — Gr., Var. Lect., parallela Scripturæ Loca, studio et labore S. Curcellæi, 12mo. *old calf*, 8*s* *Amst., Elzevirii*, 1658

"A very beautiful and correct edition."—*Harwood.*

4680 — Gr., parallela Scripturæ Loca annotata sunt, studio et labore S. Curcellæi, 12mo. *calf, neat*, 6*s* *Amst., apud D. Elzevir*, 1675

In this Edition, which is a very valuable one, *all* the various readings are placed at the bottom of the Text.

4681 — Gr., opera ac studio J. Gregorii, folio, *old calf, neat*, 7*s* 6*d* *Oxonii*, 1703

Formed on Bp. Fell's edition, and contains a preface supposed to have been written by him.

4682 — Gr., auctore Joh. Leusden, Professore, thin 12mo. *calf, neat*, 5*s* *Amst., Wetstein*, 1717

4683 — Gr., 12mo. *old calf, very neat*, 5*s* *Londini, J. Tonson*, 1714

"*Theo. Dillingham, Donum Tho. Tooke, S. T. P.*, 1719." Michael Maittaire's 1st Edition "Elegantly executed."—*Dibdin.*

4684 — Græcè, edidit G. D. T. M. D., *maps and plates*, thick 12mo. *fine copy in calf*, 7*s* 6*d* .. *Amst., Wetstein*, 1735

"This Edition, which is very elegantly printed, was revised by the famous J. J. Wetstein, and contains many corrections and improvements."—*Dibdin.*

4685 — Gr., cum Versione Latina Ariæ Montani, auctore J. Leusden, Professore, 12mo. *old calf*, 4*s* 6*d* .. *Amst., Wetstein*, 1741

With the autograph of Dr. Charles Sutton.

4686 — Gr., cum Vers. Lat. Ariæ Montani, auctore J. Leusden, Professore, *map*, 12mo. *calf*, 6*s* .. .. *ib.*, 1741

This is Leusden's last edition, and a very nicely printed volume it is.

4687 — Græcè, royal 8vo. *beautifully bound in purple Turkey morocco, extra, gilt edges*, £2 2*s* .. .. *Oxonii*, 1763

This sumptuous volume was printed with Baskerville's Type, at the Clarendon Press in Oxford.

4688 TESTAMENTUM NOVUM, Gr., Bowyer, editio 2nda, 4to. *old calf, neat*, 12*s* .. .. *Londini, J. Nicholls*, 1783

"Vir doctus, et Stephanorum tum in arte suâ, tum in Græcarum literarum Scientia æmulus."—*Masch.* For his "Conjectural Emendations," 4to., see *Bowyer.* No. 625.

4689 — Gr., textum ad fidem codicum Versionum et Patrum recensuit et lectionis varietatem adjecit D. J. J. Griesbach, 2 vols. 8vo. LARGE PAPER, *a fine copy in russia*, £2 2*s* *Halæ Saxonum*, 1796-1806

The fine paper copies, of which this is one, were printed at the expense of the Duke of Grafton, at that time Chancellor of the University of Cambridge. These are most beautiful books, and are only procurable at very high prices.—See *Horne's Introduction.*

4690 — Gr., cum Scholiis Theologicis et Philologicis, edidit E. Valpy, 3 vols. 8vo. *boards*, 10*s* (*pub. at* £2 12*s* 6*d*) .. 1816

4691 — Græcè, accedunt parallela S. Scripturæ loca necnon Vetus Capitulorum Notatio et Canones Eusebii, 12mo. *cloth*, 3*s* 6*d* *Oxonii*, 1856

Edited by Bp. Lloyd. This is one of the most beautiful and correct editions of the Greek Testament ever published.

4692 — Greek and English in parallel columns, by Professor Scholefield, 12mo. *cloth, new*, 7*s* 6*d* .. *Cambridge*, 1857

An excellent edition, the Greek is from Stephens's third edition of 1550.

4693 — Gr., 12mo. *cloth*, 3*s* .. *Oxonii, e typog. Acad.*, 1859

4694 — Latinè, per Des. Eras. Rotero. Novissime recognitum, small thick 8vo. *old calf*, RARE, 15*s* *Antverpiæ, apud M. Cæsarem*, 1536

"Erasmus, the author of this Latin Version of the New Test., died July 12th, 1536, the same year that this book was printed." *MS. note.* On a page is written "Edward Haddon, his booke, and hand." The Apocalypse is illustrated by many curious woodcuts.

4695 — Latinè, 12mo. *old red morocco*, 2*s* .. *no date*

At the end in MS. "*Gulielmus Leman me jure tenet*, 1679."

4696 — à Sebastiano Castalione Latinè redditum, 12mo. *engraved title page*, 3*s* .. .. *Londini, S. Mearne*, 1682

4697 — Vulgatæ Editionis, Sixti V. Pont. Max. jussu recognitum, et Clem. VIII. auctoritate editum, 18mo. *old purple morocco gilt, gilt edges*, 5*s* .. .. *Lut. Par.*, 1703

4698 TESTAMENT, IN ENGLISH, with Marginal References, small thick 8vo. *fine copy in old red morocco, gilt leaves*, £1 1*s* *Imprinted at London by T. Vautroullier for Christ. Barker, no date*

This edition, which has the whole of the New Testament complete, wants the title page, 3 leaves of the Epistles, at the beginning, and one leaf of the Table at the end, the numerals go as far as 848. It is the Genevan Version, and probably the edition of 1575.

4699 — Translated faithfully into English out of the authentical Latin, with Annotations by Members of the English College of Rhemes, 4to. *MS. title, nicely bound in calf*, 18*s* 1582

Wants pages 277 to 280, and 481 and 2, in all 3 leaves.

4700 — Translated into English out of the authentical Latin at the English College at Rhemes, 4to. *old binding*, 12*s* *Antwerp, by Daniel Vervliet*, 1600

This is the 2nd Edition of the Douay Testament, with "a New Table of Heritical Corruptions, and other Tables and Annotations somewhat augmented."

4701 TESTAMENT, by William Tyndale, with a Memoir of his Life and Writings by George Offor, *portrait*, small 8vo. *morocco, elaborately tooled and gilt, gilt edges*, £1 1*s* .. *Bagster*, 1836

This is the first translation of the New Testament from Greek into English, and a correct reprint of the very rare edition of 1526.

4702 — in English, 12mo. *bound, neat*, 1*s* 6*d* *Cambridge*, 1844
4703 — en FRANCAISE, 12mo. *old panelled calf*, 2*s* *Amst., Wetstein*, 1710
4704 — le meme, et Les Pseaumes de David, *set to music*, 12mo. *neat*, 3*s* 6*d* .. .. *Amst., Wetstein*, 1710
4705 — une autre edit., 8vo. *bad condition, large type*, 2*s* *Londres*, 1735
4706 — GERMAN, nach der Deutschen Uebersetzung Dr. M. Luthers, 8vo. *cloth*, 2*s* 6*d* .. .. *Cöln*, 1857
4707 — SYRIAC, 4to. *neat*, 12*s* .. .. 1823
4708 — SYRIAC, Vetus et Novum Test., 2 vols. 4to. *neat*, £1 5*s* *Londini*, 1816—23
4709 — in the BENGALI Language, 8vo. *bound, neat*, 9*s* *Calcutta*, 1837
4710 — (SECHUANA Version) 12mo. *neat*, 3*s* 6*d* *London*, 1840

"This language is spoken by the Bechuana tribes of Southern and Central Africa."—See *Bible of every Land*.

4711 — ÆTHIOPICÈ, ad Codicum MSS. fidem edidit T. P. Platt, 4to. *calf, as good as new*, 10*s* .. *Londini*, 1830
4712 THACKERAY'S (W. M.) English Humourists of the Eighteenth Century, post 8vo. *cloth*, 2*s* 6*d* .. .. 1858
4713 — Newcomes, original edition, 48 *plates*, 24 numbers, 12*s* (*cost* 24*s*) 1853—55
4714 THADDÆI (Joh.) Conciliatorium Biblicum, *fine portrait of the author*, 12mo. *old binding*, 3*s* *Amst., Janson*, 1648
4715 THEMISTII Philosophi Orationes, Gr. et Lat., argumentum per Georgium Remum, 4to. *old vellum*, 5*s* *Francofurti*, 1614

"*Ex Libris Joannis Baptæ de Rocoles Biterrens. J. V. D. et Amicorum*, 1687."

4716 THEOCRITI aliorumque Poetarum Idyllia, ejusdem Epigrammata, Gr. et Lat., observationes H. Stephani, 18mo. *vellum, a fine clean copy*, 5*s* .. *Excudebat H. Stephanus*, 1579

"Edition recherchée et assez rare."—*Brunet.*

4717 — Gr. et Lat., cum Scholiis Græcis, 8vo. *old calf, neat*, 3*s* 6*d* *Londini, Innys*, 1729

A very neat edition which does not now often occur for sale.

4718 — Gr. et Lat., cum Notis Variorum et Th. Kiessling, thick 8vo. *half vellum, neat*, 9*s* .. .. *Lipsiæ*, 1819

"Editio Optima."—*Hebenstreit.*

4719 THEODORITI Cyrensis Episcopi de Curatione Græcarum, &c., *Parisiis*, 1519, see No. 3693.
4720 THEODORUS—Rubenii (Alberti Petri Pauli F.) Dissertatio de Vita Fl. Mallii Theodori, V. C. Quæstoris Sacrii Palatii, &c. 18mo. *parchment, neat*, 5*s* .. *Ultrajecti*, 1694

"In qua non tantum Theodori, sed et Ausonii dignitates, ac illorum temporum historia illustrantur."—This Theodorus was born A.D. 350, died 410. This little volume written by the son of the illustrious painter, Peter Paul Rubens, is dedicated by the learned Grævius, who published it, to our no less learned Dr. Richard Bentley.

4721 THEODOSIUS Mathematicus—Clavius's Commentary on the Sphericks of Theodosius Tripolitæ; or, Spherical Elements, Englished by Edmund Stone, 6 *plates*, 8vo. *old calf, neat, scarce*, 6*s* *J. Senex*, 1721

Necessary in all parts of Mathematicks, wherein the nature of the Sphere is concerned. "This mathematician flourished probably under Trajan, about A.D. 100."—*Dr. A. Clarke.*

4722 THIERRY (Augustin) Histoire de la Conquête de l'Angleterre par les Normands, 4 vols. 12mo. *sewed*, 7*s* 6*d* *Bruxelles*, 1835

4723 — the same in English, by W. Hazlitt, *portrait*, 2 vols. post 8vo. *cloth*, 4*s* (*cost* 7*s*) .. .. *D. Bogue*, 1847

4724 THOMAS of Erceldoune, called the Rhymer, his curious early Metrical Romance of Sir Tristrem, edited by Sir Walter Scott, see *Scott*.

4725 THOMAS (William, *of Ubley, Somerset*,) Preservative of Piety, small 4to. *old calf, neat*, 4*s* 6*d* .. .. 1662

A most excellent book. I. Of Four Christian Duties. II. Of Four Family Duties.

4726 THOMPSON and Orme's Historical Sketch of the Translation and Circulation of the Scriptures from the Earliest Period to this Time, *Perth*, 1815.—Greville Ewing's Lecture on the XV. Chap. of Acts, *Glasgow*, 1804.—Thomas Chalmers's Address to the Inhabitants of Kilmany, *Edinburgh*, 1815.—with 6 other Scotch Tracts.—in 1 vol. 8vo. *hf. cf. nt.*, 7*s*

4727 THOMPSON'S (Henry) Arnold, Newman, and Neale's History of Roman Literature, *plates*, crown 8vo. *cloth, new*, 10*s* 6*d* *Ency. Metropolitana*, 1852

4728 THOMSON'S (James) Poetical Works, *portrait and plates*, 4 vols. 12mo. *old calf, neat*, 7*s* 6*d* .. .. 1762

4729 — Seasons, with his Life, an Index and a Glossary, and Notes to the Seasons by Percival Stockdale, *portrait and plates after Stothard*, royal 8vo. *calf, neat*, 10*s* 6*d* .. .. 1793

4730 — Seasons and Life, *plate*, 24mo. *old calf*, 1*s* .. 1800

4731 THOMSON'S (Richard) Illustrations of the History of Great Britain, 2 vols. 18mo. *cloth*, 5*s* .. *Edinburgh*, 1828

There is a large Introduction containing judicious critiques on all the best Historians.

4732 THORESBY'S (Ralph) Ducatus Leodiensis; the Topography of the Town and Parish of Leedes, in Yorkshire, with Pedigrees of the Nobility and Gentry, *fine portrait, by Vertue and numerous plates*, folio, *good copy in old calf*, £2 2*s* .. 1715

4733 THORNBURY'S (Geo. W.) Art and Nature at Home and Abroad, 2 vols. post 8vo. *cloth*, 9*s* 6*d* (*pub. at* 21*s*) .. 1856

4734 THORNDIKE (Herbert) Two Discourses—I. Of the Primitive Government of Churches.—II. Of the Service of God at the Assemblies of the Church, now inlarged with a Review, thick 8vo. 732 pages, *old calf, scarce*, 9*s* *Cambridge, R. Daniel*, 1650

"The clergy sought from his works, as it were from an armory, the weapons for refuting their opponents." Thorndike in his own day commanded much admiration and respect. He assisted Bp. Walton in his Polyglot Bible, was of the Savoy Conference, and was engaged in the revision of the Liturgy.

4735 THORNTON'S (Colonel, *of Thornville-Royal, Yorkshire,*) Sporting Tour through various parts of France in 1802, *portrait and* 80 *plates, many in mezzotint,* 4to. *boards,* £1 1*s (pub. at* £5 5*s)* 1806

"Containing a concise description of the Sporting Establishments, mode of Hunting, and other Field amusements, with observations on the Agriculture, Husbandry, and Commerce, and the Customs and Manners of the French people."

4736 THOROLD'S (I.) Origin and Use of Coat Armour, shewing the Antiquity of Arms, 12mo. *half calf, neat, scarce,* 3*s* 6*d* *Yarmouth, for the Author, no date.*

Not in Lowndes, being a local book, it is scarcely known.

4737 THORPE'S (Mr. Thomas, *of London, Bookseller,*) Catalogues, a bundle of XI. of them, published from 1833 to 1844, 8vo. *sewed, clean and neat,* £1 1*s*

Chiefly of Autograph Letters and Correspondence.

4738 — Catalogues of Manuscripts, 17 of them, containing some singularly rare and curious Collections, £1 1*s* .. 1835-43

4739 — Catalogue of his most valuable Collection of Curious Books, thick 8vo. 849 pages, *half morocco, neat,* 7*s* 6*d* .. 1842

4740 — A nice Collection of them, Romances and Novels, Facetiæ, Early Voyages and Travels, Bibliotheca Theologica, B. Britannica, B. Scotica, B. Hibernica, B. Anglo-Poetica et Dramatica, B. Classica, B. Hispanica, &c. in 1 vol. royal 8vo. *nice cloth,* 7*s* 6*d* *No date.*

These Catalogues contain a fund of bibliographical information.

4741 THOUGHTS on the Manners of the Great, 1788.—Strictures on Two Discourses by Dr. Samuel Cooper, occasioned by the Death of his eldest Daughter, 1787.—Hey's Happiness and Rights, 1792.—Linguet's Political Speculations, 1778.—Essay on Landscape, 1783.—Mendoza's (Daniel) Art of Boxing, *plates,* in 1 vol. 12mo. *calf, neat,* 4*s* .. .. V.Y.

4742 THUANI (Jac. Aug.) Historia sui Temporis, 5 tom. 8vo. *vellum, rare,* 12*s* .. .. *Parisiis,* 1604—1606

De Thou's own Edition. Lord Chancellor Hardwicke is said to have given up the Seals, in order that he might the more diligently and uninterruptedly peruse this great work.

4743 THUCYDIDIS Historia, Græcè, 2 vols. 18mo. *cloth,* 5*s* *Oxonii, Parker,* 1859

4744 — Historico Greco, tradotto per Francesco di Soldo Strozzi, 4to. *fine clean copy in vellum,* 15*s* *Vinegia, Gabriel Giolito,* 1564

Sir Christopher Hatton's copy, with 2 of Giolito's devices. This forms part of the Collana of the Italians. "Traduction Estimée."—*Brunet.*

4745 — Eight Bookes of the Peloponnesian Warre, interpreted with Faith and Diligence by Thomas Hobbes, *engraved title by T. Cecill,* folio, *original binding,* 9*s* .. .. 1634

"A Version still valuable for its remarkable fidelity."—*Sir James Mackintosh.*

4746 THURLOW'S (Lord Edward) Poems, post 8vo. *calf, ornamental binding,* 8*s* .. .. .. *Bulmer,* 1813

"Son of the Bp. of Durham, and nephew of the great Lord Thurlow," in MS. on the title page.

4747 TICOZZI (Stefano) Dizionario dei Pittori dal rinnovamento delle Belle Arti fino al 1800, *Monograms,* 2 tom. *Milano,* 1818.—Claussin, Catalogue raisonné de toutes les Estampes qui forment l'Œuvre de Rembrandt, *portrait, Paris,* 1824—in 1 vol. 8vo. *half calf, new and neat,* 12*s* .. .. .. V.Y.

4748 TIGHE'S (Mrs. Henry) Psyche and other Poems, 5th edition, *portrait by Scriven*, 8vo. *half calf, neat*, 5*s* 6*d* .. 1816

4749 TILL'S (Will.) Essay on the Roman Denarius and English Silver Penny, showing their derivation from the Greek Drachma of Ægina, *plate*, 12mo. *cloth*, 4*s* (*pub. at* 7*s* 6*d*) 1837

4750 TILLOTSON'S (Archbishop, John) Works; being Fifty-four Sermons and Discourses, with the Rule of Faith, *portrait*, folio, *old calf, neat*, 7*s* 6*d* .. .. .. 1701

4751 — Sermons, *portrait*, 12 vols. 8vo. *half bound, neat*, £1 1*s* 1742

"Art, eloquence, and perspicuity, appear in the utmost perfection in Tillotson's Sermons, and when I would labour to compose a sermon, I would prepare my mind, and consequently my style, with reading some few of those discourses beforehand."—*Wotton on studying Divinity.*

4752 TIMBS'S (John) Things not Generally Known, familiarly explained, a book for Old and Young, *plates*, 12mo. *cloth, new*, 3*s* 6*d* 1858

4753 TIRABOSCHI (Girolamo) Biblioteca Modenese, o Notizie della Vita e delle Opere degli Scrittori natii Stati del Serenissimo Signor Duca di Modena, vols. 1 and 2 only, 4to. *boards, uncut*, 10*s* .. .. .. *Modena*, 1781-82

4754 TODD'S (Henry J.) Account of the Deans of Canterbury from Henry VIII., with a Catalogue of the MSS. in the Church Library, 8vo. *half russia, neat*, SCARCE, 6*s* *Canterbury*, 1793

4755 TOLOMEI (Claudio) delle Lettere di, libri sette, small 8vo. *calf, very neat*, 7*s* 6*d* .. *Venetia, Guerra*, 1596

An edition not in Haym. These letters are addressed to various learned men from about 1540 to 1555.

4756 TOM BROWN'S School Days, by an Old Boy, 12mo. *cloth, new*, 5*s* *Cambridge*, 1860

4757 TOMLINE'S (Bp. George) Refutation of Calvinism, 8vo. *boards*, 3*s* .. .. .. .. 1811

4758 — Elements of Christian Theology, vol. 1 only, 8vo. *boards*, 3*s* 1818

On the Authenticity and Inspiration of the Scriptures; History of the Jews; contents of the several Books of Old and New Testaments.

4759 TOMLINS'S (Sir Thomas E.) Law Dictionary, 3rd edition, 2 large vols. 4to. *boards*, £1 1*s* .. .. 1820

The 4th edition of 1835, which is the last, is published at 4 Guineas.

4760 TOMLINSON'S (Chas.) Cyclopædia of Useful Arts, Mechanical and Chemical, Manufactures, Mining, and Engineering, 40 *steel engravings and* 2477 *wood cuts*, 2 thick vols. royal 8vo. *half calf, neat*, £1 10*s* (*cost* £2 16*s*) .. .. 1852

4761 — Illustrations of Useful Arts and Manufactures, *numerous plates*, 4to. *cloth*, 3*s* .. .. .. 1858

4762 TONDI (Matteo) Elementi di Orittognosia, 41 *plates*, 4 parts in 2 vols. 8vo. 2nd edition, *boards*, 16*s* .. *Napoli*, 1827

With a MS. Alphabetical Index added.

4763 TONE'S (Theobald Wolfe) Memoirs, written by himself, comprising his Negociations with the French for the Liberation of Ireland, *portrait*, 2 vols. 8vo. *boards*, 7*s* 6*d* (*pub. at* 24*s*) 1827

4764 TOOKE'S (John Horne) Diversions of Purley, *plates*, 2 vols. 4to. *half morocco, top edges gilt, very neat, uncut*, 18*s* 1798

*A Fine Copy of the best Edition* of this "highly esteemed work," usually priced 24*s*.

4765 TOOKE'S Catalogue of his Library, (*priced, with purchasers' names,*) sold by King and Lochée, May, 1813, 8vo. *boards*, 3*s* 6*d* 1813

4766 TORELLI (Conte Pomponio, *detto il perduto, nell' Academia de gli illustre Signori innominati di Parma*) RIME AMOROSE, 4to. 84 leaves, *fine clean copy in parchment*, £1 11*s* 6*d* *Parma, Seth Viotti*, 1575

It is somewhat singular that this very rare little volume is not to be found in Haym, Brunet, or De Bure.

4767 TORRIANO (Gio.) Italian Reviv'd, with a new Store House of Choice Dialogues, intended for Travellers into Italy and the Levant, 8vo. *old calf, curious*, 5*s* .. 1673

Has also an Appendix of ITALIAN PROVERBS, the Addresses to Dignitaries, Nobles, Gentry, &c., and "Mescolanza Dolce di Varia Historiette."

4768 TORSHELL (Samuel) Case of Conscience concerning Flying in Times of Trouble, 1643.—Hypocrite Discovered and Cured, 1644. —Helpe to Christian Fellowship, 1644.—3 Treatises in 1 vol. small 4to. *neat*, 4*s* .. .. .. 1643-4

4769 TOSCANELLA'S Translation of Agricola della Invention Dialettica, see *Agricola, No.* 32.

4770 TOURNEFORT'S (Jos. P.) Compleat Herbal, with large Additions from Ray, Gerarde, Parkinson, and others, 500 *plates illustrating above* 4000 *plants*, 2 vols. 4to. *old calf, neat*, £1 5*s* 1719

4771 TOURNEFORT (Pitton de) Relation d'un Voyage du Levant, *numerous plates of Natural History, Antiquities, &c.* 3 vols. 8vo. *old calf, neat*, 15*s* .. .. *Lyon*, 1717

"These Travels bear too high a character to be particularly pointed out, they comprise the Archipelago, Constantinople, the Black Sea, Armenia, Georgia, the Frontiers of Persia and Asia Minor; and are rich and valuable in the rare junction of Antiquarian and Botanical knowledge."—*Stevenson.*

4772 TOUR through the Island of Great Britain, *maps*, 4 vols. 12mo. *calf, gilt, very nice copy*, 12*s* .. .. 1778

Originally begun by the celebrated Daniel de Foe, continued by Mr. Richardson, author of Clarissa Harlowe.

4773 TRACTS—De Arboribus Pomiferis, 35 *plates*, containing a great variety of Specimens.—Museum Calannianum, Magnificent Museum of Natural History, 1797.—Burke's Speeches for the Better Security of the Independence of Parliament, &c., 1780.—Burke's Letter to a Noble Lord on the Attacks made upon him and his Pension, 1796.—Rules for Drawing Caricatures, with an Essay on Comic Painting, *plates*, 1788.—Gifford's Letter to Erskine on the War with France, 1796.—Political State of G. Britain in 1787.—Memoirs of the Life and Writings of Bishop Lowth, 1787.—Lieut. Gen. J. Burgoyne's Heiress, a Comedy, dedicated tc the Earl of Derby, 1787.—in 1 vol. 8vo. *calf, very neat*, 10*s*

"Mr. Debrett, the publisher, gave £200 for the copy-right of the Heiress; being, we believe, the first instance known of such a price having been either obtained or required."—*Baker's Biographia Dramatica.*

4774 TRACTS for the Times, vol. 1, for 1833-4, 8vo. *cloth*, 5*s* 6*d* (*pub. at* 8*s* 6*d*) .. .. .. .. 1840

4775 TRACTS, in 1 vol., 4to.—1. Lord Chief Justice Hale's Judgment of the Nature of True Religion, published by Richard Baxter, 1684.—2. Turretin's Oration concerning the different Fates of the Christian Religion, with Dr. Nicholls's Letter of Thanks to him, in Latin and English, 1709.—3. Seasonable Recommendation and Defence of Reason in the Affairs of Religion, 1670.—4. George (Villiers,) Duke of Buckingham's Short Discourse upon the Reasonableness of Men's having a Religion, 1685.—5. Rust's (Dr. George, *Bishop of Dromore,*) Remains, published by Mr. Henry Hallywell, 1686.—6. Origen, a Letter of Resolution concerning Origen and the Chief of his Opinions, 1661, "*This is also in the Phœnix, a Collection of scarce Tracts.*"—7. Mercurius Theologicus; the Monthly Instructor briefly Explaining and Applying all the Doctrines and Duties of the Christian Religion by a Divine of the Ch. of England, *sold by P. Bishop, in Exon,* (*Exeter*) 1701.

Here are 12 numbers of Mercurius Theologicus, and I can no where find these Tracts mentioned. This is a curious and valuable collection of Tracts, £1 1*s*.

4776 TRAGEDIES, a Collection of, *plates*, 4 vols. 12mo. *old calf, neat,* 12*s* .. .. .. .. 1745

24 Plays by Dryden, Lillo, Cibber, Otway, Mallet, Lee, Southern and others.

4777 TRANSACTIONS of the Provincial Medical and Surgical Association, vols. 1 and 4 to 12, *cloth;* then New Series, vols. 13, 14, 15, *in cloth;* then vols. 16 to 19, *sewed*, and 2 Reports—together 14 vols. in *cloth*, 5 Parts and 2 Reports, 8vo. £1 10*s* 1836—1853

4778 TRAPEZONTIO (George) Dialettica, tradotta da O. Toscanelli, see *Agricola*, No. 32.

4779 TRAPP'S (John) Commentary or Exposition upon the Four Evangelists and the Acts of the Apostles, thick small 4to. *old binding,* 6*s* .. .. .. 1647

4780 — Commentary on the Epistles and the Revelations, thick small 4to. *old calf, neat,* 6*s* .. .. .. 1647

"Trapp's Annotations contain many useful remarks with much quaint wit."—*Bickersteth.*

4781 TRENCH (Dean) on the Study of Words, 9th edition, 12mo. *cloth, new,* 4*s* .. .. .. .. 1859

4782 TRENT COUNCIL. Canones et Decreta Sacrosancti Œcumenici et Generalis Concilii Tridentini sub Paulo III., Julio III., et Pio IV., Pontif. Max., 4to. *limp vellum,* RARE, 12*s* *Lugduni, apud. Guil. Rouillium, M.D. LXVI.*

4783 — Catechismus ad Parochos ex Decreto Concilii Tridentini editus, et Pii V., Pont. Max. jussu promulgatus, 8vo. *old calf,* 6*s* *Lugduni, permissu Superiorum,* 1676

4784 — Jurieu's (Dr. Peter) History of the Council of Trent Englished, *frontispiece,* 1684.—C. Luzancy's Reflexions on the Council of Trent—in 1 vol. 8vo. *old calf, scarce,* 8*s* *Oxford,* 1679

4785 TRIAL of Frederick Calvert, Esq., Baron of Baltimore, Ireland, for Rape on Sarah Woodcock, March, 1768, 8vo. *half bound,* 3*s* .. .. .. .. 1768

4786 TRIMMER'S (Mrs.) Economy of Charity, 2 vols. 12mo. *boards*, 3*s* .. .. .. .. 1801

4787 — History of England, *plates*, 2 vols. 18mo. *bound*, 2*s* 1832

4788 TRITHEMII (Johanni) Steganographia, cum Clave, small 4to. *half bound, neat, scarce*, 10*s* 6*d* .. *Darmbstadii*, 1621

Trithemius one of the most learned men of the XVth Century, Abbot of Spanheim, and most perfect master of Natural Magic, was born in 1462, and died in 1516. This, "On the various methods of Writing in Cyphers," is one of his most curious works.

4789 TROJANO (Massimo) Dialoghi, tradotti nella Lingua Castigliana da M. Giovanni Miranda, nell' uno e nell' altro Idioma, â benefitio comune, *fine portrait by "Nicolaus Nellius*, 1568," 4to. *above* 200 *pages, sewed*, 9*s* *Venetia, Bolognino Zaltieri*, 1569

With this autograph in an old hand, "Harancourt." "Opera molto utile e necessaria pronuncia Castigliana."

4790 TROLLOPE'S (T. A.) Girlhood of Catherine de' Medici, *portrait*, small 8vo. *cloth*, 5*s* 6*d* (*pub. at* 10*s* 6*d*) .. 1856

4791 TROWER'S (W. J.) Exposition of the Epistles, 12mo. *cl.*, 2*s* 1847

4792 TRYON'S (Thomas) Knowledge of a Man's Self the Surest Guide to the True Worship of God and good Government of the Mind and Body, *portrait by White*, 8vo. *old calf*, 3*s* 1703

4793 TUCCARO (Archange) Trois Dialogues de l'exercice de Sauter et Voltiger en l'air, *plates cut in wood*, 4to. *half bound, neat and clean*, 10*s* 6*d* .. *Paris, Cl. de Monstrœil*, 1599

"Livre assez rare, Vend 70 Fr. Mac-Carthy."—*Brunet*. This copy has the 197 leaves described by Brunet, but is deficient of the 4 introductory and the title page.

4794 [TUCKER'S (Abraham)] Light of Nature Pursued by Edward Search, Esq., i.e. (Abr. Tucker) 5 vols. 8vo. *half calf, neat*, £1 5*s* .. .. .. .. 1768

"A vast mine of thought."—*Blackwood's Magazine*. "The 'Light of Nature' is a work, which after much consideration, I think myself authorized to call the most original and profound that has ever appeared on Moral Philosophy."—*Sir James Mackintosh.*

4795 TUPPER'S (Martin F.) Proverbial Philosophy, illustrated edition, *antique bevelled cloth, gilt edges*, £1 11*s* 6*d* .. 1857

Elegant illustrations by Cope, Horsley, Corbould, Birket Forster, Leitch, Pickersgill, Humphreys and others.

4796 — smaller edition, *portrait*, 18mo. *cloth, gilt, gilt edges*, 5*s* 1858

4797 TURKEY; The Roving Englishman in Turkey, 12mo. *cl.*, 1*s* 6*d* 1855

4798 TURNER'S (Dawson) Synopsis of the British Fuci, 2 vols. in 1, 12mo. *calf, neat*, 7*s* 6*d* .. *Yarmouth*, 1802

*Dillwyn* pronounces this an "admirable" work.

4799 — Muscologiæ Hibernicæ Spicilegium, 16 *coloured plates*, small 8vo. *boards, uncut*, 8*s* .. .. *Yermuthæ*, 1804

4800 — another copy, *nicely bound in calf, grained*, 9*s* *ib.*, 1804

Mr. Martin in his Catalogue of Privately Printed Books says, there were but 250 copies of this book printed.

4801 — List of Norfolk Benefices, continued from Blomefield's History, royal 4to. *stiff cover*, 4*s* (*pub. at* 7*s* 6*d*) *Norwich, C. Muskett*, 1847

Only 50 copies printed on this sized paper, intended to be added to the 4to Editions of Blomefield's Norfolk.

4802 — Descriptive Index of the Contents of 5 MS. volumes Illustrative of the History of Great Britain, in his Library, royal 8vo. *cloth, privately printed*, 5*s* .. *Great Yarmouth*, 1851

4803 TURNER'S (Dawson) Catalogue of his Library, sold by Sotheby and Wilkinson, in March, 1853, 8vo. *sewed*, 3*s* 6*d* 1853

4804 — Catalogue of the remaining Library, Engravings, Pictures, &c. sold by Puttick and Simpson, May, 1859, 8vo. *sewed*, 3*s* 1859

4805 TURNERI (Roberti, *Devonii Oratoris et Philosophi in Academia Ingoldstadiensi,*) Epistolæ, 12mo. of 433 pages, *old calf, neat*, 10*s* 6*d* *Col. Agrippinæ*, 1615

Many of these Letters, of which there are 200, were written in the reign of Queen Elizabeth, 1591. This is the most complete Edition. Some extracts are made from it in Strype's Annals. Turner was a scholar of Edward Campion's, and wrote his Life, See *Wood's Athenæ Oxon.*

4806 TURNER'S (Sharon) Sacred History of the World, 3 vols. 8vo. *half russia, neat*, £1 8*s* .. .. 1834

4807 [TURTON (Dr. T.)] Vindication of the Literary Character of the late Professor Porson from the Animadversions of Bishop Thomas Burgess, by Crito Cantabrigiensis, 8vo. *calf, gilt*, 10*s* 6*d* *Cambridge*, 1827

This is on the celebrated controverted Passage, 1 John V, 7. There are two other Tracts at the end, on the same subject, by Clemens Anglicanus, and Dr. Turton, 1829-1833. "*From the author*, to the North Erpingham Theological Society." "From that Society to their Secretary, William Tilney Spurdens," since deceased.

4808 TWEDDELL'S (John) Remains, being his Correspondence, Prolusiones Juveniles, &c., with a Memoir of him by Robert Tweddell, *maps and plates*, thick 4to. *boards*, 10*s* 6*d* (*pub. at* £3 3*s*) 1816

Dr. Samuel Parr has pronounced highly laudatory encomiums on Tweddell, which may be seen in Field's Life of the Doctor. V. 2, p 417.

4809 TWISDEN'S (Sir Roger) Historical Vindication of the Church of England in Point of Schism, as it stands Separated from the Roman, and was Reformed I. Elizabeth, original edition, 4to. *old calf*, 6*s* .. .. .. *R. Daniels*, 1657

"A most elaborate historical work, written in opposition to Saunders and others of that stamp."—*Nicolson.*

4810 TWISSE (Dr. Will.) Riches of God's Love unto the Vessells of Mercy, with Henry Jeanes's Vindication of Dr. Twisse against Goodwin's Redemption Redeemed, folio, *nice copy in calf*, *scarce*, 14*s* .. .. .. *Oxford*, 1653

4811 TWO RECTORS, 12mo. *boards*, 3*s* (*pub. at* 7*s*) .. 1824

4812 TYRANNY—The Second Part of the Display of Tyranny, Remarks upon the Illegal Proceedings (under Judge Jefferies) in the Courts of Westminster and Guildhall, London, from 1678 to 1688, small 8vo. *wormed*, 3*s* .. .. .. 1690

4813 TYTLER'S (Alex. Fraser) Essay on the Principles of Translation, 8vo. *new calf, gilt*, 7*s* .. .. *Edinburgh*, 1813

This volume contains many excellent rules for the translation both of prose and poetry, deduced from a comparative view of the structure of various languages, and illustrated by numerous examples from well known writers, which are here collated with their originals.

4814 — Elements of General History, Ancient and Modern, with Dr. Nares's Continuation to 1820, *maps*, 3 vols. 8vo. *bds.*, 15*s* 1821-2

4815 — Questions on Select Sections of Tytler's Elements of History, for the Use of the Roy. Military College, 8vo. *half cloth*, 3*s* 1837

4816 — Elements of General History, with Continuation by Turner, 12mo. *bound*, 3*s* 6*d* (*pub. at* 6*s* 6*d*) .. 1846

4817 TYTLER'S (M. F.) Lives of Celebrated Admirals, *frontispiece*, 12mo. *cloth*, 3*s* 6*d* .. .. .. 1847

Rodney, Howe, Earl St. Vincent, Saumarez, Collingwood, Sir Sidney Smith, Exmouth.

4818 TYTLER (P. F.) Lives of Scottish Worthies, *plates*, 3 vols. 18mo. *cloth*, 7*s* 6*d* (*cost* 15*s*) .. .. *Fam. Lib.*, 1831

4819 — Historical View of the Progress of Discovery on the more Northern Coasts of America, the Natural History by Wilson, *map and plates*, 12mo. *cloth*, 2*s* 6*d* .. *Edinb.*, 1832

4820 VBALDINO (Petruccio, *Cittadin Fiorentino*) delle brevi dimostatione et precetti Morali, Politici et Iconomici, scritti al comun beneficio degli huomini civili, 4to. *limp vellum, clean as new*, RARE, 10*s* 6*d* .. *No place or printer's name*, 1592

Haym mentions 4 of this author's works, but not this; it consists of 200 maxims. Baretti says, Ubaldini was a nobleman of Florence who lived many years in England in the service of Edward VI. He was in great favour at our Court in the reign of Q. Elizabeth, as late as 1588. See also *Walpole's Anecdotes.*

4821 ULLOA'S (Don Geo. Juan and Don Antonio de) Voyage to South America, with the Natural History of the Country, translated from the Spanish, *map and plates*, 2 vols. 8vo. *a fine copy in old calf, gilt*, 10*s* .. .. .. 1758

4822 — another edition, with Mr. Adams', of Waltham Abbey, Account of the Brazils, *maps, charts, and plates*, 2 vols. 8vo. *good copy in old calf*, 8*s* .. .. .. 1772

4823 — another, the 5th edition, *maps and plates*, 2 vols. 8vo. *boards*, 7*s* .. .. .. .. 1807

"Ulloa's Travels may be selected as the most interesting and satisfactory work of its kind; they are the unacknowledged source of much that has been published in other forms."—*Retrospective Review.*

4824 UNION, Select Scotch and English Poems, 12mo. 1st edition, *calf, neat*, 3*s* .. .. .. *Edinburgh*, 1753

4825 — another copy, 12mo. 2nd edition, *calf*, 2*s* .. 1759

"A small but choice collection of Poems edited by Dr. Thomas Warton."—*Lowndes.*

4826 UNIVERSAL MAGAZINE, *portraits and plates*, 8 vols. 8vo. *half bound, clean*, 10*s* .. .. .. 1774—78

4827 URQUHART'S (D. H., *Prebendary of Lincoln*) Commentaries on Classical Learning, 8vo. *calf, neat*, 5*s* .. 1803

4828 URSINI (Fulvii) Familiæ Romanæ quæ reperiuntur in Antiquis Numismatibus ab urbe condita ad tempora divi Augusti, adjunctis Familiis XXX., ex libro Antoni Augustini Ep. Ilerdensis, folio, *numerous cuts of coins*, folio, *old calf, gilt edges*, 15*s* *Romæ, Francisci Tramezini*, 1577

4829 USSHERII (Jacobi Archiepisc.) Annales Veteris Testamenti, una cum Rerum Asiaticarum et Ægyptiacarum Chronico, folio, *old calf, very neat*, 12*s* .. .. *Londini*, 1650

"A work perfect in its kind."—*Wotton on the Study of Divinity.*

4830 — de Græcâ SEPTUAGINTA, interpretum versione Syntagma; cum Libri ESTHERÆ edit. Origenicâ et Vetere Græcâ altera, *nunc primùm in lucem productâ*; accesserunt de CAINANE dissertatio; et Epistola ad L. Capellum, small 4to. *old binding*, SCARCE, 10*s* *Londini*, 1655

This is a very uncommon piece of the Archbishop's, Dr. Elrington, p. 271 of his Life, says, "This was the last work published by Abp Ussher." "If ever man deserved the character of a giant in learning it was James Ussher."—*Dr. Elrington.*

4831 USSHER. Britannicarum Ecclesiarum Antiquitates Historia, thick folio, *old calf, neat,* £1 5s .. .. *Londini,* 1687

To this edition is added "Gravissimæ quæstiones de Christianarum Ecclesiarum Successione et Statu Historica Explicatio," in 191 pages.

4832 — Opusculæ duo; de Episcoporum et Metropolitanorum origine, et de Asia Proconsulari; accessit Vet. Eccles. Gubernatio Patriarchalis; aut, de Antiqua Ecclesiæ Britannicæ Libertate, et Privilegiis, 8vo. *old calf,* 4s .. *Londini,* 1688

4833 — Life and Death, a Funeral Sermon for him at Westminster Abbey, April 17, 1656, by Dr. N. Bernard, 8vo. *old binding,* 3s .. .. .. .. 1656

4834 — Life, with 300 Letters between him and the most eminent men of his time, published by Dr. Parr, *portrait,* folio, *good copy in old calf,* 15s .. .. .. 1686

"This volume forms the best monument yet erected to his memory, and from the very names of his correspondents, gives us a high idea of the respect in which he was held, and the high place he filled in the literary world."—*Chalmers's Biog. Dict.*

4835 — Life, with an Account of his Writings, by Dr. C. R. Elrington, *fine portrait by Finden,* 8vo. *cloth,* 6s 6d *(pub. at* 12s) *Dublin,* 1848

A valuable contribution to the literature of that period, by a most able man.

4836 VADE MECUM; a Manual of Essayes, Morall, Theologicall, interwoven with Moderne Observations, Historicall, Politicall, 18mo. *old calf, very neat,* SCARCE, 5s .. .. 1629

By D. T., "probably Daniel Tuvil."—*Lowndes.*

4837 VALENTIA'S (Lord) Voyages and Travels to India, Ceylon, the Red Sea, Abyssinia, and Egypt, in 1802 to 1806, *numerous fine plates,* 3 vols. 4to. *elegantly half bound in red morocco,* £2 2s *(pub. at* £9 9s*)* .. .. .. 1809

Mrs. Nassau's original subscriber's copy of these interesting travels, finely printed by Bulmer; the 69 plates are by Angus, Landseer, and other eminent engravers.

4838 — another edition, 3 vols. 8vo. *the plates in* 4to. *half russia, gilt* 16s .. .. .. .. 1811

These interesting Travels in the East were chiefly written by Mr. Salt, Ld. Valencia's Secretary.

4839 VALENTINE VOX, the Ventriloquist, by Henry Cockton, 40 *plates by Cruikshank,* 8vo. (*wants title*) *cloth,* 5s .. 1850

4840 — another edition, 12mo. *cloth,* 2s 6d .. .. 1854

4841 — another, *plates,* post 8vo. *cloth,* 4s 6d .. *No date.*

4842 VALERII Flacci Argonautica, small 8vo. *old parchment,* 10s 6d *Venetiis, in Ædibus Aldi,* 1523

Burmann says this edition was superintended "Non e vulgo correctorum, sed per virum eruditum."

4843 VALERIUS Maximus, 18mo. *calf, very neat,* 4s *Amst., Elzevir,* 1650

4844 — alia editio, 24mo. *old calf,* 2s .. .. *ib.,* 1671

4845 VALERY'S Italy and its Comforts, a Manual for Tourists, *map,* 12mo. *cloth,* 3s (*pub. at* 7s 6d) *Paris, Renouard,* 1841

4846 VALLÆ (Georgii) In Ciceronis Partitiones Commentaria, small 8vo. *very curious and perfect specimen of old stamped oak binding,* 10s 6d *Parisiis, Rob. Stephani,* 1533

At the end, "Eutropii de Gestis Romanorum libri X.," *Parisiis, apud S. Colinæum,* 1531, a very early edition.

4847 VALPY'S Latin Vocabulary, 12mo. *cloth, new,* 2*s* 1844
4848 — Manual of Latin Etymology, 4to. *cloth, new,* 5*s* (*pub. at* 7*s*) 1852

With a MS. note of thanks from the author to a friend.

4849 — Primitive and Leading Words of the Greek Language, 12mo. *cloth,* 3*s* (*pub. at* 6*s*) .. .. .. 1854
4850 VALUATIONS of all the Ecclesiastical Preferments in England and Wales, 12mo. *old calf, neat,* 3*s* 6*d* .. 1680
4851 VANDALIÆ et Saxoniæ Historia, Alberti Cranzii Continuatio ab A. C. 1500, ubi ille desint, folio, *old calf, very neat,* 12*s* *Witteбergæ,* 1586

Accessit Metropolis seu Episcoporum in Viginti Diœcesibus Saxoniæ, catalogus, ad 1585, cum Præfatione Dav. Chrytræi.

4852 VAN HALEN'S (Don Juan) Narrative of his Imprisonment in the Dungeons of the Inquisition at Madrid, and his Escape in 1817, with his Journey to Russia, *portraits and plates,* 2 vols. 8vo. *boards,* 7*s* 6*d* (*pub. at* 24*s*) .. .. 1827

"These pages present a most dismal picture. The escape is most interesting in its details."—*Literary Gazette.*

4853 VANIERII (Jacobi) Prædium Rusticum, 12mo. *calf, neat,* 2*s* 6*d* *Parisiis,* 1746

"This is his principal Latin Poem, which raised him to the first rank of modern Latin poets."—*Dict. Hist.*

4854 VAN MOOCK (S. J. M.) Dictionnaire Française-Hollandais, 2 vols. 8vo. *half calf, neat,* 7*s* .. .. *Arnhem,* 1832
4855 VAN SWIETEN (Gerard) Commentaries upon the Aphorisms of Dr. Herman Boerhaave, 11 vols. 8vo. *calf, neat,* £1 1*s* 1744
4856 VARCHI (Benedetto) l'Hercolano, Dialogo, 4to. *vellum, much damaged by damp,* 5*s* .. *Venezia, Filippo Giunti,* 1570

"His chief merit is in the elegance of his Italian style, which is still reckoned a model."—This dialogue on Language is his principal philological work. See *Tiraboschi.*

4857 VARENI (Bernhardi) Descriptio Regni Japoniæ et Siam, 8vo. *old calf,* 3*s* 6*d* .. .. *Cantab.,* 1673
4858 VARILLAS (M. *Historiographe de France*) La Pratique de l'Education des Princes, 4to. *old calf, gilt,* 10*s* 6*d* *Paris,* 1684

This is a "Histoire de Guillaume de Croy, surnommé Le Sage, Seigneur de Chièvres, Gouverneur de Charles d'Autriche qui fut Empereur cinquième du nom."—*Book-Plate of Lord Walpole of Woolterton.*

4859 — Histoire des Revolutions arriveés dans l'Europe en Matiere de Religion, 1374—1547, 3 vols. 12mo. *old binding,* 5*s* *Paris,* 1686

Brunet does not mention this author, which is somewhat singular. Our Bishop Burnet replied to him at the time.

4860 — une autre edition, 3 vols. 12mo. *old calf,* 7*s* 6*d* *Paris,* 1688
4861 VARLEY'S (W.) Observations on Colouring and Sketching from Nature, 8vo. *boards,* 2*s* .. *For the Author,* 1820
4862 VASARI'S (Giorgio) Lives of the most Eminent Painters, Sculptors, and Architects, translated from the Italian, *portraits,* 5 vols. post 8vo. *cloth,* 17*s* 6*d* .. *H. G. Bohn,* 1850
4863 VELLEIUS PATERCULUS, Historia Romana, cum Notis G. Vossii, 18mo. *old calf, neat,* 3*s* .. *Amst., Elzevir,* 1664
4864 — cum Notis Variorum et Burmanni, 8vo. *good copy in vellum,* 7*s* *Lugd. Bat.,* 1719

4865 VELLEIUS PATERCULUS, 8vo. *vellum*, 7s 6d *Lugd. Bat.*, 1719

The edition of 1719 is a very excellent one; both Ernesti and Harwood give it a very high character. It contains the pure text of the Editio Princeps.

4866 VELVET Cushion, by J. W. Cunningham, Vicar of Harrow, post 8vo. *half calf, neat*, 3s .. .. 1814

"This work, frequently reprinted, occasioned much controversy."—*Lowndes.*

4867 VENEER'S (S.) Exposition of the XXXIX. Articles of the Church of England, *frontispiece*, 2nd edition, 2 vols. 8vo. *old calf, neat*, 7s 6d .. .. *C. Rivington*, 1730

4868 VENETIA et SAVOIA.—Avviso di Parnasso, nel quale si racconta la povertâ, e miseria, dove è guiuta la Republica di Venetia et il Duca di Savoia, scritto da un curiosa Novellista Spagnolo, con alcune annotationi per Valerio Fulvio, tradotto dalla lingua Spagnuola, in Italiana, 4to. *old boards*, 10s 6d *In Antopoli, nella Stamperia Regia*, 1621

This curious little volume has 2 other tracts in it. I. entitled, Castigo Essemplare de' Calunniatori, Avviso di Parnasso di Valerio Fulvio Savoiano, dedicated to Charles Emanuel Duke of Savoy, 20 pages; and II. Vita di F. Bartolomeo dalla Casa, Vescovo di Chiapa, 1538. Both these Tracts are printed at *Antopoli*, (most likely a feigned name as it is not in Dr. Cotton's list) in the same year as the first Tract, 1621.—Neither of these Treatises are to be found in *Haym.*

4869 — Sketches from Venetian History, compiled from Sismondi and Daru, *plates*, 2 vols. 18mo. *cl.*, 5s (*cost* 10s) *Fam. Lib.*, 1831

4870 — Venice under the Yoke of France and of Austria, with Memoirs of the Courts, Governments, and People of Italy, by a Lady of Rank, 2 vols. 8vo. *boards*, 9s (*pub. at* 21s) .. 1824

Contains anecdotes of the Buonaparte family.

4871 VENTOUILLAC'S (L. T.) French Librarian; or Literary Guide to the best French Works, with Bibliographical Notices, 8vo. *half morocco, uncut, top edges gilt*, 10s .. .. 1829

"Contains much interesting information respecting French literature."—*Lowndes.*

4872 VENUTI (Abate Ridolfino) descrizione Topografica delle Antichita di ROMA, *numerous plates*, 2 vols. 4to. *fine copy in Italian vellum, gilt*, £1 18s .. .. .. *Roma*, 1824

This, the 3rd and best edition, is by Stefano Piale; the plates are by Piranesi.

4873 VERGILII (Polydori, *Urbinatis*) Anglicæ Historicæ libri XXVI., 2 *clever wood cut borders by Hans Holbein*, folio, *calf, neat*, £1 1s *Basileæ, apud Io. Bebelium*, 1534

This book is interesting as being the 1st edition and dedicated to K. Henry VIII., and published during the time he was Dean of Wells. The purity of his language is generally allowed, and he excelled most of the writers of his age for elegance and clearness of style. It is necessary to supply a chasm of almost 70 years in our History, including particularly the lives of Edw. IV. and V.

4874 — de Rerum Inventoribus libri VIII., small thick 8vo. *newly bound in calf, neat*, 7s 6d .. .. *Argentorati*, 1606

4875 VERNON'S (E. J.) Guide to the Anglo-Saxon Tongue, the Grammar after Rask, post 8vo. *cloth*, 3s 6d (*pub. at* 5s 6d) 1850

4876 VERSTEGAN'S (Richard) Restitution of Decayed Intelligence in Antiquities, concerning the Most Noble and Renowned English Nation, *fine impressions of the plates*, small 4to. FIRST EDITION, *old binding*, RARE, £1 4s *Antwerp, by Robert Bruney*, 1605

With the book-plate of Edmund Horrex. This first edition, dedicated to King James I. with Introductory Complimentary Verses, is a very scarce little book; the impressions of the plates in it being much superior to the more recent ones; but it is not only curious but very valuable as containing the rudiment of Mr. Somner's Anglo-Saxon Dictionary, the surnames of our ancient Families, &c. *Oldys* has analysed it well. See his *British Librarian.*

4877 VERSTEGAN'S (Richard) Restitution of Decayed Intelligence in Antiquities, *plates*, 8vo. *calf, neat, scarce, 7s 6d* 1653

This is a valuable and a learned work, see Bishop Nicolson. It has much commendatory Poetry by Thomas Shelton, Cornelius Kilian, Richard Stanihurst, and others.

4878 VERTOT (M. l'Abbé de) Historie Critique de l'Etablissement des Bretons dans les Gaules, et de leur dépendance de Rois de France, 2 vols. 12mo. *old calf, 6s* .. .. *Paris,* 1720

With the autograph of "*Caesaris De Missy, Berolinensis.*"

4879 — History of the Knights Hospitallers of St. John of Jerusalem, now of Malta, Englished, 5 vols. 12mo. *half calf, neat, 7s 6d* *Edinburgh,* 1770

4880 VETUS TESTAMENTUM Græcum, ex Versione Septuaginta interpretum, 3 vols. 12mo. *cloth, 14s* *Oxonii, e typog. Acad.*, 1848

4881 VETUSTISSIMORUM et Sapientiss. Comicorum L., quorum opera integra non extant, Sententiæ, quæ supersunt, Gr. et Lat., cum uniuscujusque Poetæ Vita, &c. per Jac. Hertelium, small thick 8vo. of 864 pages, *old binding, 8s* .. *Basiliæ,* 1560

The Sententiæ of Menander, Philemon, Diphilus, Apollodorus, Posidippus, Epicharmas, Cratinus, Plato, Phrynichus, Pherecratis, Theopompus, Alexides, Antiphanes, Eubulus, and many other uncommon authors are here collected.

4882 VIALE (Salvador) Dianomachia, Poemetto Eroi-comico, *plates*, 8vo. 250 pages, *sewed, 3s* .. .. *Parigi,* 1823

4883 VICUS (Æneas) Ex libris XXIII. Commentariorum in Vetera Imperatorum Romanorum Numismata, *portrait of Cæsar and* 4 *plates,* 4to. *parchment, (wants the engraved title which is written in) very neat, and clean, 10s* .. *Venetiis, Aldus,* 1560

Collates by Renouard; a fine, large, and tall copy in a handsome roman type.

4884 VIDÆ (M. Hieronymi, *Albæ Episc. et Comitis*) Constitutiones Synodales eidem Civitati ac Diocesi præscriptæ, 4to. *limp vellum,* VERY RARE, *injured by damp, 10s 6d* *Cremonæ, apud V. Conctum,* 1562

This rare Treatise was printed at this elegant latin Poet's birth-place 4 years before his death which happened at his See at Alba. He attended the Council of Trent in his Episcopal character, and this volume contains the Constitutions consequent upon that event.

4885 VIENNA—Lines Engraven in Letters of Gold upon the Gates of Vienna, recording the Successes of the Austrians against the Turks and French, *broadside, printed in red, 3s 6d* 1684

4886 VIETA (Francisci) Angulares Sectiones, opera Alexandri Andersoni *Scoti,* 4to. *limp vellum, a fine copy, 7s 6d* *Parisiis,* 1615

Dedicated to Charles, Prince of Wales, by this learned Scotch Mathematician, who has added to this book Demonstrations of his own. Not in *Lowndes.*

4887 VILLEGAS (Alfonso) Nuovo Legendario della Vita di Maria Vergine, immacolata Madre di Dio, delli Santi Patriarchi, et Profete dell' Antico Testamento, folio, 90 *wood cuts, old vellum, neat, 12s* *In Venetia, G. Ciotti,* 1596

This is Villega's Flos Sanctorum translated into Italian by D. Guilio Cesare.

4888 VILLEQUIER—La Charge du Seigneur de Villequier, comme il l'a baillé par escrità Mons. le Duc Casimir, et response de mondit Seigneur le Duc à la dite Charge, 1577.—Response faite par tres-illustre et Excellent Prince Monsr. Guillaume Landgrave de Hessen, au Sieur de Villequier Ambassadeur du Roy de France, 18 Mars, 1577.—Apologie des Eglises de France, contre les fausses Accusations de Villequier, Vers les tres-illustres Princes d'Alemagne, 1567.—Recueil de tout ce qui s'est Negotié en la Compagnie du tiers Estat de France, en l'assemblee generalle des trois Estats, assignez par le Roy en la Ville de Bloys, 15 Nov., 1576.—Sommaire discours, des justes causes et raisons, qui ont contraint les Estats Generaux des Pays bas de pourvoir à leur deffence, contre le Seigneur Don Jehan d'Austriche, *En Anvers, par Guillaume Sylvius*, 1577.—S'Ensuyvent les Lettres de Don Jean d'Autriche et autres, desquelles est faite mention au present discours ; sur prinses à diverses fois et en divers lieux, trad. d'Espagnol en François.—L'Union des Etats Generaux des Pays Bas, assemblez a Bruxelles, dont l'original est signé, tant par les Prelats, Nobles, Villes, &c.—Brieve et Veritable Histoire de la Prinse d'Anvers et du cruel Meurtre, embrasement de feu, et autres actes inhumains des Espagnols, le 4 jour de Novembre, 1576, trad. de Flamand en François, 1577.—8 Tracts in 1 vol. small 8vo. *old vellum*, VERY RARE, £2 2*s*

With the exception of one, these VERY RARE Tracts relating to the Massacre of St. Bartholomew and other matters, have no places where printed mentioned, or the printer's names.

4889 VINCI'S (Leonardo da) Treatise on Painting, Englished with a Life of the Author, *portrait and plates*, 8vo. *old calf, very neat*, 6*s* 1721

4890 — another edition, *portrait and plates, fine copy in calf, gilt*, 7*s* 6*d* 1796

4891 VINDICIÆ Gallicæ, adversus Alexandrum Patricium Armacanum, 18mo. *old binding*, 2*s* 6*d* .. .. *Parisiis*, 1638

4892 VINNII (Arnoldi) in IV. libros Institutionum Imperialium commentarius, 2 vols. in 1, 4to. *old calf*, 6*s* .. *Lugduni*, 1683

4893 VINTIMIGLIA (Giovanni, *Messinese*) de Poeti Siciliani Libro Primo, 4to. 453 pages besides the Index, *old limp vellum*, 10*s* 6*d* *Napoli, Sebast. d'Alecci*, 1663

According to Haym, it appears that this is all that was published of this work. "Nel quale si tratta de' Poeti Bucolici, e dell' origine, e progresso della Poesia nell' Isola di Sicilia."

4894 VIPERANI (Io. Antonii) de Rege et Regno liber, ejusdem Viperani de Historia scribenda liber, 8vo. *old vellum*, 7*s* 6*d* *Antverpiæ, C. Plantini*, 1569

An author I cannot find mentioned in bibliographical books.

4895 VIRGILII OPERA, nunc emendatiora, 18mo. *old calf, neat*, £1 5*s* *L. Bat., Elzevir*, 1636

The *true* edition, as described by Dibdin.

4896 — Nic. Heinsii recensuit, 18mo. *neat*, 3*s* 6*d* *Amst., Elzevir*, 1676

"A very correct edition" *in MS* "Universally allowed to be the most correct and ample of Heinsius's Editions."—*Dibdin.*

4897 — cum Notis Variorum et Masvicii, *plates after Houbraken*, 2 vols. 4to. *old calf, gilt*, £1 1*s* .. *Leovardiæ*, 1717

"This is certainly a sumptuous edition, various readings and the Erythræan Index are contained in this beautiful work."—*Dr. Dibdin.*

4898 — Codex Antiquissimus in Bibliotheca Mediceo-Laurentiana adservatus, 4to. *calf, very neat*, 10*s* 6*d* *Florentiæ, typis Mannianis*, 1741

This is a fac-simile of the famous CODEX MEDICEUS, printed throughout in CAPITAL LETTERS. It is conceived to be more ancient than the CODEX VATICANUS, which is 1300 years old.

4899 VIRGILII OPERA, ad usum Delphini, accessit Clavis Metrico-Virgiliana, operâ J. Carey, 8vo. *bound*, 5*s* (*cost* 12*s*) *Londini*, 1822

4900 — ad fidem editionis C. G. Heyne, small 8vo. *boards*, 6*s* *Harding, Mavor, et Lepard*, 1824

"An edition as accurate in its readings and punctuation, as it is beautiful in type, paper, and printing, a worthy companion to the Horace and Terence, published by the same firm."—*Dr. Dibdin.*

4901 — 18mo. *cloth*, 2*s* 6*d* .. *Oxonii, Parker*, 1859

4902 — HEXAGLOTT VIRGIL'S GEORGICS (in Latin, Spanish, German, English, Italian, and French) edited by Mr. Sotheby, royal folio, *handsomely half bound in Turkey morocco*, £2 2*s* 1827

But few copies of this splendidly printed volume, by William Nicol, were struck off at 5 Guineas per copy, this was the late Bp. of London, Dr. Blomfield's, copy.

4903 — Georgicks and Bucolicks, Latin and English, with Notes by John Martyn, F.R.S., *plates*, 2 vols. 8vo. *boards, uncut, fine state*, 14*s* .. .. .. 1746—49

"When a schoolmaster, I recommended this work (the Bucolics) to my scholars, as I also did the Georgics by Martyn, and not only allowed, but advised them to bring these books to lesson. The notes must have assisted, and the English translation on the sides, could protect no boy from my searching questions."—*Dr. Parr's Catalogue*, p. 227.

4904 — Bucolica et Georgica, ex antiquis monumentis illustrata, cura et studio H. Justice, royal 8vo. *calf, neat*, 6*s* *Hagæ Comitum*, 1757

4905 — l'Opere, cioè la Bucolica, la Georgica et l'Eneida, nuovamente da diversi excellentis. auttori tradotte in versi sciolti, et con ogni diligentia raccolte da M. Lodovico Domenichi, 8vo. *vellum, scarce*, 15*s* .. .. *Fiorenza, i Giunti*, 1556

This is the 1st edition. Andrea Lori did the Bucolics;—Bernardino Daniello the Georgics;—Alessandro Sansedoni, Hippolito de' Medici, Bernardino Borghesi, Lodovico Martelli, Tommaso Porcacchi, Allessandro Piccolomini, G. Betussi, L. Ghini, B. Minerbetti, L. Domenichi, B. Danielo, and P. Mini the Æneid. The volume contains above 700 pages.

4906 — L'Opere, cioè, la Bucolica, la Georgica, e l'Eneide, commentate in Lingua Volgare Toscana, da Giovanni Fabrini, Carlo Malatesta e Filippo Venuti, large folio, *Italian vellum, clean and neat*, £1 1*s* *Venezia, Paolo Baglioni*, 1710

This has the Latin Text, as well as the Commentaries. From Lord Calthorpe's collection.

4907 — L'Eneide di, tradotta in Rime Volgare per Giovan Paulo Vasio, small thick 8vo. *unpaged* (*title page in MS.*) *calf, very neat*, 10*s* *Venezia*, 1532 or 1538

As this book wants the printed title page, we cannot ascertain its date, but it is one of the above, as there were but 2 editions by Vasio, or rather as Haym asserts, by Tommasino Cambiatore, of Reggio.

4908 — Works, translated into English Verse by Christopher Pitt and Joseph Warton, with Notes, &c., by Holdsworth, Spence, and others, *plates*, 4 vols. 12mo. *very nice set in old calf, gilt*, 8*s* 1763

"A work of the first excellence, and has not been *exceeded* by any subsequent attempt."—*Dr. A. Clarke.*

4909 — Holdsworth's Remarks and Dissertations on Virgil, published with Notes, &c., by Mr. Spence, and two Vocabularies, *maps and plates*, 4to. *good copy in calf*, 10*s* 6*d* *Dodsley*, 1768

"An ingenious and judicious work."—*Lowndes.* "He made more journeys to Italy than perhaps any gentleman of his age; and studied Virgil's works in particular, on the very spot where he wrote them."—*Spence's Anecdotes.* At the end is the Latin Poem "Muscipula."

4910 VIRGILIUS.—Vuillichius (Jodocus) Chronologia in Æneida Virgilii, —de Verborum et de rerum copia comparanda, 2 vols. in 1, sm. 8vo. *old rough calf, scarce,* 6*s* *Francforti, par I. Eichorn,* 1551

The last Treatise is dedicated to Sir Philip Sidney.

4911 VITALIS (Lud.) Lectiones Variæ Juris Civilis, 12mo. *vellum,* 4*s* *Lipsiæ,* 1597

4912 VITRUVIO, I Dieci libri dell' Architettura, tradutti et commentati da Monsignor D. Barbaro, Patriarca d'Aquileia, *plates,* large folio, *stained, old calf, neat,* £1 5*s* *In Venezia, per F. Marcolini,* 1556

This is Barbaro's first edition in folio, which Brunet says is "la plus belle." "Edizione rara, e Stimata."—*Haym.*

4913 — il Medesimo, *plates,* 4to. *vellum,* 10*s* 6*d* *In Vinetia, F. de Franceschi Senese,* 1584

4914 — il Medesimo, *numerous plates,* 4to. *old calf, gilt,* 10*s* 6*d* *ib.,* 1584

4915 VIVIANI (Vincentio) de Maximis et Minimis Geometrica divinatio in V. Conicorum Apollonii Pergæi adhuc desideratum, folio, *old binding,* 9*s* .. .. *Florentiæ,* 1659

"Cet ouvrage savant se rencontre difficilement. Vendu 15 fr. Labey."—*Brunet.* Apollonius Pergæus flourished about 30 years later than Archimedes, and 60 after Euclid.—Vincentio Vivani, born at Florence in 1621, was the disciple of the illustrious Galileo. In restoring the 5th Book of Apollonius's Conic Sections it was found that he had more than *divined;* as he seemed superior to Apollonius himself. See *Chalmers,* &c.

4916 VIVIS (Joannis Ludovici) Linguæ Latinæ Exercitatio, *Lugduni, apud Gryphium,* 1542.—Catonis Disticha de Moribus, cum Scholiis D. Erasmi, eadem Græcè, à Maximo Planude à Latino Versa, *Lugduni, apud G. Beringum,* 1544.—Philippi Melancthonis de Corrigendis studiis Sermo; Rodolphi Agricolæ de formandis Studiis Epistola doctiss.; De Miseriis Pædagogorum Oratio, *Parisiis, R. Stephani,* 1537.—in 1 vol. 8vo. *very fine clean copies, in the original calf gilt,* 18*s* .. .. V.Y.

L. Vivis was invited into England in 1523, by Cardinal Wolsey, he was afterwards appointed tutor to the young Princess, afterwards Queen Mary, daughter to K. Henry VIII.

4917 VIZANI (Pompeo, *Gentilhuomo Bolognese,*) I due Ultimi libri delle Historie della sua Patria, small 4to. *very fine copy, in old calf, gilt,* 7*s* 6*d* .. .. *Bologna, G. Rosii,* 1608

These are books XI. and XII., and carry the history from 1531 to 1598. Books I. to X. were printed in 1596.

4918 VLIELAND'S (J. N.) Complete Course of Study, for Englishmen to obtain the French Language at Home (*with the Tables,*) 8vo. *boards,* 5*s* 6*d* (*pub. at* 16*s* 6*d*) .. .. 1827

4919 — French Chit Chat, 12mo. *cloth,* 2*s* .. *Norwich,* 1834

4920 — another edition, 12mo. *cloth,* 2*s* 6*d* .. .. 1850

4921 — Le Glaneur Français, 12mo. *cloth,* 1*s* 6*d* .. 1845

4922 — First Studies in Italian, 12mo. *cloth,* 1*s* *Norwich,* 1839

4923 VOCABULA Rei Nummariæ Ponderum et Mensurarum Græca, Latina, Ebraica quorum intellectus omnibus necessarius est, collecta ex Budei, J. Camerarii et Phil. Melancthon Annotationibus; additæ sunt appellationes Quadrupedum, Insectorum, Piscium, &c., collectæ à P. Ebero et C. Peucero, 12mo. *fine copy in old calf,* 12*s* .. .. *Witebergæ,* 1552

At the end of this rare little volume is another Tract entitled "Priscorum Numismatum ad Nurembergensis Monetæ Valorem facta æstimatio Bibibaldo Pirckeymero authore." *Tubingæ, per Huldenrichum Morhardum,* 1533. It contains besides three Treatises by Andrew Alciat, Budæus, and Philip Melancthon, on the same subjects.

4924 VOGAN'S (Thomas S. L.) Sermons, with his Bampton Lecture Sermons, 8vo. *half cloth*, 6*s* (*pub. at* 12*s*) *Oxford*, 1837

4925 — Nine Lectures on the Holy Sacrament of the Lord's Supper, 8vo. *half cloth*, 3*s* (*pub. at* 5*s*) .. .. 1849

4926 VOGLERI (V. H.) Introductio Universalis in Notitiam cujuscunque generis bonorum Scriptorum, 4to. *boards*, 3*s* *Helmestadii*, 1670

4927 VOGT, Apparatus Literarius, collectio 2da, small 8vo. *old calf, neat*, 3*s* .. .. .. *Witebergæ*, 1718

4928 VOITURE'S Familiar and Courtly Letters, Englished by Dryden, Cheek, Dennis, and others, with Letters by Wycherly, Congreve, Tom Browne, and others, *fine portrait by Vdr. Gucht*, 2 vols. sm. 8vo. *old calf, scarce*, 5*s* .. .. .. 1701

4929 VOLTAIRE, le Micromégas, avec une Histoire des Croisades, et plan de l'Hist. de l'Esprit humain, 12mo. *sd., uncut*, 3*s* *Londres*, 1752

4930 — Siecle de Louis XV., 2 vols. 12mo. *old binding*, 3*s* *Lausanne*, 1769

4931 — Age of Lewis XIV., Englished by M. Chambaud, *portrait*, 2 vols. 12mo. *calf*, 3*s* 6*d* .. .. .. 1753

4932 — History of the War of 1741, 8vo. *old calf, neat*, 3*s* 1756

4933 VOLTERRANI (R.) Commentariorum Urbanorum libri XXXVIII., thick folio, *vellum*, RARE, £2 2*s* *Imgressum Romæ, per I. Besicken*, 1506

This early work, of which we can find no account, is finely printed on a thick paper, on 547 leaves, and a treatise at the end on the Œconomics of Xenophon, on 11 unpaged leaves. It is dedicated to Pope Julius 2nd., and is divided thus, Loca et Populi, Homines Clari, Pontifices Romani, Principes Romani, Animalia, Plantæ, Morbi ac Medicinæ, &c., &c.

4934 VON TEMPSKY'S (G.F.) Mitla; Adventures in Mexico, Guatemala and Salvador, in 1853, by J. S. Bell, *coloured plates*, 8vo. *cloth*, 6*s* (*cost* 18*s*) .. .. .. 1858

4935 VULCANII (Bonaventuræ) Thesaurus Utriusque Linguæ, Latino-Græca et Græco-Latina, *portrait, L. Bat.*, 1600.—Onomasticon Vocum Latino-Græcarum, in 1 vol. folio, *half bound, neat*, 9*s* *Lugd. Batavorum, J. Patii*, 1600

4936 VULGAR ERROURS in Practice Censured, also the Art of Oratory, 8vo. *bound*, 2*s* 6*d* .. .. *R. Royston*, 1659

4937 WADDINGTON'S (George) Visit to Greece in 1823 and 1824, *map*, post 8vo. *boards*, 3*s* 6*d* (*pub. at* 8*s* 6*d*) *Murray*, 1825

4938 WAKE (Isaac) Rex Platonicus, 12mo. *old calf, neat*, 10*s* *Oxoniæ*, 1627

This is a copious account of King James the First's Visit to Oxford, Aug. 27, 1605, and is very curious as having many autographs, shewing it to have been first possessed by Nicholas Langford, from whom it passed to Roger Jones, from him to Robert Jones, then to Robert Sharrock, O. Foyle, Philip Fell, Stephen Cooke, 1648, Will. Nicholson, James Ubard, and Thomas Ryves, 1650. "Isaac Wake, the author of this curious little volume, was public orator of the University of Oxford. One of the most curious passages it contains, is that which relates to the little spectacle exhibited at St. John's College, when James entered the University from Woodstock; and it is the more remarkable, as it is supposed to have given rise to the Macbeth of Shakspeare, which did not appear till a year afterwards."—*Sir E. Brydges.*

4939 WAKEFIELD'S (Priscilla) Introduction to Botany, *coloured plates*, 12mo. *boards*, 3*s* (*pub. at* 7*s*) .. .. 1812

4940 WAKEMAN'S (W. F.) Handbook of Irish Antiquities, Pagan and Christian, *numerous illustrations*, 12mo. *cloth, gilt, neat*, 3*s* 6*d* *Dublin*, 1848

4941 WALCHNER (F.A.) Handbuch der Gesammten Mineralogie, thick 8vo. of 631 pages, *sewed*, 6*s* .. *Carlsruhe*, 1829

4942 WALCHNER, Handbuch der Gesammten Mineralogie (Geognosie) *plates*, 8vo. *sewed*, 2*s* 6*d* .. *Carlsruhe*, 1830

4943 WALDEGRAVE'S (James, Earl) Memoirs, from 1754 to 1758, *portrait*, 4to. *half bound*, 6*s* (*pub. at* 25*s*) .. 1821

"With Doddington may be read a book that has lately been published with a biographical and critical preface, by Mr. Fox, afterwards Lord Holland—the Memoirs of Lord Waldegrave. It is very deserving of perusal."—*Professor Smythe.*

4944 WALES.—COMMENTARIOLI BRITANNICÆ Descriptionis Fragmentum, Auctore HUMFREDO LHUYD, *Denbyghiense, Cambro-Britanno*, sm. 8vo. *old vellum* (*wormed*) 12*s* .. *Col. Agrip.*, 1572

An excellent work, "much followed by Camden."—*Bp. Nicolson.* At Bindley's sale 22*s*, Townley's, £2 2*s*.

4945 — idem, small 8vo. *nice copy in the original calf*, £1 5*s* *Coloniæ Agrip. apud Jo. Birckmannum*, 1572

On the title page of this copy is the autograph of "*Thom. Tanner*," an excellent antiquary, Archdeacon of Norfolk, and afterwards Bp. of St. Asaph. At the end are two considerable Tracts. 1. Academiarum Orbis Christiani libri duo, authore JAC. MIDDENDORPIO, 420 pages, *Coloniæ*, 1572. 2. Germaniæ ex Variis Scriptoribus per brevis explicatio, autore BILIBALDO PYRKHEYMERO, *Witebergæ*, 1571.

4946 — VIRUNNII (PONTICI) Britannicæ Historiæ libri VI., quibus prefixus est Catalogus Regum Britanniæ, per DAV. POUELUM, small 8vo. *old vellum*, RARE (*wants title*) 10*s* *Londini, apud E. Bollifant*, 1585

With the dedication to Sir Henry Sydney, and the Catalogue of the Kings from Brute to Cadwallader.

4947 — ITINERARIUM CAMBRIÆ, auctore SIL. GIRALDO, *Cambrense*, cum Annotationibus DAV. POUELI, small 8vo. *old vellum*, 15*s* *Londini, apud E. Bollifant*, 1585

"Giraldus Cambrensis, the oldest Topographer of Wales, everywhere quoted at large by Camden, as an author of undoubted credit and reputation. The edition of 1585 has Dr. Powell's learned notes."—*Bp. Nicolson.*

4948 — WALES ILLUSTRATED, Views in North and South Wales, of Castles, Towns, Seats of the Nobility, &c., with Descriptions, *numerous plates*, 2 vols. 4to. *half bound in purple morocco, top edges gilt*, £1 11*s* 6*d* (*cost* £3 3*s*) .. 1830

4949 WALKER'S (Chas. V.) Electrotype Manipulation, the Art of Working in Metals, 2 parts, in 1 vol. 12mo. *cloth*, 2*s* 1845

4950 WALKER'S (Clement) Relations and Observations, Historical and Politick, upon the Parliament begun A.D. 1640, *full length portrait of Oliver Cromwell, in armour, directing the felling the Royal oak, by W. Marshall*, parts 1 and 2, small 4to. *fine copy in old calf, gilt, scarce*, 12*s* .. .. 1648-49

This is the first edition of Walker's History of Independency, which the 2nd part is called, it "gives an admirable idea of the character of the times, parties, and persons." *Bp. Warburton.*

4951 WALKER'S (George, *of Nottingham*,) Sermons on Various Subjects, 2 vols. 8vo. *calf, gilt*, 5*s* 6*d* .. .. 1790

4952 WALKER'S (John) Pronouncing English Dictionary, with Key to the Classical Pronunciation of Proper Names, and additional Words by Dr. Young, *portrait*, 8vo. *cloth, new*, 5*s* *Dublin*, 1858

4953 — Key to the Classical Pronunciation of Greek, Latin, and Scripture Proper Names, *portrait*, 8vo. *boards*, 2*s* 6*d* .. 1807

4954 WALKER'S (John) Attempt towards Recovering an Account of the Numbers and Sufferings of the Clergy of the Ch. of England, sequestered during the Grand Rebellion, folio, *old calf, neat, scarce*, £1 11*s* 6*d* .. .. .. 1714

4955 WALKER'S (John) Selection of Curious Articles from the Gentleman's Magazine, vols. 3 and 4 only, 8vo. *boards*, 6*s* 1814

6*s* will be given for vols. 1 and 2 of the same edition.

4956 WALKER'S (John, M.D.) Life of, by Dr. John Epps, 8vo. *half cloth*, 4*s* 6*d* (*pub. at* 12*s*) .. .. .. 1831

4957 WALKER'S (Joseph Cooper) Historical Memoir on Italian Tragedy, with Biograpical Notices of the Principal Tragic Writers of Italy, *portraits and plates*, 4to. *half, calf neat*, 9*s* .. 1799

"Many notices of scarce dramas may be gleaned from this work, as the author seems to have laboured with great and exemplary diligence in the illustration of his subject." *Lowndes.*

4958 WALKER'S (Robert, *of Shingham, Norfolk,*) Analysis of Researches into the Origin and Progress of Historical Time, from the Creation to the Accession of C. Caligula, 8vo. *boards, uncut*, 4*s* 6*d* .. .. .. .. 1796

Contains Strictures on Sir Isaac Newton's Chronology, and Mr. Falconer's Chronological Tables.

4959 WALKER'S Maps of Suffolk, England and Wales, Devonshire, Dorsetshire, Somersetshire, and Cornwall, *in cloth for the pocket, mounted on canvas*, 1*s* 6*d each*

4960 WALLACE (Sir William, *Knight of Ellerslie,*) The Metrical History of, by Henry, commonly called Blind Harry, 3 vols. 12mo. *half bound, uncut*, 10*s* 6*d* .. .. *Perth*, 1790

This is a good edition, with notes, illustrations, and a glossary, it is faithfully transcribed from a MS. in the Advocates' Library, and the old orthography is preserved.

4961 WALLENSTEIN (Duke of Friedland) his Life, by Lt. Col. Mitchell, *portrait*, 8vo. *half calf, neat*, 5*s* 6*d* .. .. 1838

4962 WALLER'S (Edmond) Poems, &c. to several Persons, 4th edition with Additions never before printed, small 8vo. *original binding*, 7*s* 6 *d* .. .. .. .. 1682

This Edition has his Speech at the Conference of both Houses, corrected from Rushworth's collections.

4963 — Poems, with his Life, *portrait*, 10th Edit., 12mo. *old calf, neat*, 4*s* .. .. .. .. 1722

With Book-plate of Thos. Stradling, of St. Donat's Castle, Esq.

4964 — Works, published by Mr. Fenton, *fine portrait and plates*, 12mo. *old calf, gilt*, 3*s* 6*d* .. .. *Tonson*, 1730

4965 WALPOLE'S (Honble. Fred., R. N.) Ansayrii or Assassins, with Travels in the further East, in 1850-51, including a Visit to Nineveh, 3 vols. 8vo. *cloth, new*, 10*s* 6*d* (*pub. at* 2 *guineas*) 1851

4966 WALPOLE (Horace, Earl of Orford) Catalogue of Royal and Noble Authors, 2 vols. small 8vo. *calf, neat*, 6*s* .. 1759

The 2nd edition of a most amusing literary work.

4967 — Modern Anecdotes of the Ancient Family of Kinkvervankotfdarfprakengotchdernscstate for Christmas, 1779, 12mo. *half bound*, 3*s* .. .. .. .. 1779

This is a Satire on Horace Walpole's Castle of Otranto.

4968 WALPOLE. Il Castello di Otranto, Storia Gotica, *plates*, 8vo. *calf, neat*, 5s .. .. *Londra, Molini*, 1795

4969 — Castle of Otranto and Old English Baron, by Clara Reeve, *plates*, 18mo. *cloth, gilt edges*, 2s 6d .. .. 1826

4970 — Memoirs of Horatio, Lord Walpole, connected with the History of the Times from 1678 to 1757, by Archdeacon W. Coxe, 2 vols. 8vo. *boards*, 8s .. .. .. 1808

4971 — Walpoliana, *portrait, fac-simile of hand-writing and view of Strawberry Hill*, 2 vols. in 1, 12mo. *half russia, neat*, 5s

4972 WALPOLE (Lord, *of Woolterton*,) Answer to the latter part of Lord Bolingbroke's Letters on the Study of History, 8vo. *both parts, half bound, scarce*, (*not in Lowndes*,) 5s .. 1763

4973 WALSHE (Capt. A.) Military Catechism and Hand-book on Regimental Standing Orders, Guards, Drill, Military Law, and Finance, 8vo. *cloth*, 5s 6d (*pub. at* 10s) .. .. 1852

4974 WALSINGHAM'S Arcana Aulica; or, Manual of Prudential Maxims, with Sir Robert Naunton's Fragmenta Regalia; Observations on Q. Elizabeth, her Times and Favourites, 18mo. SCARCE, 12s 1694

With this autograph, "*E. Libris J. Newton.*" Sir Isaac Newton lived at this time.

4975 St. WALSTAN, Confessor, his Life by F. C. Husenbeth, D.D., V. G., Provost of Northampton, 12mo. *sewed*, 1s *Norwich*, 1859

4976 WALTON'S (Brian, *Bp. of Chester*) Memoirs of his Life and Writings, by the Rev. Henry J. Todd, *portrait*, 2 vols. 8vo. *half cloth*, 7s (*pub. at* 21s) .. .. .. 1821

Editor of the London Polyglot Bible, 6 vols., 1657, with his own Vindication of it, and notices of his coadjutors in that illustrious work.

4977 WALTON'S (Isaac) and Charles Cotton's Complete Angler, with Lives of the Authors and Notes by Sir John Hawkins, *plates by Ryland after Wale*, 4th Edit., crown 8vo. *calf, neat*, 10s 6d 1784

This is a very good Edition of the esteemed Angler, copiously illustrated, with notes.

4978 — Complete Angler, edited by Ephemera, *plates*, post 8vo. *cloth, new*, 2s 6d .. .. .. 1853

4979 — Complete Angler, 2 *plates*, 48mo. *cloth*, 3s (*cost* 6s) *Pickering*, 1825

4980 — Life of Dr. Sanderson, Bishop of Lincoln, with Bp. Sanderson's Cases of Conscience, *portrait by White*, 8vo. *old calf*, 7s 6d 1678

4981 — Lives of Dr. Donne, Sir Henry Wotton, Hooker, Herbert, and Bp. Sanderson, *portraits*, 48mo. *cloth*, 4s (*cost* 6s) *Pickering*, 1827

4982 — Lives, another edition, *portraits, autographs, and plates*, small 8vo. *antique morocco, extra, gilt, leaves*, 18s
*W. Nicol, at the Shakspeare Press*, 1847

A most elegantly executed volume, both as regards printing, embellishment, and binding.

4983 WALTON (William) Complete Calculator and Universal Ready Reckoner, 8vo. *half calf, very neat, scarce*, 15s .. 1824

The best and most comprehensive Ready Reckoner extant, on all sums from a penny to £80,000.

4984 WANDERINGS in some of the Western Republics of America, by George Byam, late 43rd Light Infantry, *plate*, post 8vo. *cloth*, 3s 6d (*pub. at* 7s 6d) .. .. .. 1850

4985 WANLEY'S (Nathaniel) Wonders of the Little World; a General History of Man, 4to. *remarkably fine clean copy in old calf, neat,* 18*s* .. .. .. .. 1774

Accounts of surprising Escapes, Strange Discoveries of long concealed Murders, &c. A most extraordinary and amusing common-place book of thousands of marvellous stories of former times, extracted from a great variety of old authors. Every story, however incredible, vouched by its authority.

4986 WANOSTROCHT, Recueil Choisi, 12mo. *bound,* 2*s* 1829

4987 WARBURTON'S (Bp.) Alliance between Church and State, 3rd edition, 8vo. *old calf,* THICK PAPER, 4*s* 6*d* .. 1748

"One of the finest pieces that is to be found in any language of scientific reasoning applied to a political subject."—*Bp. Horsley.* "On this 3rd Edition he exerted his whole strength, and has left it in a condition to brave the utmost efforts of future criticism." See *Chalmers's Biog. Dict.*

4988 — Letters from a late Eminent Prelate (Warburton) to one of his Friends (Bp. Hurd) *portraits,* 8vo. *boards,* 5*s* 1809

4989 WARD'S (Edward) Hudibras Redivivus; a Burlesque Poem on the Times, with the Apology, *portrait by W. Sherwin,* 2 vols. in 1, 3rd edition, 4to. *calf, neat,* 18*s* .. .. 1715

The author of this Poem, who was a violent antagonist of the Whigs, then in power, was fined and set in the pillory.—*Smollett's History.* See also the *Retrospective Review,* vol. 3.

4990 WARD'S (James) History of Gold as a Commodity and as a Measure of Value, *map of Victoria,* 12mo. *sewed,* 1*s* .. 1856

4991 WARD (N. B.) on the Growth of Plants in Closely Glazed Cases, 8vo. *cloth,* 5*s* .. .. *Van Voorst,* 1842

4992 WARD'S (Thomas) England's Reformation, from the time of King Henry VIII. to the end of Oates's Plot, a Poem, in 4 Cantos, 12mo. *neat,* 4*s* .. .. .. 1719

4993 WARD'S (William, *of Serampore*) Farewell Letters to a few Friends in Britain and America on returning to Bengal in 1821, post 8vo. *boards,* 3*s* .. .. *New York,* 1821

4994 WARDER'S (Joseph) True Amazons; or, the Monarchy of Bees, *portrait by Hulsbergh,* small 8vo. *original sheep,* 2*s* 1713

4995 WARE (Jac. *Eq. Aur.*) de Scriptoribus Hiberniæ libri duo, small 4to. *old binding,* 6*s* .. .. *Dublinii,* 1639

Dedicated to Lord Thomas Wentworth, the then Lord Lieut. of Ireland. With the Earl's arms at the back of the title.

4996 WARING'S (Edw. Scott) Tour to Sheeraz, by the Route of Kazroon and Feerozabad, with a History of Persia, *portraits,* 4to. *boards,* 7*s* 6*d (pub. at* 36*s)* .. .. *Bulmer,* 1807

"This work is chiefly confined to the manners, laws, religion, language, and literature of the Persians; on all of which it is instructive and interesting."—*Stevenson.*

4997 WARKWORTH'S (Dr. John) Chronicle of the first 13 years of King Edward IV., Edited from a MS. by J. O. Halliwell, Esq., 4to. *cloth,* 4*s* .. .. *Camden Soc.,* 1839

4998 WARNER'S (Rev. Richard) Literary Recollections, 2 vols. 8vo. *boards,* 6*s* .. .. *Longmans,* 1830

4999 WARTON'S (Dr. John) Death-bed Scenes and Pastoral Conversations, 2 vols. 8vo. *boards,* 12*s* (*pub. at* 24*s*) .. 1827

Large Letter Edition, quite out of print.

5000 WARTON'S (Thomas) Poems, 8vo. *calf, neat,* 3*s* 1777

5001 WARWICK'S (Arthur) Spare Minutes, square 12mo. *cloth,* 3*s* 6*d* 1637, *reprinted* 1829

250 copies only printed. See the *Retrospective Review* for a character of this admirable little work.

5002 WATERLAND'S (Dr. Daniel) Summary View of the Doctrine of Justification, 8vo. *sewed,* 2*s* 6*d* .. *reprinted,* 1807

5003 WATKINS'S (Dr. John) Universal Biographical Dictionary, very thick 8vo. *cloth,* 9*s* .. .. .. 1823

5004 — another edition, thick 8vo. *half russia, gilt, very neat,* 10*s* 6*d* 1825

This is a very useful book.

5005 — another, with the Supplement, thick 8vo. *boards,* 15*s* (*pub. at* 25*s*) .. .. .. *Longmans,* 1829

5006 WATSON'S (Bp. R.) Apology for the Bible in Refutation of Tom Paine, 12mo. *sewed,* 1*s* 6*d* .. .. 1796

5007 — Two Apologies, one for Christianity, the other for the Bible, with a Defence of Revealed Religion, 8vo. *boards,* 3*s* 6*d* 1816

In answer to Gibbon and Tom Paine.

5008 — Anecdotes of his Life, Written by Himself, *fine portrait,* 4to. *calf, very neat,* 7*s* 6*d* .. .. .. 1817

Mr. Joseph John Gurney's copy, with his Book-plate.

5009 WATTS'S (Mrs. Alaric) New Year's Gift and Juvenile Souvenir, 12mo. *morocco,* 2*s* .. .. .. 1834

5010 WATTS'S (Dr. Isaac) Works, with his Life, by Burder, *portrait and plates,* 6 vols. large 4to. *boards,* £1 12*s* (*pub. at* £9 9*s*) 1810

5011 — Humble Attempt towards the Revival of Practical Religion among Christians, particularly Protestant Dissenters, 12mo. *old calf, neat,* 3*s* .. .. .. 1731

5012 — on Humility and the contrary Vice, 8vo. *old calf,* 1*s* 6*d* 1737

5013 — on the Improvement of the Mind, Rules for the Attainment of Useful Knowledge, with an Account of his Life, 12mo. *cloth, new,* 3*s* (*sells* 5*s* 6*d*) .. .. *Norwich,* 1822

"Whoever has the care of instructing others, may be charged with deficiency in his duty, if this book is not recommended."—*Dr. Johnson in his Life of Dr. Watts.*

5014 WAY'S (Albert, Esq.) Illustrations of Domestic Customs during the Middle Ages, ornamental Fruit-Trenchers inscribed with Posies, 8vo. presentation copy, *sewed,* 2*s* 6*d* 1845

5015 WAYLAND SMITH; a Dissertation on a Tradition of the Middle Ages, from the French of Depping and Michel, with Additions by S. W. Singer, and the amplified Legend of Oehlenschlager, 12mo. *cloth,* 4*s* 6*d* .. .. *W. Pickering,* 1847

"One of the most interesting of the old Sagas of the North. Sir Walter Scott having made use of it in Kenilworth has given it universal celebrity."—*Singer.*

5016 WEBB'S (Daniel) Inquiry into the Beauties of Painting and into the Merits of the most Celebrated Painters, 1761.—Remarks on the Beauties of Poetry, in 1 vol. small 8vo. *nice copies in old calf, gilt,* 4*s* 6*d* .. .. .. 1762

5017 — Inquiry into the Beauties of Painting, post 8vo. *calf, gilt, a nice old copy,* 3*s* 6d .. .. .. 1777

5018 WEBSTER'S (John) Dramatic Works, edited with an Introduction and Notes by William Hazlitt, 4 vols. foolscap 8vo. *cloth*, £1 *J. R. Smith*, 1858

For criticisms on Webster's Plays, see *Retrospective Review*, vol. 7, and Charles Lamb's Works. Mr. J. Russell Smith, deserves the thanks of the reading public for producing his Library of Old Authors, in which creditable work, Webster appears.—Webster had become scarce and difficult to procure.

5019 WEBSTER'S (Dr. Noah) Dictionary of the English Language, by Barker, of Thetford, 2 thick vols. 4to. *cloth*, £1 12*s* (*pub. at* £5 5*s*) .. .. .. .. 1831

5020 — another edition, by Worcester, with Walker's Key to the Classical Pronunciation of Classical and Scripture Proper Names, large 8vo. *boards*, 15*s* .. .. .. 1856

5021 WEEMSE'S (John) Treatise of the Foure Degenerate Sonnes, the Atheist, the Magician, the Idolater, and the Jew, being vol. 4 of his Works, 4to. *old calf*, 3*s* .. .. 1636

5022 WEEVER'S (John) Antient Funeral Monuments of Great Britain, Ireland, and Isles adjacent, with the dissolved Monasteries, *portrait, plates, & index*, 4to. *hf. russia, gilt, good copy* £1 11*s* 6*d* 1767

Best edition of a book extremely useful to the antiquary, and containing information nowhere else to be found.

5023 WEISMANNI (C. E.) Introductio in Memorabilia Ecclesiastica Historiæ Sacræ Novi Testamenti, vol. 1 only, thick 4to. of 1100 pages, *very fine copy in white vellum*, 12*s* *Stuttgardiæ*, 1718

"We find in the History of Weismann, both the piety of Milner and the historical fulness and accuracy of Mosheim."—*Conybeare's Bampton Lectures.* This volume extends over 15 Centuries.

5024 WELCHMAN (Edw.) XXXIX. Articuli Eccles. Ang. text. S.S. et Patrum primævorum Testimoniis confirmati, et Notis illustrati, 8vo. *interleaved*, 2*s* 6*d* .. .. *Oxonii*, 1730

5025 — alia editio, 8vo. *boards*, 3*s* .. *Cantabrigiæ* 1819

Added is the Edward VIth's Catechism, and the Articles of 1552 and 1571.

5026 — On the Articles, in Latin and English, 8vo. *half calf, very neat*, 4*s* .. .. .. .. 1817

5027 WELLINGTON'S (Arthur, Duke of) Life, with his Political and Military Services in Flanders, India, Ireland, Denmark, Spain, and Portugal, by F. L. Clarke, *portraits and plates*, vols. 1 and 3, 8vo. *half calf, neat*, 6*s* .. .. *No date.*

5028 — his Life and Character, by Lord Ellesmere, 12mo. *sewed*, 1*s* 1852

5029 WELLS'S (Edward) New Sett of 41 Maps both of Antient and Present Geography, engraved by Burghers, Sutton Nicholls, Cole, Smith, &c. *coloured*, atlas folio, *old calf, gilt*, 15*s* *No date.*

Dedicated to his Highness William Duke of Gloucester.

5030 — Rich Man's Duty to Contribute liberally to the Building, Repairing, and Adorning Churches, 18mo. *morocco, gilt leaves*, 3*s* 6*d* (*cost* 5*s*) .. .. .. *Oxford*, 1840

5031 WELLS (Nath. Armstrong) The Picturesque Antiquities of Spain, royal 8vo. *numerous plates, cloth, uncut*, 7*s* 6*d* (*pub. at* 21*s*)

5032 WELWOOD'S (Dr. James) Memoirs of the most Material Transactions in England for the last Hundred Years, preceding the Revolution of 1688, 8vo. *original edition, old calf*, 3*s* 6*d* 1700

"This author, strongly attached to republican principles, is recommended by the Earl of Chatham, in his Letters to his nephew, Mr. Pitt."—*Lowndes.*

5033 WELWOOD'S Memoirs, 12mo. *calf, very neat,* 3*s* .. 1710
5034 — another edition, 8vo. *boards,* 4*s* .. .. 1826

Baron Maseres edited this edition of what he styles "a most valuable and excellent work."

5035 WEMMERS (Jacobi) Lexicon Æthiopicum, cum ejusdem linguæ Institutionibus Grammat. et Indice Vocum Latinarum, 4to. *fine copy in old calf,* VERY RARE, £1 5*s* .. *Romæ,* 1638

For an Ethiopic New Testament, see No. 4711.

5036 WESLEY (John) Survey of the Wisdom of God in the Creation; a Compendium of Natural Philosophy, 2 vols. 12mo. *old calf,* 4*s* 6*d* .. .. *Bristol, William Pine,* 1763
5037 WEST'S (Mrs.) Letters to a Young Lady, 3 vols. 12mo. *half calf, neat,* 6*s* .. .. .. .. 1806
5038 WEST'S Guide to the Lakes in Cumberland, Westmorland, and Lancashire, *map and plate,* 8vo. *boards,* 4*s* .. 1789
5039 WEST INDIES—Sketches and Recollections of the West Indies by a Resident, post 8vo. *boards,* 3*s* 6*d (pub at* 9*s)* 1828
5040 — a Winter in the West Indies, by Joseph John Gurney, *plates,* 8vo. *cloth, scarce,* 5*s* .. .. .. 1840
5041 WESTMINSTER MAGAZINE, *portraits and plates,* 5 vols. 8vo. *half bound, clean and neat,* 10*s* .. .. 1773-79
5042 WESTMINSTER SCHOOL—Sacred Exercises, in 4 books, compiled particularly for the Use of Westminster School, dedicated to Pearce, Bp. of Rochester, 8vo. *old calf, neat,* 3*s* 6*d* 1764
5043 WESTON'S (Stephen) Fragments of Oriental Literature, *with an outline of a painting on a curious Chinese vase,* 8vo. *boards,* 3*s* 6*d* 1807
5044 WEYLAND (John, F.R.S) Principles of Population and Production, with a View to Moral and Political Consequences, 8vo. *calf extra, grained,* 6*s* .. .. .. 1816

From Lord Calthorp's Collection, for another work on this subject, see *Ricardo* in the Appendix.

5045 WHATELY'S (Abp. Richard) Logic and Rhetoric, and Samuel T. Coleridge on the Science of Method, small 8vo. *cloth, new,* 5*s* 1855
5046 WHEAR (Deg.) Relectiones Hyemales de Ratione et Methodo Legendi Historias, Civiles et Ecclesiasticas; accessit Gab. Naudæi Bibliographia Politica, 12mo. *old calf, neat,* 3*s* 6*d Cantabrigiæ,* 1684
5047 — idem, 12mo. *a nice copy in old calf,* 5*s* .. *ib.,* 1684

Degory Whear is recommended by John Locke as a guide, and the little Treatise by Naudé, who was Librarian to Cardinal Mazarine, is very scarce in the original.

5048 WHEATLEY'S (Charles) Rational Illustration of the Book of Common Prayer of the Church of England, 8vo. *old calf, very neat,* 4*s* 6*d* .. .. .. 1741
5049 — new edition, 8vo. *cloth,* 5*s* *Oxford, Clarendon Press,* 1846

The substance of every thing Liturgical in Bp. Sparrow, L'Estrange, Drs. Comber and Nichols, and all former ritualists, commentators, &c. This is the best book on the subject.

5050 WHELER (George) and Dr. Spon, of Lyons, Journey into Greece, *map and numerous curious plates,* folio, *old calf, scarce,* 15*s* 1682

"Valuable for its plates of the Antiquities of Greece and Asia Minor, and of Medals, Inscriptions, &c."—*Stevenson.* "A very valuable production chiefly for antiquaries and artists."—*Pinkerton.*

5051 WHEWELL'S (Professor) Astronomy and General Physics, considered with reference to Natural Theology, post 8vo. *cloth, new,* 5*s* .. .. .. *W. Pickering,* 1837

5052 — another edition, 12mo. *cloth,* 3*s* 6*d* .. *ib.,* 1847

5053 WHISTLECRAFT (Orlando, *of Thwaite, Suffolk*) on the Climate of England, with Meteorological Tables, 8vo. *half cloth,* 4*s* 6*d* (*pub. at* 9*s*) .. .. .. .. 1840

5054 WHISTON'S (Will.) New Theory of the Earth, with a Discourse on the Mosaic History of the Creation, *plates,* 8vo. *old calf, neat,* 3*s* 6*d* .. .. .. .. 1696

5055 — Memoirs of his Life and Writings, by Himself, 3 vols. 8vo. *calf, neat,* 12*s* .. .. .. .. 1749

The 3rd part, which rarely occurs, contains the "Liturgy of the Church of England, reduced nearer to the primitive standard."

5056 WHITBY'S (Dr. Daniel) Paraphrase and Commentary on the New Testament, *fine portrait by Vdr. Gucht,* 2 vols. folio, 4th edition, *a good sound copy in old calf,* £1 4*s* .. 1718

"Divines of every denomination concur in pronouncing Dr. Whitby's Commentary to be, upon the whole, the best upon the New Testament that is extant in the English language."—*Horne's Introduction.*

5057 — Disquisitiones Modestæ, in Cl. Bulli defensionem Fidei Nicenæ, 8vo. *old calf, neat,* 3*s* .. .. *Londini,* 1720

5058 WHITE (Dr. Francis, *Deane of Carlisle*) Replie to Jesuit Fisher's Answere to certain Questions proposed by King James I., *finely engraved title page,* folio, *old calf,* 7*s* 6*d* *Adam Islip,* 1624

5059 WHITE'S (Henry Kirke) Remains and Life, by Robert Southey, *portrait and plates,* 2 vols. 8vo. *calf, neat,* 7*s* 6*d* 1813

5060 WHITE'S (Hugh) Gospel Promotive of True Happiness, 12mo. *cloth,* 2*s* .. .. .. *Dublin,* 1843

5061 — Profession and Practice, 12mo. *cloth,* 2*s* .. *ib.,* 1839

5062 WHITE'S (Rev. T. H.) Fragments of Italy and the Rhineland, thick 12mo. *cloth,* 4*s* (*pub. at* 7*s* 6*d*) *W. Pickering,* 1841

5063 WHITE'S (Rev. W., *of Hardingham, Norfolk*) Dissertation on the Disorder of Death, 8vo. *half cloth,* 7*s* *Norwich,* 1819

From the author to Dr. Wingfield.

5064 WHITWORTH'S (Lord Charles) Account of Russia as it was in 1710, small 8vo. *good copy in calf,* 12*s* *Strawberry Hill,* 1758

This very curious account of the Russian Empire, as it began to emerge from barbarism, is accompanied by a preface of 24 pages, written by the Hon. Horace Walpole, afterwards Earl of Orford, at whose private press at Strawberry Hill, it was printed.

5065 WHO'S WHO in 1855, 18mo. *cloth,* 1*s* 6*d*

5066 WHOLE Duty of Man, *frontispiece,* 8vo. *fine copy in old claret morocco, gilt, gilt edges,* 10*s* 6*d* .. .. 1704

With the autograph of "*S. Walpole,*" great grandmother to the Earl of Orford. The author of this excellent Treatise has never been satisfactorily ascertained, but it has been attributed to Abps. Sancroft, Frewen, and Sterne, Bp. Fell, Dr. Allestry, and various others.

5067 WICQUEFORT (Conseiller aux Conseils d'Estat) l'Ambassadeur et ses Fonctions, thick 4to. *old calf, gilt,* 9*s* *Cologne,* 1690

With the reflections at the end, and a Discourse on the Election of the Emperor and the Electors. Also MS. marginal remarks by one of the Lords Walpole, of Woolterton, some of whom were engaged in diplomatic missions.

5068 WILARS de Honecort's (an Architect of the 13th Century) Facsimile of his Sketch Book, with Commentaries by Lassus and Quicherat, translated and edited by Professor Willis of Cambridge, *portrait and numerous plates*, thick 4to. *cloth*, £2 10*s* *Oxford, Parker*, 1859

This handsome and most curious book is illustrated with 73 large plates, and 43 woodcuts. Professor Willis says of it, "The Manuscript which is the subject of the present volume, is a most valuable monument of the state of the art of delineation in the 13th Century. It exemplifies the manner in which the artists carried on their studies, and that they copied from the antique."—*Preface.*

5069 WILBERFORCE (H. W.) Parochial System, an Appeal to English Churchmen, 12mo, *cloth*, 2*s* .. *Rivington*, 1838

5070 WILBERFORCE'S (Bp. of Oxford) Eucharistica, 24mo. *cloth*, 2*s* 6*d* .. .. .. *Oxford*, 1856

5071 WILD (Marquard) Apologie pour la Vieille Cité d'Avenche, ou Aventicum en Suisse au Canton de Berne, *plates of antiquities*, 8vo. *sewed, uncut*, 5*s* .. .. *Berne*, 1710

5072 WILD (R., D.D.) Iter Boreale, with large Additions of several other Poems, small 8vo. *old binding*, 10*s* 6*d* .. 1668

Iter Boreale records the "Matchless march of the Lord General George Monck from Scotland to London, in the winter of 1659." This is an earlier edition than is described by the Bibliotheca Ang. Poetica.

5073 WILKIE'S (Sir David) Life, with his Journals, Tours, Critical Remarks on Works of Art, and Correspondence by Allan Cunningham, *portrait*, 3 vols. 8vo. *cloth*, 14*s* *(pub. at 36s)* 1843

"A work of great interest."—*Gentleman's Magazine.*

5074 WILKINS (Bishop John) Discovery of a New World, or the Probability of the Moon's being a Habitable World, *engraved title*, 8vo. *calf, neat*, 3*s* 6*d* .. .. .. 1684

5075 — Mathematical and Philosophical Works, with an Account of his Life and Works, 2 vols. 8vo. *calf, neat*, 8*s* .. 1802

CONTENTS.—That there may be another habitual world in the moon.—That our earth is one of the planets.—Mercury, the Secret and swift messenger.—Mathematical Magic.—On a Philosophical Language.

5076 WILLAN'S (R. and N.) Life of Christ from the Narrations of the Four Evangelists, *map*, 8vo. *calf, neat*, 3*s* 6*d* .. 1803

5077 WILLEMENT'S (Miss) Scripture Lessons for my Infant Class, *plates*, 18mo. *cloth, gilt*, 1*s* 6*d* .. .. *Norwich*

5078 WILLIAM of Malmesbury's Chronicle of the Kings of England to the Reign of K. Stephen, with Notes and Illustrations by Dr. Giles, *plate*, post 8vo. *cloth*, 3*s* *(cost 5s)* *H. G. Bohn*, 1847

5079 WILLIAM III.—Names of the Lords Spiritual and Temporal who Voted the Settling the Crown on the Prince and Princess of Orange, *broadside*, RARE, 5*s* .. *J. Newton*, 1689

5080 — True List of the Parliament, October, 1690, with MS. Corrections and Additions, *broadside, curious*, 5*s* *Tho. Braddyll*, 1690

5081 — Parchment and Paper, Table of the Prices to be paid for, settled by the Lords of the Treasury, July 31, 1695, signed, William Lowndes, *broadside*, 2*s* 6*d* *C. Bill and Newcomb's Executrix*, 1695

5082 — Life, containing an Account of his Family, Birth, Marriage, Will, Death, &c. *map, portraits, medals, &c.* 8vo. *old calf, neat*, 4*s* 1703

5083 WILLIAMS (Dr. Edward) Christian Preacher, Discourses on Preaching, with an Appendix on the Choice of Books, 12mo. *half calf, neat*, 3*s* .. .. .. .. 1824

5084 — another edition, 12mo. *cloth*, 3*s* 6*d* .. .. 1843

There is an Appendix on the choice of books, with criticisms on them, a very useful little work.

5085 WILLIAMS (John) Lord Keeper of the Great Seal, Bp. of Lincoln, and Abp. of York, his Life by Ambrose Philips, *fine portrait by Vander Gucht*, 8vo. *calf, gilt*, 6*s* .. *Cambridge*, 1700

A narration of many remarkable occurrences in Church and State in the time of James 1. and Charles I.

5086 WILLIAMS'S (T.) Song of Songs, which is by Solomon, a new Translation, with Commentary and Notes, 8vo. *boards*, 3*s* 6*d* 1801

"In page 100 to 109 is given an interesting account of nearly 40 Expositors and Commentators on this book. See also *Monthly Review*, v. 47."—*Horne's Introduction*.

5087 WILLIATT (And.) de Universali et Novissima Judæorum Vocatione, small 4to. *sewed, scarce*, 6*s* *Cantabrigiæ, John Legatt*, 1590

Dedicated to William Cecil, Lord Burleigh, who was then Chancellor of the University of Cambridge.

5088 WILLIS'S (Browne) Notitia Parliamentaria; a History of the Counties, Cities, and Boroughs in England and Wales, 8vo. *old calf, neat*, 5*s* .. .. .. 1715

Bedford, Berks, Bucks, Cambridge, and Cheshire.

5089 WILMOT (Dr. S. G.) On Stricture of the Urethra, sm. 8vo. *cloth, new*, 7*s* 6*d* .. .. .. *Dublin*, 1858

5090 WILSON'S (Arthur) History of Great Britain; being the Life and Reign of King James the First, *portrait by Vaughan*, small folio, *old calf, neat*, 8*s* .. .. .. 1653

Arthur Wilson, Esq, was born at Great Yarmouth, Norfolk. Mr. Joseph John Gurney's copy, with his Book-plate.

5091 WILSON'S (Rev. E.) Sermons for Sunday Evenings, 12mo. *cloth*, 2*s* 6*d (pub. at 5s)* .. .. .. 1832

5092 — Doctrine of Apostolical Succession Explained and Vindicated, 8vo. *sewed*, 1*s* .. *Norwich, C. Muskett*, 1845

5093 [WILSON] De Animi Tranquillitate dialogus Florentio Voluseno Scoto autore, 8vo. *old binding, scarce*, 5*s* *Edinburgi, R. Freebairn*, 1707

This allegory, dedicated to K. James IV., is "adorned with many pleasing incidents and adventures, and abounds with genius and learning."—*Warton*. Lowndes does not mention this edition.

5094 WILSON'S (Capt. Henry) Account of the Pelew Islands in the W. Pacific Ocean, by George Keate, *portrait, map, and fine plates*, 4to. *in old calf, gilt*, 10*s* 6*d* .. .. 1788

Sir Lambert Blackwell's copy, and a very fine one.

5095 WILSON'S (Dr. James P.) Essay on the Probation of Fallen Men, *portrait*, 8vo. *bound*, 2*s* 6*d* *Philadelphia, Geddes*, 1827

With an autograph of Mr. J. J. Gurney.

5096 WILSON'S (Thomas, *Bp. of Sodor and Man*,) Works, with his Life by C. Crutwell, *portraits of him and his son*, 2 vols. in 1, folio, *old calf, neat*, £1 1*s* .. .. *Bath*, 1782

5097 — Short and Plain Instruction for the Better Understanding the Lord's Supper, 5th edition, 12mo. *nice copy in calf*, 3*s* 1740

5098 WILSON'S Essay towards an Instruction of the Indians, with Private and Family Prayers, 12mo. *old calf, very neat*, 3*s* 1742

5099 — Maxims of Piety and Christianity, 12mo. *bound*, 2*s* *Bath, Cruttwell*, 1815

5100 — Sacra Privata, Private Meditations, Devotions, and Prayers, 12mo. *cloth*, 6*s* .. *Oxford, J. H. Parker*, 1854

This is the 1st complete edition.

5101 — Parochialia; Instructions to the Clergy, 18mo. *morocco, elegant stamped gilt edges*, 5*s* (*cost* 8*s*) *Oxford, J. H. Parker*, 1840

5102 — Parochialia, 18mo. *plain morocco, gilt edges*, 3*s* (*cost* 5*s* 6*d*) *Oxford*, 1840

The works of this most excellent prelate and Christian man, are held in great and deserved esteem.

5103 — Life, by Hugh Stowell, *portrait*, 8vo. *boards*, 4*s* 6*d* (*pub. at* 10*s* 6*d*) .. .. .. *Rivington*, 1829

5104 WILSON'S (Rev. Tho.) Nozrani, in Egypt and Syria, *map and plan of Jerusalem*, 1st edition, 12mo. *cloth*, 3*s* 6*d* (*pub. at* 6*s*) *Norwich, C. Muskett*, 1846

5105 WILTS.—Hatcher (Henry) Memoirs of his Life, Character, and Writings, by John Britton, F.S.A., *portrait*, royal 8vo. *stiff cover*, 4*s* .. .. .. *For the author*, 1847

Henry Hatcher was the author of a History of Salisbury.

5106 WINCHESTER—Historical and Descriptive Guide to the City of Winchester, *plates*, 12mo. *boards*, 1*s* 6*d* *Winchester*, 1829

5107 WINGATE'S (Edmund) Plain Method for Attaining the Knowledge of Common Arithmetic, by James Dodson, *frontispiece*, 8vo. *calf, very fine copy*, 4*s* 6*d* .. .. .. 1751

5108 WINKLEMANN (Giovanni) Storia delle Arti del Disegno presso gli Antichi, tradotta del Tedesco, per l'Abate Carlo Fea, 126 *plates*, 3 vols. 4to. *fine copy in Italian vellum*, £1 18*s* *In Roma*, 1783

Winklemann's works were highly recommended by the King of Prussia, in an address lately delivered by his Majesty to a Society of Arts.

5109 WINTER'S (Christ. T.) Six Months in British Burmah in 1857, *plates*, post 8vo. *cloth*, 4*s* 6*d* (*pub. at* 10*s* 6*d*) .. 1858

5110 WISEMAN'S (Cardinal) Three Lectures on the Catholic Hierarchy, crown 8vo. *sewed*, 1*s* .. .. .. 1850

5111 WITHER'S (George) Hymns and Songs of the Church, with an Introduction by Edward Farr, and the Musical Notes by Orlando Gibbons, *portrait after Hole*, foolscap 8vo. *cloth*, 5*s* *J. R. Smith*, 1857

5112 — Hallelujah, or Britain's Second Remembrancer; in Praiseful and Penitential Hymns, Spiritual Songs, &c., with an Introduction by Edward Parr, *portrait*, fcap. 8vo. *cloth*, 6*s* *ib.*, 1857

"So few copies of the original are known to exist, that the copy from which this reprint has been taken cost 21 guineas."

5113 WITHERING'S (Dr. William) Arrangement of British Plants according to the Linnæan System, with an easy Introduction to the Study of Botany, *plates*, 4 vols. 8vo. *calf, gilt*, 12*s* 1818

5114 WITICHINDI Saxonis Rerum ab Henrico et Ottone I. Impp. Gestarum libri III., unà cum aliis quibusdam raris et antehac non lectis diversorum autorum historiis, ab Anno 800 usq. ad præsentem ætatem, folio, LARGE PAPER, *half calf, neat,* 15*s* *Basiliæ, apud Jo. Hervagium,* 1532

Contains 10 rare Tracts. 1. Henrici IIII. Ducis Bavarii Vita. 2. Epistolæ Hen. IV. ad Pont. et alios Principes. 3. Gesta Imp. Henrici VII. 4. Caroli Magni Vita. 5. Æneæ Sylvii Historia Bohemica. 6. Rerum Magunciacarum Chronicon, etc. "Edition peu commune, où l'on trouve encore d'autres monumens de l'histoire d'Allemagne."—*Du Fresnoy.*

5115 WODEHOUSE'S (Rev. Canon) Letter to the Bishop of Norwich (Dr. S. Hinds) with his Lordship's Answer, 8vo. *sewed,* 1*s* *Norwich, C. Muskett,* 1851

5116 WOLF'S (John Christopher) Life and Adventures, small 8vo. *calf, neat,* 3*s* 6*d* .. .. .. 1785

Mr. Wolf was principal Secretary of State at Jaffanapatnam, in Ceylon, this book, therefore, contains a description of the island, by him and Mr. Eschelskroon.

5117 WOLFF (Rev. Dr. Joseph, Missionary) Sketch of the Life and Journal of, in Palestine and Persia, 12mo. *boards,* 1*s* 6*d* *Norwich,* 1827

5118 — Researches and Missionary Labours among the Jews, Mohammedans, and other Sects, 1831 to 34, *map,* 8vo. *half cloth,* 7*s* (*pub. at* 12*s*) .. .. .. 1835

5119 — Journal, containing an Account of his Missionary Labours, from 1827 to 31, and from 1835 to 38, 8vo. *cloth,* 5*s* 1839

"Rev. J. D. Parmeter, from his friend, Joseph Wolff, D.D., LL.D."

5120 — Narrative of a Mission to Bokhara, in 1843 and 1845, to ascertain the fate of Col. Stoddart and Capt. Conolly, *portrait,* 8vo. *cloth,* 7*s* 6*d (pub. at* 14*s)* .. .. 1846

5121 WOOD'S (James) Elements of Algebra, by Lund, 12th edition, *boards, uncut,* 5*s* (*pub. at* 12*s* 6*d*) *Cambridge,* 1845

5122 WOOLSEY (Thomas, *Cardinal, once Archbishop of York, and Lord Chancellor of England*) Life and Death, by his Gentleman Usher, William Cavendish, Esq., *portrait,* small 8vo. *half calf, neat,* 5*s* .. .. .. .. 1667

Bought out of the Duke of Sussex's library, in 1844, with H. R. H. Book-plate. "A most interesting piece of biography, in elegant and simple language, bearing evidence of a most exemplary impartiality, and describing with fidelity and accuracy all that came under the author's own observation."—*Retrospective Review.*

5123 — another edition, with Notes and other Illustrations by S. W. Singer, *several portraits,* 8vo. *boards,* 9*s* .. 1827

Cavendish was Gentleman Usher to the Cardinal. At the end "Extracts from the Life of Queen Anne Boleigne," by George Wyatt, Esq., and "a Parallel between Card. Wolsey and Abp. Laud," 1641, and "Who wrote Cavendish's Wolsey."

5124 — his Rise and Fall, as related by Cavendish, 12mo. *sewed,* 1*s* 1855

5125 WOMAN. Can Woman Regenerate Society? 12mo. *cloth,* 2*s* *J. W. Parker,* 1844

5126 WOOD'S (Anthony à) Athenæ Oxonienses; an exact History of all the Writers and Bishops who have had their Education in Oxford, from 1500 to 1690, with the Fasti or Annals of the University, 2 vols. in 1, folio, *old calf, neat,* 16*s* 1691

This first edition was burnt before the public theatre in Oxford, and Wood banished the University for expressions contained in it reflecting on Hyde, Earl of Clarendon, the Chancellor of the University. See *Chalmers's Biog. Dict.*

5127 WOOD'S Athenæ Oxonienses, to 1695, 2nd edition, with the addition of 500 new Lives from Wood's MS., by Bp. Tanner, 2 vols. royal folio, *good copy in calf, new backs, gilt,* £1 5*s* 1721

"Dr. Tanner, the author of Notitia Monastica, supplied a great part of the additions and corrections to this second edition."—*Lowndes.* "Wood's Athenæ is an invaluable work, both as regards biography and bibliography, and should be in every English library."—*Lowndes.*

5128 WOOD'S (Rev. Basil) Family Record; or Memoirs of several deceased Members of his Family, *portrait,* post 8vo. *cloth,* 2*s* (*pub. at* 6*s*) .. .. .. .. 1834

5129 WOOD'S (Jas.) Elements of Optics, 8vo. *boards,* 2*s* *Cambridge,* 1811

5130 WOOD'S (Neville) Ornithologist's Text Book, being Reviews of Ornithological Works, with Discussions on topics of Interest, 12mo. *cloth,* 3*s* .. .. .. 1836

5131 WOOD'S (Will.) Catalogue of his extensive Collection of Books on Natural History, *coloured plate,* 8vo. *cloth,* 5*s*—*half calf, very neat,* 6*s* .. .. .. .. 1832

Very useful, as containing *collations* of the various works.

5132 WOODHOUSE'S (Robert) Elementary Treatise on Astronomy, 8vo. *boards,* 4*s* .. .. .. *Cambridge,* 1812

5133 WOODS'S (Dr. Leonard) Letters to Unitarians and Reply to Dr. Ware, 2nd edition, with an Appendix, 8vo. *boards,* 4*s* *Andover, Massachusetts,* 1822

5134 WOODWARD'S (Sam.) Synoptical Table of British Organic Remains, *plate of fossil turtle,* 8vo. *cloth,* 3*s* (*pub. at* 5*s*) 1830

5135 — Outline of the Geology of Norfolk, *coloured plates,* 8vo. *cloth,* 3*s* 6*d* .. .. .. *Norwich,* 1833

5136 WOOL. Memoirs of Wool, Woollen Manufacture and Trade, in England, from the Earliest Times, by John Smith, 2 vols. 8vo. *calf, neat,* 9*s* .. .. .. 1747

"An invaluable and erudite work."—*Lowndes.*

5137 [WOOLNOR'S (Henry)] True Originall of the Soule, edited by Elias Palmer, 18mo. *bound, scarce,* 3*s* .. .. 1641

5138 WORDSWORTH, a Critical Essay on his Poetry, 12mo. *sewed,* 1*s* .. .. .. .. 1853

5139 WORRELL and Brooke's Bibliotheca Legum Angliæ; a Catalogue of Ancient Law Writers, 2 vols. 18mo. *old calf, neat,* 5*s* .. .. .. .. 1788

5140 WORTHINGTON'S (Dr. John, *Master of Jesus College, Cambridge*) Scripture Catechism, 12mo. *old calf,* 1*s* 6*d* .. 1673

5141 — Miscellanies on the Millenium, a Dissertation de Ecclesiæ and de voce Merachépheth, also his Epistles to Mr. Hartlib, 8vo. *old calf, neat,* 5*s* .. .. .. 1704

Highly commended by Archbishop Tillotson.

5142 WORTHINGTON'S (William) Essay on the Scheme and Conduct of Man's Redemption, 8vo. *old calf, neat,* 3*s* 6*d* 1743

"To his excellent friend Dr. Daniel Duncan, from the author."

5143 — another edition, 8vo. *calf, neat,* 3*s* 6*d* *Edw. Cave,* 1748

5144 WOTTON'S (Dr. William) Thoughts on a Proper Method of Studying Divinity, 8vo. *sewed,* 2*s* .. *Oxford,* 1818

This is a valuable list of Books, with critiques, which he recommends to the study of the clergy.

5145 WOWER (Joan. a) de Polymathia Tractatio; integri operis de Studiis Veterum, editio nova cum prefatione Jac. Thomasii, cum autoris vita, small 8vo. *old calf,* 3*s* 6*d* *Lipsiæ,* 1665

5146 WRAXALL'S (Lascelles) Handbook to the Naval and Military Resources of the Principal European Nations, 8vo. *cloth, new,* 4*s* .. .. .. .. 1856

5147 WRAXALL'S (Sir Nath. W.) Tour in the North of Europe, Copenhagen, Stockholm, and Petersburgh, *map,* 8vo. *beautiful copy in bright calf, gilt,* 5*s* .. .. .. 1766

5148 — History of France, from the Accession of Henry III., in 1574, to the Death of Henry IV., in 1610, 3 vols. 4to. *half russia, very neat,* 15*s* .. .. .. 1795

"A work, from which the reader will derive the greatest assistance, while engaged with the original works of De Thou and Davila. The particulars are brought together with great diligence."—*Professor Smyth.*

5149 — Memoirs of the Courts of Berlin, Dresden, Warsaw, and Vienna, in 1777, 78, 79, 2 vols. 8vo. *half russia, neat,* 6*s* 1806

5150 — Posthumous Memoirs of his own Time, *portraits,* 3 vols. 8vo. *cloth,* 12*s* .. .. .. .. 1836

5151 WREN'S (M.) Monarchy Asserted, or the State of Monarchical and Popular Government, 8vo. *original binding,* 5*s* *Oxford,* 1659

Dedicated to Dr. Wilkins, Warden of Wadham College, Oxford, by Matthew Wren, successively Bp. of Hereford, Norwich, and Ely, this is an answer to Harrington's Oceana.

5152 WRIGHT'S (Edward) Travels in France and Italy, in 1720 to 22, *plates of Antiquities, &c., by Vdr. Gucht,* 2 vols. 4to. *old calf, very neat,* 7*s* 6*d* .. .. .. 1730

5153 — another edition, 2 vols. in 1, 4to. *a fine copy, old calf, gilt,* 10*s* 6*d* .. .. .. .. 1764

5154 WRIGHT'S (Josiah) Hellenica; a History of Greece, in Greek, as related by Diodorus, and Thucydides, 12mo. *cloth,* 2*s* (*cost* 3*s* 6*d*) *Cambridge,* 1857

5155 WRIGHT'S (Sir Martin) Introduction to the Law of Tenures, royal 8vo. *calf, neat,* 5*s* 6*d* .. .. 1768

5156 WRIGHT'S (Thomas) Biographia Britannica Literaria; a Biography of Literary Characters of England and Ireland arranged Chronologically (Anglo-Saxon Period) 8vo. *cloth, new,* 7*s* (*pub. at* 12*s*) 1842

5157 — (Anglo-Norman Period) 8vo. *cloth, new,* 7*s* (*pub. at* 12*s*) 1842

5158 — Narratives of Sorcery and Magic, 2 vols. post 8vo. *cloth,* 10*s* 6*d* (*pub. at* 21*s*) .. .. .. 1851

Mr. Wright's name is a guarantee for this being a most amusing and recondite book.

5159 WYCHERLEY'S (Will.) Plays, *plates, by Pine,* 2 vols. 12mo. *old calf, very neat,* 6*s* .. .. .. 1720

"A writer of infinite spirit, satire, and wit."—*Pope.* Lord Lansdowne has drawn his character as a writer in an elegant manner.

5160 WYCLIFFE'S (Dr. John) Translation of the New Testament in English, circa 1380, small 4to. *extra vellum,* **Black Letter,** *uncut,* £1 11*s* 6*d* .. .. .. *Pickering,* 1848

Now first printed from a contemporary MS. formerly in the Monastery of Sion, Middlesex, lately in the collection of Lea Wilson, Esq., F.S.A. A very valuable relic, and a curious specimen of the Old English Language, beautifully printed at Chiswick, by Charles Whittingham.

5161 WYCLIFFE'S Life and Opinions, with a View of the Papal System in Europe to the commencement of the 14th Century, *portrait*, 2 vols. 8vo. *half cloth*, 9*s* (*pub. at* £1 1*s*) .. 1831

"To the Rev. T. Smith, with the kind regards of the author, Nov. 4, 1831.

5162 — Life, by C. Webb Le Bas, *portrait*, 12mo. *cloth*, 3*s* 6*d* (*pub. at* 6*s*) .. .. .. .. 1832

5163 WYKEHAM—The Life of William of Wykeham, Bishop of Winchester, 1324 to 1404, by Bishop Robert Lowth, *plates*, 8vo. *first edition, old calf, scarce*, 7*s* 6*d* .. .. 1758

This excellent Life is "a model in its way."—*Quarterly Review*.

5164 WYNNE'S (Edward) Eunomus; Dialogues concerning the Law and Constitution of England, 5th Edit., with Notes, &c. by Mr. Bythewood, 2 vols. 12mo. *law calf, neat*, 10*s* .. 1822

5165 XENOPHONTIS Opera, Græcè et Latinè, H. Stephani annotationes, thick folio, *old calf, gilt, by Johnson, stained at the end*, 21*s* *Excudebat H. Stephanus*, 1561

Dr. Harwood says this first edition "is the most beautiful and correct of H. Stephens's editions of the Greek Classics." "Belle Edition."—*Brunet*.

5166 — Expeditio Cyri, Græcè, 18mo. *cloth*, 2*s* *Oxonii, Parker*, 1859

"The Greek and Latin languages have nothing in their kind more perfect than those admirable performances, the Expedition of Cyrus and the Commentaries of Cæsar."—*Spelman*.

5167 — Memoirs of Socrates, with the Defence of Socrates before his Judges, Englished by Sarah Fielding, 8vo. *nice copy in old calf, gilt*, 5*s* .. .. .. *Bath*, 1762

"Done with equal judgment and accuracy."—*Dr. Clarke*.

5168 — Minor Works; Memoirs of Socrates, the Banquet, Hiero, and Economics, translated into English, 8vo. *calf, neat*, 4*s* 1813

5169 — Works, translated into English, 4 vols. 8vo. *calf, very neat*, 24*s* 1811

Contains Spelman's translation of the Expedition of Cyrus into Persia; the Hon. Maurice Ashley's Cyropædia; Smith's History of the Affairs of Greece; Memoirs of Socrates; The Banquet; Hiero; and Economics, by Welwood, Bradley, Graves, and others.

5170 — della Vita di Ciro Re de Persi, tradotto in lingua Toscana da Jacopo di Messer Poggio (Bracciolini) Fiorentino, small 8vo. *old vellum*, 10*s* 6*d* *Tusculano, per Alexandro da Paganini*, 1527

Few books were printed at Toscolano before this.

5171 XIMENES—History of the Administration of Cardinal Ximenes, Great Minister of State, in Spain, Englished by W. Vaughan, *fine portrait by T. Cross*, small 8vo. *nice copy in old calf*, 6*s* 1671

Dedicated to Sir Henry Herbert, Knt., Master of the Revells, and to Cardinal Richelieu, by the author the Sieur M. Baudier of Languedoc.

5172 YARMOUTH—Repertory of Deeds and Documents Relating to Great Yarmouth, Norfolk, 4to. *half vellum*, £1 1*s* 1855

A very rare Tract, only 100 copies printed by order of the Town Council.

5173 YARRELL'S History of British Birds, *illustrated by 550 wood engravings, remarkably well drawn and engraved*, 3 vols. 8vo. *boards*, last edition, £4 14*s* 6*d* .. .. 1856

5174 — another copy, *nicely bound in russia, gilt leaves*, £6 1856

The very best Scientific History of British Birds

5175 YATES'S (John) Ibis ad Cæsarem; a submissive appearance before Cæsar, in Answer to Mr. Montague's Appeal on the Points of Arminianism and Popery maintained by him, 4to. *half calf, neat,* 4*s* 6*d* .. .. .. *R. Mylbourne,* 1626

5176 YATES'S (Rev. W.) Account of New Zealand and of the Church Miss. Society's Mission, *portrait of Rev. S. Marsden and plates,* post 8vo. *cloth,* 5*s (pub. at* 10*s* 6*d)* .. 1835

5177 YEAR BOOK—Reports of Cases Decided in the 1st year Edw. V.—1st and 2nd Richard III.—1st to 16th, 20th, and 21, Henry VII.—12th, 13th, 14th, 18th, 19th, 20th, 26th, and 27th Henry VIII. all in NORMAN FRENCH, very thick folio, **Black Letter,** *in a very fine clean state, interiorly, and the old stamped binding, sound and good,* £3 3*s*
*Printed by Richard Tottill at various times between* 1555 *and* 1574

As each year in this very interesting old YEAR BOOK has a separate pagination, there are 29 different paginations in it. On a fly leaf is the autograph of —— Polhill, and the margins of the book, which are very ample, are largely annotated in a very beautiful minute character, apparently by the same hand. Altogether the volume consists of 552 leaves.

5178 YELDHAM (Stephen) Homœopathy in Acute Diseases, 8vo. *cloth,* 4*s* .. .. .. *H. Bailliere,* 1849

5179 YORK—Catalogue of the Library of H.R.H. the late Duke of York, sold by Sotheby, royal 8vo. *sewed,* 3*s* .. 1827

5180 YORKSHIRE—Deed between *Sir John Ramsden,* of Longley in Com. York, Knt., and Richard Shan, of Potterton, Leasing the Manor House to him, signed by *Richard Shan,* witnessed by *Edward Woodhouse, Jo. Watmoughe,* and another, *on parchment with seal, complete,* 10*s* 6*d* *dated* 9*th Car.* 1, 1633

5181 — History of the Cathedral and Metropolitical Church of St. Peter, York, *plates,* 12mo. *neat,* 3*s* .. *York,* 1768

5182 — History of Pontefract, by George Fox, *plan and plates,* 8vo. *half cloth,* 6*s* .. .. .. *Pontefract,* 1827

5183 — Parker (J. H., Esq., *of Oxford,*) Architectural Notes of the Churches and other Ancient Buildings in the City and Neighbourhood of York, with Notices of the Painted Glass by John Browne, *plates,* 8vo. *sewed,* 3*s* 6*d* .. *No date.*

Presentation copy, on thick paper, very few copies so printed.

5184 — Raine's (James) Catterick Church in the County of York, with Remarks and Notes, 13 *plates by Anthony Salvin,* 4to. *half cloth, scarce,* 9*s* .. .. .. .. 1834

A correct copy of the contract for its building in 1412. "The extreme scarcity of documents in English at the period of this indento, may be judged of on referring to Hallam's Middle Ages, Ch. 9, p. 2, p. 575. Edit. 1826."

5185 — Thorpe (Sergeant, *Judge of Assize for the Northern Circuit,*) his Charge delivered to the Grand Jury at Yorke Assizes, March 20, 1648, clearly Epitomizing the Statutes, small 4to. *sewed,* 4*s* 1649

5186 YONGE'S (James) 25 Sermons, 2nd series, (the 1st Sermon taken out) 8vo. *cloth,* 2*s* .. .. *Exeter,* 1832

5187 YOUNG'S (Arthur) Six Months' Tour through the North of England, *plates,* 4 vols. 8vo. *nice old calf, gilt,* 12*s* .. 1770

5188 — Farmer's Tour through the East of England, *plates,* 4 vols. 8vo. *calf, neat,* 15*s* .. .. .. 1771

5189 YOUNG'S Six Weeks' Tour through the Southern Counties of England and Wales, *plates*, 8vo. *calf, neat*, 3*s* 6*d* 1768

The 3 last articles uniformly bound in peculiarly nice fresh old calf, gilt.

5190 YOUNG'S (Dr. Edward) Night Thoughts on Life, Death, and Immortality, 2 vols. 8vo. *calf neat*, 6*s* .. .. 1749

5191 — another edition, 12mo. *calf, neat*, 2*s* 6*d* .. 1755

5192 YOUNG'S (Thomas) Egyptian Dictionary in the Ancient Enchorial Character, with a Memoir of the Author, and a List of his Works, *portrait*, 8vo. *boards*, 7*s* 6*d* .. .. 1831

5193 ZENOBII Compendium Veterum Proverbiorum, ex Tarræo et Didymo Collectum, opus luculentum et utile, Græcè, small 8vo. *old vellum, very rare*, £3 3*s* .. .. *Haganoæ*, 1535

On the title page is this autograph, "Gulielmi Cæcilii." This William Cecil was afterwards the celebrated great Lord Burleigh, Lord High Treasurer to Queen Elizabeth, who, being of St. John's College, Cambridge, at the age of 19, shortly after this book was printed, delivered a Greek Lecture there, at a time when there were few masters of Greek in his country. Highly interesting. Dr. Clarke says this little volume is "liber rarissimus." Zenobius flourished 200 years after Christ.

5194 ZIMMERMANN'S (Dr. J. G.) Essay on National Pride, Englished, with his Life, by S. H. Wilcock, 8vo. *calf, gilt*, 3*s* 1797

5195 ZOOLOGICAL GARDENS, Regent's Park; a Popular Guide to, by D. W. Mitchell, *plan and plates*, 12mo. *stiff cover*, 2*s* 1853

5196 ZOOLOGIST, Sept. 1845, Nov. 1846, *sewed*, 1*s each*

5197 ZORNLIN'S (R. M.) World of Waters, Recreations in Hydrology, *plates*, 12mo. *cloth, neat*, 3*s* 6d .. .. 1850

5198 ZOTTI Grammaire Italienne et Française, par Veneroni, thick 12mo. *bound*, 4*s* (*pub. at* 8*s*) .. .. .. 1838

5199 ZOUCHE'S (Richard) Dove; or Passages of Cosmography, a Poem, reprinted from the original edition of 1613, with a Memoir and Notes by R. Walker, *portrait*, 8vo. *cloth*, 4*s* *Oxford*, 1839

"Seth Stevenson, Esq., Norwich, from his friend, the Editor." In Mr. Stevenson's writing, "Acknowledged, Oct 8, 39."

Zouche was Regius Professor of Civil Law, and Judge of the High Court of Admiralty, temp. Car. I.

5200 ZUCCHI (Bartolomeo) L'Idea del Segretario, parte quarta, 4to. 472 pages, *unbound, quite clean*, 6*s*
*Vinetia, presso la Compagnia Minima*, 1600

These Letters d'Essortatione, di Consolatione, di Preghiere, di Raccomandatione, di Difesa, &c, are written by Tasso, Annibal Caro, Jacopo Bonfadio, Aldo Manutio, and hundreds of others of the most eminent Italians.

5201 ZUINGERI (Theodori) Dissertatio Medica de adquirenda Vitæ Longevitate, 8vo. *old calf*, 2*s* .. *Basileæ, No date.*

# APPENDIX.

5202 ABBOTT'S (Jacob) Mary Bell, a Story; Wallace, a Story; *plates*, 2 vols. 18mo. *cloth*, 1*s each* .. .. 1855

5203 ACTS of the Commons of England for the Abolishing of Deans, Deans and Chapters, Canons, Prebends, &c., and also Archbishops and Bishops, 4to. *original binding*, 5*s* *R. Cotes*, 1649

5204 ÆSOPI Fabulæ, Luciani dialogi, Isocrates Orationes II., et Cebetis Tabula, Gr. et Lat., 12mo. 2*s* *Edinb., Ruddimanni,* 1723

5205 AIKIN'S (Dr. John) England Delineated; a Geographical Description of every County in England and Wales, *maps,* 8vo. *boards,* 3*s* .. .. .. .. 1803

5206 ALARDI (Lamperti) Pathologia Sacra Novi Testamenti, 12mo. *vellum wrapper, autograph of "Sam. Torshel,"* 3*s* *Lipsiæ,* 1635

5207 ALBASPINI (Gabr. *Aurelianensis Episcopi*) de Veteribus Ecclesiæ Ritibus, notæ in Concilium Eliberitanum, quosdam alios antiquos Canones, et aliquot Tertulliani libros, 4to. *old binding, much wormed,* 5*s* .. .. *Lut. Par.,* 1623

5208 ALPHABETIC Writing, Conjectural Observations on the Origin and Progress of, 3 *plates,* 8vo. *sewed, uncut,* 3*s* 6*d* 1772

Anonymous, but written by the Rev. Charles Davy, cited in *Todd's Johnson's Dict.*

5209 ALTING (Jac.) Historia Academiarum et Promotionum Acad. in populo Hebræorum, 12mo. *bound,* 2*s* 6*d* *Amst., Janson,* 1652

5210 AMAMÆ (Sixt.) Anti-Barbarus Biblicus, thick 8vo. of 1156 pages, *old calf,* 4*s* .. .. .. *Amst.,* 1628

5211 AMERICA and the Americans, by a Citizen of the World, 8vo. *boards,* 4*s* 6*d* (*pub. at* 12*s*) .. *Longman,* 1833

5212 — *Bibliothecæ Americanæ Primordia,* an Attempt towards laying the Foundation of an American Library [by White Kennett, Bishop of Peterborough] 4to. *original binding,* VERY SCARCE, £1 11*s* 6*d* .. .. *London, J. Churchill,* 1713

"The books named in this Catalogue were left by will to the Society for the Propagation of the Gospel in Foreign Parts. It is to be regretted that many of the volumes have been irretrievably lost, by incautiously lending them."—*Lowndes.* This copy formerly belonged to that judicious antiquary "THOMAS TANNER," afterwards Bp. of St. Asaph, as it has his autograph, and who says "EX DONO R. V. DNI KENNET."

5213 — Caldcleugh (Alex.) Travels in South America, in 1819-21, Brazil, Buenos Ayres, and Chili, *map and plates,* 2 vols. 8vo. *nice copy in calf,* 12*s* (*pub. at* 30*s*) *Murray,* 1825

"The author has added considerably to our stock of information concerning several parts of South America."—*Quarterly Review.* From Lord Calthorpe's Collection.

5214 — Spizelii (Theophili) Elevatio Relationis Montezinianæ de repertis in America tribubus Israeliticis; et discussio argumentorum pro Origine Gentium Americanarum Israelitica a Menasseh Ben Israel, 8vo. *original binding,* VERY SCARCE, £1 1*s* *Basileæ,* 1661

This book is not to be found in Bp. White Kennett's *Biblioth. Americanæ Primordia,* but at page 245, we read that Mr. John Dury published an Epistle to Mr. Thoroughgood, "concerning his conjecture that the *Americans* are descended from the *Israelites,* with a History of a *Portugal Jew, Antonie Monterinos,* attested by *Menasseh Ben Israel* to the same effect." This evidently relates to this book.

5215 AMESII (Guil.) Bellarminus Enervatus, 4 vols. in 1, thick 12mo. *vellum, stained,* 3*s* .. .. *Amst., Janson,* 1658

5216 AMMIANUS MARCELLINUS, Roman Historie, now translated from the Latine into English by Dr. Philemon Holland, *of the Citie of Coventrie,* folio, *original binding,* 12*s* *Adam Islip,* 1609

Dedicated to the "Maior and Aldermen of Coventrie." "The character of the Roman Nobles, by A. Marcellinus, translated by Edward Gibbon, will be found in this Roman History, chap. 31." This History extends from A.D. 97, to A.D. 377, through Constantius, Julianus, Jovianus, Valentinianus, and Valens reigns. From Lord Calthorpe's Collection.

5217 AMORY'S (Thomas) Memoirs of the Lives of Several Ladies of Great Britain, 2 vols. 12mo. *good copy in old calf*, 8*s* 1769

"An excellent notice of this Unitarian Romance will be found in the *Retrospective Review*, vol. 6."—*Lowndes.*

5218 ANACREONTIS Odæ, Græcè, accedunt Variæ Lectiones curâ Edv. Forster, sm. 8vo. *cf.*, *nt.*, 10*s* 6*d* *Londini, typis G. Bulmer*, 1802

"A very beautiful edition, printed in a large type, on thick wove paper, with elegant vignettes." "In point of typographical splendour it confers great credit on the printer."—*Dibdin.*

5219 — Odes, translated from the Greek by D. H. Urquhart, 12mo. *boards*, 2*s* .. .. .. 1787

5220 ANDREWS (Lanc. *Episc. Winton.*) Preces Privatæ, Græcè et Latinè, 12mo. *old calf, neat*, SCARCE, 6*s* *Oxonii, e Th. Sheld.* 1675

5221 — Learned Discourse of Ceremonies Retained and Used in Christian Churches, 12mo. *much injured by damp*, 2*s* .. 1653

5222 ARCHITECTURE. Bloxam's (M. H.) Principles of Gothic Ecclesiastical Architecture, 228 *woodcuts*, 12mo. *cloth*, 4*s* (*cost* 6*s*) .. .. .. .. 1846

5223 — Glossary of Terms used in Grecian, Roman, Italian, and Gothic Architecture, third edition, with the Companion, *numerous engraved plates and hundreds of woodcuts*, 3 vols. 8vo. *cloth*, £1 1*s* 1840—41

5224 ARISTOPHANES Plutus, Græcè, with Critical and Explanatory Remarks by H. P. Cookesley, 8vo. *bds.*, 3*s* 6*d* (*pub.* 7*s* 6*d*) 1834

5225 ARISTOTELIS, Epitome Doctrinæ Moralis, ex Ethicorum Aristot. collecta per Th. Golium, 8vo. *old calf*, 3*s* 6*d*
*Londini, Danielis, pro Edv. Story, Bibliopola Cantabrigiensi*, 1662

5226 ARTICLES. Ten Discourses on some of the Principal Articles of the Church of England, by W. Hancock, 12mo. *bds.*, 1*s* 6*d* 1830

5227 ATHENÆI Dipnosophistarum; sive Cœnæ Sapientum libri XV., NATALE DE COMITIBUS *Veneto, nunc primum* è Græca in Latinam linguam vertente, thick 8vo. of 1174 pages, *wormed*, 5*s*
*Basileæ, apud H. Petri*, 1556

Early translations of Athenæus are rare, there are none in English, Italian, or German, and none in French earlier than 1680.

5228 ATTERBURY (Bp. F.) Sermons, vol. 2 only, 8vo. *calf, neat*, 2*s* 1734

5229 AUSTIN (Will., Esq.,) Hæc Homo, wherein the Excellency of the Creation of Woman is described, 12mo. *limp vellum*, 6*s*
*For Ralph Mabb*, 1637

5230 BALDUINI (Frid.) Idea Dispositionum Biblicarum, 8vo. *old binding*, 2*s* .. .. .. *Wittebergæ*, 1622

5231 BALZAC'S Politics in Select Discourses, Englished, with an Account of his Life and Writings by Basil Kennett, 8vo. *old panelled calf, neat*, 2*s* 6*d* .. .. .. 1709

5232 BARETTI'S (Joseph) Italian-English and English-Italian Dictionary and Grammar, corrected by F. Damiani, 2 vols. in 1, 4to. *old calf, neat*, 10*s* .. .. .. .. 1798

Autograph of "Fredk. Bevan, Emanuel College, Cambridge," late of Carleton Rode, Norfolk.

5233 S. BARNABÆ Apostoli (A.D. 34) Epistola Catholica et Hermæ (A.D. 65) Pastor, 18mo. *stained*, 2*s* 6*d* *Oxoniæ*, 1685

5234 BASTWICK (Joh.) Elenchus Religionis Papisticæ, 8vo. *much stained by damp*, 3*s* .. .. .. *Londini*, 1627

5235 BAXTER'S (Rich.) Gildas Salvianus, the Reformed Pastor, shewing the Nature of the Pastoral Work, 2nd edition, thick 8vo. of 634 pages, *old calf, neat*, 6*s* .. .. 1657

This edition has a large Appendix answering objections to the former edition. Autograph of "Fredk. Bevan, Easton."

5236 BEACHCROFT'S (R. P.) Plain Scriptural Sermons, 2 vols. 8vo. *boards*, 6*s* .. .. .. .. 1816

5237 BEAUSOBRE and L'Enfant's Introduction to the Reading of the Holy Scriptures, 4to. *old calf, neat*, 3*s* .. 1734

5238 BECMANI (Christ.) Manuductio ad Latinam Linguam anno 1608; nec non de originibus Latinæ Linguæ, thick 8vo. of 1350 pages, *old calf*, 6*s* .. .. .. *Hanoviæ*, 1629

"Becmannus in Præfatione multa habet de Latinitate notatu digna."—*Morhoff.*

5239 BEDÆ (Venerab.) Epistolæ duæ, necnon Vitæ Abbatum Wiremuthensium et Girwiensium; accessit Egberti Archiepisc. Ebor. Bedæ Æqualis Dialogus de Ecclesiastica Institutione, ex Antiq. Cod. MSS. et Notis illustravit Jac. Waræus, 8vo. *old binding*, 5*s* *Dublinii*, 1664

5240 BELL'S (Charles) System of Dissections, explaining the Anatomy of the Human Body, the Manner of Displaying the parts, and their Varieties in Disease, 30 *plates*, 2 vols. in 1, royal folio, *boards*, 15*s* . .. .. .. 1810

5241 BELLARMINUS (Rob. *Cardinalis*) de Scriptoribus Ecclesiasticis, et brevi Chronologia ab Orbe condito ad an. 1630, thick 8vo. of 600 pages, *old calf*, 6*s* .. .. *Parisiis*, 1630

5242 BENNET'S (Dr. Tho.) Directions for Studying, and on the 39 Articles of Religion.—S. Hieronymi Epistola ad Nepotianum de Vita Clericorum.—Welchman, 39 Articuli Eccles. Ang., in 1 vol. 8vo. *calf*, 3*s* .. .. .. 1724-27

5243 BERGERAC (Cyrano de) Satyrical Characters and handsome Descriptions, in Letters, Englished, 8vo. *old binding*, 4*s* 1658

For an account of this singular and amusing work, see *Retrospective Review*, vol. I.

5244 BERKENHOUT'S (Dr.) Letters to his Son at the University, 8vo. *boards*, 2*s* .. .. .. *Cambridge*, 1790

5245 BERTRAM—The Book of Bertram the Priest concerning the Body and Blood of the Lord, Latin and English, 12mo. *old calf, scarce*, 5*s* .. .. .. .. 1686

This edition has a large Historical Dissertation of 125 pages concerning the author of this work.

5246 BEVEREGII (Guil.) Institutiones Chronologicæ, 4to. *old calf*, 9*s* *Londini*, 1669

In the same volume, Jacobi Usserii Chronologia Sacra, accurante Tho. Barlow, *Oxoniæ*, 1660.—Jac. Usserii de Romanæ Ecclesiæ Symbolo Apostolico Vetere, aliisque Fidei formulis, *Oxonii*, 1660.

5247 — Codex Canonum Ecclesiæ Primitivæ vindicatus ac illustratus, 4to. *old calf, stained*, 4*s* 6*d* .. *Londini*, 1678

5248 BEVEROVICII (Joh.) de Vitæ Termino, Fatali an Mobili? sm. 8vo. *old calf*, 4*s* .. .. .. *Dordrechti*, 1634

At the end two other Treatises by Beverovicius. 1. Medicinæ Encomium. 2. Reputatio Argumentorum, quibus necessitatem Medicinæ impugnat *Mich. Seigneur de Montaigne.*

5249 BEZA (Theod.) de Hæreticis a Civili Magistratu puniendis, adversus M. Bellium, 8vo. *vellum*, 5*s* .. *R. Stephani*, 1554

This rare work was written by Beza in defence of the Execution of Servetus, and in answer to *Castalio*, who under the name of *Bellius* published a tract "*de Hereticis gladio non puniendis.*"

5250 BIRD'S (Dr. Golding) Lectures on Electricity and Galvanism, *cuts*, 12mo. *cloth*, 3*s* (*cost* 5*s* 6*d*) .. *Longmans*, 1849

5251 BISCOE'S (Richard) History of the Acts of the Apostles, 8vo. *cloth*, 9*s* 6*d* .. .. *Oxford, the Clarendon*, 1840

5252 BLACK'S (Wm.) Practical Treatise on Brewing, 5th edit., 8vo. *cloth*, 5*s* 6*d* (*pub. at* 10*s* 6*d*) .. *Longmans*, 1854

5253 BLASII (Gerardi, M.D.) Anatome Animalium, 60 *plates*, 4to. *old vellum*, 9*s* .. .. *Amstelodami*, 1681

5254 BLOUNT (Edw.) Ars Aulica; or the Courtiers Arte, 12mo. *old vellum wrapper*, 4*s* .. .. *M. Bradwood*, 1607

5255 BODLEIAN LIBRARY—CATALOGUS Universalis Librorum in Bibliotheca Bodleiana, accessit APPENDIX Librorum, auctore THOMA JAMES, *Oxoniæ*, 1620.—Catalogus Interpretum S. Scripturæ juxta numerorum ordinem, quo extant in Bibliotheca Bodleiana, *Oxoniæ*, 1635.—APPENDIX ad Catalogum Librorum in Bib. Bodleiana, qui prodiit A.D. 1620, editio secunda, *Oxoniæ*, 1635.—in 1 vol. thick 4to. *old calf, very neat, and rare*, £2 2*s* *Oxoniæ*, 1620-35

This is a very curious and complete copy of the 2nd edition of Dr. Thomas James's Catalogue of the Bodleian Library. The 1st part, which is dedicated to K. James I. and Prince Charles, consists of 539 pages, besides the Proemium, signed Tho. James, 5 leaves. The 1st Appendix has 36 pages. The Cat. Interp. S. Scripturae, has 55 pages, and the 2nd Appendix, done by John Rouse, 208 pages.

5256 BOLINGBROKE'S (Henry St. John, Lord Viscount) Works, vols. 1, 3, 4, 5, 4to. *old calf, gilt, a fine copy*, £1 10*s* 1754

Lord Calthorpe's copy, with his book-plate.

5257 BOXHORNII (M. Z.) Quæstiones Romanæ, accedunt Plutarchi Questiones Romanæ, Gr. et Lat., cum Boxhornii Commentario, 4to. *unbound*, 2*s* 6*d* .. .. *L. Bat.*, 1637

5258 BOYER'S French-English and English-French Dictionary, 8vo. *bound*, 2*s* 6*d* .. .. .. 1761

5259 BRADLEY'S (John) Impartial View of the Truth of Christianity, with the History of the Life and Miracles of Apollonius Tyanæus, 12mo. *old calf*, 2*s* 6*d* .. .. 1699

With an account of Josephus's Testimony concerning Christ; Of the Oracles of the Sibylls; and Reflexions on Blount's Oracles of Reason.

5260 BRADY'S (Dr. Robert) Introduction to the Old English History in Three Tracts, with an Appendix of Records to the End of Henry III., and a Glossary, small folio, *old calf, neat*, 10*s* 6*d* 1684

This volume usually accompanies Dr. Brady's Tory History of England, it is an answer to Sir William Petyt, Selden, and Atwood's 3 Treatises; the Glossary expounds words used in Ancient Records, Laws, and Histories.

5261 BRAGGE'S (Francis) Practical Observations upon the Miracles and Parables of our blessed Saviour, 4 vols. 8vo. *old calf, neat*, 12*s* 1710

5262 BRIGHTWELL'S (Miss) Stories about Birds, *coloured plate,* 18mo. *cloth, gilt,* 2*s* 6*d* .. .. .. 1859

5263 BRISSONII (Barnabæ) de Formulis et Sollemnibus populi Romani Verbis, thick 4to. above 800 pages, *old calf, neat,* 12*s* *Francofurti,* 1592

5264 — another indifferent copy, 4to. *old binding,* 5*s* *ib.,* 1592

5265 BRYANT'S (Jacob) Observations upon some Passages in Scripture, which the Enemies to Religion have thought most Obnoxious, and attended with Difficulties not to be surmounted, *portrait inserted,* 4to. *half calf, neat,* 12*s* .. .. 1803

In the same volume also by Bryant, "Dissertations on the wind Euroclydon; the Island Melita; an Account of Egypt in its most early state; and of the Shepherd Kings," *Cambridge,* 1767, *with maps and plates of coins, &c.* Two very learned works, the latter sold for £1 4*s* at the Roxburghe sale: at Gosset's, £1 2*s*; at Heath's, £1 3*s*

5266 BUDDICOM'S (R. P.) Sermons on Important Points of Faith and Duty, 2 vols. 12mo. *boards,* 5*s* (*pub. at* 10*s*) 1822

5267 BUXTORFII (Johan.,) Tiberias, sive Commentarius Masorethicus, 4to. *old calf,* 5*s* .. .. *Basileæ,* 1620

5268 — Institutio Epistolaris Hebraica, cum Epistolarum Hebraicarum Centuria, 8vo. *old calf,* 4*s* .. .. *ib.,* 1629

5269 — de Abbreviaturis Hebraicis, cui accesserunt operis Talmudici brevis recensio, cum ejusdem librorum; Item Bibliotheca Rabbinica, 8vo. *old binding,* 4*s* .. .. *ib.,* 1640

5270 — (J. *Filii*) Tractatus de Punctorum, Vocalium, et Accentuum, in Vet. Test. Hebr. Originè, Antiquitate et Authoritate, 4to. *old calf,* 5*s* .. .. .. *ib.,* 1648

5271 — (Joh. *Filii*) Anticritica; seu Vindiciæ Veritatis Hebraicæ, adversus L. Capellum, thick 4to. *calf, above* 1000 *pages, old binding,* 7*s* 6*d* .. .. .. *ib.,* 1653

5272 BYRON'S Poetical Works, 200 *engravings by Kenny Meadows, B. Foster, and others,* large 8vo. *cloth, elegant,* 8*s* (*cost* 15*s*) 1858

5273 CÆSAR'S Commentaries, in English, by Professor Duncan, 8vo. *boards,* 3*s* 6*d* (*pub. at* 9*s* 6*d*) .. .. 1824

5274 — Julius Celsus de Vita et Rebus Gestis C. Julii Cæsaris, 12mo. *neat,* 2*s* 6*d* .. .. .. *Londini,* 1697

5275 CAMOENS Poems, translated from the Portuguese, with Remarks on his Life and Writings by Lord Strangford, *portrait,* 12mo. *boards,* 3*s* .. .. .. .. 1804

5276 CAMPANELLA (Thomas, *an Italian Friar, and Second Machiavel*) his Advice to the King of Spain for Attaining the Universal Monarchy of the World, Englished by Ed. Chilmead, 4to. *old calf,* 5*s* .. .. .. .. 1659

Published with an admonitory Preface by William Prynne, of Lincolne's Inne, Esq., to warn the English people against the evil tendency of this tract, which was written about the end of Q. Elizabeth's reign, with a particular view to the subjugation of England.

5277 CAMPIANI (Edmundi) RATIONES DECEM quibus fretus Certamen Adversariis obtulit in Causa Fidei, cum Vita et Epistolæ, 12mo. *original binding,* £1 11*s* 6*d* .. *Cosmopoli,* 1581

This would appear to be the FIRST EDITION, and is, of course, EXCESSIVELY RARE. These reasons, which the Roman Catholics, according to *Wood,* count an Epitome of all their doctrines, were first printed in the house of one *Stonor,* a Catholic gentleman, living near to Henley in Oxfordshire, an. 1581, and were so difficult to procure in Q. Elizabeth's time, that Lord Burleigh who wished Bp. Aylmer to answer them, could not meet with a copy for that purpose.

5278 CANTING CREW. A New Dictionary of the Terms, Ancient and Modern, of the Canting Crew, in its several Tribes, Gypsies, Beggars, Thieves, Cheats, &c., by B. E. Gent, 8vo. *old binding, scarce*, 7*s* 6*d*
*London, for W. Hawes, at the Rose, in Ludgate Street, no date*

5279 CAPELLI (Jacobi) Observationes in Novum Testamentum, cum Lud. Cappelli Spicilegio, 4to. *old calf*, 3*s* *Amst., Elz.*, 1657

5280 CARDINALS. History of the Cardinals of the Roman Church, from their first Creation to Pope Clement the Ninth, with a Full Account of his Conclave, Englished by J. H., small folio, *original binding*, 7*s* 6*d* .. .. 1670

From the Italian, by the author of "Il Nipotismo di Roma."

5281 CARR'S (William, *Gentleman, Consul at Amsterdam*) Remarks of the Government of several parts of Germanie, Denmark, Sweedland, the United Provinces, &c., 12mo. *old binding, curious*, 3*s* 6*d*
*Amsterdam*, 1688

5282 CARTER'S (Matt.) Honor Redivivus; or the Analysis of Honor and Armory, *Arms*, 8vo. 3rd edition, *bound*, 3*s* 6*d* 1673

This is the best edition, but it is much stained by damp.

5283 CARY'S (H.) Law of England, a Guide for all Persons concerned in Ecclesiastical Courts, 12mo. Black Letter, *bound*, 2*s*
*For the Author*, 1646

5284 CAVE (Guil.) Chartophylax Ecclesiasticus, quo propè M.D. Scriptores Ecclesiastici breviter indicantur, 8vo. *old binding*, 3*s*
*Londini*, 1684

5285 CAXTON (WILLIAM) The GAME OF CHESS reproduced in Facsimile from a Copy in the British Museum, with a few Remarks on Caxton's Typographical Productions by Vincent Figgins, 23 *curious woodcuts*, 4to. Black Letter, 184 *pages, half morocco*, £1 1*s* .. .. *John Russell Smith*, 1860

5286 — another copy, *in antique calf, very appropriately bound*, £1 8*s* 1860

This is a great curiosity, a facsimile of the first book printed in England, by William Caxton, shortly after 1474, when the first edition was put forth. The paper upon which this is printed was made expressly for it, with the reed and water marks imitated from the original, and Mr. Figgins says, "My motive in producing this book has been partly to enable my contemporaries better to appreciate the industry of our worthy countryman, William Caxton, but more especially to assist in raising funds for the completion and endowment of a benevolent institution for decayed Printers, at Wood Green, Tottenham." As this is very praiseworthy, I give the notice such publicity as this Catalogue will afford.

5287 CERVANTES (Miguel) Les Nouvelles de, où sont contenuës plusieurs rares advantures et memorables exemples d'Amour, de Fidelité, de force de Sang, de Jalousie, &c. thick 8vo. of 695 pages, *vellum, neat*, 10*s* 6*d* .. .. .. *Paris*, 1633

Not in Brunet, with the autograph of "*E. Macro, ex dono D. Petr. Fernandez, Lusitani, M.D.*, 1705."

5288 — Dialogue between Scipio and Berganza, two Dogs of Toledo, with the Comical History of Rincon and Cortado, 12mo. *old calf*, 2*s* 6*d* .. .. .. .. 1767

5289 CHAMBERS'S (Sir William) Treatise on the Decorative part of CIVIL ARCHITECTURE, with Notes and an Essay on the Principles of Design in Architecture by John B. Papworth, *plates*, imperial 4to. LARGE PAPER, *cloth*, £2 18*s* (*pub. at* £4 14*s* 6*d*) .. .. .. 1826

This fine edition is illustrated by 53 *plates*, to which Mr. Papworth has added 9 *more* illustrative of Grecian Architecture. "Mr. Chambers's Treatise on Civil Architecture, is the most sensible book, and the most exempt from prejudices, that ever was written on that science."—*Horace Walpole*. "An accurate and precise Treatise, equally acceptable to the Architect, the Connoisseur, and the Builder."—*Lowndes*.

5290 CHAMBERS'S (W. & R.) Edinburgh Journal, vols. 1 to 9 and 11, royal 8vo. *cloth*, 21*s* (*cost* 45*s*) .. .. 1844-49

5291 CHAPPELL (Will., Bp. of Cork) Preacher; or, the Art and Method of Preaching, with a List of Books recommended, 12mo. *old binding, curious*, 5*s* .. .. .. 1656

This is the 1st English translation of this curious little volume.

5292 CHARLES I. [Dr. Peter Heylin's] Observations on [Hamon L' Estrange's] Historie of the Reign of King Charles, for Rectification of some Mistakes, 12mo. *bound*, 4*s* .. 1656

5293 CHARLES I. and II.—a volume of 7 Tracts, the titles of which follow:—

1.—Lachrymæ Cantabrigienses in *Obitum* HENRIETTÆ Caroli Imi Regis et Martyris *Filiæ*, Ducissæ Aurelianensis (Orleans) *Cantabrigiæ*, 1670
2.—Musarum Cantabrigiensium Threnodia, (*wants the title*) *No date.*
3.—Academiæ Cantabrigiens.s ΣΩΣΤΡΑ. sive, ad Carolum II. reducem, de Regnis ipsi, Musis per ipsum feliciter restitutis Gratulatio, (*wants a leaf at the end*) .. .. .. *Cantab.*, 1660
4.—Anagrammata Regia; in honorem maximi et mansuetissimi Regis Caroli conscripta, opusculum Regiis *Nuptiis* destinatum *Londini*, 1626
5.—Eucharistica Oxoniensia in Caroli e Scotia reditum Gratulatoria *Oxoniæ*, 1641
6.—Britannia Rediviva, (*wants title*) .. .. *ib.*, 1660
7.—Genethliacum illustrissimorum Principum Caroli et Mariæ a Musis Cantabrigiensibus celebratum (not in *Lowndes*) *Cantab.*, 1631

a singularly curious collection, in 1 vol. small thick 4to. *old calf, very neat*, £2 2*s* .. .. .. V.Y.

5294 CHEPMELL'S (Dr. Edward C.) Domestic Homœopathy, with Rules for Diet and Regimen, &c., 12mo. *cloth*, 2*s* 6*d* (*pub. at* 5*s*) .. .. .. .. 1850

5295 CICERONIS Epistolæ ad Atticum, ad Brutum et ad Q. Fratrem, J. M. Bruti in easdem Scholia, 12mo. *neat*, RARE, 5*s* *Lugduni, Gryphii*, 1571

5296 — de Oratore, cum P. Melancthonis castigationibus et Scholiis, 8vo. *old calf, neat*, 6*s* .. *Londini, Joannes Kingston*, 1573

5297 — de Oratore, de Claris Oratoribus, Oratoriæ Partitiones, et Topica, curante Alex. Stewart, 8vo. *calf, very neat*, 6*s* (*cost* 15*s*) *Edinburgi*, 1812

5298 CLAGETT'S (Dr. Will.) Discourse on the Operations of the Holy Spirit, with a Confutation of Dr. J. Owen on that subject, 8vo. *bound*, 3*s* .. .. .. .. 1678

5299 CLARKE'S (Dr. ADAM) BIBLE, containing the Old and New Testaments, with a Commentary and Critical Notes, 8 vols. 4to. *newly and neatly half bound in brown russia, marbled leaves, a very capital set of the original edition*, £7 7*s* .. 1836

5300 CLARK'S (Sa. *of Bennet Fink*) Mirrour or Looking-Glasse both for Saints and Sinners, held forth in about 2000 Examples, 2nd edition, much enlarged, *old binding*, RARE, 10*s* 6*d* 1654

With *brilliant impressions* of his *portrait* and of the engraved title by *R. Gaywood.*

5301 COCUS (Robt.) Censura quorundam Scriptorum, quæ sub Nominibus Sanctorum et Veterum Auctorum, à Pontificiis citari solent, 4to. *old binding, curious*, 7*s* 6*d* *Londini, R. Field*, 1623

In Lowndes, under *Cooke*. This author "who writes himself Cocus, became a man learned in the Church, singularly well studied in the disquisition of antiquity, especially for discerning the proper works of the fathers from the forged and counterfeit."—*Wood's Athenæ Oxon.*

5302 COLE'S (E.) English Dictionary, containing many Thousands of Hard Words not in any other, 8vo. *bound*, 3*s* .. 1696

5303 COMMON PRAYER. A Survey of the Booke of Common Prayer, by way of 197 Quæres grounded upon 58 places, with a View of LONDON MINISTERS exceptions, small 8vo. *extremely scarce*, £1 11*s* 6*d* .. .. *Anno Domini*, 1610

This is the 2nd Edition, "Reviewed, corrected, and augmented," of this VERY RARE little volume. In Lowndes is a "Defence of the Minister's reasons for refusal of Subscription to the B. of C. Prayer, 1607," *but this is not mentioned.* It is annotated by some one of the period.

5304 COMSTOCK and Hoblyn's Manual of Natural Philosophy, 281 *woodcuts*, 12mo. *cloth*, 3*s* 6*d* (*cost* 6*s*) .. 1847

5305 CONSTANTINI Porphyrogennetæ Imperatoris Opera, in quibus Tactica nunc primùm prodeunt, Gr. et Lat., Joannes Meursius edidit, thick 8vo. *good copy in old calf*, 7*s* 6*d* *L. Bat., Elz.*, 1617

Son of Leo the wise, born at Constantinople in 905. He was so attached to literature, that he neglected the concerns of his empire. Poisoned by his son for living too long.

5306 CRESTS. Book of Family Crests, all the Bearings properly Blazoned and Explained, 4000 *engravings*, Dictionary of Mottoes, &c., 2 vols. 12mo. *cloth*, 8*s* 6*d* (*pub. at* 21*s*) *Washbourne*, 1840

5307 CROSS'S (Walter) Taghmical Art, the Art of Expounding Scripture by the Points, usually called Accents, 8vo. *old binding, curious*, 3*s* .. .. *For the Author*, 1698

5308 CUMBERLAND (Rich.) de Legibus Naturæ, quinetiam Elementa Philosophiæ Hobbianæ refutantur, 4to. *old calf*, 4*s* *Londini*, 1672

"Bp. Cumberland being told by some of his friends that he would weary himself out by intense application, replied, *It is better to wear out than to rust out.*"—*Bp. Horne.*

5309 CURTIS'S (John H.) Treatise on the Physiology and Pathology of the Ear, *plates*, 8vo. *boards*, 4*s* (*pub. at* 7*s* 6*d*) *Longmans*, 1836

5310 DARES Phrygius, de Bello Trojano, Latino Carmine à Josepho (Hall) Exoniensi elegantiss. redditi, curâ et Studio Jo. Mori, 8vo. *old binding, scarce*, 6*s* .. .. *Londini*, 1675

"Editio præclara."—*Hebenstreit.* Cannot find it in Lowndes. This copy belonged to *Francis Blomefield*, the Norfolk Historian, and has his *autograph* and Book-plate.

5311 DAVIES (J., *of Kidwelly*,) Instructions for History; with a Character of the most considerable Historians, Ancient and Modern, sm. 8vo. *old calf*, 10*s* .. .. .. 1680

This should be in Lowndes, but it is not, it is a very scarce little book.

5312 DAVISON'S (John) Discourses on Prophecy, its Structure, Use, and Inspiration, 8vo. *cloth*, 9*s* .. *Oxford, Parker*, 1856

5313 DELILLES'S French Grammar.—1. Accidence.—2. Syntax, written in French, 12mo. *bound*, 3*s* .. .. 1853

5314 DES CARTES (Renati) Epistolæ, *plates*, 3 parts in 2 vols. 4to. *old binding*, 10*s* .. .. *Lond., et Amst.*, 1668-83

"A man of an astonishing depth of mind and compass of thought."—*Dr. A. Clarke.*

5315 — Life, containing the History of his Philosophy and Works, 8vo. *old calf*, 3*s* .. .. .. .. 1693

5316 DIBDIN'S (Dr. T. F.) Typographical Antiquities, *portraits*, 4 vols. 4to. *very fine set, newly half bound in brown russia, marbled leaves*, £6 6*s* .. .. .. .. 1810-19

5317 DICKENS'S Little Dorrit, in 20 numbers complete, 40 *plates*, 8vo. original edition, 10*s* (*pub. at* 20*s*) .. .. 1857

5318 DICTIONARY. (Old) Withal's Dictionary in English and Latin, for Children, recognized by Dr. Evans, Abr. Fleming, William Clerk, and B. R., thick small 8vo. of 623 pages, Black and Roman Letter, *old binding*, RARE, £1 1*s* *London, Tho. Purfoot*, 1623

This appears to be the *last* edition of a book, which was *first* printed by Wynkyn de Worde.

5319 — Cockeram's (Henry) English Dictionarie, or Interpreter of Hard Words, 4th edition, 12mo. *old vellum*, 5*s* .. 1632

5320 — Bulloker (Dr. John) English Expositour, Interpreting the hardest Words and Terms of Art in our Language, by a Lover of the Arts, 12mo. 3*s* 6*d* .. .. *Cambridge*, 1680

The last edition of a work first printed in 1616.

5321 DIOGENES, *numerous humorous plates*, vols. 1 and 2, 4to. *cloth*, 5*s* .. .. .. .. 1853

5322 DODWELL'S (Archdeacon) Athanasian Creed, Vindicated and Explained, 12mo. *sewed*, 1*s* 6*d* .. *Oxford*, 1802

5323 DORRINGTON'S (Theophilus) Reform'd Devotions in Meditations, Hymns, and Petitions for Every Day in the Week; contains also An Holy Office, Before, At, and After Receiving the Sacrament, by Dr. Edward Lake, 18mo. *old calf*, 3*s* 6*d* 1724

5324 DRUSII (Joan.) Opuscula, quæ ad Grammaticam spectant, *Franek.*, 1609.—I. Drusii in librum primum Hasmonæorum Comment. sive Notæ, 1600.—Alberici Gentilis ad primum Macbæorum disputatio, *dedicated to Toby Matthews, Bp. of Durham, Franek.*, 1600.—Liber Hasmonæorum qui vulgo prior Machabæorum, Gr. et Lat., cum Notis J. Drusii, in 1 vol. 4to. *old calf, neat*, 10*s* *Franekeræ*, 1600-9

5325 — Annotationes in Nov. Test., *Franek.*, 1612.—Drusii ad Voces Ebraicas Nov. Test. Comment. duplex, nec non Vitæ, operumque I. Drusii editorum, per Abel Curiandrum, 2 vols. in 1, *old binding*, 6*s* .. .. .. *ib.*, 1616

"Drusius was the most noted critic, linguist, and theologist of his day, well versed in the Rabbins, &c."—*Walchius.*

5326 [DU MOULIN (Lud.)] Jugulum Causæ, 2 parts in 1 vol. thick 8vo. of above 700 pages, *old binding*, 6*s* *Londini*, 1671

5327 DUNLOP'S (John) Philosophy of Artificial and Compulsory Drinking Usages in Great Britain and Ireland, 12mo. *cloth*, 2*s* 6*d* 1839

5328 DWIGHT'S (Dr. Timothy) Sermons, 2 vols. 8vo. *boards*, 12*s* (*pub. at* 24*s*) .. .. .. *Edinburgh*, 1828

5329 EGYPT, a Description of the Land, People, and Produce, *map and 53 engravings*, 12mo. *cloth*, 3*s* (*pub. at* 5*s* 6*d*) 1839

5330 ELECTRIC Science, its History, Phenomena, and Applications, by F. C. Bakewell, *plates*, 8vo. *cloth*, 2*s* 6*d* .. 1853

5331 EPICURUS'S Morals, faithfully translated, with an Apologie for Epicurus by W. Charleton, *fine head*, small 4to. *old binding*, 3*s* 6*d* .. .. .. .. 1656

5332 EPISCOPIUS'S (Dr. Simon) Popish Labyrinth, with an Account of Episcopius's Life and Death, as also of the Life and Death of James Arminius, *portrait of each*, small 8vo. *old calf, scarce*, 6*s* .. .. .. .. 1673

5333 EPISTOLÆ Clarorum Virorum, sm. 8vo. *old vellum*, 6*s* *Coloniæ*, 1569

Some of these Letters are written by Hermolaus Barbarus, as far back as 1484, some as late as 1563, by many illustrious persons.

5334 ESPERNON. Histoire de la Vie du Duc d'Espernon, par Guil. Girard, *portrait*, folio, *a fine copy in vellum*, 12*s* *Paris*, 1655

Jean Louis de la Vallette duc d'Espernon was a Peer and Colonel General of France, and Governor of Guienne, the History extends from 1570 to 1642. Charles Cotton translated this Life into English, in 1670. Espernon was the last Knight of the Garter elected in the reign of Cha. I.

5335 EUSTACE'S (John C.) Classical Tour through Italy, An. 1802, *map and plans*, 4 vols. 8vo. *calf*, (*Lord Calthorpe's copy*,) *a very nice one*, £1 1*s* .. .. .. 1815

5336 EUTICHII Patriarchæ Alexandrini Ecclesiæ suæ Origines, Arabicæ, nunc primum typis edidit ac Versione et Commentario auxit Jo. Selden, 4to. *old binding*, 6*s* .. *Londini*, 1642

"Among the Arabians, no author acquired a higher reputation than Eutychius, Bishop of Alexandria."—*Mosheim.*

5337 FAMILY HERALD, a Domestic Amusing Magazine, full of Tales, Bon Mots, &c., 1855, 1856, 1857, 3 vols. 4to. *cloth*, 3*s* *each*

5338 FARINDON'S (Anthony) Sermons, with his Life, by the Rev. Thomas Jackson, 4 vols. thick 8vo. *cloth*, *good as new*, £1 8*s* (*pub. at* £2 8*s*) .. .. .. 1849

These highly esteemed Sermons were originally printed in folio, in 1672-4. This edition, the only reprint there is, has a preface by Mr. James Nichols, who says Mr. Jackson has a most accurate knowledge of the literature of the age in which Farindon lived, and therefore, was very competent to write his Life and edit his works.

5339 FEARNE (Dr. H.) Certain Considerations of Present Concernment touching this Reformed Church of England, in Answer to An. Champny, 8vo. *unbound*, 3*s* .. .. 1653

5340 FENESTELLA de Magistratibus, Sacerdotisque Romanorum.—POMPONIUS LÆTUS itidem de Magistratibus et Sacerdotiis, small 8vo. *old calf, very scarce*, 9*s* *Lutetiæ, Rob. Stephani*, 1549

A curious and scarce edition, and what is singular, is, that Mr. Greswell does not enumerate it in his Lives and Works of the Stephani.

5341 FLUTE, a word or two on the, by W. N. James, 12mo. *boards*, 3*s* 6*d* (*pub. at* 8*s*) .. .. *Edinburgh*, 1826

5342 FORMULARIES of Faith, put forth by Authority, temp. Henry VIII., 8vo. *cloth*, 7*s* *Oxford, the Clarendon*, 1856

Contains reprints of these scarce books; 1. Articles about Religion, 1536. 2. The Institution of a Christian Man, 1537. 3. A Necessary doctrine and Erudition for any Christian Man, 1543.

5343 FOSTER'S (John) Essay on the different Nature of Accent and Quantity, with the Greek Poem of MUSURUS, and a Latin Version and Notes, 2nd edition, 8vo. *nice copy, old calf, gilt,* 7*s* 6*d* *Eton,* 1763

The best edition of "an admirable work."—*Lowndes.* Has sold for 22*s* and 23*s* at sales.

5344 FRANCE, Travels in, during 1814-15, comprising a Residence at Paris during the stay of the Allied Armies, and at Aix, at Buonaparte's landing, 2 vols. 8vo. *half calf, neat,* 6*s* *Edinb.,* 1816

5345 FRANCIS'S (G.) Dictionary of the Arts, Sciences, and Manufactures, 1100 *engravings,* 8vo. *cloth,* 5*s* (*cost* 10*s*) 1849

5346 FULLER (Nich.) Miscellanea Sacra, thick 8vo. of 787 pages, *old calf,* 7*s* 6*d* .. .. *Argentorati,* 1650

"The best edition of this learned work was published at Strasburg, in 1650. It includes a considerable number of curious and important discussions. The book ought to have a place in every critical library. The author was one of the best oriental scholars of his time." See *Orme's Bibliotheca Biblica.*

5347 FYSSHYNGE—The Treatise of Fysshynge wyth an Angle, attributed to Dame Juliana Berners, *plates,* 8vo. *calf, very neat, scarce,* 7*s* 6*d* *Pickering,* 1826

Reprinted from Wynkyn de Worde's Edition of the Book of St. Alban's, of 1496, with Baskerville type.

5348 GALE'S (Theophilus) Court of the Gentiles, a complete copy with the Treatise of DIVINE PREDETERMINATION, 5 parts in 2 thick vols. 4to. *a fine copy in calf,* VERY SCARCE, £3 13*s* 6*d* 1672-78

5349 GALLAUDET'S (Thomas H.) Discourses on Various Points of Christian Faith and Practice delivered in the Chapel of the Oratoire, Paris, in 1816, 8vo. *boards,* 3*s* 6*d* .. 1818

5350 GARDINER (Rich., *Herefordensis,*) Orationes, Epistolæ et Carmina, 8vo. *old binding,* 3*s* .. .. *Oxoniæ,* 1668

5351 GARNET—True and Perfect Relation of the Whole Proceedings against the late most barbarous Traitors, Garnet, a Jesuite, and his Confederates, with the Lords Commissioner's Speeches, and of all that passed at Garnet's Execution, 4to. *old vellum, stained,* 9*s* .. .. .. .. 1606

This is the genuine and original account of the trials of those concerned in the Popish Plot.

5352 GOLDSMITH'S Animated Nature, *numerous coloured plates,* 4 small vols. *cloth,* 5*s* 6d (*cost* £1 2*s* 6*d*) .. .. 1839

5353 GRADUS ad Parnassum; sive, novus Synonemorum, Epithetorum, Versuum ac Phrasium Poeticarum Thesaurus, 8vo. *bound,* 3*s* 6*d* (*cost* 7*s* 6*d*) .. .. .. *Londini,* 1817

5354 GRAMMARS.—Harris (Ri.) Latin Grammar, *wants title,* 1624.—Tabulæ Joannis Murmellii in Artis Componendorum Versuum Rudimenta, *Coloniæ, Io. Gymnicus,* 1535.—De Syllabarum et Carminum ratione, libri II., authore Rod. Gualthero, *Tiguri, Chr. Froschover,* 1542.—Du Moulin's Elements of Logic, by Nat. Delaune, Bach. of Arts in Cambridge, 1624.—in 1 vol. small thick 8vo. *curious,* 12*s* .. .. .. V.Y.

I possess a very curious collection of old English, Greek, Latin, and Hebrew Grammars, which I have not time now to catalogue, but which may be seen at my house. They appear to have been put together about 150 years ago.

5355 GREEN'S (Robert, *of Clare Hall,*) Demonstration of the Truth and Divinity of the Christian Religion, 8vo. *calf,* 2s *Cambridge,* 1711

5356 GREEN (Will., *Hardingham, Norfolk,*) Poetical Parts of the Old Test., newly translated from the Hebrew, with Notes, Critical and Explanatory, 4to. *calf, very neat,* 6s *Cambridge,* 1781

"These translations are, in general, very accurate and elegant specimens of biblical interpretation, the notes discover much good taste and sound criticism."—*Orme.*

5357 GREGORII Magni Episc. Romani de Cura Pastorali liber verè aureus, editus a Jer. Stephano, small 8vo. *limp vellum,* 6s *Londini,* 1629

5358 GROTII (Hugonis) Annales et Historiæ de Rebus Belgicis, folio, *a fine copy in vellum,* 10s 6d .. *Amst., Jo. Bleau,* 1657

With *a very fine impression of the portrait of Grotius, by W. Delff,* and this autograph, "*Christoph Schrader.*" From Lord Calthorpe's collection.

5359 GUAZZO (Stefano, *Gentil'huomo di Casile*) Lettere del, small thick 8vo. *limp vellum,* 5s .. *Vinegia, B. Barezzi,* 1596

5360 HAKEWILL (Dr. Geo. *Archdeacon of Surrey,*) Apologie, or Declaration of the Power and Providence of God in the Government of the World, *engraved title by T. Cecill, mounted,* folio, *old calf,* 7s 6d *Oxford, W. Turner,* 1630

Highly spoken of by Dr. Johnson in his Life of Milton. "The production of an uncommonly liberal and enlightened mind, well stored with various and choice learning, collected both from Ancient and Modern authors."—*Dugald Stewart.*

5361 HARRINGTON (I.) Art of Law-Giving, in 3 books, with an Appendix concerning an House of Peers, sm. 8vo. *old calf,* 5s 1659

5362 HARROD'S (Henry) Gleanings among the Castles and Convents of Norfolk, *plates,* 8vo. LARGE PAPER, *cloth,* 25s *Norwich,* 1857

5363 HAWKER'S (Rob.) Morning and Evening Portions, 2 vols. 12mo. *cloth,* 3s .. .. .. .. 1846

5364 HEART'S EASE, by the Author of the Heir of Redclyffe, 2 vols. 12mo. *cloth,* (vol. 1 wants title) 4s *(pub. at 12s)* 1854

5365 HERALDRY—Clarke's (Hugh) Introduction to Heraldry, *plates,* 12mo. *cloth,* 5s (*pub. at* 7s 6d) .. .. 1854

5366 HERODOTI Historia, Græcè, cum Vita Homeri, 2 vols. 18mo. *cloth,* 6s .. .. *Oxonii, Parker,* 1858

5367 HEWITT'S (W.) Essay on the Encroachments of the German Ocean along the Norfolk Coast, *plates,* 8vo. *cloth,* 5s *Norwich,* 1846

5368 HEYLIN (Dr. Peter, *Chaplain to Cha. I. and II.*) his Life, by Geo. Vernon, sm. 8vo. *old binding,* 3s 6d .. 1682

5369 HOBLYN'S (R. D.) Manual of Chemistry, 75 *engravings,* 12mo. *cloth,* 2s 6d (*pub. at* 4s 6d) .. .. 1841

5370 HOME CIRCLE, *numerous engravings,* vols. 8, 9, 10, *cloth,* 2s *each,* (*cost* 4s *each*)

5371 HOMERI Ilias et Odyssea, 2 vols. 18mo. *cloth,* 6s 6d, *separately* 3s 6d and 3s .. .. *Oxonii, Parker,* 1859

5372 HOOKER and ARNOTT'S British Flora; comprising the Phænogamous or Flowering Plants and the Ferns, 12 *plates,* thick 12mo. *cloth,* 8s 6d (*cost* 14s) .. .. *Longmans,* 1850

5373 HOOPER'S (Dr. George, *Bp. of Bath and Wells* in 1720) Works, 2 vols. 8vo. *cloth,* 8s .. *Oxford, the Clarendon,* 1855

Contents—Sermons, a Discourse on Lent, On Ancient Measures, de Valentinianorum hæresi conjecturæ, Emendationes et Observationes in Tertullianum.

5374 HOWELL'S (James, Esq.) Dodona's Grove, or the Vocall Forrest, with England's Teares for the present Wars and the Pre-eminence of Parliaments, 3 Tracts in 1 vol. 12mo. *plates, old calf,* 4*s* *Cambridge,* 1645

5375 — Instructions and Directions for Forren Travell, *a portrait of Prince Charles, and plate of a Sphere,* 12mo. *old calf,* 4*s* 1650

5376 — Phil Anglus; som sober Inspections made into the Carriage and Consults of the late Long Parliament, sm. 8vo. *stained,* 3*s* 1660

5377 HUNT (Nicholas, *Master of Arts*) Judiciary Exercises, or Practicall Conclusions whereby any one of meane capacity may readily finde out the Christian Names of Men and Women, their titles of honour, &c., with Arithmetical Recreations, small thick 12mo. *old calf,* RARE, 10*s* .. .. .. 1631

This is a very curious little book, not in *Lowndes.*

5378 ILLUSTRATED BOOKS.—BERLIN and its TREASURES, *illustrated by* 110 *plates,* 4to. *half calf, neat,* £1 11*s* 6*d* (*cost* £2 12*s* 6*d*) .. .. .. 1848

5379 — The DANUBE, by Dr. Will. Beattie, illustrated in a Series of 150 Views by W. H. Bartlett, 4to. *half calf, gilt,* £1 11*s* 6*d* (*cost* £2 10*s*) .. .. .. 1844

5380 — FRANCE, illustrated by 270 fine engraved plates, after Allom, descriptions by G. M. Wright, 4 vols. in 2, 4to. *half bound in green morocco,* £2 12*s* 6*d* (*cost* £5 5*s*) .. 1847

5381 — HINDOSTAN, its Landscapes, Palaces, Temples, Tombs; the Shores of the Red Sea, and Himalaya Mountains, illustrated in 100 Views by Turner, Stanfield, &c., descriptions by Emma Roberts, 2 vols. 4to. *half calf, gilt,* 28*s* (*pub. at* £2 8*s*) 1845-7

5382 — IRELAND. Scenery and Antiquities of Ireland, by J. S. Coyne, illustrated with 160 plates by W. H. Bartlett, 2 vols. 4to. *half calf, gilt,* £2 2*s* (*cost* £3 18*s*) .. 1846

5383 — LONDON INTERIORS, with their Costumes and Ceremonies, *numerous well engraved plates,* 2 vols. in 1, 4to. *nicely half bound in green morocco, extra gilt leaves,* £1 8*s* (*cost* £2 10*s*) 1841

5384 — PALESTINE. Stebbing's (Dr. Henry) Christian in Palestine, illustrated by 80 plates, from drawings by Bartlett, 4to. *fine copy, half bound in green morocco, extra gilt leaves,* £1 8*s* (*cost* £2 10*s*) .. .. .. .. 1850

5385 INSECT LIFE, Episodes of, *numerous beautifully coloured plates,* 3 vols. 8vo. *cloth, elegant,* £1 11*s* 6*d* (*pub. at* £3 3*s*) *Reeves's Edition,* 1849-50-51

5386 — History of Insects, 36 *nicely coloured plates,* square 18mo. *cloth, gilt edges,* 3*s* .. .. .. 1842

5387 IRVING'S (Washington) Sketch Book, 2 vols. 8vo. *half russia, nice copy,* 12*s* .. .. .. .. 1820

5388 JAMES (Tho.) Bellum Papale, sive Concordia discors Sixti V. et Clementis VIII. circa Hieronymianum Edit. S. Bibliorum, sm. 8vo. *neat, scarce,* 9*s* .. .. *Londini,* 1678

5389 JOHNSON'S (Dr. Samuel) Plan of a Dictionary of the English Language, addressed to Lord Chesterfield, 4to. ORIGINAL EDITION, 34 pages, *sewed,* 5*s* .. .. *Knapton,* 1747

5390 JOURNAL of the Royal Agricultural Society of England, Nos. 42 and 43, being vol. 19, part 2, and vol. 20, part 1, *sewed, good as new,* 9*s* *(cost* 20*s)* .. .. .. 1858-9

These numbers are immediately in continuation of the set at page 167 of this Catalogue.

5391 JUELLI (Joan., *Episc. Sarisb.*) Apologiæ Ecclesiæ Anglicanæ, *Cantab.*, 1683.—Tertulliani Apologeticus et Minucii Felicis Octavius, in 1 vol. 12mo. *neat,* 4*s* 6*d* .. *ib.*, 1686

5392 KAMES (Henry Home, Lord) Principles of Equity, 8vo. *half calf, very neat,* 7*s* 6*d* .. .. *Edinburgh*, 1800

5393 — Sketches of the History of Man, 3 vols. 8vo. *calf, very neat, Lord Calthorpe's copy,* £1 1*s* .. *Edinburgh*, 1807

5394 KENDALL (Georgii) Fur pro Tribunali, Examen dialogismi cui inscribitur Fur Prædestinatus,—de Doctrina Neo-Pelagianâ Oratio, 1654.—Tuissii Vita et Victoria, de Scientia brevicula dissertatio, in 1 vol. sm. 8vo. *scarce,* 6*s* *Oxoniæ*, 1657

This is an answer to Abp. Sancroft's *Fur Prædestinatus*, see Nos. 262 and 4147 in this Catalogue.

5395 KERSEY'S (John) Elements of that Mathematical Art called Algebra, with Lectures on the Geometrical Construction of Algebraical Equations, &c. by Dr. E. Halley, *portrait by Faithorne,* folio, *old calf,* 7*s* 6*d* .. .. .. .. 1725

"An ample and complete work."—*Dr. Hutton.* Very honourable mention is made of it in the Philos. Transact. V. 8.

5396 KOPKE (Balth.) Dialogus de Templo Salomonis, 12mo. 2*s* *Amst.*, 1698

5397 LA CHAMBRE (Le Sieur) Characteres des Passions, thick 12mo. above 600 pages, *fine copy, old vellum,* 6*s* *Amst.*, *Ant. Michell*, 1658

The type much like Elzevirs; dedicated "a Monseigneur Sequier, Chancelier de France," to whom he was Physician.

5398 LARDNER'S (Dr. Dionysius) Handbook of Natural Philosophy, *hundreds of illustrations,* 4 vols. post 8vo. *cloth,* 14*s* (*pub. at* 20*s*) .. .. .. 1855-56

Mechanics, Optics, Hydrostatics, Pneumatics, Heat, Electricity, Magnetism, Acoustics.

5399 — Animal Physics, or the Body and its Functions familiarly explained, 520 *illustrations,* post 8vo. *cloth,* 7*s* 6*d* (*pub. at* 12*s* 6*d*) .. .. .. .. 1857

5400 — and Walker's Manual of Electricity, Magnetism, and Meteorology, 2 vols. 12mo. *cloth,* 5*s* *Cab. Cyclopædia*

5401 LAURIE'S (Dr. I.) Elements of Homœopathic Practice of Physic, thick 8vo. 852 *pages, cloth,* 7*s* 6*d* (*pub. at* 16*s*) 1847

5402 LAUS ASINI, Laus Pediculi, cum aliis festivis opusculis, thick 12mo. *old calf, clean and neat,* 10*s* 6*d* *Lugd. Bat.*, *Elzevir*, 1629

Daniel Heinsuis, Professor of Greek at Leyden, a man of profound learning, is the author of this humorous and satirical little volume. *Selden* speaks of him as "tam severiorum quam amœniorum literarum sol."

5403 LAW BOOKS. Archbold's (John F.) Law and Practice of Bankruptcy, by Flather, 5th edition, 12mo. *law calf,* 8*s* 1834

5404 — — 10th edition, thick 12mo. *boards,* 15*s* (*pub. at* 26*s*) 1844

5405 — — Pleading and Evidence in Criminal Cases, by Jervis, 5th edition, 12mo. *boards,* 7*s* (*pub. at* 19*s*) — 1834

5406 — — Peel's Acts, Lord Lansdowne's Act, &c., on Poaching, Smuggling, &c., 2 vols. 12mo. 2nd edition, *boards,* 5*s* 1830

5407 LAW BOOKS. Archbold's Practice of the Court of King's Bench, Common Pleas, and Exchequer, in Personal Actions and Ejectment, by Chitty, 3rd edition, 2 vols. 12mo. *law calf*, 6*s* .. .. .. .. 1833

5408 — — 8th edition, by Chitty, 2 thick vols. 12mo. *boards*, £1 4*s* (*pub. at* £2 8*s*) .. .. .. 1845

5409 — — Poor Law, to April, 1850, with Forms, 6th edition, 12mo. *boards*, 8*s* (*pub. at* £1 3*s*) .. .. 1850

5410 — Ayckbourn's Chancery Practice, 2nd edition, 12mo. *boards*, 4*s* (*pub. at* 14*s*) .. .. .. 1846

5411 — Barnewall and Cresswell's King's Bench Reports, vol. 6, parts 1, 2, 3, *sewed*, 8*s* (*pub. at* 20*s*) .. 1826-7

5412 — Burn's Justice of the Peace, by Bere and Chitty, vols. 1 and 3, 8vo. *boards*, 12*s* .. .. .. 1837

5413 — Cabinet Lawyer, 9th edition, 12mo. *law calf*, 5*s* 1835

5414 — Chitty's Forms of Practical Proceedings in the Courts of King's Bench, Common Pleas, and Exchequer, 12mo. *boards*, 5*s* (*cost* 18*s*) .. .. .. .. 1834

5415 — — 6th edition, part 1, 8vo. *boards*, 3*s* (*pub. at* 11*s*) 1845

5416 — — Practice of the Law, in all its Departments, 3 vols. in 6 parts, royal 8vo. 2nd edition, *cloth*, £1 10*s* (*pub. at* £6) 1834-35

5417 — Crabb's Conveyancer's Assistant, 2 vols. 8vo. *boards*, 8*s* (*cost* 32*s*) .. .. .. .. 1835

5418 — Doctor and Student; Dialogues on the Laws of England, by W. Muchal, 8vo. *law calf*, 6*s* .. .. 1787

"This book by Christopher St. Germain, is a work of considerable authority."—*Lowndes.*

5419 — Fry's Poor Law Acts of 1851, 12mo. *boards*, 1*s* 6*d*

5420 — Gilbert's (Lord Chief Baron) Law of Evidence, by Sedgwick, 8vo. *law calf*, 5*s* .. .. .. 1801

5421 — Gray's Country Attorney's Practice in the Superior Courts at Westminster, 5th edition, 12mo. *boards*, 4*s* (*cost* 9*s*) 1841

5422 — — Country Solicitor's Practice in the Court of Chancery, 3rd edit., 12mo. *boards*, 4*s* (*pub. at* 10*s*) .. 1840

5423 — Hayes's (Will.) Short Introduction to Conveyancing, 12mo. *law calf, neat*, 3*s* 6*d* .. .. .. 1834

5424 — Law Journal Reports, *Analytical Digest* of Cases published in, Vol. V. to IX., New Series, and all the Reports from 1835 to 1840, in 1 vol. 4to. *boards*, 10*s* (*cost* 30*s*) .. 1843

5425 — Lunatics and Lunatic Asylums, 8 and 9 Vict., c. 100, 126; also Poor Removal Act, 8 and 9 Vict., c. 117, 12mo. *boards*, 3*s* .. .. .. .. 1845

5426 — Roscoe's Digest of the Law of Evidence on the Trial of Actions at Nisi Prius, 12mo. 3rd edition, *law calf*, 4*s* 1834

5427 — Shelford's Law of Railways, with Statutes and Forms, 2nd edition, 12mo. *boards*, 10*s* (*cost* 21*s*) .. 1846

5428 — Sheppard's Precedent of Precedents in Conveyancing, by T. W. Williams, 8vo. *boards*, 4*s* (*pub. at* 16*s*) .. 1825

5429 — Theobald's Practical Treatise of the Poor Laws as altered by the Poor Law Amendment Act, thick 8vo. *boards*, 12*s* (*pub. at* £1 11*s* 6*d*) .. .. .. 1836

5430 LAW—Sugden's Law of Vendors and Purchasers of Estates, 5th edition, royal 8vo. *boards*, 6*s* .. .. 1818

5431 — Coventry's (Tho.) Conveyancers' Evidence, (no other edition) royal 8vo. *boards*, 6*s* *(pub. at 12s)* .. .. 1832

5432 LEECH (Humfrey, *M. of Arts and Minister*) Triumph of Truth; or, Declaration of the Doctrine concerning Evangelicall Counsayles, sm. 8vo. *original limp parchment*, RARE, £1 1*s* .. 1609

No place, but said to be printed at *Douay.* "With relation of sondry occurrents, and particularly of D. KING, the Vice-Chancellor, his exorbitant proceedings against H. L., also the *motives* which perswaded him to renounce the faction of hereticall congregations, and to embrace the unity of the *Catholique* Church." See *Wood's Athenæ Oxon. This is a very curious piece of personal history.*

5433 LINDLEY'S (Professor John) School Botany, *numerous cuts*, 8vo. 3*s* (*pub. at 5s 6d*) .. .. .. 1847

5434 — Elements of Botany, with Glossary of Technical Terms, *numerous plates*, 8vo. *cloth*, 6*s* *(cost 12s)* .. .. 1849

5435 LINDEBORN (Joan.) Jesus sub Pontio Pilato passus, 12mo. *vellum*, 2*s* 6*d* .. .. .. *Coloniæ*, 1689

5436 LINGENDES (Rev. Patris de, *e Soc. Jesu*) Concionum in Quadragesimam, 3 vols. 8vo. *old calf*, 10*s* 6*d* .. *Parisiis*, 1664

5437 LIPSIUS (Justus) Discourse of Constancy, Englished by R. G., *plate*, 12mo. *old calf*, 2*s* 6*d* .. .. 1654

5438 LIVES and Deaths of the Holy Apostles, with the Two Evangelists, Saint Mark and Luke, *cuts*, 12mo. Black Letter, *neat, but some leaves torn*, 5*s* .. .. .. *No date.*

This is an old chap book, printed for Dorman Newman, at the King's Arms in the Poultry.

5439 LONDON—Merchant Tailors' School—The School's Probation; or Rules and Orders for Certain Set Exercises to bee performed by the Scholars on Probation Days, 8vo. *old calf, neat*, 6*s* *Lond., Will. Du-Gard*, 1652

"Made and approved by learned men," the orders are signed by John Overall, Dean of St. Paul's, and John Dove, John Spencer, Nicolas Felton, and John Childerley, Doctors in Divinity.

5440 — Patience and its Perfect Work, under Sudden and Sore Tryals, sm. 8vo. *old calf*, 5*s* .. .. .. 1666

"Meditated and written *that week* the deplorable *fire* was at *London*, and upon *that occasion.*"

5441 LONGINUS, Gr. et Lat., G. Langbaenii, *frontispiece by W. Marshall*, 12mo. *old calf*, 5*s* .. *Oxonii, Guil. Webb*, 1638

"The 'Notarum Auctarium,' 118 pages, the exclusive performance of Langbain, is a very acceptable acquisition, and has always been welcomed by the lovers of Longinus." *Dibdin.*

5442 LYDYAT (Tho.) Tractatus de Variis Annorum formis, sm. 8vo. *very fine copy in limp vellum*, 12*s* *Londini, Norton*, 1605

5443 — Emendatio Temporum compendio facta, ab initio Mundi ad 1608, contra Scaligerum et alios, 12mo. *stained by damp*, 3*s* *Hagæ*, 1654

For an account of Lydyat, and "his curious and valuable publications." See *Wood's Athenæ Oxon.*

5444 LYNDE (Humfrey, *Knight,*) Via Tuta; the Safe Way, leading all Christians to the True Faith, 12mo. *old calf*, 3*s* 1628

5445 MASON'S (W.) English Garden; a Poem with a Commentary and Notes by Dr. W. Burgh, small 8vo. *calf, neat*, 2*s* 6*d* *York*, 1783

5446 MARTINII (Petri) Grammatica Hebræa, et Comment. de recta Ling., Ebrææ Sixt. Amama, 8vo. *old binding,* 3*s* 6*d* *Amst.,* 1611

5447 — Grammatica Hebræa et Chaldea, 8vo. *old stamped binding,* 4*s* *Rupellæ,* 1591

5448 — (Matth.) Cadmus Græcophænix; id est Etymologicum, thick 8vo. *calf, neat,* 6*s* .. .. *Bremæ,* 1625

5449 MAYER'S (John) Treasury of Ecclesiastical Expositions on Matthew to John, and Acts, 4to. *old binding,* 7*s* .. 1622

5450 MEN OF GENIUS—Exposition of the False Medium and Barriers Excluding Men of Genius from the Public, *portrait,* post 8vo. *boards,* 3*s* 6*d* .. .. .. 1833

5451 MENTZERUS (Balth.) Papismi Labem, gnesios Lutheranis Epistolis eluta, 8vo. *old calf,* 3*s* 6*d* .. *Londini,* 1719

5452 — Exegesis Augustanæ Confessionis, *portrait, Wittebergæ,* 1704.—Succincta Epitome Errorum Calvinianorum authore J. Fewerbornio, *ib.,* 1700, in 1 vol. thick 8vo. *half vellum,* 6*s* V. Y.

5453 MIDDLETON'S (Dr. C.) History of the Life of Cicero, *fine head of Cicero and vignettes by Gravelot,* 2 vols. 4to. *a very fine copy in old calf,* LARGE PAPER, 12*s* *Printed for the Author,* 1741

From Lord Calthorpe's collection, with his Lordship's book-plate and crest, a very handsome book.

5454 MILLAR'S (John) Historical View of the English Government from the Settlement of the Saxons in Britain, 4 vols. 8vo. *calf, very neat,* (Lord Calthorpe's copy) 24*s* .. 1818

5455 MOLINÆI (Petri) Vates, seu de præcognitione futurorum et bonis malisque Prophetis, small thick 8vo. *old calf,* 4*s* *L. Bat.,* 1640

5456 — de Cognitione Dei tractatus, 18mo. *nt,* 2*s* *Londini, Jo. Bill,* 1624

5457 MONTGOMERY'S (Robert) Woman, the Angel of Life, a Poem, post 8vo. *boards,* 3*s* 6*d* *(pub. at* 7*s* 6*d)* .. 1833

5458 MORE. Epistola H. Mori ad V. C. (Vincent Cane) Apologiam complectitur pro Cartesio, *Londini, Flesher,* 1664.—Renati Des-Cartes Principia Philosophiæ; Dioptrice et Meteora, *plates;* Passiones Animæ, in 1 vol. 8vo. *old cf,* 6*s* *Lond. Jo. Hart,* 1664

5459 MORGAN'S (William) Homœopathic Treatment of Indigestion, Constipation, and Hæmorrhoids, *plate,* 8vo. *cloth,* 2*s* 6*d* 1852

5460 NEALE'S (Rev. W. H.) Mahommedan System of Theology; the History and Doctrines of Islamism Contrasted with Christianity, 8vo. *calf, neat,* 5*s* 6*d* *(cost* 12*s)* *For the Author,* 1831

This is an examination of Mr. Forster's "elaborate work," Mahometanism Unveiled.

5461 NICHOLS'S (B. C.) Practical Sermons, second series, post 8vo. *cloth, new,* 4*s* *(pub. at* 6*s)* .. .. .. 1857

5462 NORFOLK Archæology, *numerous plates,* vol. 4, 8vo. VERY SCARCE, *cloth, as good as new,* 24*s* .. *Norwich, C. Muskett,* 1855

5463 NORWICH—The Fan, a Heroi-Comical Poem, in three Cantos, 4to. *sewed,* 2*s* 6*d* *For James Carlos, Bookseller, Dove Lane, Norwich,* 1749

5464 NOTES and QUERIES, No. 311 to 322, (Oct. 13 to Dec. 29) and Index of vol. 12, in 12 numbers, 2*s* 6*d*

5465 — vols. 1 to 4 of 2nd series, with the *Indexes* complete in numb., 21*s*

5466 — No. 105 to 115 of vol. 5, 2nd Series, 10 numbers, 2*s*

These last three articles are all in immediate continuation of each other.

5467 PAPISTS—The Practical Divinity of the Papists, Discovered to be Destructive of Christianity and Men's Souls, 4to. 450 pages, *old calf,* 4*s* .. .. .. .. 1676

5468 [PARKER (Sam., *Bp. of Oxford,*)] Reproof to [Andrew Marvell's] Rehearsal Transposed, thick 8vo. *old calf,* 3*s* 6*d* 1673

5469 PARLIAMENT—Arrest of the Five Members by Charles the First, a Chapter of English History re-written by John Forster, post 8vo. 400 pages, *new,* 12*s* .. .. *Murray,* 1860

The *Original Broadsides,* published by the Parliament relating to the subject of this book of Mr. Forster's, lately ably reviewed in the *Times,* are to be found in this Catalogue, Nos. 985 and 986, and singularly curious they are.

5470 PICTORIAL BIBLE, being the Authorized Version of 1611, reprinted with original Notes by Dr. John Kitto, *illustrated with steel engravings and many hundred wood cuts,* 4 vols. imperial 8vo. *cloth,* £2 8*s* .. .. .. 1855

This edition has additional notes based on the discoveries of the most recent travellers, Layard, Lepsius, and others.

5471 POPE'S (Alexander) Works, containing his Juvenile Poems and Translations, with Bp. Warburton's Notes, *plates,* 6 vols. 12mo. *old calf, neat,* 8*s* .. .. .. 1764

5472 REGISTRAR GENERAL'S 1st, 5th, 6th, and 7th Annual Reports of Births, Deaths, and Marriages in England, 4 vols. 8vo. *cloth,* 10*s* .. .. .. 1839-43, 4, 5

5473 REID'S (Dr. Thomas) Inquiry into the Human Mind on the Principles of Common Sense, 8vo. *half calf, neat,* 8*s* 1801

5474 — Essays on the Powers of the Human Mind, *portrait,* 3 vols. 8vo. *calf, gilt, very neat,* £1 1*s* .. *Edinburgh,* 1808

5475 RICARDO'S (David) Principles of Political Economy and Taxation, 8vo. *calf gilt, neat,* 9*s* .. .. .. 1819

5476 RUSSELL'S (Lady Rachel) Letters, with the Trial of her Husband, Lord William Russell, for High Treason, *portraits,* 8vo. *old sprinkled calf, neat,* 6*s* .. .. .. 1793

This edition contains an introduction vindicating the character of Lord Russell against Sir John Dalrymple, and others.

5477 SHAKESPEARE RESTORED, 4to. *stiff cover,* *Norwich, Charles Muskett,* 1853

Of this rarity there were but 100 copies printed, and not published. It is the Tragedy of MACBETH, with various readings, by Hastings Elwin, Esq., of Thorpe near Norwich, it elicited warm commendation from the Quarterly and a few other Reviews, to which it was sent, but beyond these but few copies have found their way into private hands.

5478 SPENSER'S (Edmund) Works, with a Glossary, *plates,* vols. 1 to 5, 12mo. *old calf, neat,* 7*s* (*Lord Calthorpe's copy*) 1715

Has all the Fairy Queen, the Shepherd's Calendar, and the Glossary.

5479 STEELE'S (Sir R.) Christian Hero, 12mo. *boards,* 1*s* 6*d* *Oxford,* 1802

5480 SWINBURNE'S (Henry) Travels through Spain in 1775-6, *plates,* 1779.—Travels in the Two Sicilies, 1777 to 1780, *plates,* 2 vols. together 3 vols. 4to. *fine copies in calf,* £1 10*s* 1783-85.

5481 TAYLOR'S (Capt. Meadows) Confessions of a Thug, post 8vo. *boards,* 2*s* .. .. .. .. 1858

5482 VOSSII (Ger. Jo.) Latina Grammatica, sm. 8vo. *old calf, neat,* 3*s* 6*d* *Amst., Jansson,* 1650

# PORTRAITS.

*"But no invention has better answered the end of perpetuating the memory of illustrious men than the modern art of engraving, which I shall, without scruple, prefer to the boasted art of the Egyptians; and I would much rather be possessed of a good collection of prints of my countrymen, than a collection of their mummies, though I had a pyramid for its repository."*—GRANGER'S PREFACE.

| | | s. | d. |
|---|---|---|---|
| Agrippa H. Cornelius | *Th. Burnford* | 1 | 0 |
| Alabaster Dr. Will. *small,* | *Thompson* | 0 | 6 |
| Bacon Francis, Lord | *out of Lodge* | 1 | 0 |
| Barrett Rev. W. G., Miss. | *Cochran* | 0 | 6 |
| Barrington John Shute 1st Visct. | *proof* | 2 | 0 |
| Bastwick Dr. John . . . | *Page* | 0 | 6 |
| Beale Mary, Artist . . . | *Wright* | 0 | 6 |
| Beatoun Cardinal, 1546 . . | *Lodge* | 1 | 0 |
| Beckford Alderman . . . . . . | | 0 | 6 |
| Becon Thomas, Reformer | *Maddocks* | 0 | 6 |
| Beman Rev. Dr., Troy, U.S. | *Cochran* | 0 | 6 |
| Bennett Rev. W. Dursley . | *Ridley* | 0 | 6 |
| Blackstone Judge . . . . | *Hall* | 1 | 0 |
| Blake Rob., Admiral to Cromwell . . | | 1 | 6 |
| Bodley Sir Thomas ob. 1602 . | *Lodge* | 1 | 0 |
| Bowers Rev. James, Haverhill, Suff. | *Freeman* | 0 | 6 |
| Brome Alex., Poet . . | *Richardson* | 1 | 0 |
| Brougham and Vaux, Lord | *Roffe* | 1 | 0 |
| Browne Rev. John, Biggar | *Freeman* | 0 | 6 |
| Brydges Sir. S. Egerton . . | *Cooper* | 1 | 6 |
| Bullen Queen Ann, 1536 . | *Lodge* | 1 | 0 |
| Bunyan John . . . . . | *Beilby* | 1 | 0 |
| Buonarotti Michael Angelo | *Sherwin* | 2 | 0 |
| Burder Rev. John, Stroud | *Freeman* | 0 | 6 |
| Burghley Will. Cecil, Lord . | *Lodge* | 1 | 0 |
| Cæsar Sir Julius, 1636 . . . . | | 1 | 0 |
| Caius Marius, *fine* . . . . | *J. E.* | 1 | 0 |
| Camden Lord, *very fine, whole length, judicial robes.* . . . | *Ravenet* | 10 | 6 |
| Campbell Rev. W. Miss. | *Woodman* | 0 | 6 |
| Cato Street Conspirators, 7 of them | | 2 | 0 |
| Cavendish Thomas, Voyager | *Page* | 0 | 6 |
| Cellini Benvenuto, Artist . | *Quinton* | 1 | 0 |
| Chesterfield Earl . . | *F. Bartolozzi* | 2 | 0 |
| ——— another . . | *J. Vitalba* | 2 | 0 |

| | | s. | d. |
|---|---|---|---|
| Clarendon Ed. Hyde Earl | *M. Burghers* | 2 | 6 |
| ——— another . . | *out of Lodge* | 1 | 0 |
| Cobbett Will. *fine, proof* | *F. Bartolozzi* | 7 | 6 |
| Coke Sir Edward . . . | *Trotter* | 0 | 6 |
| Cope Rev. Dr. R. Penryn . . | *Dean* | 0 | 6 |
| Corder William, 1828 . . . . . | | 0 | 6 |
| Cranmer Archbishop, 1556 | *Lodge* | 1 | 0 |
| Crump Rev. H. J., Mill Hill | *Cochran* | 0 | 6 |
| Darnley H. Stuart, Lord, 1567 | *Lodge* | 1 | 0 |
| Defoe Daniel, Novelist | *Vdr. Gucht* | 2 | 0 |
| Devonshire E. Cecil, Countess | *Lodge* | 1 | 0 |
| Digby Sir Kenelm, 1665 . . | *ib.* | 1 | 0 |
| Dilworth Thos., Schoolmaster | *Burgh* | 1 | 0 |
| Dimsdale Baron Thomas . | *Cook* | 0 | 6 |
| Dorset Thomas Sackville, Earl | *Lodge* | 1 | 0 |
| ——— another by . . | *A. Walker* | 1 | 0 |
| Drake Sir Francis 1596 . . | *Lodge* | 1 | 0 |
| Earlom R., Engraver, *mezz.* | *Lupton* | 2 | 0 |
| Eaton Daniel Isaac . . . . . . | | 0 | 6 |
| Eccles Rev. Will., Leeds . . . . | | 0 | 6 |
| Edwards Bryan, author of History West Indies. . . . | *Holloway* | 2 | 0 |
| ——— E., lives of painters | *Cardon* | 2 | 0 |
| ——— G., Naturalist, *fine proof* . . | | 3 | 0 |
| ——— Rev. James, Petworth | *Freeman* | 0 | 6 |
| ——— Jonathan, President | *Walker* | 0 | 6 |
| ——— Thomas, Cambrian Shakspere | *Chapman* | 0 | 2 |
| Elizabeth Queen, ob. 1603 . | *Lodge* | 1 | 0 |
| Elphinstone J., Schoolmaster | *Caldwal* | 1 | 0 |
| Elwes John, Esq, Miser | *A. Smith* | 1 | 0 |
| Ely Rev. John, Leeds . . | *Cochran* | 0 | 6 |
| Emery Mr., Comedian . . | *Ridley* | 1 | 0 |
| Emlyn Thomas, Arian | *I. Hopwood* | 1 | 6 |
| Emmet Robert, Esq., *proof,* | *Heath* | 2 | 6 |
| Englefield Sir H. C., Bart. | *C. Picart* | 3 | 6 |

| | s. | d. |
|---|---|---|
| Erasmus, *fine* . . . . *Holloway* | 5 | 0 |
| Erskine Lord . . . . . . . . | 0 | 6 |
| Essex R. Devereux, Earl, 1646 *Lodge* | 1 | 0 |
| —— Tho. Cromwell, Earl, 1540 *ib.* | 1 | 0 |
| Euler Leonard . . . . *Blake* | 2 | 0 |
| Evans, Rev. Will., Bristol *Ridley* | 1 | 0 |
| Evelyn John, *mezz.* : *Worlidge* | 2 | 0 |
| Fairfax Lord, *etching* . . *T. W.* | 2 | 6 |
| Farish Will, Jacksonian Professor Camb. 3 quarter, *mezz. proof H. Dawe* | 7 | 6 |
| Farmer Rev. Dr. R., *proof* *Reading* | 2 | 6 |
| Fayette, *proof.* . . . *B. le Clair* | 2 | 6 |
| Fell John, Bp. of Oxford *Richardson* | 2 | 0 |
| Fellowes Rev. Rob. . . . . . . . | 1 | 0 |
| Fenelon, Abp. of Cambray, *Smith* | 1 | 0 |
| Ferguson Dr. Adam, *fine proof, Lane* | 5 | 0 |
| Ferguson James, F. R. S. *T. Cook* | 1 | 0 |
| Ferino, *déposé à la Bibliotheque Nationale.* *Elizabeth Herhan* | 2 | 6 |
| Fielding Sir John, Knight, *fine mezz.* *J. R. Smith* | 12 | 0 |
| Fitzgerald Lord Edward *Singleton* | 1 | 0 |
| Fitzpatrick General Rich. . . . . . | 1 | 6 |
| Fitzwilliam W. Wentworth, Earl *Hicks* | 0 | 6 |
| Flamsteedius Johannes, Astronom. Professor *G. Vertue* | 4 | 0 |
| Flatman Thomas, Poet *A. Walker* | 1 | 6 |
| Fletcher Rev. Alex. of Down *Ridley* | 0 | 6 |
| —— Andrew, of Saltoun, *proof* . | 2 | 6 |
| —— Rev. J., Madeley *pf. Spilsbury* | 2 | 6 |
| —— Rev. R., Manchester *Cochran* | 0 | 6 |
| Flower Benjamin, 1798 . . *Birrell* | 1 | 6 |
| Folkes Martin, Pres. R. Soc. . . . | 1 | 6 |
| Follett Sir W. Webb, Sol. & Attorney General . . . . . *Ryall* | 1 | 0 |
| Foote Jesse . . . . . . . . . . | 2 | 0 |
| —— Samuel, Comedian . . . . | 1 | 0 |
| Fordyce George, M.D. *S. Phillips* | 1 | 6 |
| —— James, D.D. . . *Trotter* | 1 | 0 |
| Forman Simon, Astrologer, 1552 . | 1 | 0 |
| Forrest Capt. T., 1779, *an early Sharp* | 3 | 0 |
| Fortescue John Lord . . . . . | 2 | 0 |
| Foster James D. D. . . . *Ravenet* | 2 | 0 |
| Foster Sir Michael, Judge *Neagle* | 1 | 0 |
| Fothergill J., M.D. *fine mezz. V. Green* | 5 | 0 |
| Fox C. J., *in attitude speaking in the House,* 1782 . . . . . . . | 1 | 6 |
| Francis Sir Philip, Bart. *proof* . . | 1 | 6 |

| | s. | d. |
|---|---|---|
| Frampton Tregonwell, Esq., father of the turf, *folio, mezz.* . . . *Jones* | 5 | 0 |
| Frank, Professor A. H. of Halle *Blood* | 0 | 6 |
| Franklin Dr. Benjamin . . . . . | 1 | 0 |
| —— another, different engraver *prf.* | 1 | 6 |
| Freeman Rev. J. J., Walthamstow *Cochran* | 0 | 6 |
| Frend Will., Fellow of Jesus Coll. Cambridge, *proof* . . *Birrell* | 1 | 6 |
| Fréron . . . . . . . *Jenkins* | 1 | 0 |
| Fuller Isaac, Painter . *Chambars* | 1 | 0 |
| Fulton Robert, Esq., Engineer *Leney* | 1 | 0 |
| George IV. King, 8vo. . . *Thomson* | 1 | 0 |
| —— another, 4to. . . . . . | 2 | 0 |
| Gill John, D. D.. . . . . *Kitchen* | 1 | 6 |
| Goethe, *profile* . . . . . . . . | 0 | 6 |
| Gresham Sir Thomas, 1579 *Lodge* | 1 | 0 |
| Grey Lady Jane, ob. 1554 . . *ib.* | 1 | 0 |
| Hale Sir Matthew, Judge *Trotter* | 1 | 0 |
| Hallifax George Saville, Marquis *Bannerman* | 1 | 0 |
| Hamilton James, Duke of, 1649 *Lodge* | 1 | 0 |
| Hawkwood Sir John, military, 1393 | 0 | 6 |
| Heber Bishop Reginald . . . . | 0 | 6 |
| —— another . . . *Woolnoth* | 1 | 0 |
| Henderson Rev. Dr. E., Highbury *Cochran* | 0 | 6 |
| Hercules, fm. Marlboro' Gem *Worlidge* | 1 | 0 |
| Hill Rev. Micaiah Missionary *Dean* | 1 | 0 |
| Hill Rev. Rowland . . . . . . . | 0 | 6 |
| —— another, larger . . . *Bond* | 1 | 0 |
| Holland Dr Philemon . *Thompson* | 0 | 6 |
| Holmes John, Esq., F. S. A., East Retford, Norfolk . . *Sharp* | 1 | 0 |
| Holt Lord Chief Justice . *Audinet* | 1 | 0 |
| Horn, the Parson of Brentford . . | 1 | 0 |
| Horne George, Bishop of Norwich . | 0 | 6 |
| Howe Rev. James, Berbice . . . | 0 | 6 |
| Huntly George Gordon, Marquis, 1649 *Lodge* | 1 | 0 |
| Irving Washington . . . *Roffe* | 1 | 0 |
| Jenkyn Rev. Dr., Pres. Coward Coll. *Dean* | 0 | 6 |
| Jones Rev Morgan, Treevach *Ridley* | 0 | 6 |
| Keppel Honorable Augustus . . | 1 | 0 |
| —— George, Earl of Albemarle | 1 | 0 |
| King Lieutenant . . *W. Skelton* | 0 | 6 |
| Littleton Sir Thomas, Judge *Trotter* | 1 | 0 |

| | s. | d. |
|---|---|---|
| Leicester R. Dudley, Earl, 1588 *Lodge* | 1 | 0 |
| ——— T. W. Coke, Earl 1843 *Smith* | 2 | 0 |
| Manchester Duchess of . *Goldar* | 1 | 0 |
| Mann Rev. Tho., West Cowes *Cochran* | 0 | 6 |
| Mannering Rev. E., London . *ib.* | 0 | 6 |
| Marlborough Sarah, Duchess *Goldar* | 1 | 0 |
| Martyr Peter, (Vermilli) . *Meyer* | 0 | 6 |
| Marvell Andrew, friend of Milton 1660 *Etching* . . *Cipriani* | 3 | 0 |
| Mary Queen of Scots, 1587 *Lodge* | 1 | 0 |
| Monk General, Duke of Albemarle | 2 | 0 |
| Montesquieu, French Writer *Chapman* | 1 | 0 |
| Montrose James Graham, Marquis 1650 . . . . . . *Lodge* | 1 | 0 |
| Moore Rev. William, Truro . *Dean* | 0 | 6 |
| Morton Rev. William, Missionary *ib.* | 0 | 6 |
| Mulgrave Constantine Phipps, 1st Ld. | 1 | 0 |
| Murray James Stuart, Earl of, 1570 *Lodge* | 1 | 0 |
| Napier of Merchiston, 1600 . . . | 1 | 6 |
| Nash Richard, Beau, 1760 *J. June* | 1 | 0 |
| Naylor James, Fanatic, 1656 *Grave* | 1 | 6 |
| Neal D., Hist. of Puritans *Vd. Burgh* | 1 | 0 |
| Necker, Father of Mad. de Stael. *proof* *B. C. Clair* | 1 | 6 |
| Nelson Horatio, Admiral *Maddocks* | 0 | 6 |
| ——— another, 4to. . . . *Evans* | 2 | 0 |
| Neville R. Aldworth, Esq. *J. Basire* | 1 | 6 |
| Newcastle Marg., Duchess *Kellaway* | 0 | 6 |
| Newland Abraham . . . . . . | 1 | 0 |
| Newton Rev. John, Cardiphonia, &c. *Ridley* | 0 | 6 |
| ——— another, *proof* . *Horsburgh* | 1 | 0 |
| Nichols J., Printer, 4to., *prf. C. Heath* | 5 | 0 |
| Nicholson Will., Esq. *proof* *Blood* | 1 | 0 |
| Nixon Rbt., Cheshire Prophet *Harding* | 1 | 0 |
| Northcote James, Painter, *Etching, proof on India Paper, Prince Hoare* | 10 | 6 |
| Nugent Dr. Thomas, Translator of Voltaire, *proof* . . . . . | 2 | 6 |
| Nugent Robert, Earl, 1788 . . . | 1 | 0 |
| Oates Titus. . . *sold by T. Rodd* | 1 | 6 |
| Occom Rev. S., Missionary *Ridley* | 0 | 6 |
| Ogden Dr. Sam. . . . . . *Scott* | 1 | 6 |
| Ogilby John, Poet, *proof* . *Edwards* | 1 | 6 |
| Ogilvie Dr. John, F.R.S., Edin. *Heath* | 1 | 0 |
| Oliver Peter, Painter, temp. Ch. I. *Etching, small folio fine* | 7 | 6 |

| | s. | d. |
|---|---|---|
| Omai, a native of Ulaietea, *whole length, fine* . . *F. Bartolozzi* | 7 | 6 |
| Opie John, Painter . . . *Meyer* | 1 | 6 |
| Orford Sir Robert, 1st Earl *Wright* | 0 | 6 |
| ——— Horatio, Lord Walpole *Page* | 0 | 6 |
| Paganini, Violinist, 1831 . . . . | 1 | 0 |
| Paine Thomas, *fine impression, rare, plate destroyed* . . . *Sharp* | 5 | 0 |
| Paley Dr. Will. . . . *Englehart* | 2 | 0 |
| Palmer Elihu, Principles of Nature, *Tunbridge* | 2 | 0 |
| Paoli, Pasqual de, General, *mezz. fine* | 2 | 0 |
| Par, Queen Catharine, 1548 *Lodge* | 1 | 0 |
| Parisiensis, (Matthæi) historici, ob. 1259 . . . . . *Richardson* | 1 | 0 |
| Park Mungo, African Traveller *Ridley* | 1 | 0 |
| Parker Matthew, Abp. of Canterbury *Kellaway* | 0 | 6 |
| ———another, folio, *fine G. Vertue* | 3 | 6 |
| Parnell Dr. Tho., Archdeacon of Clogher, *mezz., fine T. Davies* | 7 | 6 |
| Parr Old, aged 152 years . *Condé* | 2 | 0 |
| Parsons Father Robert, S. J., ob. 1610 | 1 | 0 |
| Pascal, Blaise . . . . *Audinet* | 1 | 0 |
| Pearson John, Bp. of Chester *Page* | 0 | 6 |
| Penn William, Quaker *W. Grainger* | 1 | 6 |
| —— from a model . . . . *Proof* | 2 | 0 |
| Pennant Thomas, Antiquary *Chapman* | 1 | 0 |
| ———*fol. very fine*, 1778 *I. K. Sherwin* | 7 | 6 |
| Percy Rev. J. W., Woolwich *Blood* | 0 | 6 |
| ——— Tho., Bp. of Dromore *Proof* | 2 | 0 |
| Perouse J. F. G. de la, Voyager *Heath* | 2 | 6 |
| Perrault, Charles de l'Acad. Fr. *fine Edelinck* | 6 | 0 |
| Peterborough, Cha. Mordaunt, Earl *Noble* | 1 | 0 |
| Peters Hugh, *satirical* . . . . . | 1 | 6 |
| Petre Edward, called Father Peters | 1 | 6 |
| Phillip Arthur, Commander in Chief, N. S. Wales . . . *Sherwin* | 1 | 0 |
| Pinkerton John . . . . *Ridley* | 1 | 0 |
| Pitt William, *folio very fine J. Gillray* | 21 | 0 |
| Plunket Rt. Hon. W., Cunningham, *proof* . . . . . . *Heath* | 2 | 0 |
| Pocock Sir George . . . *Aliamet* | 1 | 0 |
| Polwhele Rev. Rich., Hist. of Devon | 1 | 0 |
| Pomarra, King of Taheite *Freeman* | 0 | 6 |
| Pope Sir William, of Roxton *Godefroy* | 1 | 0 |

| | s. | d. |
|---|---|---|
| Porson Rich, Greek Professor, Camb. *Maddox* | 0 | 6 |
| Poussin Nicolas, Painter . *Corner* | 2 | 0 |
| Price Rich. D.D., F.R.S. *folio, very fine* *Holloway* | 10 | 6 |
| Priestley Dr. Joseph . . *Bromley* | 0 | 6 |
| Prior Matthew, Poet . . . *Cook* | 0 | 6 |
| Puffendorff . . . . *Vdr. Gucht* | 1 | 0 |
| Pye Henry James, Poet Laureate *Chapman* | 1 | 0 |
| Quarles Francis, Poet . . *Wright* | 0 | 6 |
| Quick John, Comedian, 1760 . . . | 1 | 0 |
| Quin, Comedian, 1760 . *Bromley* | 1 | 0 |
| Racine John, French Poet *Collyer* | 1 | 0 |
| Raffles Rev. Tho., Liverpool *Blood* | 0 | 6 |
| Raikes R. Esq., Gloucester *Bromley* | 1 | 0 |
| Raleigh Sir Walter, 1618 *P. Audinet* | 3 | 0 |
| ——— another . . . *from Lodge* | 1 | 0 |
| Ramsden Mr, Optician . *C. Knight* | 1 | 0 |
| Rapin de Thoyras, Historian *G. Vertue* | 3 | 0 |
| Rataffe, Prince of Madagascar *Freeman* | 0 | 6 |
| Ravenet, French Engraver . . . | 1 | 0 |
| Rawdon Lord, now Marquis of Hastings. *mezz. proof* *J. Baldrey* | 3 | 0 |
| Ray John,. F. R. S, Naturalist *Roffe* | 0 | 6 |
| —— another . . . . . . . . . | 1 | 0 |
| Raymond Lord Chief Justice *Audinet* | 1 | 0 |
| Raynal Abbé, French Writer *fine head* . . . . . . *Trotter* | 3 | 0 |
| Reed Gen., President of Pennsylvania | 1 | 0 |
| Regnier, Déposé à la Bib. Nat. *folio, fine* . . . *Eliz. G. Herhan* | 5 | 0 |
| Reid Thomas, D. D., F. R. S., Edinb. *Ridley* | 1 | 0 |
| —— Will. Hamilton, *etching* *Barlow* | 1 | 0 |
| Rembrandt's head of himself, in fur cap, from Duke of Argyle's collection, *fine* . *by T. Worlidge* | 15 | 0 |
| Rennell Major James, *proof* *Ridley* | 1 | 6 |
| Rennie John, F. R. S., Engineer . | 0 | 6 |
| Repton Humphrey . . . *Cooke* | 0 | 6 |
| Richardson Jonathan, Portrait Painter, 1745 *etched, by C. Bretherton* | 2 | 0 |
| ——— Samuel, Novelist . *Page* | 2 | 0 |
| ——— Wm., Prof. of Humanity, Glasgow . . . . . *Ridley* | 1 | 0 |
| Richmond Rev. Legh . . . . . | 0 | 6 |
| Ritson Joseph, Critic *proof* *Gillray* | 3 | 6 |
| Robinson Hon. F., M. P., Chancellor of Exchequer . . . . . . | 2 | 0 |
| ——— Robert, Author of History of Baptism, *proof* . . *Neagle* | 2 | 0 |
| Rollin, French Historian . . . . | 0 | 6 |
| Roscoe William, Historian, *proof, folio* *C. Picart* | 5 | 0 |
| Roubiliac L. F., Sculptor *Chambars* | 2 | 0 |
| Rousseau J. J., *proof* . . *Barlow* | 1 | 6 |
| Rubens Peter Paul, Painter . . . | 1 | 6 |
| Russell Alex., M. D., F. R. S., *proof* | 2 | 0 |
| Ryder Henry, Bp. Lich. and Cov. . | 1 | 0 |
| —— Sir W., Mayor of London, 1600 | 1 | 0 |
| Rysbrack Michael, Sculptor *Chambars* | 1 | 6 |
| Ryves Bruno, Chaplain to Charles I., *proof* . . . . . *R. Earlom* | 3 | 0 |
| Sabatier, French Writer *Forestier* | 1 | 0 |
| Sadler James, Æronaut . . *Taylor* | 2 | 0 |
| Saunders Rev. Thos., Coventry *Ridley* | 0 | 6 |
| Saunderson Nicholas, Mathematician, Camb. . . . . *Vdr. Gucht* | 3 | 0 |
| Sawbridge Alderman . . . *Proof* | 2 | 0 |
| Scott Rev. James. Missionary *Dean* | 1 | 0 |
| —— Rev. T., Cleckheaton *Freeman* | 0 | 6 |
| —— Sir Walter . . . *Engelmann* | 0 | 6 |
| Scrimgeour Rev. J., Edinb. *Ridley* | 0 | 6 |
| Secker Abp. Thomas . . . . . | 1 | 0 |
| Selden John, ob. 1654 . . *Birch* | 1 | 0 |
| Seneca Statua di *In Roma, de Poilly* | 2 | 6 |
| Seward Wm., Biographer . *Ridley* | 2 | 0 |
| Sewel Wm., Dutch Dict., 1728 *Amst.* | 1 | 0 |
| Sewell J., Bookseller, Cornhill *Ridley* | 1 | 0 |
| Seymour Jane, Queen, ob. 1537 *Lodge* | 1 | 0 |
| Sharpe Granville . . . . *Blood* | 1 | 0 |
| Shaw Dr. . . . . . . . . . . | 1 | 0 |
| Sheldon John, Prof. Anat. Roy. Acad. *Freeman* | 1 | 0 |
| Shenstone Will., Poet . . *J. Hall* | 1 | 0 |
| ——— another . . . . *Clamp* | 1 | 0 |
| Sheridan Richd. Brinsley, Dramatist | 1 | 0 |
| ——— Thos., Eng. Dict,, 1788 . | 2 | 0 |
| Sherlock Thos., Bp. of London, 1756 *sitting, book in right hand, folio, fine, after Vanloo by Ravenet* . . | 10 | 6 |
| Shipley Jonathan, Bp. of St. Asaph *Reading* | 1 | 6 |
| Shirley James, Dramatist, *proof on India* . . . . *Worthington* | 2 | 6 |

| | | s. | d. |
|---|---|---|---|
| Shippen Will. . . . . . | *Harding* | 2 | 0 |
| Shortland Lieut. . . . | *Shirwin* | 0 | 6 |
| Shovel Sir Cloudesley, Admiral | *Penny* | 0 | 6 |
| Sidney Sir Philip, 1586 . . | *Lodge* | 1 | 0 |
| Slatterie Rev. Jos., Chatham | *Dean* | 1 | 0 |
| Sloane Sir Hans, M.D. and Naturalist | *Prescott* | 1 | 6 |
| Smeaton John, F.R.S., Civil Engineer *proof* . . . . . . | *Bromley* | 2 | 6 |
| ——* *large folio, proof, no letters* | | 15 | 0 |
| * Standing, right hand on a globe, not in Bromley's heads. | | | |
| Smellie Will., Surgeon, 1763 | *Freeman* | 1 | 6 |
| Smith Dr. Adam . . . . | *Ridley* | 1 | 6 |
| —— Rev. David, Brentwood . | *ib.* | 0 | 6 |
| —— Rev. Geo., London . . | *Dean* | 0 | 6 |
| —— Rev. Dr. J. P., Div. Tutor, Old Coll., Homerton . . . | *Blood* | 0 | 6 |
| —— Dr. W., Dean of Chester | *Freeman* | 1 | 0 |
| Smollett Dr. Tobias, Novelist | *Holl* | 1 | 0 |
| Soane John, Architect . . | *Blood* | 1 | 6 |
| Socrates, *fine, af. Rubens by T. Trotter* | | 2 | 0 |
| Somerset Edward Seymour, Duke of, 1552 . . . . . . | *Lodge* | 1 | 0 |
| Soult Marshal, *coloured lithograph* | *Bouvier* | 2 | 6 |
| South Dr. Robert . . | *G. Vertue* | 1 | 0 |
| Southern T., Dramatist, *prf., no letters* | | 3 | 0 |
| Southgate, Richard, F.A.S. . . . | | 2 | 0 |
| Spelman Sir Henry . . . | *Wright* | 0 | 6 |
| Spencer Rev. Edward, of Winkfield, Wilts. . . . . . | *Freeman* | 0 | 6 |
| —— Thos., drowned at Liverpool | | 0 | 6 |
| Staines Sir W., Lord Mayor of Lond. | | 1 | 6 |
| Stanhope Earl, *proof, no letters* . . | | 3 | 0 |
| Stanley Edw. G., Lord . | *Robinson* | 1 | 0 |
| —— Thos., Lives of Philosophers | | 1 | 0 |
| Stanyan Abraham, Esq. . . | *Cook* | 1 | 0 |
| Stapleton Sir Robert, Translator of Juvenal, *fol., brilliant* | *P. Lombart* | 15 | 0 |
| Steadman Rev. Dr. . . . . . . | | 0 | 6 |
| Steel Richard, M.A., 1692 | *Hopwood* | 1 | 0 |
| Steevens Geo., Commentator | *Cooke* | 2 | 0 |
| Steinkopff, Rev. C. F., Lutheran | | 1 | 0 |
| Stephen Rev. J. . . . . . . . . | | 0 | 6 |
| Sterne Lawrence, Novelist . | *Scott* | 1 | 0 |

| | | s. | d. |
|---|---|---|---|
| Steuben Major Gen., Baron | *B.B.E.* | 1 | 0 |
| Stewart Athenian, Architect, *from sketch by Sir Joshua Reynolds* . | | 3 | 0 |
| Stillingfleet Bishop . . | *John Hall* | 1 | 0 |
| Stowe John, *proof on India, no letters* | | 3 | 0 |
| Strafford Thomas Wentworth, Earl of | | 1 | 0 |
| Strachan Will., Printer . . | *Leney* | 2 | 0 |
| Struensee Count, beheaded 1772, *proof* | *Etched by W. Nicholls* | 2 | 0 |
| Stuart Dr. Gilbert, Author . . . | | 1 | 0 |
| Styles Rev. John, Brighton | *Ridley* | 0 | 6 |
| Sunderland Dorothy Sidney, Countess | | 1 | 0 |
| Ste. Susanne, Déposé à la Bibliotheque Nationale, *folio, fine* | *G. Fiesinger* | 4 | 0 |
| Sussex H.R.H. the Duke of, *proof* | *C. Warren* | 5 | 0 |
| Swartz Christ. F., Missionary | *Ridley* | 1 | 0 |
| Swedenborg Eman., Baron | *Battersby* | 2 | 0 |
| Swift Jonathan, Dean of St. Patrick | *J. Basire* | 2 | 0 |
| —— Owen . . . . . . | *Harland* | 1 | 0 |
| Swinburne Henry, Traveller | *Mne. Bovi* | 2 | 0 |
| Symonds Dr. Charles, Prebendary of St. David's, Author, *prf.* | *R. Grave* | 2 | 6 |
| Taylor Edward, of Norwich, Musical Prof., Gresham Coll. | *H. E. Dawe* | 2 | 0 |
| Torrington Geo. Byng, Visct. | *Goldar* | 1 | 0 |
| Townley Rev. Henry, London | *Cochran* | 0 | 6 |
| Victoria Her Most Gracious Majesty | | 5 | 0 |
| Vignola Giacomo Barozzio, Architect | *W. Sherwin* | 2 | 0 |
| Volney C. F. . . . . . . . . . | | 0 | 6 |
| Wade Rev. Dr. Arthur, Warwick | *Meyer* | 1 | 0 |
| Walcot Dr. (Peter Pindar) | *Mackenzie* | 1 | 6 |
| Walsingham Sir Francis . | *Lodge* | 1 | 0 |
| Washington George, Pres. U. States *folio, fine* . . . . . | *Nutter* | 5 | 0 |
| Watts Lieut. . . . | *W. Sherwin* | 0 | 6 |
| Wellington Duke of . . | *Woolnoth* | 1 | 0 |
| Wilde Matthew, Esq., Norwich, *Photograph* . . . . . . | *Fitt* | 3 | 6 |
| William IV. King, at 14. . | *Roffe* | 1 | 0 |
| Woolsey Cardinal, 1530 . | *Lodge* | 1 | 0 |
| Wood Alderman, twice Lord Mayor | | 0 | 6 |
| Zeno . . . . . . . . . | *J. E.* | 1 | 6 |

J. FLETCHER, PRINTER, MARKET PLACE, NORWICH.

www.ingramcontent.com/pod-product-compliance
Lightning Source LLC
LaVergne TN
LVHW020126110826
845151LV00001B/286

* 9 7 8 1 4 2 5 5 4 0 6 2 3 *